$32^{\underline{25}}$ H

011366

Duane Comforth

624-0205

David Colson

Tom
377-1117

Strategic
Marketing
Problems

Fourth Edition

Strategic Marketing Problems

Cases and Comments

ROGER A. KERIN
Southern Methodist University

ROBERT A. PETERSON
University of Texas

ALLYN AND BACON, INC.
Boston London Sydney Toronto

Series Editor: Jack Peters
Production Coordinator: Sandy Stanewick
Composition Buyer: Linda Cox
Designer: Judith Ashkenaz
Editorial-Production Services: Total Concept Associates
Cover Coordinator: Linda K. Dickinson
Cover Designer: Colleen Crowley

Library of Congress Cataloging-in-Publication Data

Kerin, Roger A.
   Strategic marketing problems.

   1. Marketing—Decision, making—Case studies.
2. Marketing—Management—Case studies.
I. Peterson, Robert A.   II. Title.
HF5415.135.K47   1987   658.8   86–22180
ISBN 0–205–10333–2
ISBN 0–205–10553–X (International Edition)

Printed in the United States of America
10 9 8 7 6 5 4 3 2 1   91 90 89 88 87 86

To our families

To our families

Contents

vii

Preface

DECISION MAKING IN MARKETING is first and foremost a skill. Like most skills, it possesses tools and terminology. Like all skills, it is best learned through practice.

This book is dedicated to the development of decision-making skills in marketing. Through textual material, concepts and tools useful in structuring and solving marketing problems are introduced. Case studies describing actual marketing problems provide an opportunity for these concepts and tools to be employed in practice. In every case study, the decision maker must develop a strategy consistent with the underlying factors existing in the situation presented, and must consider the implications of that strategy for the organization and its environment.

This fourth edition of *Strategic Marketing Problems: Cases and Comments* seeks a balance between marketing-management content and process. The book consists of eleven chapters and forty-two cases.

Chapter 1, "Foundations of Strategic Marketing Management," provides an overview of the strategic marketing-management process. The principal emphasis is on defining an organization's business and purpose, identifying opportunities, formulating strategies, budgeting, controlling the marketing effort, and developing contingency plans.

Chapter 2, "Financial Aspects of Marketing Management," provides an overview of concepts from managerial accounting and managerial finance that are useful in marketing management. Primary emphasis is placed on such concepts as cost structure, relevant versus sunk costs, margins, contribution analysis, liquidity, and operating leverage.

Chapter 3, "Marketing Decision Making and Case Analysis," introduces a systematic process for decision making and provides an overview of various aspects of case analysis. An example case and written student analysis are presented in the appendixes at the end of the book. The student analysis illustrates the nature and scope of a written case presentation, including the qualitative and quantitative analyses essential to a good case presentation.

Chapter 4, "Opportunity Analysis and Market Targeting," focuses on the identification and evaluation of marketing opportunities. Market segmentation, market targeting, and market potential and profitability issues are considered in this section.

Chapter 5, "Marketing Research," deals with the effective management of marketing information. Specifically, decisions involved in assessing the value of marketing information and managing the information acquisition process are highlighted.

Chapter 6, "Product and Service Strategy and Management," focuses on the management of the organization's offering. New-offering development, life-cycle management, product or service positioning, and product-service mix decisions are emphasized.

Chapter 7, "Marketing Communications Strategy and Management," raises issues in the design, execution, and evaluation of the communications mix. Decisions concerned with communication objectives, strategy, budgeting, programming, and effectiveness, in addition to sales management, are addressed.

Chapter 8, "Marketing Channel Strategy and Management," introduces a variety of considerations in marketing channel selection and modification and in trade relations. Specific decision areas include direct versus indirect distribution, dual distribution, cost-benefit analyses of channel choice and management, and marketing channel conflict and coordination.

Chapter 9, "Pricing Strategy and Management," highlights concepts and applications in price determination and modification. Emphasis is placed on demand, cost, and competitive influences in selecting or modifying pricing strategies for products and services.

Chapter 10, "Marketing Strategy Reformulation: The Control Process," focuses on the appraisal of marketing action for the purpose of developing reformulation and recovery strategies. Considerations and techniques applicable to strategic and operations control are introduced.

Chapter 11, "Linking Marketing and Corporate Strategy," is designed to alert the student to the expanding role of marketing concepts in the design and implementation of corporate strategy. Special attention is placed on applying marketing concepts to the investment and resource allocation decisions made by corporate strategists.

The case selection in this book represents a broad overview of contemporary marketing problems and applications. Of the forty-two cases included, twenty-nine deal with consumer products and services; the other thirteen cases have an industrial product or service orientation. Five cases introduce marketing issues in the international arena. Two-thirds of the cases are new, revised, or updated cases for this edition and many have spread-sheet applications imbedded in the case analysis. All text and case material has been classroom tested.

A Lotus 1–2–3 template and student manual are available for use with eleven of the cases in the book. The manual contains all the materials necessary to use Lotus 1–2–3 spreadsheets. It includes a sample case demonstration, instructions on using Lotus 1–2–3 with specific cases, and input and output forms. If this material is not available from your instructor or bookstore, please write to the publisher.

The efforts of many people are reflected here. First, we must thank those individuals who have kindly granted us permission to include their cases in this edition. They are prominently acknowledged both in the Table of Contents and at the bottom of the page on which their case appears. Their cases have made a major contribution to the overall quality of the book. Second, we wish to thank our numerous collaborators whose efforts made the difference between a good case and an excellent case. Third, we thank the adopters of the previous three editions of the book for their many comments and recommendations for improvements. Their insights and attention to detail are, we hope, reflected here. Finally, we wish to thank the numerous reviewers of this and previous editions for their conscientious reviews of our material. In particular we would like to thank the reviewers of this edition—Robert E. Spekman, University of Maryland at College Park; Judith D. Powell, University of Richmond; Subhash Sharma, University of South Carolina; and Gerald Albaum, University of Oregon. Notwithstanding the contributions of these many people, the authors bear full responsibility for all errors of omission and commission in the final product.

R.A.K.
R.A.P.

CHAPTER 1

Foundations of Strategic Marketing Management

THE PRIMARY PURPOSE of marketing is to create profitable exchange relationships between an organization and the public (individuals, organizations, and institutions) with which it interacts. Even though this fundamental purpose of marketing is timeless, the manner in which organizations undertake it has undergone a metamorphosis in the 1980s. No longer do marketing managers function solely to direct day-to-day operations. Rather, marketing managers must make strategic decisions as well. This elevation of marketing perspectives and practitioners to a strategic position in organizations has resulted in expanded responsibilities for marketing managers. Increasingly, marketing managers find themselves involved in charting the direction of the organization and contributing to decisions that affect long-term organizational performance. The transition of the marketing manager from being only an implementer to being a maker of organization strategy as well has prompted the emergence of *strategic marketing management* as a course of study and practice.

Strategic marketing management consists of six complex and interrelated analytical processes:[1]

1. Defining the character of the organization's business
2. Specifying the purpose of the organization
3. Identifying organizational opportunities
4. Formulating product-market strategies

1

5. Budgeting financial, production, and human resources

6. Developing reformulation and recovery strategies

The remainder of this chapter discusses each of these processes and
their relationship to each other.

DEFINING THE CHARACTER OF THE ORGANIZATION'S BUSINESS

Hewlett Packard vs. Texas Instr.

Defining the character of the organization's business is the first step in
the application of strategic marketing management. An organization
should define its business in terms of the type of customers it wishes to
serve, the particular needs of these customers, and the means or technology by which the organization will serve these needs.[2] The definition of an organization's business, in turn, specifies the market niche(s)
that the organization seeks to occupy and how it will compete. Ultimately, business definition affects the growth prospects for the organization itself by establishing guidelines for evaluating organizational
opportunities in the context of identified environmental opportunities,
threats, and organizational capabilities.

Three examples illustrate the concept of business definition in
practice. Consider the hand-held calculator industry, in which both
Hewlett-Packard and Texas Instruments seemingly competed with
each other in the 1970s. Although both firms excelled in marketing and
technical expertise, each carved out a different market niche based on
different business definitions.[3] For example, Hewlett-Packard's products were designed primarily for the technical user (customer type)
who required highly sophisticated scientific and business calculations
(customer needs). Hewlett-Packard's heavy development expenditures
on basic research (means) made the products possible. Alternatively,
Texas Instruments's products were designed for the household consumer (customer type) who required less sophisticated calculator capabilities (customer needs). Texas Instruments's efficient production
capabilities (means) made their products possible.

A second example can be found in the overnight-courier industry
by comparing Federal Express and Purolator.[4] Although both firms
compete for the same customer group—businesses that want next-
morning delivery of letters and packages—each uses very different
means for satisfying different customer needs. Federal Express satisfies
a customer's desire to ship items over distances of more than 350 miles
(customer needs) and relies on a fleet of airplanes (means) for this

purpose. By comparison, Purolator satisfies a customer's desire to ship items less than 350 miles (customer needs) and relies on a fleet of trucks (means). The differences in business definition are reflected in their respective competitive positions. Purolator captures over 75 percent of next-morning, short-haul (under 350 miles) courier volume, whereas Federal Express captures about 10 percent. Federal Express, however, captures over 53 percent of the next-morning, long-haul (over 350 miles) courier volume, where Purolator captures only about 7 percent.

Because of environmental and market changes, defining the organization's business is an ever-evolving process. However, major changes in business definition often lead to less than favorable results. An example of an organization that redefined the nature of its business, and subsequently returned to the original business definition, is Sears Roebuck and Co.[5] According to an industry observer:

> The retailing giant, which operates 866 full-line stores, is caught up in a fast-changing retailing environment where discounters and specialty stores are winning over more and more of its traditional middle-class customers—which leaves Sears scrambling to find its market niche. After tinkering with its staple goods merchandising formula throughout the 1970s—first promoting itself as an upscale, fashion-oriented department store for more affluent customers and, when that failed, experimenting with budget shops and embarking on a disastrous price-slashing binge— Sears believes it has little alternative but to try to be Sears again.

To "become" Sears again, the company developed a five-year plan to refocus efforts on attracting middle-class, home-owning families (customer type). The plan called for emphasis on "middle-of-the-road staple goods that are geared to function rather than to fashion" (customer needs) and renewed attention to product service and value (means for satisfying these needs).

SPECIFYING THE PURPOSE OF THE ORGANIZATION

The purpose of an organization is derived from its business definition. Purpose specifies the aspirations of the organization and what it wishes to achieve, with full recognition given to environmental opportunities, threats, and organizational capabilities.

From a strategic marketing management perspective, aspirations are objectives and desired achievements are goals. Objectives and goals represent statements of expectations or intentions, and they often incorporate the organization's business definition. For example, consider the marketing objectives outlined in the Speer Electric case in this text. Speer Electric aspires

> . . . to serve the discriminating purchasers of home entertainment products who approach their purchase in a deliberate manner with heavy consideration of long-term benefits. We will emphasize home entertainment products with superior performance, style, reliability, and value that require representative display, professional selling, trained service, and brand acceptance—retailed through reputable electronic specialists to those consumers whom the company can most effectively service.

Speer intends to achieve, in every market served, a market position of at least $1.50 sales per capita in the current year.

In practice, business definition provides direction in goal and objective setting. Capabilities of the organizational and environmental opportunities and threats set the likelihood of attainment. Goals and objectives divide into three major categories: production, finance, and marketing. Production expectations relate to the use of manufacturing and service capacity. Financial goals and objectives relate to return on investment, return on sales, profit, cash flow, and payback periods. Marketing goals and objectives relate to market share, marketing productivity, and sales volume aims. When production, finance, and marketing goals and objectives are combined, they represent a composite picture of organizational purpose. Accordingly, they must complement each other.

Finally, goal and objective setting should be problem centered and future oriented. Because goals and objectives represent statements of where the organization should be, they implicitly arise from an understanding of the current situation. Therefore, managers need an appraisal of operations, or *situation analysis,* to determine the gap between what was or is expected and what has happened or will happen. If performance has met expectations, then the question arises as to future directions. If performance has not met expectations, managers must diagnose the reasons for this difference and enact a program for remedying the situation. Chapter 3 provides an expanded discussion on performing a situation analysis.

IDENTIFYING ORGANIZATIONAL OPPORTUNITIES

Organizational opportunities and strategic direction result from matching environmental opportunities with organizational capabilities, acceptable levels of risks, and resource commitments. Three questions capture the essence of the decision-making process at this stage:

- What might we do?
- What do we do best?
- What must we do?

Each of these questions highlights major concepts in strategic marketing management. The *what might we do* question introduces the concept of environmental opportunity. Unmet needs, unsatisfied buyer groups, and new means for delivering value to prospective buyers—each represents a type of environmental opportunity. The *what do we do best* question introduces the concept of organizational capability, or distinctive competency. Distinctive competency describes an organization's principal strengths in such areas as technological expertise, market position, financial resources, and so forth. For example, the distinctive competency of the Gillette Safety Razor Division exists in three areas: (1) shaving technology and development, (2) high-volume manufacturing of precision metal and plastic products, and (3) the marketing of mass-distributed packaged goods.[6] Finally, the *what must we do* question introduces the concept of success requirements in an industry or market. Success requirements are basic tasks that must be performed in a market or industry to compete successfully. These requirements are subtle in nature and often overlooked. For example, distribution and inventory control are critical in the cosmetics industry. Firms competing in the personal computer industry recognize that the requirements for success in the 1980s include low-cost production capabilities, access to retail distribution channels, and strengths in software development.[7]

The linkage between environmental opportunity, distinctive competency, and success requirements will determine whether an organizational opportunity exists. A clearly defined statement of success requirements—What might we do? What must we do? What do we do best?—serves as a device for matching environmental opportunity with an organization's distinctive competency. If *what must be done* is inconsistent with *what can be done* to pursue an environmental opportunity, then an organizational opportunity will fail to materialize. Too often, organizations fail to recognize this linkage and embark on ventures that are doomed from the start. Exxon Corporation learned this lesson painfully after investing $500 million in the office-products market over a ten-year period. After the company abandoned this venture in 1985, a former Exxon executive summed up what was learned: "Don't get involved where you don't have the skills. It's hard enough to make money at what you're good at."[8] Alternatively, many organizations clearly establish the linkages necessary for success previous to any action. A Hanes Corporation executive illustrates this point by specifying his organization's new-venture criteria:

> . . . products that can be sold through food and drugstore outlets, are purchased by women, sell for less than $3, can be easily and distinctly packaged, and comprise at least a $500 million retail market not already dominated by one or two major producers.[9]

When one considers Hanes's impact with its L'eggs line of women's hosiery, it is apparent that whatever Hanes decides it might do in the future will be consistent with what Hanes can do best, as illustrated by past achievements in markets whose success requirements are similar. An expanded discussion of these points and others is found in Chapter 4.

In actuality, organizational opportunities emerge from existing markets or from newly identified markets. Opportunities also arise for existing, improved, or new products and services. Matching products and markets to form product-market strategies is the subject of the next set of decision processes.

FORMULATING PRODUCT-MARKET STRATEGIES

Product-market strategies consist of plans for matching existing or potential offerings of the organization with the needs of markets, informing markets that the offering exists, having the offering available at the right time and place to facilitate exchange, and assigning a price to the offering. In practice, a product-market strategy involves the selection of specific markets and profitably reaching them through a program called a marketing mix.

Using the format of matching offerings and markets, a classification of product-market strategies appears in Exhibit 1.1. A few brief comments on each strategy illustrate their operational implications and requirements.

Market-Penetration Strategy

A market-penetration strategy dictates that the organization seeks to gain greater dominance in a market in which it already has an offering. This strategy involves attempts to either increase present buyers' usage or consumption rate of the offering, attract buyers of competing

EXHIBIT 1.1
Product-Market Strategies

		Markets	
Offerings	*Extension*	*Existing*	*New*
Existing		Market penetration	Market development
New		New offering development	Diversification

Source: This classification is adapted from H. Igor Ansoff, *Corporate Strategy* (New York: McGraw-Hill Company, 1964), Chapter 6. An extended version of this classification is presented in G. Day, "A Strategic Perspective on Product Planning," *Journal of Contemporary Business* (Spring 1975): 1–34.

offerings, or stimulate product trial among potential customers. The mix of marketing activities might include lower prices for the offerings, expanded distribution to provide wider coverage of an existing market, and heavier promotional efforts extolling the "unique" aspects of an organization's offering over competing offerings.

Several organizations have attempted to gain dominance by promoting more frequent and varied usage of their offering. For example, the Florida Orange Growers Association advocates drinking orange juice throughout the day rather than for breakfast only. Airlines stimulate usage through a variety of reduced-fare programs and various family-travel packages, designed to reach the primary traveler's spouse and children.

Marketing managers should consider a number of factors before adopting a penetration strategy. First, they must examine market growth. A penetration strategy is usually more effective in a growth market. Attempts to increase market share when volume is stable often result in aggressive retaliatory actions by competitors. Second, they must consider competitive reaction. Recently, Proctor and Gamble implemented such a strategy for its Folger's coffee in selected East Coast cities only to run head-on into an equally aggressive reaction from General Foods's Maxwell House Division. According to one observer of the competitive situation:

> When Folger's mailed millions of coupons offering consumers 45 cents off on a one-pound can of coffee, General Foods countered with newspaper coupons of its own. When Folger's gave retailers 15 percent dis-

counts from the present list price of $2.93 per pound, General Foods met them head-on. [General Foods] let Folger's lead off with a TV blitz that introduced tidy Ms. Olson to all those East Coast housewives thought to be distraught because their husbands say they make terrible coffee. Then [General Foods] saturated the airwaves with sagacious rejoinders from Cora, who tells the customers at her coffee counter: "When you find a good thing, stick with it."[10]

Third, they must consider both the capacity of the market to increase usage or consumption rates and the availability of new buyers. Both are particularly relevant when viewed from the perspective of the costs of conversion involved in gaining buyers from competitors, stimulating usage, and attracting new users.

Market-Development Strategy

A market-development strategy dictates that an organization introduce its existing offering to markets other than those it is currently serving. Examples include introducing existing products to different geographical areas (including international expansion) or different buying publics. For example, Saga Corporation, a California-based restaurant and food-services company that operates Black Angus Steak Houses and Straw Hat Pizza outlets, among other restaurant chains, plans to expand its geographical coverage and open Black Angus Steak Houses in the Midwest. O. M. Scott and Sons Company employed this strategy when it moved from the home lawn-improvement market to large users of lawn-care products, such as golf courses and home construction contractors.

The mix of marketing activities used will often vary to reach different markets with differing buying patterns and requirements. Reaching new markets often requires modified versions of the basic offering, different distribution outlets, or a change in sales effort and advertising.

L'eggs Products, Incorporated, mentioned earlier as a division of Hanes Corporation, had long been a marketer of women's stockings sold through department stores and specialty shops. However, it recognized a change in hosiery-purchasing behavior that favored supermarket and drug outlets, with no one brand being foremost in these outlets. Through innovative packaging and sales promotion (the L'eggs display unit), expansion of distribution to cover supermarkets and drugstores, cents-off coupons on stockings and pantyhose, and a $10 million advertising allocation that was almost twice the advertising expenditure for the total hosiery industry, L'eggs became the largest selling nationally branded hosiery.

As with the penetration strategy, market development involves a careful consideration of competitive strengths and weaknesses and retaliation potential. Moreover, because the firm seeks new buyers, it must understand their number, motivation, and buying patterns to develop marketing activities successfully. Finally, the firm must consider its strengths, in terms of adaptability to new markets, to evaluate the potential success of the venture.

Product-Development Strategy

A product-development strategy dictates that the organization should create new offerings for existing markets. The approach taken is one of creating totally new offerings—*product innovation*—or enhancing the value of existing offerings—*product augmentation.* Texas Instrument's development of Speak & Spell is an example of product innovation, as is the cash management account developed by Merrill Lynch in the financial-services industry. The product-augmentation approach represents a slightly different version of product development in that the product itself is unchanged; instead, complementary items or services are added to it. Product-augmentation strategies are evident in the personal computer industry, as exemplified by programming services, application aids, and training programs for buyers. Cookbooks and training classes typically accompany the purchase of a microwave oven.

Either product innovation or product augmentation can be successful, provided the offering is a solution to a clearly understood problem faced by potential buyers, the problem is significant enough to a sizable number of buyers, and the offering can be communicated to buyers. Accordingly, considerable research is necessary—on the offering itself *and* on the buyer it is designed to serve.

Important considerations in planning a product-development strategy concern the market size and volume necessary to be profitable, the magnitude and timing of competitive response, the impact of the new product on existing offerings, and the capacity (in terms of human and financial investment and technology) of the organization to deliver the offering to the market(s). The failure of DuPont's attempt to introduce Corfam successfully has been attributed to the magnitude of competitive response generated by Leather Industries of America (a trade association) and to the fact that the company could not develop competitive prices for the product because of an inability to lower production costs.

The potential for *cannibalism* must be considered with the new product development strategy.[11] Cannibalism occurs when sales of a new product or service come at the expense of existing products already marketed by the firm. For example, Anheuser-Busch estimated that 20 to 25 percent of the volume for its Michelob Light came from the existing Michelob brand because of the low-calorie appeal among current customers. Cannibalism of this degree is likely to occur in many new product-development programs. The issue faced by the manager is whether its extent detracts from the overall profitability of the organization's total mix of offerings.

Diversification

Diversification involves the development or acquisition of offerings new to the organization and their introduction to publics not previously served by the organization. Many firms have adopted this strategy in recent years to take advantage of growth opportunities. Yet this is often a high-risk strategy because both the offering and the public or market served are new to the organization.

Consider the following examples of diversification.[12] General Foods announced a $39 million write-off when its entry into the business of fast-food chains failed. Rohr Industries, a subcontractor in the aerospace industry, reported a $59.9 million write-off on a mass-transit diversification. Singer's effort to develop a business machines venture over a ten-year period was abandoned while still unprofitable.

These examples highlight the importance of understanding the link between market success requirements and an organization's distinctive competency. In each of these cases, a bridge was not made between these two concepts and the opportunity was not realized.

Still, diversifications can be successful. Successful diversifications typically result from an organization's attempt to apply its distinctive competency in reaching new markets with new offerings. Therefore, even though Borden has offerings ranging from milk to glue and Proctor and Gamble has offerings ranging from cake mixes to disposable diapers, each firm has relied on its marketing expertise and extensive distribution system for success.

Strategy Selection

A recurrent issue in marketing management is determining the consistency of these product-market strategies with the organization's mission and capacity, market capacity and behavior, environmental forces, and competitive activities. Proper analysis of the factors depends on the availability and evaluation of information describing each. For example, information is necessary on the size of markets and how they behave in terms of buying behavior and requirements for buying. Information on environmental forces such as social, legal, political, and economic changes is necessary to determine the future viability of the organization's offerings and markets served. In recent years, for example, organizations have had to change or adapt their product-market strategies because of political actions (deregulation), social changes (increase in employed women), economic fluctuations (income shifts and the decline in disposable personal income), and population shifts (city to suburb; northern to southern United States), to name just a few of the environmental changes. Competitive activities must be monitored to ascertain their existing or possible strategies and performance in satisfying buyer needs. Considerations in the acquisition and management of information are discussed in Chapter 5.

In practice, the strategy selection decision is determined by a comparative cost-benefit analysis between alternative strategies and the probabilities of success. For example, a manager may consider the costs and benefits involved in further penetrating an existing market versus introducing the existing product to a new market. A careful analysis of competitive structure, market growth, decline or shifts, and *opportunity costs* (potential benefits *not* obtained) represents important considerations. The product or service itself may dictate a strategy change. If the product has been purchased by all of the buyers it is going to attract in an existing market, opportunities for growth beyond replacement purchases are reduced. This would indicate a need to search out new buyers (markets) or to develop new products or services for present markets.

The probabilities of success of each of these four strategies must be considered. In this regard, A. T. Kearny, a management consulting firm, has provided rough probability estimates of success for each strategy.[13] For example, the probability of a successful diversification is one chance in twenty. The success probability for introducing an existing product into a new market (market-development strategy) is one in four. There is a fifty-fifty chance of success for a new product being introduced into an existing market (product-development strategy). Finally, minor modification of an offering directed toward its existing market has the highest probability of success (market-penetration strategy).

A useful technique for gauging potential outcomes of alternative marketing strategies is to array actions, the responses to these actions, and the outcomes in an orderly manner for decision making. This implies, for any action taken, that certain responses can be anticipated, each with its own specific outcomes. Exhibit 1.2 shows *decision tree* format, so named because of the branching out of responses from action taken.

As an example, consider a situation where a marketing manager must decide between two marketing strategies (e.g., a market-penetra-

EXHIBIT 1.2

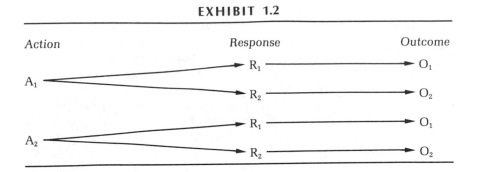

tion strategy versus a market-development strategy). Suppose the manager recognizes that competitors may react either aggressively or passively to either strategy. This situation can be displayed vividly using the decision tree scheme shown in Exhibit 1.3.

This representation allows the manager to consider actions, responses, and outcomes simultaneously. From the decision tree, a manager can note that the highest profits will result *if* a market-development strategy is enacted *and* competitors react passively. The manager must resolve the question of competitive reaction because an aggressive response will plunge the profit to $1 million, which is less than either outcome under the market-penetration strategy. The manager must rely on informed judgment to assess subjectively the likelihood of competitive response. Chapter 3 presents a more detailed description of decision analysis.

The Marketing Mix

Matching offerings and markets requires recognition of the other marketing activities available to the marketing manager. Combined with the offering, these activities form the marketing mix.

A marketing mix typically includes activities controllable by the organization. These include the kind of product, service, or idea offered (product strategy), how it will be communicated to buyers (promotion strategy), the method for distributing the offering to buyers (channel strategy), and the amount buyers will pay for the offering (price strategy). Each of these individual strategies is described later in this book. Suffice it to say that each element of the marketing mix has its complement in terms of stimulating a market's willingness and ability to buy. For example, promotion—personal selling, advertising, sales promotion, and public relations—informs and assures buyers that the offering will meet their needs. Marketing channels satisfy buyers' shopping patterns and purchase requirements in terms of point-of-

EXHIBIT 1.3

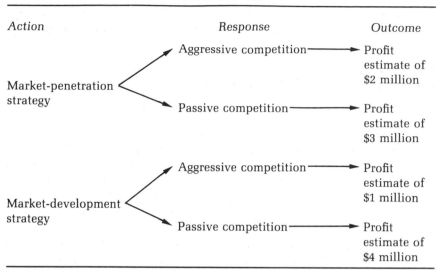

Action	Response	Outcome
Market-penetration strategy	Aggressive competition	Profit estimate of $2 million
	Passive competition	Profit estimate of $3 million
Market-development strategy	Aggressive competition	Profit estimate of $1 million
	Passive competition	Profit estimate of $4 million

purchase information and offering availability. Price represents the value or benefits provided by the offering.

Determination of an appropriate marketing mix depends on the success requirements of the markets at which it is directed. The "rightness" of a product, promotion, channel, or price strategy can be interpreted only in the context of markets served. Thus it is common to observe markedly different marketing mixes being used by organizations in the same industry (e.g., Avon and Revlon in the cosmetics industry, Volkswagen and Ford in the automobile industry).

In addition to being consistent with the needs of markets served, a marketing mix must be consistent with the organization's capacity, and the individual activities must complement each other. Several questions offer direction in evaluating an organization's marketing mix. First, is the marketing mix *consistent*? Do the individual activities complement each other to form a whole as opposed to fragmented pieces? Does the mix fit the organization, the market, and the environment into which it will be introduced? Second, are buyers more *sensitive* to some marketing mix activities than others? For example, are they more likely to respond favorably to a decrease in price or an increase in advertising or other combinations? Third, what are the *costs* of performing marketing mix activities? Do the costs exceed the benefits in terms of buyer response? Can the organization afford the marketing mix expenditures? Finally, is the marketing mix properly *timed*? For example, is promotion scheduled to coincide with product availability? Is the entire marketing mix timely with respect to the nature of the markets and environmental forces?

The implementation of marketing strategy is as much an art as a science. Implementation requires an integration of markets, environmental forces, organizational capacity, and coordination of marketing mix activities.

An example of strategy implementation with less than successful results is that of A&P's WEO (Where Economy Originates) program. Prior to implementing the program, A&P had watched its sales volume plateau with shrinking profits, while other chain supermarkets continued to increase sales volume and profits. When the WEO program was initiated, it emphasized discount pricing (price strategy) with heavy promotional expenditures (promotion strategy). The program increased sales volume by $800 million, but produced a profit loss of over $50 million. In the words of one industry observer at the time:

> Its competitors are convinced that A&P's assault with WEO was doomed from the start. Too many of its stores are relics of a bygone era. Many are in poor locations [distributional strategy]. . . . They are just not big enough to support the tremendous volume that is necessary to make a discounting operation profitable [capacity] . . . stores lack shelf space for stocking general merchandise items, such as housewares and children's clothing [product strategy].[14]

The product-market strategy employed by A&P could be classified as a market-penetration strategy. Its implementation, however, could be questioned in terms of internal consistency, costs of the marketing mix activities, and fit with organizational capacity. Moreover, the retail grocery industry was plagued by rising food costs at the time, illustrating the destructive effect of environmental forces on strategy success.

BUDGETING FINANCIAL, PRODUCTION, AND HUMAN RESOURCES

The culmination of all strategic decisions is reflected in the master budget for the organization. A well-prepared budget quantitatively expresses marketing strategy and also integrates the goals of all functional areas of the organization.

The sales forecast is the foundation of the master budget. Financial, production, and human resource allocation, depicted in dollar terms, illustrate how the sales goals will be achieved. The end result is the profit or loss projection.

A complete description of the budgetary process is beyond the scope of this section. However, Chapter 2, "Financial Aspects of Marketing Management," provides an overview of cost concepts and behavior. It also describes useful analytical tools for dealing with the financial dimensions of marketing management.

DEVELOPING REFORMULATION AND RECOVERY STRATEGIES

Reformulation and recovery strategies form the cornerstone of adaptive behavior in organizations. Strategies are rarely timeless. Changing markets and competitive behavior require periodic, if not sudden, adjustments in strategy.

Marketing audit and control procedures are fundamental to the development of reformulation and recovery strategies. The marketing audit has been defined as follows:

> A marketing audit is a comprehensive, systematic, independent, and periodic examination of a company's—or business unit's—marketing environment, objectives, strategies, and activities with a view of determining problem areas and opportunities and recommending a plan of action to improve the company's marketing performance.[15]

The audit process directs the manager's attention toward both the strategic fit of the organization with its environment and operational aspects of the marketing program. Strategic aspects of the marketing audit address the synoptic question, Are we doing the right things? Operational aspects address an equally synoptic question, Are we doing things right?

The distinction between strategic and operational perspectives, as well as the implementation of each, is examined in Chapter 10. Suffice it to say here that marketing audit and control procedures underlie the process of defining the organization's business and purpose, identifying opportunities and strategic direction, and formulating product-market strategies and marketing mix activities.

The intellectual process of developing reformulation and recovery strategies during the planning process serves two important purposes. First, it forces the manager to consider the "what if" questions. For example, "What if an unexpected environmental threat arises that renders a strategy obsolete?" or "What if competitive and market response to a strategy is inconsistent with what was originally expected?" Such questions focus the manager's attention on the sensitivity of results to assumptions made in the strategy development process. Second, preplanning of reformulation and recovery strategies, or *contingency plans,* leads to a faster reaction time in terms of implementing remedial action. Marshaling and reorienting resources is a time-consuming process itself without the additional time lost in planning.

LINKING CORPORATE
AND MARKETING STRATEGY

This introduction is intended to illustrate the nature and scope of strategic marketing management. The concepts and analytical processes described are also useful in the development of corporate strategy. As marketing executives continue to play a greater role in charting corporate strategy, these concepts and processes are being applied to the investment or resource-allocation decisions made by corporate strategists. Such concepts as business definition, opportunity analysis, product-market relationships, among others described in the following chapters, are frequently applied in the development of corporate strategy. Additional concepts useful in forging the link between corporate and marketing strategy are introduced in Chapter 11.

NOTES

1. This sequence of analytical processes was influenced by the work of D. Abell and J. Hammond, *Strategic Market Planning: Problems and Analytical Approaches* (Englewood Cliffs, N.J.: Prentice-Hall, 1979), p. 9.

2. D. Abell, *Defining the Business* (Englewood Cliffs, N.J.: Prentice-Hall, 1980).

3. See, for example, "Hewlett-Packard: Where Slower Growth Is Smarter Management," *Business Week* (June 9, 1975): 50–58.

4. "Next-Day Service Delivers Billions in Courier Profits," *Dallas Times Herald* (January 3, 1984): B-1.

5. "Sears' Strategic About-Face," *Business Week* (January 8, 1979): 80–83.

6. "Gillette Safety Razor Division: The Blank Cassette Project," ICCH No. 9-511-044.

7. "The Coming Shake-Out in Personal Computers," *Business Week* (November 22, 1982): 72–83.

8. "Exxon's Flop in Field of Office Gear Shows Diversification Perils," *Wall Street Journal* (September 3, 1985): 1ff.

9. "Hanes Expands L'eggs to the Entire Family," *Business Week* (June 14, 1975): 57ff.

10. H. Menzies, "Why Folger's Is Getting Creamed Back East," *Fortune* (July 17, 1978): 69.

11. For an extended treatment of this topic and additional examples, see R. Kerin, M. Harvey, and J. Rothe, "Cannibalism and New Product Development," *Business Horizons* (October 1978): 25–31.

12. These examples given in R. Biggadike, "The Risky Business of Diversification," *Harvard Business Review* (May–June 1979): 103–111.

13. These estimates reported in "The Breakdown of U.S. Innovation," *Business Week* (February 16, 1976): 56ff.

14. E. Tracy, "How A&P Got Creamed," *Fortune* (January 1973): 104. Items in brackets added for illustrative purposes.

15. P. Kotler, W. Gregor, and W. Rodgers, "The Marketing Audit Comes of Age," *Sloan Management Review* 18 (1977): 25–43.

ADDITIONAL READINGS

Abell, Derek F. "Strategic Windows." *Journal of Marketing* (July 1978): 137–145.

Biggadike, E. Ralph. "The Contributions of Marketing to Strategic Management." *Academy of Management Review* (October 1981): 25–35.

Cory, E. Raymond. "Key Options in Market Selection and Product Planning." *Harvard Business Review* (September–October 1975): 119–128.

Carman, James M., and Langeard, Eric. "Growth Strategies for Service Firms." *Strategic Management Journal* (January–February 1980): 7–22.

Shapiro, Benson. "Rejuvenating the Marketing Mix." *Harvard Business Review* (September–October 1985): 28–34.

Stevenson, Howard. "Defining Corporate Strengths and Weaknesses." *Sloan Management Review* (Spring 1976): 51–68.

CHAPTER 2

Financial Aspects of Marketing Management

MARKETING MANAGERS ARE ACCOUNTABLE for the impact of their actions on profits. Therefore, they need a working knowledge of basic accounting and finance. This chapter provides an overview of several concepts from managerial accounting and managerial finance useful in marketing management: (1) fixed and variable costs, (2) relevant and sunk costs, (3) margins, (4) contribution analysis, (5) liquidity, and (6) operating leverage.

FIXED AND VARIABLE COSTS

An organization's costs divide into two broad categories: variable costs and fixed costs.

Variable Costs

Variable costs are expenses that are uniform per unit of output within a relevant time period (usually defined as a budget year); yet the total variable cost fluctuates in direct proportion to the output volume of units produced. In other words, as volume increases, total variable costs increase.

Variable costs are divided into two categories. One category is cost of goods sold. For a manufacturer or a provider of a service, cost of goods sold consists of materials, labor, and factory overhead applied directly to production. For a reseller (wholesaler or retailer), cost of goods sold consists primarily of the costs of merchandise. A second category of variable costs consists of expenses that are not directly tied to production, but that nevertheless vary directly with volume. Examples include sales commissions, discounts, and delivery expenses.

Fixed Costs

Fixed costs are expenses that do not fluctuate with output volume within a relevant time period (the budget year), but become progressively smaller per unit of output as volume increases. The decrease in per-unit fixed cost results from the increasing output over which fixed costs are allocated. Note, however, that no matter how large volume becomes, the *absolute* size of fixed costs remains unchanged.

Fixed costs divide into two categories: programmed costs and committed costs. Programmed costs result from attempts to generate sales volume. Marketing expenditures are generally classified as programmed costs. Examples include advertising, sales promotion, and sales salaries. Committed costs are those required to maintain the organization. They are usually nonmarketing expenditures such as rent and administrative and clerical salaries.

It is important to understand the concept of fixed cost. Remember that total fixed costs do not change during a budget year, regardless of changes in volume. Thus, once fixed expenditures for a marketing program are made, they remain the same whether or not the program causes unit volume to change.

Despite the clear-cut classification of costs into variable and fixed categories, cost classification is not always apparent in actual practice. Many times costs have a fixed and variable component. For example, selling expenses often have a fixed component (e.g., salary) and a variable component (e.g., commissions or bonus) that are not always evident at first glance.

RELEVANT COSTS AND SUNK COSTS

Relevant Costs

Relevant costs are expenditures that (1) are expected to occur in the future as a result of some marketing action, and (2) differ among marketing alternatives being considered. In short, relevant costs are future expenditures unique to the decision alternatives under consideration.

The concept of relevant cost can be illustrated by an example. Suppose a manager considers adding a new product to the product mix. Relevant costs include potential expenditures for manufacturing and marketing the product plus salary costs arising from the time sales personnel give to the new products at the expense of other products. If this additional product does not affect the salary costs of sales personnel, then salaries are not a relevant cost.

Sunk Costs

Sunk costs are the direct opposite of relevant costs. Sunk costs are past expenditures for a given activity and are typically irrelevant in whole or in part to future decisions. In a marketing context, sunk costs include past research and development expenditures (including test marketing) and last year's advertising expense. These expenditures, although real, will neither recur in the future nor influence future expenditures. When marketing managers attempt to incorporate sunk costs into future decisions affecting new expenditures, they often fall prey to the *sunk cost fallacy*—that is, they attempt to recoup spent dollars by spending still more dollars in the future.

MARGINS

Margins are another useful concept for marketing managers. Margin refers to the difference between selling price and the "cost" of a product or service. Margins are expressed on a total volume basis or on an individual unit basis in dollar terms or as a percentage. Three margins are described here: gross, trade, and net profit margins.

Gross Margin

Gross margin, or gross profit, is the difference between total sales revenue and total cost of goods sold, or, on a per unit basis, the difference between unit selling price and unit cost of goods sold. Gross margin is expressed in dollar terms or as a percent.

Total Gross Margin	Dollar amount	Percentage
Net sales	$100	100%
Cost of goods sold	− 40	−40%
Gross profit margin	$ 60	60%

Unit Gross Margin		
Unit sales price	$1.00	100%
Unit cost of goods sold	−0.40	−40%
Unit gross profit margin	$0.60	60%

Gross margin analysis is a useful tool because it implicitly includes unit selling prices of products or services, unit costs, and unit volume. A decrease in gross margin percentages or dollars is of immediate concern to a marketing manager because such a change has a direct impact on profits, providing other expenditures remain unchanged. Changes in total gross margin should be examined in depth to determine if the change was brought about by fluctuations in unit volume, changes in unit price or unit cost of goods sold, or a modification in the sales mix of the firm's products or services.

Trade Margin

Trade margin is the difference between unit sales price and unit cost at each level of a marketing channel (e.g., manufacturer→wholesaler→retailer). A trade margin is frequently referred to as *markup* or *mark-on* by channel members, and it is often expressed as a percentage.

Trade margins are occasionally confusing since the margin percentage can be computed on the basis cost or selling price. Consider the following example. Suppose a retailer purchases an item for $10 and sells it at a price of $20—that is, a $10 margin. What is the retailer's margin percentage? Retailer margin as a percentage of selling price is:

$$\frac{\$10}{\$20} \times 100 = 50 \text{ percent}$$

Retailer margin as a percentage of cost is:

$$\frac{\$10}{\$10} \times 100 = 100 \text{ percent}$$

Differences in margin percentages show the importance of knowing the base (cost or selling price) on which the margin percentage is determined. Trade margin percentages are usually determined on the basis of selling price, but practices do vary between firms and industries.

Trade margins affect the pricing of individual items in two ways. First, suppose a wholesaler purchases an item for $2 and seeks to achieve a 30 percent margin on this item based on selling price. What would be the selling price?

$2.00 = 70 percent of selling price, or

Selling price = $2.00/0.70 = $2.86

Second, suppose a manufacturer suggests a retail list price of $6 on an item for ultimate sales to the consumer. The item will be sold through retailers whose policy is to obtain a 40 percent margin based on selling price. For what price must the manufacturer sell the item to the retailer?

$$\frac{x}{\$6.00} = 40 \text{ percent of selling price,}$$

where x = retailer margin. Solving for x indicates that the retailer must obtain $2.40 for this item. Therefore, the manufacturer must set the price to the retailer at $3.60 ($6.00 − $2.40).

The manufacturer's problem of suggesting a price for ultimate resale to the customer becomes more complex as the number of intermediaries between the manufacturer and final consumer increases. This complexity is shown by expanding the example to include a wholesaler between the manufacturer and retailer. The retailer receives a 40 percent margin on the sales price. If the retailer must receive $2.40 per unit, then the wholesaler must sell the item for $3.60 per unit. In order for the wholesaler to receive a 20 percent margin, the manufacturer must sell the unit for $2.88:

$$\frac{x}{\$3.60} = 20 \text{ percent wholesaler margin on selling price,}$$

where x = wholesaler margin. Solving for x shows that the wholesaler's margin is $0.72 for this item. Therefore, the manufacturer must set the price to the wholesaler at $2.88.

This example shows that a manager must work backward from the ultimate price to the consumer through marketing channel members to arrive at a product's selling price. Assuming that the manufacturer's cost of goods sold is $2.00, we can calculate the following margins, which incidentally show the manufacturer's gross margin of 30.6 percent.

	Unit Cost of Goods Sold	Unit Selling Price	Gross Margin as a Percentage of Selling Price
Manufacturer	$2.00	$2.88	30.6%
Wholesaler	$2.88	$3.60	20.0%
Retailer	$3.60	$6.00	40.0%
Consumer	$6.00		

Net Profit Margin (Before Taxes)

The last margin to be considered is the net profit margin before taxes. This margin is expressed as a dollar figure or a percent. Net profit margin is the remainder after cost of goods sold, other variable costs, and fixed costs have been subtracted from sales revenue. The place of net profit margin in an organization's income statement is shown as follows:

	Dollar Amount	Percentage
Net sales	$100,000	100%
Cost of goods sold	−30,000	−30%
Gross profit margin	$ 70,000	70%
Selling expenses	−20,000	20%
Fixed expenses	−40,000	−40%
Net profit margin	$ 10,000	10%

Net profit margin dollars represent a major source of funding for the organization. As will be shown later, net profit dollars influence the *working capital* position of the organization; hence the dollar amount ultimately affects the organization's ability to pay its cost of goods sold plus selling and administrative expenses. Furthermore, net profit also affects the organization's *cash flow* position. Cash flow is discussed in Chapter 11.

CONTRIBUTION ANALYSIS

Contribution analysis is an important concept in marketing management. Contribution is the difference between total sales revenue and total variable costs, or, on a per-unit basis, the difference between unit selling price and unit variable cost. Contribution analysis is particularly useful in assessing relationships between costs, prices, and volumes of products and services.

Break-even Analysis

Break-even analysis is one of the simplest applications of contribution analysis. Break-even analysis identifies the unit or dollar sales volume at which an organization neither makes a profit nor incurs a loss. Stated in equation form, total revenue = total variable costs + total fixed costs. Since break-even analysis identifies the level of sales volume where total costs (fixed and variable) and total revenue are equal, it is a valuable tool for evaluating an organization's profit goals and assessing the riskiness of actions.

Break-even analysis requires three pieces of information: (1) an estimate of unit variable costs; (2) an estimate of the total dollar fixed costs to produce and market the product or service unit (note that only relevant costs apply); and (3) the selling price for each product or service unit.

The formula for determining the number of units required to break even is as follows:

$$\text{Unit break-even} = \frac{\text{Total dollar fixed costs}}{\text{Unit selling price} - \text{unit variable costs}}$$

The denominator in this formula (unit selling price − unit variable costs) is called *contribution per unit.* Contribution per unit is the dollar amount that each unit sold "contributes" to the payment of fixed costs.

Consider the following example. A manufacturer plans to sell a product for $5.00. The unit variable costs are $2.00, and total fixed costs assigned to the product are $30,000. How many units must be sold to break even?

Fixed costs = $30,000

Contribution per unit = unit selling price − unit variable cost
= $5 − $2 = $3

Unit break-even = $30,000/$3 = 10,000 units

This example shows that for every unit sold at $5, $2 is used to pay variable costs. The balance of $3 "contributes" to fixed costs.

A related question is what the manufacturer's dollar sales volume must be to break even. The manager need only multiply unit volume break-even by the unit selling price to determine the break-even dollar volume: 10,000 units × $5 = $50,000.

A manager can calculate a dollar break-even point directly without first computing break-even unit volume. To do this, the *contribution margin* must be determined. The contribution margin is computed as:

$$\text{Contribution margin} = \frac{\text{Unit selling price} - \text{unit variable cost}}{\text{Unit selling price}}$$

Using the figures from our example, the contribution margin is 60 percent:

$$\text{Contribution margin} = \frac{\$5 - \$2}{\$5} = 60 \text{ percent}$$

The dollar break-even point is:

$$\text{Dollar volume} = \frac{\text{Total fixed cost}}{\text{Contribution margin}} = \frac{\$30,000}{0.60} = \$50,000$$

Sensitivity Analysis

Contribution analysis can be applied in a number of different ways, depending on the manager's needs. The following illustrations show how break-even points in our example vary by changing selling price, variable costs, and fixed costs.

1. *What would break-even volume be if fixed costs are increased to $40,000 while the selling price and variable costs remain unchanged?*

Fixed costs = $40,000

Contribution per unit = $3

Unit break-even volume = $40,000/$3 = 13,333 units

Dollar break-even volume = $50,000/0.60 = $66,667

Note that the difference between the dollar break-even with the contribution margin and the result of simply multiplying unit selling price by break-even unit volume (13,333 × $5 = $66,665) is due to rounding.

2. *What would break-even volume be if selling price is dropped from $5 to $4 while fixed and variable costs remained unchanged?*

Fixed cost = $30,000

Contribution per unit = $2

Unit break-even volume = $30,000/$2 = 15,000 units

Dollar break-even volume = $30,000/0.50 = $60,000

3. *Finally, what would break-even volume be if unit variable cost per unit is reduced to $1.50, selling price remains at $5, and fixed costs are $30,000?* 30.000

Fixed cost = $30,000

Contribution per unit = $3.50

Unit break-even volume = $30,000/$3.50 = 8,571 units

Dollar break-even volume = $30,000/0.70 = $42,857

Contribution Analysis and Profit Impact

No manager is content to operate at the break-even point in unit or dollar sales volume. Profits are necessary for the continued operation of the organization. A modified break-even analysis is used to incorporate a profit goal.

Because "contribution per unit" is the dollar amount available to pay fixed costs using simple break-even analysis, the profit goal can be regarded as an additional fixed cost. The break-even formula can be modified to incorporate the dollar profit goal, as follows:

$$\frac{\text{Unit volume to}}{\text{achieve profit goal}} = \frac{\text{Total dollar fixed cost} + \text{Dollar profit goal}}{\text{Contribution per unit}}$$

Suppose a firm has fixed costs of $200,000 budgeted for a product or service, the unit selling price is $25, and the unit variable costs are $10. The profit goal is $20,000. How many units must be sold to achieve the profit goal?

Fixed cost + profit goal = $200,000 + $20,000 = $220,000

Contribution per unit = $25 − $10 = $15

Unit volume to achieve profit goal = $220,000/$15 = 14,667 units

Many firms specify their profit goal as a percentage of sales rather than as a dollar amount ("Our profit goal is a 20 percent profit on sales"). This objective can be incorporated into the break-even formula by including the profit goal in the contribution-per-unit calculation. If the goal is to achieve a 20 percent profit on sales, then each dollar of sales must "contribute" 20 cents to profit. Using our example, each unit sold for $25 must contribute $5 to profit. The break-even formula incorporating a percent profit on sales goal is as follows:

$$\text{Unit volume to achieve profit goal} = \frac{\text{Total dollar fixed cost}}{\text{Unit selling price} - \text{unit variable cost}}$$

The unit volume break-even point to achieve a 20 percent profit goal is 20,000 units:

Fixed cost = $200,000

Contribution per unit = $25 − $10 − $5 = $10

Unit volume to achieve profit goal = $200,000/$10 = 20,000 units

Contribution Analysis and Market Size

An important consideration when using contribution analysis is the relationship of break-even unit or dollar volume to market size. Consider a situation in which a manager has conducted a break-even analysis. The unit volume break-even point is 50,000 units. This number has meaning only when compared with the potential size of the market segment sought. Suppose the market potential is 100,000 units. Therefore, the manager's product or service must capture 50 percent of the market sought to break even. An important question to be resolved is whether such a percentage can be achieved. A manager can assess the feasibility of a venture by comparing the break-even volume with market size and market capture percentage.

Contribution Analysis and Performance Measurement

A second application of contribution analysis lies in performance measurement. For example, a marketing manager may wish to examine the performance of products. Consider an organization with two products, X and Y. A description of each product's financial performance follows:

	Product X (10,000 volume)	Product Y (20,000 volume)	Total (30,000 volume)
Unit price	$10	$3	
Sales revenue	$100,000	$60,000	$160,000

	Product X (10,000 volume)	Product Y (20,000 volume)	Total (30,000 volume)
Unit variable cost	$4	$1.50	
Total variable cost	$40,000	$30,000	$70,000
Unit contribution	$6	$1.50	
Total contribution	$60,000	$30,000	$90,000
Fixed cost	$45,000	$10,000	$55,000
Net profit	$15,000	$20,000	$35,000

The net profit figure shows that Product Y is more profitable than Product X. However, Product X is four times more profitable than Product Y on a unit-contribution basis and generates twice the contribution dollars to overhead. The difference in profitability lies in the allocation of fixed costs to the products. When measuring performance, it is important to consider which products contribute most heavily to the organization's total fixed costs ($55,000 in this example) and then to total profit.

Should a manager look only to net profit, a decision might be made to drop Product X. However, Product Y must then cover total fixed costs. If the fixed costs remain at $55,000 and only Product Y is sold, then this organization will experience a *net loss* of $25,000, assuming no change in Product Y volume.

Cannibalization Assessment

A third application of contribution analysis involves the assessment of cannibalization effects. Cannibalization is the process by which one product or service sold by a firm gains a portion of its revenue by diverting sales from another product or service also sold by the firm. For example, sales of Brand X's new gel toothpaste may be at the expense of sales of Brand X's existing opaque white toothpaste. The problem facing a marketing manager is to assess the financial effect of cannibalization. Contribution analysis is useful in this instance.

Consider the situation concerning the two types of toothpaste, and suppose we have the following data:

	Existing Opaque White Toothpaste	New Gel Toothpaste
Unit selling price	$1.00	$1.10
Unit variable costs	−0.20	−0.40
Unit contribution	$0.80	$0.70

This situation suggests that the gel toothpaste can be sold at a slightly higher price, given its formulation and taste, but that the variable costs are also higher. Hence, the gel toothpaste has a lower contribution per unit. Therefore, for every unit of the gel toothpaste sold instead of the opaque white toothpaste, the firm "loses" $0.10. Suppose further that the new gel toothpaste was expected to sell one million units in the first year after introduction and that, of that amount, 500,000 units would be diverted from the opaque white toothpaste, which was expected to sell one million units. Given these data, what is the effect on Brand X's total contribution dollars?

One approach for assessing the financial impact of cannibalization is shown below:

1. Brand X expects to lose $0.10 for each unit diverted from the opaque white toothpaste to the gel toothpaste.

2. Given that 500,000 units will be cannibalized from the opaque white toothpaste, then the total contribution *lost* is $50,000 ($0.10 × 500,000 units).

3. However, the new gel toothpaste will sell an additional 500,000 units at a contribution per unit of $0.70, which means that $350,000 ($0.70 × 500,000 units) in additional contribution will be generated.

4. Therefore, the net financial effect is a positive increase in contribution dollars of $300,000 ($350,000 − $50,000).

Another approach to assessing the cannibalization effect is as follows:

1. The opaque white toothpaste alone is expected to sell one million units with a unit contribution of $0.80. Therefore, contribution dollars will equal $800,000 ($0.80 × 1,000,000 units).

2. The gel toothpaste is expected to sell one million units with a unit contribution of $0.70.

3. Given the cannibalism rate of 50 percent (i.e., one-half the gel's volume is diverted from the opaque white toothpaste), the combined contribution is:

Product	Unit Volume	Unit Contribution	Contribution Dollars
Opaque white toothpaste	500,000	$0.80	$400,000
Gel toothpaste: Cannibalized volume	500,000	$0.70	350,000

Product	Unit Volume	Unit Contribution	Contribution Dollars
Incremental volume	500,000	$0.70	350,000
Total	1,500,000		$1,100,000
Less original forecast volume for opaque white toothpaste	1,000,000	$0.80	800,000
Total	+500,000		+$300,000

Both approaches arrive at the same conclusion: Brand X will benefit by $300,000 by introducing the gel toothpaste. The manager can use the approach with which he or she is more comfortable in an analytic sense.

It should be emphasized, however, that the incremental fixed costs reflected in advertising and sales-promotion costs or any additions or changes in manufacturing capacity must be considered to complete the analysis. If the fixed costs approximate or exceed $300,000, then the new product should be viewed in a very different light.

LIQUIDITY

Liquidity refers to an organization's ability to meet short-term (usually within a budget year) financial obligations. A key measure of an organization's liquidity position is its *working capital*. Working capital is the dollar value of an organization's current *assets* (e.g., cash, accounts receivable, prepaid expenses, inventory) minus the dollar value of *current liabilities* (e.g., short-term accounts payable for goods and services, income taxes).

A manager should be aware of the impact of marketing actions on working capital. Marketing expenditures precede sales volume; therefore, cash outlays for marketing efforts reduce current assets. If marketing expenditures cannot be met out of cash, then accounts payable are incurred. In either case, working capital is reduced. In a positive vein, a marketing manager's creation of sales volume, with corresponding increases in net profit, contributes to working capital. Since the timing of marketing expenditures and sales volume is often lagged, a marketing manager must be wary of marketing efforts that unnecessarily deplete working capital and must assess the likelihood of potential sales, given a specified expenditure level.

OPERATING LEVERAGE

A finance concept closely akin to break-even analysis is operating leverage. *Operating leverage* refers to the extent to which fixed costs
and variable costs are used in the production and marketing of products and services. Firms that have high total fixed costs relative to total
variable costs are defined as having high operating leverage. Examples
of firms with high operating leverage include airlines and heavy-equip-
ment manufacturers. Alternatively, firms with low total fixed costs
relative to total variable costs are defined as having low operating
leverage. Firms typically having low operating leverage are residential
contractors and wholesale distributors.

   If a firm has high operating leverage, its total profits will increase
at a faster rate than increases in sales volume once break-even volume
is achieved, in comparison to a firm with a low operating leverage.
However, these same firms with high operating leverage will incur
losses at a faster rate once sales volume falls below break-even.

   Exhibit 2.1 illustrates the effect of operating leverage on profit.
The base case shows two firms that have identical break-even sales
volumes. The cost structures of the two firms differ, however, with one
having high fixed/low variable costs and the other having low fixed/
high variable costs. Note that when sales volume is increased 10 percent, the firm with high fixed/low variable costs achieves a much
higher profit than the firm with low fixed/high variable costs. When
sales volume declines, however, just the opposite is true. That is, firms
with high fixed/low variable costs incur losses at a faster rate than
firms with high variable/low fixed costs once sales fall below break-
even.

   The message of operating leverage should be clear from this example. Firms with high operating leverage benefit more from sales
gains than do firms with low operating leverage. At the same time,
firms with high operating leverage are more sensitive to sales-volume
declines since losses will be incurred at a faster rate. Knowledge of a
firm's cost structure will therefore prove valuable in assessing the
gains and losses from changes in sales volume brought about by marketing efforts.

SUMMARY

This note provides an overview of basic accounting and financial concepts. Yet a word of caution is necessary. Financial analysis of marketing actions is a necessary but insufficient criterion for justifying
marketing programs. A careful analysis of other variables impinging on

EXHIBIT 2.1
Effect of Operating Leverage on Profit

	Base Case		10% Increase in Sales		10% Decrease in Sales	
	High-Fixed-Cost Firm	High-Variable-Cost Firm	High-Fixed-Cost Firm	High-Variable-Cost Firm	High-Fixed-Cost Firm	High-Variable-Cost Firm
Sales	$100,000	$100,000	$110,000	$110,000	$90,000	$90,000
Variable costs	20,000	80,000	22,000	88,000	18,000	72,000
Fixed costs	80,000	20,000	80,000	20,000	80,000	20,000
Profit	$0	$0	$8,000	$2,000	($8,000)	($2,000)

33

the decision at hand is required. Thus judgment enters the picture. "Numbers" serve only to complement general marketing analysis skills and are not an end in themselves.

ADDITIONAL READINGS

Droms, William G. *Finance and Accounting for Nonfinancial Managers.* Reading, Mass.: Addison-Wesley, 1983.

Mossman, Frank; Crissy, W. J. E.; and Fischer, Paul M. *Financial Dimensions of Marketing Management.* New York: Wiley, 1978.

Shapiro, Stanley J., and Kirpalani, V. H. *Marketing Effectiveness: Insights from Accounting and Finance.* Boston: Allyn and Bacon, 1984.

EXERCISES IN FINANCIAL ANALYSIS AND MARKETING DECISION MAKING

1.   Executives of Studio Recordings, Inc., produced the latest album, entitled *Sunshine/Moonshine,* by the Starshine Sisters Band. The following cost information pertains to the new album:

Album cover	$1.00/album
Songwriter's royalties	$0.30/album
Recording artists' royalties	$0.70/album
Direct material and labor	$1.00/album
Advertising	$100,000
Studio Recordings, Inc., overhead	$120,000
Selling price to record wholesaler	$4.00/album

Calculate the following:

1.   Contribution per unit
2.   Break-even volume in units and dollars
3.   Net profit if one million albums are sold
4.   Necessary unit volume to achieve a $200,000 profit

2.   The group product manager for ointments at American Therapeutic Corporation was reviewing price and promotion alternatives for two products: Rash-Away and Red-Away. Both products were designed to reduce skin irritation. However, Red-Away was primarily a cosmetic treatment, whereas Rash-Away also included a compound that eliminated the rash.

The price and promotion alternatives recommended for the two products by their respective brand managers included the possibility of using additional promotion or a price reduction to stimulate sales volume. A volume, price, and cost summary for the two products follows:

	Rash-Away	Red-Away
Unit price	$2.00	$1.00
Unit variable costs	1.40	0.25
Unit contribution	$ .60	$0.75
Unit volume	1,000,000 units	1,500,000 units

Both brand managers included a recommendation to either reduce price by 10 percent or invest an incremental $150,000 in advertising.

1. What absolute increase in unit sales and dollar sales will be necessary to recoup the incremental increase in advertising expenditures for Rash-Away? Red-Away?
2. How many additional sales dollars must be produced to cover each $1 of incremental advertising for Rash-Away? Red-Away?
3. What increase in absolute unit sales and dollar sales will be necessary to maintain the level of total contribution dollars if the price for each product is reduced by 10 percent?

3. After spending $300,000 for research and development, chemists at Diversified Citrus Industries have developed a new breakfast drink. The drink, called ZAP, will provide the consumer with twice the amount of Vitamin C currently available in breakfast drinks. ZAP will be packaged in an eight-ounce can and will be introduced to the breakfast drink market, which is estimated to be equivalent to 21 million eight-ounce cans nationally.

One major management concern is the lack of funds available for advertising. Accordingly, management has decided to use newspapers (rather than television) to promote the product in the introductory year in major metropolitan areas that account for 65 percent of U.S. breakfast drink volume. Newspaper advertising would carry a coupon that would entitle the consumer to receive 20 cents off the price of the first can purchased. The retailer would receive the regular margin and be reimbursed by Diversified Citrus Industries. Past experience indicated that for every five cans sold during the introductory year, one coupon will be

returned. The cost of the newspaper advertising campaign (excluding coupon returns) will be $250,000. Other fixed overhead
costs are expected to be $90,000 per year.

Management has decided that the suggested retail price to
the consumer for the eight-ounce can would be 50 cents. The only
unit variable costs for the product are 18 cents for material and 6
cents for labor. The company intends to give retailers a margin of
20 percent off the suggested retail price and a broker's fee of 10
percent of the retailers' cost of the item.

1. At what price will Diversified Citrus Industries be selling
   their product?
2. What is the contribution per unit for ZAP?
3. What is the break-even unit volume in the first year?
4. What is the first year break-even share-of-market?

4. Max Leonard, vice-president of marketing for Dysk Computer,
   Inc., must decide whether to introduce a mid-priced version of
   the firm's DC6900 minicomputer product line—the DC6900-X
   minicomputer. The DC6900-X would sell for $3,900, and the unit
   variable costs are $1,800. Projections made by an independent
   marketing research firm indicated that the DC6900-X would
   achieve a sales volume of 500,000 units next year in its first year
   of commercialization. One-half of the first year's volume would
   come from competitors' minicomputers and market growth. However, a consumer research study indicated that 30 percent of the
   DC6900-X sales volume would come from the higher-priced
   DC6900-Omega minicomputer, which sold for $5,900 (unit vari-
   able costs were $2,200). Another 20 percent of the DC6900-X sales
   volume would come from the economy-priced DC6900-Alpha
   minicomputer, priced at $2,500 (unit variable costs were $1,200).
   The DC6900-Omega unit volume was expected to be 400,000 units
   next year, and the DC6900-Alpha was expected to achieve a
   600,000 unit sales level. The fixed cost of launching the DC6900-X
   was forecast to be $2 million during the first year of commercial-
   ization. Should Mr. Leonard add the DC6900-X model to the line
   of minicomputers?

5. A marketing manager for the Dental Products Division of a large
   firm is considering whether to introduce Product A, a toothpaste
   with stain remover compounds, or Product B, a toothpaste with
   added decay prevention compounds. The manager's assistant
   prepared the following table, which includes the profit expecta-

tions to each of three possible market share possibilities developed from marketing research.

Market Share

	20%	10%	5%
Introduce Product A	$20 million	$10 million	− $8 million
Introduce Product B	$15 million	$9 million	− $3 million

The estimated profit loss identified for the 5 percent market share estimate prompted the manager to review ten case studies of previous product introductions. The review indicated that three new product introductions achieved a 20 percent market share, five new products achieved a 10 percent market share, and two new products recorded a 5 percent market share.

1. What is the expected monetary value for Product A? for Product B? Given the data provided, should the marketing manager introduce Product A or Product B?
2. Concern over whether either would achieve the market share projections prompted consideration of a test market. What is the maximum amount of money that the manager should budget for a test market?

CHAPTER 3

Marketing Decision Making and Case Analysis

SKILL IN DECISION MAKING is a prerequisite to being an effective marketing manager. Indeed, Nobel Laureate Herbert Simon viewed managing and decision making as being one and the same.[1] Another management theorist, Peter Drucker, has said that the burden of decision making can be lessened and better decisions can result if a manager recognizes that "decision making is a rational and systematic process and that its organization is a definite sequence of steps, each of them in turn rational and systematic."[2]

One objective of this chapter is to introduce a systematic process for decision making. Another objective is to introduce basic considerations in case analysis. Just as decision making and managing can be viewed as being identical in scope, so the decision-making process and case analysis go hand in hand.

DECISION MAKING

No simple formula exists that can assure a correct solution to all problems at all times. However, a systematic decision-making process can increase the likelihood of arriving at correct solutions.[3] The decision-making process described here is called DECIDE:[4]

Define the problem.
Enumerate the decision factors.

Consider relevant information.
Identify the best alternative.
Develop a plan for implementing the chosen alternative.
Evaluate the decision and the decision process.

A definition and discussion of the implications of each step follow.

Define the Problem

The philosopher John Dewey observed that "a problem well defined is half solved." What this statement means in a marketing setting is that a well-defined problem outlines the framework within which a solution can be derived. This framework includes the *objectives* of the decision maker, a recognition of *constraints,* and a clearly articulated *success measure* or goal to assess progress toward solving the problem.

Consider the situation faced by El Macho Foods, a marketer of Mexican foods. The company had positioned its line of Mexican foods as a high-quality brand and used advertising effectively to convey that message. Shortly after the company's introduction of frozen dinners, two of its competitors began cutting the price of their frozen dinner entrees. The firm lost market share and sales as a result of these price reductions; this led to reductions in the contribution dollars available for advertising and sales promotion. How might the problem be defined in this situation? One definition of the problem leads to the question: Should we reduce our price? A much better definition of the problem leads one to ask: How can we maintain our quality brand image (objective) and regain our lost market share (success measure), given limited funds for advertising and sales promotion (constraint)?

The two problem definitions provide two additional points for consideration. The first problem definition actually states a response to an immediate issue facing the company. It does not articulate the broader and more important considerations of competitive positioning. Hence, the problem statement fails to capture the significance of the issue raised. The second definition, in comparison, provides a broader perspective on the immediate issue posed and allows the manager greater latitude in seeking solutions.

In a case study, the analyst is frequently given alternative courses of action to consider. A narrow view of the case situation would lead to the analysis of these different options. Such an approach often leads to the selection of alternative A or alternative B without regard for the significance of the choice in the broader context of the situation facing the company or the decision maker.

Enumerate the Decision Factors

Two sets of decision factors in combination affect the outcome. These are (1) *alternative courses of action* and (2) the *uncertainties* in the competitive environment. Alternatives are controllable decision factors because the decision maker has complete command of them. Alternatives are typically product-market strategies or changes in the various elements of the organization's marketing mix described in Chapter 1. Uncertainties are uncontrollable factors that the manager cannot influence. In a marketing context, uncertainties often include actions of competitors, market size, and buyer response to marketing action.

The recent bankruptcy of Braniff Airlines illustrates how the combination of an action and uncertainties can spell disaster. Braniff embarked on a major expansion program after the airline industry was deregulated. The expansion resulted in new aircraft and additional routes (action) that, combined with escalating fuel costs and a decline in passenger traffic (environmental uncertainties), produced enormous losses, ultimately resulting in bankruptcy.

Case analysis provides an opportunity to relate alternatives to uncertainties. In fact, they *must be* related. Any expected outcome, financial or otherwise, of a chosen course of action is unrealistic if it is considered apart from the environment into which it is introduced.

Consider Relevant Information

The third step in the decision-making process involves the consideration of relevant information. *Relevant* information, like relevant costs discussed in Chapter 2, consists of information that relates to the alternatives identified by the manager that will affect future events. More specifically, relevant information might include characteristics of the industry or competitive environment, characteristics of the organization (e.g., competitive strengths and position), and characteristics of the alternatives themselves.

Identifying relevant information is difficult for both the practicing manager and the case analyst. There is frequently an overabundance of facts, figures, and viewpoints available in any decision setting. Choosing what matters and what does not is a skill that is best gained through experience. Analyzing many and varied cases is one way to develop this skill.

Two words of caution are necessary. First, the case analyst often considers *everything* in a case as "fact." However, many cases—and actual marketing situations—contain conflicting data. Part of the problem to be addressed in any case and marketing situation requires the use of judgment in assessing the validity of the data presented. Second, in many instances relevant information must be created. An example of creating relevant information is the blending together of several pieces of data, as evidenced in the calculation of a simple break-even point.

It should be clear at this point that even though the consideration of relevant information is the third step in the decision-making process, relevant information will also affect the two previous steps. As the manager or case analyst becomes increasingly involved in considering and evaluating information, the problem definition may be modified or the decision factors may change.

At the conclusion of the first three steps, the manager or case analyst has completed a *situation analysis*. The situation analysis should produce an answer to the synoptic question. Where are we now? Specific questions that relate to the situation analysis are found in Exhibit 3.3 at the end of this chapter.

Identify the Best Alternative

Identifying the best alternative is the fourth step in the decision-making process. The selection of a course of action is not a simple choice of alternative A over other alternatives but, rather, a considered evaluation of identified alternatives and the uncertainties apparent in the problem setting.

A framework for identifying the best alternative is *decision analysis*, which was introduced in Chapter 1. Decision analysis, in its simplest form, matches each alternative identified by the manager with the uncertainties existing in the environment and assigns a quantitative value to the outcome created by each match. Managers implicitly use a *decision tree* and a *payoff table* to describe the relationship among alternatives, uncertainties, and potential outcomes. The use of decision analysis and the application of decision trees and payoff tables can be illustrated by referring back to the situation faced by El Macho.

Suppose that at the conclusion of step 2 in the DECIDE process (enumerate decision factors), El Macho executives identified two alternatives: (1) reduce the price on frozen dinners, or (2) maintain the price. They also recognized two uncertainties: (1) competitors could maintain the lower price, or (2) competitors could reduce the price further. Suppose further that at the conclusion of step 3 in the DECIDE process (consider relevant information), El Macho executives examined the changes in market share and sales volume brought about by the pricing actions. They also calculated the contribution per unit of frozen dinners for each alternative for each competitor response. They performed a contribution analysis because the problem was defined in terms of contribution to advertising and sales promotion in step 1 of the DECIDE process (define the problem).

Given two alternatives, two competitive responses, and the calculation of contribution for each combination, four unique financial outcomes were identified. The situation described can be displayed in the decision tree shown in Exhibit 3.1.

It is apparent from the decision tree that El Macho will generate the largest contribution if the firm maintains its price on frozen dinners *and* competitors maintain their lower price. However, if El Macho maintains its price and competitors reduce their price on frozen dinners further, the lowest contribution among the four outcomes identified will be generated. The choice of an alternative obviously depends on the uncertainties in the environment and the likelihood of their occurrence.

A *payoff table* is a useful tool for displaying the alternatives, outcomes, and uncertainties facing a firm. In addition, a payoff table includes another dimension—management's subjective determination of the probability of the occurrence of an uncertainty. Suppose, for example, that El Macho management believe that competitors are most likely to maintain the lower price regardless of El Macho's action. This belief is based on the assumption that competitors are also operating with slim contribution margins. Therefore, they believe that there is a 10 percent chance that competitors will reduce the price of frozen din-

EXHIBIT 3.1
Decision Tree

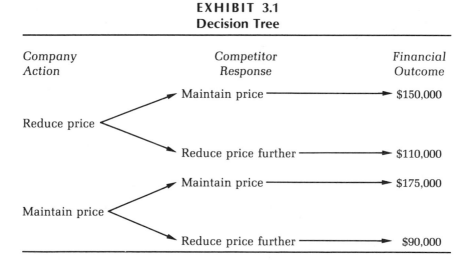

Company Action	Competitor Response	Financial Outcome
Reduce price	Maintain price	$150,000
	Reduce price further	$110,000
Maintain price	Maintain price	$175,000
	Reduce price further	$90,000

ners even further.[5] Since only two uncertainties are identified, the subjective probability of competitors maintaining their price is 90 percent
(note that the probabilities assigned to the uncertainties must total 1.0,
or 100 percent). Given these probabilities, the payoff table for El
Macho Foods is shown in Exhibit 3.2.

The payoff table allows the manager or case analyst to compute
the "expected value" of each alternative. The expected value is calculated by multiplying the outcome for each uncertainty by its probability of occurrence and then totaling across the uncertainties for each
alternative. The expected value of an alternative can be viewed as the
value obtained if the manager were to choose the same alternative
many times under the same conditions.

The expected value of the price-reduction alternative equals the
probability that competitors will maintain prices, multiplied by the
financial contribution if competitors maintain prices, plus the probability that competitors will further reduce prices, multiplied by the
financial contribution if competitors further reduce prices. The calculation is:

$$(0.9)(\$150,000) + (0.1)(\$110,000) = \$135,000 + \$11,000 = \$146,000$$

The expected value of maintaining the price is:

$$(0.9)(\$175,000) + (0.1)(\$90,000) = \$157,500 + \$9,000 = \$166,500$$

Therefore, El Macho management should maintain its price because of
the higher average contribution of $166,500. The higher contribution is
obtained because competitors are expected to maintain their prices
nine times out of ten. Under the same conditions (same outcomes,
same probability estimates), El Macho would achieve an average con-

EXHIBIT 3.2
Payoff Table

	Uncertainties	
Alternatives	Competitors Maintain Price (Probability = 0.9)	Competitors Reduce Price (Probability = 0.1)
Reduce price	$150,000	$110,000
Maintain price	$175,000	$ 90,000

tribution of $146,000 if the price-reduction alternative were chosen. A rational management would therefore select the price-maintenance alternative.

Familiarity with decision analysis is important for four reasons. First, decision analysis is a fundamental tool for considering "what if" situations. By displaying alternatives, uncertainties, and outcomes in this manner, a manager or case analyst becomes sensitive to the dynamic processes present in a competitive environment. Second, decision analysis forces the case analyst to quantify outcomes associated with specific actions. Third, decision analysis is useful in a variety of settings. For example, Ford Motor Company used decision analysis in deciding whether to produce its own tires; Pillsbury used decision analysis in determining whether to switch from a box to a bag for a certain grocery product.[6] Fourth, an extension of decision analysis can be used in determining the value of "perfect" information. This topic is discussed in Chapter 4.

Develop a Plan for Implementing the Chosen Alternative

The selection of a course of action must be followed by a plan for its implementation. Simply deciding what to do will not make it happen. The execution phase is critical and forces the case analyst to consider resource allocation and timing questions. For example, if a new product launch is recommended, then it is important to consider how managerial, financial, and manufacturing resources will be allocated to this course of action. If a price reduction is recommended, it will be important to monitor whether the reduced prices are reaching the final consumer and not being absorbed by resellers in the marketing channel. Timing is crucial, since a marketing plan takes time to develop and implement.

As a final note, it is important to recognize that strategy formulation and implementation are not necessarily separate sequential processes. Rather, an interactive give-and-take process occurs between formulation and implementation until the case analyst realizes that "what might be done can be done," given organizational strengths and market requirements. Another reading of the discussion on the marketing mix in Chapter 1 will highlight these points.

Evaluate the Decision and the Decision Process

The last step in the decision-making process involves evaluating the decision made and the decision process itself. With respect to the decision itself, two questions should be asked. First, *Was a decision made?* This seemingly odd question refers to a common shortcoming in many case analyses, whereby a case analyst does not make a decision but, rather, "talks about" the situation facing the organization. Failure to act decisively can have even more disastrous results in a business setting. The unwillingness or inability of Woolco's management to decide whether to be a variety, discount, or medium-priced store chain in the 1960s resulted in the closing of 336 stores in 1983 as a result of highly unprofitable operations.[7]

The second question asks: *Was the decision appropriate, given the situation identified in the case setting?* This question speaks to the issue of insufficient information on the one hand and the failure to consider and interpret information on the other. In many marketing cases, and indeed in actual business situations, *all* the information necessary to make a decision is simply not available. Though a source of frustration, incomplete information requires that assumptions be made. A case analyst is often expected to make assumptions to fill in gaps, but such assumptions should be logically developed and articulated. Merely making assumptions to make the "solution" fit a preconceived notion of a correct answer is a death knell in case analysis and business practice.

The case analyst should constantly monitor how he or she applies the decision-making process. The mere coincidence that one's decision was right is not sufficient reason to think that the decision process was appropriate. For example, we have all found ourselves lost while looking for an address of a home or business. We somehow find it but are again at a loss when asked to direct someone to the same address. This analogy applies to arriving at a "correct" solution. The case analyst may arrive at the solution but be unable to outline (map) the process involved.

After a class discussion of a case, a written case assignment, or a group presentation, the case analyst should critically examine his or her performance. The following questions might be helpful:

1. Did I define the problem adequately?
2. Did I identify all pertinent alternatives and uncertainties?
3. Did I consider information relevant to the case?
4. Did I recommend the appropriate course of action? If so, was my logic consistent with the recommendation? If not, were my assumptions different from other assumptions? Did I overlook an important piece of information?
5. Did I consider how my recommendation could be implemented?

Honest answers to these questions will improve the chances of making better decisions in the future.

CASE ANALYSIS

How do I prepare a case? This question is voiced by virtually every student exposed to the case method for the first time. In actuality, the question also expresses the problem, How do I approach a marketing problem?

A major difficulty in preparing a case for presentation—or, more generally, resolving an actual marketing problem—is in structuring your thinking process to address relevant forces confronting the organization. The previous discussion of the decision-making process should be of help in this regard. The remainder of this chapter provides some useful hints to assist you in preparing a marketing case.

Approaching the Case

In approaching a marketing case, you should read the case once to become acquainted with the situation in which the organization finds itself. This first reading should provide some insights into the problem requiring resolution as well as background information on the environment and organization.

A second reading of the case should follow. Here you should take careful notes with particular emphasis on key facts or assumptions. At this juncture, you should determine the relevance and reliability of the quantitative data provided in the case in the context of what you see as the issues or problems facing the organization. Valuable insights often arise from analyzing two or more bits of quantitative information concurrently.

You should avoid three pitfalls during the second reading. First, *do not rush to a conclusion.* If you do so, it will quickly become apparent that information has been overlooked or possibly distorted to fit a preconceived notion of the answer. Second, *do not "work the numbers"* until their meaning and derivation are understood. Third, *do not confuse supposition with fact.* Many statements are made in a case, such as "Our firm subscribes to the marketing concept." Is this a fact, given an appraisal of the firm's actions and performance, or a supposition?

Formulating the Analysis

The previous remarks should provide some direction in approaching a marketing case. The marketing case analysis worksheet shown in Exhibit 3.3, provides a framework for organizing information. Four analytical categories are shown with illustrative questions pertaining to each. You will find it useful to consider each analytical category when preparing a case.

Nature of the Industry, Market, and Buyer Behavior

The first analytical category focuses on the organization's environment. It is here that the context in which the organization operates should be established. Specific topics of interest include: (1) an assessment of the structure, conduct, and performance of the industry and competition and (2) an understanding of who the buyers are, and why, where, when, how, what, and how much they buy.

The Organization

Second, you should develop an understanding of the organization's financial, human, and material resources, its strengths and weaknesses, and the reasons for its success or failure. Of particular importance is an understanding of what the organization wishes to do. The "fit" between the organization and its environment represents the first major link to be drawn in case analysis. This link is the situation analysis, since it is an interpretation of where the organization currently stands.

A Plan of Action

You should be prepared to identify possible courses of action on the basis of the situation analysis. More often than not, several alternatives are possible, and each should be fully articulated. Each course of action typically has associated costs and revenues. These should be carefully determined and realistically reflect the magnitude of effort expected in their pursuit.

Potential Outcomes

Finally, the potential outcomes of all courses of action identified should be evaluated. On the basis of the appraisal of outcomes, one course of action or strategy should be recommended. It should be emphasized, however, that your evaluation must illustrate not only why the recommendation was preferred but also why other actions were dismissed.

Even though it is always useful to consider each of the analytical categories just described, the method of arranging them may vary. There is no one way to analyze a case, just as there is no single correct way to attack a marketing problem. Just be sure to cover the bases.

EXHIBIT 3.3
Marketing Case Analysis Worksheet

Specific Points of Interest

Nature of industry, market,
and buyer behavior

1. What is the nature of industry structure,
   conduct, and performance?
2. Who are the competitors, and what are
   their strengths and weaknesses?
3. How do consumers buy in this industry or
   market?
4. Can the market be segmented? How? Can
   the segments be quantified?
5. What are the requirements for success in
   this industry?

The organization

1. What are the organization's mission,
   objectives, and distinctive competency?
2. What is its offering to the market? What is
   its past and present performance? What is
   its potential?
3. What is the situation in which the
   manager or organization finds itself?
4. What factors have contributed to the
   present situation?

A plan of action

1. What actions are available to the
   organization?
2. What are the costs and benefits of each
   action in both qualitative and quantitative
   terms?
3. Is there a disparity between what an
   organization wants to do, should do, can
   do, and must do?

Potential outcomes

1. What will be the buyer, trade, and
   competitive response to each course of
   action?
2. How will each course of action satisfy
   buyer, trade, and organization
   requirements?
3. What is the potential profitability of each
   course of action?
4. Will the action enhance or reduce the
   organization's ability to compete in the
   future?

Communicating the Analysis

Three settings exist for communicating case analyses: (1) class discussion, (2) group presentation, and (3) written reports.

Class Discussion

Discussing case studies in the classroom setting can be an exciting experience, provided each student actively *prepares* for and *participates* in the discussion. Preparation means more than simply reading the case prior to the scheduled class period. Rather, the case should have been carefully analyzed using the four analytical categories described earlier. Four to five hours of preparation are usually required for each assigned case. The notes developed during the preparation should be brought to class.

Participation involves more than talking. Other students should be carefully watched and listened to during a class discussion. Attentiveness to the views of others provides opportunities to build on previous comments and analyses. Furthermore, most class discussions follow a similar format. Class analysis begins with a discussion of the organization and its environment. This discussion is first followed by a discussion of the alternative courses of action and then by a consideration of possible implementation. Knowing where the class is in the discussion is important both for organizing the multitude of ideas and analyses presented and preparing remarks for the subsequent steps in the class discussion.

Immediately after class discussion, you should prepare a short summary of the analysis developed in class. This summary includes specific facts, ideas, analyses, and generalizations developed. The summary is useful in comparing and contrasting case situations.

Group Presentations

Group presentation of a case requires a slightly different set of skills. In this setting a group of three to five students conduct a rigorous analysis of a case and present it to classmates. Role playing may be featured in this setting; class members serve as an executive committee witnessing the analysis and interpretation of a task force or project team.

If the instructor asks students to form groups, consider the following advice. First, do not form groups solely on the basis of friendship. Rather, try to develop a balanced team where various skills complement each other (financial skills, oral presentation skills, and so on). Second, seek out individuals who are committed and dependable. Finally, organize the efforts of the group around individual interests and skills.

A polished presentation is very important in this setting. Therefore, group members should rehearse the presentation, and each group member should seriously critique the performance of other group members. A text on oral presentations or guidelines for effective speaking can be consulted. At the very least, the following steps should be taken. First, prepare an outline of the presentation (including important exhibits) and distribute it to the class. Second, use transparencies to highlight important points and unique analyses. But *do not* read transparencies to your audience.

Written Reports
The content of written analysis of a case assignment is similar to what you *should* have been doing when preparing for class discussion. The only difference is in the submission of the analysis; a written report should be carefully organized, legible (typically typed), and grammatically correct.

There is no one correct approach for organizing a written case analysis. However, it is usually wise to think about the report as falling under three major headings: (1) identification of the strategic issues and problems, (2) analysis and evaluation, and (3) recommendations.[8] The first heading should contain a focused paragraph that defines the problem and specifies the constraints and options available to the organization. Material under the second heading should provide a carefully developed assessment of the industry, market and buyer behavior, the organization, and the alternative courses of action. *Analysis and evaluation should represent the bulk of the written report.* This section *should not* contain a restatement of case information. It *should* contain an *assessment* of the facts, quantitative data, and management views. The last heading should contain a set of recommendations. These recommendations should be documented from the previous section and should be *operational* given the case situation. By all means, commit to a decision!

A case and a written student analysis of the case is presented in the appendix at the end of the book. It is recommended that you carefully analyze the case before reading the student analysis.

NOTES

1. Herbert A. Simon, *The New Science of Management Decision* (New York: Harper & Row, 1960).

2. Peter Drucker, "How to Make a Business Decision," *Nation's Business* (April 1956): 38–39.

3. There are a variety of systematic approaches to the decision-making process. For a review, see Ernest R. Archer, "How to Make a Business Decision: An Analysis of Theory and Practice," *Management Review* (February 1980): 54–61.

4. DECIDE acronym copyright © 1981, 1973 by William Rudelius. It is used here with permission. For another description of DECIDE, see William Rudelius, W. Bruce Erickson, William J. Bakula, Jr., and Jeanne Hanson, *An Introduction to Contemporary Business,* 3rd ed. (New York: Harcourt Brace Jovanovich, 1981), Chapter 4.

5. A frequent issue in developing these subjective probabilities is how to select them. One source is past experience. In Chapter 1, for example, the "probability of success" for alternative strategies was described by A. T. Kearney. Alternatively, case information can lead to probability estimates. At the very least, when two possible uncertainties exist, a subjective probability of 0.5 can be assigned to each. This means that the two uncertainties have an equal chance of occurring. These probabilities can be revised up or down, depending on case information.

6. These examples and others are found in Jacob W. Ulvila and Rex V. Brown, "Decision Analysis Comes of Age," *Harvard Business Review* (September–October 1982): 130–141.

7. "Finally, Woolworth Wields the Axe," *Business Week* (October 11, 1982): 118–119.

8. For an expanded discussion on these headings, see A. J. Strickland III and Arthur A. Thompson, Jr., *Cases in Strategic Management* (Plano, Tex.: Business Publications, Inc., 1982), 13–18.

ADDITIONAL READINGS

Decision-Making Process and Decision Analysis

Archer, Ernest R. "How to Make a Business Decision: An Analysis of Theory and Practice." *Management Review* (February 1980): 54–61.

Simon, Herbert A. "Rational Decision Making in Business Organizations." *American Economic Review* (September 1979): 493–513.

Ulvila, Jacob, and Brown, Rex V. "Decision Analysis Comes of Age." *Harvard Business Review* (September–October 1982): 130–141.

Case Analysis Approaches

Peter, J. Paul; Donnelly, James H., Jr.; and Tarpey, Lawrence X. *A Preface to Marketing Management,* 3rd ed. Plano, Tex.: Business Publications, Inc., 1985. Section II: "Analyzing Marketing Problems and Cases."

Ronstadt, Robert. *The Art of Case Analysis,* 2nd ed. Dover, Mass.: Lord Publishing Company, 1980.

CHAPTER 4

Opportunity Analysis and Market Targeting

THE DEVELOPMENT AND IMPLEMENTATION of marketing strategy is a complicated and challenging task. At its pinnacle, marketing strategy involves the selection of markets and the development of programs to reach these markets. This is done in a manner that simultaneously benefits both the markets selected (satisfying the needs or wants of buyers) and the organization (typically in dollar profit terms).

Within this framework, a necessary first task is *opportunity analysis* and *market targeting*. This chapter describes analytical concepts and tools that the marketing manager will find useful in performing opportunity analyses and selecting market targets.

OPPORTUNITY ANALYSIS

Opportunity analysis consists of three interrelated processes:

- Opportunity identification
- Opportunity-organization matching
- Opportunity evaluation

Opportunities arise from identifying new types or classes of buyers, uncovering unsatisfied needs of buyers, or creating new ways or means for satisfying buyer needs. In short, opportunity analysis focuses on finding a market niche(s) for the organization.

An example from the computer industry highlights the *opportunity identification* process in practice.[1] Historically, computer buyers have responded to advances in computer technology. Buyer needs in the early 1970s consisted of increased computer capabilities, and the means for satisfying these needs required heavy research and development expenditures by manufacturers. Accordingly, large sophisticated and centralized computer installations were the growth segment. However, in the late 1970s buyer needs shifted toward "distributed" computer capability, exemplified in the desire to have computers where data originate or information is needed. These shifted needs prompted the development of "plug-compatible" computer equipment that easily tied into existing computer facilities. Such new equipment required little in the way of research and development expenditures. This transformation of buyer needs (full office automation) prompted new ways to satisfy these needs (plug-compatible equipment) that has become a viable market niche for many small manufacturers. Only recently have large manufacturers attempted to compete in this market niche.

Opportunity-organization matching determines whether an identified market niche is consistent with the definition of the organization's business, purpose, and distinctive competency. This determination usually requires a self-assessment of the organization's purpose, strengths, and weaknesses and an identification of the requirements for success to operate profitably in the market niche. For example, the Gillette Company never took advantage of the market opportunity for feminine hygiene sprays, even though the aerosol technology and marketing experience in introducing feminine products existed. This situation allegedly occurred because Gillette executives could not bring themselves to use certain parts of the female anatomy in their business conversations.[2] The product simply was inconsistent with Gillette's business definition. Similarly, no steam locomotive manufacturers entered the field of diesel locomotives, and most manufacturers of safety razor blades avoid producing electric shavers. The main cause for all of these actions is usually the difficulty or unwillingness to modify organizational strategy.

Opportunity evaluation typically consists of two distinct phases—one qualitative and one quantitative. The qualitative dimension focuses on matching attractiveness of an opportunity with the potential for uncovering a market niche. Attractiveness is dependent on (1) competitive activity; (2) buyer requirements; (3) market demand and supplier sources; (4) social, political, economic, and technological forces; and (5) organizational capabilities.[3] Each of these factors, in turn, must be tied to its impact on the types of buyers sought, the needs of buyers, and the means for satisfying these needs. Exhibit 4.1 shows an opportunity evaluation matrix and illustrative questions

EXHIBIT 4.1

Opportunity Evaluation Matrix: Attractiveness Criteria

Market Niche Criteria	Competitive Activity	Buyer Requirements	Demand/Supply	Political, Technological, and Socioeconomic Forces	Organizational Capabilities
Buyer type	How many and which firms are competing for this user group?	What affects the willingness and ability to buy?	Do different buyer types have different levels of effective demand? How important are adequate sources of supply?	How sensitive are different buyers to these forces?	Can we gain access to buyers through marketing mix variables? Can we supply these buyers?
Buyer needs	Which firms are satisfying which buyer needs?	Are there needs not being satisfied? What are they?	Are buyer needs likely to be long term? Do we have or can we acquire resources to satisfy buyer needs?	How sensitive are buyer needs to these forces?	Which needs can our organization satisfy?
Means for satisfying buyer needs	What are the strategies being employed for satisfying buyer needs?	Is the technology for satisfying needs changing?	To what extent are the means for satisfying buyer needs affected by supply sources? Is the demand for the means for satisfying buyer needs changing?	How sensitive are the means for satisfying buyer needs to these forces?	Do we have the financial, human, technological, and marketing expertise for satisfying buyer needs?

useful in the qualitative analysis of a market opportunity. The quantitative stage yields estimates of market potential, organization sales potential, and sales forecasts. It also produces budgets for financial, human, marketing, and production resources as necessary to assess the profitability of a market opportunity.

WHAT IS A MARKET?

Still, the identification and evaluation of an opportunity does not necessarily imply that a *market* exists for the organization. While definitions vary, a market may be considered as the prospective buyers (individuals or organizations) willing and able to purchase the existing or potential offering (product or service) of an organization.

Several managerial implications arise from this definition of a market. First, the definition focuses on buyers, not on products or services. People and organizations whose idiosyncrasies dictate whether and how products and services will be acquired, consumed, or used make up markets. Second, by highlighting a buyer's willingness and ability to purchase a product or service, the concept of *effective demand* is introduced. Even if buyers are willing to purchase a product or service, exchange cannot occur unless they are able to do so. Alternatively, if buyers are able to purchase a product or service but are unwilling to do so, then again exchange will not occur. These relationships are important to grasp because a marketing strategist must ascertain the extent of effective demand for an offering to determine whether a market exists. Third, use of the term *offering*, rather than product or service, expands the definition of what organizations provide for buyers. Products and services are not purchased for the sake of a purchase; they are purchased for the values or benefits that buyers expect to derive from them. It is for this reason that the late Charles Revson of Revlon Cosmetics continually reiterated that his company did not sell cosmetics but, rather, hope. This expanded definition of an offering requires strategists to consider benefits provided by a product or service apart from its tangible nature.

A further distinction must be made when considering what is meant by a "market." Frequently one hears or reads about the automobile market, the soft drink market, or the health-care market. These terms can be misleading because each is a composite of multiple minimarkets. Consider, for example, the "coffee market." Exhibit 4.2 shows how the "coffee market" might be viewed by a marketing strategist for Maxwell House Coffee or Folger's Coffee. Exhibit 4.2 shows that multiple markets exist for coffee. For competitive purposes, it is much

EXHIBIT 4.2
Market Structure for Coffee

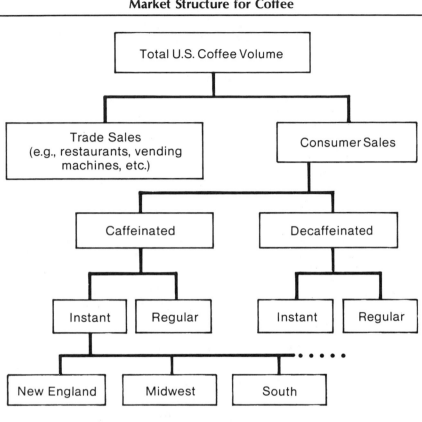

more useful to consider consumer sales of instant decaffeinated coffee in the Midwest than the "coffee market" in its entirety.

When a market is viewed as shown in Exhibit 4.2, the marketing manager can better gauge marketing opportunities. For example, the manager can more effectively identify who is competing in the caffeinated versus the decaffeinated market, monitor changes in sales volume for instant decaffeinated coffee, and appreciate differences in buyer taste preferences in the South versus the Pacific Coast.

Finally, the concept of *market share* becomes more meaningful. Market share can be defined as the sales of a firm, product, or brand divided by the sales of the "market." Obviously, market definition is critical in calculating this percentage.[4] For example, consider Brand X, an instant, decaffeinated coffee brand with annual sales of $1 billion.

Based on the definition of the market, the brand's share will range from 12.5 percent to 50 percent as shown in the following table.

Market Definition	Dollar Sales	Brand X Sales	Market Share
U.S. coffee market	$8 billion	$1 billion	12.5%
U.S. decaffeinated coffee market	$4 billion	$1 billion	25.0%
U.S. instant decaffeinated coffee market	$2 billion	$1 billion	50.0%

MARKET SEGMENTATION

A useful concept for structuring markets is *market segmentation*—the breaking down or building up of potential buyers into groups. These groups are typically termed *market segments*. Each segment is thought of as possessing some sort of homogeneous characteristic relating to its purchasing or consumption behavior, which is ultimately reflected in its responsiveness to marketing programs.

Market segmentation came about from the recognition that, in general, an organization cannot be all things to all people. While Henry Ford is reputed to have said that buyers of his automobiles could have any color they desired as long as it was black, most marketers now agree that such an undifferentiated marketing strategy is no longer appropriate. For a variety of reasons, the idea that an organization can effectively apply one marketing strategy to all possible buyers is no longer viable.

At the other extreme, unless the organization is highly specialized and sells only to, say, one buyer, it is not feasible to treat each potential buyer as unique. Thus, as Enis has so aptly written, market segmentation "is a compromise between the ineffectiveness of treating all customers alike and the inefficiency of treating each one differently."[5]

Segmentation offers two principal benefits with regard to the development of marketing strategy. First, needs, wants, and behaviors of specific groups of buyers are more precisely determined. More specifically, answers to the following six fundamental questions are made possible for each buyer segment:

1. *Who* are they?
2. *What* do they want to buy?

3. *How* do they want to buy?
4. *When* do they want to buy?
5. *Where* do they want to buy?
6. *Why* do they want to buy?

Second, a more proper allocation of resources is possible in designing marketing mix activities to satisfy the needs, wants, and behaviors of buyers.

Simultaneously, though, these advantages must be considered in view of their costs. Research costs are associated with identifying appropriate market segments. Likewise, there are added expenses incurred in designing more than one or different marketing strategies, including the design of offerings, salesperson training, and possibly multiple channel selection.

A variety of measures are useful for segmenting markets. A brief listing would include the following:

- Socioeconomic characteristics such as sex, occupation, income, family life cycle, education, or geographic location
- Buying and usage characteristics such as end use versus intermediate use, buying for another versus buying for self, size of purchase, or volume of consumption
- Benefits sought from products or services, such as status, economy, taste, convenience of use

Measures used for segmenting markets vary depending on their relative contribution to the manager's knowledge of buyer behavior and effective demand exhibited. Whichever measure is selected, it must meet a number of important requirements. First, the measure should assist in the identification of distinct groups of prospective buyers. Second, the groups identified should be economically accessible to a product or service organization through existing or possible marketing programs. Finally, the groups should be large enough in terms of sales volume potential to support the costs of the organization serving it.

OFFERING-MARKET MATRIX

A useful procedure for investigating markets is to construct an *offering-market matrix*. Such a matrix relates offerings to selected groups of buyers. Exhibit 4.3 shows an illustrative matrix for calculators. Four

EXHIBIT 4.3
Product-Market Matrix for Calculators

Computational characteristics	Market segments (usage groups)			
	Business	Scientific	Home	School
Simple (arithmetic operations only)				
Moderate (arithmetic operations + squares + square root)				
Complex (all of above + trigonometric functions)				
Very complex (all of above + programmable features				

possible user groups (or market segments) are business, scientific, home, and school. By displaying offerings and user groups in this manner, gaps in the calculator market may be identified. In other words, it may be possible to identify which user groups are not being satisfied. Furthermore, competitors and their product offerings can be assigned to specific *cells*. Knowing where competitors are active provides a basis for determining if a market opportunity exists. Recognition of gaps in the market and knowledge of competitive activities in specific offering-market cells should assist in gauging the effective demand for an organization's offering and in the likelihood of developing a profitable marketing program. Regardless of whether the organization is investigating a potential or existing market, development of an offering-market matrix is often a prerequisite for market targeting.

MARKET TARGETS

After a market has been segmented, it is necessary to select the segment(s) on which marketing efforts will be focused. Market targeting (or target marketing) is merely the specification of the segment(s) the organization wishes to pursue. Once the manager selects the target market(s), the organization must then decide which marketing strategies to employ.

Two frequently used approaches are *differentiated* marketing and *concentrated* marketing. In a differentiated marketing approach, the organization simultaneously pursues several different market segments, usually with a unique marketing strategy for each. An example of this type of marketing is the strategy of Coca-Cola, which simultaneously markets a variety of soft drinks—Coca-Cola Classic, Mr. Pibb, Tab, and Fresca to name a few—to various market segments. A concentrated marketing approach exists when an organization focuses on a single market segment. An extreme case would be where an organization markets a single product offering to a single market segment. More commonly, an organization will offer a product line to a single segment. For many years Gerber proclaimed that "babies are our only business."

DETERMINING SALES POTENTIAL AND PROFITABILITY

Before an organization can employ target marketing, however, it is necessary to evaluate how much various possible market segments are worth. This is done by first determining the market potential of a segment and then estimating its sales potential—the sales a particular organization might expect to obtain from the segment. From the sales estimate it is possible to compute the potential profitability of the segment.

Market potential analysis provides a quantitative assessment of the unit or dollar sales volume in a specific, defined market segment. Once determined, it serves as the basis for estimating what the sales potential might be within the market segment. Sales potential is due, to a great extent, to the marketing program.

Profitability analysis follows from determining market-sales potential by deducting the likely costs of marketing programs from the estimated revenues. Market segments that provide the greatest profit contribution represent viable market targets for the organization.

NOTES

1. This example was drawn from "More Tumult for the Computer Industry," *Business Week* (May 30, 1977): 58–66.

2. W. Corley, "Gillette Co. Strategies as its Rivals Slice at Fat Profit Margins," *Wall Street Journal* (February 2, 1972): 1ff.

3. D. Abell and J. Hammond, *Strategic Market Planning: Problems and Analytical Approaches* (Englewood Cliffs, N.J.: Prentice-Hall, 1979), Chapter 2.

4. See, for example, Yoram Wind and Vijay Mahajan, "Market Share: Concepts, Findings and Directions for Future Research," in B. Enis and K. Roering, *Review of Marketing: 1981* (Chicago: American Marketing Association, 1981), pp. 31–42.

5. Ben M. Enis, *Marketing Principles: The Management Process,* 2nd ed. (Pacific Palisades, Calif.: Goodyear, 1977); p. 241.

ADDITIONAL READINGS

Bonoma, Thomas, and Shapiro, Benson. *Segmenting the Industrial Market.* Lexington, Mass.: Lexington Books, 1983.

Cook, James. "Where's the Niche?" *Forbes* (September 24, 1984): 54.

Day, George; Shocker, Allan; and Srivastava, Rajendra. "Customer-Oriented Approaches to Identifying Product Markets." *Journal of Marketing* (Fall 1979): 8–19.

Garda, Robert. "Strategic Segmentation: How to Carve Niches for Growth in Industrial Markets." *Management Review* (August 1981): 15–21.

Haley, Russell. "Benefit Segmentation—Twenty Years Later," *Journal of Consumer Marketing* 1, No. 2 (1984): 5–14.

Rothchild, William. "Surprise and Competitive Advantage." *Journal of Business Strategy* (Winter 1984): 10–18.

Wilson, Aubrey, and Atkin, Bryan. "Exorcizing the Ghosts in Marketing." *Harvard Business Review* (September–October 1976): 117–127.

Wind, Yoram. "Issues and Advances in Segmentation Research." *Journal of Marketing Research* (August 1978): 317–337.

Sorzal
Distributors

SORZAL DISTRIBUTORS IS an importer and distributor of a wide variety of South American and African artifacts. It is also a major source of southwestern Indian—especially Hopi and Navajo—authentic jewelry and pottery. Although the firm's headquarters is located in Phoenix, Arizona, there are currently branch offices in Los Angeles, Miami, and Boston.

Sorzal (named after the national bird of Honduras) originated as a trading post operation near Tucson, Arizona, in the early 1900s. Through a series of judicious decisions, the firm established itself as one of the more reputable dealers in authentic southwestern jewelry and pottery. Over the years, Sorzal gradually expanded its product line to include pre-Columbian artifacts from Peru and Venezuela and tribal and burial artifacts from Africa. By their careful verification of the authenticity of these South American and African artifacts, Sorzal Distributors developed a national reputation as one of the most respected importers of these types of artifacts.

In the late 1970s Sorzal further expanded its product line to include items that were replicas of authentic artifacts. For example, African fertility gods and masks were made by craftspeople who took great pains to produce these items so that only the truly knowledgeable buyer—a collector—would know the difference. Sorzal now has native craftspeople in Central and South America, in Africa, and in the southwestern United States who provide these items. Replicas account for only a small portion of total Sorzal sales; the company agreed to enter this business only at the prodding of the firm's clients, who desired an expanded line. The replicas have found most favor among gift buyers and individuals looking for novelty items.

Sorzal's gross sales are about $12 million and have increased at a constant rate of 20 percent per year over the last decade. Myron Rangard, the firm's national sales manager, attributed the sales increase to the popularity of its product line and to the expanded distribution of South American and African artifacts:

> For some reason, our South American and African artifacts have been gaining greater acceptance. Two of our department store customers featured examples of our African line in their Christmas catalogs last year. I personally think consumer tastes are changing from the modern and abstract to the more concrete, like our products.

Sorzal distributes its products exclusively through specialty shops (including interior decorators), firm-sponsored showings, and a few exclusive department stores. Often the company is the sole supplier to its clients. Mr. Rangard recently expressed the reasons for this highly limited distribution:

> Our limited distribution has been dictated to us because of the nature of our product line. As acceptance grew, we expanded our distribution to specialty shops and some exclusive department stores. Previously, we had to push our products through our own showings. Furthermore, we just didn't have the product. These South American artifacts aren't always easy to get and the political situation in Africa is limiting our supply. Our perennial supply problem has become even more critical in recent years for several reasons. Not only must we search harder for new products, but the competition for authentic artifacts has increased tenfold. On top of this, we must now contend with governments not allowing exportation of certain artifacts because of their "national significance." Increasingly, our people are feeling like Indiana Jones in the movie *Raiders of the Lost Ark* or the *Temple of Doom!*

The problem of supply has forced Sorzal to add three new buyers in the last two years. Whereas Sorzal identified five major competitors a decade ago, there are eleven today. "Our bargaining position has eroded," noted David Olsen, director of procurement. "We have watched our gross margin slip in recent years due to aggressive competitive bidding by others."

"And competition at the retail level has increased also," injected Mr. Rangard. "Not only are some of our specialty and exclusive department store customers sending out their own buyers to deal directly with some of our Hopi and Navajo suppliers, but we are often faced with amateurs or fly-by-night competitors. These people move into a city and dump a bunch of inauthentic junk on the public at exorbitant prices. Such antics give the industry a bad name."

In recent years several mass-merchandise department store chains and a number of upper-scale discount operations have begun to sell merchandise similar to that offered by Sorzal. Even though product quality was often mixed and most items were replicas, occasionally an authentic group of items was found in these stores, according to company sales representatives. Subsequent inquiries by both Rangard and Olsen revealed that other competing distributors had signed purchase contracts with these outlets. Moreover, the items were typically being sold at retail prices below those charged by Sorzal's dealers.

Late one spring morning, Mr. Rangard was contacted by a mass-merchandise department store chain concerning the possibility of carrying a complete line of Sorzal products. The chain was currently selling a competitor's items but wished to add a more exclusive product line. A tentative contract submitted by the chain stated that it would buy at 10 percent below Sorzal's existing prices, and that its initial purchase would be for no less than $250,000. Depending on consumer acceptance, purchases were estimated to be at least $1 million annually. An important clause in the contract dealt with the supply of replicas. Inspection of this clause revealed that Sorzal would have to triple its replica production to satisfy the contractual obligation. Soon after executives of Sorzal Distributors began discussing the contract, the president mentioned that accepting the contract could have a dramatic effect on how Sorzal defined its business.

Case

Apple Computer, Inc.

EDWARD REUTEMANN, NEWLY APPOINTED manager for home computer markets at Apple Computer, Inc., was faced with a problem. It was November 1982, and since February of that year Mr. Reutemann had been studying the market potential for personal computers in the home market. Very soon he had to present his recommendations to the board of directors concerning whether or not Apple should aggressively enter the home computer market, and if so, how. Mr. Reutemann defined the home computer as "a computer purchased with personal disposable income for use primarily in the home."

INDUSTRY AND COMPANY BACKGROUND

In 1982 the personal computer (or microcomputer) market was a young one, and represented the fastest-growing segment of the dynamic computer industry (see Exhibit 1). The power and versatility of the IC (integrated circuit) silicon chip of the personal computer only began to be realized in 1974. As stated in *Business Week*:

> Since 1976 when Apple Computer, Inc. rolled out its strange little machine, built around a microprocessor chip, the market for personal com-

This case was made possible by the cooperation of Apple Computer, Inc. It was prepared by graduate students Roger A. Olsen and Mui Jin Tan under the supervision of Dr. Stuart U. Rich, professor of marketing, College of Business Administration, University of Oregon. The case was designed for class discussion rather than to illustrate either effective or ineffective handling of an administrative situation.

This case is reproduced with the permission of its author, Dr. Stuart U. Rich, professor of marketing, and director, Forest Industries Management Center, College of Business Administration, University of Oregon, Eugene, Oregon.

EXHIBIT 1
Apple Computer, Inc.: Computer Sales of Major Industry Sectors

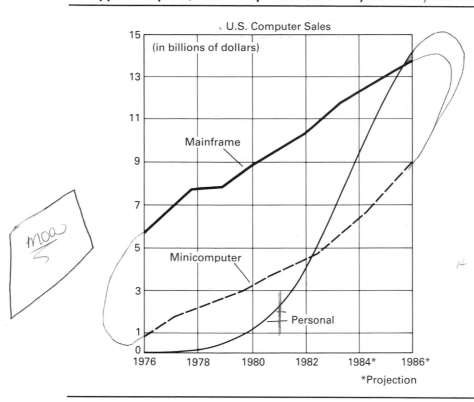

U.S. Computer Sales (in billions of dollars)

Source: International Data Corporation.

puters has grown from scratch to $6.1 billion in worldwide sales this year [1982]. By 1986 sales are expected to climb to $21 billion, according to InfoCorp, a California marketing research firm. The personal computer has made it possible for Apple, Commodore International, and Tandy, despite the recession, to turn in a string of record quarterly profits.[1]

The technology of the market was rapidly changing toward making a more powerful (more memory capacity and capabilities) computer at lower prices, with more and better software. In addition, because consumers were becoming better educated and trained in computer usage and because of the increased variety and pricing patterns of personal computers, they now tended to shop for the best buy for their dollars. Most personal computers now had some form of word processing that was standard or could be added.

The personal computer market was a highly competitive one, with over 150 manufacturers and 8,000 computer retail outlets in the United States in 1982. The number of manufacturers had been increasing so rapidly that they had to compete aggressively with one another to get their computers on the retailers' shelves, in spite of the corresponding rapid growth in retail outlets. Apple, in order to differentiate itself from the numerous manufacturers in the market, and to make the retailer more willing to stock its machines, had been advertising heavily. It spent $15 million on advertising in 1981, the highest in the industry. The company increased its consumer awareness factor from 20 percent to 80 percent that year. Its primary advertising audience was men, with income of $35,000 and up, in business and management positions.[2]

Apple was a pioneer in the personal computer market. In fact, it was cited as one of the greatest success stories of the 1970s. The company was started in 1976 by two college dropouts, Steve Jobs and Steven Woznick, who built their first personal computer in a garage with money obtained from the sale of their VW bus and calculator. Since then the company had risen to become one of the largest manufacturers of personal computers, with 1982 sales projected at $589 million and a market value of $1.2 billion. Even with that year's recession, Apple's third-quarter sales had risen 80 percent and profits 70 percent. The founders were smart enough to attract highly qualified top executives to lead their company, and successfully hired away experienced managers from companies such as Intel, Fairchild, Atari, and National Semiconductor. An example of this was the current president and CEO of Apple, Mr. A. C. Markkula, Jr., who had previously been marketing manager for Intel. The prior experiences of these top executives helped Apple minimize any rapid expansion problems and personnel problems with its organization and production during its first five years.

Since its inception, the company had a philosophy that it was primarily a personal computer company, producing quality personal computers, not a home entertainment or software developer. The common industry definition of personal computers was systems costing less than $15,000. Personal computers, including Apple's, normally consisted of a keyboard containing the electronic computer circuits, that was attached to a television set, which was used as a display screen, or was attached to a monitor screen built specifically for the computer. The IC chip was that part of the computer circuit that had storage and memory capabilities. Apple currently bought its IC chips from outside suppliers. However, IBM, Hewlett-Packard, and Commodore produced their own chips, and some industry observers felt that these companies would be better able to reduce the prices of their computers because of the vertical integration of chip production into their computer production process.

To make fuller use of the computer, a consumer might have to spend hundreds of dollars more for additional equipment (known as *peripherals*), such as more internal computer memory, which extended the machine's capabilities; disk devices for storing data; and printers. (These peripherals and the computer itself are known as *hardware*.) Apple's first computer hardware, the Apple II, was a resounding success and remained the best industry seller through 1982. Apple had tried to duplicate this success with the more powerful Apple III in 1980 too quickly and ran into technical problems. Apple had to recall it and debug it before reintroducing it in late 1981. In 1982 Apple was currently selling the Apple III, with 128K (measurement of memory size),[3] at a suggested retail price of $2,995.

To serve its customers fully, Apple also sold software with its computers. A complete computer system consisted of both hardware and software. (*Software programs* are instructions that tell the computer how to compute a mortgage or how to play a space war game.) Software in 1982 generally ranged in price from a few dollars to a few thousand dollars, depending on the sophistication of the application. Software programs came in three forms: as cartridges similar to those containing video games that plug into the computer, on cassette tapes, or on flexible disks about the size of 45 rpm records. The most popular form was the flexible disk (*floppy disk*), since it was the most efficient and most reliable.

There were two kinds of software in the personal computer market. The most familiar type was applications software that instructed the computer to perform specific tasks. The second type—the operating system—made up the guts of the machine and formed its internal logic structure. The key to applications software lay in the operating system software, because software written for one operating system would not work on a computer with a different internal structure. In 1982 there were three standard operating systems in the industry: CPM (Control Process Mode), MS-DOS (Disk Operating System), and Apple's DOS system. Apple's DOS system had become the standard for the early eight-bit systems.[4] Although Apple II and Apple III could be converted to CPM, there was an additional cost of between $400 and $450. In the more powerful sixteen-bit machines, the leaders were CPM and MS-DOS. IBM had adopted the CPM system as its principal operating system for personal computers. There was a trend toward moving to the sixteen-bit computer in the upper-end market, which included the professional and business users.

Apple had been particularly successful in having other entrepreneurs develop software and peripherals used with the Apple II and Apple III. This had been particularly helpful during the earlier years, when resources were needed to develop the company's Apple II and III markets. In fact, Apple was said to owe much of its success to an ingenious business forecasting program called VISICALC, which initially had been available only on Apple. There was more software available for Apple computers than for any other personal computers. Apple produced some of its own software and most of its peripherals, too. IBM, Apple's greatest competitor, was known for writing and supporting its own software, and in 1982 IBM was expected eventually to produce more business and professional software than Apple. (Mr. Markkula was reported to have said at this time, "Apple's three biggest competitors are IBM, IBM, and IBM.")

NEW PRODUCTS

Apple planned to introduce new products starting in early 1983 to help its overall market mix and to compete more effectively at both the upper and lower ends of the market. The new Apple IIe would replace the five-year-old Apple II with the same good features but with a slightly better memory, normally purchased options standard, and all at about the same price, $1,995. Another new product was the Lisa, which would be a computer that was more "user-friendly" (easier for the novice to use) than the Apple II. It was supposed to reduce learning time from twenty hours to twenty minutes so as to overcome the new user's hesitancy and fear of computers. It was planned to be introduced in 1983 and was designed for the higher-end users. It had a much greater memory capability than the Apple II, which was the most powerful Apple the company currently had in 1982. The Lisa was to be priced to compete with IBM's and Xerox's personal computers, primarily in the business, small business, and industrial segments. Finally, it was rumored that yet another new product, code-named the Macintosh, would be introduced at some later date than the Lisa, and would incorporate the technical features of the Lisa, but would sell at a lower price.

DISTRIBUTION

Apple tried to maintain its high quality and dealer service and its training image by being selective in the development of its retail outlets. However, a Business Week interview with more than forty leading hardware, software, and peripheral equipment makers, industry consultants; and analysts indicated that Apple lagged behind IBM and Tandy in service and support.[5] In 1981, because of displeasure with some Computerland franchise operations, Apple had terminated its blanket computer contract with the company. After that, each store had to sign a separate contract agreeing to Apple's terms of service and training, thus giving Apple more control over its distribution outlets. Apple's distribution system in 1982 included four types of outlets: stereo/electronic retailers; computer specialty stores; franchised computer specialty stores (similar to the second type); and office equipment stores. During 1982 the company opened outlets in several department store chains, but Apple's management was somewhat concerned about the ability of these retailers to service and support the end user (the computer buyer). Apple also sold direct. It had recently hired its own sales force of 300 to service and sell to the *Fortune* 1,000 largest companies, after it had worked out financial arrangements with local retailers who had feared this might cut into their sales.

Apple depended almost entirely on retailers to sell its products. Management felt that this freed Apple from the necessity of having a large sales force and capital expenditure for its own stores, and allowed the company to concentrate on producing quality products. Selling through retail outlets had also solved many of Apple's rapid growth problems in sales. There were 1,300 Apple outlets in 1982. At that time, Radio Shack (Tandy) had the most distribution outlets (6,180), with Atari second with 2,500 outlets. Radio Shack's outlets consisted of some 6,000 electronics stores of its own ("supermarkets" of electronic equipment), plus its separate chain of 180 computer centers. It also had a small national accounts sales force to call on major corporations. Atari's outlets were independent and chain retailers and mass merchandisers. In 1982 IBM used several different distribution channels: the sales force of its Data Processing Division (which also sold the company's mainframe computers and minicomputers), the Computerland chain of franchised computer stores, Sears's office equipment and supply stores (called Sears Business Systems Centers), and finally its own retail stores (called IBM Product Centers). By the latter part of 1982, IBM had 38 of these IBM Product Centers, and was reported to be planning to add 100 more during the coming year.

One problem that had been created in the industry by the rapidly falling prices of computers was that of the decreasing profit margins to retailers. Apple usually gave its retailers a 37.5 percent margin, which was about standard for the whole market for computers over $1,000. However, after deducting for servicing, training, royalties, and other overhead costs, the effective margin for retailers was only about 17 percent. Since prices were decreasing because of better technology and increasing competition among the manufacturers, the margins were getting smaller for retailers and they were beginning to face a cost-profit squeeze. Most retailers and authorized dealers were unwilling to sell computers in the lower end of the market. Only the mass merchandisers such as K-Mart and Dayton-Hudson were willing to carry the cheap computers, since they did not require as much support and service.

THE UPPER- AND LOWER-END COMPUTER MARKETS

With advancing technology and falling prices, a whole new lower-end segment of the personal computer market was created in 1981. This consisted of computers costing less than $1,000, such as the Atari 400, and the VIC-Commodore 20. The lower-end market was currently dominated by only five companies: Atari, Commodore, Radio Shack, Timex/Sinclair and TI (Texas Instruments). Their respective 1981 market shares were as follows: Atari, 25 percent; Commodore, 25 percent; Radio Shack, 19 percent; Timex/Sinclair, 15 percent; TI, 11 percent; others, 5 percent. Although competition was not yet as great in the lower-end market as it was for larger personal computers, in which dozens of companies were involved, the competition was stiff nevertheless. Because of the smaller profit margins of these cheaper computers, the retailers were consistently offering discounts on these computers in hopes of making money on the equipment that was attached to the computer and on the software, as well as on the volume of units sold.

The upper-end market was dominated by some twelve or so manufacturers, with the three largest being Apple, IBM, and Commodore, with market shares of 26 percent, 17 percent, and 12 percent respectively.[6] The other major competitors were Tandy, Hewlett-Packard, Xerox, TI, and Nippon Electric Corporation (NEC). IBM and Xerox had entered the market in 1981. Xerox sold only business and professional personal computers, and did not intend to go into the home, hobby, or entertainment market. IBM, however, had been seriously thinking of going into the home market, where the large market potential had not yet been tapped fully. Hewlett-Packard had always been strong in the scientific and industrial market, having the most scientific and industrial software available. Hewlett-Packard had so far concentrated in this market and the business market. Apple sold to all market segments—that is, the business, small business, industrial/scientific, and education markets. Apple was strongest in the business and small business markets and was rapidly increasing its position in the education market. Although there was more competition in the business and small business markets after the entrance of Xerox and IBM (when IBM entered the market, stock prices of existing personal computer companies fell sharply, but recovered later), Apple management stated that it welcomed the competition. Apple was fully committed to the end users and was looking for the best way to reach, service, and educate them.

As more companies entered the market, Apple felt there would be more advertisements and education of potential users about computers. Moreover, with IBM joining the market, Apple felt this helped legitimize the personal computer as a powerful and useful tool for people to use. It also brought respectability and a sense of quality to the personal computer market. Apple further felt that the "pie" (total market) for personal computers had been expanded by these new entries, and that Apple would benefit, even if it had the same share of the pie, because its slice would be that much bigger.

APPLE'S ORGANIZATION

Apple Computer, Inc., was organized along functional lines (see the organization charts in Exhibits 2 and 3). Given the company's rapid growth, the chart had changed twice in the past year, and with the newly announced hiring mandate of increasing the work force from 3,600 to 4,900 within the next year, it could well change again soon.[7] Apple's work force had been increasing rapidly since the company was incorporated in 1977. Apple prided itself on being an innovative and creative company. It had actively hired "young blood" with creative ideas into the company; Mr. Reutemann was one of them. The average age of its employees was only twenty-eight.

As shown in the organization charts, the home computer market fit, along with four other existing market divisions (business, small business, education, and industrial and scientific), into the larger division of markets marketing. This large division was responsible for developing Apple's marketing strategy for those five market segments. Mr. Reutemann, in addition to some sales work with large department store chains, had been intensively studying the potential for Apple's computers in the home market.

THE MEMORANDUM

In order to clarify his thoughts on the issue of entering the home computer market, Mr. Reutemann had written a memorandum to three of

EXHIBIT 2
Apple Computer, Inc.: Apple's Overall Organization Chart

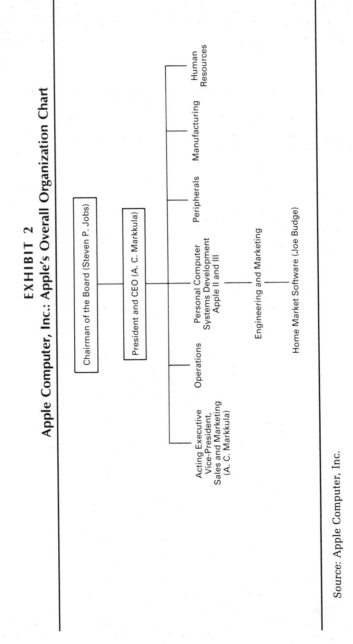

Source: Apple Computer, Inc.

EXHIBIT 3
Apple Computer, Inc.: Apple's Organization Chart of Sales and Marketing

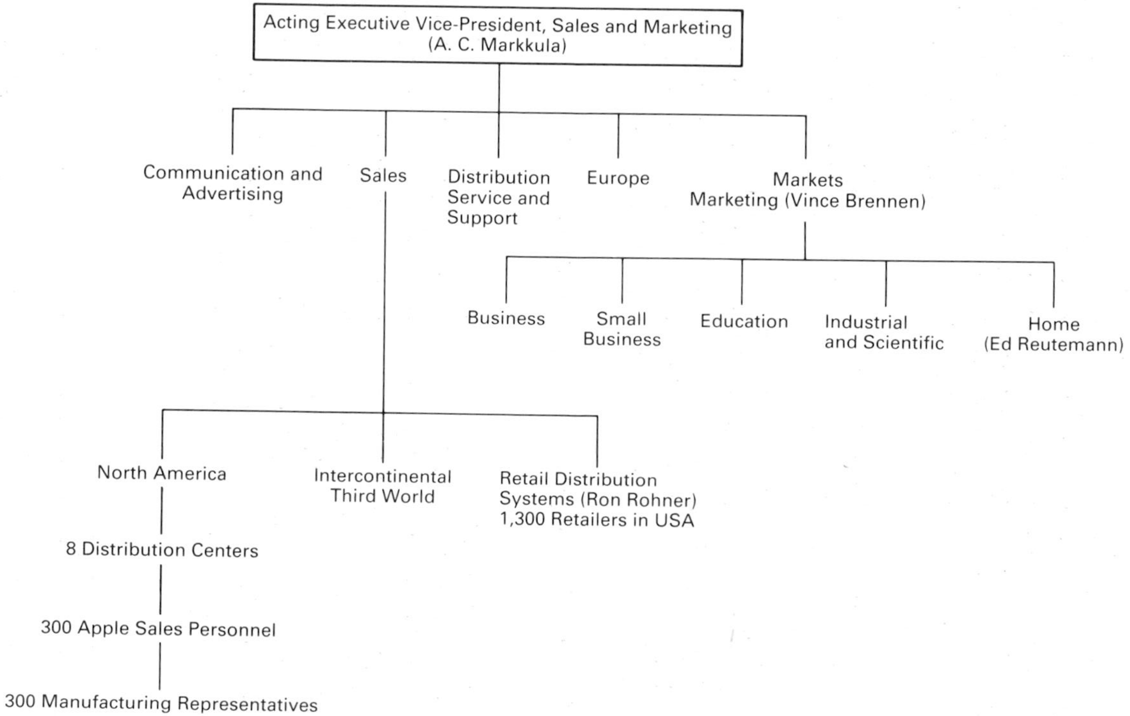

Acting Executive Vice-President, Sales and Marketing
(A. C. Markkula)

Communication and Advertising

Sales

Distribution Service and Support

Europe

Markets Marketing (Vince Brennen)

Intercontinental Third World

Business

Small Business

Education

Industrial and Scientific

Home (Ed Reutemann)

Retail Distribution Systems (Ron Rohner) 1,300 Retailers in USA

North America

8 Distribution Centers

300 Apple Sales Personnel

300 Manufacturing Representatives

Source: Apple Computer, Inc.

77

his Apple co-workers to expedite a meeting he had scheduled with
them to discuss this issue. The memorandum outlined the various market segments that Apple was already in, as well as relevant marketing
information and data. He hoped that this would provide a common
basis from which the discussion should flow. The three associates invited to the meeting were people whose opinions Mr. Reutemann valued and whose advice had helped him formulate his thoughts to date
on the issue. They were:

> *Mr. Joe Budge from personal computer systems development
> (PCSD), consumer software marketing.* This division sold soft-
> ware for the current Apple IIs and IIIs, and Mr. Budge's exper-
> tise was in software development for home use.

> *Mr. Ron Rohner, manager of retail distribution systems.* Mr. Roh-
> ner was responsible for developing efficient and effective dis-
> tribution systems and, in particular, working with current re-
> tailers.

> *Mr. Vince Brennen, developing markets manager.* Mr. Brennen
> was Reutemann's immediate superior and was responsible for
> developing new markets for the Apple computer.

The memorandum was as follows:

Apple Computer, Inc.
Home Computer Market
2025 Mariani Ave.
Cupertino, CA 95051

Memorandum to: Messrs. Budge, Rohner, and Brennen

Subject: Background information on the five personal computer markets: business and small business, education, industrial and scientific, and home.

From: Ed Reutemann

This is a short background piece on the industry, our market segments,
and its users. I thought it would be appropriate for all of us to have the
same information and data prior to our meeting: reference the home
computer market.

In 1979, we, for all intents and purposes, wrote off the home computer
market and decided to concentrate on the business and small business;
education; and industrial and scientific markets. We have been very successful, especially in the business, small business, and recently, the education areas. In addition, by pricing ourselves in the higher end of the

market we have produced higher returns for both the company and the retailer, and have made ourselves one of the forerunners in the personal computer market. However, the recent lowering of computer manufacturing costs, extreme price competition, higher consumer demand for personal computers, and market projections calling for an explosion in the home market area has caused us (and many other manufacturers) to re-think earlier decisions on the home computer market. I have been asked to look into this possibility, and have put together some information and pertinent data on the five markets (business and small business; industrial and scientific; education; and home), with greater details on the home computer, to help us in discussing the issue as follows:

Business and Small Business Segments

The business and small business areas together represent the largest segment in the whole personal computer market and for us also. It is also our most competitive market with IBM and Xerox entering recently. This market developed largely because at the early stages of development for personal computers, only businesses could afford the high prices at which these computers sold, usually over $3,000. Hence, most manufacturers, Apple included, concentrated on meeting the needs of this segment by providing a wide range of business and professional softwares.

Presently, we have the largest number and range of computer software for the business and small business segment. It has been estimated that the number of units installed in these market segments was 38 percent of the total personal computer market in 1979, and is expected to rise to 42 percent of the market in 1984. This is also the most profitable segment for us and our distributors. From our marketing surveys, we have also found that business/small business users require less training and support, per computer purchased, since retailers deal with one purchasing agent per company and usually can train employees in a group situation. Dollar add-ons (both hardware and software) for this segment are the largest. Businesses also buy the largest average system size of any of the personal computer markets. [See Exhibit 4.]

Industrial and Scientific Segment

This is the smallest and most specialized segment in the market. In addition, this is normally the higher-end market as this segment requires more complex and sophisticated hardware and software. Software is normally specialized and customized to the user's specifications because of the uniqueness of each user's applications. Most industrial and scientific customers write their own software or commission someone to do it for them. They seldom buy pre-packaged software popularly bought by the business segment, and it is very difficult to make software on a large

EXHIBIT 4
Apple Computer, Inc.: 1981 First-Year Add-On Sales of
Computer Stores

Customer Type	Percentage of Sales	Typical System Price	Twelve-Month Add-Ons	Number of Visits	Weeks to Close Sale
Business/ professional	40.8	$9,460	$2,882	3.60	4.30
Industrial/ scientific	15.2	6,192	1,372	2.80	4.30
Home/hobby	27.1	2,100	1,810	2.75	5.45
Education	16.9	4,017	814	2.10	7.50

Source: Douglas W. Stinson, "Marketing Computers for Mass Appeal," *Home Computers/A Special Lebhar-Friedman Report*, p. 3.

scale for this market. The scientific/industrial users mainly buy just the hardware.

Education Segment

This is one of the more rapidly growing sections of the industry with the increased emphasis on computer literacy in schools and the work-place. Computer manufacturers are scrambling to get their computers into the classroom, because that could potentially lead to more home sales. As you all know, we are proposing an "Apple Bill" to Congress so that we can receive a tax break for donating one of our computers to every elementary and secondary school in the nation. The bill should be passed early next year. We, Texas Instruments, and others are also looking into the possibility of forming partnerships with educational publishers to develop educational programs to run on our computers. We have also set up several successful and popular computer summer camps and courses to educate and promote the personal computer among the young consumers. The typical customers in this segment are teachers, parents, students, and educational institutions. Educational users normally buy a more fully equipped computer than the home buyer, but less than the previous three market segments. This segment also buys more software than the home and industrial/scientific users in terms of dollars.

Home Segment

The home user typically buys the basic no-frills computer to learn on, and then advances by buying additional equipment and software as his or her computer knowledge increases. This market is characterized by three types of customers. The first type wants a computer that has full expansion capabilities so that he or she can use it not only for games but also for business and other more sophisticated applications. The second kind is not sure if he or she will fully use the computer and is hesitant to spend too much on one just to find out. Finally, there is the user who just wants a computer for entertainment. The home market can be divided into those computers selling above $1,000 for the first type of customer, and the below-$1,000 computers for the remaining two types of customers. The home buyer normally requires the most support and service by the retailers. Hence, if we should decide to sell a new computer below $1,000 our present retailers and dealers will be unwilling to do so because the lower profit margins in the machines will not justify the amount of support and service they will have to provide to buyers of computers in this price range. However, our surveys also show that these home buyers buy a larger percentage of add-ons [see Exhibit 4] than the three other market segments, which means that the retailers may be able to improve their profits through add-on sales, and then may be persuaded to sell a cheaper Apple computer, below $1,000.

The lower-end market (created in 1980) consists of computers priced at less than $1,000. This market is expected to grow at a 60 percent rate per year over the next five years. In comparison, sales of computers costing $1,000 to $5,000 (in which we, IBM, Commodore, and Radio Shack are the major competitors) are projected to grow at a slower 38 percent rate over the next five years.

It is generally felt that computers below $500 are essentially game machines with hardly any capabilities presently for upgrading, and would be suited for the third type of customer mentioned above. Customers who buy in this less-than-$500 range normally buy a brand new computer when they want to advance to a more powerful computer. Exhibit 5 shows the estimated home market sales forecasted for the less-than-$500 and greater-than-$500 computers in the U.S. (with the corresponding decrease in cost and price over time based on similar trends in hand-held calculators and TV sets). As you all can see, the potential is high for this segment, but so are the risks. However, I think Apple realized this when they hired me to study the home market.

THE MEETING

After free coffee and donuts (a benefit of working for a high-technology firm), the meeting was called to order. Mr. Reutemann began:

"Thank you for coming together today. I assume that you all got my memorandum on this topic, so let's use that as a jumping-off place. I guess my concern can be summarized by the fact that, like it or not, we're already in the home computer market to some degree. I see us having to become further involved in a more diversified way in this

EXHIBIT 5
Home Market for Computers

A. Units Shipped (thousands)

Price Category	1981, Actual	1982, Estimated	1983, Estimated	1984, Estimated	1985, Estimated	Five-Year Total	Percentage of U.S. Households in 1981
Under $500	540	1,520	2,700	4,200	6,300	15,260	18%
Over $500	200	280	560	1,120	2,140	4,300	5%
Total units	740	1,800	3,260	5,320	8,440	19,560	23%

B. Average Retail Price per Unit (dollars)

Price Category	1981, Actual	1982, Estimated	1983, Estimated	1984, Estimated	1985, Estimated		
Under $500	$285	245	185	165	167		
Over $500	$1,290	811	800	750	730		

C. Retail Dollar Value of Units Sold (millions of dollars)

Price Category	1981, Actual	1982, Estimated	1983, Estimated	1984, Estimated	1985, Estimated		
Under $500	$154	372	500	693	1,052		
Over $500	$258	227	448	840	1,562		
Total dollar value	$412	599	948	1,533	2,614		

Source: Apple Computer, Inc.

market in order to stand a chance of getting a decent piece of this exploding market. If we don't get into the home computer market in a purposeful way, we risk difficult times ahead in the slower growing markets—that is, business and small business; industrial and scientific; and education. This doesn't take into account increased competition for these last three markets from IBM, HP, [Hewlett-Packard], Xerox, and others; this is especially true in the office systems area, where we're currently top dog.

"Also, the home computer market seems to be a natural for us to go into to get a pull-through effect for our more expensive and more powerful computers like Mac and Apple IIe when they're introduced. It seems to fit with what Steve (Jobs) and Mark (A. C. Makkula) seem to be saying about making Apple the computer every family can own. We're getting a good deal of pressure for the higher end of the other markets from IBM, Xerox, and HP, but Lisa should take care of the competition there, and then some. However, we've left the $0–$1,250 range for computers void of Apple products.

"Now, we know Atari, Commodore, Tandy, Texas Instruments, and Timex/Sinclair are killing each other at the less-than-$500 area, but the $500–$1,250 range has really only the Atari 800 and the VIC-Commodore 80, and their prices don't include the extras most people need and eventually get. Now, with the market for home computers projected by 1985 to grow to 8 million units and the price of computers falling, we'd better start thinking about that price range and fast."

"I agree with you, Ed, on many of the points," interrupted Ron Rohner from Retail Distribution Systems, "but you left out some very important problems with this scenario. First of all, we only have 1,300 retail distributors, and most of those are specialty computer stores or franchises. They only want items with large enough margins to make a profit and at least stay in business. You know the grumbling we're getting about the drop in price for Apple IIs because of price competition. Only by some creative packaging deals were we able to quiet them down. And the discounting by unauthorized dealers is also hurting us. Frankly, I don't see the home computer market as one that our present dealers would be interested in pursuing.

"We already know from our own surveys that it takes as much dealer time to sell a $500 machine as a $5,000 machine, and as much time to train and service a user, but the margin is not there for our dealers to make the $500 machine worthwhile in the long haul.

"Last, and most important, our current dealers are noted for their service and quality, and with only 1,300 retailers, we don't have enough to service the home market. That means going to mass marketers like J. C. Penney and K-Mart, and you know they're basically discounters and could care less about service, advice, or training these users. Our current dealers couldn't stand the price wars that would result and our customers would suffer and probably blame us. There goes the image of the quality leader in personal computers that we've worked hard to establish. I also think that. . . ."

"Ron, if you don't mind, I'd like to add to what you've said about problems with the home market," interrupted Joe Budge of Personal Computer Systems Development. "Right now, I can't justify most people buying a home computer; there just aren't enough services or software programs designed for their use to cost-justify the purchase. The boom predicted for services like news, stock quotes, electronic banking, etc., has not materialized as fast as the experts predicted, although banking is really pushing for home banking by home terminals as a way to save processing costs. The costs of the above services are fine for businesses, but the home market is too price-sensitive to purchase in the quantities originally predicted.

"Neither has the cable TV market grown as was predicted; in fact, they have a lousy market penetration of U.S. homes. TV is also a bad two-way communication medium and would require a great deal of capital investment to get into substantially more homes. TV, cable, and the computer would seem to be a good mix on the surface, but there are problems.

"The phone company has a better distribution system and penetration of the home market, in fact the best, and is an excellent two-way communication medium, but it can't handle TV pictures. Rumor has it that AT&T agreed to the divesting of its local phone companies to get into the home computer and telecommunications market more heavily. It has a great distribution system in its Phone Store system, and its sales force is highly trained and educated.

"One more thing to consider is software development. If we make our new home computer compatible with our old machines, we get the benefits of all the existing software packages being able to be used by it. However, we also inherit all the limitations of the old system and technology that's five years old. A completely new software system and technology would give us a unique new product, but make our old software and equipment incompatible. If software were incompatible, it would take another two years to develop an adequate amount of software packages to make our new system truly competitive. It's a trade off—new, unique technology, or two years of additional sales using an older software system."

"Joe!" Ed interrupted, "That's my point too. People need to be educated about computer use and there are enough programs available to market our program gradually. Remember the surge in number is predicted toward 1984 and 1985, so we have some working time.

"We need to stress five areas in which computers can be used in the home effectively and efficiently. Obviously, a program like VISI-CALC can save enough money in staff salaries and typing costs to justify both itself and the computer system several times over in a year for a business. What we need to help justify home computers are those things that are hard to price, or services of great potential in the near future. The areas that we should be stressing are:

1. *Education:* The main emphasis of our marketing, since parents know computers are the way of the future and computers can help their children learn. We're selling computer literacy and self-improvement under this area and all in the family can benefit.

2. *Entertainment:* Obviously, many people buy computers, at least the cheaper ones, for the games they offer. We need to tread lightly on these because of our image; we don't want to be a game company. We already know the Apple II has a large assortment of game cartridges developed by independent software companies, and that people do want to be entertained when they're at home. However, while we need some of the manual dexterity games, like Space Invaders, or Pac-Man, I think we ought to concentrate on the strategy-type games that require mental dexterity and logic like Wizardry Cult; this will appeal to our most 'esoteric' group of people. That's the group we want. Right, Vince?" (Vince Brennen, developing markets manager, smiles and nods.)

3. *Personal Record Keeping:* We need to stress the use of a computer to help in keeping track of things like addresses, insurable items, and serial numbers, income tax records, etc., as well as showing how software programs on taxes, investments, and businesslike activities can be used in the home to do volunteer and church group activities like mailing lists and letters.

4. *Telecommunications:* Although recognizing the problems that Joe has mentioned are real and must be overcome, this is still an area of high potential, especially the information services like *The Source* or *Dow Jones.* Computer shopping, banking, and electronic mail are definitely in the near future—within ten years. We can't afford to ignore them, and miss the boat.

5. *Home Management Potential:* The potential for the computer to control the environment of the home is a real high probability item. It can do this now, but not while in use processing the other four areas I've just mentioned. So, recognizing the limitations here, we need to stress the future potential of this product. Perhaps more home builders will add the wiring necessary to do this in the future—if we ever get out of this recession."

"I agree with you on numbers 1, 2, and 3, but 4 and 5 are too hard to sell now," Joe said. "Besides that, I'd like to see education split into two separate categories—computer literacy and education—and number 4 hidden (if you still want to use it) under entertainment. I agree with you that the game part needs to be downplayed. Because of our image, we can't afford to lose the other markets because of the home market."

Vince Brennen finally spoke. "Good point," he said. "We're a personal computer company trying to reach into the high end of the home computer market. This new market has to complement our middle and higher-end product lines and image or it's a no-go from Steve and Mark's viewpoint. Ed, you need to be sure that we can pull this off. Joe and Ron have some serious concerns about pricing, distribution, image, technological changes, and software development that must be answered before we can go ahead.

"In addition, I'm concerned about several areas, but just like you, I can't see how we can stay out of the market, if for no other reason than the decrease in computer prices brought about by competition and by decreased manufacturing costs. There are some other points in favor of this market, however.

"It's easier for us to move down the price range than for Atari, Commodore, and TI to move up it. We have the quality name in personal computers, while they're still striving to become respectable and taken for a serious product.

"The technological changes, especially in the predicted boom areas of telecommunication and electronic text, concern me the most, since we have little control over that area. Can you get a better handle on that? Speaking of concerns, a while ago I sidestepped the concerns over distribution. Mass merchants scare the heck out of me! We've dealt with department stores with good success, but mass merchants are different and they could be a problem. Are there other ways for us to channel our product to the home market that would fit our company better?

"Finally, how do we educate the masses out there who know nothing of computers and are scared to death of those little noisy boxes."

Reutemann thanked his three co-workers, went to his office, plopped in his chair, and reached for his aspirin bottle. It seemed that the meeting had raised more questions, in addition to a large headache, than it had answered.

NOTES

1. "The Coming Shakeout in Personal Computers," *Business Week* (November 22, 1982): 72.

2. Madeline Dreyfack, "Apple's Personal Touch," *Marketing and Media Decisions* (Spring 1982): 50.

3. In the world of digital computers, each piece of information is called a *bit* (for binary di*git*). Clusters of bits, forming the equivalent of a single letter in ordinary language, are called *bytes*. The size of a computer's memory is generally described in K (1 K = 1,024 bytes). See "The Computer Market Moves In," *Time* (January 3, 1983): 31, 39.

4 See note 3.

5. "The Coming Shakeout in Personal Computers," *Business Week* (November 22, 1982): 74.

6. "Can John Young Redesign Hewlett-Packard?" *Business Week* (December 6, 1982): 72–73.

7. "Apple Computer Inc. to Boost Work Force," *Wall Street Journal* (November 2, 1982): 32.

Jones Blair Company

MR. ALEXANDER BARRETT, president of Jones Blair Company, slumped back in his chair as his senior management executives filed out of the conference room. "Another meeting and still no resolution," he thought. The major point of disagreement among the executives was where and how to deploy corporate marketing efforts among the various trade paint markets served by the company. He asked his secretary to schedule another meeting for next week.

THE PAINT INDUSTRY

The market for paint coatings can be divided into _trade sales_ and _industrial sales_. Trade sales, known as _shelf goods_, include products sold primarily to households, contractors, and professional painters. Industrial sales include sales of numerous products for original application by manufacturers. Principal industrial customers include manufacturers of furniture; appliances; transportation equipment (autos, ships, trucks); construction components; and farm implements. Most coatings sold to industrial customers are special formulations designed to meet specific needs and application methods. Total sales of paint coatings in the United States are divided equally between trade and industrial sales.

This case was prepared by Professor Roger A. Kerin, Edwin L. Cox School of Business, Southern Methodist University, as a basis for class discussion and is not designed to illustrate effective or ineffective handling of administrative situations. Certain names and all market and sales data are disguised and are not useful for research purposes.

Market Outlook for Trade Paint Sales

Industry sources estimate U.S. trade sales of paint and allied products (brushes, paint thinners, etc.) to be $5.1 billion in 1984, with projected sales of $5.8 billion in 1986. The average annual growth rate in dollar sales during the 1980s is considerably below the growth rate observed in the 1960s and 1970s. The rate of increase in paint volume could slow down further in the late 1980s, for a variety of reasons. First, there will be increased use of materials such as aluminum, plastics, and other nonwood products that require little or no painting. Second, producers of coatings have developed more durable products, and industrial paint users have developed more efficient application techniques. Third, improvements in paint quality have reduced the amount of paint necessary per application and the frequency of repainting. Counteracting these factors, industry observers foresee increasing demand for miscellaneous products such as paintbrushes, rollers, and other paint sundries.

Paint manufacturers in general have had to contend with a cost-price squeeze in recent years, and there is no end in sight. Cost of raw materials and increased competition is expected to remain a major threat to industry profitability.

Competition

There were an estimated twelve hundred paint manufacturers in the United States in 1985, compared with sixteen hundred manufacturers in 1968. The increased concentration of paint manufacturing is due to business failures and increased acquisition of regional manufacturers by national firms. Still, because of a readily available technology and differences in paint formulations associated with regional climate needs, a large number of regional manufacturers compete effectively against national manufacturers.

The four largest paint producers—Sherwin-Williams, DuPont, PPG Industries, and SCM Corporation (through its Glidden-Durkee division)—account for about 30 percent of the total U.S. market. Sherwin-Williams, the largest producer, concentrates on the trade sector, although its sales of industrial finishes are significant. Other important producers include DeSoto, Inc. (with virtually all production sold to Sears); United Technologies Corporation (as a result of the mid-1979 acquisition of Carrier Corporation, which had acquired Inmont Corporation, a paint producer, in December 1977); Celanese; Cook Paint & Varnish; Grow Chemical; Benjamin Moore; Pratt & Lambert; Dutch

Boy; and Standard Brands Paint (which serves the do-it-yourself market on the West Coast and certain sections of the Southwest).

About 50 percent of trade paint sales are private brands. Montgomery Ward, K-Mart, and Sears are major suppliers. Sears is committed to hold its share of the paint business, if not increase it.

Paint stores and hardware stores selling paint have been able to compete in the paint business despite the presence of private brands and mass merchandisers. Industry sources estimate that paint stores were the recipient of about 36 percent of exterior and interior paint sales; hardware stores and lumber yards received 14 percent. These figures have remained unchanged in the last decade. Furthermore, paint and hardware stores and lumber yards in nonmetropolitan areas have outdistanced mass merchandisers as a source of paint. This is largely attributable to a lack of mass-merchandise distribution in these areas and to paint store customer relations and service.

Trade Sales Purchase Behavior

Approximately 45 percent of trade sales are accounted for by households. Contractors and professional painters account for another 35 percent. The remainder are accounted for by government purchases, exports, and miscellaneous commercial applications.

Approximately one in four households purchases interior house paint in any given year. About 15 percent of U.S. households purchase exterior house paint. Industry observers believe that a majority of the paint purchased by the general public was applied by the purchaser.[1] The popularity of do-it-yourself painting has necessitated an expanded product line of paint and sundry items carried by retail outlets, which partially accounts for the development of manufacturer-owned and -operated retail outlets such as Sherwin-Williams.

Contractors are typically involved in large-scale painting jobs such as new home and building construction. Professional painters, by comparison, typically paint the exterior and interior of individual homes or serve in a maintenance capacity for property management firms.

"Paint has become a commodity," commented Mr. Barrett. "Household purchasers view paint as paint—a covering—and try to get the best price. But there are a significant number of people who desire service as well in the form of information about application, surface preparation and durability," he added. He conceded that "once paint is on the wall, you can't tell the difference between premium-priced and competitively priced paint.

"There is a difference between contractors and professional painters, however," he continued. "Pot and brush guys [professional painters] do seek out quality products, since their reputation is on the line and maintenance firms don't want to have to paint an office each time a mark is on a wall. They want paint that is durable, washable, and will cover in a single coat. Contractors want whitewash in many instances and strive for the lowest price, particularly on big jobs."

JONES BLAIR SERVICE AREA

Jones Blair markets its products in over fifty counties in Texas, Oklahoma, New Mexico, and Louisiana. Dallas–Fort Worth (DFW), with a population of 3 million, is the major urban center in the company's service area. DFW, the business and financial center for the Jones Blair service area, is a city that has benefited from recent migration because of its prosperous economy.

A similar pattern of growth has occurred in the entire fifty-county service area. The population growth rate has exceeded the DFW growth based on the 1980 U.S. census. The total population in the fifty-county service area is 6 million.

Competition at both retail and manufacturing levels has accelerated in recent years. Sears and K-Mart have multiple outlets in DFW, as does Sherwin-Williams. Competition for retail selling space in paint stores, lumberyards, and hardware stores has also increased. "Our research indicates that one thousand of these outlets now operate in the fifty-county service area, and DFW houses three hundred of them," noted Mr. Barrett. "When you consider that the typical lumberyard or hardware store gets 10 percent of its volume ($30,000) from paint and the typical paint store has annual sales of $125,000 with three brands, you can see that getting and keeping widespread distribution is a key success factor in this industry. Over twelve hundred outlets had operated in the area in 1970; about six hundred were situated in DFW or its suburbs at the time."

Competition at the manufacturing level has increased as well. The major change in competitive behavior has occurred among paint companies that sell to contractors serving the housing industry. The companies have aggressively priced their products to capture a higher percentage of the home construction market. "These companies have not pursued the three hundred or so professional painting firms in DFW and the one hundred painters in rural areas or the household market as yet," said Mr. Barrett. "They have not been able to gain access to retail outlets, but they may buy their way in through free goods, promotional allowances, or whatever means are available to them.

"We believe that mass merchandisers control 50 percent of the household paint market in the DFW metropolitan area. Price seems to be the attraction, but we can't quarrel with their quality," noted Mr. Barrett.

The estimated dollar volume of paint and allied products sold in Jones Blair's service area was $55 million (excluding contractor sales). DFW was estimated to account for 60 percent of this figure, with remaining paint and allied product volume being sold in rural areas. Do-it-yourself household buyers were believed to account for 70 percent of non-contractor-related volume in DFW and 90 percent of volume in rural areas. A five-year summary of paint and allied product sales in the Jones Blair service area is shown in Exhibit 1.

JONES BLAIR COMPANY

Jones Blair Company is a privately held corporation that is involved in trade paint sales under the Jones Blair brand name. In addition to producing a full line of paints, the company sells paint sundries (brushes, rollers, thinners, etc.) under the Jones Blair name, even though these items are not manufactured by the company. The company also operates a very large industrial-coatings division, which sells its products nationwide.

Company trade paint and allied products sales volume in 1984 was $4.67 million, and net profit before taxes was $450,000. Dollar sales have increased at an average annual rate of 10 percent per year over the past decade. Paint gallonage, however, has remained stable over the past five years (see Exhibit 2). "We have been very aggressive in raising our prices to cover increased material and labor costs, but I'm afraid we've crossed the threshold," Mr. Barrett said. "We are now the highest-priced paint in the markets we serve." At present, cost of goods sold, including freight expenses, was 60 percent of net sales.

EXHIBIT 1
Paint and Allied Product Sales Volume: 1980–1984

Year	Total Dollar Sales (millions)	DFW Sales	Rural Sales
1980	$43.2	$33.2	$10.0
1981	$46.2	$33.7	$12.5
1982	$49.4	$33.8	$15.6
1983	$52.4	$33.9	$18.5
1984	$55.0	$33.0	$22.0

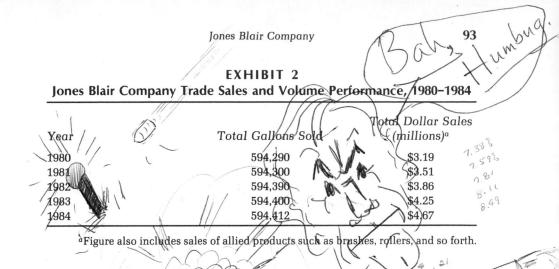

EXHIBIT 2
Jones Blair Company Trade Sales and Volume Performance, 1980–1984

Year	Total Gallons Sold	Total Dollar Sales (millions)[a]
1980	594,290	$3.19
1981	594,300	$3.51
1982	594,390	$3.86
1983	594,400	$4.25
1984	594,412	$4.67

[a]Figure also includes sales of allied products such as brushes, rollers, and so forth.

Distribution

The company distributes its products through two hundred independent paint stores, lumberyards, and hardware outlets. Forty percent of its outlets are located in DFW. The remaining outlets are situated in rural areas in the fifty-county service area. Jones Blair sales are distributed evenly between DFW and rural accounts. Exhibit 3 shows the account and sales volume distribution by size of dollar purchase per year.

Retail outlets in rural areas with paint and sundry purchases exceeding $15,000 annually carry only the Jones Blair product line. However, except for fourteen outlets in DFW (those with purchases greater than $30,000 annually), which carry the Jones Blair line exclusively, DFW stores carry two or three lines with Jones Blair's line being premium priced. "Our experience to date shows that in our DFW outlets, the effect of multiple lines has been to cause a decline in gallonage volume. The rural outlets, by comparison, have grown in gallonage

EXHIBIT 3
Account and Sales Volume Distribution by Dollar Purchase per Year

Dollar Purchase/Year	Accounts			Sales Volume		
	Urban	Rural	Total	Urban	Rural	Total
$30,000+	7%	10%	17%	28%	28%	56%
$15,000–$30,000	14%	20%	34%	13%	13%	26%
Less than $15,000	19%	30%	49%	9%	9%	18%
Total	40%	60%	100%	50%	50%	100%

volume. When you combine the two, you have flat gallonage volume," remarked Mr. Barrett.

Promotional Efforts for Trade Sales

Jones Blair employs eight sales representatives, who are responsible for monitoring Jones Blair inventories of paint and sundry items in each retail outlet, as well as for order taking, assisting in store display, and coordinating cooperative advertising programs. A recent survey of Jones Blair paint outlets indicated that the sales representatives were well liked, helpful, and knowledgeable about paint. Commenting on the survey findings, Mr. Barrett said, "Our reps are on a first-name basis with their customers. It is not uncommon for our reps to discuss business and family over coffee during a sales call, and some of our people even 'mind the store' when the proprieter has to run an errand or two." Sales representatives were paid a salary and a 1 percent commission on sales.

The company spends approximately 3 percent of net sales on advertising and sales promotion efforts. Approximately 55 percent of advertising and sales-promotion dollars are allocated to cooperative advertising programs with retail accounts. The cooperative program, whereby Jones Blair pays a portion of an account's media costs based on the amount purchased from Jones Blair, applies to newspaper advertising and seasonal catalogs distributed door to door in a retailer's immediate trade area. The remainder of the advertising and sales promotion budget is spent on in-store displays; on corporate brand advertising on outdoor signs; and in regional magazines; on premiums; and on advertising production costs. Exhibits 4 and 5 show Jones Blair print advertisements.

PLANNING MEETING

Senior management executives of Jones Blair Company assembled again to consider the question of where and how to deploy corporate marketing efforts among the various trade paint markets served by the company. Mr. Barrett opened the meeting with a statement that it was absolutely necessary to resolve this question at the meeting in order for the tactical plan to be developed.

Vice-President of Advertising Alex, I still believe that we must direct our efforts toward bolstering our presence in the DFW market. I just received the results of our DFW consumer advertising awareness study. As you can see [Exhibit 6], awareness is related to paint pur-

EXHIBIT 4
Jones Blair Print Advertisement

EXHIBIT 5
Jones Blair Print Advertisement

EXHIBIT 6
Percentage of DFW Population Who Were Aware of
Paint Brands and Purchased Paint
in the Last Twelve Months

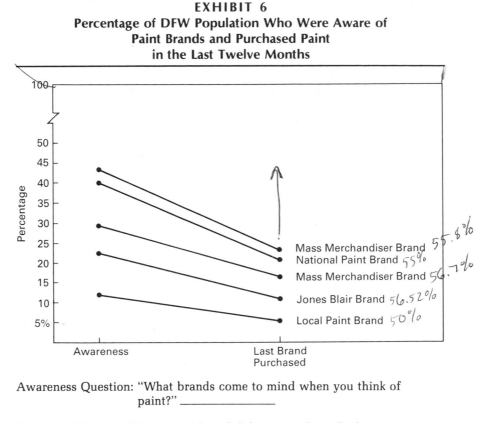

Mass Merchandiser Brand 55.8%
National Paint Brand 55%
Mass Merchandiser Brand 56.7%
Jones Blair Brand 56.52%
Local Paint Brand 50%

Awareness Question: "What brands come to mind when you think of paint?" _____

Last Brand Bought: "What paint brand did you purchase the last time you bought paint?" _____

Note: Sample size N = 400. Percentages are subject to a 5 percent sampling error.

chase behavior. Furthermore, industry research on paint purchase behavior indicates that a majority of consumers decide ahead of time what brand they will buy before shopping for paint and do think about paint they have seen advertised when choosing a brand. It seems to me that we need an awareness level of at least 30 percent to materially affect our market share.

Preliminary talks with our ad agency indicates that an increase of $150,000 in corporate brand advertising beyond what we are now spending, with an emphasis on television, will be necessary to achieve this awareness level. Furthermore, this television coverage will reach rural consumers as well.

Vice-President of Operations   I don't agree. Advertising is not the way to go, and reference to the DFW market alone is too narrow a focus. We have to be competitive in the household paint market, period. Our shopper research program indicated that dealers will quickly back off from our brand when the customer appears price-sensitive. We must cut our price by 20 percent on all paint products to achieve parity with national paint brands. Look here. In today's newspaper, we advertise a price-off special on our exterior paint, and our price is still noticeably higher than a mass merchandiser's everyday price. With both ads on the same page, a customer would have to be an idiot to patronize one of our dealers.

Vice-President of Sales   Forget the DFW market. We ought to be putting our effort into the rural market, where half of our sales and most of our distributors exist right now. I hate to admit it, but our sales representatives are actually on a milk run. We have only added five new accounts in the last five years; our account penetration in rural areas is only 17 percent. I'm partially at fault, but I'm ready to act. We should add one additional sales representative whose sole responsibility is to develop new retail account leads and presentations or call on professional painters. I've figured the cost to keep one rep in the field at $40,000 per year.

Vice-President of Finance   Everyone is proposing a change in our orientation. Let me be the devil's advocate and favor pursuing our current approach. We now sell to both the home owner and professional painter in DFW and rural markets through our dealers. We have been and will continue to be profitable by judiciously guarding our margins and controlling costs. Our contribution margin is 35 percent. Everyone suggests that increasing our costs will somehow result in greater sales volume. Let me remind you, Alex, we have said that it is our policy to recoup noncapital improvement expenditures within a one-year time horizon. If we increase our advertising by an incremental amount of $150,000, then we had better see the incremental sales volume as well. The same goes for additional sales representatives and, I might add, the across-the-board cut in prices.

Mr. Barrett   We keep going over the same ground. All of you have valid arguments, but we must prioritize. Let's quit pushing our pet projects and think about what's best for all of us.

Increased advertising seems reasonable, since national paint firms and mass merchandisers outspend us tenfold. You are right in saying people have to be aware of us before they will buy, or even consider, Jones Blair. But I am not sure what advertising will do for us given that about 75 percent of the audience is not buying paint. Your reference to DFW as being our major market has been questioned by others. Can't we take that $150,000 of incremental advertising and apply it toward newspapers and catalogs in rural areas?

The price cut is a more drastic action. We might have to do it just to keep our volume. It would appear from our sales representatives' forecast that the demand for paint in our area will not increase next year despite the population growth. Any increases will have to come out of a competitor's hide. Moreover, since our costs are unlikely to decline, we must recoup gross profit dollars from an increase in volume. Is this possible?

The idea of hiring additional representatives has merit, but what do we do with them? Do they focus on the retail account side or on the professional painter? Our survey of retail outlets indicated that 70 percent of sales through our DFW outlets went to the professional painter, while 70 percent of sales through our rural outlets went to households. These figures are identical to the 1977 survey of retail outlets. Our contractor sales in DFW and rural areas are minimal. We would need a 40 percent price cut to attract contractors, not to mention the increased costs, expertise, and headaches of competitive bidding for large jobs.

Now that I've had my say, let's think about your proposals again.

NOTE

1. "Targeting the Do-It-Yourselfer," *Decorative Products World* (September 1982): 41–46.

Forney Engineering Company

IN EARLY 1979, executives at Forney Engineering Company were in the process of outlining the marketing plan for ECS 1200.[a] ECS 1200 is a microprocessor-based distributed process control system with analog capabilities for use in large industrial plants. The major question under consideration was the identification and selection of industrial users most likely to provide the necessary sales volume to support a concerted marketing effort.

INDUSTRIAL PROCESS CONTROLS

Trends

The primary trend in industrial process control has been the continued development and application of computerized controllers. First introduced in 1970, programmable computerized process controllers' dollar volume is currently growing 67 percent annually. The growth of com-

The assistance of Forney Engineering Company in the preparation of this case is gratefully acknowledged. This case was prepared by Tim Nicolaou, graduate student, and Professor Roger A. Kerin, Southern Methodist University, as a basis for classroom discussion and is not designed to illustrate appropriate or inappropriate handling of administrative situations. All market and cost data given in the case are provided solely for discussion purposes, are not useful for research, and do not necessarily reflect company estimates or opinions.

[a]ECS 1200 is a registered trademark of Forney Engineering Company.

puterized controllers is due to a variety of benefits they provide. For example, they can be often adapted to changing processes, the average downtime is twenty minutes, the control panel size is small, and software logic can support complex algorithms.

Before computerized controllers were developed, electronic controllers dominated industry shipments. Pneumatic controllers were used almost exclusively in the mid-1950s and early 1960s. Even though rapid technological change has been characteristic of the industry in the 1970s, upwards of 40 percent of the process controller dollar volume is accounted for by pneumatic controllers. Although industry size estimates vary dramatically between different industry sources, a commonly held opinion is that the dollar value of process controllers shipments is $800 million per year.

A second trend in industrial process controls concerns the evolutionary nature of system configurations. In the early 1970s, four categories of process controllers were available. Each is described here.

Analog Control   A control system consisting of electronic or pneumatic single-loop analog controllers, where each process loop is controlled by a single device. Each controller is tuned and adjusted manually by operators.

Supervisory Control   An analog control system, but with provision for allowing controller setpoints to be adjusted remotely. Typically, setpoints are adjusted by a large supervisory host computer. This method is also known as digitally directed analog (DDA).

Direct Digital Control (DDC)   A control system in which all control outputs are generated by a control computer. In a DDC system, no additional intelligence exists between the central computer and the process.

Distributed Control   A control system where total plant control is divided into several areas of responsibility. Each area is managed by its own control system. The individual systems communicate with each other via a data highway or communications medium of some kind.

These clearly defined categories have been modified in recent years, resulting in hybrid control systems that only vaguely resemble the traditional category configuration. As the industry continues to evolve, industry observers are suggesting that many control systems will become less salable, if not obsolete, in a four- to five-year span.

Competitive Manufacturers

Estimates of the number of manufacturers competing in the process control industry vary because of confusion in classifying products and system configurations. In 1977, industry observers typically estimated that twenty companies competed for a $400 million market growing at an annual rate of between 80 and 100 percent. In 1979, seven manufacturers appeared to dominate: Honeywell, Foxboro, Fisher Controls, Taylor Instruments, Leads and Northrup, Beckman, and Rosemount, Inc. Process control systems provided by Honeywell and Foxboro will be described briefly. System configurations of other manufacturers are summarized in Exhibit 1.

Honeywell markets its Total Distributed Control system—the TDC 2000.[b] This system was the first distributed control system combining both DDC and supervisory control. Honeywell pioneered the distributed control process or strategy and made it commonplace in the process control industry. Despite these efforts, new technologies such as light- and touch-sensitive CRT screens have made it possible for other manufacturers to introduce simpler operator-machine interfaces.

Foxboro markets its Spec 200[c] system. This system includes an analog controller that can be coupled with a supervisory or host computer. A configuration of this type gives the user the reliability of an analog controller with the flexibility of a supervisory computer. The system is distributed because each controller is autonomous. The supervisory computer is used to gather information for the operator in the central control room. Both Foxboro and Honeywell allow the combination of digital and analog control, but digital or sequential control is offered only if the host computer is purchased.

THE COMPANY

Forney Engineering Company was founded in 1927 to provide burner control and furnace safety systems for the electric utility industry. In 1965, Forney was acquired by the Foster Wheeler Corporation, an engineering, manufacturing, and construction organization serving power and process industries throughout the world. Foster Wheeler Corporation, with headquarters in New York, recorded net sales of $1.5 billion in 1978.

---

[b]Trademark of Honeywell.

[c]Trademark of Foxboro Company.

EXHIBIT 1
Configurations of competing process control systems

Manufacturer	Strategy: Distributed	Strategy: Centralized		Capabilities: Process Control Graphics		
		Supervisory	DDC	Analog	Digital	
Honeywell	*[a]	*Host[a]		*	*Host	
Foxboro		*Host		*	*Host	*Host
Beckman		*		*	*	*
Taylor Instruments				*		*
Rosemount				*		*
Leeds and Northrup			*	*		*
Bailey				*		
Arco Bristol			*	*		*
EMC Controls		*	*	*	*	*
Fisher Control				*	*	*
Centum		*	*	*	*	*
Moore Products				*		
Powell Industries		*	*	*		*
Robertshaw Controls		*	*	*		*
Westinghouse			*	*	*	*
Fisher and Porter		*	*	*	*	*
Hibachi		*	*	*	*	*

Source: Estimates made by casewriter from industry publications.

[a]Reference to "host" in the exhibit (indicated by an asterisk) means that the control systems require additional minicomputer or mainframe computer to provide the option noted.

Forney has expanded its product line since its inception to include burner hardware and various control systems designed primarily for the utilities industry. The product line includes: burner control, combustion control, feedwater control, fuel safety, diesel monitoring, environmental monitoring and control, programmable material handling, and sequencing control systems. According to company literature, Forney is committed to maintaining its position as the prime supplier of burner control and furnace safety systems for steam generators in industrial and electric utility applications and of control systems for marine boilers, turbines, and auxiliary equipment.

Forney is divided into four divisions. The *Power and Process Division* stemmed from the company's original product lines. This division is responsible for burner management and combustion safety systems, auxiliary control systems for fossil or nuclear plants, heavy-duty dampers, and desuperheating equipment.

The *Manufacturing Division* is responsible for Forney's custom-made production effort. This division is responsible for fabrication, assembly, finishing, and quality control of all Forney products.

EXHIBIT 2
CQ III Programmable Logic System

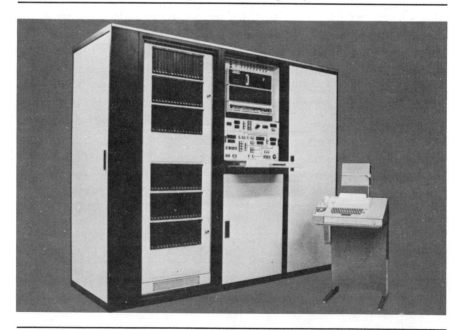

Forney International was created in 1965 to expand the company's foreign opportunities. Forney equipment is currently operating in thirty foreign countries.

The *Industrial and Marine Division* was formed to combine Forney's control expertise and experience with new technologies. The result has been the development of process control systems ranging from electromechanical controls to the CQ III,[d] a digital control system.

The CQ III is a centralized minicomputer-based system that utilizes a simplified programming language (see Exhibit 2). The CQ III language is designed to give a user the capability of implementing and controlling any digital process. An example of a digital application would be a conveyer belt with several storage bins. The status of the entire conveyer system can be represented in two-state logic. The belt is either on or off, or storage bins are full or empty. This characteristic exists in every digital control system.

Most activity is expended on CQ III–related installation in the electric utility industry. Exhibit 3 shows the wide variety of CQ III applications in a typical electric utility generating plant. Forney executives estimated that the company accounted for 3 to 4 percent of the total process control industry volume. Almost all of their process control sales volume was in the electric utilities industry.

THE ECS 1200

Despite the variety of CQ III applications, many processes in utility and industrial plants cannot be controlled with a digital system. Temperature control is a process where a full range of values must be monitored. Processes such as this require an analog signal capability. While the CQ III has some analog capability, its technical limitations preclude Forney from competing for total plant control applications.

The ECS 1200 was designed to overcome this shortcoming. The ECS 1200 is a microprocessor-based distributed control system in which analog control loops are software emulated and driven using direct digital control. A typical ECS 1200 system consists of one central operator station with a number of remote processors controlling a subsystem in a plant. A communications link exists that allows the various remote processors to pass information throughout the control system.

The ECS 1200 also allows sequential control using CQ III language without the support of a host computer. This innovation will make the ECS 1200 the only system that combines both analog and

---

[d]Trademark of Forney Engineering Company.

EXHIBIT 3

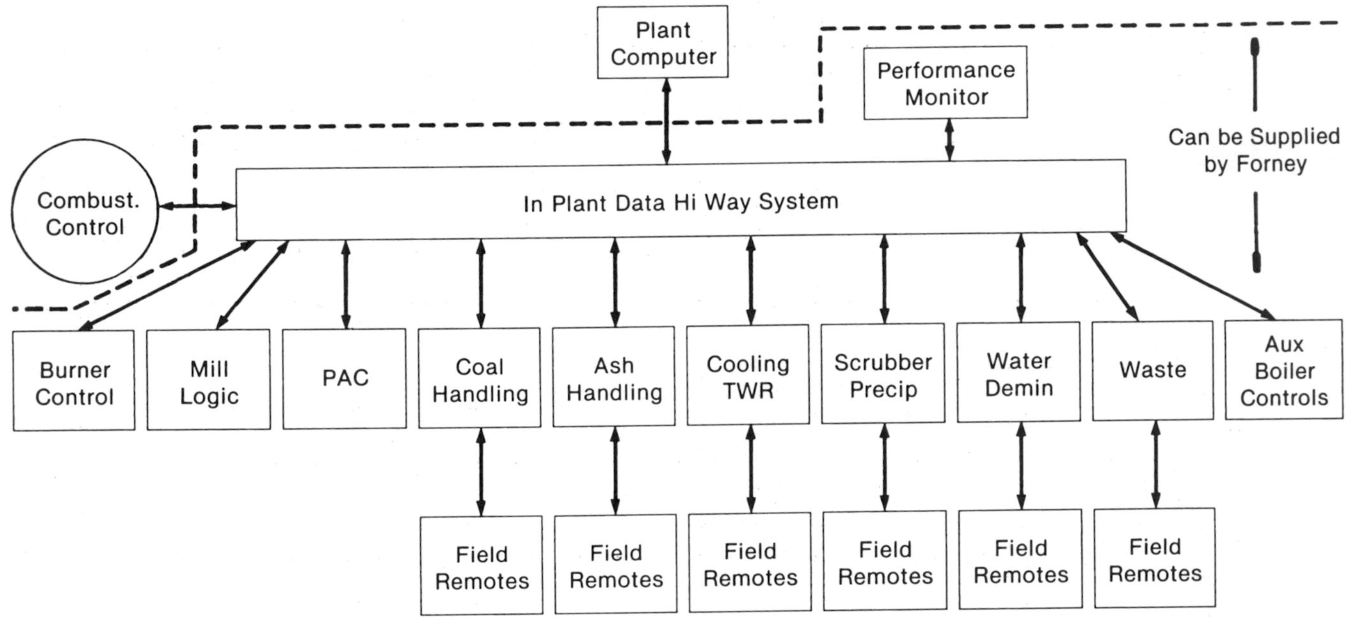

CQ III Applications in a Typical Electric Utility Generating Plant digital control in a remote processor. Another significant feature of the ECS 1200 is its CRT screen, which will replace the conventional keyboard for a majority of manual operations. This feature makes the ECS 1200 the simplest operator interface system available.

INDUSTRIAL PROCESS CONTROL APPLICATIONS

Industrial process controls find applications among a variety of users. Applications exist in the following industries: (1) chemical; (2) oil refining and petrochemical; (3) electric utility; (4) wastewater and environmental; (5) mining, cement, and metallurgy; (6) paper and pulp; and (7) food processing. While specific applications vary between industries for both analog and digital controls, the justification for improved process control systems is similar. Every industry seeks energy conservation, additional throughput, improvements in manpower utilization, plant operation stabilization, and high-quality production.

Two industries appear to offer the greatest opportunities for industrial process control applications, according to Forney executives. These are electric utilities and the hydrocarbon processing industry, which includes oil refining, petrochemical gas processing, and solid fuel processing. Each will be described.

Electric Utility Industry

Demand for electricity is correlated with changes in population, standard of living, and gross national product. Prior to 1974, the industry was actively involved in new plant construction. Between 1972 and 1974, the industry was building approximately seventy new plants per year. However, the industry has been relatively depressed since 1974 because of inflation and increased fuel costs.

Several trends are evident in the industry. First, total demand for electricity has reached a plateau and is projected to increase only 3 percent per year over the next twenty years. Second, plants are larger in terms of megawatts of generating capacity. Third, this trend toward larger plants has reduced the actual number of new plants being built. Projections through the year 2000 suggest that the number of new plant completions will be lower than pre-1974 levels (see Exhibit 4). Fourth, plant construction costs will increase dramatically in the next decade. Projections for the 1980s indicate that a nuclear power plant will cost approximately $2 billion to build and a fossil fuel plant will cost from $557 million to $1 billion. Fifth, the actual time for planning and constructing power plants is increasing. For example, a nuclear plant

EXHIBIT 4
Estimated Number of New Generating Plants to be Built
(Completed): Fossil Fuel versus Nuclear Fuel, 1976–2000

Plant type	Years				
	1976–1980	1981–1985	1986–1990	1991–1995	1996–2000
Fossil	14	10	15	15	20
Nuclear	5	9	9	12	13
Total	19	19	24	27	33

Source: Estimates made by casewriter from industry trend data.

might require two to three years in the planning and bidding stage and ten years to build. A fossil fuel plant might require two years to plan and let bids and four years to build. Finally, increasing environmental and regulatory requirements have raised industry concerns about the building of new generating plants, particularly nuclear plants. The ultimate impact on the scheduling and planning of nuclear plants remains open to question. However, if nuclear plant construction declines, it is possible that fossil fuel plant construction will increase.

Hydrocarbon Processing Industry

Demand for products produced by firms in the hydrocarbon processing industry is correlated with changes in population, gross national product, and energy and chemical usage. Composite output growth in this industry is between 2 and 3 percent annually.

Several trends are emerging in the industry as a whole. First, major growth in this industry is occurring in foreign countries. Exhibit 5 gives a breakdown of plants to be in operation by year in the United States and abroad. Second, the costs of plants is increasing. For example, ammonia plants will cost about $200 million and oil refineries $500 million in the next twenty years. Other types of hydrocarbon processing plants typically fall between these figures. A third trend is toward solid fuel processing, such as coal gasification. Several pilot plants are in operation, but their role in the industry has yet to be fully determined. A fourth trend, at least in the United States, has been toward longer planning periods prior to actual construction. The lengthening of planning time horizons is a result of increased environmental and regulatory considerations. Two to four years are invested in planning

EXHIBIT 5
Estimated Number of Hydrocarbon Processing Plants
to Be Built (Completed) in the United States
and Abroad, 1978–1982

	Year				
	1978	*1979*	*1980*	*1981*	*1982*
Plants in the United States					
Ammonia/ethylene	10	6	1	1	1
Oil refineries	0	0	7	7	7
Other petrochemical[a]/gas processing	0	0	1	1	1
Total U.S.	10	6	9	9	9
Plants abroad					
Ammonia/ethylene	78	35	27	14	9
Oil refineries	2	2	12	12	12
Other petrochemical[a]/gas processing	10	8	7	9	5
Total abroad	90	45	46	35	26
Total plants worldwide	100	51	55	44	35

Source: Estimates made by casewriter from published industry sources, interviews with industry observers, and published estimates of energy needs.

[a]Figures do not include pilot plans investigating coal gasification, liquefication, and solvent refining in the United States.

and bidding time in the United States, compared with about half that time abroad. Construction time periods are about four years.

MARKETING EFFORTS IN THE INDUSTRIAL PROCESS CONTROL INDUSTRY

Marketing efforts in this industry are long-term, often difficult, and extremely competitive. Manufacturer experience, engineering expertise, and technical superiority all play significant roles in the marketing process. Marketing efforts are long-term, given the lengthening planning process preceding the actual construction of plants. A critical concern of sales representatives is knowing when and where plans are underway. It has been estimated that about two-thirds of a project's life in the hydrocarbon processing industry is spent in a secret or planning phase, when sales representatives are not allowed to contact decision makers.[1] Moreover, it is during this time that specifications for plant operations are developed.

Marketing efforts are difficult because many individuals are involved in the purchasing process. Furthermore, the bidding process on new projects can take up to five months. During this period, company management and technical staff review suppliers, prepare bid invitations, issue invitations, review proposals, and finally award contracts.

Marketing efforts are competitive because the number of potential contracts is limited and rewards for a successful bid are high. Current estimates are that process control systems represent from 2 to 4 percent of total plant cost. Furthermore, technical change is a constant threat.

Manufacturers differentiate themselves along a number of dimensions. For example, several firms produce small controls, priced from $5,000 to $10,000, with limited capabilities. Others, such as Honeywell, provide more complicated systems that control an entire plant's process systems. Also, firms such as Foxboro and Honeywell provide "turnkey" process control systems and emphasize hardware capabilities. Others, such as Forney Engineering Company, offer custom-made process control systems and emphasize engineering expertise. This distinction is apparent in the petrochemical industry, where the "purchase" is often for hardware only, with little systems engineering sought. Some firms seek value-added increases due to production of control systems, whereas others seek value-added increases arising from the design of control systems. Each of these dimensions plays an important role in the determination of bid invitations and bid success.

By early 1979, technical aspects of the ECS 1200 control system were well in hand. Even though the capabilities of the system made it suitable for applications in the electric utilities and the hydrocarbon processing industry, Forney executives had to decide which industry should be sought out first, since limited sales and engineering personnel precluded simultaneous coverage of both industries. The hydrocarbon processing industry represented a new market for Forney, whereas the electric utilities industry represented an opportunity for increased penetration of an existing market. The tentative sales goal for the ECS 1200 was $50 million per year over the life of the system.

NOTE

1. This estimate was obtained from *1979 HIP Market Data,* prepared by *Hydrocarbon Processing* magazine, 1979, p. 35.

Show Circuit Frozen Dog Dinner

EXECUTIVES OF TYLER Pet Foods (TPF), Inc., looked forward to their meeting with representatives of Marketing Ventures Unlimited, a marketing and advertising consulting firm. The purpose of the meeting was to review the program for TPF's entry into the household dog food market in the Dallas–Fort Worth, Texas, metropolitan area (DFW). TPF had sought out the consulting firm's services after discussions with food brokers who cited the tremendous potential for TPF in the household dog food market.

THE COMPANY AND THE PRODUCT

Tyler Pet Foods, Inc., is a major distributor of dog food for show-dog kennels in the United States. TPF has prospered as a supplier of a unique dog food for show dogs called Show Circuit Frozen Dog Dinner. Show Circuit was originally formulated by a mink rancher as a means of improving the coats of his minks. After several years of research he perfected the formula for a specially prepared food and began feeding his preparation to his stock on a regular basis. After a short period of time, he noticed that their coats showed a marked improvement. Shortly thereafter, a nearby kennel owner noticed the improve-

The cooperation of Tyler Pet Foods, Inc., in the preparation of this case is gratefully acknowledged. This case was prepared by Professor Roger Kerin, Southern Methodist University, Dallas, as a basis for class discussion and is not designed to illustrate effective or ineffective handling of an administrative situation. Certain names have been changed.

ment and asked to use some of the food to feed his dogs. The dogs' coats improved dramatically and a business was born.

Show Circuit contains federally inspected beef by-products— beef, liver, and chicken. Fresh meat constitutes 85 percent of the product's volume, and the highest-quality cereal accounts for the remaining 15 percent. The ingredients are packaged frozen to prevent spoilage of the fresh uncooked meat.

PACKAGING, PRICING, AND DISTRIBUTION MODIFICATIONS

TPF executives recognized that modifications in packaging Show Circuit were necessary to make the transition from the kennel market to the household dog food market. After some discussion, it was decided that Show Circuit would be packaged in a fifteen-ounce plastic tub with twelve tubs per case.

Because of the costs of producing Show Circuit, a recommended retail price of 99 cents per tub was set. The cost of production, freight, and packaging of the meal was $6.37 per case, which represented total variable costs. The suggested price to retailers was $9.00 per case.

The discussions with food brokers indicated that distribution through supermarkets would be best for Show Circuit because of the need for refrigeration. Food brokers would represent Show Circuit to supermarkets and would receive a 7 percent commission for their services.

THE MEETING

TPF executives listened attentively to the presentation made by representatives from Marketing Ventures Unlimited. Excerpts from their presentation follow.

During the course of the meeting, TPF executives raised a number of questions. The questions were primarily designed to clarify certain aspects of the program. One question that was never asked but that plagued TPF executives was: Will this program establish a place in the market for Show Circuit? This direct question implied several subissues:

1. Was the market itself adequately defined?

2. What position would Show Circuit attract in the market? Should it be targeted toward all dog food or toward specific segments?

3. Could the food brokers get distribution in supermarkets, given the sales program?

4. Could TPF at least break even in the introductory year and achieve a 15 percent return on sales in subsequent years?

TPF executives realized that they had to answer these questions and others before they accepted the proposal. The total cost of the marketing plan proposal was $200,000.

MARKETING VENTURES UNLIMITED PROPOSAL

The following is an excerpted version of the proposal presented to TPF.

The Situation

Our goal is to introduce and promote effectively the sale of Show Circuit dog food in the market area of north Texas. Show Circuit is the costliest dog food to prepare and will be available through supermarkets and chain store outlets.

Show Circuit will be the first completely balanced frozen dog food available in a supermarket. It is of the finest quality and has been used and recommended by professional show-dog owners for years.

Yet, in spite of this history, Show Circuit is essentially a new product and is unknown to the general public. The fact that Show Circuit will be the only dog food located right next to "people food" in the frozen food section is an advantage that must be capitalized upon. The fact that Show Circuit will be the most expensive dog food in the supermarkets can easily be turned into an advantage. Show Circuit's history of blue-ribbon winners is another plus. So, in essence, to market Show Circuit successfully, we must accomplish three objectives:

- Make the public aware of the brand name of Show Circuit, what the packaging looks like, and the fact that Show Circuit is a high-quality dog food.

- Rationalize any objection to spending 99 cents for 15 ounces of dog food.

- Teach the public to shop for dog food in the frozen food section.

The Environment

Sales of dog food will total $3 billion this year. Still, fewer than half the dogs in the United States are regularly fed prepared dog food, which means the dog food industry has yet to tap its full potential.

This optimism is well founded. The dog food industry has been growing rapidly. The dog population, spurred on by the owners' desire for companionship or need for protection, is growing steadily and is expected to continue growing. Also, the trend in using convenience foods (e.g., frozen dinners) in the household contributes to a lack of the table scraps that used to be served to the dog, a fact that will only improve the prospects of the prepared dog foods. One more important trend is that homemakers continue to invest their pets with human qualities and view them as members of the family. About 30 percent of all dogs are fed exclusively from the table.

Supermarket chains, which dispensed around $2.5 billion in dog food nationally, are amenable to opening up required shelf footage for these products, especially since they receive a gross profit margin on pet foods that is superior to the gross profit margins of eighteen other departments located in most supermarkets. Approximately 84 percent of total dog food sales are made in supermarkets. Pet shops and health food stores account for most of the remaining 16 percent. These percentages also apply to the DFW market.

Finally, the DFW market is growing rapidly in both population and median income. Furthermore, the dog and human populations are highly correlated. Our estimate that the Dallas–Fort Worth area has 1.5 percent of the U.S. population (and 1.5 percent of the dog population) makes this a great area for launching the product.

The Competition

Essentially, ten brands of dog food command 45 percent of the $3 billion dog food industry. These ten brands are as follows.

Brand	Sales (millions)
Dog Chow	$254
Alpo	$200
Puppy Chow	$167
Kal Kan	$140
Milk Bone	$137
Gravy Train	$116
Mighty Dog	$ 91
Dog Meal (Hi Pro)	$ 87
Ken-L-Ration	$ 72
Cycle	$ 68

In addition to market share, the forms of the competition will be a major consideration in planning Show Circuit's marketing strategy. Until Show Circuit's program breaks, there are four major forms of dog food: dry (cereal), moist (patties and pouches), wet (canned), and snacks (milk bones). Competitive data described in the presentation are shown in Exhibit 1.

The Problems and Opportunities

Introducing a New Dog Food in a New Form   This is an opportunity to educate the consumer. Until now, dog foods consisted of four categories: canned, dry, moist, and snack-type. Canned dog foods average about 75 percent moisture and 25 percent solid materials. They are marketed either as complete foods or as supplementary foods.

Dry meals are usually produced as flakes, small pellets, or large chunks containing about 10 percent moisture and 90 percent solids. They are chewy, usually well-rounded, and more economical than canned or semi-moist foods.

Moist foods come in chunk or patty form and are about 25 percent moisture and 75 percent solids. They require no refrigeration and are made to look tempting to humans. This category has shown the greatest percentage increase in recent years.

Dog food snacks are available in a wide variety of ingredients and, while tasty, are not recommended as a complete food. All three forms are marketed in the same area of the store. The consumer must be taught to shop for his dog food in another part of the store—the frozen food section.

Overcoming Objections to Frozen Dog Food   An objection must be anticipated regarding the thawing time and freezer space. Therefore, we should state on the container the thawing time, suggestions for quick thawing, how long the food will keep in the refrigerator, plus a gentle reminder to pull that container out of the freezer in the morning. Microwave instructions are a possibility.

Dog Food That Is Not Appealing to Humans   We can quickly turn this problem into an asset in our advertising ("the first dog food made to appeal only to dogs").

High Cost   While people seemingly give price little consideration, they might be hesitant in spending 99 cents (see Exhibit 2). However, the fact that it is so costly to produce should be turned into a positive advantage in the advertising. Backed up with introductory coupons, the price factor should not remain a formidable barrier.

EXHIBIT 1
Statistics on the Dog Food Industry

Total Dog Food Sales (at manufacturer prices) $3 billion

Top Five Dry Dog Food Brands/Market Share[a]

Brand	Producer	Market Share (%)
Dog Chow	Ralston Purina	14.7
Puppy Chow	Ralston Purina	9.7
Gravy Train	General Foods	6.7
Dog Meal (Hi-Pro)	Ralston Purina	5.1
Come 'N Get It	Carnation	3.4
Total		39.6

Top Five Moist Dog Food Brands/Market Share[b]

Brand	Producer	Market Share (%)
Gaines Burgers	General Foods	34.8
Top Choice	General Foods	25.0
Ken-L-Ration Special Cuts	Quaker Oats	15.0
Moist & Meaty	Benco	6.0
Ken-L Burgers	Quaker Oats	5.4
Total		86.2

Top Five Canned Dog Food Brands/Market Share[c]

Brand	Producer	Market Share (%)
Alpo	Grand Met USA	24.2
Kal Kan	Mars	16.9
Mighty Dog	Carnation	11.0
Ken-L-Ration	Quaker Oats	8.6
Cycle	General Foods	8.2
Total		68.9

Top Three Dog Snack Food Brands/Market Share[d]

Brand	Producer	Market Share (%)
Milk Bone	Nabisco Brands	49.8
Jerky Treats	Heinz	12.9
Bonz	Ralston Purina	12.2
Total		74.9

[a]Total sales volume for dry dog food category: $1.725 billion.
[b]Total sales volume for moist dog food category: $186 million.
[c]Total sales volume for canned dog food category: $827 million.
[d]Total sales volume for snack dog food category: $275 million.

EXHIBIT 2
Representative Prices of Dog Food Brands in Dallas–Fort Worth Supermarkets

Canned Dog Food		*Dry Dog Food*	
Mighty Dog	$0.45/6.5 oz.	Dog Chow	$2.59/5 lbs.
Cycle	$0.49/14 oz.	Gravy Train	$5.39/10 lbs.
Alpo	$0.50/14 oz.	Chuck Wagon	$5.39/10 lbs.
Moist Dog Food		*Snack Dog Food*	
Gaines	$1.79/36 oz.	Milk Bone	$1.09/16 oz.
Ken-L-Ration	$3.39/72 oz.		

We see Show Circuit seizing upon four opportunities:

1. The opportunity of being first to tap the vast market potential of frozen dog food

2. The opportunity of being first to be able to claim to produce an organic dog food

3. The opportunity of laying the groundwork for entering the frozen cat food business

4. The opportunity of being able to enter the dog food market when major competitors are under investigation

Creative Strategies

Positioning   Show Circuit will be positioned as the finest dog food available at any price, the most expensive dog food in the supermarket, and the only thing you will feed your dog if he is truly a member of the family.

Concentration   We believe our advertising should be directed to singles and young marrieds between the ages of twenty-one and thirty and people fifty years old and over. The reason is that single adults, young marrieds, and childless (older) couples regard their dogs as a part of the family. The dog sleeps on the bed and has free run of the house or apartment. When children enter the picture, the dog goes into the back yard.

Concepts   Because Show Circuit is such a unique product, there are a variety of concepts that can easily be applied, each with adequate justification:

1. The luxurious fur coat
2. The most expensive dog food
3. The world's finest dog food
4. The guilt concept (shouldn't your dog eat as well as you do?)
5. Now your dog can eat what show champions have been eating for years.

All these will be touched on as the campaign progresses.

Creative Directions   Initially, the campaign will focus attention on product identification and an introductory coupon offer.

Newspapers will supply a smaller, more retentive audience with facts to justify all claims and the 99-cent price. They will also supply the coupon, proven crucial to a successful introduction in the pet food market. The container and coupon will be prominently displayed, and copy will emphasize Show Circuit's quality and explain why it is worth 99 cents for 15 ounces. Special-interest ads will appear in the society, sports, television, and dining-out sections. This unusual media positioning is warranted by the product's unique qualities. Also, positioning in these sections will pull a relatively low promotional budget out of the mass of food-section advertising.

Radio and television will provide access to a mass audience. Prime objectives are to register effectively the brand name and the package design in the viewer or listener's memory. Because of the proven subliminal qualities of these media, an imaginative and all-important emotional approach will be taken.

Geographical Directions   The entire campaign has been designed to accommodate product introduction outside the DFW market area. When the product goes national, the television spot is ready, the introductory ads are ready, the radio spots are ready, and the immediate follow-up is ready.

Sales Packet

The sales packet given to brokers should include, in the most persuasive form possible, the following categories of information:

1. Profits available in the dog food category
2. Chain store acceptance of dog food
3. Market potential

4. An answer to price objection

5. Information about Show Circuit

6. Information about the container

7. User endorsements

8. Promotional schedule

9. Order information

10. Reprints of ads and TV storyboard

11. Sample shelf strip

The packet is designed to persuade the chain store frozen-food buyer to provide freezer space to Show Circuit. Two major problems have to be overcome. Because of the organizational modes of chain store buying departments, we will not be dealing with the regular pet food buyer. Instead, it will be necessary to persuade the frozen-food buyer to stock Show Circuit. The other major problem involves the usual higher markup for frozen foods. It will be necessary to persuade the buyer that greater product turnover will compensate for the lower markup for Show Circuit.

Creative Strategy by Media

Creative strategies will differ by media. It is decided that print media will be utilized to position the product against its competition by comparing product advantages against canned, dry, and semimoist categories. The print campaign will open with an attention-getting ad with a brief product history.

Television will carry the brunt of the attack. The most pressing problem is seen as the difficulty of finding the food in the supermarket, so it is decided to emphasize location in the TV spot.

In order to give the campaign continuity, each ad will show the container. At the top of each of the ads designed to position the competition, the artwork reproduced on the container will be used.

No single breed of dog will be associated with the product. Both the container and the ads will show a variety of breeds from show dogs to mongrels.

The myth/fact format in newspapers will be utilized to take advantage of the current publicity dealing with the nutritional value of all-meat dog food and the growing trend toward more natural foods (see Exhibit 3).

EXHIBIT 3
Show Circuit Print Advertisement

The copy block dealing with Show Circuit will turn the problem of Show Circuit being frozen into a product advantage.

Media Plan

General Media Strategy   Advertising objectives are as follows:

1. Create awareness of new brand.
2. Obtain distribution through grocery outlets.
3. Motivate trial through coupon redemption.
4. Motivate trial through emotional impact of television.

Collateral Advertising   Accomplishment of objective 2 is the main purpose of collateral advertising. The sales packet, containing fact sheets, shelf strips, the TV storyboard, and testimonial letters gives the food broker an impressive story to tell to the supermarket buyer. This is recognized as the critical stage of the campaign, for without sufficient distribution, consumer advertising will be delayed.

Newspaper Magazine   The primary purpose of newspaper advertising is distribution of coupons into the market. This will be accomplished by half-page ads in major north Texas newspapers. As a secondary means of distribution, one full-page ad will be placed in *Better Homes and Gardens* for distribution throughout most of the north Texas market area (see Exhibit 4). We expect that one out of ten sales will involve a coupon redemption.

EXHIBIT 4
Show Circuit Print Advertisement

The second phase of coupon distribution will be effected through thirty-inch ads in the same newspapers. A final coupon distribution will be made through a thirty-inch ad midway through the campaign. Newspaper insertion will be coordinated with TV flights.

Television   The bulk of the budget will be placed in TV production and time. Three two-week flights will be spaced throughout the ninety-day campaign (i.e., two weeks on and two weeks off). A sizable portion of the time budget will be spent on the "Tonight" show aired on channel 5. Fixed space will be purchased within the first half hour of the program. The remainder of the budget will reach daytime and nighttime audiences through channels 8 and 11. Each flight will begin on a Monday, and newspaper advertising will be placed the following Thursday week.

Television Spots

Two basic approaches were taken toward the development of a thirty-second TV spot. The first approach attempts to capitalize on the love of pet owners for their dogs. A somewhat frowzy, middle-aged, semi-greedy woman is shown enjoying a steak dinner—in contrast to an unappetizing cylinder of canned dog food. The spot ends on a close-up of the product. The storyboard for this spot is shown in Exhibit 5.

A second TV spot will emphasize location of the food in the supermarket. A description of the video and audio characteristics of this spot are as follows:

Video	*Audio*
Supermarket/long establishing shot of small boy with bulge under jacket	Announcer: There are many things to remember about new Show Circuit Frozen Dog Food.
Close-up of boy, as puppy pops out of top of jacket	Remember, although it's new to you, champion show dogs have eaten it for years.
Manager walks by, boy hides dog, looks relieved	Remember, it contains all the vitamins your dog needs.
Close-up of sign indicating pet foods	Remember, Show Circuit is a perfectly balanced diet of meat and cereal. Remember, it doesn't come in a can.

EXHIBIT 5
Show Circuit Television Spot

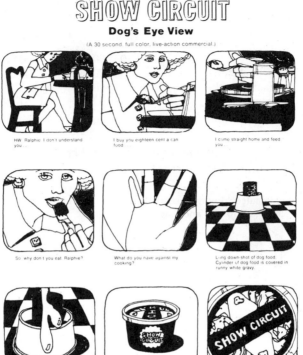

SHOW CIRCUIT

Dog's Eye View

(A 30 second, full color, live-action commercial.)

HW: Ralphie. I don't understand you...

I buy you eighteen cent a can food...

I come straight home and feed you...

So, why don't you eat Ralphie?

What do you have against my cooking?

Long down-shot of dog food. Cylinder of dog food is covered in runny white gravy.

VO: It's a crying shame what some people feed their dogs.

VO: Now your dog can eat what show dogs have eaten for years. Show Circuit, a nutritious dog dinner so different it's found in the frozen food section... next to people food.

HW: Ralphie, think of all the hungry dogs in the world who would love to have your food.

Video	Audio
Dolly shot of boy looking at competitive brands	
Close-up of boy and dog (sync)	Boy: I don't see it anywhere, Sparky.
Boy walks out of store past frozen food compartment. People turn to stare. Tilt down and zoom in on product.	Announcer: But most important, remember you find Show Circuit in the frozen (bark) food section where you shop for other members of your family.

Product Budget

The budget for the program described is $200,000 and is allocated as follows:

Item[a]	Amount	Percentage
Television	$106,000	53.00
Newspaper/magazine	82,000	41.00
Collateral (sales packet)	8,500	4.25
Miscellaneous	3,500	1.75
Total	$200,000	100.00

We see this cost as being the only incremental cost associated with the launch in the Dallas–Fort Worth market.

---

[a]Amounts allocated to individual items include production costs and 15 percent agency fee for placement for TV and magazines.

CASE

TenderCare Disposable Diapers

TOM CAGAN WATCHED as his secretary poured six ounces of water onto each of two disposable diapers laying on his desk. The diaper on the left was a new, improved Pampers, introduced in the summer of 1985 by Procter & Gamble. The new, improved design was supposed to be drier than the preceding Pampers. It was the most recent development in a sequence of designs that traced back to the original Pampers, introduced to the market in 1965. The diaper on his right was a Tender-Care diaper, manufactured by a potential supplier for testing and approval by Cagan's company, Rocky Mountain Medical Corporation (RMM). The outward appearance of both diapers was identical.

Yet the TenderCare diaper was different. Just under its liner (the surface next to the baby's skin) was a wicking fabric that drew moisture from the surface around a soft, waterproof shield to an absorbent reservoir of filler. Pampers and all other disposable diapers on the market kept moisture nearer to the liner and, consequently, the baby's skin. A patent attorney had examined the TenderCare design, concluding that the wicking fabric and shield arrangement should be granted a patent. However, it would be many months before results of the patent application process could be known.

As soon as the empty beakers were placed back on the desk,

This case was written by Professor James E. Nelson, University of Colorado. This case is intended for use as a basis for class discussion rather than to illustrate either effective or ineffective administrative decision making. Some data are disguised. © 1986 by the Business Research Division, College of Business and Administration and the Graduate School of Business Administration, University of Colorado, Boulder, Colorado 80309-0419.

Cagan and his secretary touched the liners of both diapers. They agreed that there was no noticeable difference, and Cagan noted the time. They repeated their "touch test" after one minute and again noted no difference. However, after two minutes, both thought the TenderCare diaper to be drier. At three minutes, they were certain. By five minutes, the TenderCare diaper surface seemed almost dry to the touch, even when a finger was pressed deep into the diaper. In contrast, the Pampers diaper showed little improvement in dryness from three to five minutes and tended to produce a puddle when pressed.

These results were not unexpected. Over the past three months, Cagan and other RMM executives had compared TenderCare's performance with ten brands of disposable diapers available in the Denver market. TenderCare diapers had always felt drier within a two- to four-minute interval after wetting. However, these results were considered tentative because all tests had used TenderCare diapers made by RMM personnel by hand. Today's test was the first made with diapers produced by a supplier under mass manufacturing conditions.

ROCKY MOUNTAIN MEDICAL CORPORATION

RMM was incorporated in Denver, Colorado, in late 1982 by Robert Morrison, M.D. Sales had grown from about $400,000 in 1983 to $2.4 million in 1984 and were expected to reach $3.4 million in 1985. The firm would show a small profit for 1985, as it had each previous year.

Management personnel as of September 1985 included six executives. Cagan served as president and director, positions held since joining RMM in April 1984. Prior to that time he had worked for several high-technology companies in the areas of product design and development, production management, sales management, and general management. His undergraduate studies were in engineering and psychology; he took an M.B.A. in 1981. Dr. Morrison currently served as chairman of the board and vice-president for research and development. He had completed his M.D. in 1976 and was board certified to practice pediatrics in the state of Colorado since 1978. John Bosch served as vice-president of manufacturing, a position held since joining RMM in late 1983. Lawrence Bennett was vice-president of marketing, having primary responsibilities for marketing TenderCare and RMM's two lines of phototherapy products since joining the firm in 1984. Bennett's background included an M.B.A. received in 1981 and three years' experience in groceries product management at General Mills. Two other executives, both also joining RMM in 1984, served as vice-president of personnel and as controller.

Phototherapy Products

RMM's two lines of phototherapy products were used to treat infant jaundice, a condition experienced by some 5 to 10 percent of all newborn babies. One line was marketed to hospitals under the trademark Alpha-Lite. Bennett felt that the Alpha-Lite phototherapy unit was superior to competing products because it gave the baby 360-degree exposure to the therapeutic light. Competing products gave less complete exposure, with the result that the Alpha-Lite unit treated more severe cases and produced quicker recoveries. Apart from the Alpha-Lite unit itself, the hospital line of phototherapy products included a light meter, a photo-mask that protected the baby's eyes while undergoing treatment, and a "baby bikini" that diapered the baby and yet facilitated exposure to the light.

The home phototherapy line of products was marketed under the trademark Baby-Lite.® The phototherapy unit was portable, weighing about 40 pounds, and was foldable for easy transport. The unit when assembled was 33 inches long, 20 inches wide, and 24 inches high (see Exhibit 1). The line also included photo-masks, a thermometer, and a short booklet telling parents about home phototherapy. Parents could rent the unit and purchase related products from a local pharmacy or durable medical equipment dealer for about $75 per day. This was considerably less than the cost of hospital treatment. Another company, Acquitron, Inc., had entered the home phototherapy market in early 1985 and was expected to offer stiff competition. A third competitor was rumored to be entering the market in 1986.

Bennett's responsibilities for all phototherapy products included developing marketing plans and making final decisions about product design, promotion, pricing, and distribution. He directly supervised two product managers, one responsible for Alpha-Lite and the other for Baby-Lite. He occasionally made sales calls with the product managers, visiting hospitals, health maintenance organizations, and insurers.

TenderCare Marketing

Right now most of Bennett's time was spent on TenderCare. Bennett recognized that TenderCare would be marketed much differently than the phototherapy products. TenderCare would be sold to wholesalers, who in turn would sell to supermarkets, drugstores, and mass merchandisers. TenderCare would compete either directly or indirectly with two giant consumer goods manufacturers, Procter & Gamble and Kimberly-Clark. TenderCare represented considerable risk to RMM.

Because of the uncertainty surrounding the marketing of TenderCare, Bennett and Cagan had recently sought the advice of several

EXHIBIT 1
Print Advertisement for Home Phototherapy Unit

Now you can give jaundiced infants the Home Field advantage.

Q: Is jaundice the most commonly treated problem of newborns?
A: Yes. Anywhere from 5-15% of the babies in your community are treated for jaundice.

Q: What is the prescribed treatment for this problem?
A: Proper exposure to special blue lights will effectively treat jaundiced infants.

Q: Can this treatment only be done in a hospital?
A: No. BABY-LITE Home Phototherapy Unit is specifically designed for portability and safe, effective use in the home. The unit provides a controlled, comfortable environment for the baby.

Q: Why is phototherapy at home important to families?
A: Home phototherapy offers the privacy and convenience of the home for nursing and parent-infant bonding, while it shortens expensive hospital stays and avoids readmissions.

BABY-LITE
Home Phototherapy Unit

Rocky Mountain Medical Corporation

marketing consultants. They reached formal agreement with one, a Los Angeles consultant named Alan Anderson. Anderson had had extensive experience in advertising at J. Walter Thompson. He also had had responsibility for marketing and sales at Mattel and Teledyne, specifically for the marketing of such products as IntelliVision,® the Shower Massage,® and the Water Pik.® Anderson currently worked as an independent marketing consultant to several firms. His contract with RMM specified that he would devote 25 percent of his time to Tender-Care the first year and about 12 percent the following two years. During this time, RMM would hire, train, and place their own marketing personnel. One of these people would be a product manager for Ten-derCare.

Bennett and Cagan also could employ the services of a local marketing consultant who served on RMM's advisory board. The board consisted of twelve business and medical experts who were available to answer questions and provide direction. The consultant had spent over twenty-five years in marketing consumer products at several large corporations. His specialty was developing and launching new products, particularly health and beauty aids. He had worked closely with RMM in selecting the name TenderCare,® and had done a great deal of work summarizing market characteristics and analyzing competitors.

MARKET CHARACTERISTICS

The market for babies' disposable diapers could be identified as children, primarily below age three, who use the diapers, and their mothers, primarily between ages eighteen and forty-nine, who decide on the brand and usually make the purchase. Bennett estimated there were about 11 million such children in 1985, living in about 9 million households. The average number of disposable diapers consumed in these households was thought to range from 0 to 15 and to average about 7.

The consumption of disposable diapers is tied closely to birth rates and populations. However, two prominent trends also influence consumption. One is the disposable diaper's steadily increasing share of total diaper usage by babies. Bennett estimated that disposable diapers would increase their share of total diaper usage from 75 percent currently to 90 percent by 1990. The other trend is toward the purchase of higher-quality disposable diapers. Bennett thought the average retail price of disposable diapers would rise about twice as fast as the price of materials used in their construction. Total dollar sales of disposable diapers at retail in 1985 were expected to be about $3.0 billion, or about 15 billion units. Growth rates were thought to be about 14 percent per year for dollar sales and about 8 percent for units.

Foreign markets for disposable diapers would add to these figures. Canada, for example, currently consumed about $0.25 billion at retail, with an expected growth rate of 20 percent per year until 1990. The U.K. market was about twice this size and growing at the same rate.

The U.S. market for disposable diapers was clearly quite large and growing. However, Bennett felt that domestic growth rates could not be maintained much longer because fewer and fewer consumers were available to switch from cloth to disposable diapers. In fact, by 1995, growth rates for disposable diapers would begin to approach growth rates for births, and unit sales of disposable diapers would become directly proportional to numbers of infants using diapers. A consequence of this pronounced slowing of growth would be increased competition.

COMPETITION

Competition between manufacturers of disposable diapers was already intense. Two well-managed giants—Procter & Gamble and Kimberly-Clark—accounted for about 80 percent of the market in 1984 and 1985. Bennett had estimated market shares at:

	1983	1984	1985
Pampers		32%	28%
Huggies		24	28
Luvs		20	20
Other brands	21%	24	24
		100%	100%

Procter & Gamble was clearly the dominant competitor with its Pampers and Luvs brands. However, Procter & Gamble's market share had been declining, from 70 percent in 1981 to about 50 percent today. The company had introduced its thicker Blue Ribbon® Pampers recently in an effort to halt the share decline. It had invested over $500 million in new equipment to produce the product. Procter & Gamble spent approximately $40 million to advertise its two brands in 1984. Kimberly-Clark spent about $19 million to advertise Huggies in 1984.

The 24 percent market share held by other brands was up by some 3 percentage points from 1983. Weyerhaeuser and Johnson & Johnson manufactured most of these diapers, supplying private-label brands for Wards, Penneys, Target, K-Mart, and other retailers. Generic disposable diapers and private brands were also included here, as well as a number of very small, specialized brands that distributed only to local markets. Some of these brands positioned themselves as low-cost alternatives to national brands; others occupied premium ("designer") niches with premium prices. As examples, Universal Converter entered the northern Wisconsin market in 1984 with two brands priced at 78 and 87 percent of Pampers' case price. Riegel Textile Corporation's Cabbage Patch® diapers illustrated the premium end, with higher prices and attractive print designs. Riegel spent $1 million to introduce Cabbage Patch diapers to the market in late 1984.

Additional evidence of intense competition in the disposable diaper industry was the major change of strategy by Johnson & Johnson in 1981. The company took its own brand off the U.S. market, opting instead to produce private-label diapers for major retailers. The company had held about 8 percent of the national market at the time and decided that this simply was not enough to compete effectively. Johnson & Johnson's disposable diaper was the first to be positioned in the industry as a premium product. Sales at one point totaled about 12 percent of the market but began to fall when Luvs and Huggies (with similar premium features) were introduced. Johnson & Johnson's advertising expenditures for disposable diapers in 1980 were about $8 million. The company still competed with its own brand in the international market.

MARKETING STRATEGIES FOR TENDERCARE

Over the past month, Bennett and his consultants had spent considerable time formulating potential marketing strategies for TenderCare. One strategy that already had been discarded was simply licensing the design to another firm. Under a license arrangement, RMM would receive a negotiated royalty based on the licensee's sales of RMM's diaper. However, this strategy was unattractive on several grounds. RMM would have no control over resources devoted to the marketing of TenderCare: the licensee would decide on levels of sales and advertising support, prices, and distribution. The licensee would control advertising content, packaging, and even the choice of brand name. Licensing also meant that RMM would develop little marketing expertise, no image or even awareness among consumers, and no experience in dealing with packaged-goods channels of distribution. The net result would be that RMM would be hitching its future with respect to TenderCare (and any related products) to that of the licensee. Three other strategies seemed more appropriate.

The "Diaper Rash" Strategy

The first strategy involved positioning the product as an aid in the treatment of diaper rash. Diaper rash is a common ailment, thought to affect most infants at some point in their diapered lives. The affliction usually lasted two to three weeks before being cured. Some infants are more disposed to diaper rash than others; however, the ailment probably affects a majority of babies at some point in their diapered lives. The ailment is caused by "a reaction to prolonged contact with urine and feces, retained soaps and topical preparations, and friction and maceration" (Nelson's *Text of Pediatrics*, 1979, p. 1884). Recommended treatment includes careful washing of the affected areas with warm water and without irritating soaps. Treatment also includes the application of protective ointments and powders (sold either by prescription or over the counter).

The diaper rash strategy would target physicians and nurses in either family or general practice and physicians and nurses specializing either in pediatrics or dermatology. Bennett's estimates of the numbers of general or family practitioners in 1985 was approximately 65,000. He thought that about 45,000 pediatricians and dermatologists were practicing in 1985. The numbers of nurses attending all these physicians was estimated at about 290,000. All 400,000 individuals would be the eventual focus of TenderCare marketing efforts. However, the diaper rash strategy would begin (like the other two strategies) where approximately 11 percent of the target market was located—California. Bennett and his consultants agreed that RMM lacked resources sufficient to begin in any larger market. California would provide a good test for TenderCare because the state often set consumption trends for the rest of the U.S. market. California also showed fairly typical levels of competitive activity.

Promotion activities would emphasize either direct mail and free samples or in-office demonstrations to the target market. Mailing lists of most physicians and some nurses in the target market could be purchased at a cost of about $60 per 1,000 names. The cost to print and mail a brochure, cover letter, and return postcard was about $250 per 1,000. To include a single TenderCare disposable diaper would add another $400 per thousand. In-office demonstrations would use registered nurses (employed on a part-time basis) to show TenderCare's superior dryness. The nurses could be quickly trained and compensated on a per-demonstration basis. The typical demonstration would be given to groups of two or three physicians and nurses and would cost RMM about $6. The California market could be used to investigate the relative performance of direct mail versus demonstrations.

RMM would also advertise in trade journals such as the *Journal of Family Practice*, *Journal of Pediatrics*, *Pediatrics*, and *Pediatrics Digest*. However, a problem with such advertisements was waste coverage because none of the trade journals published regional editions. A half-page advertisement (one insertion) would cost about $1,000 for each journal. This cost would be reduced to about $700 if RMM placed several advertisements in the same journal during a one-year period. RMM would also promote TenderCare at local and state medical con-

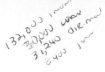

ventions in California. Costs per convention were thought to be about $3,000. The entire promotion budget as well as amounts allocated to direct mail, free samples, advertisements, and medical conventions had yet to be decided.

Prices were planned to produce a retail price per package of 12 TenderCare diapers at around $3.80. This was some 8 to 10 percent higher than the price for a package of 18 Huggies or Luvs. Bennett thought that consumers would pay the premium price because of TenderCare's position: the pennies-per-day differential simply would not matter if a physician prescribed or recommended TenderCare as part of a treatment for diaper rash. "Besides," he noted, "in-store shelf placement of TenderCare under this strategy would be among diaper rash products, not with standard diapers. This will make price comparisons by consumers even more unlikely." The $3.80 package price for 12 TenderCare diapers would produce a contribution margin for RMM of about 9 cents per diaper. It would give retailers a per-diaper margin some 30 percent higher than that for Huggies or Luvs.

The Special-Occasions Strategy

The second strategy centered around a "special-occasions" position that emphasized TenderCare's use in situations where changing the baby would be difficult. One such situation was whenever diapered infants traveled for any length of time. Another occurred daily at some ten thousand daycare centers that accepted infants wearing diapers. Yet another came every evening in each of the 9 million market households when babies were diapered at bedtime.

The special-occasions strategy would target mothers in these 9 million households. Initially, of course, the target would be only the estimated one million mothers living in California. Promotion would aim particularly at first-time mothers, using such magazines as *American Baby* and *Baby Talk*. Per-issue insertion costs for one full-color, half-page advertisement in such magazines would average about $20,000. However, most baby magazines published regional editions where single insertion costs averaged about half that amount. Black and white advertisements could also be considered; their costs would be about 75 percent of the full-color rates. Inserting several ads per year in the same magazine would allow quantity discounts and reduce the average insertion cost by about one-third.

Lately Bennett had begun to wonder if direct mail promotion could instead be used to reach mothers of recently born babies. Mailing lists of some 1–3 million names could be obtained at a cost of around $50 per 1,000. Other costs to produce and mail promotional materials would be the same as those for physicians and nurses. "I suppose the real issue is, just how much more effective is direct mail over advertising? We'd spend at least $250,000 in baby magazines to cover California while the cost of direct mail would probably be between $300,000 and $700,000, depending on whether or not we gave away a diaper." Regardless of Bennett's decision on consumer promotion, he knew RMM would also direct some promotion activities toward physicians and nurses as part of the special-occasions strategy. Budget details were yet to be worked out.

Distribution under the special-occasions strategy would have TenderCare stocked on store shelves along with competing diapers. Still at issue was whether the package should contain 12 or 18 diapers (like Huggies and Luvs) and how much of a premium price TenderCare could command. Bennett considered the packaging and pricing decisions interrelated. A package of 12 TenderCare diapers with per-unit retail prices some 40 percent higher than Huggies or Luvs might work just fine. Such a packaging/pricing strategy would produce a contribution margin to RMM of about 6 cents per diaper. However, the same pricing strategy for a package of 18 diapers probably would not work. "Still," he thought, "good things often come in small packages, and most mothers probably associate higher quality with higher price. One thing is for sure—whichever way we go, we'll need a superior package." Physical dimensions for a TenderCare package of either 12 or 18 diapers could be made similar to the size of the Huggies or Luvs package of 18.

The Head-On Strategy

The third strategy under consideration met major competitors in a direct, frontal attack. The strategy would position TenderCare as a noticeably drier diaper that any mother would prefer to use anytime her baby needed changing. Promotion activities would stress mass advertising to mothers using television and magazines. However, at least two magazines would include a dollar-off coupon to stimulate trial of a package of TenderCare diapers during the product's first three months on the market. Some in-store demonstrations to mothers using "touch tests" might also be employed. Although no budget for California had yet been set, Bennett thought the allocation would be roughly 60:30:10 for television, magazines, and other promotion activities, respectively.

Pricing under this strategy would be competitive with Luvs and Huggies, with the per-diaper price for TenderCare expected to be some 9 percent higher at retail. This differential was needed to cover additional manufacturing costs associated with TenderCare's design. TenderCare's package could contain only 16 diapers and show a lower price than either Huggies or Luvs with their 18-count packages. Alternatively, the package could contain 18 diapers and carry the 9 percent higher price. Bennett wondered if he really wasn't putting too fine a point on the pricing/packaging relationship. "After all," he had said to Anderson, "we've no assurance that retailers or wholesalers would pass along *any* price advantage TenderCare might have due to a smaller package. Either one or both might instead price TenderCare near the package price for our competitors and simply pocket the increased margin!" The only thing that was reasonably certain was TenderCare's package price to the wholesaler. That price was planned to produce about a 3 cent contribution margin to RMM per diaper, regardless of package count.

Summary of the Three Strategies

When viewed together, the three strategies seemed so complex and so diverse as to defy analysis. Partly the problem was one of developing criteria against which the strategies could be compared. Risk was obviously one such criterion; so were company fit and competitive reaction. However, Bennett felt that some additional thought on his part would produce more criteria against which the strategies could be compared. He hoped this effort would produce no more strategies; three were plenty.

The other part of the problem was simply uncertainty. Strengths, weaknesses, and implications of each strategy had yet to be given much thought. Moreover, each strategy seemed likely to have associated with it some surprises. An example illustrating the problem was the recent realization that the Food and Drug Administration (FDA) must approve any direct claims RMM might make about TenderCare's efficacy in treating diaper rash. The chance of receiving this federal agency's approval was thought to be reasonably high; yet it was unclear just what sort of testing and what results were needed. The worst-case scenario would have the FDA requiring lengthy consumer tests that eventually would produce inconclusive results. The best case could have the FDA giving permission based on TenderCare's superior dryness and on results of a small-scale field test recently completed by Dr. Morrison. It would be probably a month before the FDA's position could be known.

"The delay was unfortunate—and unnecessary," Bennett thought, "especially if we eventually settle on either of the other two strategies." In fact, FDA approval was not even needed for the diaper rash strategy if RMM simply claimed (1) that TenderCare diapers were drier than competing diapers and (2) that dryness helps treat diaper rash. Still, a single-statement, direct-claim position was thought to be more effective with mothers and more difficult to copy by any other manufacturer. And yet Bennett did want to move quickly on TenderCare. Every month of delay meant deferred revenue and other postponed benefits that would derive from a successful introduction. Delay also meant the chance that an existing (or other) competitor might develop its own drier diaper and effectively block RMM from reaping the fruits of its development efforts. Speed was of the essence.

FINANCIAL IMPLICATIONS

Bennett recognized that each marketing strategy held immediate as well as long-term financial implications. He was particularly concerned with finance requirements for start-up costs associated with the California entry. Cagan and the other RMM executives had agreed that a stock issue represented the best option to meet these requirements. Accordingly, RMM had begun preparation for a sale of common stock through a brokerage firm that would underwrite and market the issue. Management at the firm felt that RMM could generate between $1 and $3 million, depending on the offering price per share and the number of shares issued.

Proceeds from the sale of stock had to be sufficient to fund the California entry and leave a comfortable margin remaining for contingencies. Proceeds would be used for marketing and other operating expenses as well as for investments in cash, inventory, and accounts receivable assets. It was hoped that TenderCare would generate a profit by the end of the first year in the California market and show a strong contribution to the bottom line thereafter. California profits would contribute to expenses associated with entering additional markets and to the success of any additional stock offerings.

Operating profits and proceeds from the sale of equity would fund additional research and development activities that would extend RMM's diaper technology to other markets. Dr. Morrison and Bennett saw almost immediate application of the technology to the adult incontinent diaper market, currently estimated at about $300 million per year at retail. Underpads for beds constituted at least another $50 million annual market. However, both of these uses were greatly dwarfed by another application, the sanitary napkin market. Finally, the technology could almost certainly be applied to numerous industrial products and processes, many of which promised great potential. All these opportunities made the TenderCare situation that much more crucial to the firm: making a major mistake here would affect the firm for years.

CHAPTER 5

Marketing Research

EFFECTIVE MANAGEMENT OF INFORMATION is a prerequisite for successful decision making. Put simply, the better the information, the better the decision, because decisions are made in an environment of uncertainty, and information reduces uncertainty. Hence, the less uncertainty, the less risky a decision.

Marketing managers are faced with three information-related tasks. They must first determine the kind and amount of information necessary for making a correct decision. They must then compare the costs of acquiring this information with its value in reducing uncertainty. Finally, managers must be able to organize, interpret, and evaluate information as it relates to the decision at hand.

Marketing research is one source of information for the marketing manager. Although definitions vary, marketing research can be thought of as a systematic procedure for providing marketers with actionable decision-making information. As such, marketing research facilitates decision making by providing information that is useful in both the identification and the solution of marketing problems.

Typically, the marketing manager is not directly involved in the practice of marketing research. Technical functions such as data collection, sampling, scaling, or statistical analysis are more likely to be performed by marketing-research specialists. Still, it is imperative that the marketing manager be familiar with both the procedures and the techniques of marketing research. Only this familiarity will enable the manager to ascertain the true value of the information provided by marketing research.

Because the decision-making process directly interfaces with the marketing-research process (the latter being a subset of the former), the marketing manager must be able to evaluate the following:

- Value of marketing-research–based information
- Marketing-research information acquisition process

APPRAISING THE VALUE OF INFORMATION

From a conceptual perspective the value of information is reflected by the extent to which information can reduce decision-related uncertainty. Alternatively, the value of information is reflected by the degree to which the chances of making a correct decision are increased by use of information. Implicit in this perspective is the notion that the information being referred to is incremental information. Hence, information value implicitly refers to the value of incremental information—discrete units of information not currently available to the decision maker.

Given this perspective, information is potentially more valuable in certain decision situations than in others. Since the value of information may be defined as information benefits minus information costs, value increases as benefits increase or costs decrease. Additionally, though, information is potentially more valuable in a decision situation in which there is a great deal of *uncertainty* present and the consequences of an incorrect decision, or the *amount at stake,* are substantial.

Quantitative Appraisal

As indicated in Chapter 3, decision analysis can be used to determine the value of information. To review, decision analysis is used to link together uncertainties in the environment and the alternatives available to a manager. Decision analysis can be extended to identify the upper limit to spend for research information as well.

Returning to the El Macho example in Chapter 3, it was determined, using decision analysis, that El Macho management should maintain its prices, *given* the subjective probabilities of competitor actions and the attendant outcomes (payoffs) assigned to each alternative competitive reaction linkage. The analysis used to arrive at that decision is reconstructed in Exhibit 5.1.

Exhibit 5.1 also shows how the expected monetary value of "perfect" information (EMVPI) can be calculated. Simply speaking, EMVPI is the difference between what El Macho would achieve in contribution dollars if its management knew for certain what competitors would do and the average contribution dollars realized without such information. In other words, if El Macho *knew for certain* that competitors would maintain the price, the "maintain price" alternative would be selected. However, if El Macho management *knew for certain* that competitors would reduce their price, then the "reduce price" alternative would be chosen. Assuming El Macho management faced this decision ten times and knew what competitor reaction would be

EXHIBIT 5.1
Decision Analysis and the Value of Information

Payoff Table Uncertainties

Alternatives	Competitors maintain price (probability = 0.9)	Competitors reduce price (probability = 0.1)
A_1: Reduce price	$150,000	$110,000
A_2: Maintain price	$175,000	$ 90,000

Calculation of expected monetary value (EMV)

$EMV_{A1} = 0.9(\$150,000) + 0.1(\$110,000) = \$146,000$
$EMV_{A2} = 0.9(\$175,000) + 0.1(\$90,000) = \$166,500$

Calculation of expected monetary value of perfect information (EMVPI)

$EMV_{certainty} = 0.9(\$175,000) + 0.1(\$110,000) = \$168,500$
$EMVPI = EMV_{certainty} - EMV_{best\ alternative}$
$EMVPI = \$168,500 - \$166,500 = \$2,000$

each time, El Macho management would make the appropriate decision each time. The result would be an EMV of $168,500. The difference between $168,500 and $166,500 (the best alternative without such information) is viewed as the upper limit to pay for "perfect" information.

Qualitative Appraisal

Still the question remains: What constitutes good decision information? Intuitively, certain types of information would seem to be more valuable than other types of information. Therefore, we need to address those explicit characteristics that make information valuable for decision making.

One such characteristic is the cost of information. While cost (especially absolute cost) may be an overriding concern when determining if a particular kind or form of information is to be utilized in a specific decision context, cost is probably too simplistic to be the only characteristic taken into account. The value of information for decision making can be also evaluated according to five other characteristics. To be maximally useful for decision making, information must possess the characteristics of (1) accuracy, (2) currency, (3) sufficiency, (4) availability, and (5) relevancy. The extent to which information possesses these characteristics determines its practical value in the decision-making process.

Accuracy refers to the degree to which information reflects reality. In other words, information must closely approximate the true state of affairs. While no one would disagree with this statement, frequently there is a tendency to overlook the more subtle question, How much accuracy is required for a given decision to be correctly made? Specifically, the level of accuracy required is best viewed in a relative context—the consequence of making an incorrect decision. If a television manufacturer is in the process of launching a new videotape console—the success or failure of which may determine the future of the firm—there is a need for highly accurate decision information. Alternatively, if the decision relates to whether a restaurant should offer flat or round toothpicks, then less accurate information will suffice. Hence, the accuracy criterion should be considered in a relative sense: How accurate must the data be for the specific decision at hand? Stated somewhat differently, How much inaccuracy can be tolerated before it will affect the decision alternative selected? In brief, information accuracy must be assessed relative to the importance of the decision and the probability and consequences of an incorrect decision.

Currency is the degree to which information reflects events in the present time period. More to the point, information must be up to date. Information on clothing styles or automobile travel behavior in the 1970s may be obsolete for decision making today. The clothing fashion cycle is so rapid that what was in style last fall is "ancient history" this year. Likewise, the life-style changes endured by many U.S. citizens as a result of gasoline and oil price fluctuations have rendered much previous automobile travel information obsolete. Because of the rapidity of environmental changes influencing marketing, information that is not current possesses little likelihood of being decision-actionable.

Sufficiency refers to whether there is enough information to make a correct decision. Hence, the extent to which information is useful for decision making also depends on its completeness and its detail. If information is not sufficient, complete, or detailed enough to permit a decision to be made, it is of little value to a decision maker. Although aggregated information on the existence or size of a market may be available, the lack of detailed information on its geographical, demographic, or attitudinal composition may preclude effective decision making as to what, if any, marketing activities should be directed toward that market.

Availability refers to having information accessible (in hand) when a decision is being made. A marketing manager faced with making a promotion budget decision by the end of July needs appropriate information before the end of July. Even if the information were perfect, it would be of no value if it was not available until August 1. Information must be available when a decision is being made. Tomorrow is too late.

Relevancy refers to the pertinency and applicability of information to the decision issue at hand. This is perhaps the single most important information characteristic. Even if information possesses all the other characteristics of good information, it is of no use unless it is relevant. Although trade-offs frequently must be made among the other characteristics—the requirement of accuracy often being relaxed to ensure availability—relevancy should be the one characteristic immune to compromise. It is the one essential information ingredient for successful decision making.

Finally, bad information—information that does not possess the characteristics just mentioned—may be worse than no information at all. Even if a decision maker does not have information, there is always a chance of making a correct decision. While good information does not insure good decisions (judgment is still required), bad information will normally result in poor decisions. The decision maker has little opportunity to make a correct decision if the underlying information is incorrect. The decision to introduce a new recipe for Coca-Cola is a classic example of how bad information can lead to a poor decision. Coca-Cola marketing research focused heavily on taste tests (which favored the new recipe over the old) but failed to consider the emotional bond to the original Coca-Cola. As a result, marketing-research experts have labeled the research effort "bad research," and industry executives have criticized Coca-Cola for neglecting to use a "large dose of judgment" in designing the research and interpreting the results.[1]

MANAGING THE INFORMATION ACQUISITION PROCESS

The manager should play an active role in the marketing-research, information acquisition process. Specific responsibilities are:

1. Delineating information requirements by defining the problem to be studied

2. Devising the best way to obtain the information

3. Determining the amount to spend for the information

4. Deciding on the types of analysis to best solve the problem

5. Developing actionable marketing strategies from the information

Delineate Information Requirements

The most critical and difficult task a manager faces is the specification of information needed to make a decision. The kinds and amounts of information needed is based on an understanding of the problem confronting the manager. Consider the situation faced by the Gerber Products Company several years ago when it introduced a cereal for infants. Despite optimistic sales forecasts, actual sales performance was disappointing. Was the problem a less-than-expected sales volume, or was this merely evidence of a still more basic problem? If low sales volume was defined as the problem, then a manager would ask the fairly general question: Why has the sales volume failed to meet the forecasts? Alternatively, sales volume could be viewed as a result of more basic underlying factors such as the elements of the marketing mix, market capacity, or competitive behavior. Stated in this way, information can be specified for all or any of these factors. In the Gerber example, executives first examined existing company information on the distribution of the cereal and learned that the item was being distributed through only 25 percent of the outlets originally planned for the cereal.[2]

This example illustrates two important points. First, issues facing organizations many times represent the tip of the iceberg or are symptomatic of more fundamental problems. By addressing the sales-volume question, executives could collect information on a wide variety of topics. However, specification of the problem in terms of factors that could influence sales volume would enable a more disciplined and productive information collection process to be implemented. This means that a model must be specified that identifies both factors influencing the problem under investigation and the relationship between these factors. The idea of models and model building should not connote highly sophisticated or mathematical representations of a phenomenon. Rather, simple (not simplistic) models often provide valuable insight and structure for thinking about a problem. For example, sales volume for a new product can be modeled as follows:

> The number of people in the target market *times* the fraction who become aware of the product *times* the fraction who find it available *times* the share of purchases that triers devote to the new brand *times* the sales rate for the product class [emphasis in original].[3]

Second, implicit in the Gerber example was that existing or readily available information was sought out first. The lesson here is that once a problem is defined, existing sources of information should be examined first. Not only is this information readily available, but it is often the most inexpensive and relevant information available. Only if it is inadequate should additional data be collected.

Devise the Best Means for Obtaining Information

The cost of information will depend on the means for obtaining it. Determining the best means for getting the information necessary for decision making depends on the manager's information requirements, potential or available funds, time constraints, and an appraisal of information usefulness once obtained. Managers are often called on to decide if information should be (1) either generated internally, from available organizational data or collected by organizational personnel, or (2) acquired from external sources through standardized information services provided by them or collected by them, especially for the problem under investigation. Internal and external information sources often complement each other. However, it is not uncommon to find conflicting information from the two sources, and managers sometimes obtain redundant information when both sources are used.

Determine the Cost of Information

Money and time represent two major costs of information. Information has a monetary cost in that the data specified must be paid for as a direct expense. The cost of time is reflected in that the time spent to gather the material dictates when the decision can be made. An important determinant in evaluating expenditures of money and time for information acquisition is the value of the information. Therefore, the manager must evaluate its accuracy, currency, sufficiency, availability, and relevancy to arrive at a decision about the amount of money and time that should be allocated to obtain it.

Decide on the Types of Analysis and Interpretation

Since marketing managers must ultimately make a decision based on the information provided by research, they should be involved in specifying the types of analyses performed on it. For example, a manager should specify how the information should be organized. In examining the sales of a product, it might be useful to have sales data organized by geographical location of the sale, the type of intermediary selling the product, buyer characteristics, and so forth.

An important consideration in specifying the type of analysis is the selection of those factors that best present the information and assist the manager in focusing on critical aspects of the decision to be made. In this way, information becomes relevant, and a manager will not become inundated by an impressive but meaningless volume of information.

Deciding on how to interpret marketing-research data is often a difficult task, even after the manager has specified how research data is to be presented. Consider the research conducted by Brown-Forman Distillers Corporation on Frost 8/80, a new brand of whiskey, which was clear as opposed to being amber or pale brown like other whiskeys. The firm employed eight research firms and spent $500,000 studying virtually every aspect of the product and its potential market. The product failed despite development and marketing expenditures of $6.5 million on the brand. In retrospect, the executive who directed the sales for the brand placed the blame on the interpretation of research data:

> The research we had done probably was all right, but we misread it. The brand came off high on "uniqueness," and we interpreted this to mean the people would be anxious to try it. As it turned out, uniqueness was our biggest problem. The product looked like Vodka but tasted like whiskey. It upset people. They didn't know what to make of it. As far as I'm concerned, that was it in a nutshell.[4]

Develop Actionable Strategies

A final responsibility of the manager is the development of actionable marketing strategies based on the information available. Even though this responsibility is considered last in the present discussion, it follows directly from specifying the information requirements and permeates every aspect of the information-acquisition process. A quote from Mark Twain sums up the importance of knowing in advance the reason for collecting information: "Collecting data is much like collecting garbage. You must know in advance what you are going to do with the stuff before you collect it."[5]

If the information obtained is not actionable, in that it does not lend itself to effective decision making, then its costs has exceeded its value. By specifying in advance, either implicitly or explicitly, what various informational inputs will lead to in terms of specific actions, the entire marketing-research, information-acquisition process becomes a worthwhile venture.

NOTES

1. "How Coke's Decision to Offer 2 Colas Undid 4½ Years of Planning," *Wall Street Journal* (July 15, 1985): 1ff; "Coke's Switch a Classic," *Advertising Age* (July 15, 1985): 1ff.

2. "The Low Birthrate Crimps the Baby-food Market," *Business Week* (July 13, 1974): 44–50.

3. J. D. C. Little, "Decision Support Systems for Marketing Managers," *Journal of Marketing* 43 (1979): 9–27.

4. F. Klein, "An Untimely End," in *Paths to Profit,* ed. J. Barnett (Princeton, N.J.: Dow Jones Books, 1973), pp. 36–42.

5. This quote, attributed to Mark Twain, is found in William Rudelius, W. Bruce Erickson, and William Bakula, Jr., *An Introduction to Contemporary Business* (New York: Harcourt Brace Jovanovich, 1976), p. 142.

ADDITIONAL READINGS

Andreason, Alan. "'Backward' Market Research." *Harvard Business Review* (May–June 1985): 176–182.

Deshpande, Rohit. "The Organizational Context of Market Research Use." *Journal of Marketing* 46 (1982): 91–101.

Greenberg, Barnett; Goldstucker, Jac; and Bellenger, Danny. "What Techniques Are Used by Marketing Researchers in Business." *Journal of Marketing* 41 (1977): 62–68.

Krum, James. "B for Marketing Research Departments." *Journal of Marketing* 42 (1978): 8–12.

Lodish, L. M., and Reibstein, D. J. "New Gold Mines and Minefields in Market Research." *Harvard Business Review* (January–February 1986): 168ff.

Penn, William. "Problem Formulation in Industrial Marketing Research." *Industrial Marketing Management* 7 (1978): 402–409.

Peterson, Robert, and Kerin, Roger. "The Effective Use of Marketing Research Consultants." *Industrial Marketing Management* 9 (1980): 69–73.

Southwestern Montana Coors, Inc.

LARRY BROWNLOW WAS just beginning to realize the problem was more complex than he thought. The problem, of course, was giving direction to Manson and Associates regarding which research should be completed by February 20, 1979, to determine market potential of a Coors beer distributorship for southwestern Montana. With data from this research, Larry would be able to estimate the feasibility of such an operation before the March 5 application deadline. Larry knew his decision on whether or not to apply for the distributorship was the most important career choice he had ever faced.

LARRY BROWNLOW

Larry was just completing his M.B.A. and, from his standpoint, the Coors announcement of expansion into Montana could hardly have been better timed. He had long ago decided the best opportunities and rewards were in smaller, self-owned businesses and not in the jungles of corporate giants.

Because of a family tragedy some three years ago, Larry found himself in a position to consider small business opportunities such as the Coors distributorship. Approximately $200,000 was held in trust

This case was prepared by Professor James E. Nelson, University of Colorado, for educational purposes only. It is designed for classroom purposes and neither for research nor for illustrating effective nor ineffective handling of administrative problems. Some data are disguised. Copyright © 1977 by the Endowment and Research Foundation at Montana State University. Used by permission. Revised 1986.

for Larry, to be dispersed when he reached age thirty. Until then, Larry and his family lived on an annual trust income of about $18,000. It was on this income that Larry decided to leave his sales engineering job and return to graduate school for his M.B.A.

The decision to complete a graduate program and operate his own business had been easy to make. While he could have retired and lived off investment income, Larry knew such a life would not be to his liking. Working with people and the challenge of making it on his own, Larry thought, were far more preferable than enduring an early retirement.

Larry would be thirty in July, about the time money would actually be needed to start the business. In the meantime, he had access to about $7,500 for feasibility research. While there certainly were other places to spend the money, Larry and his wife agreed the opportunity to acquire the distributorship could not be overlooked.

COORS, INC.

Coors' history dated back to 1873, when Adolph Coors built a small brewery in Golden, Colorado. Since then, the brewery had prospered and become the fifth-largest seller of beer in the country. Coors' operating philosophy could be summed up as "hard work, saving money, devotion to the quality of the product, caring about the environment, and giving people something to believe in."

Company operation is consistent with this philosophy. All facilities are still located in Golden, which is centrally located to the sixteen western states in which Coors is marketed. Coors is still family-operated and -controlled. The company had recently issued its first public stock, $127 million worth of nonvoting shares. The issue was enthusiastically received by the financial community despite its being offered at the bottom of the 1975 recession.

Coors' unwillingness to compromise on the high quality of its product is well known both to its suppliers and to its consuming public. Coors beer requires constant refrigeration to maintain this quality, and wholesalers' facilities are closely controlled to ensure proper temperatures are maintained. Wholesalers are also required to install and use aluminum can recycling equipment. Coors was one of the first breweries in the industry to recycle its cans.

Larry was aware of Coors' popularity with consumers. From both personal experience and published articles, Coors consumers were characterized as almost fanatically brand-loyal despite the beer's premium price. As an example, ticket counter employees at the Denver airport regularly reported seeing out-of-state passengers carrying one or more cases of Coors on board for home consumption in non-Coors states. Local acceptance, Larry thought, would be no less enthusiastic.

Because of this high consumer acceptance, the Coors company spent less on advertising than competitors. Consumer demand seemed to pull the product through the distribution channel.

MANSON RESEARCH PROPOSAL

Because of the press of studies, Larry had contacted Manson and Associates in January for their assistance. The firm was a Spokane-based general research supplier that had conducted other feasibility studies in the Pacific Northwest.

Larry had met John Rome, senior research analyst for Manson, and discussed the Coors opportunity and appropriate research extensively in the January meeting. Rome promised a formal research proposal (Exhibit 1) for the project which Larry now held in his hand. It certainly was extensive, Larry thought, and reflected the professionalism he expected. Now came the hard part—choosing the more relevant research from the proposal because he certainly couldn't afford to pay for it all. Rome had suggested a meeting for Friday, which gave Larry only three more days to decide.

Larry was at first overwhelmed. All the research would certainly be useful. He was sure he needed estimates of sales and costs in a form allowing managerial analysis, but what data in what form? Knowledge of competing operations' experience, retailer support, and consumer acceptance also seemed crucial for feasibility analysis. For example, what if consumers were excited about Coors and retailers indifferent or the other way around? Finally, several of the studies would provide information also useful in later months of operation in the areas of promotion and pricing, for example. The problem now appeared more difficult than before!

It would have been nice, Larry thought, if he only had some time to perform part of the suggested research himself. There just was too much in the way of class assignments and other matters to allow him that luxury. Besides, using Manson and Associates would give him research results from an unbiased source. There would be plenty for him to do once he received the results anyway.

INVESTING AND OPERATING DATA

Larry was not completely in the dark regarding investment and operating data for the distributorship. In the past two weeks he had visited two beer wholesalers in his hometown of Pullman, Washington, who

EXHIBIT 1
Manson and Associates Research Proposal

January 16, 1979

Mr. Larry Brownlow
1198 West Lamar
Pullman, WA 99163

Dear Larry:

It was a pleasure meeting you last week and discussing your business and research interests in Coors wholesaling. From further thought and discussion with my colleagues, the Coors opportunity appears even more attractive than when we met.

Appearances can be deceiving, as you know, and I fully agree some formal research is needed before you make application. Research that we recommend would proceed in two distinct stages and is described below:

Stage One Research Based on Secondary Data and Manson Computer Models:

Study A: National and Montana per Capita Beer Consumption for 1978, 1979, 1980, 1981, and 1982.
Description: Per capita annual consumption of beer for the total population and population age twenty-one and over in gallons is provided.
Source: Various publications, Manson computer model
Cost: $500

Study B: Population Estimates for 1975–1985 for Five Montana Counties in Market Area.
Description: Annual estimates of total population and population age twenty-one and over is provided for the period 1975–1985.
Source: U.S. Bureau of Census, Sales Management Annual Survey of Buying Power, Manson computer model
Cost: $750

Study C: Coors Market Share Estimates for 1980–1985.
Description: Coors market share for the five-county market area based on total gallons consumed is estimated for each year in the period 1980–1985. This data will be projected from Coors' experience in Idaho, Colorado, California, Oklahoma, and Texas.
Source: Various publications, Manson computer model
Cost: $1,000

Study D: Estimated Liquor and Beer Licenses for the Market Area 1980–1985.
Description: Projections of the number of on-premise sale operations and off-premise sale operations is provided.

EXHIBIT 1 *(continued)*

Source: Montana Department of Revenue, Manson Computer Model

Cost: $500

Study E: Beer Taxes Paid by Montana Wholesalers for 1977 and 1978 in the Market Area.

Description: Beer taxes paid by each of the five presently operating competing beer wholesalers is provided. This can be converted to gallons sold by applying the state gallonage tax rate (10.5 cents per gallon).

Source: Montana Department of Revenue

Cost: $400

Study F: Financial Statement Summary of Wine, Liquor, and Beer Wholesalers for 1978.

Description: Composite balance sheets, income statements, and relevant measures of performance provided for 416 similar wholesaling operations is provided.

Source: Robert Morris Associates Annual Statement Studies 1979 ed.

Cost: $25

Stage Two Research Based on Primary Data:

Study G: Consumer Study

Description: Study G involves focus group interviews and a mail questionnaire to determine consumer past experience, acceptance, and intention to buy Coors beer. Three focus group interviews would be conducted in three counties in the market area. From these data, a mail questionnaire would be developed and sent to 300 adult residents in the market area utilizing direct questions and a semantic differential scale to measure attitudes toward Coors beer, competing beers, and an ideal beer.

Source: Manson and Associates

Cost: $4,400

Study H: Retailer Study

Description: Group interviews would be conducted with six potential retailers of Coors beer in one county in the market area to determine their past beer sales and experience and their intention to stock and sell Coors. From these data, a mail questionnaire would be developed and sent to all appropriate retailers in the market area to determine similar data.

Source: Manson and Associates

Cost: $2,400

Study I: Survey of Retail and Wholesale Beer Prices

Description: Study I involves in-store interviews with a sample of fifteen retailers in the market area to determine retail

EXHIBIT 1 *(continued)*

and wholesale prices for Budweiser, Hamms, Michelob, Olympia, and a low-price beer.
Source: Manson and Associates
Cost: $1,000

Examples of the form of final report tables are attached [Exhibit II]. This should give you a better idea of the data you will receive.

As you can see, the research is extensive and, I might add, not cheap. However, the research as outlined will supply you with sufficient information to make an estimate of the feasibility of a Coors distributorship, the investment for which is substantial.

I have scheduled 9:00 next Friday as a time to meet with you to discuss the proposal in more detail. Time is short, but we firmly feel the study can be completed by February 20, 1979. If you need more information in the meantime, please feel free to call.

Sincerely,

John Rome
Senior Research Analyst

---

handled Olympia and Hamms beer to get a feel for their operation and marketing experience. It would have been nice to interview a Coors wholesaler, but Coors management had strictly informed all their distributors to provide no information to prospective applicants.

While no specific financial data was discussed, general information had been provided in a cordial fashion because of the noncompetitive nature of Larry's plans. Based on his conversations, Larry had made the following estimates:

Inventory		$120,000
Equipment:		
Delivery trucks	$76,000	
Forklift	10,000	
Recycling and miscellaneous equipment	10,000	
Office equipment	4,000	
Total equipment		100,000
Warehouse		160,000
Land		20,000
Total investment		$400,000

A local banker had reviewed Larry's financial capabilities and saw no problem in extending a line of credit on the order of $200,000. Other family sources also might loan as much as $200,000 to the business.

As a rough estimate of fixed expenses, Larry planned on having four route salesmen, a secretary, and a general warehouse man. Salaries for these people and himself would run about $95,000 annually plus some form of incentive compensation he had yet to determine. Other fixed or semifixed expenses were estimated at:

Equipment depreciation	$20,000
Warehouse depreciation	8,000
Utilities and telephone	8,000
Insurance	6,000
Personal property taxes	5,000
Maintenance and janitorial	2,800
Miscellaneous	1,200
	$51,000

According to the two wholesalers, beer in bottles and cans outsold keg beer by a three-to-one margin. Keg beer prices at the wholesale level were about 45% of prices for beer in bottles and cans.

MEETING

The entire matter deserved much thought. Maybe it was a golden opportunity, maybe not. The only thing certain was that research was needed, Manson and Associates was ready, and Larry needed time to think. Today is Tuesday, Larry thought—only three days until he and John Rome would get together for direction.

EXHIBIT 2
Examples of Final Research Report Tables
Table A: National and Montana Resident Annual Beer
Consumption, 1978–1982
(Gallons)

Year	U.S. Consumption		Montana Consumption	
	Based on Entire Population	Based on Population over Age 21	Based on Entire Population	Based on Population over Age 21
1978				
1979				
1980				
1981				
1982				

Source: Study A.

Table B: Population Estimates for 1975–1985 for Five
Montana Counties in Market Area
(Montana has no drinking age requirement.)

County	Entire Population					
	1975	1977	1979	1981	1983	1985
A						
B						
C						
D						
E						

County	Population Age 21 and Over					
	1975	1977	1979	1981	1983	1985
A						
B						
C						
D						
E						

Source: Study B.

Table C: Coors Market Share Estimates for 1980–1985

Year	Market Share (%)
1980	
1981	
1982	
1983	
1984	
1985	

Source: Study C.

Table D: Liquor and Beer License Estimates for Market Area for 1980–1985

Type of License	1980	1981	1982	1983	1984	1985
All beverages						
Retail beer and wine						
Off-premise beer only						
Veterans beer and liquor						
Fraternal						
Resort beer and liquor						

Source: Study D.

Table E: Beer Taxes Paid by Beer Wholesalers in the Market Area, 1977 and 1978

Wholesaler	1974 Tax Paid ($)	1978 Tax Paid ($)
A		
B		
C		
D		
E		

Source: Study E.

Note: Montana beer tax is 10.5 cents per gallon.

154

Table F: Financial Statement Summary for 416 Wholesalers of Wine, Liquor, and Beer in 1978

Assets   *Percentage*

Cash and equivalents
Accounts and notes receivable net
Inventory
All other current
    Total current
Fixed assets net
Intangibles net
All other noncurrent   ____

    Total   100.0 *Ratios*
                           Quick
                           Current
                           Debts/worth

Liabilities

Notes payable—short term   Sales/receivables
Current maturity long-term debt   Cost sales/inventory
Accounts and notes payable—trade   Percentage profit before
Accrued expenses   taxes
All other current   based on total assets
    Total current
Long-term debt
All other noncurrent
Net worth   ____

    Total liabilities and net worth   100.0

Income Data
Net sales   100.0
Cost of sales
    Gross profit
Operating expenses
Operating profit
All other expenses net   ____

    Profit before taxes

Source: Study F (Robert Morris Associates, © 1979)

Note: Robert Morris Associates cannot emphasize too strongly that its figures *may not* be representative of the entire industry, for the following reasons:

1. The only companies with a chance of being included in Table F are those for whom their submitting banks have recent figures.
2. Even from this restricted group of potentially includable companies, those that are chosen, and the total number chosen, are not determined in any random or otherwise statistically reliable manner.
3. Many companies in Table F have *varied* product lines. Bankers have categorized them by their *primary* product line, and some "impurity" in the data will be introduced.

Thus the figures should not automatically be considered as representative norms.

Table G: Consumer Questionnaire Results

	Yes %	No %	%
Consumed Coors in the past:			
Attitudes toward Coors:			%
Strongly like			
Like			
Indifferent/no opinion			
Dislike			
Strongly dislike			
Total			100.0
Weekly beer consumption:			%
Less than 1 can			
1–2 cans			
3–4 cans			
5–6 cans			
7–8 cans			
9 cans and over			
Total			100.0

	Yes	No %
Usually buy beer at:		%
Liquor stores		
Taverns and bars		
Supermarkets		
Corner grocery		
Total		100.0
Features considered important when buying beer:		%
Taste		
Brand name		
Price		
Store location		
Advertising		
Carbonation		
Other		
Total		100.0

Intention to Buy Coors:

	%
Certainly will	
Maybe will	
Not sure	
Maybe will not	
Certainly will not	___
Total	100.0

Semantic Differential Scale[a]

	Extremely	Very	Somewhat	Somewhat	Very	Extremely	
Masculine	___	___	___	___	___	___	Feminine
Healthful	___	___	___	___	___	___	Unhealthful
Cheap	___	___	___	___	___	___	Expensive
Strong	___	___	___	___	___	___	Weak
Old-fashioned	___	___	___	___	___	___	New
Upper-class	___	___	___	___	___	___	Lower-class
Good taste	___	___	___	___	___	___	Bad taste

Source: Study G.

[a] Profiles would be provided for Coors, three competing beers, and an ideal beer.

157

Table H: Retailer Questionnaire Results

Brands of beer carried:	%		Beer sales:	%
Olympia			Olympia	
Budweiser			Budweiser	
Rainier			Rainier	
Hamms			Hamms	
Brand E			Brand E	
Brand F			Brand F	
Brand G			Brand G	
Others			Others	
Total	100.0		Total	100.0

Semantic Differential Scale[a]

	Extremely	Very	Somewhat		Somewhat	Very	Extremely	
Masculine	——	——	——		——	——	——	Feminine
Healthful	——	——	——		——	——	——	Unhealthful
Cheap	——	——	——		——	——	——	Expensive
Strong	——	——	——		——	——	——	Weak
Old-fashioned	——	——	——		——	——	——	New
Upper-class	——	——	——		——	——	——	Lower-class
Good taste	——	——	——		——	——	——	Bad taste

Intention to sell Coors:
%

Certainly will ——
Maybe will
Not sure
Maybe will not
Certainly will not ——

Total 100.0

Source: Study H.

[a]Profiles would be provided for Coors, three competing beers, and an ideal beer.

Table I: Retail and Wholesale Prices for Selected Beers in the Market Area

Beer	Wholesale[a] Six-Pack Price (dollars)	Retail[b] Six-Pack Price (dollars)
Budweiser		
Hamms		
Michelob		
Olympia		
Low Price Special		

Source: Study I.

[a]Price that the wholesaler sold to retailers.

[b]Price that the retailer sold to consumers.

_____ CASE _____

Soft and Silky

IN JANUARY 1986, Phoebe Masters, product manager for hand and
body lotions, was considering whether to introduce a new package
design for the firm's Soft and Silky shaving cream. The major questions were whether a 5½-ounce or an 11-ounce aerosol container
should be introduced and whether the cost of additional research
could be justified. Timing was critical because the incidence of wom-
en's shaving would increase during the spring months and reach its
peak during the summer months.

THE COMPANY AND THE PRODUCT

Soft and Silky is marketed by a manufacturer of women's personal-
care products. The firm's line of products includes facial creams, hand
and body lotions, and a full line of women's toiletries. Products are
sold by drug and food-and-drug stores through rack jobbers. Rack jobbers are actually wholesalers who set up retail displays and keep them
stocked with merchandise. They receive a margin of 20 percent off the
sales price to retailers.

Soft and Silky was introduced in the spring of 1978. The product
was viewed as a logical extension of the company's line of hand and
body lotions and required few changes in packaging or manufacturing.
The unique dimension of the introduction was that Soft and Silky was
positioned as a women's shaving cream. The positioning strategy was
successful in differentiating Soft and Silky from existing men's shaving
creams. Moreover, rack jobbers were able to obtain product placement
in the women's personal-care item section of drug and food-and-drug
stores, thus emphasizing the product's positioning statement. Furthermore, placement apart from men's shaving cream minimized direct

This case was prepared by Professor Roger A. Kerin, Edwin L. Cox School of
Business, Southern Methodist University, as a basis for class discussion rather than to
illustrate appropriate or inappropriate handling of administrative situations. Data presented in the case are not useful for research purposes.

price comparisons with men's shaving creams, since Soft and Silky was premium priced—$2.55 per 5½-ounce tube at retail. Retailers receive a 40 percent margin on their selling price.

Soft and Silky is sold in a tube as opposed to an aerosol container. This packaging plan was adopted because the firm did not have the technology to produce aerosol containers in 1978. Furthermore, the firm's policy in 1978 was to utilize existing manufacturing capacity whenever possible. As of 1986, all products sold by the firm are packaged in tubes, bottles, or jars.

Soft and Silky had experienced a profitable sales growth from its introduction. Although the market for women's shaving cream was small, the premium price and unique positioning had produced a "customer franchise," in Ms. Master's words. "We have a unique product for the feminine woman who considers herself special."

The unit volume for Soft and Silky for the period 1978–1985 is shown in Exhibit 1. The Soft and Silky income statement for 1985 is shown in Exhibit 2. Advertising and promotional expenses had increased, as a percentage of sales, each year since 1981.

WOMEN'S SHAVING

Research on women's shaving commissioned by Ms. Masters over the last several years has produced a number of findings useful in preparing annual marketing plans for Soft and Silky. The major findings and selected marketing actions prompted by these findings are described next.

Leg-Hair Removal and Shaving Frequency   Women use a variety of methods for leg-hair removal. The most popular method is simply soap and water. Shaving cream is the next most used method, followed by electric razors. Women typically have their own razors, use double-edge razors, and purchase their own supplies of blades.

EXHIBIT 1
Soft and Silky Unit Volume, 1978–1985

Year	Volume	Year	Volume
1978	220,000	1982	452,237
1979	242,000	1983	565,300
1980	278,700	1984	678,356
1981	347,875	1985	814,028

EXHIBIT 2
Soft and Silky Income Statement for the Period
Ending December 31, 1985

Sales		$993,114
Cost of goods sold (incl. freight)[a]		325,611
Gross profit		$667,503
Assignable costs		
Advertising and promotion	$311,648	
Overhead and administrative costs	195,000	506,648
Brand contribution		$160,855

[a]For analysis purposes, treat the cost of goods sold as the only variable cost.

Shaving frequency varies by season, with summer months producing the greatest shaving activity. However, over 80 percent of women shave at least once per week, with working women shaving more frequently than nonworking women.

Attitudes toward Shaving   Women view shaving as a necessary evil. When queried about their ideal shaving cream, women typically respond that they want a product that contains a moisturizer, reduces irritation, and makes shaving easier. It appears that four of five women use a moisturizer after shaving.

These specific results resulted in a change in the Soft and Silky ingredient formulation in 1982. Prior to 1982 the product contained no moisturizers; however, in 1982 moisturizers were added to the product and emphasized in the package and in media advertising.

Market Size and Competitive Products   Industry sources estimate the dollar value of women's "wet shaving" products to be over $95 million in 1985, at manufacturer's prices. Razors account for the bulk of this figure.

There are no shaving creams positioned as a "woman's only" cream currently available in the drug and food-and-drug stores served by the company. Ms. Masters offered two reasons for this situation. "First, the market just isn't that large. I don't think two competing products would or could be profitable. Second, the shelf space battle in food and food-and-drug stores is increasing. One only has to visit one of these stores to see that the shelves are already congested. I doubt that health and beauty aid buyers in these stores want to add another brand, particularly since shaving cream for women is not a big-turnover item.

"However, since men's shaving creams are a substitute for Soft and Silky, we have to consider them as competitors," she added. The average retail price per ounce of men's shaving cream packaged in nonaerosol containers and the price per ounce in aerosol containers are shown in Exhibit 3.

NEW PACKAGE DESIGN

The idea for a new package design was provided by Ms. Masters's assistant, Heather Courtwright. Ms. Courtwright had observed that shaving creams for men were frequently packaged in tubes and aerosol containers. These two packages were frequently displayed side by side in the men's shaving area of drug and food-and-drug stores. The aerosol containers were often more expensive on a container basis since they were typically packaged in 11-ounce cans, but were often cheaper on a per-ounce basis than nonaerosol or tube containers.

Her observations were brought to Ms. Masters's attention in late 1985. After discussing the possibility of changing the package design, Ms. Masters directed Ms. Courtwright to investigate the idea further. Ms. Masters's response was prompted by two recent developments. First, the annual average unit sales volume increase for Soft and Silky had plateaued in recent years. Perhaps a change in packaging or another package might bolster sales volume, she thought. Second, the growth of Soft and Silky had strained manufacturing capacity. Historically, production of Soft and Silky had been easily integrated into the firm's production schedules. However, growth in the entire line of hand and body lotions coupled with Soft and Silky volume had aggravated production scheduling. Given current economic conditions, the firm had no capacity-expansion plans for the next three years.

EXHIBIT 3
Retail price comparisons

Container Type/Size	Average Retail Price/Ounce	Retail Price Range/Ounce
Nonaerosol—4 oz.	$0.42	$0.32–$0.44
Nonaerosol—10 oz.	$0.21	$0.18–$0.25
Aerosol—6 oz.	$0.27	$0.24–$0.30
Aerosol—11 oz.	$0.16	$0.08–$0.23

Ms. Courtwright contacted a firm specializing in "contract fill-ing." A contract filler purchases the cans, propellants, caps, and valves from a variety of sources. The firm assembles these components, in-cluding the product fill (i.e., shaving cream), into the final aerosol prod-uct. The production method is called pressure filling. In this method, the cap and valve are inserted in the can and then sealed. At the same time a vacuum is created in the container. The product fill and propel-lant are then injected under high pressure through the valve into the can.

The estimated delivered cost from the contract filler and the freight cost to retailers for an 11-ounce aerosol can, including the shav-ing cream, was $0.29. A minimum order of 50,000 11-ounce cans would be required. The retail price would be set at $2.85 per 11-ounce can, reflecting Soft and Silky's premium price strategy. The estimated de-livered cost and the freight cost to retailers for a 5½-ounce aerosol can, including shaving cream, was $0.20. The carton would be the same as an 11-ounce can carton and the retail price would be $1.85. A 50,000-unit minimum order would be required.

PRELIMINARY TESTS

In November 1985, Ms. Courtwright requested $15,000 to assess con-sumer response to the aerosol container. Ms. Masters approved the request on the basis of the cost data provided and the recognition that use of a contract filler would require no incremental investment in manufacturing capability.

Ms. Courtwright commissioned a large marketing-research firm to conduct four focus-group studies.[a] Two focus groups would involve current users of Soft and Silky and two focus groups would involve nonusers of Soft and Silky, but users of shaving cream. The principal information sought from these focus group studies were:

1. Are present customers and noncustomers receptive to the aerosol can?

2. At what rate would present customers convert to the aerosol can and would noncustomers switch over to Soft and Silky?

3. Where, in drug and food-and-drug stores, do customers and noncustomers expect to find the aerosol can?

4. Is the price acceptable?

---

[a] A *focus-group* interview consists of a moderator questioning and listening to a group of eight to twelve consumers.

In addition to these questions, the marketing-research firm was asked to examine analogous situations of package changes and report these findings.

In late December the marketing-research firm presented its findings. They were:

1. Customers and noncustomers were unanimously in favor of the aerosol can. The 11-ounce can was the favorite since it would require fewer purchases.

2. Half of Soft and Silky customers said they would convert to the 11-ounce can while 25 percent said they would convert to the 5½-ounce can.

3. One-fourth of the noncustomers said they would switch over to the aerosol can irrespective of can size. These consumers' preference for the aerosol over the tube package was their principal reason (in addition to price) for not buying Soft and Silky previously.

4. Customers expected to find the aerosol can next to the tube container. Noncustomers expected to find the aerosol container next to the men's shaving cream.

5. The pricing was acceptable and actually favored by current customers. Noncustomers thought the price was somewhat high, but liked the moisturizing benefit and would try the product.

In addition to these findings, the marketing-research firm presented ten products case histories in which marketers of men's shaving cream had introduced a new package.[b] Two statistics were highlighted: sales growth with the combined packages and the cannibalization rate for the existing package. According to the report:

> It is difficult to draw one-to-one comparisons between the experience of other shaving creams and Soft and Silky, given its unique market position. We have tried to do so after examining ten product design changes. Our estimates [Exhibit 4] are broken down into a "high" and a "low" forecast for each package size. Seven out of ten studied experienced the "high" situation presented; three experienced the "low" situation. We see the 11-ounce package as producing the largest increase in ounces sold. Even with the cannibalism effect operating, we believe that an additional package will produce higher sales, in ounces, than the forecasted volume of 5,372,587 ounces (976,834 5½-ounce tubes) for 1983. Only a market test will indicate what will actually occur.

----

[b] There was no distinction made by size of package, whether the package change was from aerosol to nonaerosol or vice versa, or previous sales performances.

JANUARY 1986

Ms. Masters and Ms. Courtwright studied the research firm's findings carefully. They particularly noted the recommendation made. The recommendation emphasized the need to conduct a market test to determine the best package design.

The test market recommendation emphasized the introduction of the new package design in a limited cross-section of drug and food-and-drug stores, including heavy-volume and low-volume stores. Test stores would be isolated geographically from nontest stores. The new package would be placed among men's shaving creams, and the test

EXHIBIT 4
Soft and Silky forecasts by size of aerosol container

Forecast A: Low estimate for 5½-ounce aerosol package addition

5½-oz. tube package volume		4,900,000 ounces
5½-oz. aerosol package volume:		
Cannibalized volume	472,587	
Net new volume	250,000	722,587 ounces
		5,622,587 ounces

Forecast B: High estimate for 5½-ounce aerosol package addition

5½-oz. tube package volume		5,200,000 ounces
5½-oz. aerosol package volume:		
Cannibalized volume	172,587	
Net new volume	300,000	472,587 ounces
		5,672,587 ounces

Forecast C: Low estimate for 11-ounce aerosol package addition

5½-oz. tube package volume		4,500,000 ounces
11-oz. aerosol package volume:		
Cannibalized volume	872,587	
Net new volume	400,000	1,272,587 ounces
		5,772,587 ounces

Forecast D: High estimate for 11-ounce aerosol package addition

5½-oz. tube package volume		5,200,000 ounces
11-oz. aerosol package volume:		
Cannibalized volume	172,587	
Net new volume	600,000	772,587 ounces
		5,972,587 ounces

would run for three months beginning April 1, 1986. One-half of the stores would carry the 5½-ounce aerosol container. The test would include a full complement of promotional aids, including newspaper and point-of-purchase displays and approximate full-scale introduction.

Ms. Courtwright noted that the estimated cost for the test market would be $22,000, which included the cost of gathering marketing-research data on the cannibalization rate and incremental sales growth. No other incremental costs would be charged against the products. Sales and marketing efforts for the existing package would remain unchanged during the course of either test.

Late in the evening of January 28, 1986, Ms. Masters found herself considering whether the 5½-ounce or the 11-ounce aerosol container should be introduced since she believed it unwise to introduce both sizes, given the uncertainty of market acceptance. She also wondered whether the test market proposal should be adopted. Ms. Masters was confident that the existing package would produce sales of 976,934 units (a 20 percent increase) in 1986, given the product's sales history. "Perhaps I should have told Heather to forget the whole matter last fall," she thought to herself.

CASE

Anderson Clayton Foods, Inc.

IN LATE SUMMER 1985, Mr. Timothy Summers was hired as vice-president of marketing and sales for the Consumer Products Division of Anderson Clayton Foods. Shortly after his arrival, Mr. Summers faced his first major decision. Upon reviewing correspondence between his predecessor and senior Anderson Clayton Foods executives, he noticed that funds for syndicated market data services had been approved for the Consumer Products Division, although no action had been taken. The decision he faced was whether to purchase the services provided by A. C. Nielsen Company Food Index or by Selling Areas–Marketing, Incorporated (SAMI), since both could not be obtained because of budget restraints. Intracompany correspondence revealed that there was some disagreement between sales and marketing personnel as to which service should be selected, even though industry executives recognize both services as important sources of market data for food companies.

THE COMPANY

Anderson Clayton Foods is a producer and marketer of food items for institutional use and for retail sale. The company recorded sales of $505 million in the fiscal year ending June 30, 1985.

This case was made possible through the cooperation of Anderson Clayton Foods, Inc. The case was prepared by Professor Roger A. Kerin, Edwin L. Cox School of Business, Southern Methodist University, as a basis for class discussion, and is not designed to illustrate effective or ineffective handling of administrative situations. Names of individuals have been disguised.

The company is structured in three business divisions, with each division being identified by its basic product line. The *Consumer Products Division* generated approximately $80 million in sales and comprised two major branded retail product lines: Chiffon Margarine and Seven Seas Salad Dressings. The *Dairy Division* had sales of approximately $125 million. The third division, the *Oil Products Division,* had sales of approximately $300 million in 1985.

Anderson Clayton Foods marketed the products of all three divisions in the United States through its own sales force and a network of food brokers. The consumer products division sold its products in fifty-five sales territories identified by Anderson Clayton Foods.

THE CONSUMER PRODUCTS DIVISION

As vice-president of marketing and sales for the consumer products division, Mr. Summers had reporting to him the product manager for Chiffon Margarine, Brock Jensen, and for Seven Seas Salad Dressings, Janet Donaldson. Both Mr. Jensen and Ms. Donaldson had joined the company in 1983. Mr. Jensen had been employed by a major marketing-research firm for the three years prior to his joining Anderson Clayton Foods as product manager. Ms. Donaldson had joined the company upon completing her graduate studies and had been promoted to product manager just prior to Mr. Summer's appointment.

Also reporting to Mr. Summers was Philip Kendrick, the sales manager for both Chiffon Margarine and Seven Seas Salad Dressings. Mr. Kendrick was a career employee of Anderson Clayton Foods, having worked for the company for thirty-three years. He had joined the company out of high school as an assistant territory sales manager and had worked his way up through the ranks to his current position, which he had held for five years.

The Margarine Category

In 1985, sales for the total margarine industry were approximately 2 billion pounds, up 1 percent from the previous year. Growth in the margarine category had averaged less than 2 percent per year for the past five years, and industry observers expected this rate of growth to continue for the foreseeable future. In general, sales growth of margarine mirrored U.S. population growth.

Anderson Clayton Foods executives viewed the margarine industry as being segmented into three basic types of brands: (1) nationally advertised brands, (2) regionally advertised brands, and (3) private labels. As Chiffon Margarine had been in national distribution since

1956 and was advertised on network television, Anderson Clayton Foods executives considered Chiffon Margarine as competing within the nationally advertised brands segment, even though its sales tended to cluster in the midwestern and southwestern United States. The nationally advertised segment made up about 52 percent of total industry sales. Major brands in this segment were Imperial, Parkay, Bluebonnet, Fleishmann's, and Shedd's. In the 1985 fiscal year, Chiffon Margarine recorded an estimated 3 percent market share of total pounds sold, which represented sales of $30 million. Chiffon Margarine typically obtained a 20 percent gross margin on sales. The Chiffon Margarine soft tub product line is shown in Exhibit 1. Anderson Clayton Foods also marketed a Chiffon one-pound stick product.

Research conducted in previous years revealed that the margarine category was one in which brand loyalty was very low; however, consumers did have a favorite brand. Consumers generally selected a segment (advertised brand, regional brand, private label) in which to buy and then shopped for the best deal within the category. Similarly, the retail trade viewed margarine as a high-turnover, low-margin item

EXHIBIT 1
Chiffon Margarine Product Line

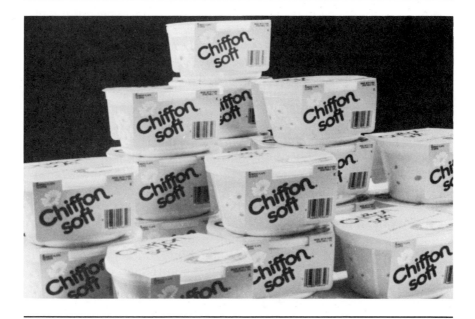

Source: Courtesy of Anderson Clayton Foods, Inc.

that was frequently given a "feature" price to serve as a traffic builder for the store. In order to gain these feature prices, margarine manufacturers frequently offered trade promotion allowances.[a] This industry practice in the margarine category resulted in marketing budgets heavily weighted toward trade promotion spending. Approximately 80 percent of the advertising and promotion budget for branded margarine was spent on trade promotions; 20 percent was spent on advertising and consumer promotions.

Early talks between Mr. Summers and Mr. Jensen indicated that Mr. Jensen was trying to find a way to move his brand away from dependence on these trade promotions as the means of volume generation. Mr. Jensen's rationale for his objective was that even though trade allowances were sometimes fully reflected in the retail price of the product, too often the trade would take the allowance and reflect only a portion of the allowance at retail. This practice increased the trade's profit on margarine but did not provide the consumer with the incentive to purchase that the manufacturer had intended in offering the allowance.

The Salad Dressing Category

Sales for bottled salad dressings in 1985 amounted to 400 million pounds, an increase of 5 percent over 1984 volume. The past five-year annual growth of the category was 3 percent, with expectations of 3 percent annual growth for the next five years. Bottled salad dressings were produced by over a hundred manufacturers, although 85 percent of the industry's volume was captured by the brands produced by five companies. Major brands were Kraft and Wishbone. Kraft captured a market share near 40 percent, and Wishbone's market share was 20 percent. Seven Seas Salad Dressings recorded sales of $50 million in the 1985 fiscal year, with a 40 percent gross margin on sales. In terms of pounds, Seven Seas' market share was 12 percent; however, sales were highest in the midwestern and the northeastern United States. The Seven Seas Salad Dressings product line is shown in Exhibit 2 (a total of eighteen flavors are offered, with six flavors sold in eight-ounce and sixteen-ounce sizes).

The marketing dynamics of the bottled salad dressing category differed from those for margarine. For example, the growth rate was higher as a result of new product introductions and the attendant promotional support, flavor variations, and the introduction of a number of gourmet salad dressings such as Paul Newman's Own Salad Dress-

---

[a] Typical trade promotion allowances in the industry included off-invoice allowances, quota programs, shelf tags, and cooperative advertising allowances.

EXHIBIT 2
Seven Seas Salad Dressing Product Line

Source: Courtesy of Anderson Clayton Foods, Inc.

ing. Furthermore, the retail trade viewed the category as one in which the responsibility for moving the product off the shelf was the manufacturer's. Trade efforts were therefore held to a relatively smaller part of the promotion mix. A typical promotion support budget for a nationally advertised salad dressing would have 60 percent of the dollars allocated to advertising and consumer promotions and 40 percent allocated to trade promotions.

Views on the Use of Market Data Services

Mr. Summers desired input from his staff about the choice between Nielsen and SAMI for market data even though he already knew what differences of opinion would emerge. He called Kendrick, Jensen, and Donaldson together to ask their opinions about which data service would most benefit the Consumer Products Division in determining, implementing, and monitoring marketing strategy.

Philip Kendrick preferred SAMI to Nielsen. He pointed out that SAMI is much more trade-oriented than the Nielsen Retail Food Index.

SAMI's warehouse withdrawal data were, in his opinion, a good measure of sales volume to retailers and an indicator of the effectiveness of short-term trade promotions. Strengths of SAMI, in Mr. Kendrick's estimation, included its more frequent data reports (every twenty-eight days) and its coverage of actual shipments making up 77 percent of the total food sales in the United States. In addition, SAMI has a second service, called SARDI, which measures product distribution at retail.

"I saw some figures the other day that showed that 23 percent of the retail grocery stores do 80 percent of the country's total volume," Mr. Kendrick declared. "Since SAMI covers the major market areas we are in, SAMI is the service that will be the biggest help to our sales organization.

"My salespeople find that wholesalers to whom they sell our products are interested only in sales figures for their own market," Mr. Kendrick continued. "They don't care what's happening in the rest of the country as long as they are doing O.K. in selling to their customers. SAMI data are more local than Nielsen's figures, so they're more useful to us in making competitive deals."

From his previous experience in the food industry, Mr. Summers knew that SAMI data were especially useful for charting market behavior where trade deals were used in local areas to stimulate sales. In these situations SAMI allowed for early response to problem areas, permitted quicker lowering of competitive prices, and created good opportunities for effective sales calls at a retail outlet's buying office. Moreover, SAMI data were also useful for measuring short-term effectiveness of marketing programs. Nevertheless, Mr. Summers was also of the opinion that SAMI data tended to overstate deal effectiveness whenever there was trade inventory accumulation during deal periods. This, despite being one of the objectives of a trade deal, was a danger in relying exclusively on SAMI data, Mr. Summers thought. Still, he appreciated Philip Kendrick's point of view that SAMI was valuable in salesperson-buyer negotiations. Moreover, Mr. Summers knew that major retail stores already had access to and examined SAMI data continuously. This was not true for the Nielsen Retail Food Index.

Brock Jensen favored contracting with the A. C. Nielsen Company for the Retail Food Index. Jensen made the point that Nielsen's data represent estimates of retail sales to the final customer, thus permitting the client to keep an eye on consumer reaction to products, rather than movement of products to retailers' shelves. Another advantage of Nielsen, he felt, was that the Retail Food Index could be used to project sales and brand share at the national level. "This capability is important for measuring the long-run effectiveness of our advertising and trade promotions. Nielsen data can also be customized according to our company's particular data needs," Jensen said.

Janet Donaldson supported Jensen's preference for the Nielsen data service. She said that the Nielsen breakdown of retail sales by store type and size provided necessary information about Anderson Clayton Foods' product distribution. "The several kinds of data secured by Nielsen allow better tracking of competitive activity and of the competitive environment," she declared. "We would also get prompt service here at Anderson Clayton Foods because one of Nielsen's ten client service offices is located near our office."

Summers felt Jensen and Donaldson had reasons for promoting the selection of the Nielsen Retail Food Index that were as good as Philip Kendrick's reasons for advocating the choice of SAMI. Summers knew that Nielsen's statistically selected sample of the market tended to give accurate readings of total volume and trend, including competitive position. He also recognized that, with the Retail Food Index, Anderson Clayton Foods would be able to detect over- or undersupply at the retail level sooner than with measurements of warehouse withdrawals. Nielsen data permitted determination of velocity of brands, sizes, and types of products relative to those of the competition. This capability permitted the use of the data as a sales tool. Summers also was aware of the variety of ancillary services available to Nielsen clients.

Of primary importance to Mr. Summers was choosing the data source that would provide the best market information for Anderson Clayton Foods's Consumer Products Division. Moreover, he wanted to choose the service that would best satisfy the information needs required for promotional planning and budgeting for Chiffon Margarine and Seven Seas Salad Dressings. Even though both product lines had the same level of promotional expenditures, their relative emphasis on consumer and trade promotion differed, he thought, and that difference should be reflected in the service selected. Summaries of the Nielsen Retail Food Index and SAMI are found in Appendixes A and B, respectively.

A. C. Nielsen Company

The A. C. Nielsen Company is the world's largest marketing-research operation. Perhaps best known for the scientific measurement of television audiences, A. C. Nielsen provides more than sixty fact-finding services for its clients. One of these services is the Nielsen Retail Index. This service measures consumer sales every sixty days through its professional field force, who conduct audits of invoices and inventories in 1,300 typical chain and independent food stores. Exhibit A.1 illustrates the scope of information furnished in bimonthly reports. Exhibit A.2 shows data breakdowns available. These data are entered directly into a computer system that automatically checks the accuracy and logic of the data, including comparisons with data from previous periods. The data are then processed, projected, and summarized for the entire country, the Retail Index territories, client sales areas, and any other client-specified market breakdowns.

Every two months these data are charted and presented to the client by a Nielsen client-service representative within four to seven weeks after the close of the two-month audit period. The Nielsen client-service representative analyzes the charts for the client, drawing attention to the most important data and providing an interpretation of the figures in terms of client goals and plans. One such chart is Exhibit A.3, which shows the client's brand sales (market share) relative to

EXHIBIT A.1
Compete List of Data Secured Every Sixty Days
in Food Stores

1. Sales to consumers	8. Prices (wholesale and retail)
2. Purchases by retailers	9. Special factory packs
3. Retail inventories	10. Dealer support (displays, local advertising, coupon redemption)
4. Average monthly sales	
5. Store count distribution	11. Total food store sales (all commodities)
6. All commodity distribution	
7. Out-of-stock stores	12. Major media advertising (from other sources)

This material is drawn from A. C. Nielsen Company brochures. Exhibits are presented through the courtesy of the A. C. Nielsen Company.

EXHIBIT A.2
Data Breakdowns Available

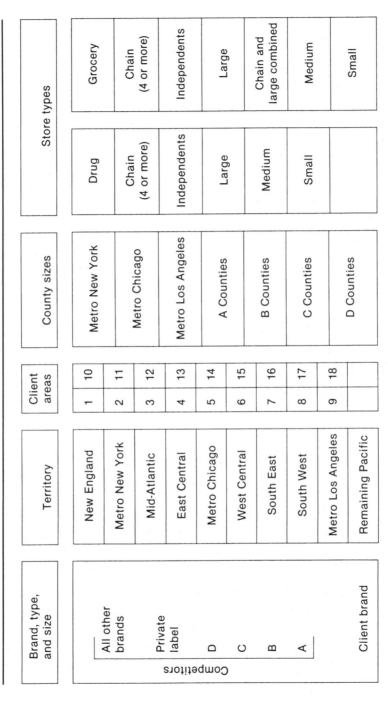

Brand, type, and size		Territory	Client areas		County sizes	Store types			
		New England	1	10	Metro New York	Drug	Grocery		
Competitors	All other brands	Metro New York	2	11	Metro Chicago	Chain (4 or more)	Chain (4 or more)		
	Private label	Mid-Atlantic	3	12	Metro Los Angeles	Independents	Independents		
	D	East Central	4	13	A Counties	Large	Large		
	C	Metro Chicago	5	14	B Counties	Medium	Chain and large combined		
	B	West Central	6	15	C Counties	Small	Medium		
	A	South East	7	16	D Counties		Small		
		South West	8	17					
		Metro Los Angeles	9	18					
Client brand		Remaining Pacific							

EXHIBIT A.3
Consumer Sales: All Brands
(in thousands of dollars)

	Jan. Feb.	Mar. Apr.	May June	July Aug.	Sept. Oct.	Nov. Dec.	Jan. Feb.
Total	$1,205	$1,310	$1,530	$1,800	$1,460	$1,270	$1,120
Miscellaneous brands	$289 24%	341 26%	488 32%	612 34%	409 28%	228 16%	134 12%
Competitor C	$145 12%	170 13%	184 12%	216 12%	190 13%	203 16%	179 16%
Competitor B							
Competitor A	$253 21%	275 21%	337 22%	396 22%	336 23%	292 23%	246 22%
Your brand	$301 25%	314 24%	337 22%	396 22%	350 24%	356 28%	348 31%

competitive brand sales share over time. Information provided by the Nielsen Retail Index System can also be used to

- Measure sell-in to the retailer.
- Evaluate in-store position.
- Analyze and correct distribution problems.
- Evaluate pricing strategies.
- Monitor consumer deal activity.
- Determine retailer promotional activity.
- Track advertising efforts.
- Monitor competitive marketing efforts.
- Analyze marketing variables by individual store.
- Analyze sales and marketing efforts by sales area.
- Supplement other marketing data.

One of the most illuminating aspects of the data provided by the Retail Index is its use for evaluating changes in a manufacturer's pro-

motion activity and resultant consumer response. Two examples illustrate this point.

Consider first the situation where a manufacturer modifies an
advertising effort for Brand A. If the manufacturer monitors only shipments from the factory for Brand A before and after the change, it
would appear that the change adversely affected volume (see Exhibit
A.4). However, upon inspection of consumer sales provided by the
Retail Index, it becomes apparent that the change in fact had a positive
effect on Brand A sales.

The Retail Index is also valuable for assessing both the short- and
the long-term effects of a trade promotion such as a cents-off or two-
for-one deal. Exhibit A.5 shows how a successful one-cent promotion
would be identified over time through continuous monitoring by the
Retail Index. Exhibit A.6 illustrates an unsuccessful one-cent promotion when charted over time.

EXHIBIT A.4
A Change in Advertising (Quantity, Type, Copy, Media)

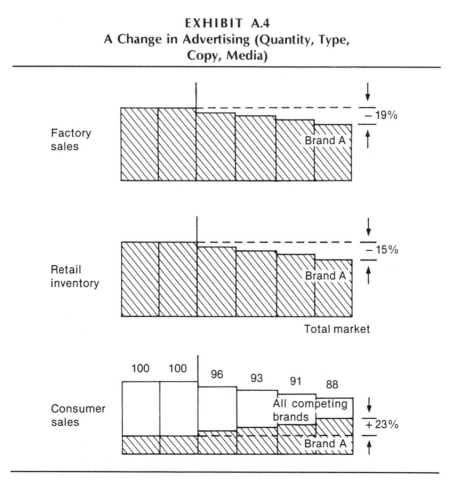

EXHIBIT A.5
A Successful Promotion: Brand B, Metropolitan New York

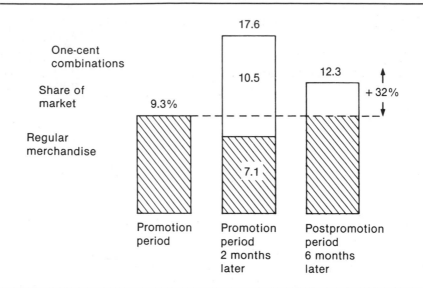

One-cent combinations

Share of market

Regular merchandise

17.6

10.5

12.3

9.3%

7.1

+32%

| Promotion period | Promotion period 2 months later | Postpromotion period 6 months later |

EXHIBIT A.6
An Unsuccessful Promotion: Brand L, Metropolitan New York

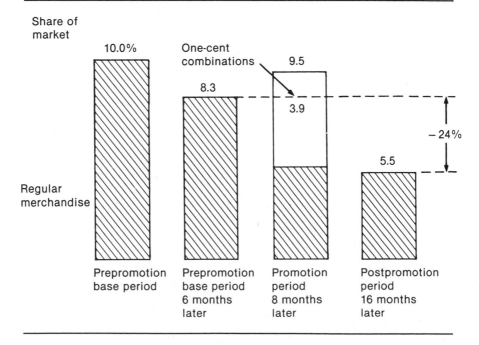

Share of market

10.0%

One-cent combinations

9.5

8.3

3.9

5.5

−24%

Regular merchandise

| Prepromotion base period | Prepromotion base period 6 months later | Promotion period 8 months later | Postpromotion period 16 months later |

The foundation for the Nielsen Retail Index is found in the sampling plan used for selecting retail outlets and the ongoing relations with these outlets. The design of the Retail Index sample is such that it meets the two critical criteria for a probabilistic sample. First, it provides an accurate picture of the universe so that the resultant data can be relied on for marketing decisions. Equally important, it provides this necessary accuracy at a realistic cost by maintaining the most efficient cost/sample size relationship possible. The A. C. Nielsen Company uses disproportionate sampling for the Retail Index by relating the sample selection to the stores' volume rather than store count. By then stratifying the universe according to geography, population, and store type and size, the sample reflects the unprojected purchases of an equivalent of 1.6 million households—or 4.6 million people, who spend about $3.5 billion annually in these sample stores.

Once the sample stores have been designated, Nielsen makes contracts with each store and, in the case of chains, with their headquarters, for the privilege of taking in-store inventories and auditing the invoices of all goods coming into the store. Cooperating organizations receive regular financial payments as well as regular reports on space allocation and other trends in the retail grocery store business. All the individual store data are kept confidential, as is the identity of the sample stores.

APPENDIX B
Selling Areas–Marketing, Inc. (SAMI)

Selling Areas–Marketing, Inc. (SAMI) is owned by Time, Inc. SAMI audits sales volume of packaged goods items sold in grocery stores at the wholesale level rather than at the retail level. Specifically, warehouse withdrawals to retail grocery outlets in SAMI-defined markets are audited every four weeks (twenty-eight days) and results are provided to the warehouse owners (food operators) every twelve weeks and to manufacturers every four weeks. Information is provided on sixty-seven product groups (e.g., baby foods) and over four hundred categories that are subdivisions of these product groups. For example, for baby foods, the categories are cereal, juice, formula, strained, junior, milk/cereal-based, and miscellaneous.

SAMI data are derived from warehouse withdrawal data provided by food operators in thirty-nine major markets. These markets (shown in Exhibit B.1) account for approximately 77 percent of national food sales. Food operators include chains, wholesalers, health and beauty aid rack jobbers, and frozen-food warehouses; and their movement includes the volume retailed by chain supermarkets, mom-and-pop stores, independent supermarkets, and food discounters. Generally speaking, the auditing procedure is as follows:

> At the end of each four-week period, the food distributor sends to SAMI's production headquarters in Chicago a record in computer processable form of case movement, price, etc., for all brands, sizes, and flavors shipped. SAMI then codes and processes this data and produces reports showing movement in dollars, equivalents, units, etc., for all items in a given category. Specific safeguards are provided in the coding, processing and analysis stages to ensure the accuracy of the data.

SAMI services are unique in that both the food operator and manufacturer receive information for planning and control purposes. Food operators receive five basic reports.

1. An *Executive Report* provides total measured market volume plus the individual food operator's share of this market by product group and category.

This material is drawn from Selling Areas–Marketing, Inc., brochures. Exhibits are presented through the courtesy of Selling Areas–Marketing, Inc.

EXHIBIT B.1
Market Areas

Albany–Schenectady–Troy	Miami
Atlanta	Milwaukee
Baltimore–Washington	Minneapolis–St. Paul
Birmingham–Montgomery–Huntsville	Nashville–Knoxville
Boston–Providence	New Orleans
Buffalo	New York
Charlotte	Norfolk–Richmond
Chicago	Oklahoma City–Tulsa
Cincinnati–Dayton–Columbus	Philadelphia
Cleveland	Phoenix–Tucson
Dallas–Fort Worth	Pittsburgh
Denver	Portland, Oregon
Des Moines–Omaha	Raleigh/Greensboro–Winston Salem
Detroit	St. Louis
Houston	Salt Lake City–Boise
Indianapolis	San Antonio–Corpus Christi
Jacksonville–Tampa	San Francisco
Kansas City	Seattle–Tacoma
Los Angeles–San Diego	Syracuse
Memphis–Little Rock	

2. An *Item Detail Report* provides total measured market volume plus the individual food operator's share of this market for every item in every measured category.

3. An *Exception Report* shows items carried by at least three other food operators but not by the particular operator.

4. An *Exception Report–Penetration* shows its items of which the food operator has a market share of at least three times its all-commodity volume share.

5. The *Top 500 Report* shows the top 500 items in each category in dollar volume terms.

Several manufacturer report formats are available. Most commonly used are:

1. The *Standard Dollar Report* shows sales and shares for all brands, sizes, flavors, and so on in a given category for each market purchased.

2. A *Brand Trend Report* shows trends in sales volume by brand and item over one or two years by four-week periods.

3. A *Ranking Report* lists the products in a particular category in rank order based on sales volume.

There is great flexibility in the SAMI reporting system. Categories can be subdivided by class (e.g., the strained baby-food category can be broken apart by vegetables, fruits, meat, etc.). Categories and classes can be combined into any universe desired by a client.

Several other reports are available, such as trends projected to regions and the total United States. Other reports summarize an individual brand's share of market in each of thirty-nine markets on one page. Computerized charts are also available by market, region, or total United States.

EXHIBIT B.2
Use of SAMI Information by Sales Personnel

A) To close brand distribution gaps by providing the importance of his brand in his customer's marketing area. The SAMI figures show how great the volume and share is without the customer's support— obviously, it will be greater when he also carries the brand.

B) To close item distribution gaps— sizes, flavors, etc., using the same reasoning as above, SAMI figures enable the salesman to compare each item in his line with each competitive item, and to point out the competitive comparisons which most strongly prove his customer's need to take on a specific item in order to maximize sales in the product area.

C) To increase shelf facings or encourage more favorable shelf positioning. If the salesman's brand is doing as well as or better than another which receives preferential on-shelf treatment, he has all the arguments necessary to improve his shelf placement.

D) To demonstrate expert knowledge about a product group with the aim of reorganizing a client's stocking and shelf arrangement plan for the category. SAMI shows consumer demand and each of the salesman's customers intends his layout and merchandising to reflect consumer preferences.

E) To prove the effectiveness of his consumer deals. SAMI will document rate of sell-through and amount of increase.

F) To show the effect of new sizes and flavors on the brand's franchise and on the total market, and its profitability.

G) To disprove competitive claims based on less specific, local and up-to-date data.

H) To keep on top of competitive consumer deals, new items, case allowance, distribution, etc.

I) To see local size, flavor, price preferences and to dispel incorrect assumptions about them.

EXHIBIT B.2 *(continued)*

J) To keep tabs on private label in a category and to point out, where applicable, a chain's over-emphasis on same.

K) To determine the relative effectiveness of alternative deals or promotional expenditure for a brand.

L) To spot competitive weakness and capitalize on them. Also SAMI will show competitive strengths by size, flavor, etc., and thereby suggest new possibilities for a brand.

M) To demonstrate the effectiveness of advertising campaigns, co-op allowances, etc.

N) To prepare a factual new product introduction sheet. SAMI will even show a customer what items he should drop to take on new ones.

O) To see and sell against seasonal trends in the market; in general, to keep up to date with the local, competitive situation.

P) To cut down unproductive time in buyer appointments. No need to "prove" the accuracy or applicability of data.

Q) To be alerted to items which may be dropped. Planning may enable the salesman to develop meaningful reasons for continued stocking. In other cases, it will make sense to initiate such discontinuation so that he can hope to influence the new use of the vacated shelf space.

R) To encourage his customer to think in terms of units, cases, dollars, sizes, flavors, etc., whichever illustrates his brand's performance most favorably.

S) To gain the confidence of his customer by citing fresh local statistics and by using data the customer also receives and upon which he relies.

Source: The Facts of SAMI, a brochure published by Selling Areas–Marketing, Inc. 1978.

SAMI data are useful both for sales efforts and for corporate planning purposes. Exhibit B.2 lists possible uses of SAMI information for sales personnel.

SAMI's usefulness for corporate planning is reflected in two quarterly services available to a manufacturer. The *Category Size and Trend Report* shows, for each SAMI category, total U.S. dollar volume through food stores for the most recent fifty-two-week period and the four prior years. Subscribers to this service are eligible for two "dividend" services. The *Four-Week Category Trend Report,* provided about one month after each four-week SAMI reporting period, shows the percentage changes in dollars and tonnage for each category with the corresponding year-ago period. A second service is the *Where the Action Is* presentation. In this instance, a SAMI representative personally presents highlights of trends indicated by data by product groups and categories. The SAMI presenter of *Where the Action Is* attempts to cite underlying reasons behind trends and define their significance to the client. A second quarterly service is the *SAMI New Product Service*. This comprehensive report not only presents the growth patterns of all new products introduced in food stores, but also indicates, at an early stage, the impact of these new products.

Wyler's Unsweetened Soft Drink Mixes

AS MR. KENNETH OTTE sat in his office in Northbrook, Illinois, in early August 1977, he felt a bit like Jack in the children's story "Jack and the Beanstalk." He was facing a major challenge against a dominant foe, General Foods' Kool-Aid powdered soft drink mix, the giant of the unsweetened drink mix category.

The question Mr. Otte was considering was whether to recommend a major national introduction of Wyler's Unsweetened Soft Drink Mix against Kool-Aid in 1978 or to continue testing the product. He knew RJR Foods's Hawaiian Punch was considering a national introduction of an unsweetened soft drink mix, and because of Kool-Aid's dominant position in the market—a 92 percent share and virtually unchallenged in its fifty-year existence—he questioned whether there was room for two additional brands in the market. If he waited another year, it might be too late. If, however, he introduced a new product in 1978 and Hawaiian Punch did too, then perhaps neither product would be successful.

The question was more complex than whether or not to introduce the product nationally. Wyler's Unsweetened Soft Drink Mix was just

---

This case was prepared by Associate Professor Don E. Schultz and Mr. Mark Traxler of Northwestern University as a basis for class discussion and is not designed to illustrate appropriate or inappropriate handling of administrative situations. Revised 1982. Reprinted with permission.

completing a test market under Mr. Otte's direction. There was certainly time to make changes and adjustments to the program should he decide to continue testing or launch a national introduction. But the question was: What changes should he investigate or recommend prior to a January meeting with the Wyler sales and broker force?

Management had requested a review of the situation and Mr. Otte's recommendations by October 1, 1977. Since a national introduction in 1978 would require substantial marketing expenditures, Mr. Otte had several questions facing him. Should he recommend a national program for 1978? If not, what recommendation should he make? Another test market? A fine tuning of his present program? Major changes? What?

As Mr. Otte prepared to develop his recommendation, he reviewed the entire situation of the category, the product, competition, and test market results. Did he have enough ammunition to challenge Kool-Aid?

WYLER FOODS

Wyler Foods is a Chicago-based company that manufactures consumer products. Their line includes instant soups, bouillon powders and cubes, and powdered soft drink mixes, among other products.

The original company was organized in the late 1920s and in 1930 introduced "Cold Kup" soft drink mix, a presweetened mix in a pouch. It was available in four flavors. About the same time, Peskin Company introduced "Kool-Aid," an unsweetened soft drink mix. Peskin was later acquired by General Foods and Wyler was purchased by Borden. Wyler continued to concentrate on the presweetened soft drink mix market. In 1954 a powdered lemonade mix was introduced very successfully. By 1977 the lemonade flavor accounted for approximately 40 percent of all Wyler soft drink mix sales.

Wyler and Kool-Aid continue to do battle in the soft drink mix market, with Wyler dominant in the presweetened market and Kool-Aid in the unsweetened area. In the early 1960s Kool-Aid entered the presweetened market with an artificially sweetened product using cyclamates. This sweetener was banned by the federal government in 1969 and Wyler, with its sugar sweetening, rapidly gained ground in the mix market. As a result of the ban, Wyler moved up to a 20 percent share of the presweetened market. In 1972 Wyler introduced an industry "first" by packaging presweetened soft drink mixes in cannisters equivalent to ten to fifteen quarts. With this innovation, Wyler's share of the presweetened market increased to over 40 percent. Shares have declined slightly from this level as increased competitive pressures have segmented the market. Wyler did not have an unsweetened entry until initiating the market test described in this case.

SOFT DRINK MIX MARKET

The liquid refreshment market, comprised of hot, cold, and alcoholic beverages, is limited in growth by the "share of belly" concept, which suggests that human beings can consume just so much liquid in a given year. All entries in the soft drink mix market are competing with all other potable refreshments for some space in an unexpandable belly. The level of per-capita liquid consumption, under this concept, is tied to the U.S. population growth rate or changing consumer preferences.

The soft drink mix business, the twelfth-largest dry grocery product category, accounts for about 10 percent of all soft drink sales. It has increased in both quart and dollar sales each year since 1970. This growth is due to a greater demand for more product convenience, a wider assortment of flavors, and a more economical cold beverage alternative to carbonated drinks and single-strength canned drinks. In 1977 soft drink mixes are expected to produce sales of 14.5 million Wyler equivalent cases.[a] Mr. Otte noted industry predictions that with a 5 percent volume growth in 1978, soft drink mixes would generate 15.2 million Wyler equivalent cases.

In comparison with other beverage categories, soft drink mixes are inexpensive, with unsweetened drink mixes the least expensive of all. Mixes cost less than half as much as carbonated beverages and single-strength canned drinks. Unsweetened mixes are least expensive due to the economy of adding one's own sugar. The typical cost per four-ounce serving of unsweetened powdered mix is 3 cents, while the cost of presweetened powdered mix is 4.7 cents. By comparison, the cost per four-ounce serving of carbonated soft drinks and of chilled orange juice is 11.7 cents.

The powdered drink mix market divides as follows. In terms of case volume, the market is divided into 52.4 percent presweetened and 47.6 percent unsweetened. In terms of dollar sales, the split is 74.6 percent presweetened and 25.4 percent unsweetened. The major difference is the cost per quart of the sweetened product versus the unsweetened.

Soft drink mix sales are highly seasonal. Sales peak during the summer months (May–August) and drop off almost entirely during the remainder of the year. Many grocers, particularly those in the northern

---

[a] One case contains 288 two-quart foil pouches, or the equivalent of 576 quarts of liquid beverage.

climates, do not stock soft drink mixes during the winter months after the summer inventory is sold. An attempt to overcome this extreme seasonality was initiated in 1976 by Wyler's. Their "second-season" promotion strategy, which promotes to both the consumer and the trade, was designed to encourage year-round product usage.

Soft Drink Mix Buyer

The buyer profile for soft drink mix users shows that about two-thirds of all U.S. households purchase the product. The primary purchaser is the female homemaker between the ages of eighteen and forty-four, with the heaviest concentration in the twenty-five to thirty-four age range. She is unemployed and has a high school education. The husband's occupation is blue-collar, clerk, or salesman. Annual household income lies between $10,000 and $20,000. The family has three or more individuals, including children under age eighteen. Powdered soft drink mix users and heavy users, who consume at least five glasses per day, are concentrated in the north-central and southern states.

More families purchase presweetened soft drink mixes than unsweetened; however, the buyer of unsweetened soft drink mixes appears to be a much heavier consumer (or purchaser at least). The presweetened mix buyer purchases the product an average of every 56.5 days, compared to the more frequent purchase pattern of the unsweetened mix buyer, who purchases every 46.7 days. Consumer panel data show that purchasers of both unsweetened and presweetened mixes pick up an average of six pouches on each shopping occasion.

Unsweetened Soft Drink Mixes

A comparison of the available and most popular flavors shows that the "red" flavors and grape are by far the fastest selling among unsweetened flavors. The available flavors for Wyler's and, in the case of Kool-Aid, the six of sixteen flavors that constitute 73 percent of their unsweetened mix volume, are shown in Exhibit 1. Representative Wyler packages are shown in Exhibit 2. The flavors listed for Hawaiian Punch are those that have been offered in the presweetened line.

Industry estimates indicate that Kool-Aid accounts for about 92 percent of the unsweetened soft drink mix segment. Private labels such as A&P's Cheri-Aid and Kroger's Flavor-Aid account for the remainder.

The out-of-store or retail price per pouch of unsweetened drink mixes ranges from 10 cents to 13 cents. The suggested retail price is 12 cents, and the typical broker price is 9.4 cents per pouch. The 12 cents price provides a 21.7 percent gross profit margin for grocery retailers, which is slightly higher than the grocery retailer storewide gross profit

EXHIBIT 1
Unsweetened Mix Flavors

Kool-Aid	Wyler's	Hawaiian Punch
Strawberry	Strawberry	Strawberry
Cherry	Cherry	Cherry
Fruit punch	Fruit punch	Red punch
Grape	Grape	Grape
Orange	Orange	Orange
Lemonade	Lemonade	Lemonade
		Raspberry

margin. The inventory turnover of soft drink mixes is higher than that of most nonperishable grocery store items during the summer peak season.

Unsweetened as well as presweetened soft drink mixes are sold to retailers through food brokers. Brokers, serving as middlemen between the producer and the retailer, receive a 7 percent commission per case for performing the distribution function.

INTRODUCTION OF WYLER'S UNSWEETENED

Target Market Selection

The target market selected for Wyler's introduction differed slightly from the one selected by Kool-Aid. The notable differences were household head's occupation and market size. Exhibit 3 summarizes the market's demographics. The primary users were children aged two through twelve, who were thought to have little influence on the purchase decision. The female homemaker bought the products she thought best for her family. Hence, most Wyler advertising was directed at mothers.

Advertising and Promotion

Wyler entered the test market with two main copy themes in advertising: (1) "double economy" stressed that Wyler's as an unsweetened drink for the entire family was economical because users added their own sugar and the entire family enjoyed it and (2) claimed that Wyler's unique flavor boosters (salt and other flavor enhancers) made Wyler's

EXHIBIT 2
Representative Packages of Wyler's Unsweetened
Soft Drink Mixes

taste better. Both executions emphasized the red flavors and vitamin C content and soft-pedaled lemonade. While the two campaigns were used in the test, they were both considered interim efforts.

The double-economy commercial was tested on two different occasions. One test indicated that the commercial generated high recall among target buyers and particularly among female homemakers between the ages of twenty-five and thirty-four. However, the other test, while identifying strong awareness of the Wyler brand name, indicated that the specific recall of Wyler's unsweetened mix was low. On the basis of these tests, a different campaign based even more strongly on flavors was being considered. This approach involved the use of Roy Clark, the television personality, who would stress the good taste of Wyler's, as spokesperson.

Kool-Aid's advertising came in three varieties with separate messages for general brand awareness, economy of use, and appeal to children. The general brand-awareness execution, a nostalgia appeal to

EXHIBIT 3
Selected Demographics of Wyler's and Kool-Aid Buyers

	Wyler's	Kool-Aid
Income	$15,000–$19,999	$15,000–$19,999
Household size	3 or more	3 or more
Age of female head	Under 45	Under 45
Age of children	12 and under	Any under 18
Occupation of household head	White-collar	Blue-collar
Market size (population)	500,000–2,500,000	Non-SMSA

mothers, said, "You loved it as a kid. You trust it as a mother." The economy-of-use execution showed children's preferences for Kool-Aid's flavor over single-strength beverages and the economy of adding one's own sugar. The execution with child appeal showed the Kool-Aid "smiling pitcher" saving the day by thwarting some dastardly deeds. Most advertising was placed in television: 70 percent network and 30 percent spot evenly divided between day and night.[b] It was anticipated that Hawaiian Punch would take advantage of their character, "Punchy," to introduce the new unsweetened mix, since he has been used extensively before.

For the 1977 test, Wyler had divided the media budget into a peak and second-season push. A total of $1,010 million was invested in spot television in the thirty-three broker areas that made up the test. From mid-April to mid-August, Wyler had purchased spot TV in prime, day, and early-fringe time. For the second season, the schedule was to be composed of day, early- and late-fringe time from September until Christmas and from late January into late March. Mr. Otte had already received a suggestion from the agency and his assistant that should the test be continued in 1978, staggered media tests should probably be undertaken since a level spending pattern had been used in the 1977 test markets.

Compared to Wyler's test program, Kool-Aid's program was spending approximately $18 million nationally in measured media in 1977. Six million dollars was being spent for presweetened, $6 million for unsweetened, and $6 million for the Kool-Aid brand. Two-thirds of the network budget was being used for weekdays and was directed toward women. The remainder was being spent on a Saturday/Sunday

---

[b] Network television provides simultaneous coverage of a nationwide market; spot television involves selecting individual stations to reach specific markets.

rotation directed at children. Spot TV funds were being allocated almost evenly between day (36 percent), night/late night (34 percent), and early fringe (30 percent). During the peak season, Kool-Aid planned on spending $13.405 million divided into $6.58 million in the second quarter and $6.825 million in the third quarter. The second-season expenditure was $4.59 million, divided into $2.57 million in the first quarter and $2.025 million in the fourth quarter. It was expected that Kool-Aid would spend about $20 million in 1978 for consumer advertising in measured media.

Mr. Otte anticipated that Hawaiian Punch, if they introduced nationally, would spend $4.7 million for television in a 1978 introduction. Two-thirds would probably be used in network (33.5 percent each for day and prime) and 33 percent for spot. Advance information indicated that this budget would break down to $3.2 million for network ($1.6 million in prime and daytime) and $1.5 million for spot television.

In addition to the consumer advertising, Wyler's spent $827,670 for consumer promotions during the tests. Expenditures included the cost of samples and coupons. Several print media, such as Sunday supplements and best-food-day newspaper sections, were being used to deliver both coupons and samples. It was still too early to determine the results of these promotions for this year.

Trade promotions during the market tests were budgeted at $292,330. Trade promotions consisted of case allowances to encourage retailers to stock Wyler's unsweetened mix. No matter how much money Wyler's spent on consumer advertising and promotion, it appeared from the tests that grocery retailers would not stock another soft drink mix without sizable case allowances since most of the soft drink mix inventory traditionally had been sold to retailers using case allowances. Mr. Otte felt that to achieve successful distribution, whether entering additional testing or going national in 1978, a case allowance of $3.60 between the end of February and the end of April would be needed. Given the seasonal nature of the market, approximately 60 percent of annual volume would be shipped during this period. This case allowance would be the highest ever offered in the unsweetened drink mix category, since typical case allowances were $2.88 for Kool-Aid. Industry sources indicated that Hawaiian Punch would offer a case allowance of $1.44.

Preliminary Test Market Results and Options

Wyler's unsweetened mix was introduced into thirty-three broker areas representing 28 percent of the U.S. population and 40 percent of total unsweetened soft drink mix category sales. Only twenty-five of the thirty-three areas had achieved adequate distribution by mid-1977.

The twenty-five successful areas comprised 17.2 percent of the U.S. population and 33.7 percent of total unsweetened mix category volume. Wyler's sold 116,000 cases in the test cities.

As Mr. Otte began to draft his recommendations for the October 1 meeting, he pondered a number of issues. First, if he decided to continue the test market in 1978, Mr. Otte was advised that he would need a minimum expenditure of $4 million for Wyler's unsweetened mix. The plan would involve $2.2 million in media advertising and $1.8 million in consumer promotions, plus the case allowances. If he decided to introduce nationally, he would of course need a substantially larger budget. The expenditure level would be part of his presentation whether or not he recommended a national introduction. Second, the amount of the case allowance was an issue needing attention. He was operating with a $25.20 case price and a 50 percent gross profit margin (excluding case allowances) in the test market at the 9.4 cent price to retailers. If the $3.60 case allowance was adopted, would this trade promotion secure increased distribution coverage and could he afford it? Third, the advertising question loomed. Should another test market or a national introduction include the revised message and claims rather than the "double economy" approach. Also, would the advertising schedule be more potent if it were staggered in a manner similar to Kool-Aid?

What to do? Should he risk another test and perhaps lose the opportunity to go national as Hawaiian Punch was contemplating, or should he develop a plan to invade Kool-Aid's territory in 1978 on a national basis? The risks and the rewards were great either way.

CHAPTER 6

Product and Service Strategy and Management

THE CORE OR FUNDAMENTAL decision in formulating a marketing mix concerns the offering of an organization. Without something to provide satisfaction for target market wants and needs, there would be nothing to price, distribute, or communicate. In essence, the ultimate profitability of an organization depends on its product or service offering(s). Accordingly, issues in the development of a product and service strategy are of special interest to all management functions and levels in an organization.

The marketing manager is basically faced with three kinds of offering-related decisions. These decisions respectively focus on:

- Modifying the offering mix
- Positioning offerings
- Branding offerings

In certain ways, offering decisions are but extensions of product-market matching strategies. Like other marketing mix decisions, offering decisions must consciously consider organization and marketing objectives, organization resources and capabilities, and competitive forces in the marketplace.

THE OFFERING PORTFOLIO

The Offering Concept

Before proceeding to a discussion of offering-related decisions, it is first necessary to define the term *offering*. In an abstract sense, an offering consists of the benefits or want satisfactions provided to target markets by an organization. More concretely, an offering consists of a tangible product or service (a *physical entity*) plus related services (e.g., delivery and setup), warranties or guarantees, packaging, and the like.

Use of the term *offering* rather than *product* or *service* provides numerous benefits for strategic marketing planning. By focusing on benefits and satisfactions *offered,* a conceptual framework is made available. This framework is potentially useful in analyzing competing offerings, identifying the unmet needs and wants of target markets, and developing or designing new products or services. It forces a marketer to go beyond the single tangible entity being marketed and to consider the entire offering or extended product or service.

In a broader view, an organization's offerings characterize its *business.* Offerings illustrate not only the buyer needs served, but also the types of customer groups sought and the means (technology) for satisfying their needs.

The Offering Mix

Seldom do organizations market a solitary offering. Rather, organizations tend to market many, or even thousands, of product or service offerings. The typical supermarket contains over 10,000 different products, while General Electric offers over a quarter million. Banks provide hundreds of services to customers, including computer billing, automatic payroll deposits, checking accounts, loans of numerous kinds, and so forth. Similarly, hospitals maintain a complete "inventory" of services ranging from pathology to obstetrics to simple food services. The totality of an organization's offerings is known as its product or service *offering mix* or *portfolio*. This mix usually consists of distinct offering lines—groups of offerings similar in terms of usage, buyers marketed to, or technical characteristics. Each offering line consists of individual offers or items.

Foremost, offering decisions concern the *width, depth,* and *consistency* of the offering portfolio. Marketing managers must continually assess the number of offering lines (the width decision) and the number of individual items in each line (the depth decision). Although this decision depends, in part, on the existing competitive or industry situation, as well as organization resources, it is perhaps most often determined by overall marketing strategy. The options are many. At one extreme, an organization can concentrate upon one offering; at another, it can offer complete lines to its customers. In between, it can specialize in high-profit and/or high-volume offerings. Furthermore, the extent to which offerings satisfy similar needs, similar buyer groups, or utilize similar technologies must be considered (the consistency decision).

MODIFYING THE OFFERING MIX

The first offering-related decision confronting the manager is modification of the offering mix. Rarely, if ever, will an organization's offering mix stand the test of changing competitive actions and buyer preferences, or an organization's desire for growth. Accordingly, the marketing manager must constantly monitor target markets and offerings to determine when new offerings should be introduced and existing offerings modified or eliminated.

Additions to the Offering Mix

Additions to the offering mix may take the form of a single offering or entire lines of offerings. An example of adding a complete line of offerings is found in General Mills's introduction, several years ago, of salty snack items called Whistles, Bugles, and Daisies.

Whatever the reason for considering new offerings, three questions should direct the evaluation of this action:

- How consistent is the new offering with existing offerings?
- Does the organization have the resources to adequately introduce and sustain the offering?
- Is there a viable market niche for the offering?

Consistency with existing offerings is influenced by a number of factors. First, offering interrelationships—whether substitute, complementary, or whatever—must be carefully taken into account in any new offering decision. Thus, there is a need to avoid situations where sales of the new offering cannibalize those of other offerings. Many sales of economy or compact automobiles came at the expense of the manufacturer's own medium-priced automobiles rather than those of its competitors. Likewise, IBM always attempts to anticipate the sales effects of any new office products it introduces and to minimize any potential deleterious sales effects on its own office product lines. Consistency may be also viewed as the degree to which the new offering fits the organization's existing selling and distribution strategies. For example, will the new offering require a different type of sales effort, such as new sales personnel or selling methods? The Metropolitan Life Insurance Company faced such a situation when it added automobile insurance to its line of life and health insurance, since the sales task involved in auto insurance differs from that for life insurance. Or will the new offering require a different marketing channel to reach the target market sought? Both the cannibalization question and the fit with sales and distribution strategies raise a fundamental third question relating to the buyers sought for the new offering. Will the new offering satisfy the target markets currently being served by the existing offering mix? If it does, then the sales and distribution issue may be overcome, but the cannibalization question remains. If it does not, then the opposite set of circumstances will result.

The second issue arising from adding new offerings relates to the adequacy of an organization's resources to introduce and sustain a new offering. In particular, the financial strength of the organization must be objectively appraised. New offerings often require large initial cash outlays for research, development, and introductory marketing programs. For example, R. J. Reynolds spent over $20 million when launching the Winston Ultra brand, and RCA spent almost $17 million to introduce the Selecta Vision Videodisc.[1] Other costs of sustaining the new offering before it returns a profit to the organization must also be measured. These costs will be determined, in part, by the speed and magnitude of competitive response to new offerings in the market and market growth itself. Atari, Inc., is a case in point.[2] Atari incurred severe capital shortages after its introduction of a coin-operated video game called Pong. Accordingly, the company was unable to satisfy the huge demand for this product, thus allowing competitors to capture potential sales, despite Atari being the innovator. Similarly, Pillsbury's introduction of a new cake mix, Pillsbury Plus, resulted in an immediate substantial share of market for the product. However, General Mills, Inc., and Proctor and Gamble Company retaliated quickly with sizable marketing expenditures and relegated Pillsbury's brand to third place in terms of market share.[3]

Finally, the question of whether a market niche exists for the new offering must be answered. An important question here is whether the new offering has a relative advantage over existing competitive offerings, or whether a distinct buyer group exists for which no offering is satisfactory. Careful market analysis is necessary to answer this question.

New-Offering Development Process

Marketing managers are often faced with new-offering decisions. Yet, the process of developing and marketing new offerings tends to be chaotic. Accordingly, managers attempt to follow some sort of structured procedure. This procedure typically includes four multifaceted steps: (1) idea generation/idea screening, (2) business analysis, (3) testing, and (4) commercialization.

Briefly, the process functions as follows. New-offering ideas are obtained from many sources—employees, buyers, and competitors—through formal (marketing research) and informal means. These ideas are screened, both from the viewpoint of organization definition and capability and from that of prospective buyers. Ideas deemed incompatible with organizational definition and capability are quickly eliminated. The match between prospective buyers and offering characteristics relate to the following factors. First, does the offering provide a *relative advantage* over existing offerings? Second, is the offering *compatible* with buyers' use or consumption behavior? Third, is the offering *simple* enough for buyers to understand and use? Fourth, can the offering be *tested* on a limited basis prior to actual purchase? Fifth, are there *immediate benefits* from the offering, once used or consumed? If the answer to these questions is yes and the offering satisfies a felt need, then the new-offering idea should pass on to the next stage. Next, these ideas are subjected to a business analysis to assess their financial viability in terms of estimated sales, costs, and profitability. Those ideas that pass the business analysis are then developed into prototypes, and various testing procedures are implemented. Marketing-related tests include product concept or buyer preference tests in a laboratory situation, or even field market tests. Offering ideas that pass through these stages are commerically introduced into the marketplace with hopes of their becoming profitable to the organization. A recent study by Booz, Allen, and Hamilton, Inc., an internationally recognized management consulting firm, indicated that it takes seven ideas to generate one successful new product. This study also reported that the two major factors contributing to success were that the new offering (1) fit market needs, and (2) fit the internal strengths of the organization.[4]

While the stages just outlined are relatively straightforward from a managerial perspective, two stages require further elaboration: the business analysis and testing stages. Sales analysis and profit analysis are two fundamental aspects of the business analysis stage. Forecasting sales volume for a new offering is an enormously difficult task. Nevertheless, preliminary forecasts of volume must be made to warrant further investigation of the offering. For the most part, profitability analyses are those related to investment requirements, break-even procedures, and payback periods. Break-even procedures can be used to determine estimates of the number of units that must be sold to cover fixed and variable costs. An extension of this procedure—and one that is frequently used in evaluating new offerings—is to compute the payback period of the new offering. *Payback* refers to the number of years required for an organization to recapture its initial offering investment. Hence, the shorter the payback period, the sooner an offering will prove profitable. Usually the payback period is computed by dividing the fixed costs of the offering by the estimated incoming cash flows from it. Though widely used, the method involves a difficulty in that it does not distinguish among offering investments according to their absolute sizes. A final method often used is the common return on investment (ROI). ROI equals the ratio of average annual net earnings (return) divided by average annual investment, discounted to the present time. Like the payback method, ROI does not distinguish among offering alternatives according to their riskiness. Risk must still be subjectively assessed.

Test marketing is a major consideration in the development and testing stage. A test market is a scaled-down version of one or more alternative marketing strategies for introducing the new offering. Test markets provide several benefits to managers. First, they provide benchmark data for assessing sales volume when the product is introduced nationwide. Second, if alternative marketing strategies are tested, then the two programs can be examined as to their relative impact under actual market conditions. In a similar vein, test markets allow the manager to assess the incidence of offering trial by potential buyers and to repeat purchasing behavior, in addition to the quantity purchased. Despite these benefits, a manager should remember that test markets of new offerings inform competitors of the organization's activities, and the magnitude and speed of competitive response might be enhanced from such knowledge.

Life Cycle Concept

An important management tool, related to the new offering development process and the management of offerings, generally, is the *life cycle* concept. The life cycle plots the sale of an offering, such as a brand of coffee, over a period of time, but may also be used to plot the sales volume of a product class, such as all coffee brands. Life cycles are typically divided into four stages: (1) introduction, (2) growth, (3) maturity-saturation, and (4) decline. Exhibit 6.1 shows the general form of a product life cycle sales volume and the corresponding stages.

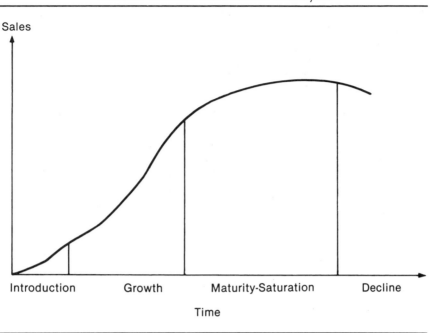

EXHIBIT 6.1
General Form of the Product Life Cycle

Sales

Introduction　　　Growth　　　Maturity-Saturation　　　Decline

Time

Recognition of the life cycle concept and strategic decisions and forces affecting the life cycle is important for several reasons. First, the sales curve can be viewed as being the result of offering *trial* and *repeat* purchasing behavior. In other words,

Sales volume = (Number of triers × Average purchase amount) + (Number of repeaters × Average purchase amount)

Early in the life cycle, management efforts are designed to stimulate trial of the offering through advertising, free samples, and obtaining adequate distribution. The vast majority of sales volume is due to trial purchases. As the offering moves through its life cycle, an increasingly disproportionate share of volume is attributable to repeat purchase volume, and management efforts are focused on retaining existing buyers of the offering through offering modifications, enhanced brand image, and competitive pricing.

Recognizing movement into advanced stages of the life cycle is a second reason for understanding the concept. These stages must be anticipated and managed. The Atari, Inc., example cited earlier illustrates the need to anticipate the growth stage, where sales volume increases at a steady rate over a relatively short time horizon. Two other inflection points are the movement into the maturity-saturation stage and the decline stage. Movement into the maturity-saturation stage is often indicated by (1) the increasing proportion of buyers that are repeat purchasers (i.e., few new buyers or triers exist), (2) the increasing standardization of production operations and product-service offerings, and (3) the increasing incidence of aggressive pricing activities of competitors. As the offering enters into and moves through this stage, management efforts typically focus on finding new buyers for the offering, significantly improving the offering, or increasing the frequency of usage among current buyers. Ultimately, the decline stage must be addressed. The decision criteria at this stage are outlined in the following discussion on modifying, harvesting, and eliminating offerings.

It should be noted that services often follow the life cycle described here.[5] *Service firms* typically follow a slightly modified pattern. For example, a restaurant modifies its menu and operations to attract new buyers as the firm approaches maturity. Examples include Mac-Donald's with its expanded menu and breakfast opening, and barbershops that evolve into hair-stylist operations featuring hair-cutting services for men *and* women. Often service firms expand their geographical scope by reproducing a simple or limited number of facilities to become multisite operators.[6] This strategy is described in the La Quinta Motor Inns case study in this text.

Modifying, Harvesting, and Eliminating Offerings

Modifying offerings is a common practice. Modification decisions are made in response to technological advances that apply to the offering—the need for finding new ways to improve the offering in terms of its quality, functions, or features, as well as price competitiveness.

Modification decisions typically focus on *trading up* or *trading down* the offering. Trading up is a conscious decision to improve an offering by adding new features and higher-quality materials, augmenting the offering with attendant services, and raising the price. Examples of augmenting products with services are found in the computer industry. Manufacturers of mainframe computers enhanced the image and suitability for use of their products through programming services, information system assistance, and user training. Trading down is the process of reducing the number of features, dropping the quality, or reducing the price of an offering.

The trading up and trading down dichotomy has been broadened in recent years because of competitive and cost pressures. In particular, many organizations have modified their offering (typically traded down) while maintaining or increasing the price. For example, many distillers have reduced the alcoholic content of their beverages without changing prices. Some airlines have added more seats, thus reducing leg room, and have eliminated certain luxury services (e.g., complimentary peanuts) in recent years. Consumer packaged-goods firms have resized their products by reducing the content of packages without reducing prices.

Modification decisions typically arise in the maturity-saturation stage of the life cycle. However, modifications might be appropriate earlier in the life cycle to stimulate trial. For example, several producers of microwave ovens recognized, early in the consumer marketing of this product, that the oven had to be augmented with cookbooks to assist buyers in scheduling meals and preparing a variety of foods.

The elimination of offerings as a specific decision is given little attention when compared with new offering or modification decisions. However, the elimination decision has grown in importance in recent years because of the realization that some offerings may be an unnecessary burden in light of potential opportunities. As an alternative to total elimination, management might consider *harvesting* the offering when it enters the late-maturity or decline stage of the life cycle. Harvesting is the "strategic management decision to reduce the investment in a business entity in the hope of cutting costs and/or improving cash flow."[7] In other words, the decision is not to abandon the offering outright but, rather, to minimize human and financial resources allocated to it. Harvesting should be considered a possibility when (1) the market for the offering is stable; (2) the offering is not producing good profits; (3) the offering has a small or a respectable market share that is becoming increasingly difficult or costly to defend from competitive inroads; and (4) the offering provides benefits to the organization, in terms of image or "full-line" capabilities, despite poor future potential.

Outright abandonment, or elimination, means that the offering is dropped from the mix of organizational offerings. Generally speaking, if the answer to each of the following questions is very little or none, then an offering is a candidate for elimination:

1. What is the future sales potential of the offering?

2. How much is the offering contributing to the overall profitability of the offering mix?

3. How much is the offering contributing to the sale of other offerings in the mix?

4. How much could be gained by modifying the offering?

5. What will be the effect on channel members and buyers?

POSITIONING THE OFFERING

A second major offering-related decision confronting the manager concerns the positioning of offerings. Positioning typically involves the creation of impressions about a product, service, or organization.[8] The positioning decision therefore involves choosing associations to be emphasized. There are a variety of positioning strategies available, including positioning by (1) attribute or benefit, (2) use or application, (3) product or service user, (4) product or service class, and (5) competitors. Positioning is important both in the introductory stage of the life cycle and in the maturity stage, when sales volume reaches a plateau.

Positioning an offering by attributes or benefits is the most frequently used strategy. Positioning an offering by attributes requires determining which attributes are important to target markets, which attributes are being emphasized by competitors, and how the offering can be fitted into this offering–target market environment. This kind of positioning may be accomplished by designing an offering that contains appropriate attributes, or perhaps by stressing the appropriate attributes if they currently exist in the offering. This latter point is evidenced by a number of cereal manufacturers, who have emphasized the "naturalness" of their products in response to the emerging natural food and nutrition interests of a sizable number of buyers.

In practice, operationalizing the positioning concept requires the development of a matrix relating attributes of the offering with market segments. Using toothpaste as an example,[9] Exhibit 6.2 shows how particular attributes may vary in importance for different market segments. Several benefits accrue from viewing the market for toothpaste in this manner. First, the marketing manager can spot potential opportunities for new offerings and determine if a market niche exists. (We might note here that the elderly market segment has not yet been exploited and question whether this segment is a viable one for an existing or new offering.) Second, looking toward offering attributes and their importance to market segments permits subjective estimation of the extent to which a new offering might cannibalize existing offerings. If two offerings emphasize the same attributes, then they can be expected to compete with each other for the same market segment. Alternatively, a different mix of attributes might appeal to a different segment. For this reason, Procter & Gamble's introduction of Crest tartar control formula toothpaste for adults did not have a major adverse

EXHIBIT 6.2
Attributes and Marketing Segment Positioning

Toothpaste Attributes	Market Segments			
	Children	Teens, Young Adults	Family	Adults
Flavor	*			
Color	*			
Whiteness of teeth		*		
Fresh breath		*		
Decay prevention			*	
Price			*	
Plaque prevention				a
Stain prevention				a
Principal brands for each segment	Aim, Stripe	Ultra Brite, McCleans	Colgate, Crest	Check-Up, Pearl Drops

aDenotes principal benefits sought by each market segment.

effect on its existing Crest toothpaste for children. Third, the competitive response to a new offering can be judged more effectively using this framework. By determining which brands serve specific markets, offerings can be evaluated in terms of financial strength and market acceptance.

Organizations can also position their offering(s) by use or application. Arm & Hammer serves as an example of this approach. After being positioned as a baking powder for many years, the product's position was later modified to being an odor-destroying agent in refrigerators and a water cleaner in swimming pools. Public television was originally positioned as a source of educational and cultural programming.

Positioning by user is a third strategy. This strategy typically associates a product or service with a user group. Federal Express positions its delivery service for the busy executive. Certain deodorant brands position themselves for females (Jean Naté by Charles of the Ritz), whereas others focus on males (e.g., Brut by Fabergé).

Products and services can be positioned by product or service class as well. For example, margarine brands position themselves against butter. Savings and Loan Associations are now positioning themselves as "banks," given new regulations.

Finally, an organization can position itself or its offerings directly against competitors. As an example, Avis positions itself against Hertz in the rental car business. Sabroso, a coffee liqueur, positioned itself against Kahlua. Often a political candidate will position him- or herself against the opponent.

The success of a positioning strategy depends on a number of factors. First, the position selected must be clearly communicated. Industry observers argue that General Motors' failure to communicate distinct positions for its different automobile lines was detrimental to the firm's competitive position in the early 1980s. Second, the development of a position is a lengthy and often expensive process, and rapid changes in the position should be avoided. Marketing of political candidates, in particular, emphasizes the importance of establishing a position and holding that position throughout a campaign. Finally, and perhaps most important, the position taken in the marketplace should be sustainable and profitable.

BRANDING OFFERINGS

A third offering-related decision made by marketing managers is whether to brand their offering and what types of brands to use. A brand is used to identify an offering and set it apart from competing offerings. The major managerial implication of branding offerings is that goodwill, derived from buyer satisfaction with an offering, can be accrued to the brand owner. Frequently, satisfied buyers will become loyal to a brand, leading to long-run sales for the organization. Loyalty to the original Coca-Cola and negative consumer response to the new Coca-Cola formula is a prime example of brand loyalty in operation.[10]

Branding applies to services as well as products. A novel approach to branding a service is evidenced by Republic Health Corporation, which has assigned brand names to various types of surgery. For example, "Step Lively" is the name given its brand of foot surgery and "You're Becoming" is the name for its cosmetic plastic surgery.[11]

Two common branding decisions confront marketing managers. The first decision arises when the organization has multiple offerings or multiple lines of offerings. For a manufacturer, the decision is whether to assign one brand name to *all* of the organization's offerings (e.g., General Electric); to assign one brand name for *each line* of offerings (e.g., Sears's appliances are Kenmore, Sears's women's clothing is Kerrybrook, Sears's tools are Craftsman); or to assign individual names to *each offering* (e.g., Tide, Cheer, and Oxydol are all laundry detergents sold by Procter & Gamble). The final decision to select a branding strategy will depend on the consistency of the offering mix. If the offerings are related, then a common (family) brand strategy is often favored. A common brand name for offerings is also selected if the organization wishes to establish a dominance in a class of offerings, as in the case of Campbell's soups. The decision to use a single brand name has certain advantages and disadvantages. Among the advantages, it is usually easier to introduce new offerings when the brand name is familiar to buyers. However, a single brand name strategy can have a negative effect on existing offerings if a new offering is a failure.

The second branding decision relates to supplying an intermediary with its own brand name. From the intermediary's perspective, the decision may be to carry, or not carry, its own brands. A potential producer of private brands, or distributor brands, should consider a number of factors when making this decision. From a production standpoint, if a producer has excess manufacturing capacity, and the variable costs of producing a distributor's brand do not exceed the sale price, then the possibility exists for making a contribution to overhead and utilizing production facilities. From a general distribution standpoint, if a distributor desires a private brand, then it must locate a producer willing to manufacture the brand. A marketing manager is then placed in the position of deciding whether to be the producer. Even though a distributor's brand will often compete directly with a producer's brand, the combined sales of the brands and the profit contribution to the producer may be greater than if a competitor obtains the rights to produce the distributor brand. However, a great danger in producing private brands is the possibility of becoming too reliant on private-brand revenue, only to have it curtailed if a distributor switches suppliers or builds its own production plant. Overreliance on distributor brands will also affect trade relationships between a producer and distributor. As a generalization, the influence of a producer, in terms of price and channel leadership, is inversely related to the proportion of its output or revenue obtained from a distributor's brand.

Distributors favor carrying their own brands for a number of reasons. By carrying a private brand, a distributor avoids price competition to some extent, since no other distributor carries an identical brand for comparison purposes. Also, any buyer goodwill attributed to an offering is accrued to the distributor, and buyer loyalty to the offering is tied to the distributor, not the producer.

NOTES

1. "New Products Struggle for Survival," *Dallas Times Herald* (November 14, 1982): 1–5ff.

2. "Atari Sells Itself to Survive Success," *Business Week* (November 15, 1976).

3. "Pillsbury's Ambitious Plans to Use Green Giant," *Business Week* (February 5, 1979): 87–88.

4. *New Products Management for the 1980s* (New York: Booz, Allen, and Hamilton, 1982).

5. R. Peterson, W. Rudelius, and G. Wood, "Spread of Marketing Innovations in a Service Industry," *Journal of Business* (October 1972): 485–96.

6. W. Sasser, R. Olsen, and D. Wyckoff, *Management of Service Operations* (Boston: Allyn and Bacon, 1978).

7. P. Kotler, "Harvesting Strategies for Weak Products," *Business Horizons* (August 1978): 15–22. The remaining discussion on harvesting is drawn from this article.

8. D. Aaker and G. Shansby, "Positioning Your Product," *Business Horizons* (May–June 1982): 56–62.

9. This example is adapted from Russell Haley, "Benefit Segmentation: A Decision-Oriented Research Tool," in B. Enis and K. Cox, eds., *Marketing Classics,* 5th. ed., (Boston: Allyn and Bacon, 1985), pp. 285–292.

10. "Coke's Brand-Loyalty Lesson," *Fortune* (August 5, 1985): 44–46.

11. "Hospital chain markets 'brand-name surgery,'" *Dallas Times Herald* (March 17, 1985): G1–G7.

ADDITIONAL READINGS

Aaker, David, and Shansby, Gary. "Positioning Your Product." *Business Horizons* (May–June 1982): 56–62.

Calantone, Roger, and Cooper, Robert. "New Product Scenarios: Prospects for Success." *Journal of Marketing* (Spring 1981): 48–60.

Day, George. "The Product Life Cycle: Analysis and Application Issues." *Journal of Marketing* (Fall 1981): 60–67.

Heany, Donald F. "Degrees of Product Innovation." *Journal of Business Strategy* (Spring 1983): 3–14.

Heany, Donald F., and Vinson, William D. "A Fresh Look at New Product Development." *Journal of Business Strategy* (Fall 1984): 22–31.

Swan, John, and Rink, David. "Fitting Marketing Strategy to Varying Product Life Cycles." *Business Horizons* (January–February 1982): 32–39.

Takeuchi, Hirotaka, and Nonaka, Ikujiro. "The New New Product Development Game." *Harvard Business Review* (January–February
1986): 137–146.

Wind, Yoram. *Product Policy: Concepts, Methods, and Strategy.* Reading, Mass.: Addison-Wesley, 1982.

Zeithaml, Valarie A.; Parasuraman, A.; and Berry, Leonard L. "Problems and Strategies in Service Marketing." *Journal of Marketing*
(Spring 1985): 33–46.

CASE

Supreme Foods of France

LATE IN APRIL 1986, Andre Belq had to prepare a budget for Spurt, a fruit-flavored concentrate that could be sprayed into a glass of water to produce a fruit-flavored beverage. The budget, which had to include forecast costs and revenues for Spurt for twelve months beginning June 1, 1986, was due May 15. The budget could include (1) costs for further consumer research, (2) expenditures for a test market based on a tentative plan that had been submitted to Mr. Belq by the firm's advertising agency, or (3) forecast revenues and costs for a national introduction in the United States.

THE COMPANY

Supreme Foods of France (SFF) is a vertically integrated multinational firm that produces and markets a wide variety of convenience and commercial foods throughout Western Europe. In addition, the company sells a variety of specialty products in the United States. These products are usually sold in the gourmet section of supermarkets.

SFF has shown consistent growth over the past decade. The company recorded sales of $700 million (U.S.) in 1985. Although most company sales were generated from European operations, sales in the United States had shown a sizable increase. The growth of U.S. sales was attributed to the increased popularity of gourmet foods, the popularity of French products, and the broadened distribution in supermarkets in the United States. In 1985 Supreme Foods of France sold its line

---

This case was prepared by Professor Roger A. Kerin, Edwin L. Cox School of Business, Southern Methodist University, as a basis for class discussion, and is not designed to illustrate appropriate or inappropriate handling of administrative situations. All company data are disguised and are not useful for research purposes.

of specialty food products through over fifty thousand U.S. supermarkets and specialty food stores through a network of food brokers.

SFF was organized into three divisions: the Commercial Foods Division, the Consumer Foods Division, and the International Division. Each division was managed by a director, to whom several product managers and marketing support managers reported. In addition, a New Ventures Department operated at the corporate level, with the responsibility for identifying ways that the company could launch new products with high growth and high profit potential. The primary tasks of the New Ventures Department consisted of exploring new markets for the company and preparing market studies. These studies also identified possible means of entry and possible positions of new products in particular markets.

HISTORY OF SPURT DEVELOPMENT

Development of Spurt began in late 1984, when the director of the International Division met with New Ventures Department executives to discuss opportunities in the $46 billion beverage market in the United States. During the course of their discussion, frequent reference was made to the apparent success of innovative package designs in launching new products in mature markets. For example, the director of the International Division noted that the Check-Up brand of toothpaste captured a sizable percentage of the toothpaste market because of the unique pump dispenser package. Gillette successfully launched Brush Plus—a device that dispenses shaving cream through a brush—and achieved a respectable share of the market. In each instance the unique packaging was considered at least partially responsible for the success of the product.

The meeting concluded with a consensus opinion that an opportunity existed for a new package design for dispensing beverages. Accordingly, the New Ventures Department went about searching for such a container.

Product Development

In early 1985 the New Ventures Department came upon a container that appeared promising. The container, which had existed in France for five years, was used for dispensing a variety of fruit-flavored concentrates. The container held fifteen ounces of concentrate and made six quarts of a beverage when added to water. A metered valve on the container assured that each time the valve was pressed, sufficient concentrate was squirted to produce an eight-ounce drink (including tap

water). Six fruit flavors were available: orange, grape, cherry, straw-
berry, raspberry, and fruit punch. The concentrate contained a vitamin
C additive as well.

Further investigation revealed that the container and concentrate
were generally well-received. The product had a long shelf life and
was ideal for storage since one container held the equivalent of
twenty-four eight-ounce drinks and required no refrigeration. Both features were welcomed by French households. Furthermore, both children and adults appeared to like the flavors. Although actual sales
statistics were not available, the product did have wide distribution in
major metropolitan areas.

Informal discussions with the container's producer indicated that
a licensing arrangement was possible whereby SSF would be given
exclusive rights to market the product in the United States. SSF would
obtain the product from the container's producer and would not have
to build its own production facility since production capacity of 1.5
million cases (twenty-four cans to one case) was available at the producer's plant. SSF sought and received approval to begin consumer
research on the product in the United States. The tentative name given
to the product was "Spurt."

Consumer Research

In late June 1985 the New Ventures Department commissioned a series
of focus group interviews on Spurt under the direction of Todd Anthony, an independent consultant in the United States. The primary
aim of these studies was to obtain qualitative information on consumers' reactions to Spurt and to learn how they viewed it relative to
canned fruit drinks such as Hi-C, carbonated soft drinks, and powdered soft drinks of the Kool-Aid variety. Anthony's report of the results were as follows:

1. Spurt is conceived first as a children's drink but also, secon-
   darily, as an all-family drink because of its excellent quality.

2. After mixing their drinks and before tasting, about half the
   respondents would buy Spurt, and half would not. Those
   who said they would buy the product were even more favorably disposed toward Spurt after tasting the product than before tasting it.

3. Spurt appears to be conceived as a high-grade Kool-Aid for
   day-to-day use, especially in the summer, rather than as a soft
   drink or canned fruit drink.

4. Consumers believe the container may in general cause many

problems: it can get plugged up, kids may make a mess with it, and mothers won't know how much is left.

5. The present flavors produce excellent-quality drinks with little noticeable aftertaste. However, further taste testing will be required to optimize the quality of the drinks.

6. The need for a vitamin C additive in fruit-based drinks is recognized by all consumers.

7. Users, especially children, appear to enjoy squirting Spurt into a glass of water.

8. Although 99 cents for twenty-four servings is considered a fair price, there is some doubt whether the can would actually produce twenty-four servings.

In summary, Anthony remarked, "We appear to have a 'superior Kool-Aid' product which would be thought of as primarily for kids' consumption, but not exclusively so, at a reasonable price. The container appears to arouse misgivings among some mothers."

In late August 1985 Todd Anthony conducted four focus groups with female heads of households with at least one child between three and fourteen years of age. After a general discussion of fruit-type drinks, each group was asked to read a concept card describing the characteristics of the product, including its price, flavors, and cost per serving. Anthony summarized his inferences from the focus groups in four points.

1. Two groups were negative in their reaction to Spurt; two groups offered a positive response. The latter two said they would buy it for their children for a special treat. They did not say that the product would necessarily become a regular item.

2. The operation of the metered valve was a mildly pleasant surprise to the respondents. For many, it had a "fun" element. However, continued use indicated that Spurt was a children's product, one that would likely be bought only with children in mind.

3. With initial trial of this product, there would be tremendous variation in the amount used of the concentrate, the use of ice, and the need to stir. The wide range of colors in the final beverage indicates that consumers will be drinking very different drinks, depending on concentrate usage. As for ice, some use it and some do not. The addition of ice to the water before spraying the concentrate necessitates stirring. Many women stirred even if no ice was used.

4. From our studies, four distinct categories of beverages are
    evident: juices, nutritious fruit drinks, carbonated soft drinks,
    and Kool-Aids. Spurt falls into the Kool-Aid category. In com-
    parison to Kool-Aids, Spurt wins on two points—more fun to
    use, and a better drink—and loses on two points—expense
    (twenty-four servings is not a believable figure) and on messi-
    ness.

In his summary, Anthony recommended that these findings represented a warning to move slowly on the project because it appeared
that Spurt was potentially a one-time novelty that even children might
not have the power to perpetuate. Soon after these results were submitted, Mr. Andre Belq, a product manager in the International Division, was assigned the product.

To supplement the research being carried out by Anthony, Mr.
Belq commissioned SSF's advertising agency in the United States to
study the relationship between Spurt and powdered soft drinks and
consumption data related to consumer preferences and shopping behavior. In-home tests conducted by the agency indicated Spurt was
highly favored over powdered soft drinks for the fruit flavors. However, when the fruit punch flavor was tested alone against Hawaiian
Punch, a canned fruit drink, Spurt lost on such features as taste, color,
and aftertaste. Additional consumer tests by the agency on product
positioning revealed that Spurt was most similar to carbonated soft
drinks, not canned fruit drinks or powdered drinks. Furthermore, consumers expected to find Spurt located in the carbonated soft drink
section of supermarkets (see Exhibit 1). Agency researchers considered
this finding important, since consumption data on beverages indicated
that powdered soft drink sales peaked in April and May and carbonated soft drink sales in June and July. Moreover, the agency estimated
that carbonated soft drinks captured 65 percent of the $46 billion bev-
erage market, powdered soft drinks captured 12 percent, and canned
fruit drinks captured 23 percent. Based on shopping behavior patterns,
shelf location, consumer preference tests, a newspaper coupon program, and a media expenditure level of $5.5 million, agency research-
ers estimated that Spurt's introductory-year volume would be 1.048
million twenty-four-can cases.

Mr. Belq's reading of the consumer test prompted him to commission another independent research agency to study Spurt. The research agency was instructed to determine the trial and repeat-
purchase rates for Spurt, given a sales price to consumers at 99 cents
and two different advertising expenditure levels—$5.5 million and $7.9
million. In late March 1986 the research agency estimated that, using a
$5.5 million advertising expenditure level, Spurt would be tried by 15
percent of the 58 million households with children. The trial rate

EXHIBIT 1
Product Positioning and In-Store Location

"Spurt most similar to . . ."	
Carbonated soft drinks	60%
Canned fruit drinks	21%
Powders	19%
Total	100%
Expected store location:	
With carbonated soft drinks	64%
With canned fruit drinks	20%
With powders	16%
Total	100%

would increase to 20 percent at the $7.9 million advertising expenditure level. The repeat purchase rate would be 35 or 40 percent of those households that tried the product. The report also noted that the average purchase for trial households would be one can. The average additional sales per repeat household per year would be three cans.[a]

Mr. Belq continued to be plagued by the question of how to position Spurt. Should he position it against powdered soft drinks, canned fruit drinks, or carbonated soft drinks? Furthermore, he was not sure whether or not he had a product with a long-term appeal or a novelty product that might be tried only once. The results from the consumer research studies were conflicting, and he was not sure whether the volume forecasts would make for a profitable product introduction. A price-cost plan prepared by Mr. Belq set the price to consumers for Spurt at 99 cents per can. The price per can to supermarkets was set at 72 cents, or $17.28 per case of twenty-four cans. These cost and price figures, plus shipping costs, food broker commissions, and licensing fees, indicated SSF could achieve a gross margin of $6.50 per case. The only relevant fixed cost assignable to Spurt would be the advertising expenditure.

---

[a] The estimates made by the advertising agency and the independent research firm are based on what are called *pretest* market test computer models. These models incorporate such variables as advertising expenditures, promotion programming, and distribution coverage in a series of equations to estimate trial and repeat rates, as well as volume forecasts. Firms that have developed these models report that the models can reduce the failure rate in test markets by as much as 50 percent. For a nontechnical description of the use, benefits, and limitations of these computer models, see R. Goydon, "Easy Numbers," *Forbes* (September 23, 1985): 180–181, and A. Stern, "Test Marketing Enters a New Era," *Dun's Business Month* (October 1985): 86–90.

Options in April 1986

In late April 1986 Mr. Belq received notice that he would have to prepare a budget for Spurt for twelve months beginning June 1, 1986. This
budget would be based on a marketing plan that could include a test
market, further consumer research, a full-scale introduction of Spurt in
the United States, or some combination of these actions.

SSF's advertising agency executives advocated a test market for
Spurt. The test market would be conducted in two cities and would
run for ten months beginning July 1, 1986. The agency recommended
that Spurt be test marketed to evaluate marketplace performance with
two strategies, under the assumption that even though Spurt was primarily a children's product, there might be an opportunity for substantial volume from consumers over twelve years old. In one city, a lower
level of advertising spending (equivalent to $5.5 million per year on a
nationwide basis) would be put into appeals directed toward children,
with minimal reinforcement of product advantages to the rest of the
family. Consequently, advertising would be directed to Saturday
morning cartoon shows and Sunday comic strips. The agency proposed a higher level of spending (equivalent to $7.9 million per year on
a nationwide basis) in the second test city. This test market would
include an exact duplicate run of the advertising program in the first
city, plus appeals directed toward an all-family audience, televised in
prime evening time. In both cities, redeemable coupons, which applied
to the purchase of Spurt, would be inserted in Sunday comic strips and
in a direct-mail program. Consumer panel data would be gathered in
both cities to assess advertising effects and trial and repeat purchase
rates to be used in drafting a national introduction program. The cost
of the test market would be $537,000.

Todd Anthony advocated further consumer research. He believed
it was necessary to replicate his and the advertising agency's studies,
since the agency's results conflicted with his observations. He believed
the positioning issue was unresolved and improper positioning could
result in Spurt's failure. Further consumer research would commence
June 1 and be completed August 1, 1986, at a cost of $15,000.

Senior executives in the New Ventures Department advocated a
national introduction. They reasoned that sufficient research had been
conducted and that the advertising agency's test market plan could be
easily expanded to a national program. Furthermore, they noted that
the container producer was talking with a United States–based food-
products firm about the possibility of using the container for a similar
type of product. Failure to act with dispatch could forever eliminate
the opportunity Spurt provided.

Frito-Lay, Inc.: O'GRADYS Potato Chips

MR. EARL SHIRLEY, product manager for O'GRADYS® brand potato chips, reached his office before dawn on Monday, June 26, 1983, to begin preparing his proposal for future action on the brand. O'GRADYS® potato chips had been in test market in Omaha, Nebraska, since January 1983, and he knew that a recommendation would soon be necessary. No sooner had he entered his office than the telephone rang. Ms. Brenda Barnes, vice-president of the Potato Products Division, was calling to request his proposal on Friday, June 30, at 9:00 A.M. Mr. Shirley knew that after he reviewed the situation for Ms. Barnes, a formal recommendation as to whether Frito-Lay, Inc., should kill the project, continue the test market, expand the test market to other cities, or introduce the product nationally would be expected. A sound rationale for each option would be part of the presentation as well.

SALTY SNACK FOOD MARKET

The salty snack food market is broadly defined to include such products as potato chips, corn chips, tortilla chips, cheese puffs, and pret-

The cooperation of Frito-Lay, Inc., in the preparation of this case is gratefully acknowledged. This case was prepared by Ms. Lucia Rohrer-Tomnitz, graduate student, under the supervision of Professor Roger A. Kerin, Edwin L. Cox School of Business, Southern Methodist University, as a basis for class discussion and is not designed to illustrate appropriate or inappropriate handling of administrative situations. Certain data are either disguised or approximations and are not useful for research purposes.

zels. In 1983 the total salty snack food market was estimated to account for sales of $5 billion at manufacturers' prices. This figure represented approximately 2.5 billion pounds sold. The salty snack food market was growing at a rate of about 6 percent per year on a dollar basis in recent years. However, the pounds sold per year had plateaued. Research indicates that 92 percent of the households in the United States consume salty snacks.

The salty snack food market can be viewed from two perspectives: (1) product class and (2) competitors. For example, potato chips represent the largest product class and account for about 46 percent of the market on a pound basis. Corn chips account for 11 percent, tortilla chips for 18 percent, cheese puffs for 10 percent, and pretzels for 12 percent of the salty snack food market. The remaining 3 percent of the market is accounted for by other specialty products. These percentages have remained stable in recent years.

Three types of competitors served the salty snack food market: (1) national brand firms, (2) regional brand firms, and (3) private brand firms. National brand firms, which distributed products nationwide, included Frito-Lay, Bordens (Guys brand potato and corn chips, and Wise brand potato chips and pretzels); Procter & Gamble (Pringles brand potato chips); Nabisco (several products such as pretzels and crackers sold under the Nabisco name, as well as Planters brand pretzels, cheese puffs, and corn and tortilla chips, and Pinata brand tortilla chips). These firms accounted for over 50 percent of the salty snack tonnage sold. The second category of competitors consisted of regional brand firms that distributed products in only certain parts of the United States. These firms, represented by Snyder, Bachman, Laura Scudder, Sunshine, and Weaver, accounted for about 35 percent of salty snack tonnage volume. Private brands were produced by regional or local manufacturers on a contractual basis for major supermarket chains (e.g., Safeway). Private brands accounted for about 15 percent of the salty snacks tonnage consumed annually.

FRITO-LAY, INCORPORATED

Frito-Lay, Inc., is a division of PepsiCo, Inc., a New York–based diversified consumer goods and services firm. Other PepsiCo, Inc., divisions in 1983 included Pizza Hut, Taco Bell, North American Van Lines, Wilson Sporting Goods Company, PepsiCo Bottling Company, and PepsiCo Foods International. PepsiCo, Inc., recorded net sales of over $7 billion in 1983.

Frito-Lay, Inc., is a nationally recognized leader in the manufacturing and marketing of salty snack foods. The company's major salty snack products and brands include potato chips (LAY'S®, RUFFLES®); corn chips (FRITOS®); tortilla chips (DORITOS®, TOSTITOS®); corn puffs (CHEETOS®); and pretzels (ROLD GOLD®). Other well-known products included BAKEN-ETS® brand fried pork skins, MUNCHOS® brand potato crisps, and FUNYUNS® brand onion-flavored snacks. In addition, the company markets a line of cookies, nuts, peanut butter crackers, processed beef sticks, GRANDMA's® brand cookies and snack bars, and assorted other snacks. Frito-Lay, Inc., net sales in 1983 exceeded $2 billion.

Given the nature of its products, Frito-Lay primarily competes in what is termed the salty snack food segment of the snack food market. In 1983 Frito-Lay captured about 46 percent of the tonnage sold. Nevertheless, its market share varied by product category. For example, the company's share of corn and tortilla chips in pounds sold was over 81 percent. By comparison, its share of potato chips was only about 32 percent on a pound basis, and its pretzels accounted for about 14 percent of pounds consumed. Frito-Lay sold about 80 percent of the total salty snack food tonnage in the southwestern United States, but only 31 percent of the total salty snack tonnage in the northeast United States.

DEVELOPMENT OF O'GRADYS® BRAND POTATO CHIPS

O'GRADYS® brand potato chips resulted from Frito-Lay's ongoing product-development program. The idea for O'GRADYS® emerged in late 1981, after Frito-Lay executives concluded that an opportunity existed for another entrant into its potato chip line, which already included LAY'S® and RUFFLES® brand potato chips. The decision to extend the line of potato chips with a new brand prompted a more formal product development effort with Frito-Lay's research and development and manufacturing staff. Mr. Rick Heller, new products manager, was given the responsibility for managing the initial product-development effort.

Product Development

Initial product development efforts focused on developing a unique potato chip. The emphasis on uniqueness was crucial in the development stage because of Frito-Lay's objective of introducing new products that would develop a category (e.g., potato chips) in a "large and meaningful" manner. *Large* in this context meant that a new product must produce incremental volume sizable enough to justify its existence. This usually meant that a new product should produce sales of $100 million annually at Frito-Lay prices. This requirement was particularly true in new product development efforts, where cannibalization of existing brands was possible. *Meaningful* meant that the new product had to be clearly differentiated in terms of product features from existing products where the consumer benefit was clear.

The objective of developing a category in a large and meaningful manner is evident in LAY'S® and RUFFLES® brand potato chips. LAY'S® is a flat chip that is particularly suitable for consumption by itself given its light flavor, thinness, and crispy texture. RUFFLES®, on the other hand, is a ridged potato chip suitable for use as a party dip chip, given its more pronounced flavor, thickness (it does not break when dipping), and crunchier texture.

The initial developmental work on O'GRADYS® resulted in a ridged potato chip. Unlike other ridged chips, it was sliced thicker and had a lattice cut. This meant that O'GRADYS® had ridges that ran at right angles to each other on each side of the chip, creating a "lattice" that could be seen when held up to the light. This feature gave the consumer a crunchier texture and ensured that O'GRADYS® (1) would never reach beyond a certain thickness in any one area of the chip, (2) would never have uncooked portions in the chip, and (3) would have an even flavor and texture throughout. After further testing, a cheese flavor was chosen for O'GRADYS® potato chips in addition to the regular flavor, comparable to LAY'S® and RUFFLES®.

O'GRADYS® was seen as a logical extension of Frito-Lay's potato chip line. The relationship to LAY'S® and RUFFLES® is depicted in Exhibit 1. As shown, O'GRADYS® was to have a stronger taste and a thicker, crunchier texture than existing brands.

Concept/Product Fulfillment Test

O'GRADYS® was submitted to a concept/product fulfillment test shortly after a prototype chip was developed. A random sample of consumers were first exposed to "concept boards" that described O'GRADYS®. Consumers were then asked to state their intention to purchase the brand and for what purpose (or "snacking occasion") the brand would be used. Consumers who reacted positively to the concept were given a product sample to take home and consume. A week later these consumers were interviewed again to identify whether or not the product had met their expectations and their purchase intentions after use. These interviews indicated that consumers were positively disposed toward O'GRADYS® because of its thicker cut, crispier texture, and more pronounced potato taste. Exhibit 2 shows the results

EXHIBIT 1
O'Gradys® Placement in the Frito-Lay Potato Chip Line

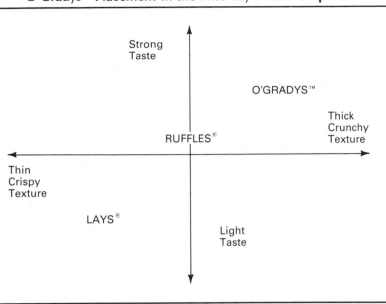

Source: Company records.

of the intention-to-buy questions for the concept/product fulfillment test.

TEST MARKET

Positive results from the concept/product fulfillment test led to a recommendation to proceed with O'GRADYS® and implement a test market under Mr. Heller's direction. Omaha, Nebraska, was chosen as the test site because Frito-Lay executives were confident it had a social and economic profile that was representative of the United States. Furthermore, Omaha, in general, represented a typical competitive environment in which to test consumer acceptance and competitive behavior. Omaha contained 1.6 million households that were identified as users of salty snack products, or 2 percent of the 78.8 million salty snack user households in the United States. Discussion among Frito-Lay marketing, sales, distribution, and manufacturing executives and the company's advertising agency indicated that the market test could begin January 9, 1983. Accordingly, a test market plan and budget was

EXHIBIT 2
Concept/Product Fulfillment Test Summary: Intention to Buy by Usage Occasion

	Usage	
	"Meal"	"Snack"
Concept test:		
Definitely would buy[a]	6%	4%
Probably would buy	40%	37%
Purchase intention after use:		
Definitely would buy	42%	33%
Probably would buy	38%	40%

[a]The five-point scale used to measure purchase intention ranged from "definitely would buy" to "definitely would not buy."

developed. The test market was scheduled to run for twelve months with a review scheduled for late June 1983.

Test Market Plan

Product Strategy

Frito-Lay executives decided to test both the cheese and regular flavored O'GRADYS® brand potato chips given the concept test results. Both would be positioned on the basis of the unique qualities of O'GRADYS®—namely, more potato flavor and a thicker, crunchier texture.

O'GRADYS® would be packaged in two sizes—a twelve-ounce package and an eight-ounce package. The twelve-ounce and eight-ounce packages were standard sizes, identical to those used for LAYS® and RUFFLES®. A 1⅛-ounce trial package would be used as well when introducing O'GRADYS® and would be discontinued later. Representative packages for O'GRADYS® are shown in Exhibit 3.

Pricing Strategy

O'GRADYS® would be priced higher than RUFFLES® or LAYS® potato chips, in part because of the slightly higher costs of production. The suggested retail prices and Frito-Lay's selling prices for the three products are shown in Exhibit 4. The gross margin for O'GRADYS® was 44 percent, irrespective of package size or flavor. The gross margins for RUFFLES® and LAYS® were 47 percent and 48 percent, respectively.

EXHIBIT 3

Representative Package Sizes for O'GRADYS®

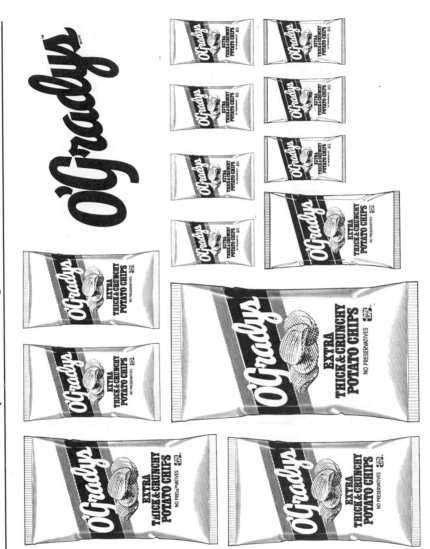

EXHIBIT 4
Potato Chip Price List

| | Brand | | |
Package Size	O'GRADYS®	RUFFLES®	LAY'S®
	Suggested Retail Price		
1⅛-ounce	$0.35	—	—
8-ounce	$1.49	$1.39	$1.29
12-ounce	$2.09	$1.99	$1.89
	Frito-Lay Selling Price to Retailer		
1⅛-ounce	$ .23	—	—
8-ounce	$1.06	$ .99	$ .92
12-ounce	$1.50	$1.425	$1.35

Advertising and Promotion Strategy

The primary audience for O'GRADYS® television advertising was mothers between the ages of twenty-five and fifty-four, since this target audience is the principal purchaser of snack foods. Secondary emphasis would be placed on reaching husbands and teens who would influence the mother's purchase behavior. The advertising message would incorporate the position sought by O'GRADYS® and read: "For those families who like potato chips, O'GRADYS® is the potato chip that's sliced thicker for crunchier texture and more potato taste." The tag line for O'GRADYS® would be: "The More Potato Potato Chip." In addition, television advertising would convey other subtle messages, including wholesomeness, heartiness, simplicity, and small-town values. Two of the television commercials to be shown during the test market are reproduced in Exhibits 5 and 6. In addition to television advertising, O'GRADYS® would be supported by newspaper advertising and supplements and in-store displays (see Exhibit 7).

Coupons were to be used to stimulate trial for O'GRADYS® during the test market as well as to generate repeat sales. Trial would be promoted through the use of 50 cent coupon inserts in newspapers, which applied to the eight-ounce and twelve-ounce packages during the first month of the test market. In-store sales and merchandising programs would be promoted as well. To stimulate repeat purchases, a 10 cent coupon was printed on every eight-ounce and twelve-ounce package that could be applied to subsequent purchases.

Distribution and Sales Strategy

Distribution and sales of O'GRADYS® was handled through

EXHIBIT 5
O'GRADYS™ Television Commercial

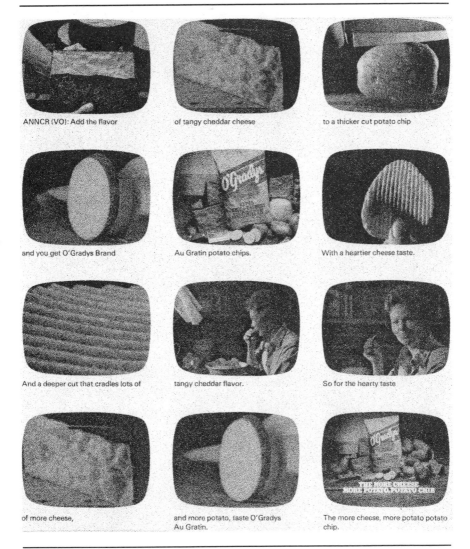

ANNCR (VO): Add the flavor

of tangy cheddar cheese

to a thicker cut potato chip

and you get O'Gradys Brand

Au Gratin potato chips.

With a heartier cheese taste.

And a deeper cut that cradles lots of

tangy cheddar flavor.

So for the hearty taste

of more cheese,

and more potato, taste O'Gradys Au Gratin.

The more cheese, more potato potato chip.

Frito-Lay's store-door delivery system. This system combines the duties of a delivery person and a salesperson. With this system, a delivery/salesperson solicits orders, stocks shelves, and introduces merchandising programs to retail store personnel. O'GRADYS™ would be sold through supermarkets, grocery stores, convenience stores, and other retail accounts that stocked Frito-Lay's salty snack products.

EXHIBIT 6
O'GRADYS® Television Commercial

VO: It's not just growing   a great potato   that makes a great potato chip.

It's how you   slice it.   Introducing O'Gradys

Sliced thicker... for the taste of more real potato.   With a deeper cut   for a serious crunch. (SFX) New O'Gradys has to be a great tasting potato chip

because there's more potato in each chip.   O'Gradys Brand.   THE MORE POTATO POTATO CHIP. The more potato potato chip. New from Frito-Lay. Super: The more potato potato chip.

Test Market Budget

The budget for the test market was set at $500,000, which was equivalent to an annual budget of $20 million for distribution nationwide. Approximately 70 percent of the budget would be spent during the first six months of the test market. Incremental expenses associated with production were negligible since the necessary machinery for produc-

EXHIBIT 7
O'GRADYS™ In-Store Display

ing O'GRADYS® was already in place and no capacity limitations were present.

Test Market Results

Mr. Earl Shirley was assigned to the brand shortly after the start of the test market. Mr. Shirley had joined Frito-Lay from PepsiCo Foods International, where he had been a marketing manager and business planner with assignments in Brazil and Asia. At the same time, Mr. Shirley was also responsible for TATOS®, another brand of potato chips in test market.

Consumer response had been monitored by an independent research firm since the beginning of the test market. This firm monitored consumer purchasing behavior through the use of a consumer panel. Each household in the panel recorded the purchase of salty snack products in a diary, including the brand name, package size, and whether or not the brand was purchased using coupons or on a deal of some type. These diaries were collected monthly, purchase data were recorded, and a report was submitted to Frito-Lay. The data provided by this firm were useful in gauging the type of purchase behavior, the incidence of trial and repeat purchase behavior, and product cannibalization in Omaha.

Type of Purchases

Information from the consumer panel indicated that the couponing program of O'GRADYS® had a major impact on purchase behavior. Exhibit 8 shows the percentage of total sales and repeat sales made on deals. Three of four purchases made during the first month were made on deals, mostly due to the 50 cent newspaper coupon insert. Subse-

EXHIBIT 8
Incidence of Deal Purchases Made

	Tracking Period					
	1/9–2/5	2/6–3/5	3/6–4/2	4/3–4/30	5/1–5/28	5/29–6/25
Percentage of repeat sales on deal	—	67	58	46	39	50
Percentage of total sales on deal	75	60	61	39	44	52

quent deal purchases were mostly repeat purchases. Although the incidence of deal purchases was high, Frito-Lay data on the Omaha market indicated that typically 25 to 40 percent of the potato chips were purchased on deals of some type. These deals consisted of coupons and in-store sales.

A change in sales mix of O'GRADYS® was also apparent over the course of the test market. During the first months after introduction, 8 percent of total O'GRADYS® sales were derived from the 1⅛-ounce "trial size" packages, 82 percent came from the 8-ounce package, and 10 percent came from the 12-ounce package size. However, the sales mix stabilized later in the test market, where 86 percent of the sales came from the 8-ounce package and 14 percent came from 12-ounce package size. These figures were identical to those for LAY'S® and RUFFLES.

Trial and Repeat Rates

Of critical concern to Mr. Shirley was the incidence of trial and repeat purchase behavior for O'GRADYS®. Exhibit 9 shows the trial and repeat rates for the regular and cheese flavors and for both flavors combined during the first six months of the test. The incidence of trial and repeat reached 33.2 percent and 40 percent, respectively, for the combined flavors by June 1983. However, some differences between the two flavors was apparent from the data. For example, the cheese flavor's trial rate was much lower than the regular flavors. However, the incidence of repeat purchase behavior had been consistently higher for the cheese flavor.

Equally important to Mr. Shirley were the "depth of repeat" data obtained from the consumer panel. *Depth of repeat* is the number of times a repeat purchaser buys a product after an initial repeat purchase. For O'GRADYS®, each repeat purchaser purchased O'GRADYS® 1.7 times after the initial repeat purchase during the six-month period. This repeat-per-repeater figure was equivalent to 3.5 on an annual basis. The average purchase during the test market had also increased. During the first month of the test, the average household purchasing O'GRADYS® bought eight ounces. However, the average purchase during the next five months was ten ounces.

Product Cannibalization

Consumer panel data also identified the incidence of product cannibalization. The data indicated that about 33 percent of O'GRADYS® volume resulted from consumer switching from RUFFLES® and LAY'S® brand potato chips. Mr. Shirley knew he would have to address this issue in his meeting with Ms. Barnes, since RUFFLES® and LAY'S® were major brands. These two brands combined

EXHIBIT 9
Trial and Repeat Rates for O'GRADYS™,
January–June 1983

	Tracking Period					
	1/9–2/5	2/6–3/5	3/6–4/2	4/3–4/30	5/1–5/28	5/29–6/25
O'GRADYS™ Regular flavor: Cumulative trial (%)	9.7	15.7	19.4	21.7	22.7	23.7
Cumulative repeat (%)	10.0	18.0	23.0	26.0	28.0	28.0
O'GRADYS™ Cheese flavor: Cumulative trial (%)	5.4	8.8	11.6	12.6	13.5	14.3
Cumulative repeat (%)	13.0	30.0	30.0	30.0	30.0	30.0
O'GRADYS™ Both flavors: Cumulative trial (%)	14.0	26.1	28.7	30.0	31.6	33.2
Cumulative repeat (%)	19.0	30.0	33.0	36.0	39.0	40.0

Notes:
(1) *Trial* refers to the percentage of households that have tried the product.
(2) *Repeat* refers to the percentage of trier households that have repurchased the product.
(3) Trial and repeat percentages for the individual flavors do not necessarily sum to the combined flavors due to switching between flavors.

captured 16 percent of total salty snack pound volume in 1983 and were supported by an annual marketing expenditure of $40 million. Each brand captured about 8 percent of total salty snack pound volume.

TEST MARKET REVIEW

Mr. Shirley's presentation, set for June 30, 1983, would conclude with his recommendation for the future marketing of O'GRADYS™. He could recommend that the test market be stopped, be continued and run for the next six months, or be expanded to other cities. Alternatively, he could recommend that O'GRADYS® be readied for a national introduction.

Timing and competitive reaction were important issues if he recommended an action beyond the outright killing of the project. Mr. Shirley knew that competitors were monitoring O'GRADYS®. There was also a high probability that these competitors were examining the chip with the intention of developing their own version. Timing was a concern for a variety of reasons. First, if Mr. Shirley continued testing the product, a competitor might launch a similar product nationally or regionally and upstage O'GRADYS®. Second, if an expanded test market or a national introduction was considered, a decision would be needed in June to implement either within six months.

Despite these issues, Mr. Shirley realized that a wrong decision had important ramifications both to the company and his career. If he recommended that O'GRADYS® be dropped and he was wrong in reading the test market data, then an opportunity would be lost. If he became overly cautious about the test market results and recommended further testing, then sizable sums of money might be wasted. If he recommended that Frito-Lay introduce O'GRADYS® nationally and the market did not support the brand, not only would a significant amount of money be lost, but his career might suffer as well. Everything, then, depended on his interpretation of the data available to him.

—————— CASE ——————

Elitch Gardens

RAYMOND MCCARTNEY, operations vice-president for Elitch Gardens, took the long way back to his office after a late lunch at the Palace Restaurant. It was 2:00, 90 degrees, Wednesday, early in August 1983. McCartney wanted to see what that meant for business.

"Pretty good for the Theatre," he thought as he went by the entrance. "It looks like a full house or nearly so, judging from the crowd outside." Theatre patrons were generally easy to spot, not just because they never strayed far from the Theatre but also because of their more formal dress and advanced years. Out of habit, McCartney looked for a patron under age thirty and met with no success. There must have been a thousand patrons in the area—sitting on benches in the shade, chatting on the entrance steps, hurrying a drink in the patio of the Palace Bar—all would soon begin filing inside for the 2:15 matinee.

The rest of the amusement park, too, looked about as he had expected. The grounds were well kept and the employees young, neat, and courteous. Most of the games appeared to be operating at about 50 percent of capacity. A few food and drink stands had some short lines, as did the Gift Shop and Miniature Golf course. The rides were by far the busiest, with five-minute lines at the Sea Dragon and Wildcat and what looked like ten-minute lines at the Twister and the Splinter. "Typical for a Wednesday," he thought. "We'll hit eight thousand easy, if it doesn't rain tonight."

ELITCH GARDENS BACKGROUND

Elitch Gardens could be described in industry terms as a traditional amusement park. The designation meant that Elitch attractions were

This case was written by Professor James E. Nelson with the assistance of MBA candidate Mary A. Marshall, University of Colorado at Denver. This case illustrates neither effective nor ineffective administrative decision-making. Some data are disguised. ©1984 by the Business Research Division, College of Business and Administration and the Graduate School of Business Administration, University of Colorado, Boulder, Colorado 80309.

evolutionary and eclectic rather than integrated along a common theme. It also meant a history—Elitch had been operating in the same north Denver location for over ninety years.

Elitch's History

Elitch opened for business on May 1, 1890, as Elitch's Zoological Gardens. P. T. Barnum was present for the occasion, along with numerous bears and lions, a camel, an ostrich, and other exotic wildlife. The main attraction, however, was the Theatre, which featured vaudeville acts and light opera. By 1897 the park had organized a summer stock company and began performing plays with great success. Success was due in large part to the company's use of experienced artists. Such acting greats as Sarah Bernhardt, Douglas Fairbanks, Harold Lloyd, Tyrone Power, and Edward G. Robinson appeared in productions before 1940. More recently, Pat O'Brien, Raymond Burr, Grace Kelly, Gene Rayburn, Lynn Redgrave, Mickey Rooney, Ginger Rogers, and William Shatner starred on stage. The 1983 season saw Noel Harrison, Gabe Kaplan, Richard Kiley, Cloris Leachman, David McCallum, and Shelley Winters in five productions.

By the early 1920s, the animals had disappeared in favor of games and rides, and the park's name was shortened to Elitch Gardens. "Gardens" had remained in the name because of the widespread use of flowers and plants to beautify park areas. Until the late 1940s, Elitch also operated a flower wholesaling and retailing business, selling the products of several greenhouses located on the grounds. Some twenty-five thousand square feet of greenhouse space still remained in 1983, under the care of twelve year-round employees. Flowers and plants were still placed in numerous places about the park. Particularly impressive were displays at the Miniature Golf course, the Sunken Gardens and Mountain at the Theatre Plaza, and the Clock (see Exhibit 1). Over three hundred hanging baskets of flowers graced ride areas, restaurant entrances, walkways, and other structures. Some patrons came to Elitch's each year for no other reason than to examine the floriculture.

Also by the early 1920s, Elitch had become known for its marvelous Trocadero Ballroom. The park had spared no expense in constructing the 75- by-200-foot dance palace, so well done that Universal Films selected it for the ballroom sequences in "The Glenn Miller Story," starring James Stewart and June Allyson. During its fifty-year existence, the Troc had hosted nearly every big band, including Les Brown, the Dorseys, Benny Goodman, Harry James, Wayne King, Guy Lombardo, and Lawrence Welk. Three generations of Denver residents had met, courted, and been otherwise entertained on its dance floor. In fact, the Troc held such fond memories for so many people that its

EXHIBIT 1
Floral Clock

demolition in 1975 brought newspaper reporters and television news teams, much formal protest, and hundreds of requests to buy pieces of the floor and decorations.

In the early 1950s, Elitch began operation of Kiddieland, a ride area for youngsters age nine and under. Kiddieland initially contained four rides, a fish pond stand, and a food stand, all in the space formerly occupied by a playground. The food stand was unique with its sunken floor, allowing employees to serve their small customers eye-to-eye. Besides turning a non-revenue-producing area into the opposite, Kiddieland was considered by management to be a success because (1) it attracted families who otherwise would not have considered Elitch as an entertainment possibility and (2) it introduced youngsters to the idea of amusement parks as a place to have fun. Kiddieland was extensively remodeled before the 1983 season to be a more interactive rather than passive ride area and was renamed Miniature Madness.

All in all, Elitch's history was both boon and bane. On the one hand, Elitch was so well established that park recognition was almost automatic. Denver residents first visited the park as children, dated at it, and then took their children and their grandchildren to it. In between these visits, residents and their families came to the park for company and other group picnics. However, Elitch's prominence and nearness to residents' hearts meant a close public involvement with park operations and, usually, an adverse reaction to change. The Trocadero experience illustrated the latter while a letter last month to a local newspaper illustrated the former:

> Sunday, July 3, my family and out-of-town guests visited Elitch Gardens. During our visit, a musical group played "Dixie" and Confederate flags were displayed at a gift redemption arcade. I deliberately walked through the park looking for an American flag but found none.
>
> I went to the guest service booth and voiced my objection to the presence of a flag which stood for dividing the country and enslaving its black people—and to the absence of a flag that stands for the independence we were celebrating that particular weekend. The employee there said that company policy was to respond to all complaints in writing within two weeks. In late July, I called and was told a response was coming. To date, I've heard nothing.

The letter had brought a quick response from Elitch's Director of Marketing, Lori Spillman. Spillman explained that American flags had proven so popular as prizes and gifts that weekend that the park's supply had simply been exhausted.

Elitch's Season

Elitch's public season ran for about 110 days each year, from the middle of May through Labor Day. Early summer weather always made season length an uncontrolled variable (cold and rain had forced the park to remain unopened for six days in 1983). After Labor Day, Elitch would open its gates only for employees of three or four large organizations, each of which "bought" the entire park for one or more days.

Elitch employed over twelve hundred people during the 1983 season at such diverse jobs as cashier, ride attendant, food service worker, and trash collector. Park revenues were expected to be about $15 million, based on an attendance projection of 1.2 million patrons. Attendance on any given day depended greatly on weather conditions, month, and day of week. For example, as many as 15,000 patrons might attend on a Saturday in July; a Tuesday in early June with similar weather could see as few as 6,000. Park management calculated that the maximum daily attendance Elitch could comfortably handle was 14,000. To increase this figure would in general require an expansion of amusement area boundaries, an expensive action that would also reduce parking space (currently at 1,950 spaces).

Elitch was open in May only on Fridays, Saturdays, and Sundays, until Memorial Day. Friday hours went from 5:00 P.M. to 11:00 P.M.; weekend hours were from 11:00 A.M. to 11:00 P.M. From Memorial Day to late August, the park was open every day from 11:00 A.M. to 11:00 P.M. During the last week in August (when public schools reopened), weekday hours reverted to the 5:00 P.M. to 11:00 P.M. schedule. However, during the entire season, Elitch was known to open as much as a half hour early and to remain open until midnight when attendance warranted.

ATTRACTIONS AT ELITCH GARDENS

Attractions at Elitch Gardens could be classified into five areas: rides, games, foods and beverages, souvenirs and gifts, and the Theatre. For 1983, the areas were expected to produce the following total revenue and gross margin percentages:

	Percentage of Total Revenue	Percentage Gross Margin
Rides	42%	26%
Games	19	32
Gate admissions[a]	18	45
Foods and beverages	17	10
Souvenirs and gifts	2	25
Theatre	2	− 5
Total	100%	

[a] Gate admission revenue was calculated at $2.50 per nontheatre patron.

McCartney was happy with this performance, except for the Theatre.

Rides

Elitch currently operated seventeen major rides with a total hourly capacity of fifteen thousand patrons. The most famous and most popular was the Twister, a three-quarter-mile roller coaster whose trains reached speeds of over sixty miles per hour. The newest was the Sea Dragon, a replica of a Viking longboat seating forty patrons and swinging to and fro at maximum heights of fifty-six feet. The Sea Dragon had begun operation in the 1982 season following the negotiation of a lease with the ride's manufacturer. Leasing was common practice in the industry, giving parks a chance to try new rides without extensive capital investment. Another popular ride (begun in 1978) was the Splinter, a water ride that floated log boats seating four patrons each through animated scenes of an old-time logging camp. The ride ended with boats climbing forty-five feet and splashing down a steep, water-filled flume.

Elitch also operated eight Miniature Madness rides for its patrons. Miniature boats, sports cars, airplanes, and the like provided thrills at a high level of safety.

All rides could be bought in two ways. When entering the park, patrons age three and over had to choose between a Pay-One-Price (POP) ticket at $8.75 or a General Admission (GA) ticket at $2.50. The POP ticket (displayed prominently on each purchaser's shirt) allowed patrons to ride any Elitch ride as many times as desired from time of arrival until 11:00 P.M. When the park remained open until midnight, POP patrons were treated after 11:00 P.M. as if they had purchased a GA ticket. The GA ticket allowed patrons to buy coupons at 10 cents each which then could be exchanged for rides. Major rides required from five to ten coupons each, while Miniature Madness rides charged either four or five coupons. About 60 percent of all patrons in 1983 would purchase POP tickets.

Elitch management followed the performance of each ride quite closely. Rides that operated below 60 percent of capacity soon caught management's attention. If subsequent operating or price changes still failed to achieve the 60 percent standard, the ride would simply be replaced.

Games

Games at Elitch Gardens were divided into carnival and electronic categories. For the 1983 season, Elitch operated eighteen carnival games where patrons could take their chances and exhibit their skills before interested onlookers. Players could, for example, hurl softballs at stacks of milk bottles or rows of stuffed cats, attempt to throw baseballs through a radar trap at a chosen speed, or bowl a rubber ball toward holes worth different point values. The last activity was called Skeeball, an extremely popular game for patrons aged eight to eighty. Over fifty Skeeball alleys were available for play in one noisy, fun-filled room. Each Skeeball player whose score exceeded displayed levels would earn tickets that could be accumulated and exchanged for prizes. It was not unusual to see a player bowl steadily for an hour or two, acquiring enough tickets for a large stuffed animal.

Elitch also operated over eighty electronic games in a nearby arcade. Players here were typically teens and preteens, along with a few parents. All faced the latest in video game technology in an atmosphere of intense noise and competition.

Elitch management considered games an important part of the park experience. Games provided a change of pace from the more physical and exhilarating rides. Games gave patrons something to do (besides leaving) whenever a rain shower passed over the park. Games were profitable and generally required far less capital investment than rides. Total game capacity at the park was about six thousand patrons per hour.

Food and Beverage Service

Elitch offered two kinds of food and beverage service. Any patron at the park could purchase snacks, meals, and beverages at the sixteen public food stands and restaurants. However, group picnic patrons could also consume catered foods and beverages at their designated picnic area.

The public eating and dining services offered a wide variety of products. Food stands sold snack-oriented products such as popcorn, hard and soft ice cream, hot dogs, hamburgers, and cotton candy. Patrons usually bought their snack or drink and consumed it while walking about the park or seated at a nearby bench. Two restaurants, The Palace and Boggio's, offered more substantial fare with seating at chairs and tables (The Palace's table tops were made from the old Trocadero floor). The Palace sold beer, wine, and mixed drinks in addition to nonalcoholic beverages. Most patrons preferred snacks over meals, leaving their dietary inhibitions in the parking lot.

Elitch's eight group picnic areas served catered foods and beverages. The smallest area could accommodate about thirty-five patrons while the largest could seat over twelve hundred. Groups reserved these areas and often contracted with the park to provide all foods and beverages. Typically, a group representative would reserve an area with Spillman and select a meal for all group members from the catered menu. Seven choices were available, ranging from fried chicken at $3.80 per serving to a deluxe buffet at $8.40. Elitch also provided beverages, ice, and almost anything else necessary to make the group picnic a success.

Most group picnics took place on weekends and required Spillman's presence to ensure that activities would come off according to expectations. Spillman would monitor the arrival of foods and beverages, explain the operation of each area's public address system, and help remove nongroup patrons from the rented areas. This last activity was usually the most troublesome. Many nongroup patrons brought their own picnic lunches and dinners (an Elitch tradition) only to find public picnic areas full. In seeking a vacant table, some of these patrons would come across a partially full group picnic area and try to claim a space. These patrons could be quite reluctant to move.

Souvenirs and Gifts

Souvenirs and gifts could be bought at five park locations. Patrons could purchase balloons, tee shirts, hats, glassware, flowers, and hundreds of other items at prices from 75 cents to $50. A special shop in the Miniature Madness area sold merchandise suited to its patrons at prices from 50 cents to $12.

The Theatre

The Elitch Summer Theatre occupied the largest building on park grounds. Built in 1891, the structure was older by some fifty years than any other in the park. Its age and distinctive architecture had led to the Theatre's inclusion in the National Register of Historic Places. The designation carried with it status, tax credits for restoration and renovation (equal to 25 percent of rehabilitation costs), and the possibility for federal grants to plan and execute any restoration and renovation. However, rehabilitation plans and work would have to be approved by the U.S. Department of Interior if tax credits or grant monies were received.

The Theatre could seat 1,479 patrons for each of its 118 performances per season. Whether or not all seats would fill for a performance depended on the date, time (matinee or evening), and the play itself. The past several seasons had seen total attendance hovering around 120,000 patrons. Elitch received $2.50 per patron under terms of its lease with the Elitch Theatre Company, now an independent organization that took total responsibility for the Theatre's productions and marketing. Elitch also received a percentage of the Theatre Company's profits, generally an uncertain revenue item of small magnitude. Against all Theatre revenue, Elitch charged building repair and maintenance costs. The net result was essentially a break-even operation.

Elitch management felt the Theatre was at a crossroads. The lease agreement would expire in January 1984, and the Theatre needed renovation or rebuilding. The 27,000-square-foot structure could be remodeled for upwards of $1.0 million, rebuilt at the same seating capacity on the same site or elsewhere (on or off park grounds) for about $1.5 million, or replaced by two or three rides and games at a cost of around $2.5 million. The problem seemed particularly complex because no one at Elitch was really expert in theater design or theater management. No one had really thought about the best way to proceed.

Other Attractions

Beyond rides, games, foods and beverages, and the Theatre, Elitch offered other attractions, all for free. A children's theater in the Miniature Madness area regularly presented short skits. Groups of musicians, magicians, jugglers, and other entertainers performed throughout the park. A troupe of singers and dancers gave twice-daily performances at the Theatre Plaza. However, equal or superior to any Elitch attraction to many patrons was simply people watching. Elitch's concentration of people of differing ages, races, and life-styles meant a wide range of emotions and behaviors available for public viewing.

STRATEGY FOR THE 1980s

McCartney returned to his office. On his desk was a sheet of paper with a single line written across the top: Obtain 10 percent real growth in revenues per year while maintaining or improving the patron's Elitch experience. McCartney felt strongly that revenue growth and patron satisfaction deserved equal emphasis. Growth without concern for satisfaction sounded too much like the 1970s, when new rides and renovation had increased park attendance to almost 1.5 million. Beyond raising revenues, the record attendance had meant long lines nearly everywhere in the park on many weekends. Long lines (greater than fifteen minutes) were simply inconsistent with profitable operations over the long term.

"The issue now," McCartney thought, "is *how* to achieve this goal." The 1970s expansion strategy could not be continued because of space limitations. Instead, he would have to emphasize control, to make sure that every Elitch attraction contributed its fair share. But control and subsequent fine tuning of Elitch operations would not by themselves produce 10 percent real growth in revenues. Nor would large price increases. Annual price increases of 12 to 15 percent would quickly change the composition of Elitch's present patron base as well as reduce overall attendance. McCartney considered both results unacceptable. "There's got to be another answer," he thought, as Spillman entered his office.

The Research Study

Spillman was carrying several sheets of paper (Exhibits 2, 3, and 4), copied, she explained, from a recently completed marketing-research study. The study had been executed by a local research agency in an effort to learn more about Elitch patrons. Over a two-week period, 353 patrons (age twelve and over, selected at random) had been asked to participate in a short interview as they were exiting the park. Three hundred (85 percent) had agreed.

Beyond providing a general understanding of Elitch patrons, results would help in reaching a decision on the possible elimination of the GA ticket. The action would reduce Elitch's labor force by some twenty positions (cashiers and ticket takers) and save about $70,000 in labor costs. Elitch would also save about $15,000 each year in ticket printing and handling costs. Several people in Elitch management also felt that park revenues would increase dramatically if every patron paid $8.75 to enter.

Spillman explained that she had not personally had time to interpret the exhibits but would do so before a meeting scheduled for Friday. The meeting would include one or two people from the research agency who would present their own interpretations and recommendations. Spillman left some more figures that she had assembled on patron arrival times and ticket purchases for July and August:

	Average Daily Purchases of:	
Arrival Time	GA Tickets	POP Tickets
Before 11 A.M.	170	650
11 A.M. to 1 P.M.	910	2,060
1 P.M. to 3 P.M.	830	1,300
3 P.M. to 5 P.M.	540	730
5 P.M. to 7 P.M.	770	780
7 P.M. to 9 P.M.	1,040	510
After 9 P.M.	470	0
Total	4,730	6,030

EXHIBIT 2
Summary of Ticket Purchases (Questions 8 and 9)

Question 8. *What kind of ticket did you purchase today?*

Ticket Type	Frequency	Percentage
POP	139	46.3%
GA	93	31.0
Group picnic (POP)	32	10.7
Theatre (GA)	36	12.0
Total	300	100.0%

Question 9. *Why did you purchase that particular type of ticket?*

Reason	Frequency	Percentage
Economy/best deal	91	30.3%
Not riding much	52	17.3
Theatre	36	12.0
Group picnic	32	10.7
Convenience	29	9.7
Short stay	18	6.0
Other	17	5.7
No reason	25	8.3
Total	300	100.0%

Note: Data in Exhibit 2 have been disguised but are useful for discussion purposes.

EXHIBIT 3
Summary of Patron's Elitch Experience
(Questions 1, 2, 3, 10, 14, and 15)

Question 1. *What is your main reason for coming to Elitch's today?* (PROBE)

Main Reason	Frequency	Percentage
General entertainment	81	27.0%
Children or family	58	19.3
Rides	39	13.0
Theatre	36	12.0
Group picnic	32	10.7
Vacation	28	9.3
Other	26	8.7
Total	300	100.0%

EXHIBIT 3 *(continued)*

Question 2. *What things did you really enjoy here at Elitch's?* (PROBE)

Elitch Feature	Frequency	Percentage
Rides (in general)	108	20.2%
Flowers, gardens	94	17.6
Rollar coasters	74	13.9
Games	51	9.6
Cleanliness	42	7.9
Log ride	33	6.2
Theatre	30	5.6
Miniature Madness	27	5.1
Food	22	4.1
Entertainment	15	2.8
Everything	38	7.1
Total	534[a]	100.1%

Question 3. *Is there anything you disliked?* (PROBE)

Elitch Feature	Frequency	Percentage
Crowds, lines	64	48.1%
Theatre-related	10	7.5
Prices too high	10	7.5
Dirty restrooms	9	6.8
Too few rides	7	5.3
Food service	5	4.0
Rude employees	4	3.0
Too little shade	4	3.0
Other	20	15.0
Total	133[b]	100.2%

Question 10. *Approximately how many rides did you ride on today?*

Number of Rides	Frequency	Percent
None	78	26.0%
1–5	78	26.0
6–10	94	31.3
11–15	34	11.3
16 and over	16	5.3
Total	300	99.9%

Ticket Type	Average Number of Rides
POP (regular)	11.0
POP (group picnic)	8.1
GA	2.4

EXHIBIT 3 *(continued)*

Question 14. *On a scale of 1 to 10 (with 10 as the highest) how would you rate the following areas at Elitch's?*

Area	Average Rating	Number Rating
Miniature Madness	8.4	136
Rides	8.4	234
Games	7.1	162
Foods	6.9	188
Entertainment	7.9	180

Question 15. *To the nearest dollar, about how much money did you spend today on:*

Area	Average Amount Spent
Rides	$ 7.30[a]
Food	3.40
Games	2.70
Souvenirs, gifts	.30
Total	$13.70

Ticket Type	Average Total Amount Spent
POP	$18.10
GA	13.30
Group picnic (POP)	9.50[c]
Theatre (GA)	2.60[d]

Note: Data in Exhibit 3 have been disguised but are useful for discussion purposes.

[a]Does not total 300 because of multiple responses.

[b]Responses received from 104 patrons.

[c]Includes an allocation of $6.25 for a POP ticket.

[d]Includes an allocation of $2.50 for a GA ticket.

EXHIBIT 4
Summary of Demographic Characteristics
(Questions 20, 21, 22, and 23)

Question 20. *What is your age?*

Age Category	Frequency	Percentage
12–17	61	20.3%
18–24	67	22.3
25–29	28	9.3
30–39	80	26.7

EXHIBIT 4 *(continued)*

Age Category	Frequency	Percentage
40–49	24	8.0
50–64	25	8.3
65 and over	10	3.3
Refused	5	1.7
Total	300	99.9%

Question 20a. *Observe respondent's sex.*

Sex	Frequency	Percentage
Male	164	54.7%
Female	136	45.3
Total	300	100.0%

Question 21. *What is your marital status?*

Marital Status	Frequency	Percentage
Single	154	51.3%
Married	146	48.7
Total	300	100.0%

Question 22. *What is your occupation?*

Occupation Categories	Frequency	Percentage
Major professionals	20	6.7%
Business managers	18	6.0
Lesser administrators	31	10.3
Skilled technicians	43	14.3
Skilled manual laborers	32	10.7
Semi-skilled laborers	30	10.0
Unskilled laborers	8	2.7
Unemployed	2	0.7
Retired	10	3.3
Students	106	35.3
Total	300	100.0%

Question 23. *Which of the following categories best represents your 1982 household income?*

Income Category	Frequency	Percentage
$50,001 and over	19	6.3%
$45,001–$50,000	9	3.0
$40,001–$45,000	17	5.7
$35,001–$40,000	25	8.3

EXHIBIT 4 *(continued)*

Income Category	Frequency	Percentage
$30,001–$35,000	27	9.0
$25,001–$30,000	23	7.7
$20,001–$25,000	25	8.3
$15,001–$20,000	21	7.0
$10,001–$15,000	15	5.0
$ 5,001–$10,000	19	6.3
$ 1–$ 5,000	28	9.3
Don't know	62	20.7
Refused	10	3.3
Total	300	99.9%

Note: Data in Exhibit 4 have been disguised but are useful for discussion purposes.

Average daily attendance during this period was about 9,400 patrons on weekdays and 13,400 on weekends. Finally, Spillman left some census data on characteristics of the Colorado and Denver–Boulder populations (Exhibit 5).

Decisions and the Data

McCartney studied all the figures for some time after Spillman left. Although the data would certainly influence his decision on the GA ticket, he realized that numbers were only one consideration. Patron reaction, park history, and many other factors would shape his eventual position. He sat thinking in silence:

> The simplest solution, I guess, is to do nothing. At the other extreme, we could get rid of the GA ticket entirely. In between, I suppose, we could sell the GA ticket only after 9 P.M. or only on weekdays. . . . And what about the POP ticket? If we do eliminate the GA ticket, we could reduce the POP ticket to, say, $7.00 in order to get patron acceptance.

Any one of a large number of decisions seemed possible.

McCartney also realized that all the figures appeared helpful in a strategic sense. In fact, he found it hard not to think about long-term questions raised by the numbers:

> Can we continue our present patron mix? Should we? What are the risks involved? How do we position Elitch against competitors?

The last question seemed quite important.

EXHIBIT 5
Selected Characteristics of the Colorado and Denver–Boulder Populations

Age Category	Colorado Percent				Denver–Boulder 1980 Percent[b]
	1970	1980	1990[a]	2000[a]	
9 and under	18.6%	14.8%	15.2%	13.4%	14.4%
10–14	10.6	7.8	6.8	7.2	7.9
15–19	10.0	9.3	6.5	6.9	9.0
20–24	9.1	10.5	7.7	6.8	10.1
25–29	7.1	10.5	9.9	7.3	10.9
30–39	11.8	16.0	20.3	17.6	16.9
40–49	11.5	10.0	13.8	18.0	10.4
50–64	12.8	12.6	11.1	14.3	12.6
65 and over	8.5	8.5	8.7	8.5	7.8
Total	100.0%	100.0%	100.0%	100.0%	100.0%
Median Age	26.2	28.6	N/A	N/A	28.9
Total population (thousands)	2,210	2,890	3,775	4,657	1,618

Sex Category	Colorado Percent 1980	Denver–Boulder Percent 1980
Male	49.5%	49.2%
Female	50.5	50.8
Total	100.0%	100.0%

Marital Status Category	Colorado Percent 1980	Denver–Boulder Percent 1980
Single	40.0%	41.5%
Married	60.0	58.5
Total	100.0%	100.0%

Occupation Category	Colorado Percent 1980	Denver–Boulder Percent 1980
Professional	13.7%	14.6%
Executive, administrative, managerial	12.2	13.4
Technician	3.7	4.1
Sales	10.9	11.0
Clerical, administrative support	17.2	19.1
Service	13.0	12.1
Farming, forestry, fishing	2.7	1.0

EXHIBIT 5 *(continued)*

Occupation Category	Colorado Percent 1980	Denver-Boulder Percent 1980
Precision production, craft, repair	13.3	12.1
Operators and fabricators	9.4	8.9
Handlers and helpers	3.9	3.7
Total	100.0%	100.0%

Source: Census publications.

[a]Census Bureau projections.

[b]Denver-Boulder population is expected to grow at an annual rate of 3%.

Competitors

Lakeside Amusement Park was located less than two miles from Elitch Gardens. Lakeside's boundaries enclosed a larger area than Elitch's, with a shallow lake occupying a substantial portion of the grounds. On paper, Lakeside's attractions looked quite similar to Elitch's. Lakeside offered twenty-six adult and fifteen "kiddie" rides, numerous carnival and electronic games, snack-oriented foods and beverages (including beer), public and group picnic areas, and souvenirs and gifts. However, Lakeside was unique in offering speedboat rides (daily) and stock car races on its one-fifth-mile paved race course (on Sunday evenings).

In actuality, Lakeside's attractions differed considerably from Elitch's. Lakeside's rides and buildings appeared to represent a lower capital investment. Lakeside employees received less extensive training, followed a less stringent dress code, and earned lower wages. Lakeside's POP ticket cost $6.50 for the 1983 season, while its GA ticket was only 50 cents.

While Lakeside was Elitch's most direct rival, many other attractions also competed for the Denver entertainment dollar. Waterworld, some ten miles north, offered water slides and other aquatic diversions at $6.00 per day. Heritage Square, about fifteen miles west, featured turn-of-the-century theme shops, rides, an opera house (dinner theater), and chuckwagon suppers, at no admission charge to the area. The Denver Zoo, only six miles away, drew thousands of area residents each summer weekend, charging $3 for adults and $1 for children. Families could always take in a movie ($4 for adults, $2.50 for children), attend a Denver Bears baseball game (ticket prices ranged from $3 to $8), or simply go for a drive in the mountains. In fact, Mc-

Cartney considered the mountains to be Elitch's biggest competition. Families could camp, fish, and hike in the wilderness or attend any number of city or resort festivals. A great deal of mountain entertainment could be reached in less than two hours of driving.

CASE

Superior Supermarkets

IN AUGUST 1986 executives of the Hall Company, which operated wholesale and retail food outlets in several south central states, met to review a series of image studies done for the company's three Superior supermarkets in Centralia, Missouri. The purpose of this meeting was to evaluate the results and prepare guidelines for changes in merchandising and promotion strategy if necessary.

The image studies were prompted by two competitive changes in the Centralia market. First, an existing competitor had recently relocated its store closer to one of the Superior supermarkets. And second, there were plans for a General Merchandise Discount Store with a grocery section to be built near another Superior supermarket.

THE COMPANY

The Hall Company is a wholesale and retail food distributor. When the company was incorporated in 1932, it included a number of wholesale food operations, brokerage houses, and produce companies. The first retail food chain was acquired in 1949; the Superior chain was purchased in 1960. The company established its first general merchandise store in 1970 and added discount food outlets in 1977. By 1986 the Hall Company distributed food and related products to corporate-owned and -operated supermarkets, discount food outlets, and general merchandise department stores. In addition, twenty-five distribution cen-

This case was prepared by Roger A. Kerin, Southern Methodist University, Dallas, and Richard N. Cardozo, University of Minnesota, as the basis for class discussion, rather than to illustrate appropriate or inappropriate handling of administrative situations. Names of locations and stores have been disguised. Copyright © Center for Experimental Studies in Business, University of Minnesota.

ters (wholesalers) supplied approximately 480 independently owned franchise supermarkets and more than 2,400 independent retailers and institutions.

The Hall Company has shown consistent growth over the past five years. In 1981 Hall had sales of $988.6 million with net earnings of $12.4 million, compared with sales of $1.3 billion and net earnings of $18.7 million in 1985.

Sales of Superior-owned and -franchised supermarkets in 1985 exceeded $150 million, about one-third of which was accounted for by corporate-owned stores. The three Superior stores in Centralia were owned and operated by Superior Division of the Hall Company.

CENTRALIA, MISSOURI

Centralia is the primary trade center in central Missouri. Its retail trade area, which encompasses the area northwest of Centralia, includes 5,450 square miles with a population of 122,527 (1980 census). During the 1980s the population of Centralia itself increased approximately 20 percent. Most of the growth occurred in the northwest and southwest sections of the city. Although agriculture produces most of the income in the trade area, industrial growth is also evident. In the last decade, industries such as meat packing, farm machinery, and mobile homes have located near the perimeter of the city. In 1985 Centralia retail sales, excluding automobiles, were estimated at $110 million. In the last ten years, retail sales have increased 83 percent. Retail sales rose 30 percent from 1982 to 1985, compared with the state average of 23 percent for the same period. Retail food sales in Centralia were expected to exceed $18.9 million in 1986. Food sales in 1985 totaled more than $18.8 million, more than double the $8.6 million sales in 1980 (see Exhibit 1).

In 1986 four major competitive food chains together accounted for approximately 86 percent of all food sales in Centralia (see Exhibit 2). The remainder of the retail food business was shared primarily by three independent stores.

Each of three chains—Henny Penny, Grand American, and Payless—operated one store; Hall operated three Superior supermarkets in Centralia. Each of the three Superior stores was smaller than the chains' stores. Grand American, Henny Penny, and Payless drew their customers from larger geographic areas than did Superior. Payless, in particular, enjoyed a strong trade from outside Centralia. Store locations are shown in Exhibit 3. Selected statistical data on Superior stores and competitors appear in Exhibit 4.

EXHIBIT 1
Total Food Sales for Selected Years: Centralia and Scott County

Year	Centralia	Scott
1980	$ 8,592,000	$ 9,261,000
1981	13,047,000	16,418,000
1982	13,252,000	16,816,000
1983	13,597,000	19,953,000
1984	18,834,000	20,150,000
1985	18,877,000	20,197,000
1986 (estimate)	18,925,599	20,248,000

Source: Company records.

HENNY PENNY

The Henny Penny supermarket on West Main Street was built about 1976 and was completely remodeled in 1985 at a cost of approximately $200,000. Some 15 percent of the store's selling space is devoted to an extensive general merchandise assortment. According to Hall executives, most of the store's customers come from a residential area of one- and two-family homes with annual family incomes in excess of $30,000. Hall officials believe that Henny Penny had captured most of the business of the middle and upper income group in Centralia, and that the store probably has the highest average sales of all the major stores.

The Henny Penny store is well managed, clean, orderly and attractive. The decor is warm, the clerks friendly, and the physical lay-

EXHIBIT 2
Estimated Share of Market for Supermarkets

	1979	1980	1981	1982	1983	1984	1985	1986
Superior	24%	29%	27%	30%	31%	22%	23%	26%
Grand American	22	11	7	6	6	6	6	12
Payless	25	25	26	28	30	34	34	27
Henny Penny	9	14	19	16	14	20	20	21
Others	20	21	21	20	19	18	17	14

Source: Company records.

Note: Share-of-market estimates were made by Hall Company executives on the basis of information they considered reliable. The total market (100 percent) represents all food sales made in Centralia.

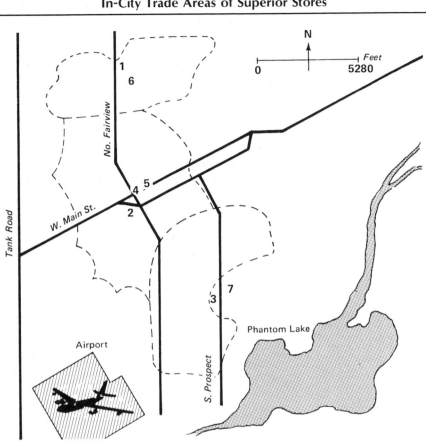

Key: 1. Superior (N. Fairview)
      2. Superior (W. Main St.)
      3. Superior (S. Prospect)
      4. Grand American
      5. Henny Penny
      6. Payless
      7. Proposed Discount Store

Note: Trade area boundaries were drawn on the basis of personal interviews with customers in each Superior store. The address of each interviewee was then plotted on the map, and boundaries drawn.

EXHIBIT 4
Centralia Store Comparison

	Weekly Food Sales/Store	Average Building Size (sq. ft.)	Average Food Selling Area (sq. ft.)	Average Food Sales/(sq. ft.)	Average Parking Spots	Average Number of Checkstands
Grand American	$ 42,500	22,000	15,400	$2.76	106	6.0+ Exp.
Henny Penny	74,250	22,500	15,750	4.72	151	8.0
Payless	100,000	110,000[a]	24,000	4.17	300+	17.0
Superior (average of 3 stores)						
W. Main	29,230	11,713	8,223	3.55	80	4.3
N. Fairview	32,214	10,842	8,090	3.98	76	5.0
S. Prospect	27,340	11,756	8,625	3.17	84	4.0
	28,134	12,540	7,954	3.54	81	4.0

	Average Number of Shopping Carts	Courtesy Counter	Average Advertising Lines/Month (1981)	Average Age of Store(s)	Average Bakery Variety[b]	Average Produce Variety[b]	Average Meat Variety[b]
Grand American	110	None	1,636	12+	—	74	84
Henny Penny	90	1	898	10+	—	60	76
Payless	300+	1	2,351 / 2,006 (all 3 stores)	10+	—	64	81
Superior (average)	63	1		12+	40	67	75
W. Main	70	1		13	21	66	75
N. Fairview	66	1		14	29	68	66
S. Prospect	52	1		10	70	66	84

Source: Conpany records.

[a]Nonfood items occupy approximately 48,000 square feet of the total of 72,000 square feet of selling space in the entire store.

[b]Variety refers to the number of separate items and the nature of the packaging. For example, rye bread is considered separate from whole wheat breads. Within the item class rye bread, there may be two types of packaging—one-pound and two-pound loaves.

out easy to shop. The merchandising strength is a balanced variety in groceries, quality meat, and produce. The store is conveniently located, with excellent parking facilities. Henny Penny's principal promotion theme is everyday low prices, as evidenced by its advertising slogan, "Save on the total." The store does not offer trading stamps. According to Hall officials, the Henny Penny store has an extremely favorable customer image.

The Henny Penny supermarket in Centralia is one of sixty-five Henny Penny supermarkets throughout Missouri and Illinois. Estimated sales in 1985 for the entire chain were $185 million.

GRAND AMERICAN

The Grand American store at the corner of Fairview and West Main opened early in 1986. This store replaced an older facility located several blocks northeast of the new site. The Centralia store is one of 148 supermarkets opened or remodeled in the last year by Grand American, one of the nation's largest food distributors and retailers. The Grand American store is the most modern store in Centralia and has the finest fixtures and decor. It has wide aisles and is relatively easy to shop.

Hall officials consider the Grand American store a major competitor. According to Hall executives, the store is highly regimented and lacks any innovative merchandising appeal. It has good variety in meat, produce, and groceries, and its dairy department is highly acceptable to the consumer. The store carries a skeleton variety of general merchandise and offers no stamps. Grand American's weekly advertising approach emphasizes a variety of items and also attempts to create a low-price image by advertising competitive prices for the wide variety of items listed in each ad. The store's customers come from residential areas similar to those from which Henny Penny customers come; however, the income distribution of Grand American customers range from $20,000 to $30,000.

PAYLESS

According to Hall officials, Payless is number one in sales volume in Centralia and is the principal competitor of the Superior supermarkets. Approximately 22 percent of Superior customers shop Payless regularly. Most of Payless's customers are middle-age and older families whose annual incomes exceed $25,000. Two-thirds of the store's selling space is allotted to general merchandise; one-third of its space contains food items. Managers of the three Superior stores maintain that "Payless's primary merchandising strength is in groceries and special purchase displays." One manager stated that "orderliness and cleanliness is sacrificed for production, and the store lacks the quality and freshness present in the other supermarkets in Centralia." Ads feature very low prices on particular items, which are displayed in large quantities at the ends of aisles in the grocery section of the store. Unlike Henny Penny and Grand American, the Payless store is part of a complex of other types of stores including several service shops, a bakery, a drug store, and a furniture store. Payless Stores Co., the regional chain that built the Centralia store and operated it for many years, had recently sold that store to an independent businessman who continued to operate the store under the Payless name.

SUPERIOR

The three Superior supermarkets in Centralia are smaller and generally older stores than those of the major competitors. According to company officials, the stores' combined sales of almost $4.4 million in 1985 represented nearly the maximum that the present physical plants could produce.

Sales for the three stores combined had increased consistently during the past five years, as indicated in Exhibit 5. Overall gross profit for the three stores was $856,100 or 19.6 percent of sales in 1985.

Hall executives pointed out, however, that much of the increase in Superior's sales, as in the sales of all food retailers, was attributable to price inflation. After adjusting for inflationary changes, executives estimated that Superior's sales had increased approximately 6 percent over the five-year period.

In 1985 sales of the three Superior stores were divided approximately as follows: grocery (including dairy), 68 percent; meat, 25 per-

EXHIBIT 5
Sales of Superior Stores in Centralia, 1981–1985

Store	1981	1982	1983	1984	1985
North Fairview	$1,109,064	$1,164,958	$1,237,865	$1,310,423	$1,356,250
West Main	1,525,447	1,605,003	1,587,712	1,581,318	1,642,585
South Prospect	964,785	1,124,112	1,253,030	1,291,968	1,379,758
Total	$3,599,296	$3,894,073	$4,078,607	$4,183,709	$4,378,593

Source: Company records.

cent; and produce, 7 percent. These figures were similar for all three stores and were typical of those for supermarkets throughout the United States. The Hall Company accounting system allocated gross profits approximately in proportion to sales. Therefore, about two-thirds of Superior stores' gross profit was attributed to the grocery department (including bakery); approximately one-fourth to meats (including delicatessen); and the remainder to produce.

Company officials believed that Superior stores offered more limited variety than the major competitors, but that Superior carried high-quality merchandise, particularly in canned goods and fresh produce. Officials recognized that the fresh meat departments of the three stores varied in consumer acceptance.

Superior stores offer S&H Green Stamps, and emphasize, "Stamps and Price" in their weekly advertising. The stores often advertise high-volume items at very low prices and occasionally feature "loss leaders."

North Fairview

Built in 1972, the North Fairview store is the oldest of the three Superior stores in Centralia. Since 1981 its sales have increased 6.6 percent beyond increases attributable to price inflation. The store is located less than two blocks from the center in which Payless is situated. Approximately 35 percent of the North Fairview store's customers come from outside Centralia.[a] Currently, the average transaction[b] amounts to $11.20.

West Main Street

The Superior supermarket on West Main Street was opened in 1969. Substantial improvements to the store were added in 1980, including an expansion of the frozen food and dairy departments and a new checkstand. In addition, a "mini-deli" was added shortly thereafter. The deli prepares baked beans, potato salad, and similar items for sale on the premises and for delivery to and sale at the Fairview and South Prospect stores.

Two competitors, Henny Penny and Grand American, are situated across the street. Although both were strong competitors, Hall

---

[a] The estimate of nonresidents patronizing stores actually meant that these customers lived approximately three to four miles away from an individual store.

[b] *Average transaction* is an approximate measure of the dollar amount spent by each shopper on each shopping trip. The average is computed by dividing the number of "totals" rung on the cash register (i.e., the number of transactions per week) into the total dollar sales volume for that week.

executives believed the West Main Street store drew most of its customers from the area south of the store, and that Henny Penny and Grand American drew fewer customers than Superior from that area. Approximately 26 percent of the West Main store's sales come from people living beyond the city limits.

When price inflation is factored out, sales have declined by 8.6 percent since 1981. Early in 1986, the average transaction was $11.60.

South Prospect

The South Prospect Superior supermarket was built in 1970 and substantially remodeled in 1981. Though no major competitors presently exist in the immediate vicinity, a discount store, which will offer general merchandise and food, is scheduled for construction across the street within the next two years. The discount store typically includes 15,000 to 20,000 square feet of selling space for food. The food section is typically operated by a lessee. Hall officials expected the lessee in Centralia to be one of the three major national chains not now operating in Centralia, each of which would offer vigorous and continuous price competition to existing food stores.

The South Prospect store has the only on-premise "scratch" bakery among the three Superior stores. Deliveries are made to the other stores daily. Company executives believe that the bakery does not offer as high quality or as much variety as the typical retail bakery shop in Centralia. Adjusting for inflationary price increases, sales have increased 26.2 percent in the last five years—the highest of the three stores. About 23 percent of the store's sales are from people who live outside Centralia. The current average transaction is $10.28.

RESULTS OF CONSUMER RESEARCH EFFORTS

In March 1986 Hall commissioned an independent marketing research firm to conduct a series of studies for the three superior stores in Centralia. Two objectives were outlined for these studies. First, Hall executives sought (1) to develop a profile of Superior shoppers and (2) to determine the shopping behavior of these customers. This information was to be used in making store modification decisions. Second, executives hoped that by questioning shoppers about what they liked and disliked about the Superior stores, Hall officials could establish what kind of retail image the stores projected. The question of store image had plagued corporate officials since 1978, when a retailing consultant to the company had concluded that the stores failed to reach their full profit potential because of the lack of a strong consumer image.

The first study consisted of a telephone survey of 150 Centralia residents who were asked to comment on the principal strengths of Superior stores, Payless, Grand American, and Henny Penny. More than 30 percent of the interviewees considered Superior's prices "above average." In contrast, some 20 percent of the respondents thought the prices at Payless and at Henny Penny were below average.

The respondents were also asked to associate the advertising slogans of the stores with the appropriate outlet. Forty percent of the respondents correctly associated the slogan "Stamps and Price" with Superior, and 60 percent of the respondents correctly named Henny Penny as the store using the slogan "Save on the Total." But "Discounts Prices" was correctly associated with Grand American by only 5 percent of the respondents, whereas 13 percent related the slogan to Superior, and 26 percent associated the slogan with Payless. Additional data from this study appear in Exhibit 6.

A second study, conducted in April 1986, consisted of asking ten housewives who were representative of the various geographic and income segments of Centralia to discuss various aspects of food shopping in Centralia. A summary of their impressions follows:

Meat. Eight of the ten housewives stated that the quality of meat was the most important determinant of store choice. They liked to see cleanliness in the meat department and bargains that were not necessarily poor cuts of meat. Meat display was also viewed as a salient consideration.

Produce. Housewives wanted home-grown produce.

Superior Bakery. Housewives generally liked the bakery and particularly the freshness of the cakes, rolls, and bread in all three stores. However, several housewives believed that bread advertised as being fresh was in fact day-old at the South Prospect store.

Consumerism. Housewives were surprisingly aware of recent packaging proposals, such as unit pricing and open coding, and favored both. The housewives did not note any displeasure in seeing both national and private brands on shelves. They typically purchased private brands, if these were less costly, and purchased them regularly if they thought the quality was acceptable.

Advertising. Eight of the ten housewives read all of the newspaper ads each week. They read the ads and compare prices regularly. Advertising emphasizing discount prices has little effect

EXHIBIT 6
Association of Particular Characteristics with Major Food Stores in Centralia
(telephone survey, n = 150)

Characteristic	Grand American	Henny Penny	Superior	Payless	Apathetic, Don't Know
Most reasonable prices	11%	36%	7%	34%	12%
Most convenience	18	21	35	25	1
Best quality meat	20	27	18	11	24
Widest variety meat	22	25	20	18	15
Best quality produce	24	35	24	11	6
Widest variety produce	24	30	14	18	14
Best store service	12	30	28	13	17
Quality canned goods	12	24	14	14	26
Best specialty games, continuity programs, and trading stamps	5	2	26	52	15
Best overall variety	6	8	2	74	10
Best store layout	27	24	14	9	26
Best bakery	—	—	42	—	58
Best deli	—	—	9	—	91

Note: Company records.

on customer intentions—they simply don't believe it. Also, discount price slogans have little impact, as all the stores proclaim to offer such reduced prices. Stamps, however, received a favorable vote by the housewives.

Stores in General. Distance does not seem to be a factor in determining customer patronage; rather, meat is the most important factor. Housewives usually shop more than one store regularly. They enjoy having store services, i.e., sewing notions, deli, and greeting card sections. Also, cents-off coupons appear to appeal to many of the housewives. In general, the housewives believed that it was the little things such as carryout service, friendliness of store personnel, well-stocked shelves, and cleanliness, that counted in generating loyal patronage.

Payless. The typical housewife comment in reference to Payless was that "you can't stick to your budget if you shop at Payless because there are so many things to buy." However, housewives didn't like the service at Payless nor did they care for the quality of meat.

Grand American. Most remarks about Grand American were in a negative vein. Housewives stated that the store was often out of stock and that the store usually over-advertises. Housewives maintain that Grand American advertised specials were not in fact specials at all.

Henny Penny. The housewives maintain that Henny Penny is winning the price war with Payless in Centralia. Henny Penny is recognized as being the best in price, courtesy, quality of merchandise, and service. In general, housewives believe Henny Penny's slogan, "Save on the Total."

Superior (combined). Almost all of the housewives liked the advertising of Superior, particularly its presentation. A strong criticism was that the stores were often out of stock. Housewives thought the Superior logo was imaginative and they liked the S&H Green Stamps.

A third study, conducted in June 1986, involved personal interviews with 587 Superior customers at the three-store sites. Customers were asked to respond to questions asked by the interviewer and to comment on the store. Responses to questions are tabulated in Exhibit 7 for each store, and for all three stores combined.

In commenting on Superior stores, shoppers stated that lower prices and greater variety were needed in the departments that required the most improvement, namely, the health and beauty aids department and the deli. Shoppers suggested that the dairy section be cleaner, the price of meat be lower, the variety of goods in the bakery be greater, the out-of-stock situation in private labels be improved, and the quality and freshness of produce be enhanced.

Questions concerning features of the Superior stores liked by shoppers generated a variety of responses. Appearance and cleanliness, friendliness, service, and trading stamps were liked most by shoppers. Prices, parking, and checkout procedures were noted as major features disliked by shoppers.

EXHIBIT 7
Results from Interviews with 587 Superior Customers,
June 1986

	S. Prospect	W. Main	N. Fairview	Superior Combined
Age of customer (years):				
Over 65	7.5%	16.8%	9.7%	10.7%
64–50	13.7	25.5	28.0	21.6
49–35	33.0	35.8	33.1	33.8
34–25	18.9	15.3	24.0	19.7
24–18	21.2	6.6	4.0	11.6
Under 18 and no response	5.7	Nil	1.2	2.6
Average persons per household	3.5	3.1	3.4	3.3
Frequency of store visits:				
4 times a week	18.1%	11.7%	9.7%	13.4%
3 times a week	19.9	21.2	22.7	21.2
2 times a week	28.2	38.0	40.0	35.0
Once a week	10.6	11.2	9.2	10.3
3 times a month	.9	1.7	5.4	2.6
2 times a month	6.0	4.5	7.0	5.9
Once a month	9.7	8.9	5.4	8.1
Other	6.5	2.8	0.5	3.5
Length of patronage:				
Less than 1 year	11.4%	10.0%	7.1%	7.6%
1–3 years	19.3	8.8	8.0	12.5
3 or more years	69.3	81.2	84.9	77.9
Proportion of total food needs purchased:				
Almost all	13.0%	12.4%	24.4%	17.0%
About $\frac{3}{4}$	18.8	14.1	13.3	15.0
About $\frac{1}{2}$	50.0	58.2	47.2	51.7
About $\frac{1}{4}$ to $\frac{1}{2}$	6.7	7.9	7.2	7.1
Less than $\frac{1}{4}$	11.5	7.3	7.8	9.2
Amount of purchase:				
$ 0–2.49	24.7%	21.6%	20.0%	21.3%
$ 2.50–4.99	20.4	15.0	21.1	19.1
$ 5.00–9.99	19.9	26.8	27.4	24.3
$10.00–14.99	13.7	11.1	8.6	11.3
$15.00–19.99	5.7	5.9	11.4	7.6
$20.00–24.99	5.7	4.6	4.6	5.0
$25.00–29.99	1.9	7.8	2.3	3.7
$30.00 and over	9.0	6.5	4.6	6.9

EXHIBIT 7 *(continued)*

	S. Prospect	W. Main	N. Fairview	Superior Combined
Departments shopped:				
All three	22.5%	17.4%	30.2%	23.4%
Grocery, meat	10.7	10.4	13.6	11.5
Grocery, produce	11.2	7.3	5.4	8.2
Meat, produce	6.5	3.7	2.2	4.3
Grocery only	33.5	45.1	29.9	35.7
Meat only	1.4	2.4	4.3	2.7
Produce only	.9	3.7	2.7	2.3
H&BA	15.2	9.2	7.5	10.9
Frozen foods	22.4	20.8	28.5	23.9
Dairy	39.6	37.6	49.7	42.3
Bakery	33.3	22.4	39.6	32.1
Other stores shopped				
most regularly:				
Grand American	7.6%	7.8%	4.9%	6.8%
Henny Penny	30.8	40.8	16.8	29.5
Payless	29.0	22.1	43.8	31.6
Superior	.6	.6	—	.4
Independent 1	5.8	—	.6	2.2
Independent 2	4.7	.6	3.7	1.8
Other	3.5	3.0	.1	3.4
None	18.0	15.0	30.1	14.3
Liked best about other				
regular store:				
Prices	33.8%	29.5%	19.5%	27.0%
Meat	8.8	22.7	7.8	11.6
Variety	10.3	9.1	6.5	8.5
Location	10.3	9.1	5.2	7.9
All other	36.8	29.6	61.0	45.0

(No one category accounted for more than 7% of the total)

Source: Company records.

EXECUTIVE APPRAISAL

Late in August 1986, Hall executives met to review the research reports. The principal objectives of the meeting consisted of an evaluation of the image studies. More specifically, they wished to define the retail image of each of their competitors—Payless, Grand American, and Henny Penny—in addition to the image of Superior. By doing so, the executives hoped to develop a strategy for strengthening or modifying their image with respect to their competitors.

The next day, after having reviewed the results of the image research, Hall Company executives directed their efforts toward evaluating alternative merchandising and promotion strategies for Superior supermarkets based on their impression of the situation. Prior to discussing alternative strategies, one Hall executive distributed a number of store comparison exhibits to, in his words, "let us know where we are now before we determine where we should or can be." Exhibit 4 provides a selected summary of Superior supermarkets' and competitive stores' operating statistics. Exhibit 8 shows selected financial data on the North Fairview, West Main, and South Prospect supermarkets, respectively.

EXHIBIT 8
Selected Operating and Financial Data

Year	Sales (000)	Gross Profit (000)	Gross Profit/ Sales	Net Profit (000)	Return on Investment
		South Prospect Store			
1981	$ 965	$190.0	19.7%	$ 2.4	1.9%
1982	1,124	221.0	19.7%	15.0	12.3%
1983	1,253	232.0	18.5%	9.2	7.8%
1984	1,292	243.2	18.8%	10.3	8.4%
1985	1,380	268.2	19.4%	15.6	N.A.
		West Main Street Store			
1981	$1,525	$295.8	19.4%	$34.6	36.6%
1982	1,605	315.0	19.6%	49.4	52.9%
1983	1,588	291.1	18.3%	22.3	22.9%
1984	1,581	290.6	18.4%	22.0	20.2%
1985	1,643	321.4	19.6%	37.2	N.A.
		North Fairview Store			
1981	$1,109	$219.8	19.8%	$22.1	33.8%
1982	1,165	224.3	19.3%	21.1	28.4%
1983	1,238	221.5	18.0%	5.6	7.4%
1984	1,310	235.2	17.9%	7.6	7.3%
1985	1,356	266.5	19.7%	21.8	N.A.

Source: Company records.

During the course of the executive meeting, four alternative points of view or strategies were expressed at one time or another. Each is described below.

Several executives favored maintaining the status quo. They contended that the image of the Superior supermarkets was most favorable, citing as reasons for this belief: (1) a recent upsurge in the stores' market share in Centralia, and (2) the apparent loyalty of a substantial percentage of Superior customers. According to a supporter of this position, "Any complaints by customers are, in reality, a figment of their imagination. If we start rocking the boat now we might lose all that we've gained over the past ten years."

Other executives advocated discontinuing S&H Green Stamps, which cost Superior stores approximately 2.25 percent of gross sales. These officials believed that customers thought stamps to be an additional cost to the store that was being passed onto the consumer as higher prices for merchandise. As one official put it:

> By dropping stamps, we would appeal to the extremely price-conscious consumer and yet maintain our present customers who favor our stores because of our merchandise. To me, at least, this means additional sales at reduced cost—or a higher-profit store. We could kill two birds with one stone: generate a low price image and increase profits.

Others found fault with this proposal, nothing that Payless offered Green Gold trading stamps and yet was regarded as one of the low-price leaders in Centralia. This observation led them to speculate that the image of the store was closely related to the merchandising strategy employed. They therefore favored a modification in the merchandise mix of the Superior supermarkets. In essence, they proposed that approximately one-third of the stores' selling space be used to house general merchandise. The only cost consisted of shelf remodeling. Since each of Superior's competitors offered nonfood items and was perceived to offer reasonable prices, these executives believed that such a strategy would work for Superior stores. Advocates of the status quo position believed that such a drastic switch in the merchandise mix would serve only to aggravate the variety problem in merchandise already carried. As one official commented, "If you allot any portion of the stores' selling space to general merchandise, you have to reduce the meat, produce, or grocery departments. Customers already think that we don't have sufficient variety—why accentuate the problem? Moreover, is it at all possible to change the image of our supermarkets?"

Another official maintained that Superior should give greater emphasis to the stores' perceived weaknesses. He contended that the Centralia shopper "lacked any knowledge of what any of the stores offered." He cited the fact that, except for the North Fairview store, Superior stores offered a competitive variety in meats—the primary complaint, next to price, of customers. "If the quality of meat is an important factor," he added, "why do shoppers frequent Payless when everyone we interview thinks their meat is terrible! In essence, I'm saying that we can create a favorable image in meat and variety in general if we promote these supposed 'weak points' heavily enough."

Another executive argued that:

> You don't build a customer store image outside the store, you start inside! Meat image starts at the meat case. We better decide to spend the money to operate a top-notch meat department if we want to establish a reputation—a good meat image. Since the quality of meat is second only to price as a factor in store selection, it's going to cost us money. The cost of better displays and better trimming less production per man hour could run between 2 and 4 percent of gross meat sales.

Another executive supported this position, and advocated that:

> In addition to improving our meat-quality image, we should strengthen and capitalize on all of our perishable departments, since quality is the second most important factor to a customer after price. This approach would mean capitalizing on our present produce advantage; improving the quality, variety, and presentation of our delicatessen department; and improving the variety and presentation of our bakery departments in all stores. Whether we keep stamps or not, we should be known and recognized as the leading quality supermarket in Centralia.

Company officials estimated that improvements in the quality of bakery and delicatessen products might cost on a continuing basis an amount equivalent to 1 percent of total gross sales. Broadening those product lines would require an additional 200–300 square feet of selling space in each store. Improved presentation would mean refixturing at a cost of approximately $3,000 to $4,000 per store.

MidAmerica BancSystem, Inc.

CHUCK SMITH WALKED BRISKLY across the lobby of the Fairview Heights bank to his office. It was 7:30 A.M., November 2, 1984. He would have at least two hours before the rush of Friday customers would begin. Friday always meant a great deal of "public relations" for Smith in terms of his exchanging greetings and small talk with customers. "Today I could do without it," Smith thought. "I'd much rather work on what the marketing committee discussed yesterday." However, he knew that many customers expected to see his door open and his face break into a smile of recognition whenever they voiced a greeting. Two hours would give him enough time to get some thoughts down on the automated teller machine (ATM) issue. The other topics that he had discussed with the committee would have to wait until the weekend.

MIDAMERICA BANCSYSTEM, INC.

MidAmerica Bank and Trust Company of Fairview Heights was one of six members of MidAmerica BancSystem, Inc., a multibank holding company under the laws of the state of Illinois. Five of the six subsidiaries were located within twenty-five miles of each other in St. Clair and Madison counties. The sixth, MidAmerica Bank and Trust Com-

This case was written by Professor James E. Nelson, University of Colorado. This case is intended for use as a basis for class discussion rather than to illustrate either effective or ineffective administrative decision making. Some data are disguised. © 1985 by the Business Research Division, College of Business and Administration and the Graduate School of Business Administration, University of Colorado, Boulder, Colorado 80309.

pany of Carbondale, was almost eighty miles away in Jackson County. St. Clair and Madison counties were due east of St. Louis, Missouri, just across the Mississippi River. Jackson County to the southeast also bordered the Mississippi.

MidAmerica BancSystem, Inc., was formed on August 31, 1982, about one year after enactment of an Illinois law permitting multibank holding companies. Prior to this date, the six subsidiary banks were considered "affiliated" in the sense that they shared a number of officers and directors. MidAmerica BancSystem, Inc., provided auditing, investment, and accounting services for its subsidiaries. It contracted with an independent organization for computer services and managed the ATM service. In short, the holding company had authority and responsibility for major financial and marketing decisions for all subsidiaries. As an example of financial decision making, senior management of the holding company had decided in late 1983 to sell $14.7 million (par value) of long-term securities at a loss of over $1.2 million. The sale made possible the purchase of higher yielding U.S. government securities with much shortened maturities. Senior management also had charged off about $2.7 million in loans (primarily agricultural) in late 1983, an amount some nine times that for 1982. Together the actions had produced a net loss of $2.9 million for 1983 (see Exhibit 1 for financial data) but promised long-term benefits in terms of liquidity, flexibility, and return.

Senior management had been less decisive in making marketing decisions. However, now that financial matters had been resolved, attention turned to marketing. A marketing committee had been formed at the request of the holding company's new chairman of the board and president, James Watt. Watt had joined the holding company in this capacity in late 1983, replacing David Charles who had served as chairman and president since 1958. Watt's previous experience included positions as senior vice-president of Essex County Bank and Trust in Boston, senior vice-president of the Bank Marketing Association in Chicago, and vice-president of Beverly Bancorporation in Chicago. Watt held an MS in marketing and thus took a keen interest in the marketing issues facing MidAmerica BancSystem, Inc. Chuck Smith chaired the marketing committee.

MARKETING ISSUES

Smith settled into his chair (the office door shut) and reread the four marketing issues he had summarized last night:

1. What should be our response to the Shop and Save proposal to allow installation of MidAmerica ATMs in twenty supermarkets in St. Clair and Madison counties?

EXHIBIT 1
Financial Data

	1981	1982	1983	1984[a]
Assets	$198,339	$211,067	$202,104	$208,093
Liabilities	183,268	195,415	189,872	194,312
Stockholders' equity	15,071	15,652	12,232	13,781
Interest income	22,687	23,399	20,807	16,871
Interest expense	14,300	15,460	12,871	10,051
Net interest income	8,387	7,939	7,936	6,820
Provision for possible loan losses	285	309	4,140	258
Net interest income after provision for possible loan losses	8,102	7,630	3,796	6,562
Other income	1,676	1,685	711	1,758
Other expenses	7,473	7,924	8,482	6,242
Income (loss) before income taxes and extraordinary item	2,305	1,391	(3,975)	2,078
Income taxes	401	43	(1,080)	803
Income (loss) before extraordinary item	1,904	1,348	(2,895)	1,275
Extraordinary item tax benefit	—	—	—	713
Net income (loss)	1,904	1,348	(2,895)	1,988
Deposit growth (%)	3.9	6.2	−2.0	−1.5
Return on assets (%)	1.0	0.6	−1.4	1.0
Return on equity (%)	12.6	8.6	−23.7	14.4
Capital to assets (%)	7.6	7.4	6.1	6.6

Note: All data are stated in thousands of dollars except data for deposit growth, return on assets, return on equity, and capital to assets.

[a]As of September 1984.

2. How can we increase use of our current ATMs?

3. How do we translate corporate financial goals into marketing goals?

   How do we make marketing goals part of the management process?

4. What should be MidAmerica's marketing strategy over the next five years?

Smith knew that senior management of the holding company considered all issues to be high-priority items.

The Shop and Save Proposal

Early in October the president of the Fairview Heights bank had paid a call on the manager of a Shop and Save supermarket located in nearby Belleville, Illinois. The purpose of the call was to see if the store had any interest in installing a MidAmerica ATM. The timing could not have been better—the store was soon to begin a remodeling project and could easily accommodate an ATM. The store's policies did not permit check cashing, nor would they allow a customer to write a check for an amount greater than that purchased. Consequently, the store manager was greatly interested in the installation, provided the system could be used by a large number of the store's customers.

This meant that the ATM had to be available to customers of banks that belonged to Magna Group, Inc., a nine-bank holding company serving many of the same market areas as MidAmerica. Contact with the marketing director for Magna had disclosed that Magna had about 60,000 cards and thirty-six ATMs in use in the two-county area. These figures greatly exceeded MidAmerica's 10,100 cards and twelve ATMs. The marketing director had shown strong interest in sharing ATM facilities currently in operation, as well as any others either holding company might add. Senior management at both organizations viewed ATMs as a highly desirable service. They also felt that a key to successful implementation of the service was convenient and widespread locations.

A letter from the marketing director summarized Magna's interest and its desire for a $1.50 charge for each interchange transaction. That is, each time a MidAmerica cardholder used a Magna ATM, MidAmerica would be billed $1.50. The same amount would be billed to Magna for each of their cardholders' transactions on a MidAmerica ATM. Smith thought that the charge could be negotiated upward or downward by 25 cents.

Smith was not sure just what sharing meant in terms of interchange usage. He estimated that MidAmerica cardholders might use Magna ATMs for between 10,000 and 30,000 transactions per month. On the other hand, Magna cardholders could use MidAmerica ATMs between 10,000 and 60,000 times per month. The most likely outcome was somewhere in between.

Once MidAmerica had obtained agreement with Magna, negotiations with chain management at Shop and Save could proceed. Chain management had become involved with the Belleville store decision and had quickly proposed that MidAmerica place ATMs in all twenty stores in St. Clair and Madison counties. The chain wanted placement in each store because of its check cashing policies and what it saw as an opportunity for increased revenues. The proposal called for Shop and Save to receive $600 per ATM per month in rent and 10 cents per each transaction beyond 2,500 per ATM per month. The proposal noted that a similar system in its Springfield, Illinois stores averaged about 10,000 transactions per ATM per month.

Smith thought that MidAmerica would be lucky to average 4,000 transactions per ATM per month initially in these stores and might reach 10,000 per month in three to five years. He thought the ratio of MidAmerica cardholder transactions to Magna cardholder transactions would be about 1:3. Shop and Save figures showed the twenty stores to average about 65,000 customers per month, although one store showed only 41,000. Smith thought that Shop and Save might come down somewhat on their rental and transaction charges; he doubted that they would move from their 2,500 figure.

MidAmerica estimates of the installed cost of each ATM were $40,000. The practical life of an ATM was considered to be about six years. Monthly fixed operating costs totalled about $400 per ATM for the computer telephone line, bookkeeping, maintenance, and the service to supply the machines with cash and to collect deposits. The computer service itself charged 40 cents per transaction.

MidAmerica currently billed each of its cardholders $1.00 per transaction. However, many banks in the St. Louis area charged only 50 cents, and some charged nothing. Smith felt that the marketing committee would soon recommend the MidAmerica charge be reduced to 50 cents, although there was some feeling among members that the charge should simply be eliminated.

"Either action should increase usage," Smith thought as he scanned a table of last month's transaction activity. The table showed that usage of cards at MidAmerica's twelve locations actually had fallen 5 percent from September of a year ago. The drop contrasted only slightly with July and August activity, which had shown no growth over usage for the previous year. The 28,400 transactions for September were based on 10,100 cards outstanding, a number that was 4 percent higher than a year ago. Something would have to be done to improve usage to at least 5,000 transactions per ATM per month. This figure was generally considered an industry standard, representing a break-even point between the cost of an ATM and the teller function for which it substituted.

Marketing Goals

The committee also had spent some time discussing marketing goals at MidAmerica. The members' lack of extensive marketing backgrounds made discussion difficult. Nonetheless, Watt and the committee felt it important that MidAmerica personnel at both the holding company and each subsidiary give marketing goals considerable thought. Marketing goals would encourage aggressive marketing actions and give focus to marketing efforts. Marketing goals would also form a standard against which performance could be measured.

This was the first time that the holding company and subsidiaries had ever set marketing goals. Most officers were familiar with financial goal setting and the holding company's financial goals for 1985: an 8 percent growth in deposits, a 1.2 percent return on assets; a 16 percent return on equity; and a 7 percent capital-to-assets ratio. Each subsidiary's financial goals departed somewhat from these figures, dependent on local market conditions and forecasts.

Neither the holding company nor the subsidiaries had translated financial goals into marketing goals. The committee had discussed some criteria for the translation, concluding that marketing goals should be consistent with financial goals and be stated in specific and measurable terms at realistic levels. The committee had even tried to write some marketing goals:

Obtain 200 Vacation Club accounts by October 1985.
Increase IRA deposits by 15 percent.
Book 150 Equity Plus loans by the end of 1985.

Each member had promised to spend more time thinking about marketing goals after yesterday's meeting. Each was also to produce a more complete list of goals by the end of next week, send it to other committee members, and be ready for a discussion at the next meeting. It would be important to get some marketing goals approved at the holding company level before expecting each subsidiary to write its own.

Also at issue was how to integrate marketing goals into the management process. The committee had touched on this matter, noting that marketing goals would be an idle exercise unless officers actually used them. A way to mandate use would be to include marketing goals and marketing performance in each officer's annual performance evaluation. Both the officer and his or her supervisor would then examine each goal and its associated performance and reach formal agreement on progress. However, one committee member strongly opposed such use because of his and MidAmerica's lack of experience with marketing goals. The other members had agreed—something else should be done.

Marketing Strategy

The last major issue discussed by the marketing committee was MidAmerica's marketing strategy over the next five years. Watt had requested that the committee study this topic and propose two options, each with clearly identified strengths and weaknesses. He had also asked for the committee's choice between the options. The committee had until December 31 to complete his request.

The first strategic option was growth via market development. This strategy would emphasize the marketing of existing financial services to new markets defined in terms of either geographic areas or market segments. Growth via new geographic areas could be done three ways. The first would be to stay in St. Clair and Madison counties and locate in such cities as Cahokia, Collinsville, and Edwardsville, for example. The second would be to expand eastward and southward to other Illinois counties. The third would be to cross the Mississippi and enter the St. Louis market area, perhaps in the St. Charles area about twenty miles west of Alton. MidAmerica could move into Missouri by means of its directors establishing a Missouri corporation in the banking industry. Alternatively, it could enter Missouri by offering a limited-service bank that would provide all of MidAmerica's services except commercial loans. A limited-service bank escaped federal and state laws prohibiting interstate banking. However, MidAmerica might be able to expand into Missouri with all of its services as soon as 1986 if an existing bill were enacted by the Illinois and Missouri legislatures. Smith thought that chances of the bill becoming law by 1986 were fifty-fifty.

Watt and the directors wanted any new market area chosen to show a deposit growth potential in excess of 8 percent per year; any new facility should show an operating profit within the first five years. Committee members thought that careful selection of new market areas could meet these criteria. However, the consequences of a mistake in their judgment could be substantial.

Less risky was a market development strategy based not on new geographic areas but on new market segments. These new segments would be in the local community where MidAmerica's reputation was strongest. Examples of new segments were professionals, commercial accounts (mostly retailing and light industry), and the military at nearby Scott Air Force Base. Potential here was probably not as great as with geographic expansion.

The second strategic option was growth via service development. This strategy would emphasize the marketing of new financial services to existing markets. New services could be aimed at either existing consumer or commercial accounts with the goal of increasing deposits, loans, or service fees. There were literally hundreds of new services that MidAmerica could add. Some of the more promising ones had been mentioned in yesterday's meeting. In-home banking would allow customers to link their home computers with the bank's system and pay bills, transfer funds, and check on account balances. Optimistic forecasts here called for about 10 percent of U.S. households to use some form of home banking by the early 1990s. Auto leasing would have MidAmerica as lessor to individual customers. Experts forecast a 10–15 percent annual growth rate for the service, reaching a level of about 40 percent of all new car deliveries in the early 1990s. Personal financial planning would use financial advisers at the bank to investigate middle-aged customers' financial objectives and resources and then recommend a financial program. A "prestige" credit card would provide increased services and higher loan limits to upscale customers. The committee recognized the need for careful research before recommending one new service over another.

The committee also recognized that a recommendation to market any new service would subject MidAmerica to the chance of failure. Costs associated with failure depended on the new service. However, in no case did the committee think that a major new service could be introduced for less than $60,000 in training, marketing, and other start-up costs.

Finally, the committee recognized that growth objectives could be met by either strategy and that MidAmerica almost certainly would not pursue one strategy to the exclusion of the other. A mix between the two would be best; the issue really was which of the two strategies should be emphasized. Further, adoption of either strategy would not mean abandonment of existing customer segments. All MidAmerica subsidiaries would be expected to continue to show growth via penetrating existing segments through the offering of present services.

HOLDING COMPANY STRATEGY

Choosing between a market development and a product development strategy was the final decision in formulating the holding company's strategy. Earlier in the year, Watt and the directors had agreed on other strategic components: profitable growth, liquidity, active asset/liability management, financial and marketing control over subsidiaries, capable personnel, and market leadership. All components were tied to a community bank orientation: suburban locations, a high profile in local community affairs, personal relationships with customers, and deposits and loans generated in the local community.

"For the next few years, our strategy could also be described as 'conservative,'" Watt had told the committee. He had gone on to explain that a conservative approach was called for because it would

1. Avoid risk and produce profits (important because of last year's loss).

   2.   Allow MidAmerica time to train and develop its associates and officers and to improve its management procedures.

   3.   Minimize the risk of costly mistakes by allowing some important industry trends to emerge.

The net effect of a conservative approach should be intermediate and long-term profitability. However, Watt noted that in the short-term the approach might mean some missed opportunities and some stronger competitors.

Watt and several other officers considered it almost certain that MidAmerica would be sold to a much larger holding company in the next five years. Industry sources predicted hundreds of such sales, beginning shortly after Congress permitted interstate banking. Bank sales and interstate banking were both parts of a broad industry trend called *deregulation* (see next section). The sale of MidAmerica would take place at a premium if MidAmerica could show capable personnel and strong performance. The present strategy should produce both characteristics by 1987.

DEREGULATION

The term *deregulation* was misleading because governments at federal and state levels would never allow banks to operate without regulation. Instead, deregulation meant reducing regulation, giving banks more freedom to pay and to charge interest rates of their choice, to develop and to market new services, and to locate limited service banks in more than one state. Deregulation had begun in the late 1970s and was expected to continue until at least 1990. Congress; federal regulatory agencies (the Federal Reserve Board, the Federal Deposit Insurance Corporation, the Comptroller of the Currency); and state regulatory agencies all expected that the trend would make banking more competitive and, hence, more efficient.

Increased competition and efficiency would cause some banks to disappear. As of October 1984, there were almost 800 banks on the Federal Reserve Board's problem list. Industry sources expected that about 60 of these would fail in the next twelve months. Already the country had seen 65 failures in 1984, making it a strong candidate for the second highest year for failures since 1937. The same sources predicted that about 2,300 or 15 percent of all U.S. banks would close, merge, or be sold over the next five years. The pace could greatly accelerate if Congress were to permit interstate banking.

Deregulation also meant the threat of other firms competing in the financial service industry. Generally these firms had large retail networks and sophisticated data processing systems. The largest was Sears. Sears had purchased Coldwell Banker (the nation's largest real estate broker) and Dean Witter (the nation's fifth-largest investment broker) for over $800 million in 1981. The purchased organizations complemented functions performed by Sears' Allstate Insurance (the nation's second-largest casualty insurer). Sears was expected to place Financial Centers at 300 of its 806 stores by the end of 1984. At each center, a Sears customer could trade securities as well as invest in a money market mutual fund and in certificates of deposit. Increased deregulation might mean that Sears could offer the nation a complete line of what used to be exclusively banking services.

Already banks had seen most of their traditional services extended to savings and loan associations, credit unions, and other institutions inside and outside the financial service industry. Consumers now could keep demand and time deposits, obtain mortgage and installment loans, and, in short, satisfy almost all financial needs at institutions other than banks. Consumers had more choices than ever before.

To some consumers, increased choice meant greater sophistication in managing their finances. Smith thought that these people might be kept by MidAmerica's strategy. They would not move a $20,000 certificate of deposit, for example, just because a competitor's interest rate was 20 basis points higher. The $40 annual difference in interest earned (before taxes) would not be worth the reduction in service. Nor would the higher rate move the deposits of unsophisticated consumers. These people placed greater importance on location and on habit than on return. However, in between these groupings were consumers that Smith worried about. These people would move for $40 per year, not caring about the loss of service or the increased inconvenience.

THE MORNING MAIL

Smith's thoughts were broken by his secretary and the morning mail. A headline on the front page of the *St. Louis Business Journal* caught his attention: "Citicorp's St. Louis 'Bank' Bid." The accompanying article explained that Citicorp, a New York bank with over $130 billion in assets, had applied to the comptroller of the currency for permission to open a limited-service bank in St. Louis. Citicorp expected to receive permission. However, it would not seek permission from Missouri regulators because Citicorp felt that the planned operation would technically not be a bank and the matter was, therefore, beyond control of the Missouri commissioner of finance. The commissioner was quoted as willing to bring suit to stop Citicorp. Lawyers for Citicorp responded that any suit would be decided in their favor because federal law superseded Missouri law.

The article also summarized fears of the St. Louis banking community that Citicorp's entry would "trigger a bidding war for consumer deposits and hurt local bank earnings." Not only that, the local bankers thought that if Citicorp entered their market, at least three or four other banks would soon follow. The net effect would be much more aggressive marketing of financial services.

A hearty "Hello!" took Smith away from the article. He looked through his now-opened door to see one of the bank's eldest customers and responded. He thought, "It must be 9:30."

CASE

Perpetual Care Hospital: Downtown Health Clinic

IN MID-APRIL 1986, Ms. Sherri Worth, assistant administrator at Perpetual Care Hospital (PCH) in charge of PCH's Downtown Health Clinic uncovered an unsettling parcel of news. During a call on the employee benefits director at a downtown department store, she was told that a firm was conducting a study to determine whether or not sufficient demand existed for a clinic located five blocks north of PCH's Downtown Health Center. The description of the clinic's services sounded similar to those offered by PCH's Downtown Health Center, and the planned opening date was May 1987.

As Ms. Worth walked back to her office, she could not help but think about the competitive clinic. Upon arriving at her office, Ms. Worth called Dr. Roger Mahon, PCH's administrator, to tell him what she had learned. He asked her to contact other employee benefit directors and query patients to see whether or not they had been surveyed. He expressed concern for two reasons. First, a competitive clinic would attract existing and potential patients of the Downtown Health Center. Second, a competitive clinic that provided similar services could hamper the Downtown Health Clinic's progress toward achieving its service and profitability objectives. They concluded their talk

This case was prepared by Professor Roger A. Kerin, Edwin L. Cox School of Business, Southern Methodist University, as a basis for class discussion, and is not intended to illustrate effective or ineffective handling of an administrative situation. All names and figures are disguised and not useful for research purposes.

with Dr. Mahon suggesting that Ms. Worth summarize the Downtown Health Clinic's performance to date so that he could speak to members of the board of trustees' executive committee on what action, if any, the DHC should take to compete for patients. He concluded their discussion by saying, "Who would have thought ten years ago that a hospital administrator would be making decisions not unlike a retail chain store executive's. But I guess it comes with the territory these days."

HEALTH CARE AND THE HOSPITAL INDUSTRY

Health care, and specifically the hospital industry, has undergone a dramatic transformation in the last decade. Until the 1960s, hospitals had been largely charitable institutions that prided themselves on their not-for-profit orientation. Hospitals functioned primarily as workshops for physicians and were guided by civic-minded boards of trustees.

Federal legislation introduced in the 1960s created boom times for the hospital industry. The Hill-Burton Act provided billions of dollars for hospital construction, to be repaid by fulfilling quotas for charity care. Additional funds were poured into expansion and construction of medical schools. Medicare and Medicaid subsidized health care for the indigent, disabled, and elderly. These programs reimbursed hospitals for their incurred costs plus an additional return on investment. The 1960s also saw dramatic increases in commercial insurance coverage, offered as employee fringe benefits and purchased in additional quantities by a more affluent public. Accordingly, health care became accessible to an overwhelming majority of U.S. citizens, regardless of where they lived or their ability to pay. Federal intervention had changed the concept of health care services from *privilege* to *entitlement.*

By the mid-1970s, however, skyrocketing health care costs had forced the federal government to reassess its role in health care. Stringent controls were placed on hospital construction and expansion, and utilization and physician review programs were implemented to ensure against too-lengthy impatient stays. By the end of the decade, hospitals were initiating voluntary cost-cutting programs to stave off additional government intervention. Despite all efforts, however, health care expenditures continued to outpace the Consumer Price Index. In 1981 Americans spent close to 10 percent of the gross national product on health care, and the government's portion was 43 percent of the $287 billion tab. Only 11 percent of all hospital services were paid for by individuals; the balance were financed by third-party payors, such as insurance companies.

The 1980s ushered in a very different health care environment, and hospitals particularly have been hard hit by the changes. On the one hand, the federal government has sought to reduce health care costs through cutbacks in subsidy programs and cost-control regulations. On the other hand, innovations in health care delivery have severely reduced the number of patients serviced by hospitals. Two of these innovations are preventive health care programs and the increase in the number of ambulatory health care services.

Preventive health care programs fall into two categories: (1) Health Maintenance Organizations (HMOs) and (2) Preferred Provider Organizations (PPOs). HMOs surfaced in the mid-1970s. An HMO encourages preventive health care by providing medical services as needed for a fixed monthly fee. HMOs typically entered into contractual relationships with designated physicians and hospitals and have been successful in reducing hospital inpatient days and health care expenditures. PPOs, which emerged in the early 1980s, have contractual arrangements between health care providers (physicians and/or hospitals) and large employer groups. Unlike HMOs, PPOs generally offer incentives for using preferred providers rather than restricting individuals to specific hospitals or physicians. PPOs are likely to have the same effect on inpatient days and health care expenditures as HMOs and Dr. Mahon had planned to design a PPO for Perpetual Care Hospital using the Downtown Health Clinic as a link to large employers in the downtown area.

A second and farther-reaching innovation is the use of ambulatory health care services and facilities. Ambulatory health care services consist of treatments and practices that consumers can use on an episodic or emergency basis. Examples include physical examinations; treatment of minor emergencies (e.g., for cuts, bruises, minor surgery); and treatments for common illnesses (e.g., colds and flu).

Ambulatory health care facilities are split into two categories: (1) minor emergency centers, known by names and acronyms such as FECs (Free-Standing Emergency Clinics) and MECs (Medical Emergency Clinics) and (2) clinics that focus on primary or episodic care.[a] Although regulation is nominal, if a clinic positioned itself as an emergency care center, expressing this focus in its name, it generally was required (or pressured by area physicians) to be staffed twenty-four hours a day by a licensed physician and to have certain basic life-support equipment.

[a] *Primary care* is the point of entry into the health care system. It consists of a continuous relationship with a personal physician who takes care of a broad range of medical needs. Primary-care physicians include general practitioners, internal medicine and family practice specialists, gynecologists, and pediatricians.

Ambulatory health care services are the fastest-growing segment of health services.[1] The first no-appointment, walk-in clinic opened in Newark, Delaware, in 1975. By 1985 there would be at least twenty-five hundred similar facilities in the United States, not including group-practice physician arrangements and HMOs. Ambulatory health care services have siphoned away a large portion of the care offered by physicians and have forced hospitals to deal increasingly with only the most acutely ill and severely injured patients.

Three factors have accounted for the growth of ambulatory health care services. First, advances in medical technology, miniaturization, and portable medical equipment have made more diagnostic and surgical procedures possible outside the traditional hospital setting. Second, consumers have adopted a more proactive stance on where they will receive their health and medical care. Consumers are choosing the hospital at which they wish to be treated, and the incidence of "doctor shopping" is on the rise. Third, the mystique of medical and health care has been altered with the growth of paramedical professionals and standardized treatment practices.

Most of the early centers emphasized quick, convenient, minor emergency care. A new wave of centers have positioned themselves as convenient, personalized alternatives to primary-care physician's practices. These operations typically employ aggressive, sophisticated marketing techniques, including branding, consistent logos and atmospherics, promotional incentives, and mass media advertising (giving rise to vernacular designations such as "Doc-in-the-Box" and "McMedical"). Although ambulatory care facilities vary considerably among communities and owners, the following characteristics appear to be universal: (1) branding, (2) extended hours, (3) lower fees than emergency rooms, (4) no appointments necessary, (5) minor emergencies treated, (6) easy access and parking, (7) short waiting times, and (8) credit cards accepted.

Even though these facilities have tapped a market need, not all have been successful. Failure rates are as high as 25 percent in some areas of the country. Many areas were already saturated with many MECs fighting aggressive market share battles.[2] According to one industry estimate, the average MEC is open sixteen hours per day, seven days per week, with two physicians on each eight-hour shift. The average visit is fifteen minutes, and the average break-even volume lies between thirty and forty-five visits per day.

PERPETUAL CARE HOSPITAL

Perpetual Care Hospital is a 600-bed, independent, not-for-profit, general hospital located on the southern periphery of a major western city.

The hospital is one of six general hospitals in the city and twenty in the county. It is financially stronger than most of the metropolitan-based hospitals in the United States. It is debt-free and has the highest overall occupancy rate among the city's six general hospitals. Nevertheless, the hospital's administration and board of trustees have had serious concerns about its patient mix, which reflected unfavorable demographic shifts. Most of the population growth in the late 1970s was occurring in the suburban areas to the north, east, and west. These suburban areas were attracting young, upwardly mobile families from the city. They were also attracting thousands of families from other states—families drawn to the area's dynamic, robust business climate.

As suburban hospitals have sprung up to serve the high-growth areas, the hospital has found itself becoming increasingly dependent on inner-city residents, who have a higher median age and higher incidence of Medicare coverage. Without a stronger, stable inflow of short-stay, privately insured patients, the financial health of the hospital would be jeopardized. Accordingly, in the summer of 1984, the board of trustees authorized a study to determine whether to open an ambulatory facility in the downtown area about ten blocks north of the hospital.

DOWNTOWN HEALTH CENTER

The charter for the Downtown Health Center (DHC) contained four objectives:

1. To expand the hospital's referral base
2. To increase referrals of privately insured patients
3. To establish a liaison with the business community by addressing employers' specific health needs
4. To become self-supporting three years after opening

The specific services to be offered by the DHC would include (1) preventative health care (e.g., physical examinations and immunizations); (2) minor emergency care; (3) referral for acute and chronic health care problems; (4) specialized employer services (e.g., preemployment examinations, worker's compensation injuries); (5) primary health care services (e.g., treatment for common illnesses); and (6) basic X-ray and laboratory tests. The DHC would be open 260 days per year (Monday–Friday) from 8:00 A.M. to 5:00 P.M. (9 hrs)

The location for the DHC would be in the Greater West Office and Shopping Complex situated on the corner of Main and West streets (see Exhibit 1). This location was chosen because a member of

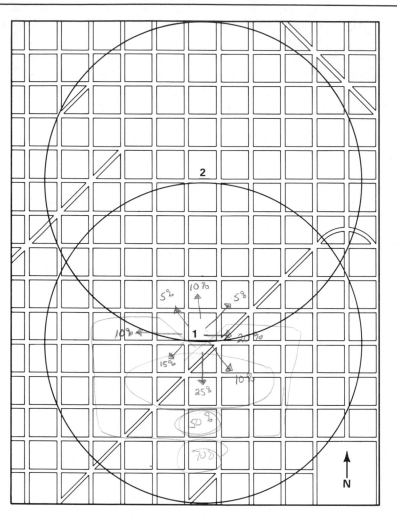

1 Original DHC and five-block service radius.
2 Planned location of competitor and five-block service radius.

the board of trustees owned the Greater West Complex and was willing to share construction, design, and equipment expenses with the hospital.

During the fall of 1984, construction plans for erecting the DHC were well underway, and the expense budget was developed (see Exhibit 2). During the winter months, PCH commissioned a study to (1) determine the service radius of the DHC, (2) estimate the number of potential users of the DHC, (3) assess responsiveness to the services offered by the DHC, and (4) review the operations of suburban ambulatory-care clinics. The results indicated that the service area would have a five-block radius, since this was the longest distance office workers would walk. Discussions with city planners indicated the service area contained 11,663 office workers during the 9:00–5:00 Monday–Friday work week. The population in the area was expected to grow 6 percent per year given new building and renovation activity. Personal interviews with 400 office workers, selected randomly, indicated that 50 percent would use or try the DHC if necessary and that 40 percent of these prospective users would visit the DHC at least once per year (see Exhibit 3 for additional findings). Finally, the study of

EXHIBIT 2
Downtown Health Center: Twelve-Month Expense Budget

Item	Expenditure
Physician coverage/260 days/ 8 hrs./5 days—$33/hr.	$ 68,640
Professional fees	21,360
Lease	38,250
Supplies	23,447
Utilities	3,315
Personnel, including fringe, (director, nurse, laboratory, X-ray technician, receptionist)	84,188
Amortization	15,324
Annual expenditure	$254,524

Note: Expenditures were based on the assumption that the DHC would have four visits per hour, or thirty-two visits per day, when operating at full capacity.

EXHIBIT 3
Profile of DHC Service Area Based on City and Survey Data

1984 Population Estimate (Source: City Planning Department)

Total office worker population in five-block radius	11,663
Expected annual growth, 1984–1989	6.0%/yr.
Sex breakdown in five-block radius:	
Male	40%
Female	60%

Results from Personal Interviews (January 1984)

Would use/try DHC if necessary for personal illness/exams	50%
Expected frequency of DHC use for personal illness/exams among those saying would use/try if necessary[a]:	
Once every other year	60%
Once per year	25%
Twice per year	10%
Three or more times per year	5%

Selected Cross-Tabulations

	Sex		
Would use or try DHC if necessary:	*Male*	*Female*	*Total*
Yes	88[b]	168	256
No	72	72	144
Total	160	240	400

	Have Regular Physician (Excluding Gynecologist)		
Would use or try DHC if necessary:	*Yes*	*No*	*Total*
Yes	58	198	256
No	130	14	144
Total	188	212	400

[a]No difference between males and females on frequency of use.

[b]Eighty-eight of the 160 males (55 percent) interviewed would use the DHC; 88 of the 256 interviewees (34 percent) who said they would use the DHC were male.

suburban ambulatory care facilities revealed the data shown in Exhibit 4. Given their locations in suburban areas, these facilities were not considered as direct competition, but did indicate that "the city's populace was attuned to ambulatory health care facilities," remarked Ms. Worth.

EXHIBIT 4

Suburban Ambulatory Care Clinics: Operations Profile

Operations	EMERCENTER #1	EMERCENTER #2	Adams Industrial Clinic	Health First	MEDCENTER
Opening	March, 1980	November, 1982	June, 1980	May, 1982	June, 1983
Patients/year	9,030	6,000	8,400	5,700	8,661
Hours of operation	10:00 A.M.–10:00 P.M. Monday–Friday	10:00 A.M.–10:00 P.M. Monday–Sunday	8:00 A.M.–5:00 P.M. Monday–Friday	5:00 P.M.–11:00 P.M. Monday–Friday; 10:00 A.M.–10:00 P.M. Saturday–Sunday	8:00 A.M.–8:00 P.M. Monday–Sunday
Physicians/8-hour shift	2	2	2	2	2
Estimated patient visits/hour	3.8/hour	3.4/hour	5.0/hour	3.0/hour	3.0/hour
Estimated average charge per visit	$30.00	$31.00	$38.00	$31.00	$32.00
Services provided:					
Preventive health care			X	X	X
Minor emergencies	X	X	X	X	X
Employer services			X		
X-ray/lab tests	X	X	X	X	X
Miscellaneous	X	X	X	X	X
Use direct mail advertising	X	X	X	X	X

These results were viewed favorably by the board of trustees and "confirmed our belief that an ambulatory facility was needed downtown," noted Ms. Worth. The DHC was formally opened May 1, 1985. However, except for the publicity surrounding the opening, no advertising or other types of promotion were planned. "Several members of the hospital staff shied away from advertising or solicitation since it hinted at crass commercialism," noted Ms. Worth.

Performance: May 1985–March 1986

A financial summary of the DHC performance through March 1986, is shown in Exhibit 5. According to Dr. Mahon:

> We are pleased with the performance to date and hope the DHC will be self-supporting by April 1987. We are getting favorable word-of-mouth from satisfied patients that will generate both new and repeat patients. We expect 410 patient visits in April (1986). In addition, we have taken steps to improve our financial standing. For example, our bad debts have been costing us 4 percent of gross revenue. With a better credit and collection procedure established just last month, we will reduce this figure to 2 percent. We plan to initiate an 8 percent across-the-board increase in charges on May 1 and will experience only a 5 percent increase in personnel and professional services expenses next year.

Records kept by PCH revealed that the DHC was realizing its objectives. For example, the referral objective was being met since the DHC has made 105 referrals to PCH and produced slightly over $189,000 in revenue and an estimated $15,000 in net profit. Almost all of these patients were privately insured. The service mix, through dominated by personal illness and examinations, did indicate that the DHC was being used for a variety of purposes. A breakdown of the reasons for patient visits for the first eleven months of operation is as follows:

Personal illness exams	53%
Worker's compensation	25%
Employment/insurance physical exams	19%
Emergency	3%
	100%

Patient records indicated that 97 percent of all visits were by first-time users of the DHC, and 113 visits were by repeat patients. Approximately 5 percent of the visits in each month from October, 1985 through March 1986 were repeat visits. "We are pleased that we are already getting repeat business because it shows we are doing our job," Ms. Worth commented. The average revenue per patient visit during the first eleven months was $33.95.[b] A breakdown of the average charge by type of visit follows. The average charge would increase 8 percent on May 1, 1986.

Personal illness/exams	$25 per visit
Worker's compensation	$39 per visit
Employment/insurance	
physical examination	$47 per visit
Emergency	$67 per visit

48% 5/1

   In an effort to monitor the performance of the DHC, patients were asked to provide selected health care information as well as demographic information. This information was summarized monthly, and Exhibit 6 shows the profile of patients visiting the DHC for the first eleven months of operation. In addition to this information, patients were asked for suggestions on how the DHC could serve the downtown area. Suggestions typically fell into three categories: (1) service hours, (2) services, and (3) waiting time. Thirty percent of the patients suggested expanded service hours with an opening time of 7:00 A.M. and a closing time of 7:00 P.M. One-half of the female patients requested that gynecological services be added. A majority of the patients expressed concern about the waiting time, particularly during the lunch hours (11:00 A.M.–2:00 P.M.). A check of DHC records indicated that 70 percent of patient visits occurred during the 11:00 A.M.–2:00 P.M. period and that one-half of the visits were for personal illnesses.

   Ms. Worth believed all three suggestions had merit and had already explored ways to expand the DHC's hours and reduce waiting time. For example, the reason for her call on the employee benefits director at a local department store was to schedule employee physical examinations in the morning or late afternoon hours to minimize crowding during the lunch hour. Nevertheless, she believed a second licensed physician might be necessary, with one physician working the hours from 7:00 A.M. to 3:00 P.M. and the other working between 11:00 A.M. and 7:00 P.M. The overlap during the lunch period would alleviate waiting times as well, she thought. Expanding from nine- to twelve-hour days would entail a 33 percent increase in personnel costs, however, as well as the cost of another physician.[c]

_____

   [b]The average charge per patient visit includes the charge for basic x-ray and laboratory tests when appropriate.

   [c]Expanded hours would be staffed by part-time personnel who would receive the same wages as full-time personnel.

EXHIBIT 5
Downtown Health Center Financial Summary

	1985								1986			Total Year to Date
	May	June	July	Aug	Sept	Oct	Nov	Dec	Jan	Feb	Mar	
Gross Revenue	4,075	8,387	8,844	9,697	11,206	11,406	11,672	11,758	12,846	13,879	14,715	118,485
Variable Expenses												
Bad debt	163	355	354	388	448	456	467	470	513	555	588	4,757
Medical/surgical supplies	6,591	798	935	643	1,063	1,213	1,661	612	976	1,580	1,078	17,150
Drugs	159	54	65	52	305	293	0	56	186	253	76	1,299
Office supplies	647	222	596	718	315	(190)	24	281	467	0	64	3,144
Total variable expense	7,560	1,429	1,950	1,801	2,131	1,572	2,152	1,419	2,142	2,388	1,806	26,350
Contribution	(3,485)	6,958	6,894	7,896	9,075	9,834	9,520	10,339	10,704	11,491	12,909	92,135

Fixed Expenses												
Personnel	7,816	7,459	6,670	5,900	6,816	11,490	7,320	6,249	6,705	8,995	7,644	83,064
Professional services[a]	10,009	6,945	7,732	7,158	7,385	6,800	7,200	7,450	7,242	7,078	7,187	82,186
Facility[b]	3,222	2,537	2,890	2,905	2,622	2,655	2,620	2,613	2,836	2,622	2,719	30,241
Miscellaneous	705	107	133	140	238	45	111	76	106	123	57	1,841
Amortization	1,277	1,277	1,277	1,277	1,277	1,277	1,277	1,277	1,277	1,277	1,277	14,047
Total fixed expense	23,029	18,325	18,702	17,380	18,338	22,267	18,528	17,665	18,166	20,095	18,884	211,379
Net Gain (Loss)	(26,514)	(11,367)	(11,808)	(9,484)	(9,263)	(12,433)	(9,008)	(7,326)	(7,462)	(8,604)	(5,975)	(119,244)
Number of Patient Visits	109	231	275	277	322	320	321	366	383	463	423	3,490
Number of Working Days	22	21	21	22	20	23	22	20	22	21	23	237

[a] Includes professional fees paid (see Exhibit 2).
[b] Includes lease payments, utilities, and maintenance.

Ms. Worth believed that scheduling was more of a problem than she or the PCH staff had expected. "You just can't schedule the walk-ins," she said, "and pardon me for saying it, but the people coming in with personal care needs have really caused the congestion." She added that the problem would get worse because the mix of patients was moving toward personal illnesses and examinations. "If the trend continues, we should have 20 percent more personal illness visits next year than last year."

Ms. Worth believed that gynecological services[d] would be a plus since 70 percent of the visits were made by women and almost all were under thirty-five years of age. She said:

> Women will or should see a gynecologist regularly at least once a year and often twice a year. We could add an additional 2,000 visits per year with a hospital gynecologist working at the DHC two eight-hour days a week by appointment. An average charge per visit would be about $52 including lab work, and the physician cost would be $35 per hour.

Ms. Worth had also given some thought to how the DHC could improve its relations with the business community. Currently, business-initiated visits (worker's compensation and employment/insurance physical examinations) accounted for 44 percent of the DHC's visits. Construction in the downtown area had stimulated worker's compensation activity and growth in employment in the five-block service radius had contributed to employment physicals. Ms. Worth believed worker's compensation visits would stabilize at about 81 per month and then decline with slowed building activity. Employment physicals accounted for 50 visits per month and were expected to remain at this level given current operating hours. Insurance physicals were not expected to increase beyond current activity levels, nor were emergency visits.

Commenting on her calls on businesses, Ms. Worth remarked:

> I have actively called on businesses under the guise of community relations because the PCH staff has not sanctioned solicitation. My guess, after talking with business people, is that we could get virtually every new employment physical if we didn't interfere with employment hours and scheduled them before 8:00 or after 5:00 P.M. Given net new employment in the area and new employees due to turnover, I'd guess we could schedule an additional 65 employment physicals every month—that is, 115 a month.

Ms. Worth added that she had also received approval to run an "informational advertisement" in the downtown weekly newspaper each

---

[d] *Gynecology* is that branch of medicine dealing with the female reproductive tract.

EXHIBIT 6
Profile of Downtown Health Center Patients:
Personal Illness/Exam Visits Only

Occupation
Clerical	48%	
Professional/technical/managerial	23	
Operators	19	
Other	10	100%

Sex
Male	30%	
Female	70	100%

½ requested gyno

Referral Source
Friends/colleagues	35%	
Employer	60	
Other	5	100%

Patient Origin
Distance:
One block	25%	
Two blocks	28	
Three blocks	22	
Four blocks	15	
Five blocks	8	
More than five blocks	2	100%

75% 90%

Direction:
North of DHC—10%, south of DHC—25%
Northeast of DHC—5%, southwest of DHC—15%
East of DHC—20%, west of DHC—10%
Southeast of DHC—10%, northwest of DHC—5%

Have Regular Physician
Yes	18%	
No	82	100%

week next year provided the advertisement did not feature prices or appear to be commercial in its presentation. The weekly advertisement would cost $5,200 per year.

Competitive Clinic

Ms. Worth's calls on local businesses and patient interviews indicated that a survey was being conducted. She believed that MEDCENTER, a privately owned suburban ambulatory facility, was the sponsor. MED-

CENTER appeared to be successful in its suburban location (see Exhibit 4) and had a reputation for being an aggressive, marketing-oriented operation. Even though MEDCENTER did not provide employer services at its suburban location, Ms. Worth thought the fact that an employee benefits director had been interviewed suggested that such services might be offered.

The location for the new clinic was five blocks directly north of the DHC. Based on the research for the DHC, Ms. Worth estimated that the number of office workers within a five-block radius of the competitive clinic would be 11,652 in 1987 and 13,590 in 1988, and would grow at an annual rate of 7 percent through 1995 because of new construction and building renovation. Ms. Worth believed the competitor's service area had the same socioeconomic profile, and the same usage and employment characteristics as the DHC's service area.

The overlap in service areas was due to the layout of the downtown area and the availability of high-quality street-level space. According to Ms. Worth, "It is possible that a third of our current personal illness/exam patients from the northern portion of our service area will switch to the new clinic and about 40 percent of potential personal illness/exam patients in this area will go to the new location." Ms. Worth went on to say that the overlap in service areas would actually cover 3,424 existing office workers in 1986.

The effect of the competitive clinic on emergency, worker's compensation, and employment/insurance exam volume was more difficult to assess. Ms. Worth did feel, however, that worker's compensation visits would not be materially affected because most construction was being undertaken in areas south, east, and west of the DHC. Emergency visits were so random that it was not possible to assess the effect of the competitive clinic. Projected employment and insurance physical volume could change with the addition of a competitive clinic, however. Ms. Worth guessed that, "At worst, we would see no increase in these types of visits over last year since we have not gotten many visits from this area."

A week after she first heard about the possibility of a competitive clinic, Ms. Worth and Dr. Mahon met to review the information on the DHC. Just before Ms. Worth completed her overview, Dr. Mahon's administrative assistant interrupted to tell him he had to leave to catch a plane for a three-day conference dealing with health care marketing. As he left the room, he asked Ms. Worth to draft a concise analysis of the DHC's position. He also asked her to specify and evaluate the alternatives for the DHC assuming MEDCENTER did or did not open a facility. "Remember," Dr. Mahon said, "PCH has a lot riding on the DHC. Making it work not only involves dollars and cents, but our image in the community as well."

NOTES

1. "FECs Pose Competition for Hospital EDs," *Hospitals* (March 1984): 77–80; *Immediate Care Centers: Fast Medicine for the '80s* (Washington, D.C.: U.S. Department of Health and Human Services, November 1984).

2. See, for example, "Urgent Care Centers Seek Niches," *Modern Healthcare* (April 1984); 110–12.

CHAPTER 7

Marketing Communications Strategy and Management

MARKETING COMMUNICATION IS the process by which information about an organization and its offerings is disseminated to selected markets. Because of the role communication plays in facilitating mutually beneficial exchange relationships between an organization and prospective buyers, the importance of communication cannot be overstated. The goal of communication is not just to induce initial offering purchases; it is also to achieve postpurchase satisfaction, thus increasing the probability of repeat sales. Even if prospective buyers possessed a pressing need, and an organization possessed an offering that precisely met that need, no exchange would occur without communication. Communication is necessary to inform buyers of the following:

- The *availability* of an offering
- The *unique benefits* of the offering
- The *where* and *how* of obtaining and using the offering

Exactly how potential buyers are informed—the actual message communicated—is one of the most subjective communication decisions. Although message development can be somewhat aided by research, there are no guaranteed message strategies available for all offerings, markets, or organizations. Each individual situation must determine whether the message is to be hard-sell, fearful, humorous, informational, or whatever.

It is the task of the marketing manager to manage the communi-

299

cation process most effectively. In doing so, managers have at their disposal specific communication activities (often called *elements, functions, tools, tasks,* or the like). These include advertising, personal selling, and sales promotion. Collectively, the activities are termed the *marketing communication mix.*[1] Elements of the communication mix range from very flexible (e.g., personal selling) to very inflexible (e.g., mass advertising), and each element has a unique set of characteristics and capabilities. Still, to a certain extent, they are interchangeable and substitutable. It is the responsibility of the marketing manager to find the most effective communication mix at the least possible cost.

Marketing managers should not limit their thinking to *which* communication activity to use when designing communication strategies. Rather, the real issue is which activity should be emphasized, how intensely it should be applied, or how communication activities can be most effectively combined and coordinated. Rare is the organization that employs only one form of communication. In a single communication strategy, all three communication activities might be simultaneously used. For instance, advertising activities might be employed to develop offering awareness and comprehension; sales promotion might be used to increase purchase intention; and personal selling might be utilized to obtain final conviction and purchase.

ANALYTICAL COMMUNICATION STRATEGY FRAMEWORK

From a managerial perspective, the formulation of a marketing communication strategy requires seven major decisions. Once the offering and target markets have been defined, the manager must consider these decisions as follows:

1. What are the information requirements of target markets as they proceed through the purchase process?
2. What objectives must the communication strategy achieve?
3. Which specific mix of communication activities should be employed in conveying information to target markets?
4. How much should be budgeted or expended for communicating with target markets?
5. In what manner should resources be allocated among various communication activities?
6. How should the communication be timed and scheduled?

7. How should the communication process be evaluated as to its effectiveness, and how should it be controlled?

Theoretically, these questions are considered distinct and are thus approached in a sequential manner. In practice, however, they are likely approached simultaneously, since they are, in fact, closely interrelated.

INFORMATION REQUIREMENTS IN PURCHASE DECISIONS

The first step in designing a communication strategy is to determine how buyers purchase a particular offering and to define the role of information in the purchase process. This often requires use of a purchase (or adoption) process model. Usually, such a model treats buyers as though they were moving through a series of sequential stages in their purchase processes, such as

Unawareness→Knowledge→Preference→Purchase

At any point in time, different buyers are in different stages of the model, and each stage requires a different communication strategy. Moreover, most models permit the marketing manager to distinguish between solitary and joint decision making. In any purchase decision, three possible roles can exist—purchaser, influencer, and user or consumer. In certain purchase situations, one individual may play all three roles. In other purchase situations, such as a joint purchase decision, the roles may be played by three different individuals. While a mother may actually purchase a breakfast cereal, her children may influence the brand purchased, and the father may actually consume the product. A similar situation could exist in an industrial setting. A purchasing agent is the buyer, an engineer is the influencer, and a technician is the user. Understanding the purchaser-influencer-user relationship is a prerequisite for successfully determining what the communication message should be as well as to whom it should be directed, and how it should be communicated.

In a similar vein, the process used by buyers to purchase an offering dictates the role of information, and hence communication strategy. To illustrate, in industrial settings purchasing procedures are often prescribed. Therefore, understanding when, where, how, and what information is employed in the purchase decision will enable an organization to direct the proper communication to the proper individual at the proper time. These remarks would also apply to communication directed toward consumers. Consider the case of consumers making a decision to buy a house. To communicate effectively, an organization must know *what* information these consumers think is necessary (price, location, or size), *where* they will seek it (newspapers, brokers, or friends), *when* they will seek it (how far in advance or on what days), and *how* they will apply the information once obtained.

Finally, the way in which buyers perceive an organization and its offering is closely related to their information needs. The perceived importance of the offering and the perceived risk in making an incorrect purchase decision influence the extent to which buyers require information, as well as their choice of information source(s). The more important or risky an offering is perceived to be (due to large dollar outlays, ego environment, or health and safety reasons), the more likely it is that buyers will seek further information from sources other than the organization providing the offering.

REASONABLE COMMUNICATION OBJECTIVES

Setting objectives for communication programs depends on the overall offering-market strategies of the organization and the stage of the life cycle in which its products are. Communication objectives will differ according to whether market penetration, market development, product development, or diversification strategy is being employed. For instance, a penetration strategy would suggest communication objectives that emphasize more frequent offering usage or that build preference for or loyalty to the offering. On the other hand, a market development strategy would encourage communication that would entail stimulating awareness and trial of the offering.

Life cycle stage plays a role in setting communication objectives in terms of the need to stimulate primary demand or selective demand. Early in the life cycle, communication efforts focus on stimulating primary demand—demand for the product or service category, such as dairy products, personal computers, or family planning. Typically, the message conveyed focuses on introducing the benefits of a product or service or overcoming objections to the product or service. Later in the life cycle, when substitute products or services exist, communication efforts focus on stimulating selective demand—demand for a particular brand or product-service provided by competitors. Typically, the message conveyed extols the benefits of a particular competitive offering and seeks to differentiate that offering from others.

Objectives must also be delineated for individual communication tools. Both general and specific communication objectives need to relate directly to the tasks that the tools are to accomplish. Communication objectives and the tasks must be reasonable—*consistent* both among themselves and with other marketing elements, *quantifiable* for measurement and control purposes, and *attainable* with an appropriate amount of effort.

COMMUNICATION MIX

Development of an appropriate communication activities mix requires the assignment of relative weights to particular communication activities, based on communication objectives. More specifically, the ultimate communication mix should be determined in part by:

- The information requirements of potential buyers
- The offering
- The nature of the target markets
- The capacity of the organization

Although no established guidelines exist for designing an optimal communication mix, several factors that influence the mix need to be considered. As a starting point, a sensitivity analysis of the effectiveness of the communication tools at various stages in the purchase-decision process ought to be undertaken. Consider the purchase-decision process for a new automobile. Through advertising, manufacturers seek to stimulate awareness of the new models and to indicate where they can be purchased. Sales personnel provide information on specific options available, financing, and delivery. Sales promotion brochures and catalogs provide descriptions of performance characteristics and other technical or salient features. Which communication tool has the greatest impact on prospective buyers? The answer to this question, while admittedly difficult to arrive at, will lead to a weighing of the importance of communication tools. The manager will achieve an effective communication mix only by understanding the information requirements of potential buyers and by matching them with the capabilities of the various communication mix elements.

Nature of the Offering

A major consideration in determining the communication mix is the organization's offering. A highly technical offering, or one with benefits not readily apparent (e.g., performance or quality), or one that is relatively expensive is likely to require personal selling. Alternatively, advertising is a potent communication tool when the offering is not complex, is frequently purchased, is relatively inexpensive, or when the benefits of the offering can be differentiated easily from competing offerings. On the other hand, sales promotion lends itself to nearly every offering type, due to the wide variety of forms it can assume. However, its main use is to induce immediate action on frequently purchased products.

Target Market Characteristics

The nature of the target market is another consideration. A target market comprising a small number of potential buyers, existing in close proximity to one another and each purchasing in large quantities, might suggest a personal selling strategy. In contrast, a mass market that is geographically scattered would generally favor emphasis on advertising.

Organizational Capacity

A third consideration is the ability or willingness of the organization to undertake certain communication activities. In brief, the organization is continually faced with *make* or *buy* decisions. If an organization decides to employ a particular communication activity, should it perform the activity internally (i.e., make), or contract it out (i.e., buy).

One such make or buy decision relates to the choice of using a company sales force or independent sales representatives.[2] This decision has both an economic and a behavioral dimension.[3] An economic dimension exists since the cost of independent representatives is variable; they are paid on sales commission only. A company sales force typically includes a fixed-cost component *and* a variable-cost element. If independent representatives fail to sell, no costs are incurred; however, if a company sales force fails to sell, the fixed costs remain to be paid. These concepts are useful in determining whether independent representatives or company representatives are most cost-effective under different sales levels.

Consider the following situation. Suppose independent representatives receive a 5 percent commission on sales, and company sales personnel receive a 3 percent commission in addition to incurring a sales salary support and administration cost of $500,000. At what sales level would independent or company representatives be less costly? This question can be resolved by setting the *cost equations* for both types of representatives equal to each other and solving for the sales level amount as follows:

$$\frac{\text{Cost of company reps}}{0.03(x) + \$500,000} = \frac{\text{Cost of independent reps}}{0.05(x)}$$

where x = sales volume. Solving for x, sales volume equals $25 million.

This calculation indicates that below $25 million in sales, the independent representative would be cheaper and above that amount, the company sales force would be cheaper. Of course, a fundamental question is the likelihood of achieving a $25 million sales level, which in turn depends on effective sales forecasting.

Behavioral dimensions of this decision focus on issues of control, flexibility, effort, and the availability of independent and company sales representatives. There is considerable difference of opinion on the advantages and disadvantages of each factor for company and independent representatives. Proponents of a company sales force argue that this strategy offers greater control, since the company selects, trains, and supervises sales personnel. The sales effort is enhanced because sales personnel are representing one company's product line and not several. Flexibility exists because the firm can change sales-call patterns and customers or transfer personnel. Finally, availability of sales personnel is evident, since an independent representative might not exist in a geographical area (a company representative could be relocated). However, proponents of independent sales representatives argue that selection, training, and supervision of sales personnel is done equally well by sales agencies and at no cost to the firm. Flexibility is improved since little dollar fixed investment in a sales force exists. Effort is increased since independent representatives live on their commissions and have no salary. Finally, availability is an issue, assuming that buyers exist in a market. Advocates of independent representatives argue that the entrepreneurial spirit of these individuals will place them where effective demand exists. These economic and behavioral dimensions were carefully considered when Apple Computer, Inc., ultimately decided to replace its network of independent representatives with its own 350-person sales force in 1984.

Another issue related to the make or buy decision concerns advertising. Often it is advantageous to have intermediaries (e.g., wholesalers, retailers, and dealers) assume advertising costs and placement. Cooperative advertising, where a manufacturer shares the costs of advertising or sales promotion, is an example in this regard.

Push versus Pull

Two summary approaches that incorporate the topics just discussed are termed *push* and *pull* communication strategies. A push communication strategy is one where the offering is pushed through a distribution channel in a sequential fashion, with each channel level representing a distinct target market. A push strategy concentrates on channel intermediaries. For instance, advertisements are likely to appear in trade journals and magazines, and sales aids and contests are likely to be used as incentives to gain shelf space and distribution. However, a principal emphasis is on personal selling to wholesalers and retailers. This strategy is typically used when: (1) an organization has easily identifiable buyers, (2) the offering is complex, (3) buyers view the purchase as being risky, (4) a product or service is early in its life cycle, or (5) the organization has limited funds for direct-to-consumer advertising.

A pull communication strategy seeks to create initial interest among potential buyers, who in turn demand the product from intermediaries, ultimately pulling the offering through a channel. A pull strategy normally employs heavy end-user (e.g., consumer) advertising, free samples, and coupons to stimulate end-user awareness and interest. Consumers might be encouraged to ask their favorite retailer for the offering to pressure retailers into carrying the product. Pennzoil Motor Oil's "Ask for Pennzoil" advertising campaign is a prime example of a pull communication strategy in practice. Conditions favoring a pull strategy are virtually opposite to those favoring a push strategy.

COMMUNICATION BUDGETING

As would be expected, the question of how much to spend on communication is difficult to answer. As with previous decisions, numerous factors have an impact on communication budget determination and must therefore be considered. Many of these factors parallel those previously mentioned. In general, the greater the geographical dispersion of a target market, the greater the required communication expenditure. The earlier an offering is in its life cycle, the greater the necessary expenditure, and so forth.

The primary rule in determining a communication budget is to *make the budget commensurate with the tasks required of the communication activities.* The more important communication is in a marketing strategy, the larger the funds that should be allotted to it. Conceptually, budget determination is straightforward—set the budget so that the marginal costs of communication equal the marginal revenues resulting from it. This, though, requires an assessment of the effectiveness of communication.

Because it is so difficult to evaluate communication effectiveness, attempts to establish a relationship between budget size and communication effectiveness have generally proved unproductive. For this reason there is no widely agreed-on criterion for establishing the size of a communication budget. Instead, numerous guidelines have been suggested. These guidelines can be roughly grouped as *formula-based* or *qualitatively based*.

The most widely used formula has been to set the communication budget as a percentage of sales. Most frequently, past sales are employed, but anticipated sales are also occasionally used. Hence, when sales increase, communication activity does not. While it creates certain conceptual problems (e.g., which should come first—sales or communication?), this procedure is commonly used as a convenient starting point because of its simplicity. A second formula-based method is to allocate a fixed dollar amount for communication per offering unit, and then to calculate the communication budget by multiplying this per-unit allocation by the number of units expected to be sold. This method is most often used by durable-goods manufacturers like automobile companies. A third approach is to treat communication as investment and to apply rate-of-return formulas in determining the communication budget. Although conceptually simple, this approach is difficult to operationalize since it requires a direct quantitative relationship between communication expenditures and sales.

In practice, the formula-based approaches tend to be rather inflexible and not marketing oriented. Therefore, they are often supplemented by qualitatively based approaches. Management may wish to maintain *competitive parity* in terms of communication budgets. The competitive parity approach simply means that an organization attempts to maintain a balance between its communication expenditures and those of its competitors. Another approach is to use *all available funds* for communication. This strategy might be employed when introducing a new offering for which maximum exposure is desired; it is also used sometimes by nonprofit organizations. A final approach is termed the *task approach*. Here, an organization budgets communication as a function of the particular marketing task that is to be accomplished.

While all of these approaches are useful, each has decided limitations. More often than not, when ultimately determining the communication budget, managers use the approaches in conjunction with one another.

Communication Budget Allocation

Once a communication budget has been settled on, it must be allocated across the communication activities. This can be accomplished by using guidelines similar to those discussed previously for general communication budget determinations.[4] Budgets must then be allocated to the respective communication activities. Advertising and personal selling will be used to illustrate necessary budgetary allocation decisions.

Advertising Budget Allocation

Advertising budget-allocation decisions revolve around media selection and scheduling considerations. Basically, there are five mass media—television, radio, magazine, newspaper, and outdoor (billboard)—that an organization can use in transmitting its advertising messages to target markets. Each of these media (i.e., *channels*) consists of *vehicles*, or specific entities in which advertisements can appear. In certain media, such as magazines, the vehicles could include *Newsweek* or *Mechanics Illustrated* or the like. The first can be thought of as a mass-appeal vehicle; the latter, a selective-appeal vehicle. Moreover, media can be treated as *vertical*—reaching more than one level of a distribution channel—or *horizontal*—reaching only one level of a channel.

Media selection is based on numerous factors, the most important of which are cost, reach and frequency, and audience characteristics. Cost frequently acts as a constraint—a thirty-second national television commercial (spot) during the Superbowl costs approximately $550,000, not to mention associated production costs. *Cost* is usually expressed as cost per thousand (CPM) readers, viewers, and so on, to facilitate cross-vehicle comparisons. *Reach* refers to the number of buyers potentially exposed to an advertisement in a particular vehicle. *Frequency* refers to the number of times these consumption units are exposed in a given time period; hence, total exposure = reach × frequency. The more closely the characteristics of the target market match those of a vehicle's audience, the more appropriate the vehicle typically is.

Other considerations include the purpose of the advertisement (image-building, price, and so on), product needs, and the editorial climate of the vehicle. Price advertisements (those emphasizing an immediate purchase) are more likely to be found in newspapers as opposed to magazines, while the opposite is true if the product must be illustrated in color and requires a detailed explanation. Finally, audience characteristics limit which advertisements are acceptable, as well as which are more appropriate. For example, it is unlikely that a tractor advertisement would appear in *Ladies Home Journal*.

The timing or scheduling of advertisements is critical to their success. Purchases of many offerings are seasonal (e.g., skis, snowblowers, and swimsuits) or are limited to certain geographical areas.

Thus, advertising budgeting must take into account purchasing patterns. For example, advertising snowblowers in Ohio during the month of July is probably not a worthwhile endeavor.

There are numerous timing strategies that a marketing manager can employ when undertaking an advertising campaign. One alternative is to *concentrate* advertising dollars in a relatively short time period. Another alternative is to spend small amounts over the long term to maintain *continuity*. A *pulse strategy* might be employed whereby an organization periodically concentrates its advertising, but also attempts to maintain some semblance of continuity.

Sales Force Budget Allocation

The sales force budgeting problem is two-faceted: How many salespeople are needed? How should they be allocated? A commonly used formula is:

$$NS = \frac{NC \times FC \times LC}{TA}$$

where

NS = number of salespeople
NC = number of customers (actual or potential)
FC = necessary frequency of customer calls
LC = length of average customer call, including travel time
TA = average available selling time per salesperson (less administrative duties)

In most instances, the time period is one business year. Although this formula can be used for nearly all types of salespeople, from retail order takers to highly creative salespeople (e.g., computer salespeople), it is more likely to be used with the latter.

Assume the number of potential customers is 2,500 and four calls should be made per customer per year. If the length of the average call and travel time is two hours, and there are 1,340 working hours per year available for selling (50 weeks $\times$ 40 hours $\times$ 67 percent available selling time per week), then

$$NS = \frac{2,500 \times 4 \times 2}{1,340} = 15 \text{ salespeople needed}$$

The formula is very flexible. By varying (1) how the various elements in this formula are defined and (2) elements, such as the frequency of calls with actual customers and potential customers, numerous strategies are possible.

A related decision concerns the allocation of salespeople. Every salesperson must have a territory, whether it be square feet of selling space, a geographic area, or a delivery route. Within this framework, two questions arise: How large should the sales territory be? and How should the sales force be organized? As to the first question, attempts should be made to equate selling opportunity with the work load associated with each sales territory.

The second question is perhaps more difficult to answer, as it must directly take into account organization and marketing objectives, offering characteristics, competitor and industry practices, and the like. Available alternatives include having salespeople specialize in certain offerings or customer types or in a combination of offerings and customer types. Each of these alternatives has definite advantages and disadvantages that must be traded off against costs when arriving at an allocation decision.

COMMUNICATION PROCESS EVALUATION AND CONTROL

As part of every communication strategy, there must be mechanisms for evaluation and control. Without them, a marketing manager would be hard pressed to manage the communication process effectively. There would be no way to determine whether a strategy had achieved its objectives, nor would there be a way to make changes in a strategy as a result of competitive activities or environmental occurrences, whether fortuitous or not.

Implicit in both mechanisms is the concept of *continuous* evaluation and control. The marketing manager must continuously monitor the execution of any communication plan or strategy to ensure that the communication objectives are being attained.

Ideally, evaluation and control could incorporate some measure of sales or profits. While this is possible for certain communication tools—the sales effectiveness of a direct-mail program can be judged in a relatively straightforward way—for others, it is not. It is nearly impossible to isolate the contribution of institutional advertising to any individual sales transaction.

Budgeting, obviously, is one form of control. It is the ultimate form of control because, by eliminating or adding to the budget of a communication activity, the activity itself is effectively eliminated or accentuated. The budgeting element is illustrated by the decision whether to, say, add an additional sales representative at a salary of $20,000, or to allocate the same amount to a direct mail sales promotion program when the product mix contribution margin is 25 percent. A simple break-even calculation ($20,000 ÷ 0.25) reveals that $80,000 in additional sales must be generated to cover the incremental cost. The issue is therefore whether the new sales representative or the sales promotion is likely to achieve this break-even sales volume. Other forms of control are also available. Some ways for controlling the sales force are outlined as follows.

Sales Force Control

Sales force control begins during the recruiting and hiring process. By setting up certain qualifications and training procedures, an organization is able to control the types and efforts of individuals who enter the sales force. Once a sales force has been established, there are two distinct control phases—motivation and evaluation.

Motivation is typically accomplished by financial and nonfinancial compensation. Financial compensation usually involves some remuneration scheme—salary, commission, bonuses, or some combination of these. The compensation plan that is used should take into consideration factors such as industry and competitive practices, communication and marketing objectives, and the nature of the sales task. Although it is always difficult to generalize, there are situations when different compensation plans seem to be more appropriate than others. Moreover, the marketing manager should be aware of generally accepted advantages and disadvantages of alternative compensation plans.[5]

Nonfinancial compensation includes use of a company car, golf club membership, and the like. Through various nonfinancial incentives, such as trips or awards, it is possible to focus sales force efforts on offerings most beneficial to the organization. Through judicious use of compensation—both financial and nonfinancial—the organization can motivate and control the sales force simultaneously.

Another widely used method of controlling the sales force consists of setting sales quotas. Monitoring sales quota performance is one way of determining the effectiveness of individual sales force personnel. Other controls include having salespeople complete periodic sales reports—reports indicating the number of present and potential customers contacted (and the results), and reports indicating how time is allocated. While these techniques are not without limitations, they at least provide some means of evaluating and controlling the sales force. Additional remarks on controlling the sales force are found in Chapter 10.

NOTES

1. Publicity is a fourth element often included in the communication mix. However, it is not considered here for two reasons. First, publicity is often uncontrollable except through the broader public relations function of an organization; hence, it is not typically the responsibility of the marketing manager. Second, even if publicity is the responsibility of the marketing manager, it is often managed as a mixture of advertising and personal selling and thus does not require separate treatment.

2. Independent representatives are autonomous individuals or firms paid commissions for selling a manufacturer's product. These individuals or companies represent several noncompeting products that are sold to one or several categories of customers. They do not carry product inventories or take legal title to goods. Their functions vary from selling only a firm's products to broader activities including applications engineering, in-store merchandising support (point-of-purchase displays, stocking), and product maintenance. Independent representatives go by a variety of names, including broker, manufacturer's representative, or sales agent.

3. These dimensions developed in B. Shapiro, *Sales Program Management: Formulation and Implementation* (New York: McGraw-Hill Book Company, 1977), pp. 250–255.

4. An alternative approach to budget determination is to build up a communication budget. By first determining individual budgets for various communication activities and then summing them, it is possible to arrive at an overall communications budget.

5. For a review of alternative compensation plans, see J. Steinbrink, "How to Pay Your Sales Force," *Harvard Business Review* 78 (1978): 111–122.

ADDITIONAL READINGS

Blasko, Vincent J., and Patti, Charles H. "The Advertising Budgeting Practices of Industrial Marketers." *Journal of Marketing* (Fall 1984): 104–110.

Doyle, Stephen, and Shapiro, Benson. "What Counts Most in Motivating Your Sales Force." *Harvard Business Review* (May–June 1980): 133–140.

Korgaonker, Pradeep, and Bellenger, Danny N. "Correlates of Successful Advertising Campaigns: A Manager's Perspective." *Journal of Advertising Research* (August–September 1985): 34–39.

Levy, Michael; Webster, John; and Kerin, Roger. "Formulating Push Marketing Strategies: A Method and Application." *Journal of Marketing* (Winter 1983): 24–34.

Jackson, Donald W., Jr.; Keith, Janet E.; and Schlacter, John. "Evaluation of Selling Performance: A Study of Current Practice." *Journal of Personal Selling and Sales Management* (November 1983): 43–51.

Kahn, Herbert L. "Your Own Brand of Advertising for Nonconsumer Products." *Harvard Business Review* (January–February 1986): 24ff.

McNiven, Malcolm. "Plan for More Productive Advertising." *Harvard Business Review* (March–April 1980): 130–136.

Reichard, Clifford. "Industrial Selling: Beyond Price and Persistence." *Harvard Business Review* (March–April 1985): 127–133.

CASE

Morgantown, Inc. (A)

LATE IN THE EVENING of August 8, 1986, Charlton Bates, president of Morgantown, Inc., called Dr. Thomas Berry, a marketing professor at a private university in the Northeast and a consultant to the company. The conversation went as follows:

Bates: Hello, Tom. This is Chuck Bates. I'm sorry for calling you this late, but I wanted to get your thoughts on the tentative 1987 advertising program proposed by Mike Hervey of Hervey and Bernham, our ad agency.

Berry: No problem, Chuck. What did they propose?

Bates: The crux of their proposal is that we should increase our advertising expenditures by $400,000. They indicated that we put the entire amount into our consumer advertising program for ads in several shelter magazines.[a]

Berry: That increase appears to be slightly above your policy of budgeting 5 percent of expected sales for total promotion expenditures, doesn't it? Hasn't John Bott [vice-president of sales] emphasized the need for more sales representatives?

Bates: Yes, John has requested additional funds. You are right about the 5 percent figure too, and I'm not sure if our sales forecast isn't too optimistic. Your research has shown that our sales historically follow the industry almost perfectly, and trade econo-

---

This case was prepared by Professor Roger A. Kerin, Southern Methodist University, Dallas, Texas, as a basis for class discussion and is not designed to illustrate effective or ineffective handling of administrative situations. All names and data are disguised.

[a]Shelter magazines feature home improvement ideas, new ideas in home decorating, and so on. *Better Homes and Gardens* is an example of a shelter magazine.

314

mists are predicting about a 13 percent increase. Yet, I'm not too sure.

Berry: Well, Chuck, you can't expect forecasts to be always on the button. The money is one thing, but what else can you tell me about Hervey's rationale for putting more dollars into consumer advertising?

Bates: He contends that we can increase our exposure and tell our story to the buying public—increase brand awareness, enhance our image, that sort of thing. He also cited data from *Home Furnishings* magazine which showed that the newly affluent baby boomers [consumers between the ages of twenty-five and forty] are almost three times more likely to buy dining room furniture and twice as likely to buy living room furniture than their elders in the next year. All I know is that my contribution margin will fall to 25 percent next year, due to increased labor and material cost.

Berry: I appreciate your concern. Give me a few days to think about the proposal. I'll get back to you soon.

After the parting remarks, Dr. Berry began to think through Charlton Bates's summary of the proposal, Morgantown's present position, and the furniture industry in general. He knew that Bates expected a well-thought-out recommendation on such issues and a step-by-step description of the logic he used to arrive at his recommendation.

THE COMPANY

Morgantown, Inc., is a manufacturer of medium- to high-priced living room and dining room wood furniture. The company was formed at the turn of the century by Bates's grandfather. Charlton Bates assumed the presidency of the company upon his father's retirement in 1982. Forecasted year-end gross sales in 1986 were $50 million; before-tax profit was $2.5 million.

Morgantown sells its furniture through 1,000 high-quality department stores and furniture specialty stores nationwide, but all stores do not carry the company's entire line. The company is very selective in choosing retail outlets. According to Bates, "Our distribution policy, hence our retailers, should mirror the high quality of our products."

The company employs ten full-time salespeople and two regional sales managers. Sales personnel receive a base salary and a small commission on sales. A company sales force is atypical in the furniture industry since most furniture manufacturers use sales agents or representatives who carry a wide assortment of noncompeting furniture lines and receive a commission on sales. "Having our own sales group is a policy my father established twenty-five years ago," noted Bates, "and we've been quite successful having people who are committed to our company. Our people don't just take furniture orders. They are expected to motivate retail salespeople to sell our line, assist in setting up displays in stores, and give advice on a variety of matters to our retailers and their sales people."

In 1985 Morgantown allocated $2.45 million for total promotional expenditures for the 1986 operating year, excluding the salary of the vice-president of sales. Promotion expenditures were categorized into four groups: (1) sales expense and administration, (2) cooperative advertising programs with retailers, (3) trade promotion, and (4) consumer advertising. The cooperative advertising budget is usually spent on newspaper advertising in a retailer's city. Cooperative advertising allowances are matched by funds provided by retailers on a dollar-for-dollar basis. Trade promotion is directed toward retailers and takes the form of catalogs, trade magazine advertisements, booklets for consumers, and point-of-view materials, such as displays, for use in retail stores. Also included in this category is the expense of trade showings. Morgantown is represented at two showings per year. Consumer advertising is directed at potential consumers through shelter magazines. The typical format used in consumer advertising is to highlight new furniture and different living room and dining room arrangements. The dollar allocation for each of these programs in 1986 is shown in Exhibit 1.

THE INDUSTRY

The household wood furniture industry is composed of over fourteen hundred firms. Industry sales at manufacturers' prices were $6.3 bil-

EXHIBIT 1
Allocation of Promotion Dollars, 1986

Sales expense and administration	$ 612,500
Cooperative advertising allowance	1,102,500
Trade advertising	306,250
Consumer advertising	428,750
Total	$2,450,000

Source: Company records.

lion in 1985 and were forecasted to reach $7.1 billion in 1986. California, North Carolina, Virginia, New York, Tennessee, Pennsylvania, Illinois, and Indiana are the major furniture-producing areas in the United States. Major furniture manufacturers include Ethan Allen, Bassett, Henredon, and Kroehler. No one firm captured over 3 percent of the total household wood furniture market.

The buying and selling of furniture to retail outlets centers around manufacturers' expositions at selected times and places around the country. At these *marts*, as they are called in the furniture industry, retail buyers view manufacturers' lines and often make buying commitments for their stores. However, Morgantown's experience has shown that sales efforts in the retail store by company representatives account for as much as one-half of the company's sales in any given year. The major manufacturer expositions occur in High Point, North Carolina, in October and April. Regional expositions are also scheduled during the June–August period in locations such as Dallas, Los Angeles, New York, and Boston.

FURNITURE-BUYING BEHAVIOR

Results of a consumer panel sponsored by *Better Homes and Gardens* and composed of *Better Homes and Gardens* subscribers provide the most comprehensive available study of furniture-buying behavior. Selected findings from the *Better Homes and Gardens* consumer panel are reproduced in the appendix following this case. Other findings arising from this research were:

- Ninety-four percent of the subscribers enjoy buying furniture somewhat or very much.
- Eighty-four percent of subscribers believe "the higher the price, the higher the quality" when buying home furnishings.
- Seventy-two percent of subscribers browse or window-shop furniture stores even if they don't need furniture.
- Eighty-five percent read furniture ads before they actually need furniture.
- Retail outlets used by subscribers:

  > Thirty-two percent use furniture specialty stores.
  > Twenty-eight percent use furniture gallery stores.
  > Fourteen percent use department stores.
  > Eight percent use Sears, Ward's, and Penney's.
  > Seven percent use discount furniture outlets.

- Ninety-nine percent of subscribers agree with the statement, "When shopping for furniture and home furnishings, I like the salesperson to show me what alternatives are available, answer my questions, and let me alone so I can think about it and maybe browse around."

- Ninety-five percent of subscribers say they get redecorating ideas or guidance from magazines.

- Forty-one percent of subscribers have written for a manufacturer's booklet.

- Sixty-three percent of subscribers say they need decorating advice for "putting it all together."

THE BUDGET MEETING

At the August 8 meeting attended by Hervey and Bernham executives and Morgantown executives, Michael Hervey proposed that Morgantown's 1987 expenditure for consumer advertising be increased by $400,000. Cooperative advertising and trade advertising allowances would remain at 1986 levels. Hervey further indicated that shelter magazines would account for the bulk of the incremental expenditure for consumer advertising.

John Bott, Morgantown's sales vice-president, disagreed with the budget allocation and noted that sales expenses and administration costs were expected to rise $50,000 in 1987. Moreover, Bott believed an additional sales representative was needed to service Morgantown's accounts since fifty new accounts were being added. He estimated that the cost of the additional representative, including salary and expenses, would be at least $50,000 in 1987. "That's about $100,000 for sales expenses that have to be added into our promotional budget for 1987," Bott noted. He continued:

> We expect sales of about $50 million in 1986 if our sales experience continues throughout the remainder of the year. Assuming a 13 percent increase in sales in 1987, that means that our total budget would be about $2,825,000 if my figures are right, or a $375,000 increase over our previous budget. And I need $100,000 of that. In other words, $275,000 is available for other kinds of promotion.

Hervey's reply to Bott noted that the company planned to introduce several new styles of living room and dining room furniture in 1987 and that these new items would require advertising to be launched successfully. He agreed with Bott that increased funding of the sales effort might be necessary and thought that Morgantown might draw funds from cooperative advertising allowance and trade promotion.

Bates interrupted the dialogue between Bott and Hervey to mention that the $400,000 increase in promotion exceeded the 5 percent percentage-of-sales policy by $25,000. He pointed out that materials cost plus a recent wage increase were forecast to squeeze Morgantown's gross profit margin and threaten the company objective of achieving a 5 percent net profit margin before taxes. "Perhaps some juggling of the figures is necessary," he concluded. "Both of you have good points. Let me think about what's been said and then let's schedule a meeting for a week from today."

As Bates reviewed his notes from the meeting, he realized that the funds allocated to promotion were only part of the question. How the funds would be allocated within the budget was also crucial. Perhaps a call to Tom Berry would be helpful in this regard, he thought.

APPENDIX A

Selected Findings from the *Better Homes and Gardens* Consumer Panel Report— Home Furnishings

Question If you were going to buy furniture in the near future, how important would the following factors be in selecting the store to buy furniture? (Base 449)

Factor	Very Important	Somewhat Important	Not Too Important	Not at All Important	No Answer
Sells high-quality furnishings	62.6%	31.0%	3.8%	1.1%	1.5%
Has a wide range of different furniture styles	58.8	29.2	8.2	2.9	.9
Gives you personal service	60.1	29.9	7.8	.9	1.3
Is a highly dependable store	85.1	12.7	1.1	—	1.1
Offers decorating help from experienced home planners	26.5	35.9	25.4	10.9	1.3
Lets you "browse" all you want	77.1	17.8	3.3	.7	1.1
Sells merchandise that's a good value for the money	82.0	15.6	.9	.2	1.3
Displays furniture in individual room settings	36.3	41.2	18.7	2.4	1.3
Has a relaxed, no-pressure atmosphere	80.0	17.1	1.6	—	1.3
Has well-informed salespeople	77.5	19.8	1.6	—	1.1
Has a very friendly atmosphere	68.2	28.1	2.4	—	1.3
Carries the style of furniture you like	88.0	10.0	.9	—	1.1

Question Please rank the following factors as to their importance to you when you purchase or shop for case-goods furniture, such as a dining room or living room suite, 1 being the most important factor, 2 being second most important, and so on, until all factors have been ranked. (Base 449)

	1	2	3	4	5	6	7	8	9	10	NA
Construction of item	24.1%	16.0%	18.5%	13.1%	10.5%	6.9%	4.9%	1.6%	.2%	1.1%	3.1%
Comfort	13.6	14.7	12.9	12.3	12.7	10.9	8.2	4.5	4.0	2.4	3.8
Styling and design	33.6	19.8	11.1	9.6	4.7	7.3	4.5	1.6	2.9	1.6	3.3
Durability of fabric	2.2	7.6	9.8	14.5	15.1	14.7	12.9	5.6	5.8	7.8	4.0
Type and quality of wood	10.9	17.8	16.3	15.8	14.7	5.8	5.3	3.1	4.9	2.0	3.4
Guarantee or warranty	1.6	3.8	1.6	5.3	8.7	10.0	13.8	25.2	14.5	11.1	4.4
Price	9.4	6.2	8.7	8.5	10.0	12.5	14.2	11.8	6.9	8.0	3.8
Reputation of the manufacturer or brand name	6.2	3.6	4.7	5.6	6.2	6.2	12.7	17.1	22.7	11.6	3.4
Reputation of retailer	1.6	1.8	1.6	2.4	4.0	7.3	7.4	13.6	22.0	34.5	3.8
Finish, color of wood	4.7	7.6	10.2	8.0	8.9	13.4	10.7	10.0	10.2	12.7	3.6

Question   Below is a list of fifteen criteria that may influence what furniture you buy. They are ranked from 1 as most important and 5 as least important. (Base 449)

	1	2	3	4	5	No Answer
Guarantee or warranty	11.4%	11.1%	26.3%	16.9%	5.3%	29.0%
Brand name	9.1	6.5	14.3	25.6	11.6	32.9
Comfort	34.7	27.8	14.5	8.5	4.7	9.8
Decorator suggestion	4.0	2.4	2.7	8.2	44.8	37.9
Material used	14.9	24.1	14.9	13.4	6.2	26.5
Delivery time	.7	.5	1.3	2.9	55.2	39.4
Size	7.6	10.7	13.6	30.9	4.0	33.2
Styling and design	33.4	17.8	21.8	13.6	2.2	11.2
Construction	34.3	23.6	13.1	11.4	2.9	14.7
Fabric	4.0	25.6	24.9	14.0	4.5	27.0
Durability	37.0	19.4	13.6	6.9	4.9	18.2
Finish on wooden parts	5.8	14.7	16.7	10.7	16.7	35.4
Price	19.4	21.8	16.0	10.9	15.4	16.5
Manufacturer's reputation	4.2	9.1	15.4	22.9	14.3	34.1
Retailer's reputation	2.2	4.7	10.5	21.2	26.5	34.9

Question   Listed below are some statements others have made about their homes and the furniture pieces they particularly like. Please indicate, for each statement, how much you agree or disagree with each one. (Base 449)

Statement	Agree Completely	Agree Some-what	Neither Agree nor Disagree	Disagree Some-what	Disagree Completely	NA
I wish there was some way to be really sure of getting good quality in furniture	61.9%	24.7%	4.7%	4.2%	3.6%	.9%
I really enjoy shopping for furniture	49.2	28.3	7.6	9.8	4.2	.9

Statement	Agree Completely	Agree Somewhat	Neither Agree nor Disagree	Disagree Somewhat	Disagree Completely	NA
I would never buy any furniture without my husband's/ wife's approval	47.0	23.0	10.9	9.8	7.1	2.2
I like all the pieces in the master bedroom to be exactly the same style	35.9	30.7	12.7	11.1	7.6	2.0
Once I find something I like in furniture, I wish it would last forever so I'd never have to buy again	36.8	24.3	10.0	18.9	9.1	.9
I wish I had more confidence in my ability to decorate my home attractively	23.1	32.3	12.5	11.6	18.7	1.8
I wish I knew more about furniture styles and what looks good	20.0	31.0	17.1	13.4	16.7	1.8
My husband/ wife doesn't take much interest in the furniture we buy	6.5	18.0	12.3	17.8	41.4	4.0

Statement	Agree Completely	Agree Some- what	Neither Agree nor Disagree	Disagree Some- what	Disagree Completely	NA
I like to collect a number of different styles in the dining room	3.3	10.5	15.2	29.8	38.3	2.9
Shopping for furniture is very distressing to me	2.4	11.6	14.3	18.0	51.9	1.8

Question   Listed below are some factors that may influence your choice of furnishings, 1 being most important, 2 being second most important, and so on until all factors have been ranked. (Base 449)

	1	2	3	4	5	No Answer
Friends and/or neighbors	1.3%	16.9%	15.8%	22.1%	41.7%	2.2%
Family or spouse	62.8	9.4	14.3	9.8	2.0	1.7
Magazine advertising	16.3	30.3	29.6	17.6	4.2	2.0
Television advertising	1.1	6.7	14.7	32.5	42.3	2.7
Store displays	18.9	37.2	22.1	14.0	5.6	2.2

Question   When you go shopping for a *major* piece of furniture or other smaller pieces of furniture, who, if anyone, do you usually go with? (Base 449—multiple response)

	Major Pieces	Other Pieces
Husband	82.4%	59.5%
Mother or mother-in-law	6.2	9.1
Friend	12.0	18.9
Decorator	4.2	1.6
Other relative	15.6	15.4
Other person	2.9	3.3
No one else	5.1	22.3
No answer	.9	3.1

Question   When the time comes to purchase a *major* item of furniture or other smaller pieces of furniture, who, if anyone, helps you make the final decision about which piece to buy? (Base 449—multiple response)

	Major Pieces	Other Pieces
Husband	86.0%	63.5%
Mother or mother-in-law	2.4	4.5
Friend	3.6	8.0
Decorator	3.1	2.7
Other relative	10.0	12.9
Other person	1.6	1.8
No one else	7.1	24.3
No answer	.9	2.2

Morgantown, Inc. (B)

IN NOVEMBER 1986 Morgantown, Inc., merged with Lea-Meadows Industries, a manufacturer of upholstered furniture for living and family rooms. The merger was not planned in a conventional sense. Charlton Bates's father-in-law died suddenly in August 1986, leaving his daughter with controlling interest in the firm. The merger proceeded smoothly, since the two firms were located on adjacent properties and the general consensus was that the two firms would maintain as much autonomy as was economically justified. Moreover, the upholstery line filled a gap in the Morgantown product mix, even though it would retain its own identity and brand names.

The only real issue that continued to plague Bates was merging the selling effort. Morgantown had its own sales force, but Lea-Meadows Industries relied on sales agents to represent it. The question was straightforward, in his opinion: "Do we give the upholstery line of chairs and sofas to our sales force, or do we continue using the sales agents?" Mr. John Bott, Morgantown's sales vice-president, said the line should be given to his sales group; Mr. Martin Moorman, national sales manager of Lea-Meadows Industries, said the upholstery line should remain with sales agents.

LEA-MEADOWS INDUSTRIES

Lea-Meadows Industries is a small manufacturer of upholstered furniture for use in living and family rooms. The firm is over seventy-five years old. The company has some of the finest fabrics and frame con-

This case was prepared by Professor Roger A. Kerin, Southern Methodist University, as a basis for class discussion and is not designed to illustrate appropriate or inappropriate handling of administrative situations. All names and data are disguised.

struction in the industry, according to trade sources. Net sales in 1986 were $3 million. Total industry sales of 1,500 upholstered furniture manufacturers in 1986 were $4.4 billion. Company sales had increased 15 percent annually over the last five years, and company executives believed this growth rate would continue for the foreseeable future.

Lea-Meadows Industries employed fifteen sales agents to represent its products. These sales agents also represented several manufacturers of noncompeting furniture and home furnishings. Often a sales agent found it necessary to deal with several buyers in a store in order to represent all lines carried. On a typical sales call, a sales agent would first visit buyers. New lines, in addition to any promotions being offered by manufacturers, would be discussed. New orders were sought where and when it was appropriate. A sales agent would then visit a retailer's selling floor to check displays, inspect furniture, and inform sales people on furniture. Lea-Meadows Industries paid an agent commission of 5 percent of net company sales for these services. Moorman thought sales agents spent 10 to 15 percent of their in-store sales time on Lea-Meadows products.

The company did not attempt to influence the type of retailers that agents contacted. Yet it was implicit in the agency agreement that agents would not sell to discount houses. All agents had established relationships with their retail accounts and worked closely with them. Sales records indicated that agents were calling on furniture and department stores. An estimated 1,000 retail accounts were called on in 1986.

MORGANTOWN, INC.[a]

Morgantown, Inc., is a manufacturer of medium- to high-priced living and dining room wood furniture. The firm was formed in 1902. Net sales in 1986 were $50 million. Total estimated industry sales of wood furniture in 1986 were $7.1 billion at manufacturers' prices.

The company employed ten full-time sales representatives who called on 1,000 retail accounts in 1986. These individuals performed the same function as sales agents, but were paid a salary plus a small commission. In 1986 the average Morgantown sales representative received an annual salary of $50,000 (plus expenses) and a commission of 0.5 percent on net company sales. Total sales administration costs were $112,500.

The Morgantown sales force was highly regarded in the industry.

---

[a]Additional background information on the company and industry can be found in the case entitled "Morgantown, Inc. (A)."

The salesmen were known particularly for their knowledge of wood furniture and willingness to work with buyers and retail sales person- nel. Despite these points, Bates knew that all retail accounts did not carry the complete Morgantown furniture line. He had therefore in- structed John Bott to "push the group a little harder." At present, sales representatives were making ten sales calls per week, with the average sales call running three hours. Remaining time was accounted for by administrative activities and travel. Bates recommended that the call frequency be increased to seven calls per account per year, which was consistent with what he thought was the industry norm.

MERGING THE SALES EFFORT

In separate meetings with Bott and Moorman, Bates was able to piece together a variety of data and perspectives on the question. These meetings also made it clear that Bott and Moorman differed dramati- cally in their views.

John Bott had no doubts about assigning the line to the Morgan- town sales force. Among the reasons he gave for this approach were the following. First, Morgantown had developed one of the most well respected, professional sales groups in the industry. Sales representa- tives could easily learn the fabric jargon, and they already knew per- sonally many of the buyers who were responsible for upholstered furniture. Second, selling the Lea-Meadows line would require only about 15 percent of present sales call time. Thus he thought the new line would not be a major burden. Third, more control over sales ef- forts was possible. He noted that Charlton Bates's father-in-law had developed the sales group twenty-five years earlier because of the commitment it engendered and the service "only our own people are able and willing to give." Moreover, our people have the Morgantown "look" and presentation style that is instilled in every person. Fourth, he said it wouldn't look right if we had our representatives and agents calling on the same stores and buyers. He noted that Morgantown and Lea-Meadows Industries overlapped on all their accounts. He said, "We'd be paying a commission on sales to these accounts when we would have gotten them anyway. The difference in commission per- centages would not be good for morale."

Martin Moorman advocated keeping sales agents for the Lea- Meadows line. His arguments were as follows. First, all sales agents had established contacts and were highly regarded by store buyers, and most had represented the line in a professional manner for many years. He, too, had a good working relationship with all fifteen agents. Second, sales agents represented little, if any, cost beyond commissions. Moorman noted, "Agents get paid when we get paid." Third, sales agents were committed to the Lea-Meadows line: "The agents earn a part of their living representing us. They have to service retail accounts to get the repeat business." Fourth, sales agents were calling on buyers not contacted by Morgantown sales representatives. He noted, "If we let Morgantown people handle the line, we might lose these accounts, have to hire more sales personnel, or take away 25 percent of the present selling time given to Morgantown product lines."

As Bates reflected on the meetings, he felt that a broader perspective was necessary beyond the views expressed by Bott and Moorman. One factor was profitability. Existing Morgantown furniture lines typically had gross margins that were 5 percent higher than those for Lea-Meadows upholstered lines. Another factor was the "us and them" references apparent in the meetings with Bott and Moorman. Would merging the sales efforts overcome this, or would it cause more problems? Finally, the idea of increasing the sales force to incorporate the Lea-Meadows line did not sit well with him. Adding a new salesperson would require restructuring of sales territories, potential loss of commission to existing people, and "a big headache."

CASE

Arrow Boat Corporation

IN OCTOBER 1985 Mr. Troy Joseph marked his first six months as vice-president of marketing for the Arrow Boat Corporation. Mr. Joseph, who had joined Arrow after five years experience with a management consulting firm, had spent much of the first six months familiarizing himself with all aspects of the company. At present, he was in the process of formulating advertising plans for 1986.

Arrow's advertising plan for the coming year was (1) to reflect the aggressive product development activities undertaken in 1985, (2) to increase top-of-mind awareness among boat owners and those likely to become involved in boating, and (3) to maintain the sales growth momentum of the previous year. The company had spent $1.7 million in 1985 for product development, which produced three breakthroughs. First, a new hull design for its seventeen- and eighteen-foot family outboard boats was perfected and would be introduced in 1986. Second, the company had developed three twenty-foot offshore (bluewater) boats (boats designed for saltwater usage) that were to be introduced in 1986. These boats were the first offshore models ever produced by the company. Third, the company had developed a new lightweight fishing boat. The emphasis on top-of-mind awareness had been prompted by a recent study conducted by Arrow Boat Corporation, which showed that the Arrow brand name awareness among new boat owners was the lowest of the ten major brand names studied. Finally, Arrow Boat Corporation sales rose 27 percent in 1985, and the company's top management wanted to repeat this growth rate in 1986.

Although the details of the 1986 advertising program and its ex-

This case was prepared by Professor Robert Peterson, University of Texas, Austin, and Professor Roger A. Kerin, Southern Methodist University, as a basis for class discussion and is not intended to illustrate effective or ineffective handling of administrative situations. All names and data have been disguised and are not useful for research purposes.

330

ecution would be left to the company's advertising director and advertising agency, it was Mr. Joseph's responsibility to make the budgeting decision. Specifically, he would have to recommend the total advertising budget to top management and determine how the budget was to be allocated.

THE COMPANY

Arrow Boat Corporation was founded in the 1950s and was one of the first companies to produce fiberglass pleasure boats. By 1986, with the product development efforts, Arrow's product line would include thirty-eight different models in five product groups varying from small fishing boats to large high-performance models powered by jet engines. A breakdown of product groups follows:

Product Group	Number of Models
Family (pleasure)	18
Offshore (blue-water)	3
Cruiser	7
Fishing	4
High-performance (jet-propelled)	6

Twenty-one of the models were outboards, (O), fourteen were inboard/outdrive (I/O), and three (in the high-performance product group) were jets.[a] The single most popular model (a seventeen-foot family outboard) accounted for 8 percent of total company sales; three other models accounted for an additional 23 percent of sales. Although complete industry statistics were unavailable, Arrow executives believed the company was one of the largest producers of fiberglass pleasure boats under eighteen feet in the United States.

In the fiscal year ending September 30, 1985, Arrow Boat Corporation had sales of $40.827 million, which represented 17,294 units sold. After-tax earnings were $1.726 million in 1985.

Distribution

Approximately 75 percent of Arrow sales occur in the continental United States. The company maintains trade relationships with 19 re-

---

[a]Traditionally, the boat segments of most interest to Arrow had been outboard (O), and inboard/outdrive (I/O). In the former, the engine purchase is separate from the boat purchase; in the latter, the engine is part of the finished product. As would be expected, I/O boats retail at a higher price than outboards; nationally, I/O boats account for 25 percent of all boats produced.

gional distributors and 800 dealers. These dealers represent several competing brands of boats and marine products. The remaining 25 percent of sales take place worldwide in more than fifty countries, either through eleven international distributors or through various licensing agreements. The largest U.S. dealer accounted for 17 percent of total company sales in 1985. This dealer was situated in the Gulf Coast region, which includes Texas, Mississippi, Louisiana, Florida, and Alabama. The next two largest dealers accounted for 16 percent of total company sales. These dealers were located in the Great Lakes region (Minnesota, Wisconsin, Indiana, Michigan, Illinois, and Ohio). All three dealers had sold Arrow boats for more than ten years.

Historically, Arrow distribution had been weakest in areas where offshore boat sales had been highest (e.g., Florida and California). However, company executives believed the introduction of the three twenty-foot offshore boats in 1986 would bolster sales in these areas.

Sales and Promotion

The Arrow Boat Corporation sales organization consists of a national sales manager, two regional sales managers, and a sales support staff. The two regional sales managers, respectively, operate east and west of the Mississippi River. Their function is to coordinate Arrow's sales effort with the sales efforts of distributors.

In the past, sales promotion activities had been limited to the development and distribution of traditional accoutrements such as Arrow jackets, banners, and cups and glasses.[b] Recently, however, Arrow has been increasingly active in boat trade and consumer shows. Trade shows are typically scheduled in the late fall and blend into consumer shows in the winter months. Both types of shows take place at multiple locations across the country, and it is during these shows that new boat models are introduced. Arrow had introduced its new hull designs and offshore boats in the fall trade shows and planned to exhibit these innovations during the winter of 1986 at consumer boat shows.

As part of its more aggressive marketing strategy for 1986, Mr. Joseph had expanded the sales promotion program. The expanded program included a promotion kit for Arrow distributors and dealers, which consisted of five packages of sales promotion materials, each organized around a seasonal theme. Included in the materials were T-shirt transfers, display posters, balloons, flags, and the like. These kits

---

[b]Sales promotion expenditures and the cost of trade and consumer boat shows were paid for out of a separate budget account, according to company accounting procedures.

were to be made available to interested distributors and dealers in February 1986.

During 1985 Arrow Boat Company spent $200,000 for advertising, the same amount that was spent in 1984. As was typical in the industry, advertising focused exclusively on print media. The percentage and dollar breakdowns of the 1985 advertising budget are shown in Exhibit 1.

Mr. Joseph was sensitive to achieving parity with other national boat manufacturers such as Arrow in terms of advertising in the six major vertical boating magazines, which reach distributors, dealers, and boat owners and boating enthusiasts. Although it was difficult to determine how much Arrow's competition was budgeting for advertising in these six magazines, the company's advertising did provide some estimates. The agency estimated that two major competitors—Wellcraft and Starcraft—spent, respectively, 0.53 percent and 0.26 percent of sales in the six vertical boating magazines in 1985. These percentages were obtained from public announcements made by the two competitors in feature articles in the industry. For comparison, Arrow spent 0.26 percent of sales in these six publications in 1985. A black and white Arrow advertisement appeared six times in each magazine during peak sales periods.

Similarly, Mr. Joseph was sensitive to the level of advertising spending in the industry as a whole. The industry average, based on

EXHIBIT 1
Advertising Budget for 1985

Budget Item	Expenditure	
National, vertical boating magazines[a]	$108,000	(54%)
Dealer catalogs/consumer brochures[b]	22,000	(11%)
Cooperative newspaper advertising with dealers[c]	40,000	(20%)
Production costs[d]	30,000	(15%)
	$200,000	(100%)

[a]Vertical magazines reach multiple distribution channel levels (distributors and dealers) and consumers. Examples of vertical boating magazines appear in Exhibit 6.

[b]Dealer catalogs/consumer brochures show Arrow's product line, including product performance specifications. These are used by distributors/dealers for point-of-sale information for prospective buyers.

[c]Cooperative advertising involved splitting newspaper advertising costs with dealers on a fifty-fifty basis. A typical coop advertisement would show Arrow products with a dealer tag line.

[d]Production costs include the costs of preparing advertisements and agency fees.

Arrow's advertising agency estimates, was 0.6 percent of sales. He knew that top management would use this figure as a reference point when he proposed the 1986 advertising budget.

Finally, Mr. Joseph was informed by his advertising agency that the major concentration of industry media dollars was spent during peak selling months. Moreover, his own observation of competitive print advertising suggested to him that advertising in the industry tended toward sameness. Most advertising featured a single model or product line. Advertisements for smaller models had a factual emphasis, whereas those for larger, more expensive, and more sophisticated models emphasized the boat's "sizzle" along with the facts.

THE BOATING INDUSTRY

The boating industry is heavily dependent on general economic conditions. This is especially true of the family (pleasure) boating segment.

Of the 500 to 1,000 full-line boat manufacturers in the United States, approximately 20 to 30 distributed their products nationally and competed directly with Arrow. No one manufacturer held more than a 10 percent industry market share.

Small local boat manufacturers are the nemesis of national boat manufacturers such as Arrow. Local manufacturers often copy the features of boats produced by national manufacturers and sell at prices below those of comparable nationally produced boats. For a variety of reasons, including expense and difficulty of prosecution, national boat manufacturers have little recourse against the small imitative firms.

Market Distribution and Seasonality

Geographically, boat sales are segmented by state and region. Exhibit 2 shows the distribution of boat registrations by state; ten states accounted for the majority of sales. Michigan and Minnesota in the Great Lakes region were the largest markets. California and Texas also represent major markets. The Great Lakes region was the dominant market for boats.

Three-quarters of retail boat sales take place between March and August, with April, May, and June being the primary purchase months. For example, family boat sales typically vary from a low of 2 percent in December to a high of 15 percent in May. Accordingly, factory shipments were heaviest in February, March, April, and May, with earlier purchase agreements representing normal operating procedure for national manufacturers. Arrow, for instance, typically built boat invento-

EXHIBIT 2
Top States and Regions in Boat Registrations

State	Percentage	Region	Percentage
Michigan	7.10	Great Lakes	27.10
Minnesota	6.80	Gulf Coast	19.40
California	6.60	Mid-Atlantic	17.70
Texas	6.50	Midwest/Mountain	9.70
Florida	5.70	East Central	9.50
Wisconsin	4.60	West Coast	7.60
New York	3.60	New England	6.40
Ohio	3.60	State/territories outside	
Louisiana	3.30	continental United States	0.60
Arkansas	3.20		100.00%
	51.00%		

Source: Company records.

ries from September through February and offered an off-season price discount program to encourage prepeak distributor purchasing.

Boat Buyer Behavior

Research on boat-buying behavior commissioned by Arrow in 1985 had produced a profile of boat owners and their reasons for purchasing boats. The study employed a nationwide random sample of boat owners.

According to the study, the typical boat owner was a married male in his mid- to late forties with two teenage children. The median annual household income of a boatowner was $30,450.

The most popular type of boat was an outboard (see Exhibit 3). This finding seemed to parallel another study Mr. Joseph had seen which indicated that fishing was by far the most popular boating activity, followed by cruising and water skiing.

Findings dealing with boat attributes and information sources yielded a few surprises. Mr. Joseph was not too surprised to see that quality of construction was easily the most important boat characteristic influencing a boat purchase (see Exhibit 4). However, he wondered how a boat buyer could presumably determine quality of construction without the assistance of a marine dealer as a salesperson. He knew that it took him a few months to distinguish between good and average construction quality—and he had been taught what to look for by Arrow's vice-president of manufacturing. He was also surprised at the

EXHIBIT 3
Primary and Secondary Boat Ownership

	Percentage Response	
Boat Type	Primary Boat	Secondary Boat
Outboard	72	38
Inboard	9	9
I/O	8	8
Sailboat	6	8
Other[a]	4	37
Total	100	100

Source: Company records.

[a]"Other" includes canoes, pontoon boats, and jet drives

relative unimportance of low price, and thought this finding might be an artifact of the study. The rankings of the information sources for selecting a brand of boat was consistent with what he expected (see Exhibit 5).

Finally, Mr. Joseph was particularly intrigued with three study findings:

- Of those present boat owners planning to purchase a boat in the next six months, 34 percent stated this boat would be an

EXHIBIT 4
Product Attributes Affecting Boat Purchases

Attribute	Relative Importance
Quality of construction	100%
Performance	81
Design purpose	78
Value	68
Smooth ride	46
Service after purchase	42
Economy of operation	29
Resale value	25
Brand	19
Amount of hspr possible	9
Low price	4
Accessories included	2

Source: Company records.

EXHIBIT 5
Source of Information on Brand of Boat Purchased

Source	Relative Information[a]
Friends and relatives	100%
Marine dealer	98
Catalog/brochure	97
Magazine advertising	93
Salesperson	86
Magazine/newspaper story	85
Newspaper advertising	69
Radio/TV advertising	67

Source: Company records.

[a]Arbitrarily assigning "friends and relatives" a 100 percent rating.

eighteen-foot or less family pleasure boat, whereas 47 percent said it would be a family cruiser type.

- All decisions, except for color, were strongly dominated by the husband.

- The typical boat owner visited a minimum of two marine dealers before making a purchase decision.

THE ADVERTISING DECISION

The 1986 advertising plan represented Mr. Joseph's first major presentation before Arrow's president and executive committee. Therefore, the presentation meant more than merely making a request for funds. He felt that the thoroughness of the advertising plan and the logic behind it would be as important as the final budget itself. He knew that the final budget would likely be a compromise between what ideally should be done and what was realistic from a funding perspective. However, he felt that if he could clearly articulate the role advertising played in the marketing of boats, then his proposal might be given more careful consideration. Furthermore, his specific recommendations on how the budget should be allocated would carry greater weight.

The budget itself would be an itemized statement like that shown in Exhibit 1. Supplementary exhibits would document the figures reported.

At Mr. Joseph's request, the advertising agency prepared a magazine summary for his consideration. Principal vertical boating magazines are shown in Exhibit 6, general interest magazines in Exhibit 7.

EXHIBIT 6
Selected Media Comparisons: Major Boating Magazines

	Boating Magazine	Yachting	National Fisherman	Small Boat Journal	Motor Boating & Sailing	Powerboat
Published	Monthly	Monthly	Monthly	Bimonthly	Monthly	11 times/year
Cost:						
1 Page B/W	$ 5,343	$ 6,610	$2,705	$1,370	$5,350	$1,733
1 Page Color	8,015	9,940	3,965	1,920	8,180	2,079
Circulation	192,000	148,447	53,456	54,919	144,608	82,920
Editorial description:	Most general boating magazine	Covers both sail and power boats, gives major events and description of new products	U.S. commercial fishing industry journal and covers new product news	Recreational watercraft under 30 feet	Boat owner/ yacht owner interested in entertainment	News and trends in the performance boating world, do-it-yourself tips

Source: Company records.

EXHIBIT 7
Selected Media Comparisons: General Interest Magazines

	Business Week	Newsweek	Time	National Geographic	Sports Illustrated	Reader's Digest
Published	Weekly	Weekly	Weekly	Monthly	Weekly	Monthly
Cost:						
1 Page B/W	$21,000	$65,000	$69,650	$74,120	$43,835	$90,500
1 Page Color	$28,000	$79,200	$87,060	$85,980	$55,235	$95,900
Circulation	814,000	3,000,000	4,600,000	10,000,000	2,300,000	17,885,000
Editorial description:	For management news as it impacts on business	National affairs news capsules	National affairs news briefs	International in scope; cultural environment, scientific information	Reports on sports, recreation, and leisure	General-interest family magazine

Note: All cost and circulation estimates are based on national distribution. Regional issues are also available which cost from 15 to 25 percent of national coverage costs.

In addition, agency personnel prepared estimates for dealer catalogs and consumer brochures that would feature the new hull designs, the three offshore boats, and the new fishing boat. A summary of the costs for catalogs and brochures is shown in Exhibit 8. Finally, the agency projected a 5 percent increase in cooperative advertising, given higher newspaper advertising costs.

EXHIBIT 8
Catalog and Brochure Cost Estimates

Catalogs		Brochures	
Units Produced	Cost	Units Produced	Cost
500	$ 9,000	2,000	$2,000
1,000	18,000	4,000	4,000
1,500	22,500	6,000	4,500
2,000	30,000	8,000	6,000
2,500	32,500	10,000	7,500
3,000	39,000	12,000	8,640

Note: Catalogs and brochures would be in color and feature new hull designs, offshore models, and the new fishing boat. Catalogs would contain over 50 pages describing boat features and pictures. Brochures would typically contain 2 to 3 pages.

La Quinta Motor Inns, Inc.: National Advertising Campaign

IN EARLY 1979 Joyce Wilson, vice-president of marketing for La Quinta Motor Inns, Inc., was composing her thoughts prior to preparing an important memo. The memo was an assignment given to all upper-level executives who had attended a management conference conducted for the company by a team of professors from well-known business schools. The memo, directed to the president and chief executive officer, Sam Barshop, was to address the continued growth rate that top management recommended for the company over the next five years. Also, managers were to discuss the impact that growth would have on their departments and the role of their departments in achieving growth objectives.

Ms. Wilson knew the 22 percent compound annual growth rate in

This case was made possible through the cooperation of La Quinta Motor Inns, Inc. The case was prepared by Professors Roger A. Kerin and M. Edgar Barrett, Edwin L. Cox School of Business, Southern Methodist University, as a basis for class discussion and is not designed to illustrate effective or ineffective handling of administrative situations. The assistance of Ms. Phyllis B. Riggins, graduate student, in the preparation of this case is gratefully acknowledged. Issues raised at the end of the case are introduced solely for discussion purposes. They do not necessarily represent the opinions of La Quinta management.

revenues and profits achieved by La Quinta during its first ten years would be a challenge to sustain. The next few years would see the chain's expansion into "frontier" areas where it lacked the recognition achieved in the Southwest. She knew some top managers occasionally questioned the efficacy of the company's recent commitment to a national advertising campaign and the narrow market segment sought out by La Quinta. The national campaign was just entering its second year, and Ms. Wilson knew her comments on the campaign and target market would have implications for the role of both the campaign and market orientation in La Quinta's future.

NOTE ON THE LODGING INDUSTRY

According to the October 1978 *Wall Street Transcript* "Roundtable Discussion" on the lodging industry, "the historic growth rate of the industry is something near two percent or a little less." Motels and motor hotels combined, however, have shown a larger growth rate than have hotels.

Occupancy rates were as high as 80 percent in the early 1960s. High occupancy rates made the industry attractive for investment, and supply began to seriously outstrip demand in the late 1960s and early 1970s. The recession of 1974 and the energy crisis that preceded it caused a slowdown in travel, and many financial institutions were forced to foreclose on lodging properties. By 1970 average industry occupancy rates approached 60 percent. The recovery proceeded slowly, and only in 1979 did industry occupancy rates approach 70 percent. Reluctance of financial institutions and investors to recreate the oversupply situation of the early 1970s served as a check during the recovery. Capacity actually declined in 1976. There were about 2.25 million lodging rooms in the United States in 1979. More than 60 percent of these rooms were over ten years old. Holiday Inns accounted for approximately 12 to 15 percent of available rooms in 1974.

Four general motel classifications have emerged in the last twenty-five years: (1) small, individually owned tourist courts; (2) budget motels, such as Days Inn and Motel 6; (3) medium-priced chains, such as La Quinta and Rodeway; and (4) large, full-service chains such as Holiday Inn. The trend is away from small, independently owned units toward largely franchised, absentee-owned motels. With regard to the second classification, "One Howard Johnson executive predicted the budget motel would be to the motel industry what the Volkswagen was to autos. . . . How did the word 'budget,' perfectly respectable when applied to cars, airline flights, and department stores, fall into such disgrace in motels? Because many a budget motel was cheap as well as less expensive. . . . In a country where a clean, well-maintained room is the bare minimum the traveler requires, anything less is an insult."

LA QUINTA MOTOR INNS

The first La Quinta Motor Inn was built by the Barshop family in San Antonio, Texas, in 1968. Sam Barshop, referred to by *Forbes* in a June 1978 article as "the reluctant motelier," was heavily involved in the family real estate business and initially considered the lodging industry a sideline. The family built its first motel in 1961 after Ramada Inns had expressed interest in a piece of family property in San Antonio. When it was announced that the 1968 World's Fair would be held in San Antonio, Sam and his brother, Phil Barshop, who had by then built other inns as franchises of Ramada and Rodeway, decided that "the occasion warranted a hotel with a different flavor." The first La Quinta Motor Inn was located across the street from Hemisfair '68. The name and architecture recalled San Antonio's Spanish Colonial heritage. Both characteristics have been retained in subsequent inns, as shown in Exhibit 1. La Quinta Motor Inns, Inc., was formed when Barshop Motel Enterprises offered stock for public sale in 1973.

Exhibit 2 summarizes the growth in the number of inns and rooms from fiscal years 1974 through 1979. Exhibit 3 shows La Quinta's income statements from 1975 through 1979.

La Quinta Service Concept

La Quinta's service concept is described in its 1978 annual report: "Because we define our primary market as the individual business traveler, we design and manage our inns to serve his or her needs: clean, quiet accommodations at a reasonable price." Every aspect of La Quinta's service is based on the company's perception of the business traveler's needs. Research conducted in early 1978 indicated that this service concept had worked effectively in attracting and satisfying these needs (see Appendix A).

The average La Quinta Motor Inn has about 120 rooms. There is a pool, color television, direct-dial telephone, a twenty-four-hour switchboard, and one-day laundry service. La Quinta leases free-standing restaurant facilities, contiguous to the inns, to national restaurant chains, such as Denny's or Jojos, who operate them. These restaurants typically provide food service twenty-four hours a day. The inns are located on premium sites on major highways close to major industrial and office complexes, large retail shopping centers,

EXHIBIT 1
La Quinta Motor Inn

and universities. Site selection is considered a key part of La Quinta's marketing strategy. According to Sam Barshop: "Part of our company's marketing monies go toward purchasing a top notch site because all the advertising and publicity in the world can't change a bad site." As of 1979, Sam or Phil Barshop had personally selected every La Quinta Motor Inn site.

The majority of inns are managed by older married couples. Their duties include filing timely reports with the home office, keeping their inns clean and in good repair, and being friendly and courteous to customers. An article on "Husband/Wife Management Teams in Texas" in *Southwest Hotel-Motel Review* describes the advantage of these teams: "A husband and wife team gets to know their guest. . . . It's sort of a personal touch. . . . It builds a very great repeat business, which is important." La Quinta managers carry this personal touch to the point of calling each regular customer by name. *Innput,* the com-

EXHIBIT 2
La Quinta Motor Inns, Inc.—Number of Motor Inns
and Rooms (Fiscal 1974–1979)

	1979	1978	1977	1976	1975	1974
Motor inns						
Company owned (50% or more)	64	55	49	49	45	36
Licensed	14	13	14	11	10	4
Total	78	68	63	60	55	40
Rooms						
Company owned (50% or more)	7,288	6,161	5,355	5,183	4,633	3,544
Licensed	1,770	1,638	1,776	1,388	1,267	596
Total	9,058	7,799	7,131	6,571	5,900	4,140

Source: Company records.
Note: Fiscal year ends May 31.

pany newspaper, is filled with letters that reflect the success of unit managers in creating this friendly feeling.

La Quinta has prospered using this service concept. Exhibit 4 shows the occupancy rate data for new and existing La Quinta Motor Inns over the last six years. The company has consistently experienced some of the highest occupancy rates in the lodging industry.

Inn Location and Site Selection

Exhibit 5 shows the location of La Quinta Motor Inns completed or under development as of late 1979. The company has expanded geographically by means of a three-part strategy. *Adjacency,* the first of these three, involves expansion to new cities of over 100,000 population within a 300-mile radius of an existing La Quinta Motor Inn property. This strategy can be observed in the existence of the various "frontier" properties, such as Casper, Wyoming, and Salt Lake City, Utah. *Clustering,* the second part of the plan, consists of the construction of several inns in one city. Dallas and Houston are both examples of cluster cities. The third part, *filling in,* is the construction of inns in other, usually smaller, cities within an established market area. Seventy-eight company-owned or -licensed inns in the La Quinta Motor Inns chain would be operating in twenty states by the end of fiscal 1979. There were twenty-five inns under development in an additional four states at the time.

EXHIBIT 3
La Quinta Motor Inns, Inc.—Income Statements (Fiscal 1975–1979)

	1979	1978	1977	1976	1975
Revenues (000s)					
Motor inn	$44,682	35,580	27,256	22,173	16,272
Restaurant rental	1,881	1,545	1,127	990	790
Restaurant and club	1,094	1,029	960	1,084	1,097
Other	1,267	1,039	780	593	389
Total revenues	48,924	39,193	30,123	24,840	18,548
Operating costs and expenses (000s)					
Motor inn direct	22,958	18,410	15,139	12,762	9,602
Restaurant and club direct	1,038	988	1,013	1,113	1,166
Selling, general and administrative	4,512	3,450	2,292	1,836	1,410
Depreciation and amortization	4,438	3,743	2,964	2,554	1,997
Total operating costs and expenses	32,946	26,591	21,408	18,265	14,175
Operating income	15,978	12,602	8,715	6,575	4,373
Other income (deductions) (000s)					
Interest, net of capitalization	(6,172)	(4,946)	(3,922)	(3,499)	(2,803)
Gain on sale of assets, principally motor inns	1,477	553	501	215	289
Partners' equity in earnings and losses:					
Operations	(2,437)	(1,719)	(897)	(385)	(45)
Sales of motor inns	(589)	—	—	—	—
Total other income (deductions)	(7,721)	(6,112)	(4,318)	(3,669)	(2,559)
Earnings before income taxes	8,257	6,490	4,397	2,906	1,814
Income taxes	3,385	2,759	1,939	1,205	707
Net earnings (000s)	$ 4,872	3,731	2,458	1,701	1,107

Source: 1979 annual report.
Note: Fiscal year ends May 31.

Price and Cost Structure

La Quinta's no-frills approach has enabled the company to minimize capital and operating costs and remain very reasonably priced. According to Sam Barshop, "La Quinta sells rooms, period . . . no atriums or meeting rooms to swell construction costs." La Quinta's price per

EXHIBIT 4
La Quinta Motor Inns, Inc.—Percentage of Occupancy
(Fiscal 1974–1978)

	1979	1978	1977	1976	1975	1974
Motor inns open one year or more	90.6%	89.1%	86.6%	82.1%	80.3%	81.4%
Overall	88.1	88.6	85.8	80.5	74.0	79.7

Source: Company records.

room is typically 20 to 25 percent below comparable rooms at motor inns with more elaborate facilities. The average daily rate per occupied room in 1979 was $20.21.

In discussing the company's cost structure, Walter Biegler, La Quinta's vice-president of finance and chief finance officer, mentioned the difficulty of performing a strict cost-profit analysis of their operations. He felt that some of the costs were actually semivariable with occupancy. Thus, he noted the variable cost component was not easy to isolate precisely. In general, however, he estimated the industry ratio of variable costs to revenue of 55 percent to be representative of La Quinta's situation.

Sales Force

La Quinta employs a small, but effective sales force under the direction of two divisional sales directors. The sales force is divided into eastern and western divisions.

The company employs eight sales representatives. These representatives made over seven thousand sales calls in 1979. Sales-call activity is heaviest during the period preceding and during new La Quinta Motor Inn openings. Sales representatives are responsible for calling on large corporations whose employees are potential customers of the entire network of La Quinta Motor Inns. Another function of the sales group is to assist unit managers in increasing occupancy rates of existing inns. Unit managers are also expected to make sales calls. The total numbers of prospective customers reached by all these efforts exceeded 25,000 in 1979.

Marketing and Advertising

Joyce Wilson joined La Quinta in 1975 to manage the newly formed marketing department. Her primary responsibilities at that time in-

EXHIBIT 5
La Quinta Motor Inn Locations as of Late 1979

ALABAMA	KANSAS	TENNESSEE
Mobile	Kansas City	Memphis
ARIZONA	Wichita	Nashville
+ Flagstaff	KENTUCKY	TEXAS
+ Kingman	Louisville	Abilene
Phoenix	LOUISIANA	Austin (3)
Tucson	New Orleans (2)	Beaumont
ARKANSAS	MISSISSIPPI	Brazosport
Little Rock (2)*	Jackson	Bryan/College Station*
CALIFORNIA	MISSOURI	+ Corpus Christi (2)
Costa Mesa*	St. Louis	+ Dallas/Fort Worth
COLORADO	NEBRASKA	(14)*****
Denver (3)*	Omaha*	Denton
FLORIDA	NEVADA	El Paso (2)*
Jacksonville*	Las Vegas	+ Galveston
++ Orlando	Reno*	Houston (7)*
Tallahassee	NEW MEXICO	Killeen
+ Tampa	Albuquerque	Laredo
GEORGIA	OHIO	Lubbock
Atlanta	+ Cincinnati	+ McAllen
Columbus*	Columbus*	Odessa*
ILLINOIS	++ Dayton	+ San Angelo
Champaign*	OKLAHOMA	San Antonio (7)
+ Moline	Oklahoma City	Texas City
INDIANA	Tulsa	Waco
Indianapolis	SOUTH CAROLINA	Wichita Falls
(2)**	Charleston*	UTAH
Merrillville	Columbia*	Salt Lake City
	Greenville*	WYOMING
		Casper*
		Cheyenne*

*Inns under development
+Licensed property
( )Number of inns located in each city

cluded assistance in formulating strategy, advertising, sales and promotion programs, and marketing research. In 1977 Ms. Sue Moore
joined La Quinta as director of advertising to manage the company's
in-house advertising agency. Creation of a marketing department and
subsequent formation of an in-house advertising agency contributed to
a more systematic approach to marketing and communications at La

Quinta. Prior to that time, responsibility for advertising was dispersed among a variety of executives and often handled on an inn-by-inn basis.

The first formal advertising campaign was launched at the beginning of the 1977 fiscal year. The campaign's objectives were to enhance local or regional awareness (markets with existing inns), communicate the broader geographical scope of the chain, and further establish La Quinta's identity, or positioning, within the industry. Space in *Media Networks*, a mix of major weekly magazines with regional editions such as *Time, Newsweek, U.S. News and World Report*, and *Sports Illustrated*, was purchased for fifteen La Quinta markets. (Markets relate to major cities and immediate environs.) Three to four full-page advertisements (depending on the market) were placed in the Southwest edition of both the *Wall Street Journal* (twenty ads scheduled throughout the year) and *Business Week* (four ads scheduled throughout the year). The rational for this selection and schedule was that these publications reached present and potential customers and would convey a "national image" for La Quinta even though their distribution was on a regional basis. Their readership also represented an "investor" audience. Two general-audience monthly magazines, *Southern Living* and *Texas Monthly*, carried three advertisements each that were scheduled for placement throughout the year. Three advertisements were placed throughout the year in in-flight magazines published by Southwest, Ozark, and Texas International Airlines since these airlines service the majority of La Quinta markets. Finally, an advertisement was placed in each of several hotel and motel reference books used by independent and corporate-travel agencies, and two advertisements were placed in *Discovery*, a quarterly magazine with a circulation of one million for Allstate Insurance Company policyholders. The total media budget for this campaign was $135,000, with an estimated cost of 1 cent per reader per year. La Quinta executives believed that this effort achieved its objective.

The objective of the fiscal 1978 campaign was to retain the regional orientation, but take a step toward national recognition of La Quinta Motor Inns as inn locations expanded beyond states in the Southwest. This step was twofold: (1) to reach "feeder" markets for La Quinta cities, and (2) to create a higher level of awareness in new markets where La Quinta was building new inns. This national effort was reflected in the selection of *Time* magazine (B edition). This edition has a selective nationwide circulation focusing on subscribers classified as manager-professionals in addition to distribution to airlines and business offices. Four two-thirds-page advertisements were scheduled for placement throughout the year. The *Media Networks* purchase was timed to coincide with inn openings and included one advertisement each in five new markets. The number of insertions throughout the year in each of the remaining magazines is as follows:

Business Week (Southwest edition): 5 insertions
Wall Street Journal (Southwest edition): 6 insertions
Southern Living: 2 insertions
Discovery: 1 insertion
Airline magazines: 3 insertions in Southwest, Ozark, and Texas
   International Airlines

Total funds invested in advertising in fiscal year 1978 declined from the previous year because of a reallocation of marketing expenditures within the company. Nevertheless, the $95,000 allocated to advertising space was viewed as getting "more bang for the bucks" by Sue Moore. The reach of the 1978 plan was 17 percent higher than the previous year, and the estimated cost per subscriber per year had been reduced to slightly over 0.6 cent. The expanded coverage was showing increased inquiries about La Quinta Motor Inns from interested companies and individuals throughout the country.

The 1979 fiscal year advertising objectives were to accelerate the momentum begun in the 1978 campaign and further direct La Quinta's advertising toward a national audience. Two-thirds-page advertisements were placed throughout the year in *Business Week* (national edition) and *Time* (B edition). Each magazine carried five insertions. Sixteen insertions were scheduled throughout the year in the *Wall Street Journal* (Southwest edition), again with the investor community in mind. Examples of fiscal 1979 advertisements are shown in Appendix B. Total funds spent for advertising were $135,000. The cost per reader per year was approximately 1 cent. Although the company did not subscribe to a readership survey service, Sue Moore noted that the amount of qualified responses in terms of sales leads was very encouraging. Typical response letters reflected several key advertising goals: company letterhead, content of letters, titles of signees, city or state origin, and often, size of company sales force. A summary of the media allocation by year is shown in Exhibit 6.

MANAGEMENT MEMO

Thinking back over the growth La Quinta Motor Inns had achieved in the last decade and the crucial question of her department's role in sustaining that growth, Joyce Wilson began to list issues she would address in her memo to Mr. Sam Barshop.

EXHIBIT 6
La Quinta Motor Inns, Inc.—Allocation of Media
Expenditures

	Fiscal 1977 June 1976– May 1977	Fiscal 1978 June 1977– May 1978	Fiscal 1979 June 1978– May 1979
Wall Street Journal (Southwest edition)	$ 18,000	$ 3,000	$ 8,000
Time		56,000	77,000
Business Week (Southwest edition)	5,000	7,000	
Media Networks	85,000	12,000	
Business Week (national edition)			50,000
Hotel and motel reference books	6,100		
Southern Living	5,000	9,700	
Texas Monthly	5,000		
Discovery	4,600	3,000	
Airline magazines	6,400	4,300	—
Total	$135,000	$95,000	$135,000

Note: These figures do not include outdoor (billboard) advertising or miscellaneous promotional efforts of individual inns in La Quinta markets. Costs associated with these efforts are assumed by individual inns.

One issue was the size of the advertising budget itself. Since 1975 La Quinta had subscribed to the policy of budgeting marketing and advertising expenditures on a per-room/per-day basis. This was a standard reporting procedure in the lodging industry. Each individual inn contributed a set amount for the marketing department, including the advertising budget. In 1975 the figure was 10 cents per room per day, which has since been raised to 12 cents per room per day for La Quinta. As a percentage of revenue, however, Ms. Wilson believed that other chains of similar or slightly larger size budgeted as much as $100,000 to $200,000 per year more for advertising than La Quinta. She knew that if she raised this issue, a sound economic justification would be necessary, since such additional funds would most likely be obtained from corporate funds rather than from individual inns.

A second issue was the national versus regional thrust of La Quinta advertising campaigns. Preliminary discussions with Ms. Moore indicated that national coverage would be proposed for the 1980 fiscal year campaign. However, company executives occasionally questioned this orientation on the grounds that La Quinta operated in forty-seven cities in twenty states. In reviewing a *Media Networks* local trade area audience plan, similar to the 1977 program, Ms. Moore determined that *Media Networks* offered their magazine combination in only thirty-two of the current La Quinta Inn cities and that one insertion for that geographical coverage would cost $87,000. Two insertions in each magazine would cost in the neighborhood of $150,000, with a volume discount, and so forth. These cities contained all but fifteen La Quinta Motor Inns currently in operation. In the past, some company executives had expressed the opinion that the regional advertising approach would be more effective due to the regional aspects of the company's operations. Ms. Wilson felt that the memo provided a unique opportunity to address this issue, as well as the decision to insert advertisements throughout the year rather than focusing only on inn opening periods.

A third advertising-related issue was the number of vehicles La Quinta used to communicate its message. Since 1977 La Quinta had systematically reduced the number of vehicles so that in 1979, only *Business Week, Time,* and the Southwest edition of the *Wall Street Journal* were used. This focused effort was not only an advertising strategy related to the target audience, but also a result of the customer profile as portrayed by the company's 1978 market research. Other lodging chains around the country spread their advertising funds across many vehicles, including magazines, hotel and motel reference books, newspapers, direct mail, airline magazines, and occasionally spot and network radio and television, but their budgets were also larger. Expense was an important issue in this regard and supported the reduction of vehicles. However, Ms. Wilson felt that other arguments should be made as well.

A broader issue was the topic of market targeting. Ms. Wilson was aware that some top-level managers had considered broadening the target market beyond the individual business traveler to include the entire family or pleasure traveler. Advocates of this strategy were concerned that La Quinta was losing these travelers by ignoring them in a direct advertising appeal. Arguments made in favor of expanding the target market were:

1. Room occupancy on weekends was lower than during the week. Friday, Saturday, and Sunday night occupancy rates were about 75 percent. If weekend occupancy were increased, overall occupancy rates would rise.

2. Broadening the target market might increase the trial of La Quinta Inns in frontier areas such as Casper, Wyoming.

Proponents of this strategy proposed that "weekend specials" of 25 percent off the average room rate be provided on Saturday and Sunday since other chains had done so. Furthermore, one-fourth of the media funds might be spent promoting the weekend business.

Such an approach was contrary to La Quinta's existing concept, but the idea was raised often enough that Ms. Wilson knew her memo must deal with it. Both she and Ms. Moore maintained that the "business travelers" appeal attracts pleasure travelers as well.

An issue related to the target market question was the creative strategy. La Quinta had rested its advertising message on four pillars: service, price, location, and no frills. If the target market were expanded, other messages would have to be communicated.

As Joyce Wilson sat back in her chair, she wondered aloud about what positions she should take on these and other issues. She was fully aware that Mr. Sam Barshop expected a thoughtful and thorough appraisal of the issues listed on her scratch pad.

APPENDIX A

Selected Results of March 1978 Customer Mail Survey[a]

1. *Average number of different occasions a traveler stayed at La Quinta during the past twelve months*   10.2 times
2. *Average number of nights stayed on most recent visit*   2.6 nights
3. *Purpose of trip (percentages exceed 100% due to multiple answers)*

Personal	9.5%
Business	79.8
Pleasure	12.2
Convention	3.5
Vacation	2.0

4. *Frequency of staying at motels or hotels*

Once a week or more	39.0%
Once every few weeks	21.7
About once a month	16.4
Less often than every few months	21.2

5. *Type of trip and payment on most recent visit*

Business trip paid for by the company	65.7%
Business trip paid for by self	16.4
Pleasure trip paid for by self	18.0

6. *Rented a car on most recent trip*

Yes	23.1%
No	75.9

7. *Mode of travel on most recent trip*

Airline	34.0%
Car	64.8

8. *Reason for choice of a particular La Quinta Motor Inn on most recent visit (percentages exceed 100% due to multiple responses)*

Close to next day's activities	47.5%
Saw it when ready to stop	5.7
Recommended by friend, relative, etc.	15.4
Specified by the company	7.3
Personal preference based on previous experience	48.1
Price	36.6
Stayed here before	40.9
Friendly and courteous personnel	27.9
Other motels full	3.1

[a]Number of respondents = 5,600 of 10,000

9. *Source of reservations*

Self	55.4%
Secretary	13.3
Company	10.4
Travel agency	2.7
Association or convention	2.2
Relative, friend, etc.	4.7
No reservations	10.4

10. *Person(s) sharing room on most recent visit (percentages exceed 100% due to multiple responses)*

Spouse	21.6%
Children	5.2
Friends	3.4
Business associates	4.1
None, stayed alone	68.9

11. *Likelihood of staying at a La Quinta Motor Inn on return visit to the city*

Extremely likely	54.2%
Very likely	30.3
Somewhat likely	11.0
Not very likely	2.6
Not at all likely	1.0

12. *Likelihood of staying at a La Quinta Motor Inn if one were available in another city visited*

Extremely likely	45.5%
Very likely	35.4
Somewhat likely	15.3
Not very likely	2.3
Not at all likely	.7

13. *First stay in a La Quinta Motor Inn*

Yes	27.0%
No	70.1

APPENDIX B
Selected La Quinta Print Advertisements

EXHIBIT B.1

66 I DON'T NEED CONVENTION MOBS, LONG CHECK IN AND CHECK OUT LINES, FANCY LOBBIES OR NIGHTCLUBS. I JUST WANT A CLEAN, QUIET ROOM AND PERSONAL SERVICE.

THAT'S WHY I STAY AT LA QUINTA. 99

At La Quinta, you'll never be jostled aside by conventioneers because we don't book conventions.

You won't be disturbed by a noisy nightclub, because we don't have nightclubs. Or any unnecessary frills for that matter.

We do have what the experienced business traveler really wants.

Comfortable, clean, quiet rooms with color TV and phone. Same-day laundry service. 24-hour coffee shop next door. Swimming pool.

And a staff trained to give you personal attention, supervised by husband and wife managers who live on the premises.

By cutting out the things you don't need, La Quinta can afford to give you lower rates. Up to 25% less in most cases.

No wonder 4 out of 5 of our guests are business travelers.

La Quinta: 7,500 rooms in 17 states. And growing.

For free directory and other information, write La Quinta Marketing, Dept.T, 1625 Regal Row, Suite 170, Dallas, Texas 75247.

Toll free reservations: 800-531-5900
From Texas: 800-292-5200

Reservations guaranteed with all major credit cards.

© 1978, La Quinta Motor Inns, Inc. Listed on American Stock Exchange (LQM)

EXHIBIT B.2

66 OUR SALESMEN ARE ON THE ROAD MORE THAN EVER. BUT OUR TRAVEL EXPENSES ARE DOWN.

WHERE ARE WE STAYING? LA QUINTA. 99

An independent survey of La Quinta guests proved 4 out of 5 are business travelers.

They know every motor inn on the road. And they prefer La Quinta over their second choice almost two to one!

Which shows us we're giving our preferred guests, business travelers, what they really want.

Metro locations close to business centers and transportation.

Big, comfortable, quiet rooms with color TV and phone. Same-day laundry service. Swimming pool. 24-hour coffee shop next door.

And a helpful, courteous staff. (Headed by husband and wife managers who live on the premises.)

We don't book conventions. Nor court the vacation trade.

By cutting out the things you don't use, La Quinta can afford to give you lower rates. Up to 25% lower in most cases!

Business travel? Think La Quinta. Now 7,500 rooms in 17 states. And growing.

For free directory, write La Quinta Marketing, Dept. B, 1625 Regal Row, Suite 170, Dallas, Texas 75247.

Toll free reservations:
800-531-5900
From Texas:
800-292-5200
Reservations guaranteed with all major credit cards.

© 1978, La Quinta Motor Inns, Inc. Listed on American Stock Exchange (LQM)

" I NEED TO BE CLOSE TO MY APPOINTMENTS.

THAT'S WHY SHE BOOKS ME AT LA QUINTA. "

We know convenience can mean time saved and money earned for the business traveler.

That's why every La Quinta is located near business centers and major thoroughfares.

That's one reason 4 out of 5 La Quinta guests are business travelers.

They prefer La Quinta because we give them what they really want:

Comfortable, quiet rooms with color TV and phone. Same-day laundry service. Swimming pool. 24-hour coffee shop next door.

And a friendly staff that has only one thing to worry about, you, because they don't have to worry about conventions (which we don't book) or nightclubs, fancy lobbies, gift shops or other frills (which we don't have).

Because we give you everything you need, and nothing you don't, we can afford to give you lower rates. Up to 25% lower in most cases.

Business travel? Think convenience and value. Think La Quinta. Now 7,500 rooms in 17 states. And growing.

For free directory and other information, write La Quinta Marketing, Dept. B, 1625 Regal Row, Suite 170, Dallas, Texas 75247.

Toll free reservations: 800-531-5900
From Texas: 800-292-5200

Reservations guaranteed with all major credit cards.

© 1978, La Quinta Motor Inns, Inc.
Listed on American Stock Exchange (LQM).

" I LIKE TO STAY AT A PLACE WHERE THE MANAGER ONLY HAS ONE THING TO WORRY ABOUT: ME.

THAT'S WHY I STAY AT LA QUINTA. "

La Quinta managers don't have to worry about the convention crowd in banquet room C. Or whether the chateaubriand is cold and the vichyssoise hot.

They don't worry about conventions, banquets, resort facilities, fancy restaurants or any other frills because we don't specialize in these at La Quinta.

What we do have is what experienced business travelers really want:

Comfortable, clean, quiet rooms with color TV and phone. Same-day laundry service. Swimming pool. 24-hour food service nearby.

Every La Quinta is located near centers of business and transportation.

And every La Quinta is managed by a husband and wife who live on the premises and whose main concern is you.

No wonder La Quinta is able to offer lower rates—up to 25% less in most cases.

No wonder 4 out of 5 of our guests are business travelers.

La Quinta. 7,500 rooms in 17 states. And growing.

For free directory, write La Quinta Marketing, Dept. B 1625 Regal Row, Suite 170, Dallas, Texas 75247.

Toll free reservations: 800-531-5900
From Texas: 800-292-5200

Reservations guaranteed with all major credit cards.

©1978, La Quinta Motor Inns, Inc.
Listed on American Stock Exchange (LQM).

Shadze New Zealand Ltd.

EARLY IN 1980, Robert Melville, manager of Shadze New Zealand Ltd., was faced with the task of preparing the annual advertising and sales promotion plan for his company's line of sunglasses. Shadze was a division of New Zealand Optical (NZO) (itself part of a multinational company based in Switzerland) which was the largest supplier of prescription optical products in New Zealand. The Shadze division had been established in 1975 when the U.S. company, Polaroid, announced it was terminating the agreement under which NZO had imported and marketed the Polaroid line of sunglasses in favor of establishing its own organization.

For the 1980 selling season, Melville faced the challenge of maintaining unit sales of Shadze sunglasses with a promotional budget that had been cut 50 percent from the previous year. He was, therefore, concerned with how the funds could be most effectively allocated among cooperative, national or regional advertising, consumer promotion, and trade promotion.

THE NEW ZEALAND SUNGLASS MARKET

In 1980, the population of New Zealand was estimated at 3.2 million. Almost 90 percent of the population was European, primarily British, with the balance Polynesian. Population growth during the preceding five years had been negligible because of the ending of the government-sponsored immigration program and a continuing decline in the birth rate. Three-quarters of the population lived on one of the two

This case was written by Visiting Associate Professor Roger A. Strang, New York University, and Dory J. Shaw, University of Southern California. Copyright© R. A. Strang.

main islands, North Island, where the largest city, Auckland, had a population of almost one million.

The island geography of New Zealand produced a relatively equable climate, and in the warmer, northern part of the country, sunglasses could be worn throughout the year. There was also a growing interest in skiing, which helped winter demand. However, 80 percent of sunglass sales were made during the spring and summer months (September to February).

Until the 1970s, sunglasses were sold almost exclusively in chemist shops (pharmacies), and they still accounted for most of the market. Sales through pharmacies in 1979 were estimated at NZ$6.5 million, or approximately 350,000 units. The dollar volume was the same as in 1978, but unit sales had declined by 10 percent, which industry leaders attributed to unseasonable weather. Melville expected that 1980 pharmacy sunglass sales would reach 380,000 units with a retail value of over $7.5 million.

In 1980 there were 1,246 chemist shops throughout New Zealand, with at least one in each town. They were generally located on main streets or in shopping centers. Most chemist shops were independently owned by a registered pharmacist, although there were several chains. Each store was relatively small in size (approximately five thousand square feet) and was staffed by the pharmacist and two to four other employees. The chemist shop product assortment usually consisted of prescription drugs, cosmetics, toiletries, gifts, camera and photo supplies, sunglasses, and other items. Most pharmacists made their own merchandising decisions, purchasing either directly from manufacturers, from drug wholesalers, or through a buying group. The oldest established of these buying groups was the Chemist Guild, to which 90 percent of the pharmacists belonged. In the past few years, two other independent buying groups had been formed, and these were expected to grow.

Other outlets that carried sunglasses included department stores and variety chains. There were approximately 100 department stores throughout the country. The 120 variety stores belonged to two chains, Woolworths and McKenzies, which had recently merged and were expected to close a number of outlets. A limited number of lower-priced sunglasses were also sold in food stores and other outlets.

Shadze's two major competitors in the New Zealand sunglass market were Polaroid and a domestic company, Solavoid. Both companies sold high-fashion premium-quality sunglasses and therefore competed with Shadze for the same sunglass consumer, although the Solavoid product line included lower-priced glasses. In 1979, Solavoid increased its market share to 37 percent of units and 39 percent of dollar sales. Although Polaroid had been the market leader in the early

1970s, its sales were only half those of Solavoid by 1979. Both Solavoid and Polaroid had aggressive marketing programs in 1979 involving national advertising as well as trade and consumer promotions. Polaroid had the advantage of an agreement with the Chemist Guild, which meant that Polaroid products were featured in the Guild's advertising.

Solavoid and Polaroid sunglasses were also distributed primarily through chemist shops, but some moves had been made to pursue other channels of distribution. Solavoid, for example, was effectively giving the pharmacies less support by also servicing department stores, boutiques, and shoe stores.

The overall number of competitors in the New Zealand sunglass market increased in 1979, with more than thirty minor brands being distributed through pharmacies. Some of these were high-fashion glasses with European designer names. Most, however, were relatively inexpensive. They were stronger in other outlets but had also increased their share of pharmacy sales. The opinion of Shadze management, however, was that the pharmacies would not substitute these other brands for the leading brands because they were generally not supported by advertising and offered none of the services provided by the major companies.

THE DEVELOPMENT OF SHADZE

At the time the decision was made to introduce the Shadze line, New Zealand Optical had no experience in the manufacturing of sunglasses since these had all previously been supplied by Polaroid. Nevertheless, they had a strong research department, which developed contact lenses as well as regular prescription lenses. They also had access to high-quality imported frames that were not available to competitors because of import limitations. Eyeglass and most sunglass frames were not manufactured in New Zealand, and their importation, together with that of many other manufactured products, was controlled by the government under a licensing system.

Shadze was initially targeted to fifteen- to twenty-seven-year-olds in urban areas. This group was believed to be the most fashion-conscious and the most likely to adopt new brand names. They also had considerable disposable income. Shadze's short-term objectives for its new product line were to sell 75,000 units and create a fashion image for the line among the target market. Shadze's long-term objectives included a 35 percent share of the quality sunglass market, the creation of a separate marketing organization, the marketing of related items under the Shadze name, and the development of export sales (this last was important in securing additional import licenses for frames which would be required to expand sales beyond 75,000 units).

Many elements of the strategy which Shadze used in 1979 were established in the introductory year. Sales presentations were made to only a selected number of the larger pharmacies throughout the country by the New Zealand Optical staff of eight technical sales representatives who operated from three regional warehouses in the main centers of Auckland, Wellington, and Christchurch. These presentations were made during a six-week period in February–March when orders were taken for September delivery. Further calls were made in September (to ensure that the stock had arrived and was properly presented), October, November, and December. During these later calls, the representative was responsible for checking stocks, for bringing any backroom inventory forward and placing it on the Shadze display stand, and for taking orders for additional sunglasses. The pharmacist could also place orders directly with Shadze by mail or telephone. Because the primary emphasis of the sales force was on sales to optometrists, different representatives were likely to make the pharmacy calls during the year. Therefore, the strategy was to develop a loyalty to the company rather than to cultivate a relationship between the pharmacist and the sales representative.

The initial offer to the pharmacists included an attractive permanent display stand together with a preselected range of sunglasses. This was offered as a discount package, which provided a greater margin than that offered by Shadze's competitors. The Shadze line was priced in a range similar to Polaroid. Five free pairs of sunglasses were provided as an additional incentive. A training film for store employees was also prepared, emphasizing customer-salesperson interaction and suggesting ways in which the employee could assist in the customer buying decision.

The introductory advertising budget for Shadze was $32,500 or approximately 10 percent of projected sales. Most of the funds ($26,000) were spent on television with the balance spent on radio.

The Shadze introduction was successful. Four hundred chemist shops agreed to stock the line. In fact, supply problems limited the units available to 55,000. These were sold out before Christmas, and the company was forced to turn away orders.

Between 1975 and 1978 a number of changes were made in the Shadze marketing strategy. The promotional emphasis shifted from television to radio, and cooperative advertising allowances and greater in-store support were offered to the trade. The biggest boost to sales was the introduction of a new lighted merchandise display stand which attracted considerably more attention in the store than the unlighted stands provided by competitors. The product line was expanded and, by 1979, included 47 models (26 plastic, 21 metal) with 139 variants. An "Autumn Collection" was also added to increase sales during the off season and to help ensure that the Shadze stand would be used all year long to sell Shadze products. The initial supply problems were solved, and sales stabilized at around 65,000 pairs annually.

Although some units were exported, there were still problems in securing an adequate supply of frames, so a decision was made to concentrate on the high-quality segment of the market. The target market was redefined as an older, more sophisticated consumer in the twenty-to-thirty-four age group. Lower-priced models were removed from the line, and prices were raised across the board. Distribution was expanded to slightly more than four hundred pharmacies, and thereafter the sales force concentrated on servicing existing accounts rather than soliciting new ones. The company also attempted to introduce several lines under the name of well-known French fashion designers, but quality and fit problems led to these being dropped after one year.

The move to a sophisticated, fashion orientation was supported by a change in advertising theme from "Shadze—You're Looking Good" to "Shadze Eye Fashion" and "Eye Styles For Fashion Lovers." Advertising stressed European styles and designs and changed from emphasizing the casual to the sophisticated. The sunglass line was also divided into three groups—street, dress, and high fashion—with the objective of encouraging Shadze customers to own more than one pair.

A new line of display stands was introduced in 1978 which were specially designed to overcome two problems. One was the problem of dust accumulation on the racks, which was emphasized by the stand lights and detracted from the appearance of the display. The second was the scratching of lenses as customers handled various models prior to purchase. The new stand had no racks and was designed so that customers had to hold each pair of glasses by the frames (see Exhibit 1). Competitors had copied the original Shadze lighted stand in the preceding year, but it was believed that the new stand offered a significant advantage once again. As a result of the substantial investment in the stands ($60,000), it was decided to eliminate television advertising and concentrate on radio.

In this year also, Shadze management reiterated its policy of selective distribution in its trade advertising and in letters to its retailers. They pointed out that many pharmacies outside their present distribution system wanted to become Shadze stockists but stated that, "We have no intention of extending our present limited distribution network as long as we continue to receive your support."

EXHIBIT 1
Shadze 1978 Display Stands

THE 1979 PROMOTION PROGRAM

Advertising and sales promotion expenditures in 1979 were increased to $62,000 over the $55,000 (excluding the cost of the new display stand) spent in 1978 (Exhibit 2). Television advertising resumed with a new 10-second commercial. The short length of the commercial reflected a desire to limit advertising expenditures to $30,000 and to achieve relatively high frequency. The media schedule was strongly skewed toward women (women purchased three times as many pairs of sunglasses as men) in the twenty-to-thirty-four target group with all the advertising being concentrated in the pre-Christmas period. It was intended to reinforce the advertising with the header cards on the display, but there were problems in achieving acceptable production quality, and, when in place, the cards tended to warp.

The 1979 sell-in to the trade was supported by elaborate audiovisual presentations in each city as well as monthly newsletters, and a double-page advertisement in the *Pharmacy Digest* (Exhibit 3). Shadze also introduced its first trade promotion aimed at the pharmacist and store employees. The Shadze Super Summer Contest offered an overseas trip for two and other prizes to those who sold the greatest number of Shadze sunglasses in the period from October 1, 1979, to January 31, 1980 (further details are given in Exhibit 4). The contest had been supported by an unusual mailer (a coconut) to pharmacists in December. The coconut was to remind them of the contest prize and an attached note both repeated the Shadze sales message and provided a recipe for a cocktail using coconut milk. Reportedly, the arrival of the

EXHIBIT 2
Shadze 1979–1980 Communications Budget

Advertising:	
TV	
Media	$30,000
Production	8,200
Display header cards	3,400
Pharmacy Digest	
Media	1,000
Production	800
Monthly mailer	1,700
	45,100
Contest:	
Prizes	4,500
Coconut mailer	1,200
Other	3,300
	9,000
Miscellaneous:	
Stand components	5,500
Other	1,000
Postage	1,100
	7,600
Total communications budget	$61,700

Source: Company records.

EXHIBIT 3
Pharmacy Digest Advertisement

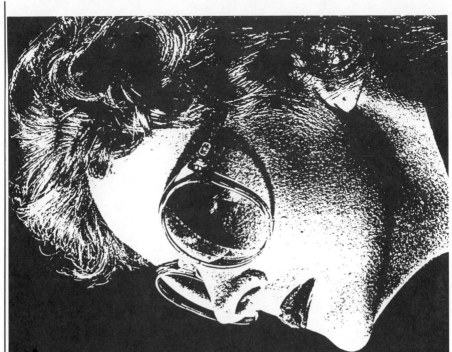

We proved it last season.
We're proving it this season.
We'll prove it again next season.

Shadze are this country's fastest-selling fashion brand of sunglasses and that means faster, surer profit for you!

Shadze select from the world market. We pick from the cream of international fashion styles. That means we can co-ordinate our range and establish frame selection on fashion from the fashion capitals.

1. **We offer a complete range of lens options** backed by optical company professionalism. Polarising lenses, CR39 solid tint, CR39 Graduatint, Cruvaara and Photochromic.

2. **Manufacturer confidence** — Shadze offer a total after sales service the like of which no other company offers.

3. **We own the sunglass fashion market**
No not puffery. It's true. As a stockist of Shadze you will know that when it comes to real fashion in sunglasses, no other company can touch us.

4. **So what's new for summer 1979-80?**
We don't want to give too much away, but the influence is Italian and colours. Dark mick plastic frames are as dead as the proverbial dodo for the new season.

5. **The Italians are coming**
They look superb. They perform superbly.
You will soon see colours and styles never before seen in New Zealand.
Guess who will bring them to you?

Who put sunglasses in pharmacy windows!
You know who. Shadze did. That's fashion.
The art of not only being first but being **right** and first.

You secure your sale at point of sale
The Shadze stand will again be the dominant one.
It stands out. It works for you. It sells Shadze fast.
And you profit fast.

We are coming soon
From the beginning of February we will be displaying the exciting SHADZE '79 range. If you wish to arrange a viewing before we contact you, please phone your Shadze distributor.

SHADZE

SHADZE

N.Z. OPTICAL (WHOLESALE) LIMITED

Quality eye-ore

365

EXHIBIT 4
1979 Trade Promotion Contest

**Win a Fantastic Holiday
For Two in
New Caledonia!**

**Share in 184
other great prizes...**

EXHIBIT 4 *(concluded)*

HERE IT IS!

HERE'S WHAT YOU CAN WIN!

OF EUROPE

SUPER SUMMER CONTEST

The biggest, brightest contest, especially for Pharmacy sales people, we've ever run.

185 prizes (and that gives your staff the biggest chance to win ever). The contest starts October 1st and runs **every month** until closing on January 31st, 1980. And every month you could win a prize!

How does the contest work?

Simple. You take your Shadze Prizecard. On it are spaces for Shadze Swing Tags to be affixed. Every time you sell a pair of Shadze to a customer, remove the swing tag and insert it on the Prizecard. When you've inserted five swing tags on the Prizecard it's completed. Put your name etc. on the card; have it signed by the manager; answer the simple question on the prizecard, and send it to us at Shadze. That's all! Your Prizecard then goes into a monthly draw which gives you a chance to win a prize. Of course we'll accept any number of completed correct Prizecards from anyone and they'll all be entered. That means the more entries you put in, the more chance you have of winning.

At the end of every month we'll take the correct entries we have received and draw out 46 Prizecards. The first entry drawn wins a Fountain Stereo; the next five drawn each win a Wella Hair Care Set; the next 40 win an L.P. Record. And that happens each month for four months. (We'll advise who the winners are each month in a special newsletter sent to every Shadze stockist.) Each winning Prizecard is put aside once you've won and held separately. So, once again, the more Prizecards you have in, the more your chance of winning.

* 160 L.P. Stero Records. You choose from our fantastic selection of Chart Topping artists.
* 20 Wella Hair Care Sets. The versatile hair dryer that lets you do it all . . . from simple drying to creative styling.
* 4 Fountain CS670 Stereos. Featuring Radio Tuner, Auto-stop Cassette Deck, 3 speed auto/manual Record Player.
* **Plus** a trip for two to New Caledonia, staying at the Nouvata Hotel. 7 days of fun in the sun with $400 spending money from Shadze. Your trip covers return air fares, transport to and from hotel and airport, plus accommodation.

And the big prize. Here's how you win that fabulous holiday.

At the end of January we will have completed the four monthly draws and 184 prizes will have been won. And that's when the big prize goes up for grabs. Into the draw for the big prize goes every monthly winning Prizecard (that's 184 of you) **plus** one entry we'll put in for every person who sent in five correctly completed Prizecards during the contest, regardless of whether or not they have already won a prize.

We'll draw from this the winner and publish the results in March Pharmacy Digest.

BONUS ENTRIES

We recognise that throughout the contest some of you will sell out of Shadze and therefore you can get bonus Prizecards entered on your behalf if you order "top up" stock. For every 5 pairs of Shadze purchased during October-January we will send a bonus prizecard to you (a different colour from the others) and all you do is fill in your name details, answer the simple question, and send it back. No swing tags on this one . . . just your name etc.

And Bonus entries go into the final draw as well, giving you an even bigger chance of winning that New Caledonian holiday.

coconut led to a number of spontaneous parties. Overall, the 1979 promotion program was viewed as successful, with more than 90 percent
of retail stocks selling through to consumers.

COMPETITIVE ACTIVITY

Both Polaroid and Solavoid allocated a large portion of their marketing
budgets to television advertising as well as radio and cooperative advertising with retailers. No information was available on the last two
items, but television advertising expenditures for the major competitive brands during the 1979–80 season were estimated as follows:

Brand	Sept.	Oct.	Nov.	Dec.	Jan.	Feb.	Total
Solavoid	$—	12,108	16,180	9,522	—	—	$37,810
Polaroid	$735	14,543	10,156	6,601	—	—	$32,035

Polaroid conducted joint advertising with the Chemist Guild. The
television time purchased under this scheme was estimated as follows:

	Sept.	Oct.	Nov.	Dec.	Jan.	Feb.	Total
Chemist Guild TV expenditure	$183,177	195,677	49,440	62,227	41,343	37,502	$506,366
Estimated Polaroid share $	—	40,000	15,000	10,000	10,000	—	$ 75,000

Solavoid, on the other hand, also undertook a national radio consumers campaign. No estimates of their radio advertising expenditures
were available, but it was known that national radio coverage cost
approximately $5,000 weekly to achieve acceptable reach and fre-
quency. There were rumors that Solavoid was also going to join with
the Chemist Guild in 1980 and substantially increase its advertising
expenditures.

Solavoid's 1979 promotional theme was "optically correct fashion
glasses." Solavoid introduced a new line of sunglasses in 1979 called
Parasol and distributed it through clothing boutiques and shoe stores.
The Solavoid line, including Parasol, used predominantly plastic
frames. Solavoid was unable to produce as full a line of fashion shapes
or colors as Shadze. Much of Solavoid's carryover stock from 1978 was
being heavily discounted through department stores.

Polaroid had also introduced a second product line in 1979
named after the British designer David Hartnell. The line was reasonably successful, but sales were less than expected as a result of prob-

lems with the shapes of the eyepieces. Polaroid also introduced nonpolarizing lenses to the New Zealand market in 1979.

Despite the disappointing sales of the David Hartnell line, Polaroid recovered a significant share of the market in 1979. However, rumors were being spread among the trade that Polaroid headquarters planned to reduce its support for the New Zealand market. The Polaroid sales force was expected to shrink in size, and the salespeople were expected to split their time between both sunglass and photographic products.

Solavoid introduced the first consumer promotion in the industry in 1979 when they offered a "champagne breakfast in Sydney" (airfares plus accommodation for two nights) as the major prize in a consumer sweepstakes. All entrants who sent in product tags were offered a cosmetic item or cigars. Shadze management estimated the cost of this promotion at $8,000. The number of entries was not known.

In addition to consumer promotions, both Polaroid and Solavoid held trade contests. More than 1,000 pharmacy sales staff entered the Solavoid contest, "Holiday in the Sun," which offered holiday prizes in Rarotonga, Honolulu, and the United States. Like the Shadze contest, entries were not accepted after the end of January. Solavoid also held a Spring Promotion dealer contest and took a four-page spread in the trade magazine, *Pharmacy Digest,* to introduce its new line.

Polaroid and Solavoid did not follow a policy of selective distribution and, as a result, according to Melville, had a harder time selling to their accounts. This was due, in part, to the lower retail margins provided by these brands. In addition, these companies often had a carryover of stock from one year to the next, whereas the Shadze line had actually sold out for the last two years. A number of pharmacists also objected to the fact that both Polaroid and Solavoid had sold their products to other types of outlets, such as department stores.

THE 1980 PROMOTION PROGRAM FOR SHADZE

Shadze's objectives for 1980–81 were to obtain 50 percent of sunglass sales among all present stockists. The total sales target for 1980–81 was 68,300 allocated by region as follows:

Region	Units	Number of Shadze Stocklists
Auckland	28,700	185
Wellington	19,100	130
Christchurch	20,500	135
Total	68,300	450

The number of models offered for sale in 1980 was increased slightly to 49, but the total number of variants dropped from 139 to 122. It was proposed that substantial price increases be taken in the coming year with an average retail price of $23 and some exclusive imported models selling for over $70. (Shadze prices were structured so that each pair sold contributed $4 to advertising, sales promotion, and profit.) In order to maintain the pharmacists' support, it was suggested that New Zealand Optical improve the payment terms available on the package deals (Exhibit 5).

As he began to prepare his promotional program for the year ahead, Melville was faced with the task of trying to achieve the objectives with a budget which had been reduced to $30,000. Since no new display stands were required, all of these funds were available for advertising and various types of promotional activity. However, Melville was aware that Solavoid would be further increasing advertising and promotional activities in the coming year and that Polaroid, although reducing its sales force, would likely expand its program with the Chemist Guild in order not to lose sales.

Melville had before him a report from the Shadze advertising

EXHIBIT 5
1980 Package Purchase Deals Offered to Buyers

	Package A	Package B
Metal sunglasses:		
Models	22	21
Variants	62	54
Units	100	62
Plastic sunglasses:		
Models	27	24
Variants	60	36
Units	60	36
Total units	160	98
Recommended retail selling price	$3,525.00	$2,152.00
Standard cost price	2,350.00	1,435.00
Prompt payment discount[a]	250.00	60.00
Total receipts	2,100.00	1,375.00
Profit	$1,425.00	$ 777.00
Margin	40%	36%

Source: Company records.

[a]Discount applicable if payment received prior to 20th of month following delivery.

agency arguing for a television campaign. The first reason was that sunglasses were a highly visual product and accordingly should be promoted on television. Second, agency executives believed that television provided authority with the consumer and the trade. Finally, they argued that television "offers sound and picture to create mood and clearly defined product positioning." The costs for television commercial time are given in Exhibit 6.

However, the national television campaign proposed by the agency was significantly beyond the allotted budget. It was possible, though, to structure a television campaign covering the Auckland re-

EXHIBIT 6
Shadze Projected Media Costs, 1980

Television Network	Time Period	10-Second Rate	Average Audience (000) Male and Female (20–34)	Male and Female Weighted[a]	Cost per Thousand Male and Female	Weighted
One	6–10 P.M.	$1,000	175	180	$5.71	$5.56
	10–close	400	90	87	4.44	4.60
Two	6–10 P.M.	840	135	135	6.22	6.22
	10–close	330	75	70	4.40	4.71

Magazine	Cost (full-page 4-column)	Readership (000) Male and Female (20–34)	Male and Female Weighted[a]	Cost per Thousand Male and Female	Weighted
New Zealand Women's Weekly	$2,000	260	290	$7.69	$6.90
New Zealand Listener	2,450	350	358	7.03	6.84

Source: Company records.

Notes:

(1) Total New Zealand population twenty–thirty-four estimated at 800,000 in 1980.

(2) Virtually all households had television sets, but Network Two reached only 70 percent of the population.

[a]Weighted in favor of females as against males on a ratio of 3:1.

gion only. Such a campaign would reach 49 percent of the total New Zealand population which accounted for approximately 51 percent of 1979–80 sales. Further cost cutting could be accomplished through the repeat use of the 1979–80 commercial (Exhibit 7). Alternatively, this commercial could be updated at a cost of $1,185. The agency felt that the commercial had not been overexposed, would not evoke negative responses by being rescreened, and would stimulate favorable recall.

However, Melville was aware that some New Zealand Optical executives were skeptical as to the value of television advertising in promoting sales of a particular brand of sunglasses. Their view was that any television advertising merely reminded consumers of the need to buy sunglasses and encouraged them to go to the store to buy a pair. The decision on which brand to purchase was made once they were in the store from among the range on display. Even if Shadze was advertised, its relative impact would be much less than that of Solavoid and Polaroid given the limited funds available and the selective distribution strategy. Melville was also concerned that mass advertising might actually harm the image of Shadze as the quality leader.

Radio advertising was suggested by the advertising agency as a compromise. Shadze had run some commercials during the introductory campaign in 1975 and again in 1978. However, these advertisements were withdrawn due to management fear of a negative consumer reaction. It was later learned that consumers in fact liked the commercial, and many displayed positive recall long after a single exposure. Melville knew that these advertisements could be revived. However, he remembered the earlier problems associated with an uncoordinated marketing effort and was not sure if the old advertisements were consistent with the new "sun sculptures" theme. They were originally produced with the objective of name and product recognition. If a new radio advertisement needed to be produced, there would be associated production costs. Yet radio was considered an effective medium with which to reach the target audience. Moreover, individual pharmacists were often willing to pay for the radio air time if they were provided with the Shadze tape and could plug their store at the end.

Shadze had never used print advertising to consumers. However, a number of magazines were available including national editions of *Time, Newsweek,* and *Readers Digest,* as well as the *New Zealand Women's Weekly* (which reached more than 30 percent of the households), and other women's publications. Another weekly magazine with a significant penetration of middle- and upper-income households was the *New Zealand Listener,* which featured articles and commentary along with program guides for radio and television. Both the *Women's Weekly* and the *Listener* were offset printed on newsprint

EXHIBIT 7
1979 Television Commercial

Client: Shadze N.Z. Limited   Length: 10-second TV commercial

Video	*Audio*
Open on typical Mediterranean scene with pavement cafe tables in foreground right on the water front with luxury yachts and glistening blue water.	Shadze music track throughout. Male voice over at end.
A casual but fashionable French-looking man is seated at a table with an aperitif on the table. There are bread sticks in a glass, toothpicks, a wine bottle with a candle in it, a packet of Galoise cigarettes. He is wearing Shadze.	
As he looks around to view the yachts, one of them swings gently round on its mooring to reveal a beautiful young lady sunning herself on the deck. She is wearing a thong swimsuit and her Shadze.	
The camera zooms in to her smiling as she lifts her Shadze.	
Cut to view of table. The man has gone. On the table are a few coins, a cigarette burns in the ash tray, his drink unfinished on the table. A waiter stands with disbelief on his face with a tray of food in his hand.	
Cut to see the man casually standing on the yacht by the girl. She smiles up through her Shadze.	Shadze of Europe. The Continentals wear little else.
Super Shadze logo.	

Source: Company records.

373

which allowed the use of color but not the same quality reproduction as a glossy magazine. However, Melville believed that print media would allow the reader more time to absorb the fashion message and could extend the reach of any broadcast campaign. Magazine advertising costs are given in Exhibit 6.

One way to increase the funds available for advertising was to reduce the retailers' margin on the package purchase deals. However, because of the increasingly competitive nature of the industry, Melville believed that it was essential not to lose trade support for Shadze. The trade competition held in 1979–1980 was very popular and proved very effective in helping Shadze achieve its sales objectives. Melville did not want to run an identical competition but, rather, some variation which related to the sun sculptures theme. Melville thought that leather wallet/billfolds might be used as secondary prizes with a trip as the main prize. If he chose to repeat the competition, Melville would have to set aside $7,000 for contest prizes and supporting materials.

However, contests were difficult to execute and time-consuming, and any complications could lead to a loss of goodwill. Also, Melville was not sure whether such competitions produced any long-term trade loyalty or just short-term enthusiasm. Another concern was that the contest might reduce the funds available for point-of-sale material. If competitors repeated their contests, Shadze "might have to put as much effort into promoting its contest as into promoting its sunglasses."

Both Polaroid and Solavoid advertised in the *Pharmacy Digest*. To remain competitive, Melville thought that Shadze should be represented in the *Pharmacy Digest* as well. It would cost approximately $850 for the development of new magazine advertisements, plus $1,000 in media costs for each insertion.

Due to the change in theme, new header cards also had to be produced. Mr. Melville, in conjunction with the advertising agency, determined that three versions of the cards would be required—one promoting the Shadze Sun Sculptures theme, one promoting the chemically hardened lens concept, and one highlighting the polarizing lens. It would cost $3,000 for sufficient cards to equip all display stands.

Another possibility was to run some type of consumer promotion. There was little enthusiasm for a price-oriented promotion since it was felt that this would harm the Shadze image. However, a contest or sweepstakes which would force the consumer to visit the Shadze stockist in order to enter was a possibility. Again, the major prize could be a holiday for two in an overseas resort which would relate to the sun sculptures theme. The cost of prizes, entry forms, and advertising was estimated at $13,000. Alternatively, the company could offer a gift with purchase such as an attractive carrying case. These were available with the Shadze name printed on them in a vinyl material with a drawstring top for 80 cents each when ordered in quantities of 5,000 or more.

Honeywell, Inc.: Spectronics Division

IN EARLY NOVEMBER 1980, Mr. Gary Null, marketing manager for Fiber Optics, scheduled a meeting with members of his management team to discuss the promotion program prepared by the division's advertising agency. The program represented the first comprehensive advertising, sales-promotion, and publicity campaign for the line of fiber optics products manufactured by the Spectronics Division of Honeywell, Inc.

The consensus of Mr. Null's team was that the proposed campaign was thorough and exciting. Nevertheless, Mr. Null realized that the campaign would have to be approved by top management. Therefore, in the memo addressed to his management team, he outlined the topics to be addressed:

1. Should we adopt the 1981 promotion campaign as presented to us?

2. If yes, how can we justify it, and at what expenditure level?

3. If no, what changes, if any, might we make in the program?

This case was made possible through the cooperation of the Spectronics Division of Honeywell, Inc. The case was prepared by Professor Roger A. Kerin and Angela Schuetze, graduate student, Edwin L. Cox School of Business, Southern Methodist University, Dallas, as a basis for class discussion rather than for illustration of appropriate or inappropriate handling of administrative situations. Certain information is disguised and not useful for research purposes.

In addition, he asked each member of the group to prepare written arguments to support the position favored.

THE FIBER OPTICS INDUSTRY: FALL 1980

The concept of fiber optics can be traced to the nineteenth century, when an English physicist demonstrated that light can be transmitted through a stream of water by internal reflection. Years later others observed that two optically dissimilar materials could be assembled to form a fiber that would transmit light. Research on optical fibers continued through the mid-twentieth century, when such other transparent fibers as glass and plastic were found to be superior conductors of light.

Although technologically complex, fiber optics can be described as the technique of transmitting light through long, thin, flexible fibers of glass, plastic, or other transparent materials. When used in a commercial application, a light source emits infrared light flashes corresponding to data. Millions of light flashes per second send streams of light through a transparent fiber. Due to a mirror effect, the fiber accelerates the movement of light. A light sensor at the other end of the fiber "reads" the data transmitted.

Fiber optic technology has been heralded as a replacement for copper wires as a means for transmitting data. Four major benefits of optical fibers over copper wire have been cited. First, they save space since optical fibers can carry more information than copper wire. Second, optical fibers do not create magnetic fields and are immune to electromagnetic fields. Third, optical fibers do not conduct electricity and thus can be used when electrical cables would be hazardous. Finally, optical fibers are small and lightweight relative to copper wire. These benefits prompted scientists to proclaim that fiber optic technology would replace copper wire in the second half of the twentieth century, and a new industry developed.

Fiber Optic Components and Systems

Fiber optic products are divided into two categories: fiber optic components and fiber optic systems. Components are the individual products necessary to emit, transmit, and detect light. There are five types of components: emitter or transmitter, fiber or cable, detector or receiver, connector, and coupler. An *emitter* is a light source. A *detector* receives the light sent by the emitter. The *fiber* or *optical cable* is a glass fiber through which light is transmitted from the emitter to the detector. A *connector* acts as a link between the emitter and detector and the optical cable. *Couplers* enable a large number of emitters and detectors to be joined into a single optical connector. When several components are assembled to form a complete, self-contained unit capable of data transmission, a fiber optic system exists.

Market for Fiber Optic Technology

The market for fiber optic technology is in its infancy. Although estimates vary, most industry forecasters believe the sales of fiber optic components and systems will exceed $100 million in 1981 and reach $1.9 billion by 1990.

The application of fiber optic technology varies by end users and by type of component. Gnostic Concepts, Inc., a major electronics research firm, made the volume estimates by user segment and component type shown in Exhibits 1 and 2.

Competitive Activity

The appeal of fiber optics technology has attracted a host of firms involved in various applications, and numerous firms have entered the

EXHIBIT 1
U.S. Fiber Optic Component Consumption by Application

Application	1981	1986	1990
Telecommunications (including telephone)	34%	38%	43%
Adjustments	27	21	19
Government/military	25	27	22
Automotive	—	—	1
Business/retail	1	2	2
Instruments	1	1	1
Satellite earth	1	1	1
Industrial	3	4	4
Cable TV	5	3	2
Computer	3	3	3
Total ($ millions)	$135	$814	$1,868

Source: Gnostic Concepts, Inc., Menlo Park, California. Printed with permission.

Note: "Adjustments" include U.S.-manufactured conponents and systems not used in U.S. equipment, minus imported parts—that is, the trade balance (exports minus imports) plus inventory change plus nonproduction use. Nonproduction uses include replacement parts, scrappage, parts for R&D and other nonproduction uses. The concept of adjustment is important in order to reconcile U.S. application requirements and U.S. production.

EXHIBIT 2
U.S. Fiber Optic Production by Component Type

Component type	1981	1986	1990
Cable	57%	53%	60%
Transmitter, receiver, repeater	38	37	30
Connector, coupler	5	10	10
Total ($ millions)	$135	$814	$1,868

Source: Gnostic Concepts, Inc., Menlo Park, California. Printed with permission.

Note: A "repeater" is a regenerative component that allows the restoration of signal after degradation due to transmission over an optical cable. Repeaters are most frequently used in medium to long cables.

Virtually all cable production is devoted to telecommunications, cable TV, and satellite earth applications.

industry as component and system suppliers. Corning Glass Works, ITT, and AT&T's Western Electric division represent major manufacturers of fiber optic cable for use in telecommunications. General Electric, AMP, Motorola, and Amphenol North America represent major firms pursuing the fiber optic component and system market. In addition, selected computer manufacturers such as IBM, DEC, and Sperry-Univac are developing fiber optic technology. Overall, competitive activity is great as the fiber optic industry evolves. The various competitors are each seeking a technological advantage while actively seeking to stimulate volume through marketing efforts. Cost considerations also loom as a critical determinant of competitive activity. Although costs vary between component and system suppliers, gross margins in the industry fall in the range of 25 to 30 percent.

SPECTRONICS DIVISION

Spectronics is a division of Honeywell, Inc., a Minneapolis, Minnesota–based *Fortune 500* company. Honeywell, Inc., is a high-technology company engaged in a variety of businesses that produce computers and controls for information processing, energy management, environmental control, industrial processes, and aerospace and defense. Honeywell, Inc., revenues in 1979 were $4.2 billion; operating profit was $478.1 million.

Spectronics is engaged in the business of optoelectronics. Optoelectronics is a branch of electronics that deals with solid-state and other electronic devices for generating, modulating, transmitting, and sensing electromagnetic radiation in ultraviolet, visible-light, and in-

frared portions of the light spectrum. Products produced by Spectronics include light-emitting and light-sensing devices, optical
switches, fiber optic devices, and a variety of optic data-transmission
ports and components for use in computers, office equipment, automobiles, and aircraft systems. Spectronics was acquired by Honeywell,
Inc., in August 1978. Spectronics's total product sales prior to the acquisition exceeded $11 million.

Sales and Marketing Efforts

Spectronics markets its full line of products through its own sales force
and selected distributors. International sales are handled through the
international sales offices of Honeywell, Inc. "The use of the term *sales*
is sort of a misnomer," said Mr. Null. "Our people are actually prob-
lemsolvers in the truest sense. The majority of our sales volume arises
from custom optoelectronic components, assemblies, and systems to
meet exact customer requirements." He continued:

> We work closely with design engineers, and virtually all of our sales and
> advertising effort is directed toward this audience. We advertise in tech-
> nical publications and try to communicate state-of-the-art applications
> of optoelectronics. I'd say the total advertising budget for Spectronics is
> modest, and a good share of that goes to updating product catalogs and
> other product-related information.

Mr. Null added, "Design engineers play an instrumental role in developing technical specifications for optoelectronic devices. Although
they do not necessarily make the final decision on the type and source
of these devices, their views carry considerable weight, given the nature of the technology. But fiber optics is different. Optoelectronics is a
mature technology; fiber optics is an emerging technology. Our sales
and advertising effort may have to be modified."

Fiber Optics

Spectronics had been developing fiber optics data-transmission systems for more than six years prior to its acquisition by Honeywell, Inc.
Principal efforts during this developmental period had focused on applying the division's engineering skills to special applications of fiber
optics for use in the military. Spectronics's largest Department of Defense contract for fiber optics was a $2.1 million Army contract for
light-emitting diode (LED) modules for forward-looking infrared systems. Secondary emphasis was placed on custom applications of fiber
optics for commercial use.
     Present product-development efforts have focused on short- to

medium-distance applications (under two miles) of fiber optics technology for local area networking in the computer industry. A "local network" is a data communications system for connecting terminals and computers that are within one building, in several buildings on the same property, or in close proximity, as opposed to long-haul networks for public switching networks such as telephone lines. However, Spectronics's products also have industrial applications and can be used in the instrumentation industry.

In May 1980 Spectronics, in conjunction with Du Pont and ITT Cannon, announced a point-to-point data link called the HDC Interface. This link is suitable for short-range data transmission between computers and uses Spectronics source and detector pairs, Du Pont plastic core cables, and electrical connectors from ITT Cannon. The HDC Interface link is shown in Exhibit 3. By late 1980 Spectronics's line of fiber optic products included fiber optic connectors, transmitters, receivers, and couplers among other fiber optic assemblies and systems.

Success in product development prompted Mr. Null to give increased attention to the marketing aspects of fiber optics. Mr. Null noted:

> Fiber optics will take us into new markets and require us to deal with different people than we have in the past. Our present customers in the computer and instrumentation markets and industrial users should be

EXHIBIT 3
HDC Interface link

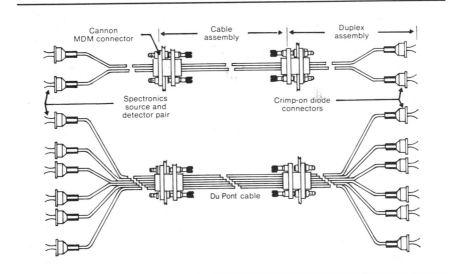

receptive to the fiber optic technology. But fiber optics will necessitate expanding into new segments of each market, such as robotics in the industrial segment. Our people who are now responsible for our other optoelectronic products will have to come up with a new customer list and develop contacts.

After talking with top management, he was given approval to commission the division's advertising agency to prepare a comprehensive promotion program for fiber optics. The next section describes the campaign recommended to Mr. Null in late October 1980.

1981 PROMOTION CAMPAIGN[a]

The proposed campaign consists of two complementary components: (1) Fiber Optics Corporate Campaign and (2) Fiber Optics Product Campaign.

Fiber Optics Corporate Campaign

Situation Analysis and Corporate Campaign
The present fiber optics market is characterized by a healthy amount of activity by a variety of participants, yet no company has forged ahead to establish itself as the industry leader. For this reason, the market appears to be primed for just such a campaign as we are proposing. The number-one "leader" position is there for the taking. It is important to note that although there are few companies that have the technology and the commitment of resources to that technology that Honeywell/Spectronics does, the leader position is open only until someone claims it.

The target firms in this campaign are North American computer and control system original equipment manufacturers (OEM). The targeted audiences in order of priority are: (a) operating management, (b) engineering management, and (c) design engineers.

The objectives for the campaign are: (1) to build a leadership identity and reputation in fiber optics for Honeywell/Spectronics; (2) to promote "currency" of fiber optics as a "today" production technology; (3) to generate awareness of affordability, ease of use, and availability of fiber optics; and (4) to further solidify perception of Honeywell/Spectronics as a single entity.

---

[a]This section is a highly condensed version of the program actually presented. However, the main points of the campaign are reported in their entirety. Selected creative work has been omitted because of space limitations.

Campaign Strategy

Approaches to leadership promotion vary greatly according to the taste, style, and resources of the advertiser. The most obvious and least effective is often the unabashed "We're Number One" technique. Very closely aligned is the product-comparison technique, which usually sacrifices impact and communicates a more subtle "We're Number One." A more prestigious approach is what we call the "Speaking for the Industry" approach. The formula is simple. By generating above-par awareness through higher-impact advertising, the market size can be increased, and Honeywell/Spectronics's market share will increase accordingly. The company with the technology and production capacity to best satisfy the market derives the greatest benefit. As Honeywell/Spectronics's marketing efforts stimulate the market, the same marketing efforts do double duty in generating awareness of Honeywell/Spectronics as the most capable fiber optics supplier. Thus our recommendations drive a program that requires promotion of fiber optics, rather than promoting our products against those of competitors.

Media Effort

The media effort will concentrate on carefully chosen publications.

Targets Target audiences fall into four subcategories, as follows:

1. *Primary target audience—operating management:* Direct advertising impressions toward managerial/administrative professionals throughout the industrial community to establish awareness of fiber optics in general and Honeywell/Spectronics in particular. Communication with these decision makers is an important support to the sales effort.

2. *Secondary target audience—engineering:* Direct advertising impressions toward engineers within the computer and control/instrumentation systems industry who are responsible for the design and specification of equipment and devices. Emphasize coverage of those engineers within the engineering management and procurement committee areas.

3. *Geographic target audience:* Advertise nationally with primary emphasis on centers of electronic activity.

4. *Seasonal targets:* Schedule advertising for maximum weight and impact to begin the campaign. Thereafter, schedule for consistent exposure throughout the year.

Media strategy To achieve the media objectives, we recommend the following strategy: Advertise in print media for a more detailed explanation of Honeywell/Spectronics's message and the most comprehensive and cost-effective coverage of the target audience.

1. Utilize business and industry trade magazines: (1) Targeted by title/function to the industry management professional or design engineer, (2) edited to be of business interest to their readers, (3) providing coverage of the target in the total United States, and (4) covering the target in the computer and controls environment conducive to the positive communication of our message.

2. Be flexible in scheduling execution to take advantage of all communication opportunities (i.e., special sections/editorial emphasis on fiber optics in selected publications).

3. Utilize two-page-spread ads in four colors for maximum impact and effectiveness.

Media recommendations and cost The publications recommended in Exhibit 4 were selected on the basis of their (1) impact in the marketplace, (2) total coverage of the target audience, (3) editorial quality and compatibility (value to reader), and (4) media efficiency.

The recommended media/insertion/cost schedule is shown in Exhibit 5. Also shown is an alternative lower-cost schedule.

Publicity and Sales Promotion

Publicity and sales promotion have been neglected by the fiber optics industry.

Objectives and Audience The objectives of publicity and sales promotion are (1) to position fiber optics as being a current or "now" technology and (2) to position Honeywell/Spectronics as the leader of the fiber optic industry. The primary audience for publicity and sales promotion efforts includes (1) engineering management, (2) design management, and (3) design engineers. The secondary audience for these efforts includes (1) the business community and (2) the general public.

Publicity Effort Fiber optics has not received the level of media exposure normally accorded a developing technology with such current and potential scope, particularly within business and mass media. The lack of coverage seems largely due to an inadequate flow of information from the companies involved in fiber optic research. In order to provide media with sufficient information to maximize Spectronics's

EXHIBIT 4
Recommended Publications for Corporate Campaign

Business Week/Industrial is an edition for subscribers in industry, specifically those employed in manufacturing as well as mining, construction, transportation, communications, and utilities. The 350,000 paid circulation is the largest available to us. Published weekly, *Business Week* earned and enjoys a unique leadership role as "the" weekly consumer business magazine.

Industry Week is published on alternate Mondays for the management (both corporate and operations) of industrial firms. *IW* reaches every industrial firm in the United States with 100+ employees. This circulation is also qualified by management function and company size.

Control Engineering is published monthly for engineers who design, develop, and apply control and instrumentation systems. Editorial is technical, informing control engineers of automatic control and data-handling systems through the practical application of new instrumentation and analytical and systems-design techniques. Special attention is given the processing industry, machinery, and manufacturing, with emphasis on exchange of information between industries. *CE* is considered the leading publication serving the control and instrumentation systems market. *CE* should be considered the basic media vehicle for this market.

Computer Design is published monthly for the digital electronics markets. Editorial is devoted to designers of digital equipment and systems. Circulation covers design engineers and engineering management throughout the total electronics OEM—circuits, components, computer equipment, subsystems, computer-based systems, and computers. We feel *CD* should be a basic buy for coverage of our target in the computer area.

EDN is published semimonthly for specifying designers of electronic products, equipment, and systems. Qualified recipients are engineers and engineering management in the electronics OEM. Editorial is technical and in depth. *EDN* offers the most efficient coverage of our basic target engineer.

Electronic Design is published bimonthly for the traditional EOEM design engineer and engineering management. Editorial covers new technology and products. *ED* provides the largest total EOEM, engineering, and engineering management circulation of candidate publications.

Electronics Products Magazine is published monthly and reports on new products, systems, and subassemblies for specifiers of electronic products in the EOEM. In terms of circulation, *EPM* resembles *ED* and *EDN*.

Electronics is published on alternate Thursdays for manufacturers and users of electronic products and equipment worldwide. *Electronics* reports and interprets new industry development/technological changes in electronics. *Electronics* is recognized as the leading publication in this field and is recommended as a basic vehicle.

(continued)

EXHIBIT 4 (*continued*)

Machine Design is published on alternate Thursdays for individuals
  performing a design engineering function. Technical editorial covers the
  following: (a) design and development; (b) current news; (c) design
  problem-solving ideas; (d) personal, professional, and management
  information; and (e) new product announcements. *MD* is the
  acknowledged leader in the product design engineering field in both
  circulation and editorial coverage. *MD* has a full-time electronics editor
  and includes an electronics feature section in each issue. *MD* has the
  greatest share of total, electronics, and exclusive advertisers of the design
  engineering publications.

Design Engineering is a technical magazine published monthly for engineers
  engaged in the design and development of products for resale and
  specialized in-plant equipment. Editorial covers (a) research and
  technology; (b) electrical/electronic power and control; (c) fluid power and
  control; (d) mechanical design and power transmission; and (e) materials
  and manufacturing. Due to the cost efficiency, *DE* would effectively add
  impact. However, it should not be considered as a replacement for *MD*
  or *DN*.

---

position, the recommended public relations program focuses on (1)
media symposia, (2) feature stories, and (3) trade shows.

1. *Media symposia:* In order to gain immediate, widespread exposure for fiber optics and Honeywell/Spectronics, the public relations program begins with a series of four media symposia across the
country. Various aspects of fiber optics technology will be addressed
by company spokesmen as well as by invited experts. The agency recommends a division of invited guests and company spokesmen between audiences comprised of: (1) technical news and trade writers
and (2) those associated with general or business news. An exhibit of
items utilizing fiber optics should be developed to serve as examples of
the technology.

2. *Feature development:* Through the symposia, Honeywell/
Spectronics will have created its own informed and receptive media
audience. This audience should not be left with only the remembrance
of its learning experience. Thus, the agency will develop an ongoing
program of feature stories. These will be for placement in trade, business, and general mass media publications.

3. *Trade shows:* In keeping with the leadership positioning, Hon-
eywell/Spectronics will design its own high-quality exhibit for trade

EXHIBIT 5
Media/Insertion/Cost Schedules

Recommended Media/Cost Schedule

Publication	One-Time Cost (1981 est.)	Number of Insertions	Total Cost
Business Week/			
Industrial	$31,648	13	$411,424
Control Engineering	5,500	12	66,000
Computer Design	6,465	10	64,650
Electronics	7,073	10	70,730
Machine Design	9,396	10	93,960
Total		55	$706,764

Alternative Media/Cost Schedule

Publication	One-Time Cost (1981 est.)	Number of Insertions	Total Cost
Industry Week	$17,472	13	$227,136
Control Engineering	5,500	12	66,000
Computer Design	6,465	10	64,650
Electronics	7,073	10	70,730
Total		45	$428,516

shows. The exhibit does not need to be large, nor does it need to alter the current exhibit policy.

A special effort will be made to gain editorial attention during major trade shows. A press kit will be developed for and distributed to the media attending each show. The agency will serve as press contact, inviting media to visit the Spectronics exhibit and arranging interviews with Spectronics spokesmen. A simple, low-cost card included in each kit will allow media to ask for information on Honeywell/Spectronics by requesting all subsequent news releases or by detailing the kinds of data that would most benefit the individual writer.

Seal Program Promotion   As the computer and control OEM industries are analyzed for sales promotion opportunities, the greatest area of opportunity rests in the marketing rather than in the engineering and specification ends of their businesses. These businesses sell their products largely on the basis of technology and benefits. The marketing of fiber optics as a value-added feature of their products would serve to promote the currency of fiber optics for these user systems.

The first step in the development of fiber optics as an OEM merchandising tool is the production of promotional vehicles available to the computer and control systems manufacturers. To this end, the agency recommends the formation of a "Fiber Optics Quality Seal." The first pass at an execution of this seal may be: "WE'VE SEEN THE LIGHT." Everything from camera-ready logo art to literature and lapel buttons could be provided to the manufacturer free or on a very low-cost basis. Exhibit 6 shows the logo/seal. Marketing of the merchandising program should, from that point forward, be an integral part of the Spectronics sales call, supported by explanatory literature and examples of other participating manufacturers.

EXHIBIT 6
Fiber Optics Quality Seal

EXHIBIT 7
Two-Page Print Advertisement

EXHIBIT 8
Two-Page Print Advertisement

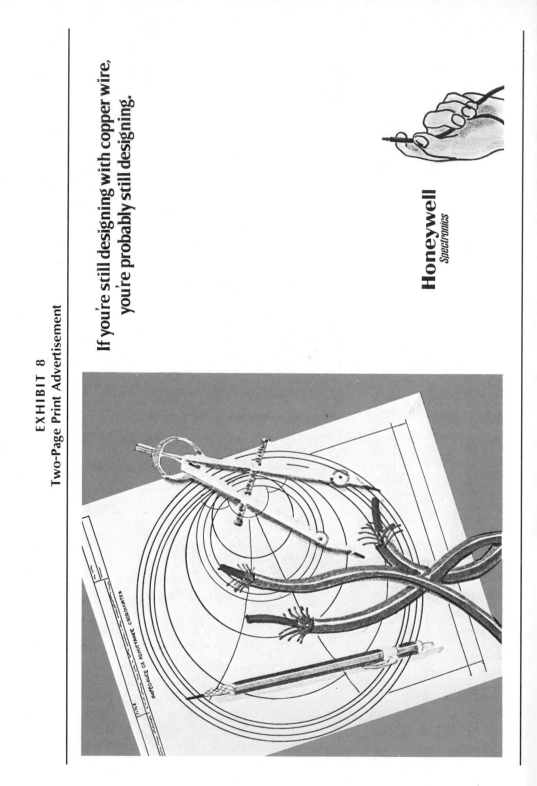

If you're still designing with copper wire, you're probably still designing.

Honeywell
Spectronics

The fee for publicity and sales promotion efforts is $63,000, which includes the out-of-pocket costs for trade shows, the four media symposia, and the seal program promotion.

Creative Directions
Creative materials will concentrate on promoting a leadership image.

Media Advertising Four-color print advertisements have been chosen to portray the leadership look. The quality and assertiveness of the advertisements will speak for the resources and commitment of a leader. The first-year campaign will promote the use of fiber optics over copper wire. The first ad will dramatically announce that the era of the old technology is over. Subsequent ads will position Honeywell/ Spectronics as the leader of the new technology and make the reader aware that fiber optics is here now, affordable, and practical. A dramatic visual will arrest the reader. Further reading will be provoked by headline techniques that tease the reader's intelligence. Body copy will play off the headline, visual, and "leader identity." Sample print advertisements (without copy) are shown in Exhibits 7 and 8.

Collateral Materials The agency will design and develop an eight-page four-color brochure. The quality of the literature will attest to the resources and commitment required of a leader. The literature will be impactful, concise, and informative. The brochure will be used in addition to available technical literature, not as a replacement.

Budget
The fiber optics corporate campaign budget is shown in Exhibit 9. The budget shows the alternative media spending levels in the context of the overall campaign.

EXHIBIT 9
Fiber Optics Corporate Campaign Budgets

	Alternative A	Alternative B
Media	$706,764	$428,516
Public relations/sales promotion	63,000	63,000
Creative		
Media advertising	40,000	40,000
Collateral advertising	30,000	30,000
Agency fee	12,000	12,000
Total	$851,764	$573,516

Fiber Optics Product Campaign

Objectives
The objectives of the product campaign are:

1. To increase top-of-mind awareness of Spectronics as a supplier of a full line of fiber optic products.

2. To support Spectronics leadership position promoted in the Honeywell campaign.

Strategy
Use four-color full-page ads in selected trade publications to speak directly to the design engineer. Each ad will be accompanied by an additional black-and-white one-third vertical page listing distribu-

EXHIBIT 10
Product Campaign Budget

Recommended Media/Cost Schedule

Publication	One-Time Cost	#Insertions	Total Cost
Electronics	$4,869	4	$ 19,476
Control Engineering	4,925	5	24,625
Computer Design	4,605	6	27,630
Electronic Design	4,440	5	22,200
EDN	4,305	6	25,830
Electronic Products Magazine	3,960	4	15,840
Total		30	$135,601

Alternative Media/Cost Schedule

Publication	One-Time Cost	# Insertions	Total Cost
Electronics	$4,869	3	$ 14,607
Control Engineering	4,925	3	14,775
Computer Design	4,605	4	18,420
Electronic Design	4,440	3	13,320
EDN	4,305	4	17,220
Electronic Products Magazine	3,960	2	7,920
Total		19	$ 86,262

tors and their telephone numbers. One ad will feature simplicity and ease of use, and the other ad will promote Spectronics's full line capabilities.

These executions will complement the Honeywell program both by gaining from its heavy exposure and, in turn, by providing an added depth targeted to the design engineer. The product campaign is designed to complement the corporate campaign and will run in parallel with it.

Media and Budget

The media chosen are more technical in orientation and thus complement the copy of the advertisements. The media and expenditure levels are slightly higher than what is now practiced. A recommended and alternative media budget is shown in Exhibit 10.

Liquid Paper Corporation

IN MARCH 1980 Ms. Susan Jackson was appointed product manager for Liquid Paper Corporation's line of typewriter ribbons and correction tapes. Upon assuming this position, she was asked to review a number of proposed marketing programs and to select from among them to develop a comprehensive advertising and sales-promotion program for the second half of the year. Time was of the essence. Although sales had been showing satisfactory growth, some production and quality problems in the latter part of 1979 had caused the program to lose momentum. Now, with these problems rectified, it was important to reenergize the sales and marketing effort. Her charge was to assess the various options available and to implement those that would allow the product to achieve budgeted sales volume and profit levels during the six-month period from July 1, 1980 through December 1980.

LIQUID PAPER CORPORATION

Liquid Paper Corporation (LPC) is a wholly owned subsidiary of the Gillette Company. Gillette is an international consumer products firm engaged in the development, manufacture, and sale of a wide range of products for personal care or use. Major product lines include blades and razors, toiletries and grooming aids, writing instruments, and small electrical appliances. The Gillette Company recorded net sales of $1.98 billion with a net income of $110.6 million in 1979.

This case was made possible through the cooperation of Liquid Paper Corporation. The case was prepared by Roger A. Kerin, Professor of Marketing, Edwin L. Cox School of Business, Southern Methodist University, as a basis for class discussion and is not designed to illustrate appropriate or inappropriate handling of administrative situations. Certain case information is disguised. Quantitative and financial data described in the case are disguised and are not useful for research purposes.

LPC was acquired by the Gillette Company in October 1979 in order to strengthen the Gillette presence in the office-supplies industry in both domestic and international markets. The company is a manufacturer and marketer of Liquid Paper typewriter correction fluid and of typewriter ribbons and correction tapes. LPC products are displayed in Exhibits 1 and 2.

LPC distributes its product line worldwide and has manufacturing facilities in the United States, Australia, Belgium, and Canada. Liquid Paper correction fluid currently accounts for an estimated 65 percent of correction fluids sold in the United States. However, total sales of correction fluid have been increasing at a declining rate in recent years as a result of the expanded use of correctable typewriter ribbons. Accordingly, LPC began developmental work on correctable ribbons in the late 1970s. A limited line of correctable typewriter ribbons was subsequently introduced, but because of production difficulties, the line achieved only marginal acceptance prior to LPC's acquisition by the Gillette Company.

EXHIBIT 1
Liquid Paper Correction Fluid Product Line

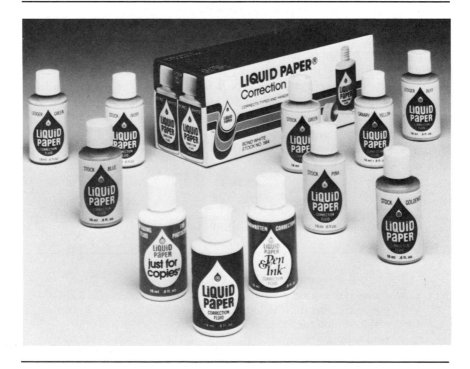

EXHIBIT 2
Liquid Paper Correctable Typewriter Ribbons and
Correction Tape Product Line

CORRECTABLE TYPEWRITER RIBBON MARKET

The correctable typewriter ribbon market came into being with the introduction of the self-correcting typewriter in the early 1970s. These self-correcting typewriters have spools for a typewriter ribbon and for correcting tape in the machine and contain a special back-space key and mechanism made specially for correctable ribbon usage. The inherent advantage of self-correcting typewriters is reflected in the market size and growth estimates for these machines and for correctable ribbons (see Exhibit 3).

EXHIBIT 3
Correctable Typewriter Ribbon Market Size Estimates
(thousands)

	1978	1980 (est.)
Correctable typewriters (units)	2,733	3,794
Correctable ribbons (unit volume)	65,592	91,056
Correctable ribbon (dollar volume at retail selling price)	$163,980	$227,640

Competitive Review

Five major manufacturers of correctable typewriter ribbons exist: IBM, Burroughs Corporation, Eaton Allen Corporation, General Ribbon Corporation, and Frankel Manufacturing Company. Exhibit 4 summarizes the competitive efforts of these companies.

Two similarities in competitive strategy are evident. First, except for IBM and LPC, all manufacturers offer a full line of correctable typewriter ribbons and correcting tapes. Second, advertising and sales-promotion programs are limited. Major manufacturers rely on personal selling efforts through either company or manufacturer's sales representatives.

Three differences are noteworthy. First, manufacturers differ in their overall marketing strategies. IBM sells its ribbons during the course of typewriter sales and service efforts. Burroughs emphasizes a comparative approach with IBM. Eaton Allen Corporation and Frankel Manufacturing Company emphasize price. General Ribbon Corporation focuses on machine dealer needs.

Second, marketing channels used to reach prospective buyers differ. IBM sells directly to prospective buyers in the course of selling and servicing typewriters. However, direct selling is augmented by a direct-mail program to solicit orders, and customers may order directly through a local supply center. General Ribbon Corporation relies on typewriter or machine dealers. Burroughs Corporation sells its ribbons through office-supply dealers and is considered the leader in indirect marketing channels (as opposed to IBM's direct distribution). Eaton Allen Corporation and Frankel Manufacturing Company also sell their ribbons through office supply dealers, but do sell directly to buyers on occasion.

Finally, pricing strategies differ. IBM is the premium-priced correctable ribbon. Burroughs Corporation is the price leader in the office supply dealer channel, while Eaton Allen and Frankel aggressively price their ribbons in this channel. General Ribbon is the price leader in the typewriter dealer channel.

In general, the correctable typewriter ribbon market is dominated by IBM. Ribbon sales through office supply dealers are dominated by full-line manufacturers led by Burroughs.

Channel Arrangements and Trade Margins

Exhibit 5 shows the marketing channel arrangements in the industry. It is estimated that direct marketers (e.g., IBM) account for 60 percent of correctable ribbon volume. Manufacturers selling through office

EXHIBIT 4
Competitive Review

	Manufacturer				
	IBM	Burroughs	Eaton Allen	Frankel	General
Manufacturer's brand name	IBM	NU-KOTE	KOR-EC-TYPE	Frankel	Distinctive quality
Marketing strategy	Adjunct to machine sales	Direct comparison to IBM	Aggressive pricing	Private labeling/pricing	Servicing machine dealers/private labeling
Channel	Direct	Supply dealers	Supply dealers	Supply dealers	Machine dealers
Price	Premium (retail) price less quantity discounts up to 30%	Standard leader through supply dealers (volume pricing structure with best pricing at a discount of 64% of retail price)	Low (similar pricing strategies to 68% of retail price)	Low with discounts up	Standard (price leader through machine dealer; similar to Burroughs)
Breadth of line	IBM typewriter ribbons only	Full line (IBM and other typewriters)	Full line	Full line	Full line
Promotional programs	Supply kit (1 year supply of ribbons with purchase)/order hotline/institutional advertising	Floor and counter displays/advertising to dealers and purchasing agents	Premium promotions, free goods/consumer premium promotions/trade advertising	No premium promotions/audio visual presentations to dealers/some advertising in trade publications	Floor and counter displays
Sales force	Machine representatives	Company representatives	Manufacturer representatives	Manufacturer and company representatives	Manufacturer representatives

supply dealers account for 25 percent, and manufacturers selling through machine dealers capture 15 percent of correctable ribbon volume.

Manufacturers selling through office supply dealers recognize all 400 wholesalers and 600 of the 12,600 office supply dealers as being key (i.e., very large and important) accounts. Moreover, they further recognize that having a manufacturer's correctable ribbon line carried by all 400 wholesalers virtually assures complete coverage of office supply dealers.

Trade margins vary by channel arrangement. For example, office supply dealers typically receive a 30 to 40 percent margin on sales to end users; wholesalers receive between 18 and 25 percent margin on sales to office supply dealers. Machine dealers typically obtain up to a 30 percent discount from the suggested retail price to end users.

EXHIBIT 5
Marketing Channels for Correctable Typewriter Ribbons

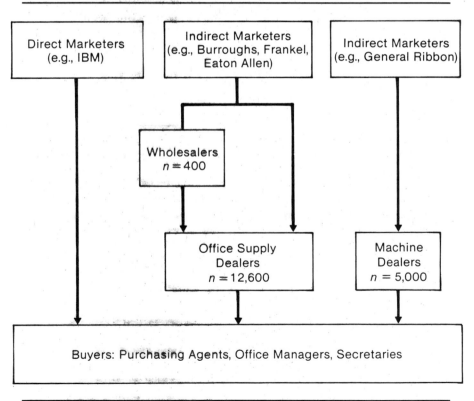

Purchasing and Use Behavior

Correctable typewriter ribbons are purchased by individual secretaries in small firms, office managers in medium-sized firms, and purchasing agents in large firms as a general rule. Major factors
considered in evaluating ribbons include darkness of print, clarity of
typed letters, incidence of ribbon twisting or jamming, neatness of the
correction, ease of installation in the typewriter, and price. Users of
typewriter ribbon are typically more concerned with ribbon performance; purchasing agents consider price more frequently in their purchase decisions. In addition, purchasing agents consider the shelf life
of ribbons since ribbons kept in storage for extended periods will oxi-
dize and become useless. The image of the manufacturer also plays a
role in ribbon-purchasing behavior.

The usage rate of correctable typewriter ribbons varies dramatically between typists. However, a common industry standard is that a
secretary will use twenty-four ribbons per year.

The kind of correctable typewriter ribbon used by typists will
vary by typewriter model. IBM typewriter models are typically used in
the industry to classify correctable ribbons. Total industry unit volume
of correctable ribbons is allocated among typewriter models in Exhibit
6. This allocation also reflects LPC's sales experience.

LPC'S SITUATION: MARCH 1980

In early March 1980 Susan Jackson began to piece together LPC's experience in the correctable ribbon business. After reviewing past documents and summarizing her notes from lengthy talks with production,

EXHIBIT 6
Distribution of Correctable Typewriter Unit Volume by
Ribbon Type

Ribbon for:	Percentage of Total Ribbon Volume
Correcting Selectric	23
Selectric II	19
Selectric 71	31
Selectric 72	10
Executive	12
Executive (with cartridge)	5

sales, and advertising personnel and selected office supply dealers, she prepared an overview of the situation as she saw it. Excerpts from this overview are outlined below.

1. Fewer than 10 percent of end users have tried LPC ribbons. This figure compares with an estimated 90 percent of end users who have tried Liquid Paper correction fluid.

2. Major competitors have significantly broader product lines in ribbons than LPC does. Thus, LPC must of necessity be the second or third line carried by office supply dealers—our major channel for reaching end users.

3. Our production problems, though now remedied, weakened LPC's relationship with office supply dealers as regards our ribbons. The number of accounts carrying our ribbons is eroding as a consequence. Our thirty-six-person sales force, though still one of the best in the business, is somewhat uneasy about emphasizing our ribbons, given our past performance.

4. LPC does not have a price or cost advantage. Our ribbons are often priced 5 to 15 percent higher than Burroughs's and higher still than Eaton Allen's. Our sales price to dealers, competitors' prices, and LPC's standard profit contribution on typical ribbons are shown in Exhibit 7.

5. LPC ribbons fit over 80 percent of all electric typewriters.

6. LPC ribbon volume in 1979 was 4 million units. Forecast 1980 ribbon volume was 5.5 million units.

7. LPC ribbon sales are short of forecasted volume levels.

ADVERTISING AND SALES PROMOTION

Pre-1980

LPC's correctable typewriter ribbons had been launched with an emphasis on advertising. Approximately $350,000 was spent for advertising media in 1979. Advertising was placed primarily in consumer/secretary magazines such as *The Secretary, Today's Secretary, Us, People,* and *McCall's.*

Approximately $260,000 was spent for sales promotion in 1979. Sales-promotion efforts consisted primarily of price-off promotions to the trade. No significant expenditures for advertising or sales promotion were made during the first quarter of 1980.

EXHIBIT 7
LPC Sale Price to Trade, Selected Prices of Competitors,
and Standard Profit Margin by Ribbon Type

			LPC	
Ribbon for:	Suggested Retail Price to End Users (IBM List Price)[a]	Burroughs Best Price[b]	Price to Trade[c]	Standard Profit Margin[d]
Correcting				
Selectric	$3.00	$1.063	$1.20	$0.5687
Selectric II	$3.00	$1.063	$1.20	$0.5875
Selectric 71	$1.75	$0.586	$0.66	$0.2818
Selectric 72	$2.50	$0.911	$1.00	$0.3995
Executive	$1.75	$0.633	$0.70	$0.3106
Executive (with				
cartridge)	$2.25	$0.99	$0.95	$0.3040

[a]Price sold to secretaries, purchasing agents, office managers.

[b]Price to office-supply dealers and wholesalers plus freight, since Burroughs does not prepay freight.

[c]Price LPC sells its ribbons to wholesalers and office supply dealers, excluding freight.

[d]*Casewriter's note:* For analysis purposes, standard profit margin is defined as selling price to the trade less direct costs of material and labor, plus assignable variable overhead to each ribbon type. Freight expenses are not included in the computation of standard profit margin. Freight expenses are estimated at 3.2 percent of the sales price.

Options, March 1980

Susan Jackson's talks with fellow LPC personnel produced a number of formal recommendations. Sales executives suggested a sales contest, advertising personnel recommended that an advertising program be launched immediately, several office-supply dealers believed that promotional allowances should be given to dealers, and other marketing personnel advocated a couponing program offering a free correctable typewriter ribbon to Liquid Paper correction fluid users. Each approach is outlined next.

Sales Contest

The sales contest focused on increasing the number of key wholesalers and office-supply dealers carrying correctable typewriter ribbons. According to the contest rules, for each new account opened with a minimum order of $500, the sales representative would receive a certain number of points, the district manager would receive a certain number of points based on the number of new accounts in his or her district, and the regional manager would receive points based on the number of new accounts in the region. In addition, points would be awarded to participants exceeding their sales quotas during the contest period. The costs of administering the sales contest, promotional materials, and awards were estimated at $7,000. The sales contest would run for two months. Approximately two months would be necessary to plan and institute the program before it could be implemented.

At the present time, LPC had distribution through 50 percent of key wholesalers, who numbered 400, and 40 percent of key office supply dealers, who numbered 600. In contrast, LPC correction fluid was carried by virtually 100 percent of all wholesale and office supply accounts.

The effect of the sales contest on improving sales performance was difficult to forecast. Each account added would, however, increase sales by another $2,500 during the remainder of the year. Thus each new account effectively represented $3,000 over the remaining six months of the calendar year.

Advertising Program

The advertising program described to Ms. Jackson included a three-pronged effort designed to reach dealers, purchasing agents, and end users. Advertising expenditures could be budgeted at three levels—$50,000, $100,000, or $150,000—for the remaining six months of 1980 (July through December). In addition, the allocation of expenditures could vary between audiences, as shown in Exhibit 8.

The magazines used for reaching specific audiences were standard in the industry. Trade magazines include *Office Products Dealer,*

EXHIBIT 8
Alternative Media Expenditures by Audience at
$150,000 Spending Level

Media	Emphasis on Trade	Emphasis on Consumer/ Secretary	Emphasis on Purchasing Agent
Trade magazines	$ 30,000	$ 10,000	$ 20,000
Consumer/secretary magazines	$ 90,000	$120,000	$ 90,000
Purchasing agent magazines	$ 30,000	$ 20,000	$ 40,000
Total media budget	$150,000	$150,000	$150,000

Geyers Dealer Topics, and Office World News. Magazines designed for purchasing agents include Modern Office Procedures, Administrative Management, and Office Product News. Consumer/secretary magazines include The Secretary, Today's Secretary, and Working Women, in addition to Us, People, McCall's, Cosmopolitan, and Ms. Selected insertion costs associated with these magazines are shown in Exhibit 9. Examples of magazine advertisements are shown in Exhibits 10 through 13.

An estimate of the sales response to the advertising program was difficult to make, in Ms. Jackson's opinion. She did believe, however, that the short-run response would not be as great as the response to trade allowances and coupons. However, the long-run effects of advertising were felt to be greater than those of the promotional efforts outlined for her.

Dealer Promotional Allowances

Discussions with several office supply dealers indicated that a promotional allowance program might be implemented. The promotional allowance of a 20 percent cash rebate program provided to office supply dealers was being considered. This 20 percent cash rebate would be earned only on net purchases (shipments less returns) and would be based on LPC's selling price to dealers. This level of discount was higher than the normal trade practice of 10 to 15 percent, but it was felt that a 20 percent figure would capture the trade's attention.

Dealers would have several options open to them. First, they

EXHIBIT 9
Magazine Insertion Cost Estimates

Magazine	Frequency	Cost per Insertion
Modern Office Procedures	Monthly	$625.00
Office Product News	Monthly	$546.00
Administrative Management	Monthly	$404.00
The Office	Monthly	$421.00
Government Product News	Monthly	$654.00
Women Who Work	Quarterly	$2,670.00
The Secretary	Monthly	$272.00
Today's Secretary	Monthly	$540.00
People	Weekly	$17,700.00
Ms.	Monthly	$5,910.00
Cosmopolitan	Monthly	$14,855.00
Geyers Dealer Topics	Monthly	$274.00
Office Products Dealer	Monthly	$291.00
Office World News	Monthly	$279.00

EXHIBIT 10
Example of Office Dealer–Oriented Advertisement

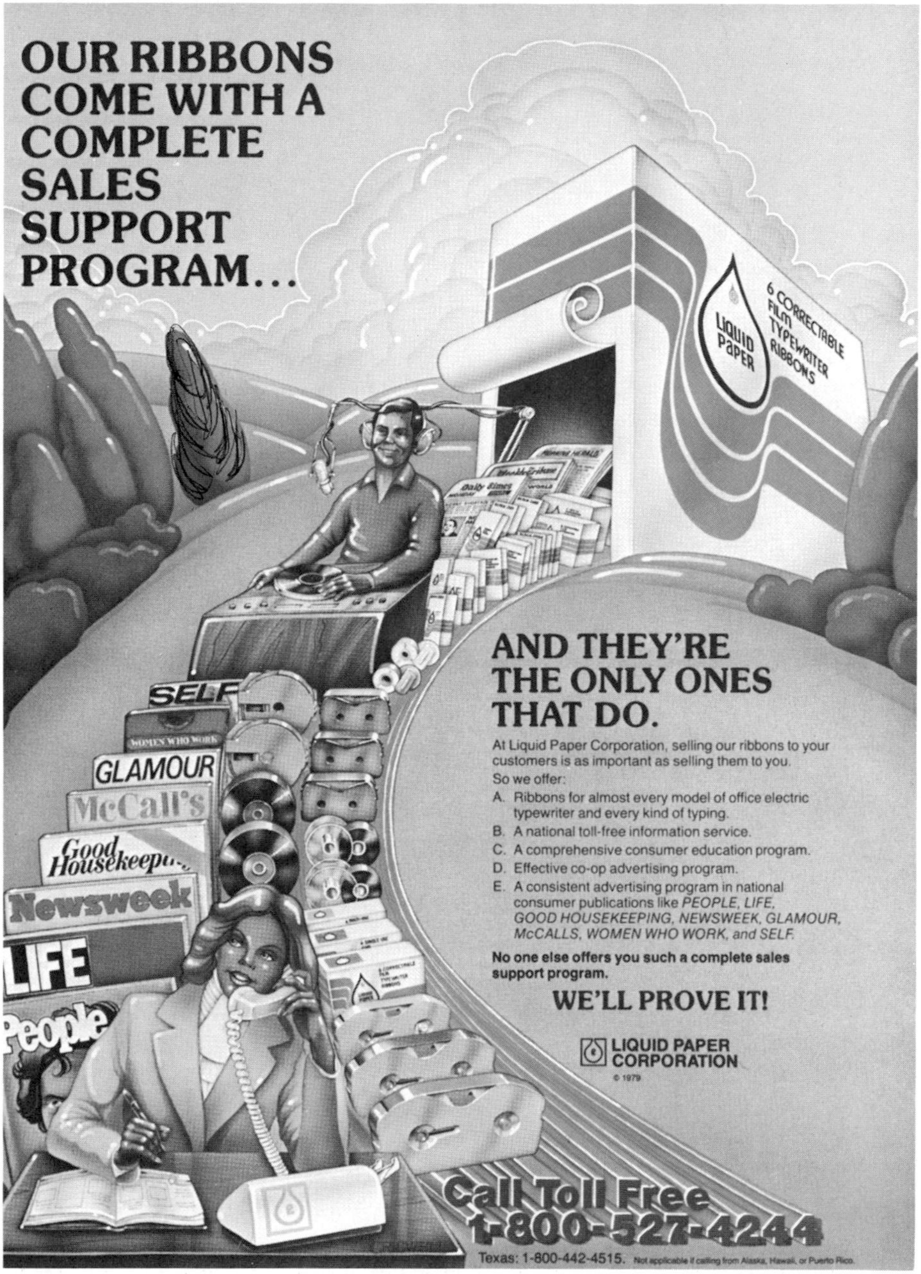

EXHIBIT 11
Example of Customer-Oriented Advertisement

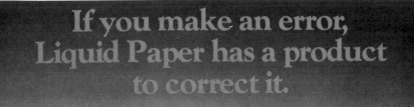

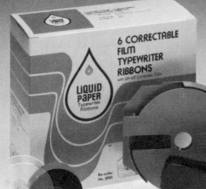

A LIQUID PAPER® Correctable Ribbon can make your ordinary office typewriter correct errors like a self-correcting typewriter. Because it lets you lift typing errors right off your paper.

Now you can make smear-free revisions on photocopies.

Make permanent corrections of typed and written errors . . . at home, at school, in the office.

For more information on these and other Liquid Paper Corporation products and where they can be purchased please call this toll-free number:
1-800-527-2250
In Texas, please call: 1-800-492-4194.

*Registered trademark of

Liquid Paper Corporation
9130 Markville Drive, Dallas, Texas 75243
©1978

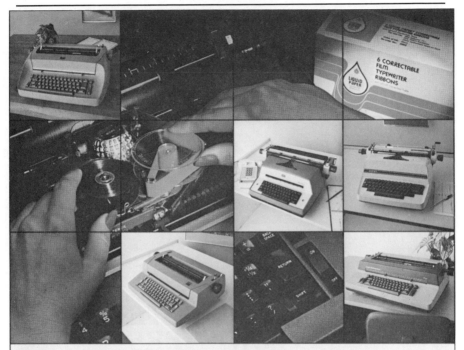

407

EXHIBIT 13
Example of Customer/Purchasing Agent-Oriented
Advertisement

could pass along some of the savings to buyers in the form of a discount. Second, dealers could use the money for sales contests instituted and managed by them. Third, they could institute a program whereby a buyer would purchase a certain number of ribbons and get one free. Finally, a dealer could keep the entire allowance.

The dealer promotional allowance program would require two months to plan and organize. The program itself would run for three months (July–September).

Ms. Jackson's past experience with a consumer packaged goods company and her personal assessment of the situation led her to speculate that sales volume with the promotional allowances could replace sales that would have occurred without the allowance. Believing that most stocking dealers (as opposed to new dealers) would participate in the program, she estimated that 90 percent of the normal unit volume sales during the three-month promotion period would include the promotional allowance of 20 percent of LPC's price to office supply dealers. She also assumed that the promotional allowance program would generate 50 percent net cumulative sales increase over the three-month promotion period. In other words, she assumed that sales volume would be 50 percent greater than would be expected without the promotion. Finally, Ms. Jackson estimated that sales would remain 20 percent above normal sales volume for the remaining three months.

[handwritten margin note: 90% of sales would be affected]

Coupon Program

The fourth option consisted of a coupon program directed primarily to the end user—the secretary. Two approaches were outlined for consideration. One approach would involve affixing a self-stick label to 700,000 Liquid Paper correction fluid boxes. The label would offer a free correctable typewriter ribbon. End users would be asked to remove the label and mail the coupon to LPC. A facsimile of the coupon is shown in Exhibit 14.

The projected administrative cost of this approach, including return mail packaging and postage costs, was $21,000, based on a redemption estimate of 3 percent. This estimate, however, did not include the cost of the free sample.

The working assumption on sales response to this coupon program was that 25 percent of those who redeemed the coupon would adopt the LPC ribbon. In other words, adoptors would purchase LPC ribbons exclusively at the industry average for the three-month period October–December.

A second approach would involve a direct-mail campaign featuring a coupon offering a free correctable typewriter ribbon (see Exhibit 15). The coupon, attached to an advertisement, would be mailed to 30,000 purchasing agents and 350,000 secretaries in small to medium-

EXHIBIT 14
Coupon on Correction Fluid Box

sized firms. A 25 cent handling charge applied to the offer would be used to defray the cost of free samples.

The estimated redemption rate for this plan was 2 percent. The cost of administration, including outgoing and return mail, would be $20,000. This cost estimate did not include the cost of the free sample. The assumed secretary and purchasing agent sales response for this program was the same as that for the self-stick label (i.e., 25 percent would become adoptors). However, it was believed that each purchasing agent who became an adoptor was equivalent to twenty secretaries in terms of sustained ribbon usage.

PROGRAM AND BUDGET CONSIDERATIONS

Ms. Jackson was pleased with the response given by LPC personnel to her request for advertising and sales-promotion proposals. Designing the integrated program and drafting the budget was her sole responsibility, however.

EXHIBIT 15
Direct-Mail Coupon

Make a Great Impression
With **LIQUID PAPER** Typewriter Ribbons.

Crisp, clean, complete print is automatic with every LIQUID PAPER typewriter ribbon. Every ribbon is unconditionally guaranteed for quality. There's a ribbon for every kind of typing you do and each type is color coded for easy ordering.

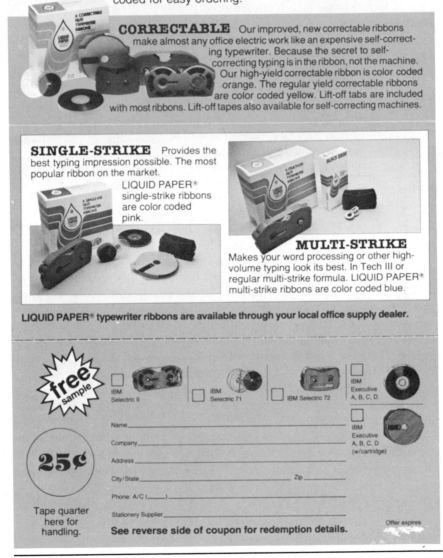

CORRECTABLE Our improved, new correctable ribbons make almost any office electric work like an expensive self-correcting typewriter. Because the secret to self-correcting typing is in the ribbon, not the machine. Our high-yield correctable ribbon is color coded orange. The regular yield correctable ribbons are color coded yellow. Lift-off tabs are included with most ribbons. Lift-off tapes also available for self-correcting machines.

SINGLE-STRIKE Provides the best typing impression possible. The most popular ribbon on the market.
LIQUID PAPER® single-strike ribbons are color coded pink.

MULTI-STRIKE
Makes your word processing or other high-volume typing look its best. In Tech III or regular multi-strike formula. LIQUID PAPER® multi-strike ribbons are color coded blue.

LIQUID PAPER® typewriter ribbons are available through your local office supply dealer.

free sample

25¢

Tape quarter here for handling.

☐ IBM Selectric II
☐ IBM Selectric 71
☐ IBM Selectric 72
☐ IBM Executive A, B, C, D
☐ IBM Executive A, B, C, D (w/cartridge)

Name_____

Company_____

Address_____

City/State_____ Zip_____

Phone: A/C (____)_____

Stationery Supplier_____

See reverse side of coupon for redemption details.

Offer expires

Program Considerations

Each proposal was neatly stacked on her desk as she began to consider which proposals should be adopted and how they would fit into an integrated advertising and sales promotion program. She believed that the proposals could be launched sequentially or simultaneously. However, if some proposals were launched after others, it would be impossible to reap the rewards of the expected sustained volume, given the time constraint she faced. Alternatively, she also realized that if too many individual proposals were introduced simultaneously, the possibility of confusion among the trade and end users could arise. Also, if two actions were combined, their interaction had to be assessed. For example, if the sales contest with the minimum order of $500 were adopted and the promotional allowance plan were launched simultaneously, then the $500 order would include the 20 percent cash rebate. Of broader concern was the possibility that she could be, in her words, "trading tomorrow for today"—that is, short-term gains at the expense of long-run benefits would haunt her next year.

Budget Considerations

Budget considerations were also important. The six-month (July–December) unit sales objective for typewriter ribbons was 3 million ribbons. The direct marketing contribution objective for this period was 12 percent of incremental full revenue sales. Unit sales in the last six months, given performance during the first six months, were estimated to be 2.4 million units[a]—600,000 units short of the sales objective. The various options would focus on achieving the incremental 600,000 units.

Ms. Jackson understood it would be necessary for her to prepare an incremental profit and loss statement for each of the proposals. In addition, if she decided to implement one or more proposals simultaneously, then a separate profit and loss statement would be needed for each combination.

Her recommendation to upper management would ultimately be prepared using the LPC approach to developing program profit and loss statements. The format is shown in Exhibit 16. The revenue and cost terms used are defined as follows:

---

[a]*Case writer's note:* For analysis purposes, consider 400,000 units as the "normal" monthly volume, given the current number of distributors, advertising and sales-promotion program, and sales effort.

EXHIBIT 16
LPC Profit and Loss Statement: Ribbons, July
1–December 31, 1980

Incremental full revenue sales	$_____
Incremental direct cost of sales	
Standard cost	$_____
Freight ($.0301 in full revenue sales in units)	$_____
Incremental profit contribution (full revenue	
sales − direct cost)	$_____
Incremental direct marketing expenses	
Advertising costs	$_____
Sales-promotion costs	$_____
Lost revenue	$_____
Incremental total direct marketing expenses	
(advertising + sales promotion + lost revenue)	$_____
Incremental direct marketing contribution	
(profit contribution − direct marketing expenses)	$_____

1. *Full revenue sales:* Full revenue sales is defined as the total number of ribbons sold times the weighted average LPC trade price (excluding discounts), whether or not ribbons are sold with dealer allowances.

2. *Standard cost:* Standard cost is defined as the average unit sales price minus the average standard profit per unit or full revenue sales times (1 − weighted average standard profit contribution).

3. *Sales promotion:* Sales promotion costs consist of the administrative expenses associated with a particular sales contest, dealer allowance, or coupon program. In addition, sales promotion costs include *lost revenue,* the cost of allowances or free samples. For example, if a 10 percent allowance were given on a ribbon priced at $2, then lost revenue would be 20 cents. If a free sample were given, the expense would be the cost of the free sample. In either instance, total lost revenue would be the dollar value allowance or the cost of the free sample multiplied by the number of units sold or provided free of charge.

S. C. Johnson— The Agree Line

AS MEL LISTON REVIEWED the latest material received from the firm's advertising agency, he felt very pleased that his recommendations on product positioning had been approved by senior management. These recommendations centered around a new targeting strategy for Agree Shampoo and Agree Creme Rinse and Conditioner that would shift marketing effort away from the "all women, aged 18 to 45" segment toward the "teenage female" segment of the market. As product manager of the Agree line at S. C. Johnson & Son, Ltd., in Brantford, Ontario, his current task was to develop a comprehensive marketing communications program aimed at the new target audience for the fiscal year (FY) 1980–1981. It was May 1980, and he would have to make strategic decisions on advertising, consumer sales promotion, and trade promotion within the next few weeks in order to finalize a plan that could be implemented by July 1, the start of the new fiscal year.

COMPANY BACKGROUND

S. C. Johnson & Son, Ltd., better known as Johnson Wax, was founded in 1886 in Racine, Wisconsin, as a manufacturer of parquet flooring. When customers became concerned with the care and protection of their flooring, Johnson began making and selling a prepared paste wax. The popularity of parquet flooring began to fade, and by 1917 the company was concentrating solely on floor wax and other wood finishing products. The Canadian operation was created in 1920, by which time there were also plants in England and Australia.

This case was prepared by Stephen B. Ash and Sandra Safran, University of Western Ontario, as a basis for class discussion and is not intended to illustrate effective or ineffective handling of administrative situations. Used with permission.

By 1980, the company had grown into a $2 billion corporation with operations in 41 countries and 110 distribution centers around the world. At that time, 78 percent of the company's sales were derived from the Consumer Products Group which comprised the U.S. Division and the International Division. The Canadian company was part of the latter group, although it had a separate management structure and research facilities. This arrangement ensured a high degree of autonomy in decisions related to marketing, finance, and research and development. Some products were developed in Canada—for example, Glade Flo-Thru Air Freshener and Super Soap—and these were frequently adopted by other subsidiaries. Other products were developed abroad and were later marketed in Canada.

Until the late 1970s, Johnson's primary emphasis was on floor and furniture care products. These were relatively mature markets that, in recent years, had suffered a slow but steady decline. Two reasons accounted for this slowdown: no-wax floors were becoming increasingly popular, and consumers' attitudes toward floor and furniture care were softening with the growth of low-maintenance chrome, glass, and wood veneer products. At this time, Johnson controlled over two-thirds of the shrinking floor market. The company responded to these trends by improving and repositioning existing products as well as by adding new products to the line. Although the company believed that these tactics helped it to maintain a market leadership position, management recognized that it would have to look farther afield in order to sustain existing sales and profitability.

NEW MARKET OPPORTUNITY

Personal care products were designated by Johnson as a key growth area at this time, and the firm began to explore the possibility of entering these markets. Market research indicated that after-shampoo products had grown recently by more than 20 percent per year despite the fact that users were apparently dissatisfied with the feel of their hair after using these oily conditioning products. Research findings suggested that consumers wanted control and softness in hair that both looked and felt clean. Owing to its wide-ranging R&D program, Johnson had developed the technology to formulate a unique creme rinse product that was 99 percent oil-free but still conditioned hair.[a] The company had recently hired personnel who were experienced in the production and marketing of hair care products.

---

[a]The 1 percent oil component was included to provide a fragrance base. At that time, a major competing brand, Tame, contained approximately 40 percent oil.

Agree Creme Rinse and Conditioner (CRC), was first launched in the United States in 1976. During the fall of that year, marketing research was undertaken in Canada to develop profiles of typical shampoo and/or CRC consumers. Findings from the "Usage and Attitude Study" indicated that 95 percent of all Canadians used a shampoo product, with women accounting for the heaviest usage. The rate of usage varied, however, from once a day to once a week or less. In addition, the study found that 40 percent of all women used CRCs "some of the time."

Agree CRC was then introduced in Canada in June 1977 and became the Canadian CRC market leader by 1979 (see Exhibit 1). Some of its success was due to Johnson's Canadian advertising budget, set at $700,000 in the launch year compared to $868,000 for all other firms in the CRC industry, including $200,000 spent by Gillette on its CRC product, Tame, the market leader prior to Agree's introduction.[b] The Johnson product was also successful because of its superior formulation, which was emphasized in its advertising (see Exhibit 2). Finally, a large-scale sampling promotion contributed to the early success of Agree CRC.[c]

The extraordinary success of Agree CRC prompted Johnson to introduce a second Agree product. Johnson entered the large, highly

---

[b]Many of Johnson's figures have been disguised, but basic relationships have not been altered significantly.

[c]During the sampling campaign, 3/4-ounce sachets were distributed in a full national mailing to approximately 3.2 million Canadian households.

EXHIBIT 1
S.C. Johnson—Agree, Creme Rinse and Conditioner, Market Shares for the Twelve Months Ending September/October 1975–1979 (percentages)

Brand	1975	1976	1977	1978	1979
Tame	23.3	23.5	18.1	13.7	11.2
Clairol (total)[a]	18.3	16.2	13.2	9.1	10.8
Alberto Culver	9.4	8.0	—	—	—
Breck Clean Rinse	4.0	3.9	—	—	—
Revlon Flex	—	5.2	11.7	11.4	13.3
Wella Balsam	—	—	5.2	6.0	7.8
Agree	—	—	—	13.5	13.8
All others	45.0	41.6	47.0	41.0	40.0

Source: Company records.

[a]Includes: Herbal Essence, Balsam, and Clairol Conditioner.

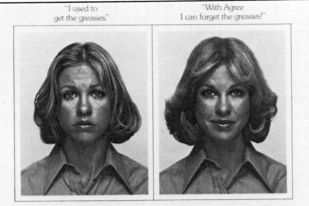

"I used to get the greasies."

"With Agree I can forget the greasies!"

New Agree
Creme Rinse & Conditioner
Helps Stop the "Greasies"

The "greasies." That's oily, greasy hair too soon after using some creme rinse and conditioners. But now there's new Agree. New Agree Creme Rinse and Conditioner *actually helps stop the greasies.*

New Agree is 99% Oil Free
Agree's® formula is very different. Some creme rinse and conditioners contain oil-up to 40% oil. And oil causes the greasies. Agree's formula is actually 99% oil free. So there's no oil to give you the greasies. Yet, be assured, Agree still gives you beautiful wet combing, great conditioning.

Does Agree Really Work?
Yes. Agree was tested. And retested. People like yourself were asked to use Agree and compare it with the leading creme rinse and conditioner. Agree was preferred. *It actually helped solve the problem of the greasies.*

Agree's Wet Combing is Proved Effective in Detangling Hair.
More tests were conducted at the Hair Care Laboratories of S. C. Johnson & Son. A laboratory instrument (commonly called an Instron) measured the force required to remove tangles. *Agree removed the tangles significantly easier than the leading creme rinse and conditioner.*

Agree Actually Conditions Hair
Shown below are actual examples of damaged and healthy looking hair. The conditioners in Agree, used regularly, will

Damaged Healthy Hair Hair

A 12 page booklet on every bottle tells you even more about new Agree

reduce fly-away, make wet combing easy and add body and shine—all signs of healthy looking hair.

Agree is pH Balanced
Most hair care experts agree that normal, healthy-looking hair is mildly acidic with a pH range from 4.0 to 5.0. Agree has a compatible pH level of 4.0 to 5.0.

Acidic Alkaline

1   4.5   10   14

The people of the Hair Care Laboratories, Personal Care Division of Johnson waxbelieve that Agree is the finest creme rinse and conditioner available in either salons or retail stores. Try Agree for yourself.

Regular Formula

New Agree

Agree
creme rinse
& conditioner
Helps stop the greasies

competitive and fragmented shampoo market early in 1978, almost a year after its Agree CRC introduction (see Exhibit 3). Agree shampoo was formulated to clean hair more thoroughly than most of the shampoos then on the market. The slogan, "Helps stop the greasies between shampoos" combined with the Agree name helped to make the new shampoo number three in the market within six months, close behind Head & Shoulders and Johnson & Johnson (J&J) Baby Shampoo.

By 1979, most other CRCs on the market were reformulated to be oil-free, thus converting Agree's main benefit into a generic one. Management recognized the potential threat posed by this move and began to consider alternative steps that could be taken to prevent any erosion of Agree's market share.

PRODUCT MANAGEMENT

S. C. Johnson employed a product management system to guide the strategic plans and activities of the firm's marketing department. Under this system, the director of marketing delegated responsibility for specific groups of products to group product managers (e.g., personal care products, furniture and floor care), who, in turn, reassigned re-

EXHIBIT 3
S.C. Johnson—Agree, Market Shares of Shampoos, Early 1978

Leading Brands	Share
Head & Shoulders	16
Johnson & Johnson Baby Shampoo	12
Clairol Herbal Essence	5
Breck Golden	6
Revlon Flex	4
Short & Sassy	3
Earth Born	3

Sales by Formula Type (Percentage)	
Dandruff medicated segment	20
Cosmetic segment (including baby shampoos)	80

Source: Company records.

Note: The total shampoo category consisted of over 150 brands and more than 700 sizes and types.

sponsibility for one or more brands within the group to product managers and assistant product managers.

Product managers at Johnson adhered to a well-defined policy governing new product development. Under this policy, a new product was permitted to lose money during its introductory year(s) but was expected to achieve annual corporate profitability goals thereafter. Because the CRC and the shampoo had been introduced at different times, the goal for the full Agree line had been set at 11 percent in FY 1979–1980. A target of 12.5 percent had been set for FY 1980–1981.

From the inception of Agree shampoo in 1978 until late 1979, Agree CRC and shampoo were handled by two separate product managers within Johnson. The rationale for this division of responsibility reflected management's belief that the competitive environments for CRCs and shampoos were quite distinct during that period. This policy resulted in the development of separate advertising and pricing strategies for Agree CRC and shampoo.

During the latter part of 1979, market analysis was undertaken by S. C. Johnson to identify and describe Agree CRC and shampoo users (see Exhibit 4). Management was quite surprised to discover that the user base for Agree was not women aged eighteen to forty-five, but primarily girls in the twelve-to-twenty-four age group. This study also showed that there was as high as 65 percent cross-usage between the Agree CRC and shampoo brands, one of the highest nationally, although they were not advertised as being essential to one another. Interestingly, earlier advertising tracking studies had indicated that approximately 24 percent of viewers of any Agree shampoo commercial recalled it as one for Agree CRC and vice versa.

In view of these research results, the product management group for Agree became increasingly convinced that consumers seemed to think about Agree products as a unit. As a result, the separate product manager positions for Agree CRC and shampoo were combined in order to achieve economies of scale and to foster better communications. As part of this integration, management decided that Agree products eventually would share a common pricing strategy together with joint trade and consumer promotions. Since Agree products would now be viewed as a family, advertising would be scheduled to alternate between shampoo and CRC. The combined FY 1979–1980 sales for these products were estimated to total $12 million at retail.

Mel Liston had recently been appointed product manager for both Agree CRC and shampoo products. As a result of the 1979 market research study, he believed that repositioning Agree would strengthen its chances for continued success. In particular, the information pertaining to the current user base for Agree products led Mel Liston to

EXHIBIT 4
S.C. Johnson—Agree, Shampoo/CRC Markets, Importance by Sex and Age Group

Group	Population (Millions)	Percentage Who Use	Frequency of Use Per Year	Number of Uses (Millions)	Adjusting Factors	Equivalent Volume Used	Percentage of Volume Represented	Percentage of Volume of Agree Used
A. Hair Conditioner Market: Importance by Sex and Age Group								
Females:								
12–18	1.35	80	200	216	1.25	270	23	32
19–24	1.37	93	157	200	1.1	220	19	10
25–34	1.96	84	134	220	1.0	220	19	13
35–54	2.60	87	98	221	0.75	166	15	15
55+	2.33	85	70	138	0.60	83	7	4
Males:								
13–34	5.2	57	53	157	1.0	157	14	24
35+	4.8	42	11	22	0.8	18	3	2
B. Shampoo Market: Importance by Sex and Age Group								
Females:								
12–18	1.35	100	260	351	1.25	439	15	23
19–24	1.37	100	239	327	1.1	360	12	8
25–34	1.96	100	208	407	1.0	407	14	11
35–54	2.60	100	175	455	0.75	341	11	12
55+	2.33	100	95	221	0.6	132	4	3
Males:								
13–34	5.2	99	175	900	1.0	900	30	37
35+	4.8	97	102	474	0.8	380	14	6

Source: Company records.

define the primary target market as girls in the twelve-to-eighteen age bracket and the secondary target market as women aged nineteen to twenty-four. New advertising copy and media schedules aimed at implementing the revised strategy for Agree were requested from Johnson's advertising agency.

Mel Liston said, "If we're going to be the 'bubble gum' shampoo, we have to gear most of our plans to this new market. We must change our thinking in order to fully exploit our knowledge of the consumer base for Agree."

THE AGREE MARKET

By May 1980, both Agree CRC and Agree shampoo were being offered on a continuous basis in three regular sizes and three formulas (see Exhibit 5). A fourth size, 50 ml, was offered each year, although mainly as a back-to-school trial size. This trial size was typically offered in

EXHIBIT 5
S.C. Johnson—Agree, Types, Sizes, and Colors of Agree Products, 1980

CRCs

Formula Name	Bottle Color	Sales Volume (Percentage)
Extra Body with Balsam	Orange	27
Regular Formula	Green	41
For Extra Oily Hair	Yellow	32

Shampoos

Formula Name	Shampoo Color (Bottle is Clear Plastic)	Sales Volume (Percentage)
Extra Gentle	Orange	29
Regular	Green	40
Oily Hair	Yellow	31

Size	Type
50 ml	Trial (promotional only)
225 ml	Regular
350 ml	Family
450 ml	Economy (introduced in Feb. 1980)

Source: Company records.

promotional packages containing other personal care products sold by a variety of companies.

At that time, there were at least 150 kinds of shampoos and 80 CRCs on the market. Less than half of them were branded, and of these, only about ten were supported by an advertising or consumer promotion. The rest were "price brands"—reasonably priced, acceptable products that were low priced to consumers and were promoted heavily to the trade. Two of the more familiar of the price brands were Unicare and Suave.

Market share estimates for the different shampoo and CRC sizes are summarized in Exhibit 6. By May 1980 the total CRC market in Canada had reached almost $37.5 million and was growing at an annual rate of approximately 20 percent. At that time, Agree CRC was the leading brand in the category, with sales of $5.2 million at retail representing almost 13.8 percent of the total CRC market in dollar terms. The total shampoo market had risen to almost $108 million, with a growth rate of about 12 percent per year. Agree was second in terms of market share, with sales amounting to $6.8 million or close to 6.3 percent of the total shampoo market. The 350-ml bottle accounted for the bulk of total Agree sales, both in the CRC and shampoo categories (see Exhibit 6).

THE CONSUMER

Company sales records indicated that by May 1980 consumers were purchasing 75 percent as much Agree CRC as shampoo. Buying habits for these two items were quite different from those associated with Johnson's other products. For example, a 1979 market research study indicated that purchase frequency was relatively high—every few weeks as opposed to every few months. If the product that the consumer wanted was not on the shelf, she would rarely postpone her purchase until the following week. Instead, she normally would switch to another brand.

According to the 1979 study, the consumer typically owned about three brands at a time. Many of the purchasers, principally women, apparently believed that they became sensitized to one particular brand after a while.[d] Consequently, they would try another brand in their "evoked brand set"—those four or five brands that they were

---

[d]As a rule, people consider their hair care requirements to be highly unique. After repeated uses of any single brand, many people gradually become concerned that the brand no longer works as effectively as it once did. It is this concern that prompts brand-switching behavior.

EXHIBIT 6
S.C. Johnson—Agree, Market Shares for Agree
Shampoo/CRC

	Share of Dollar Sales		Share of Volume Sales	
	1979–1980 to Date[a]	Percentage Change from 1978–1979	1979–1980 to Date	Percentage Change from 1978–1979
A. Shampoo				
Total market volume	107,742,000	11	6,725[b]	1
Total Agree	6.3	32	5.5	37
50 ml	0.1		0.1	
225 ml	1.5		1.1	
350 ml	4.1		3.7	
450 ml	0.7		0.6	
Head & Shoulders	16.5	22	10.8	16
J & J	7.6	2	7.9	(7)
Body on Tap	3.5	66	3.6	64
Revlon Flex	5.8	22	5.6	15
All others	60.3	6	67.4	(5)
B. CRC				
Total market volume	37,455,600	21	2,034.4	12
Total Agree	13.8	19	14.5	15
50 ml	0.3		0.5	
225 ml	2.8		2.4	
350 ml	6.1		6.5	
450 ml	4.6		5.2	
Tame	8.0	(2)	10.9	(11)
Silkience	2.9	N[c]	1.2	N[c]
Revlon Flex	10.5	43	12.0	29
Condition II	4.0	N	6.1	N
All others	60.8	10	55.3	1

Source: Company records.

[a]Based on approximately ten months of sales. FY 1979–1980 ends on June 30.

[b]Represents the liquid measure of millions of cases of twelve 350-ml bottles.

[c]New; no data for year ago.

prepared to buy at any one time. Since people tended to rotate between brands within their own set, a key objective of management was
to encourage users to come back to Agree more often, thereby ensuring
its position as the brand with the highest frequency of use in the category. Purchases tended to be made largely on impulse, particularly for
conditioners, which generally were considered to be less essential in
the household than shampoos.

SALES AND DISTRIBUTION

When Agree CRC was first introduced in 1977, Johnson's distribution
system was oriented primarily toward the food trade. However, the
launch of Agree, a personal care item, underscored the need for greater
dependency on the drug trade in order to obtain widespread distribution for this type of product. Management decided to partially realign
its field sales effort in order to place increased emphasis on the drug
trade. By 1980 more than 97 percent of the drug stores in Canada were
included as part of the Johnson distribution system. Food stores constituted the primary outlets for Agree products, followed by drug and
mass merchandising outlets, such as Woolco, K-Mart, and Zellers (see
Exhibit 7).

Johnson had clear objectives for shelf management. In particular,
it sought to have the eighteen different bottles arranged at the retail
outlet in a "billboard" or "ribbon" effect for maximum eye-catching
appeal. Inserts and shelf talkers were frequently included to increase
the likelihood of eye contact (see Exhibit 8).[e] Most retail outlets did
not, in fact, carry every size and formula of the Agree line, despite
aggressive sales force efforts to achieve this stocking pattern.

Johnson maintained its own sales force of approximately eighty
people, who were required to sell all of its products, including Agree.
By May 1980 additional penetration of distribution channels was no
longer a primary objective. However, it was recognized that continued
trade support would depend, in part, on the frequency and quality of
both consumer and trade promotions. Sales representatives were well
trained and were compensated by a salary plus incentives scheme,
where the incentives included things like free trips and prizes. Management attempted to provide strong support for the sales force
through regular meetings and discussions and by furnishing selling
aids. Some of the Johnson products which the sales group sold, for
example, "Raid" and "Off," were seasonal. In the case of Agree, how-

---

[e]*Case inserts* are written instructions indicating where to stock the brand on the
shelf. *Shelf talkers* are small signs attached to the front of a shelf on which the product
is stocked.

EXHIBIT 7
S.C. Johnson—Agree, Sales Percentage by Outlet Type

	Food	Drug	Mass Merchandise
Industry shampoo sales, 1978	43[a]	42	15
Industry CRC sales, 1978	36	42	22
Agree shampoo sales, 1979–1980	47.4	35.5	17.0
Agree CRC sales, 1979–1980	35	46.3	18.5

Source: Company records.

[a]To be read: "43% of all units sold were purchased in food stores."

ever, the variation per season was slight, averaging 3 or 4 percent higher in midsummer and 1 or 2 percent lower in winter.

PRICING

When Agree CRC was first introduced, the retail price was pegged to that of the leading brand, Tame. The regular cost to the retailer initially was $12.86 per case for one dozen 225-ml bottles and $16.94 per case for 350-ml bottles. At that time, retail selling prices ranged from $1.39 to $1.79 for the 225-ml size and from $1.79 to $2.39 for the 350-ml size. By May 1980 trade costs and suggested retail selling prices for Agree CRC were as follows:

Bottle Size	Trade Cost (per Case)	Suggested Retail Selling Prices
225 ml	$14.65	$1.59–$1.79
350 ml	$19.20	$2.09–$2.29
450 ml	$23.50	$2.59–$2.79

The suggested retail selling prices for Agree CRC provided trade margins in the 23–31 percent range.

By May 1980, trade costs and suggested retail selling prices for Agree shampoo were as follows:

Bottle Size	Trade Cost (per Case)	Suggested Retail Selling Prices
225 ml	$16.55	$1.79–$1.99
350 ml	$24.25	$2.59–$2.79
450 ml	$28.00	$2.99–$3.19

Suggested retail selling prices for Agree shampoo typically provided trade margins in the 23–27 percent range.

EXHIBIT 8
S.C. Johnson—Agree, Case Insert (Top) and Shelf Talker (Bottom)

Stock Agree next to Tame as shown for maximum shelf movement

Yellow Bottle for Extra Oily Hair   Green Bottle Regular Formula   Orange Bottle Extra Body with Balsam

"I used to get the greasies."   "With Agree I can forget the greasies."

New Agree
Creme Rinse & Conditioner ™
helps stop the greasies

The initial pricing strategy for Agree CRC was to introduce the product at a consumer price equal to that of Tame, or to Gillette Earth Born if Tame was not stocked in a particular outlet. A similar pricing strategy was pursued for Agree shampoo in that the pricing objective was parity with Johnson & Johnson Baby Shampoo, or with Clairol Herbal Essence if the former was not available. Over the next few years, Agree CRC and shampoo moved to a slight premium price relative to the top selling brands.

ADVERTISING

Mel Liston was about to set a marketing communications budget that would include expenditures for advertising, consumer promotion, and trade promotion. As a starting point, he examined the budgets for the fiscal years 1978–1979 and 1979–1980 (see Exhibit 9). In doing so, however, he recognized that some important factors had changed in the interim. For example, deal and promotional costs had been higher in FY 1978–1979 than in the following year because of the introductory expenses incurred for the launch of Agree shampoo. Although the current year was estimated to be slightly below target, his projected budget for FY 1980–1981 would still have to provide for a pretax profit level of at least 12.5 percent.

Foote, Cone & Belding, Johnson's advertising agency, was requested to prepare scripts that would direct advertising toward the new target audience. The agency created material that it felt would be effective and then made suggestions about how to use the advertising package, for example, the level of frequency required to achieve maximum impact with a particular audience. The agency commission would be included in Mr. Liston's budget as a fixed percent of his expected net revenue (see Exhibit 9).

The primary marketing objective was to maintain or increase current sales levels for Agree. To meet this goal, Mel Liston believed that it would be necessary to achieve a 90 percent awareness level for Agree within the new primary target audience of women aged twelve to eighteen. A secondary target audience was defined as women aged

EXHIBIT 9
S.C. Johnson—Agree, Mel Liston's P&L Worksheet for His 1980–1981 Budget (CRC and Shampoo Combined)

	1978–1979 ($000)	Percentage of Net Sales	1979–1980[a] ($000)	Percentage of Net Sales	1980–1981 ($000)	Percentage of Net Sales
Net sales	8,158	100	9,300	100	*12,875*	100
Cost of goods sold[b]	2,941	36	3,160	34	*4,249*	33
Gross profit	5,217	64	6,140	66	*8,626*	*67*
Advertising	1,875	23	1,578	17	*2,076*	*16*
Consumer promotion	816	10	553	6		
Deals	1,225	15	1,197	13		
Other[c]	890	11	920	10	*117p*	*10*
Total promotion	4,806	59	4,248	46		*≤ 44.5*
Functional expenses[d]	900	11	927	10		*10*
Operating profit	489	(6)	965	10		≥12.5

(handwritten annotations: "12,000,000 at retail" next to Net sales row)

Source: Company records.

[a]Projected from mid-May to June 30 year end.

[b]Includes labor, materials, standard overhead.

[c]Includes external marketing services, sales meetings, agency fees.

[d]Overhead allocations and fixed costs.

nineteen to twenty-four and he hoped to achieve at least a 60 percent awareness level for this group.

Research undertaken by the advertising agency on Canadian teens' and young women's television viewing habits indicated a national weekly reach of 99 percent for the twelve-to-eighteen age bracket and 98 percent for the nineteen- to twenty-four-year-old group, with average weekly viewing times of 21.3 and 21.5 hours, respectively. One of the tasks facing Mel Liston was to select specific programs and parts of the day (e.g., 4:00–9:00 P.M.) that achieved optimal viewing levels within the budget that he set. He felt that consumer magazine advertising was important as a support vehicle to television, since magazines provided increased reach against the light television viewer (see Exhibit 10).

The agency proposed a television commercial for each Agree product, scripts for radio advertising, and layouts for print media. Total media costs to run the television commercials on a complete network daily basis were estimated at $1.05 million for fifty-two weeks if late afternoon time slots were scheduled versus $1.6 million for a prime time insertion schedule. These figures incorporated a discount, which could range from 10 to 15 percent on a full fifty-two-week purchase. In keeping with Agree's younger image, the agency recommended a fast-paced, exciting commercial featuring a strong musical beat, which appeared to be favored by teens.

The product management group also considered radio advertising, which had been directed mainly at the "teen" segment of the Agree market during the previous two years. In FY 1979–1980, Johnson ran a seven-week radio campaign (see Exhibit 11). For FY 1980–1981, it was estimated by the agency that the media cost for twenty-seven-station national radio would amount to approximately $35,000 per week.

Since its introduction, Agree had been promoted regularly in magazines, and newspapers. During the launch periods, seven American and three Canadian magazines had carried full-page color advertisements for Agree. In Canada, Johnson had paid for the Canadian material and had received the American magazine spillover, estimated at approximately $200,000 per year, at no cost, although it was recognized that U.S. advertising would still be directed at the historical U.S. target audience, women aged eighteen to forty-five.

As Mel Liston began to work on developing a marketing communications program for FY 1980–1981, he tried to imagine a profile of a typical teen girl and the type of advertising she would be most likely to notice. Studies on women eighteen years old and over had shown that heavy users of hair products were not necessarily heavy watchers of

EXHIBIT 10
S.C. Johnson—Agree, Media Plan Excerpts

A. Quintile Analysis

The quintiles of the 1980–1981 media plan were compared with the quintiles of a television-only campaign, which would run for fifty-two weeks with a 45 percent weekly reach. The target group was women aged 12–18.

TV Watcher Quintile	TV Only % Total Impressions	Index	TV/Consumer Magazines % Total Impressions	Index
1 + 2 (light)	15.9	100	25.9	163
3 (medium)	21.5	100	33.6	156
4 + 5 (heavy)	62.6	100	40.6	70

B. Publication Costs (for full-page ads)

Publication	Cost/Insertion(s)	Total Readers Women 12–18 (000)	CPM[a] ($)
Chatelaine (E)	15,078.15	350	43.08
Flare	5,174.80	224	23.10
Homemaker's	14,614.00	176	83.03
Chatelaine (F)	4,996.85	42	118.97
Madame au Foyer	4,199.13	27	155.52
Clin d'Oeil	1,921.50	60	32.01

Source: Foote, Cone and Belding.

Note: The above analysis reflects the fact that the inclusion of consumer magazines provides increased reach against the light TV viewer. In addition, the multimedia schedule provides a more even distribution of impressions against the light, medium, and heavy quintiles.

[a]Cost per thousand impressions.

television. However, he wondered how applicable this result was, given the age disparity with the Agree primary target group. There was even less statistical information on magazine readership in the target age group. Thus, Mel Liston wondered whether or not the reading habits of the typical young female consumer would justify spending a significant part of his budget on print advertising, in either magazines or newspapers. If a decision was reached to run a print campaign, he believed that any print advertising that did appear would have to be

EXHIBIT 11
S.C. Johnson—Agree, Agree Radio Plan

Target group: Primary   Teens   12–18
Target group: Secondary   Women   19–24
Reach objective: 55% weekly
Announcements: 30 seconds
Duration: 7 weeks

Market	Number of Stations	Number of Weekly Announcements for Each Product
Vancouver	2 CKLG/CFUN	40
Victoria	1 CKDA	20
Calgary	1 CKXL	25
Edmonton	1 CHED	25
Regina	1 CJME	25
Saskatoon	1 CKOM	25
Winnipeg	2 CKRC/CFRW	35
Toronto	3 CHUM-FM/CFTR/CHUM	50
Hamilton	1 CKOC	25
Ottawa	2 CFRA/CFGO	45
Kitchener	1 CHYM-AM	30
London	1 CJBK	25
Montreal		
English	2 CKGM/CHOM-FM	40
French	2 CKLM/CKAC	30
Quebec City	2 CHOI-FM/CFLS	50
Halifax	1 CJCH	20
St. John/Moncton	2 CFBC/CKCW	20
St. John's	1 VOCM	20

Source: Company records.

young and vibrant like the ads that the agency was proposing for the coming year (see Exhibit 12).

CONSUMER PROMOTION

Johnson had introduced its Agree products with heavy consumer promotion. The CRC was introduced with a six-month sampling campaign, which consisted of a direct mailing to approximately three million potential users of a 3/4-ounce plastic sachet good for about two uses. This was followed by a second six-month campaign, which

EXHIBIT 12
S.C. Johnson—Agree, 1980–1981 Proposed Print Ad

included 400,000 3/4-ounce plastic sachets and 15 cent coupons using a cross-promotion with Close-Up toothpaste.[f] Agree shampoo was introduced by using similar sachets to 3.2 million homes, and this campaign included a fact book and another 15 cent coupon. The net effective coverage of these promotional events was approximately 50 percent of Canadian homes.

Another launch promotion for Agree consisted of 3/4-ounce pouches of free shampoo, which were attached to CRC bottles. One million of these pouches were distributed free to stores, in addition to 1.5 million 50-ml samples, which were prepriced at 39 cents each. The unit cost to Johnson was 5 cents per sachet of CRC and 7 cents per sachet of shampoo. Bulk distribution costs were estimated at $30 per thousand. Although sales for each product increased significantly during the trial period, the cost to Johnson of distributing such high quantities of free or virtually free merchandise was very high.

After Agree CRC and shampoo had been launched, other consumer promotion opportunities were considered. Refund campaigns were run twice during FY 1979–1980. Coupons that offered 50 cents off the next purchase were distributed in bulk mailings and in magazines directed toward homemakers. Cash refunds of one dollar were later offered in exchange for two Agree labels. The redemption rates were 3 percent and 2 percent, respectively. This coupon program proved rather disappointing since there was little, if any, change in sales volume during the promotion period.

In 1979, Agree in the United States had been packaged with a free Warner-Lambert razor, normally sold at $3.69. Although the perceived value of this "gift" was high, the impact on sales during the promotion period was disappointing. After calculating the total cost of the distributed premiums, this campaign was responsible for a substantial loss incurred by American Agree. A similar promotion was tried in the United States six months later. Free pantyhose were attached to Agree products. During the promotion period, sales remained relatively stable. However, the result of this promotion was less damaging to profits than the free razor campaign, since the cost to Johnson was only 40 cents per pair of pantyhose. Despite these results, Mel Liston was unwilling to describe either of the premium campaigns as a failure, since other longer-term objectives such as increases in usage frequency and brand loyalty appeared to have been met. Furthermore, in judging any sales promotion campaign, he realized, as a general rule, that most promotion events did lose money during the deal period.

One promotion being considered by Mel Liston was an "instant

---

[f]Cross-promotions are samples, coupons, and the like placed on or inside the package of a non-competing product usually sharing the same market as the promoted brand.

win" tag, whereby the purchaser would be notified if she had won a free pair of Jordache jeans. Jordache would be asked to supply the jeans free in exchange for being featured in advertising and in-store promotion. Other costs for this contest would include plastic prize tickets, special labels, backer cards, and labor. Some of these expenses would overlap into the trade promotion category. Total promotional costs for the Jordache Sweepstakes were estimated at $120,000, at least $20,000 of which would include store items such as end aisle displays.

Mel Liston believed that consumer promotions were important merchandising devices, since all customers who learned about such offers could take advantage of them. In contrast, trade promotions, particularly off-invoice allowances, were important to retailers, but the benefits from these deals were not necessarily passed along to consumers in the form of lower prices. The primary objective of a consumer promotion was to induce the consumer to buy Agree more often, perhaps every other time, rather than every fourth or fifth time.

Since the product was in the non-price-sensitive 50 percent of the market where consumers tended to buy on impulse, Mel Liston felt that nonprice promotions might be very effective. Deals such as bonus packs were nondiscretionary in that anyone who bought the product received the bonus. However, Mr. Liston wondered whether bonuses were merely a way to subsidize or reward the already loyal purchaser. In his mind, it was unclear whether or not larger amounts of an untried product would, in fact, induce trial.

As Mel Liston began to think about consumer promotion plans for the coming year, he recognized the importance of establishing a clearly defined personality for Agree CRC and shampoo. One possible promotion event consisted of a contest that would offer as the grand prize a rock group concert at the winner's school or community center. Although somewhat unusual, this type of promotion might reinforce the image he was trying to project for Agree. He said, "We want a commercial image with an underlying message which tells the kids that the music and the special Agree products are mainly for them; they're not something meant to appeal to the whole family." Other consumer promotion possibilities included couponing and redemption ideas. For example, one opportunity under consideration was cross-ruff couponing, perhaps on Pledge or Flo-Thru Air Freshener or one of the company's other home care products.

TRADE PROMOTION

Trade spending was something that companies such as Johnson felt they had to do; it was not truly discretionary. As part of each year's budget, a percentage of sales dollars was set aside in order to meet shelf space objectives. The FY 1979–1980 discretionary pool of funds was set at 7.9 percent of projected sales. Without special deals, there might be insufficient reason for stores to try to sell Agree instead of competing brands.

Johnson allocated funds to trade promotion for two main reasons. First, trade deals were viewed as essential simply to get and keep products listed. A variety of trade deals were possible such as off-invoice allowances (e.g., $1.20 off each case ordered during the deal period). During FY 1979–1980, trade spending varied widely both in the CRC and shampoo markets (see Exhibit 13).

The other reason for trade spending was related to cooperative advertising. Contributions to these programs normally were calculated according to a formula that included some percentage of a retailer's previous sales, typically around 2 percent. Advertising "slicks" (see Exhibit 14) were provided to retailers to encourage their active participation in coop advertising campaigns.[g]

To encourage retailers to sell stock at "feature prices" from time to time, S. C. Johnson provided off-invoice allowances (also called *deal money*) to the trade. Deal money was occasionally passed on to consumers as reduced prices but frequently was viewed by the retailer as a means to increase the trade margin. For example, Mel Liston estimated that only 40–50 percent of all stock sold on deal to the trade was actually retailed at the feature price. The balance was sold at the regular price, thereby increasing the retailer's trade margin. It seemed to Mel Liston that a large number of retailers were more concerned about obtaining deal money than about an extensive advertising campaign that the manufacturer might undertake to build a longer-term brand franchise.

Although advertising was sometimes cut if fourth-quarter sales were disappointing, trade deals hardly ever were cut. The risk of suffering a loss in shelf positioning was considered too great to justify a reduction in trade promotion activity. Retailers typically tried to buy and stock up at the end of a deal period to keep annual inventory costs down as much as possible. Retailer expectations regarding trade deals were not expected to change in FY 1980–1981.

THE TASK

As Mel Liston began to think about developing a comprehensive marketing communications program for the Agree line in FY 1980–1981, he

---

[g]Advertising "slicks" are reproducible copy and pictures supplied by manufacturers to participating retailers during a cooperative advertising campaign.

EXHIBIT 13

S.C. Johnson—Agree, Selected Promotional Influences for Major Brands, July–August 1979 to March–April 1980 (Three Periods)

A. Shampoo

	Agree			Head & Shoulders			Johnson & Johnson			Body on Tap			All Others		
	1979 July Aug.	Nov. Dec.	1980 Mar. Apr.	1979 July Aug.	Nov. Dec.	1980 Mar. Apr.	1979 July Aug.	Nov. Dec.	1980 Mar. Apr.	1979 July Aug.	Nov. Dec.	1980 Mar. Apr.	1979 July Aug.	Nov. Dec.	1980 Mar. Apr.
Sales share	6.4	5.4	5.7	9.5	10.8	10.1	7.3	7.3	8.6	4.0	3.3	3.9	72.7	73.1	71.7
Deal percentage of market[a]	2.8	1.2	0.4	0.1	0	0	0.5	0.8	0.4	1.5	0.5	1.0	7.5	7.0	6.4
	(43.8)	(22.2)	(7.0)	(1.0)	(0.0)	(0.0)	(6.8)	(10.9)	(4.7)	(37.5)	(15.2)	(25.6)	(10.3)	(9.6)	(8.9)
TV advertising ($000)	12.9	40.8	181.2	157.5	152.8	151.1	186.2	2	169.8	24.6	28.3	115.3	456	283	856
Radio advertising ($000)	139	3.7	0	31.3	7.0	36.2	0	0	10.9	0	0	0	5	2	15
Press advertising ($000)	0	0	17.2	13.7	16.2	7.4	0	0	0	7.1	0	11.0	105	46	220
Total advertising volume ($000)	152	45	198	203	176	195	186	2	181	31.8	28.3	126.3	566	331	1091
Advertising share[b]	13.4	4.6	11.1	17.8	31.3	10.9	16.4	0.2	10.1	2.8	5.0	7.1	49.7	58.8	60.9
Coop share:[c]															
Food	32	20	31	35	30	34	53	61	59	29	1	10			
Drug	48	44	72	64	64	86	56	57	76	41	20	31			
Mass merchandiser	83	10	59	113	46	95	64	87	102	64	29	55			
Displays share:[d]															
Food	9	6	8	16	7	8	6	14	13	3	2	4			
Drug	13	16	21	21	20	19	19	17	19	7	7	15			
Mass merchandiser	34	3	50	25	22	28	28	45	50	9	10	43			

EXHIBIT 13 (continued)

B. CRC

	Agree			Revlon Flex			Silkience			Tame			Condition II			All Others		
	1979 July Aug.	Nov. Dec.	1980 Mar. Apr.	1979 July Aug.	Nov. Dec.	1980 Mar. Apr.	1979 July Aug.	Nov. Dec.	1980 Mar. Apr.	1979 July Aug.	Nov. Dec.	1980 Mar. Apr.	1979 July Aug.	Nov. Dec.	1980 Mar. Apr.	1979 July Aug.	Nov. Dec.	1980 Mar. Apr.
Sales share	15.6	15.1	13.7	14.5	11.1	12.8	2.7	4.5	6.1	9.2	10.3	9.2	7.1	8.1	6.2	50.9	51.8	51.2
Deal percentage of market[a]	4.6 (29.5)	5.3 (35.1)	2.1 (15.3)	6.0 (41.4)	2.1 (18.9)	1.4 (10.9)	0 (0.0)	0 (0.0)	0 (0.0)	1.3 (14.1)	2.5 (24.3)	1.1 (11.9)	1.5 (21.1)	2.6 (32.1)	0.9 (14.5)	10.5 (20.6)	11.2 (21.6)	9.9 (19.3)
TV advertising ($000)	33.7	243.8	0	58.9	7.3	0	133.0	100.8	75.7	0	0	85.1	11.8	5.8	8.9	124.6	81.5	41.3
Radio advertising ($000)	47.5	0	0	0	0	0	0	0	0	0	0	0	0	0	0	1.8	0	0
Press advertising ($000)	0	0	0	0	0	0	0	19.0	30.4	0	35.1	5.2	0	10.4	28.0	71.8	7.6	99.8
Total advertising volume ($000)	81.1	243.8	0	58.9	7.3	0	133.0	119.8	106.1	0	35.1	90.3	11.8	16.2	37	198.2	89.1	141.1
Advertising share[b]	16.8	47.7	0	12.2	1.4	0	27.5	23.4	25.6	0	6.9	21.8	2.4	3.2	8.9	41.0	17.4	43.7
Coop share:[c] Food	19	9	15	19	5	14	7	14	15	13	17	17	1	7	6			
Drug	36	31	43	15	21	29	45	40	46	29	28	26	27	42	32			
Mass merchandiser	53	16	32	40	10	33	29	26	29	44	26	50	31	45	36			
Displays share:[d] Food	9	4	2	5	5	7	3	8	8	13	7	6	1	4	1			
Drug	20	15	18	17	12	19	13	24	12	22	23	5	10	14	8			
Mass merchandiser	37	22	50	6	16	21	19	13	7	34	6	18	15	35	21			

436

[a] The Neilsen Market Survey defines a deal as any package/price configuration that is different from the company's regular market configuration. The figures in the row are the proportion of brand sales that were sold on deal. For example, during July/August 1979 in the shampoo market, approximately 43.8 percent (6.4 ÷ 2.8) of Agree shampoo sales were "on deal," compared to 22.2 percent (5.4 ÷ 1.2) of sales for Agree during November–December 1979.

[b] Advertising share denotes Agree share of total advertising expenditures on the product category during each period. For example, the calculation for July–August 1979:

$$\frac{12.9 + 139.0}{(12.9 + 139.0) + (157.5 + 31.3 + 13.7)\ldots + (456.0 + 5.0 + 105.0)} = 13.4\% \text{ (rounded)}$$

[c] Coop share is supplied by A.C. Neilsen. It is a period result defined as the number of stores that did coop advertising (i.e., newspapers, flyers) weighted by their sales importance to the shampoo category. For example, in July–August 1979, food stores doing 32 percent of shampoo sales in the food trade had coop advertising on Agree.

[d] Display share is the unweighted percentage of stores that had display activity when the store was audited by A.C. Neilsen at the end of the bimonthly period. For example, at the end of August 1979, 9 percent of food stores had Agree on display. Display is defined by Neilsen as the product being somewhere in the store other than its normal shelf position.

437

EXHIBIT 14
S.C. Johnson—Agree, Example of an Advertising Slick

SP 183-1515

remembered that the first step in the process was to establish a set of clear and specific objectives against which campaign results could be measured. In addition, he understood that decisions about advertising, consumer promotions, and trade deals were highly interrelated. Thus overall success in implementing the revised positioning strategy for Agree CRC and shampoo would depend on his ability to design a well-integrated communications program. In this type of program, decisions across advertising, consumer, and trade promotion activities would have to be well coordinated with in-store merchandising to achieve a strong reinforcing effect.

Mr. Liston was frequently overheard explaining this philosophy to new people in his department. He told them that exposure was worth more than price—that is, an end aisle display with 10 cents off was more valuable to the company than a one dollar sale sitting on a shelf—but that both types of promotion might be necessary. In addition, he believed that an end aisle display with no cents off or no contest was merely a nice arrangement of stock instead of a sales booster.

The complete marketing communications plan was required by July 1, 1980. The document itself would outline decisions reached in the following areas: total communications budget for FY 1980–1981 and allocation of those funds across advertising, consumer, and trade promotion activities; message strategy; and selection and scheduling of advertising media, consumer promotions, and trade deals. In addition, the plan would outline any steps needed to coordinate the marketing communications activities proposed for FY 1980–1981. Given the importance of these decisions to the future position of Agree CRC and shampoo in the market, Mel Liston planned to consult other members of the Agree product management group before finalizing the plan.

CHAPTER 8

Marketing Channel Strategy and Management

MARKETING CHANNELS PLAY an integral role in an organization's marketing strategy. Channels not only link a producer of goods to its buyers, but also provide the means through which an organization implements its marketing strategy. The marketing channel will determine whether or not target markets sought by an organization are reached. In addition, the effectiveness of a promotional strategy is determined, in part, by the number of channel intermediaries, their geographical concentration, and their ability and willingness to perform promotion-related functions. Moreover, markup and discount policies of intermediaries will influence an organization's price strategy. Finally, product strategy is affected by the branding policies of intermediaries, their willingness to stock a variety of offerings, and their ability to augment offerings through installation or maintenance services, the extension of credit, and so forth.

To the extent that a marketing manager has alternative channels available for reaching chosen target markets, the decision facing the manager is one of selecting those channels that meet three objectives. First, among channel options, the chosen channel should provide the best coverage of the target markets sought. This means that a channel will place the organization's offerings in the right location, in the right quantity, at the right price, and at a time when buyers wish to purchase it. Second, a channel should satisfy the buying requirements of the target markets sought. Buying requirements refer to buyers' needs for information about the offering, convenience of purchase, and those services such as delivery that are incidental to purchasing. Finally, the chosen channel should maximize potential revenues returned to the organization while minimizing the costs of achieving adequate market coverage and satisfying buyer requirements.

THE CHANNEL-SELECTION DECISION

The channel-selection decision is not so much a single act as it is a process of decomposing the decision into its various components. The process of channel selection involves specifying the *type, location, density,* and *functions* of intermediaries, if any, in a marketing channel.

Before addressing specific channel-selection decisions, it is incumbent upon the marketing manager to first conduct a thorough market analysis in order to identify the target markets that will be served by a prospective marketing channel. The target markets sought and their buying requirements form the basis for all channel decisions. By working backward from the ultimate buyer or user of an offering, the manager can develop a framework for specific channel decisions and can identify alternative channel designs.

Direct versus Indirect Distribution

Exhibit 8.1 illustrates common channel designs for consumer and industrial offerings. Also indicated is the number of *levels* in a marketing channel as evidenced by the number of intermediaries between a producer and ultimate buyers or users. As the number of intermediaries between the producer and the ultimate buyer increases, the channel increases in length.

Hence, the first decision facing a manager is: Should intermediaries be used to reach target markets, or should the organization contact ultimate buyers directly through their own sales forces or distribution outlets? If the manager elects to use intermediaries, then the type, location, density, and number of channel levels must be determined.

Certain conditions usually exist in which organizations elect to contact ultimate buyers directly rather than through intermediaries. Organizations using direct distribution usually have target markets composed of a limited number of buyers who are easily identifiable and are geographically concentrated. Direct distribution is usually em-

EXHIBIT 8.1
Marketing Channel Designs

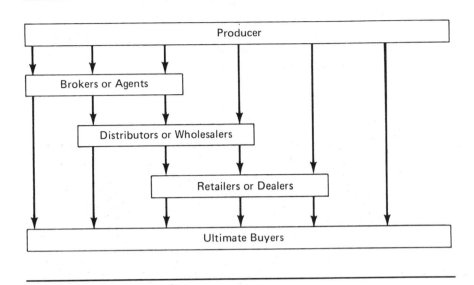

ployed when personal selling is a major component of the organization's communication program, when the organization has a wide variety of offerings for the target market, and when sufficient resources are available to satisfy target market requirements that would normally be handled by intermediaries (e.g., credit, technical assistance, delivery, postsale service, and so forth). Direct distribution must be considered when intermediaries are not available for reaching target markets, or when intermediaries do not possess the capacity to service the requirements of target markets. Certain characteristics of the offering also favor direct distribution. Typically, sophisticated technical offerings such as computers, unstandardized offerings such as custom-built machinery, and offerings of high unit value are distributed directly to buyers. Finally, the overall marketing strategy might favor direct distribution. This might occur if the organization seeks a certain aura of "exclusivity" not generated by using intermediaries, or if the organization emphasizes the "buying direct" appeal presumably important to the target markets sought. Direct distribution may also be appropriate if the organization seeks to differentiate its offering from others distributed through intermediaries.

Even though a variety of conditions favor direct distribution, an important caveat must be introduced. The decision to market directly to ultimate buyers involves the absorption of all marketing-related functions (contacting buyers, storage, delivery, and credit) typically performed by intermediaries. A marketing principle stating that "you can eliminate intermediaries, but not their functions," is particularly relevant to the manager considering direct distribution. This point is occasionally overlooked by marketing managers when they elect the direct distribution alternative. The costs of performing these functions can be prohibitive, depending on the organization's financial resources and the "opportunity cost" of deploying financial resources in other endeavors. Therefore, even though all signs favor direct distribution, the capacity of the organization to perform tasks normally assigned to intermediaries may eliminate this alternative from final consideration. A similar caveat must be noted for intermediaries who consider acquiring functions typically performed by channel members "above or below" them in the channel (e.g., a retailer who wishes to perform wholesaling functions). In recent years, many large supermarket chains have eliminated their warehousing of merchandise in favor of using independent food wholesalers. Two of the several reasons for this decision are: (1) independent wholesalers can perform these functions more cheaply, and (2) there is an "opportunity cost" of deploying resources in the wholesaling function when capital is needed to develop the "super" supermarkets now popular.

Channel Selection at the Retail Level

In the event that intermediaries are decided on as the means for reaching target markets, the channel-selection decision then focuses on the *type* and *location* of intermediaries at each level of the marketing channel. The type of intermediaries at the retail level is the first problem requiring resolution.

Consider the decision of a manufacturer of sporting goods. Since retail outlets were chosen, the question now becomes: What type of retail outlet? Should hardware stores, department stores, sporting goods stores, or a combination of these stores be selected to carry the line of sporting goods? Also, where should these retail outlets be located? A manager must determine if the retail outlets should be located in urban, suburban, and/or in rural areas, and in what parts of the country.

The type and location decision depends on the buying requirements of the target markets and the potential profitability of the outlets to the manufacturer. To the extent that retail outlets play a role in providing information about the offering to potential buyers, which of the retail outlets will most actively promote the line through point-of-purchase displays, store-sponsored advertising (including cooperative advertising), or knowledgeable sales personnel? Which of the stores will carry a reasonable inventory to attract buyers interested in selection and variety? Which outlets carry competing or complementary products? Which outlets are conveniently located for buyers? The issue of profitable retail outlets relates to the potential volume in the trade areas served by the outlets, the merchandising skill of store management, and the store's competitive environment. Each of these factors must be evaluated before a decision on the type and location of retail outlets is finalized.

Next, the density of intermediaries at the retail level of distribution must be determined. *Density* refers to the number of intermediaries carrying the organization's offering in a particular geographical area. Three degrees of density at the retail level are: *intensive distribution, exclusive distribution,* and *selective distribution.*

1. *Intensive distribution* at the retail level means that a manager attempts to distribute the organization's offerings through as many retail outlets as possible. More specifically, a manager may seek to gain distribution through as many outlets of a specific "type" (such as drugstores) or, in its extreme form, gain distribution through almost all types of retail outlets, as evidenced by the channel policies of cigarette manufacturers.

2. *Exclusive distribution* is the extreme opposite of intensive distribution in that it is typical for one retail outlet in a geographical area to carry a manufacturer's line. Usually, the geographical area constitutes the defined trade area of the retailer. Magnavox Corporation used this approach for some of its products when it utilized only 3,000 dealers among the several thousand potential retail outlets available. Automobile distribution is another familiar example of the exclusive distribution approach.

Occasionally, the exclusive distribution strategy involves a contractual arrangement between a retailer and manufacturer that gives the retailer exclusive rights to sell a line of products or product in a defined area in return for performing specific marketing functions. A common form of an exclusive agreement is a franchise agreement.

3. *Selective distribution* exists between these two extremes. This strategy implies that a manufacturer selects a few retail outlets in a specific area to carry its offering. This approach is often used for furniture, some brands of men's clothing, and quality women's apparel. Selective distribution weds some of the benefits of market coverage from intensive distribution and the control over resale evident with the exclusive distribution strategy. For this reason, selective distribution has become increasingly popular in recent years among marketers.

Also, the popularity of selective distribution has come about because of the concept of *effective distribution*. Effective distribution
means that despite the limited number of outlets at the retail level,
these outlets account for a significant fraction of the market potential.
An example of effective distribution would be a situation in which a
marketer of expensive men's wristwatches may distribute through
only 40 percent of available outlets, but these outlets account for 80
percent of the actual volume of the wristwatch market. Increasing the
density of retail outlets to perhaps 50 percent would probably increase
the percentage of potential volume to 85 percent; however, the attendant costs of this action may lead to only a marginal profit contribution at best.

The decision to select one of the three degrees of density rests on
how buyers purchase the manufacturer's offering, the amount of control over resale desired by the manufacturer, the degree of exclusivity
sought by intermediaries, and the contribution of intermediaries to the
manufacturer's marketing effort.

Intensive distribution is often chosen when the offering is purchased frequently and when buyers wish to expend minimum effort in
its acquisition. Almost by definition, these offerings are convenience
goods such as tobacco products, personal care products, and gasoline.
Limited-distribution strategies (exclusive and selective) are chosen
when the offering requires personal selling at the point of purchase.
Major appliances and industrial goods are typically distributed in this
fashion.

The density of retail distribution varies inversely with the
amount of control over resale desired by the manufacturer. As the
density of retail outlets increases, the number of intermediary levels
increases and further removes the manufacturer from the ultimate consumer. A manufacturer's control over resale declines sharply in these
cases. If control over resale is important, then more limited distribution strategies are used. Interests of intermediaries also have an impact
on the density of their offering assortments to improve their competitive advantage. Therefore, limited distribution may be forced on the
manufacturer. Further, if the nature of the offering demands considerable investment by an intermediary in terms of service capabilities,
specialized selling at the point of sale, or unique display methods,
limited distribution in the retailer's trade area may be required.

Channel Selection at Other Levels of Distribution

After having determined the nature of retail distribution, the manager
must next move to questions relating to other levels of distribution.

This decision involves specifying the type, location, and density (if any) of intermediaries that will be used to reach retail outlets. These specific selection decisions closely parallel the retail network designed earlier.

Assuming that a second-level intermediary (wholesaler or industrial distributor) is decided on, the question now becomes, What type of wholesaler? Should the manager select a specialty wholesaler who carries a limited line of items within a product line, a general-merchandise wholesaler who carries a wide assortment of products, a general-line wholesaler who carries a complete assortment of items in a single retailing field, or a combination of wholesalers? Obviously, an important consideration is whether certain types of wholesalers sell to the retail outlets desired. Often, the decision means finding whatever is available. If the types of wholesalers do not meet the requirements of the manufacturer in terms of satisfying retailers' requirements such as delivery, inventory assortment and volume, credit, and so forth, then direct distribution to retailers becomes the only viable alternative.

The location of wholesalers is determined by the location of retail outlets to the extent that geographical proximity is affected by logistical considerations such as transportation costs, fast delivery service, and the like. The density of wholesalers is influenced by the density of the retail network and wholesaler service capabilities. As a general rule, as the density of retail outlets increases, the density of wholesalers necessary to service them also increases.

Similar kinds of decisions are required for each level of distribution in a particular marketing channel; they will depend on the extent of market coverage sought and the availability of intermediaries. Suffice it to say that the number of levels in a marketing channel varies directly with the breadth of the market sought.

DUAL DISTRIBUTION

The discussion thus far has focused on the selection of a single marketing channel. However, many organizations use multiple channels simultaneously, a practice called *dual distribution*.[1] Dual distribution occurs when an organization distributes its offering through two or more different marketing channels that may or may not compete for similar buyers. For example, General Electric sells its appliances direct to house and apartment builders, but uses retailers to reach consumers.

Dual distribution is adopted for a variety of reasons. If a manufacturer produces its own brand as well as a private store brand, the store brand might be distributed directly to that particular retailer, whereas manufacturers' brands are handled by wholesalers. Also a manufacturer may distribute directly to major large-volume retailers whose service and volume requirements set them apart from other retailers, and who also use wholesalers for reaching smaller retailer outlets. Finally, geography itself might affect whether direct or indirect methods of distribution are used. The organization might use its own sales group in high-volume and geographically concentrated markets, but use intermediaries elsewhere.

The viability of the dual-distribution approach is highly situational and will depend on the relative strength of the manufacturer and retailers. If a manufacturer decides to distribute directly to ultimate buyers in a retailer's territory, retailers may drop the manufacturer's line. The likelihood of this happening depends on the importance of the manufacturer's line to the retailer and the availability of competitive offerings. If a retailer is sufficiently strong in terms of the manufacturer's volume accounted for in a market, elimination of the line could have a negative effect on sales volume.

SATISFYING INTERMEDIARY REQUIREMENTS AND TRADE RELATIONS

The role of intermediaries in channel selection has been cited several times; however, a number of specific points require elaboration. The impression given so far may be that intermediaries are relatively docile elements in a marketing channel. Nothing could be further from the truth!

Even though reference has been made to "selecting" intermediaries, the selection process in actual practice is a two-way street. Accordingly, the marketing manager must be sensitive to possible requirements of intermediaries necessary to establish profitable exchange relationships. Intermediaries are concerned with the adequacy of the manufacturer's offering in improving their product assortment for their own target markets. If the product line or individual offering is inadequate, then the manufacturer must look elsewhere. Intermediaries also seek marketing support from manufacturers. For wholesalers, support often involves promotional assistance; for industrial distributors, technical assistance is sought. As noted previously, intermediaries concerned with competition usually seek a degree of exclusivity in handling the manufacturer's offering. The ability of the intermediary to provide adequate market coverage, given an exclusive agreement, will determine whether this interest can be satisfied by the manufacturer. Finally, intermediaries expect a margin on sales consistent with the functions they are expected to perform. In short, trade discounts, fill-rate standards (i.e., ability to supply requested needs of intermediaries), cooperative advertising and other promotional support, lead-time requirements (i.e., working days from order placement to receipt), and product-service exclusivity agreements each contribute to the likelihood of long-term exchange relationships. A manager who fails to recognize these facts of life often finds that the performance of functions necessary to satisfy buyer requirements, such as sales contacts, display, adequate inventory, service, and delivery, are not being accomplished.

Conflicts often arise in trade relations. *Channel conflict* arises when one channel member (e.g., a manufacturer or intermediaries) believes another channel member is engaged in behavior that prevents it from achieving its goals. For example, H. J. Heinz Company was recently embroiled in a conflict with supermarkets in Great Britain because the supermarkets were promoting and displaying private brands at the expense of Heinz brands.[2]

Conflict can have destructive effects on the workings of a marketing channel. To reduce the likelihood of conflict, one member of the channel sometimes seeks to coordinate, direct, and support other channel members. This channel member assumes the role of a *channel captain* because of the firm's power to influence the behavior of other channel members.

Power can take four forms. First, *economic power* arises from the ability of a firm to reward or coerce other members given its strong financial position or customer franchise. IBM or Sears would have economic power. *Expertness* is a second source of power. For example, American Hospital Supply helps its customers—hospitals—manage order processing for hundreds of medical supplies. *Identification with a particular channel member* may also create power for that firm. For instance, retailers may compete to carry Ralph Lauren, or clothing manufacturers may compete to be carried by Neiman-Marcus or Bloomingdales. Finally, power can arise from the *legitimate right of one channel member to dictate the behavior of other members*. This would occur under contractual arrangements (e.g., franchising) where one channel member can legally direct how another behaves.

CHANNEL-MODIFICATION DECISIONS

Marketing channels used by organizations are subject to modification, but less so than product, price, and promotion. Shifts in geographical concentration of buyers, the inability of existing intermediaries to meet the needs of buyers, and the costs of distribution represent external reasons for modifying existing marketing channels. As an example,

Sanyo Electric, Inc., has eliminated many of its distributors because the company observed that twenty distributors covered the same market that ninety had in previous years.[3] The organization itself might initiate a channel-modification program if the product-market strategy changes as evidenced by the adoption of a market development or diversification strategy. For example, in 1982 Mitsubishi Motors of Japan decided to stop distributing its automobiles through the Chrysler Corporation dealer network given a change in Mitsubishi's product strategy. Mitsubishi now operates its own sales and service channel.[4] Whatever the reason for modifying the organization's marketing channels, at the base of the channel-modification decision should lie the manager's intent to better achieve the three channel objectives cited earlier. The approach taken for these decisions involves an assessment of both the benefits and the costs of making a change.

Qualitative Consideration in Modification Decisions

The qualitative assessment of a modification decision can be phrased in a series of questions. These questions imply that the modification decision involves a comparative analysis of the existing and new channels.

1. Will the change improve the effective coverage of the target markets sought? How?

2. Will the change improve on the satisfaction of buyer needs? How?

3. Which marketing functions, if any, must be absorbed in the change?

4. Does the organization have the resources to perform the new functions, if any?

5. What effect, if any, will the change have on other channel participants?

6. What will be the effect of a change in achieving long-range organizational objectives?

Quantitative Assessment of Modification Decision

A quantitative assessment of the modification decision considers the financial impact of the change in terms of revenues and expenses. This can be illustrated through the use of a simple example.

Suppose an organization is considering replacing its wholesalers with its own distribution centers. Wholesalers received $5 million annually from the margin on sales of the organization's offering. The organization's cost of servicing the wholesalers is $500,000 annually. Therefore, the "cost" of using wholesalers in this instance would be the margin received by wholesalers and the $500,000 for servicing them, for a total of $5.5 million. Stated differently, the organization would "save" this amount if the wholesalers were eliminated.

However, by eliminating the wholesalers, the organization will have to assume their functions. These functions would include the costs of sales to retail accounts formerly assumed by the wholesalers. Sales administration costs would be also incurred. In addition, since the wholesalers carried inventories to service retail accounts, the cost of carrying the inventory must be assumed. Expenses of delivery and torage must be determined. Finally, since wholesalers extended credit to retailers, the cost of carrying the accounts receivable must be included.

Once the costs assumed by eliminating the wholesaler have been estimated, then an evaluation of the modification decision from a financial perspective is possible. This is shown below with illustrative dollar values.

Cost of Wholesalers		Cost of Distribution Centers	
Margin to wholesalers	$5,000,000	Sales to retailers	$1,500,000
Service expense	500,000	Sales administration	250,000
Total cost	$5,500,000	Inventory cost	935,000
		Delivery and storage	1,877,000
		Accounts receivable	438,000
		Total cost	$5,000,000

Since using wholesalers costs $5.5 million and the cost of distribution centers would be $5 million, the latter opinion should be selected from a cost perspective. However, the effect on revenues must be considered. This can be determined by first addressing the questions noted earlier, and second, by translating market coverage, the satisfaction of buyer needs, and channel-participant response into dollar values.

NOTES

1. Much of this discussion is drawn from R. Weigand, "Fit Products and Channels to Your Markets," *Harvard Business Review* (January–February 1977): 95–105.

2. "Heinz Struggles to Stay at the Top of the Stack," *Business Week* (March 11, 1985): 49.

3. "Sanyo Sales Strategy Illustrates Problems of Little Distributors," *Wall Street Journal* (September 10, 1985): 31.

4. "Mitsubishi Revs Up to Go Solo," *Business Week* (May 3, 1982): 129–132.

ADDITIONAL READINGS

Davidson, William. "Channels of Distribution—One Aspect of Marketing Strategy." *Business Horizons* (February 1961): 84–90.

Gaski, John F. "The Theory of Power and Conflict in Channels of Distribution." *Journal of Marketing* (Summer 1984): 9–29.

Hlavacek, James E., and McCuisition, Tommy J. "Industrial Distributors: When, Who, and How?" *Harvard Business Review* (March–April 1983): 96–101.

Jackson, Donald J.; Krampf, Robert F., and Konopa, Leonard J. "Factors That Influence the Length of Industrial Channels." *Industrial Marketing Management* (October 1982): 263–268.

Weigand, Robert E. "Fit Products and Channels to Your Markets." *Harvard Business Review* (January–February 1977): 95–105.

CASE

Porsche AG

PETER SCHULTZ SEEMED to have everything going his way. In the three years since he became president of Porsche AG, the Porsche model 944 had become a resounding success since it was introduced in mid-1982, and Porsche sales in the United States had more than doubled. Nevertheless, Mr. Schultz had expressed concerns about Porsche's distribution effort in the United States and was contemplating a change.

Since 1969, Volkswagen of America (VWoA), a subsidiary of Volkswagenwerk AG, had handled all aspects of Porsche's automotive business in the United States, including importing, advertising, sales, and service when it established a Porsche-Audi Division. VWoA sold the Porsche line through 323 independent franchised dealers. These dealers also sold Audis, produced by a Volkswagenwerk AG subsidiary. According to industry sources, VWoA made $40 million importing Porsches into the United States in 1983.

Porsche's contract with VWoA was due to expire in August 1984, and Mr. Schultz felt the time was right to make the "single most important decision in the company's entire history": whether to change the way Porsche sold, warehoused, and repaired its cars in the United

---

This case was prepared by Professor Roger A. Kerin, Edwin L. Cox School of Business, Southern Methodist University, as a basis for class discussion and is not designed to illustrate effective or ineffective handling of administrative situations. This case is based solely on published information, which includes: "Porsche is Doing Great—So Changes Course," *Fortune* (March 5, 1984), p. 59; "Porsche to Cancel VW of America's Import Contract," *Wall Street Journal* (January 30, 1984), p. 13; "Porsche Gets Set to Go It Alone in the U.S.," *Business Week* (February 27, 1984), pp. 46–47; "Porsche to end pact with VWoA," *Automotive News* (February 6, 1984), pp. 3, 7; "Porsche casts a pall on franchise system," *Automotive News* (February 20, 1984), pp. 1, 57; "Porsche moves ahead on new set-up," *Automotive News* (May 7, 1984), pp. 1, 8; "Porsche's Civil War with Its Dealers," *Fortune* (April 16, 1984), pp. 63–64; "Porsche Forms Its Own U.S. Distribution Unit to Sell and Service Cars," *Wall Street Journal* (February 16, 1984), p. 44; *1984 Moody's International Manual* (New York: Moody's Investors Service, 1984); "Suits against Porsche could top $1 billion," *Automotive News* (March 12, 1984), pp. 1, 57; "Ad agency to drop Porsche after Porsche drops VWoA," *Automotive News* (February 6, 1984), pp. 3, 7.

States. Several factors combined to lead Mr. Schultz to consider a change. First, he had heard that successful dealers in need of cars often had to buy Porsches from other dealers at premium prices, which inflated the price paid by customers. Second, he felt a mass market retailer such as a Porsche-Audi dealer was the wrong outlet for low-volume, high-priced ($21,400–$44,000 list price) Porsche cars. Third, he believed the Japanese would soon enter the high-performance sports car market in the United States, and Porsche needed a distribution system that would compete against them. These factors led him to conclude that a new distribution arrangement was necessary to bring the Porsche factory closer to its customers. Furthermore, he believed sales in the United States would increase if customers could be assured of getting cars more readily with the special features they desired.

The new distribution plan envisioned by Mr. Schultz contained four major points:

1. Porsche AG would withdraw from its contract with VWoA in August 1984 and would stop selling its cars through the VWoA dealer network.

2. Porsche would recruit and use agents to sell its cars rather than Porsche-Audi dealers. These agents would not have to buy cars and inventory them at a fixed location as dealers do. Therefore, they would not have to tie up cash in a car inventory, incur interest costs on that inventory, and operate a dealership.

3. Porsche would operate two warehouses in the United States, one in Reno, Nevada, and the other in Charleston, South Carolina.

4. Forty distribution and repair centers would be operated in the United States, where the Porsche population was highest. These forty distribution centers would also sell Porsches. The distribution company would be called Porsche Cars North America.

THE COMPANY

Porsche AG was founded by Ferdinand Porsche in 1931. Based in Stuttgart, West Germany (Federal Republic of Germany), Porsche AG is primarily engaged in the development, manufacturing, and marketing of sports cars, in four-, six-, and eight-cylinder models, both for domestic consumption and for export. Porsche AG is also well known for its development of racing car models. For example, in 1983 Porsche cars swept nine of the first ten places at LeMans.

Porsche AG recorded net sales of $841 million with record earnings in fiscal 1983. One of the factors in this recent success was the

Porsche 944—a high-performance model with an enticing $18,450 price, well below the $33,000 average sticker prices for Porsche cars. Another factor in Porsche's record year was a more prosperous U.S. economy, since 53 percent of company sales came from the United States. The introduction of the Porsche 944 and the rebound in the U.S. economy resulted in sales of 21,831 cars in the United States in 1983, compared with 14,407 cars in 1982 and only 11,200 cars in 1981. Summary financial statements for fiscal 1983 are shown in Exhibit 1.

DISTRIBUTION PLAN

The plan envisioned for the distribution of Porsche cars in the United States was based in part on consumer research indicating that the

EXHIBIT 1
Porsche AG Financial Statement Summary
(in DM 1,000)

Income Statement Summary
(for the Year Ended July 31, 1983)

Net sales	DM	2,133,679
Gross margin		758,674
Other income		43,066
Depreciation and amortization		71,148
Operating expenses		449,919
Taxes		124,945
Net income	DM	69,600

Balance Sheet Summary
(as of July 30, 1983)

Assets:		
Current assets	DM	511,098
Fixed assets (including participatives and deferred charges)		355,452
Total assets	DM	866,550
Liabilities and equity:		
Current liabilities	DM	630,105
Long-term debt		15,700
Equity		220,745
Total liabilities and equity	DM	866,550

Note: For analysis purposes, $1.00 U.S. = DM 2.54. DM is the abbreviation for Deutschemark, the monetary unit of West Germany.

Porsche buyer was different from the so-called typical car buyer. For example, Porsche owners were not impulse buyers but, rather, approached the decision to buy a Porsche in a deliberate manner. They compared products and considered the purchase of a Porsche as an investment. Furthermore, Porsche owners were viewed as working sixty to eighty hours per week, having high standards of excellence and high expectations, and earning at least $75,000 per year. These data buttressed Mr. Schultz's opinion that Porsche customers could be better served by a different distribution arrangement. He was quoted in *Automotive News* (February 20, 1984, p. 1) as saying:

> It is our firm belief that Porsche cannot hope to be viable as a manufacturer of high-technology, high-performance sports cars that are distributed by a traditional automotive marketing organization that is basically structured to serve a volume market with traditional service and sales activities."

He added: "It must be as much fun to acquire a Porsche as it is to drive one." Details of the plan follow.

Agents versus Dealers

A central element of the new distribution plan was the change from conventional car dealers to agents who would represent Porsche Cars North America. Under the arrangement with VWoA, Porsche was inventoried and sold through Porsche-Audi dealers, which typically received a 16–18 percent margin on new Porsche cars. In addition, these dealers operated (1) a service department for routine and other car maintenance and repair needs and (2) a preowned, or used, car lot.

Under the new plan, Porsche Cars North America would sell its cars through agents that would be formed as limited partnerships. Every current Porsche dealer would be offered the opportunity to become an agent. These agents would receive an 8 percent commission on new cars sold. Each agent would receive four Porsches for demonstration purposes as part of the limited-partnership fee, but would not inventory new Porsches or operate used car lots. An agent could offer car servicing or rely on Porsche Cars North America distribution centers to perform Porsche service. Agents would be allowed to set prices for new cars; but the forty distribution centers located in areas of high Porsche ownership would list a suggested retail price and sell its cars only at the list price. According to a Porsche executive, the establishment of a fixed list price would mean that "A customer that is aware [of the list price] doesn't have to pay over list price; he has an alternative."

Distribution Centers

A second element of the new distribution plan included distribution centers. Forty distribution centers were planned, to be located in areas of high Porsche ownership. The distribution centers would assume many of the functions performed by conventional car dealers, including preparation, delivery, and service of new cars. In addition, distribution centers would operate a used car program for buyers wishing to purchase a preowned Porsche. However, used cars sales would not be handled in the usual way. The major difference would be that Porsche Cars North America would refurbish cars for the purpose of increasing their value.

Warehouse Locations

West Coast and East Coast warehouses would be operated for new cars and parts. The West Coast warehouse would be located in Reno, Nevada, and the East Coast warehouse in Charleston, South Carolina. Reno, Nevada, would also house the corporate offices of Porsche Cars North America.

Each warehouse would be situated on the premises of an airport, since parts are shipped by air and plans were underway to ship cars by air as well. The plan involved transporting 250 cars per week via Boeing 747 cargo planes. Five flights per week were planned. These cars would serve as a buffer stock for distribution centers and agents. A schematic representative of the proposed distribution system is shown in Exhibit 2.

Buyer and Agent Ordering

The ordering of new or used cars would proceed as follows. A customer would go to an agent or distribution center and arrange to buy a car. Once a car was sold, a request for the model would be made through a computer link to Reno or Charleston. The customer would then go to either location to pick up the car and drive it home. Alternatively, an agent or distribution center employee could pick up the car for the buyer.

Cost

The total cost associated with the new system would include the costs of operating the two warehouses and distribution centers as well as importing, advertising, and servicing Porsche cars in the United States. It is estimated that Porsche AG would have to invest $350 million to

EXHIBIT 2
Porsche Cars North America Three-Tiered
Distribution System

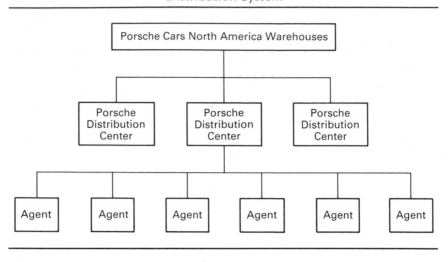

start the operation and hire at least 275 people. Approximately $22 million would be spent to set up the Reno, Nevada, warehouse alone.

DISTRIBUTION PLAN ISSUES

The plan outlined by Peter Schultz represented a significant departure from past practices and could affect long-standing relationships with Volkswagenwerk AG. For example, the management of Porsche AG and Volkswagenwerk AG shared numerous family ties. Ferdinand Porsche, the company's founder, designed the Volkswagen "Beetle" that established Volkswagenwerk AG. Ferdinand Porsche's son, Ferry, is chairman of the board of Porsche AG; his son-in-law, Anton Piëch, was Volkswagenwerk's first chairman of the board. Anton Piëch's widow and children are still active in Volkswagenwerk affairs and own a Volkswagen distributorship and retail outlets in Austria. Ferdinand Porsche's grandson, Ferdinand Piëch, is director of research and development at Volkswagenwerk's Audi subsidiary. In short, a break with Volkswagenwerk could mean severing family ties.

Another issue was the response by Porsche-Audi dealers in the United States and VWoA. When Peter Schultz presented his idea to 300 Porsche-Audi dealers on February 15, 1984, in Reno, Nevada, the response was cool. According to a *Fortune* magazine report (April 16, 1984, p. 64) ". . . the dealers felt betrayed by the abolition of franchises and insulted by Schultz's invitation for them to invest in limited partnerships that would finance Porsche centers." Within a month of Mr. Schultz's announcement, Porsche AG was put on notice that it could face legal action by Porsche-Audi dealers totaling over $1 billion in penalties. In addition, VWoA filed protests against Porsche AG with the California and Nevada Departments of Motor Vehicles.

By April 1984, Mr. Schultz had to decide whether or not to proceed with his original plan or some variation. He was fully aware of the fact that the August 31 date for renewing the distribution contract with VWoA was quickly approaching.

CASE

Carapace, Inc.

CARAPACE, INC., IS a Tulsa, Oklahoma–based firm specializing in plaster bandages used in making casts for broken bones. Carapace was established when Bill Klintworth; his father; and Jeff Nooleen, an orthopedic supplies dealer in Tulsa, Oklahoma, purchased a plaster company from its founder. Prior to the acquisition, the firm had prospered as a sole proprietorship by satisfying the bandage needs of a geographically limited market. Carapace had gross sales of $100,000 with a pretax profit of $20,000. Carapace serviced the West South Central United States through Nooleen's dealership and the efforts of one salesman. "Market acceptance was particularly high in Texas and Oklahoma due to the previous owner's reputation for high quality bandages. This reputation got our foot in the door, and by maintaining our quality, we have established potentially long-term relationships with our existing customers," remarked Klintworth.

Klintworth realized that the geographical market served by Carapace had to be expanded. Therefore, Klintworth stated that Carapace's objectives were (1) to expand the firm's market coverage from the West South Central region (Texas, Oklahoma, Arkansas, Louisiana, and Mississippi) to a national level, and (2) to capture 3 percent of the United States plaster bandage market within two years, which was well within the firm's production capacity.

Shortly thereafter Klintworth was contacted by two major distributors of orthopedic supplies concerning the possibility of selling the Carapace plaster bandage. Both sought exclusive rights to Carapace's plaster bandages. Klintworth believed that he should first review his marketing program before deciding which distributor's proposal should be accepted.

This case was written by Mr. Gregory Grimshaw, graduate student, and Professor Roger A. Kerin, Southern Methodist University, Dallas, as a basis for class discussion rather than to illustrate appropriate or inappropriate handling of administrative situations. The authors wish to thank Carapace, Inc., for its cooperation in the preparation of this case.

THE CAST MATERIAL MARKET

Plaster has been used in medicine as an immobilizer since the sixteenth century. Until several decades ago, casts were made by doctors through a process whereby they prepared a solution of plaster, then dipped strips of gauze bandages into it, and wrapped them around the limb until they hardened into a cast. Eventually, a method was developed that allowed plaster to be impregnated onto gauze and then dried and rolled, thus making it possible for plaster bandages to be mass-produced and distributed.

Plaster's Competition

Recently, synthetic materials have emerged as contenders for a portion of the estimated $15 million cast material market. For example, Merck and Company introduced a cast called Lightcast II, made of polypropylene, glass fiber, and resin, which can be as much as 50 percent lighter in weight and three times stronger than plaster. Also, because it can be immersed in water, Lightcast II permits bathing and hydrotherapy. This type of cast presents a formidable rival to the heavier plaster cast, which is still not completely waterproof.

Market Dominance

In spite of plaster's apparent drawbacks, 99.3 percent of the cast material market volume is still in plaster. The main reason for the popularity of plaster is its price. Synthetic casts are seven to ten times more expensive than plaster casts. Many doctors find it hard to pass this added expense on to their patients when other medical costs are rising. Furthermore, patients seem to prefer plaster since synthetics often make the "cast-signing" ritual difficult because of the uneven surface of synthetics. In addition to these attributes, chemical additives are constantly improving the quality of plaster casts. Resins help strengthen plaster casts and improve their water resistance. Whiteners are added to improve the cosmetic appearance. Depending on the amount of potassium sulfate used in the original plaster mixture, setting times can be varied to meet the particular needs of the user. Finally, some types of casts require the use of plaster because of its superior conforming qualities. Because of these various attributes, plaster is expected to continue to dominate the cast materials market in the foreseeable future.

Consumer Use

About six thousand tons of plaster are used for medical purposes annually. Of the 4 million casts applied in the United States per year, 75 percent were for setting fractures, and the remainder were used for the support of sprained limbs and for orthopedic immobilization.

Although figures are not available for total cast material sales, hospitals account for an estimated 50 percent of market sales volume. Remaining sales are to medical schools, orthopedic clinics, doctors' offices, veterinarians, and others. In general, a company's share of the hospital cast material market is believed to equal its share of the national market.

Hospital sales are estimated to be about 29 million units. (A unit may be anything from a 5-inch by 30-inch splint to an 8-inch by 5-yard roll.) This represents a 14.7 percent increase in volume from the previous year. Total cast material sales in dollars have grown to an estimated $7.3 million in sales to the nation's 7,451 hospitals. Exhibit 1 shows estimated average annual cast material dollar purchases for hospitals within the nation's nine geographic regions. Exhibit 2 shows hospital sales by region and market share by firm for a typical six month period. It suggests that the East North Central, the South Atlantic, and the Middle Atlantic are the three largest areas for cast material sales. Exhibit 3 shows sales by hospital size according to the number of beds, and the market shares for major marketers for the various size hospitals. The three bandage sizes that are most popular with doctors are the 4-inch by 5-yard bandage (30 percent of unit sales), the 6-inch by 5-yard bandage (30 percent of unit sales), and the 3-inch by 5-yard bandage (20 percent of unit sales). Twenty percent of unit sales are

EXHIBIT 1
Average Annual Dollar Expenditures for Casts for
Hospitals by Geographical Region

Region	Number of Hospitals in Region	Average Expenditure	Sample Size
New England	432	$1,287	26
Middle Atlantic	927	1,523	87
East North Central	1,201	1,229	90
West North Central	947	615	48
South Atlantic	1,022	986	63
East South Central	593	957	32
West South Central	1,016	505	48
Mountain	426	769	19
Pacific	887	1,081	37

Source: Company records. Data obtained from marketing research report prepared by an independent research firm.

EXHIBIT 2
Hospital Cast Material Dollar Sales by Geographical Area and Market Share by Firm

		East			Central		
	Total	Total	New England	Middle Atlantic	Total	East North Central	West North Central
Region volume ($000s)	3,696	983	278	705	1,026	737	290
Market share by firm:							
Johnson & Johnson	74.5%	62.1%	70.9%	58.6%	74.8%	75.9%	71.5%
Parke-Davis	10.2	14.8	14.2	15.0	12.5	9.1	20.4
Solar	10.0	16.6	12.8	18.2	7.6	8.4	3.3
Kendall	2.7	4.4	2.0	5.3	3.5	3.3	3.9
Acme Cotton	1.8	1.6	.0	2.2	2.5	3.1	1.0
All others	.8	.5	.1	.7	.1	.1	.0

		South			West		
	Total	South Atlantic	East South Central	West South Central	Total	Mountain	Pacific
Region volume ($000s)	1,043	504	284	256	644	164	479
Market share by firm:							
Johnson & Johnson	83.9%	86.0%	64.2%	87.7%	78.0%	81.8%	76.7%
Parke-Davis	3.8	5.4	4.3	.0	10.0	14.2	8.6
Solar	6.7	3.0	19.2	.0	10.3	.0	13.8
Kendall	2.0	1.0	5.7	.0	.1	.0	.2
Acme Cotton	2.3	1.7	3.4	2.3	.3	1.3	.0
All others	1.3	.9	3.2	10.0	1.3	2.7	.8

Source: Company records. Data obtained from marketing research report prepared by an independent research firm. Data represent a typical six month period.

accounted for by three other bandage sizes (2-inch by 3-yard, 3-inch by 3-yard, and 5-inch by 5-yard).

Competition

"Johnson & Johnson is the recognized leader in cast material sales. Due to their dominance as a supplier of hospital materials, their name alone is often enough to generate sales of cast material," according to Klintworth. Johnson & Johnson alone accounted for an estimated 81.1 percent of the hospital cast material volume. Parke-Davis was the next largest with 12.4 percent volume (see Exhibit 4). Parke-Davis distributes plaster bandages for Anchor Continental. Klintworth believed that in three or four years, Anchor Continental will distribute cast material on its own.

Several months ago Kendall decided to exit the cast material market. Owned by Colgate Palmolive, Kendall had tried to compete directly with Johnson & Johnson by modeling its packaging, product, and prices after Johnson & Johnson. Klintworth believed that Carapace should orient its product to fill the void created by Kendall's exit from the market. He noted, "With the departure of Kendall, about 3 percent of the market should be available to us, or about $450,000."

CARAPACE PRELIMINARY MARKETING STRATEGY

Product Positioning

Klintworth believed Carapace should emphasize quality, service, and its specialization in plaster bandages. The last point was especially important, since an estimated 90 percent of the market was controlled by Johnson & Johnson, Parke-Davis, and Kendall; also, all three market hundreds of other medical supplies. The advantage of specialization was emphasized in Carapace's advertising brochure:

> Just as there are specialists in the medical profession, CARAPACE is a specialist in the making of a superior plaster bandage. Other competing manufacturers consider the plaster bandage as only one of a long line of products. At CARAPACE we make only one product and we are the best at what we do.

Pricing and Cost Structure

Carapace's prices on its plaster products were established to reflect the high quality of its offering, according to Klintworth. Manufacturing

EXHIBIT 3
Cast Material Dollar Sales by Hospital Size and Market Share by Firm

	Total	*500 &* *Over*	*300–* *499*	*200–* *299*	*100–* *199*	*Under* *100*
Dollar volume (000s)	3,696	737	917	662	682	698
Market share by firm:						
Johnson & Johnson	74.5%	71.3%	74.0%	66.0%	83.6%	77.6%
Parke-Davis	10.2	11.6	13.0	15.7	5.6	4.1
Solar	10.0	8.9	7.1	16.1	3.4	15.9
Kendall	2.7	4.6	4.2	.8	3.4	0.0
Acme Cotton	1.8	2.3	1.1	1.3	4.0	.7
Others	.8	1.3	.5	.1	.1	1.8
	100.0%	100.0%	100.0%	100.0%	100.0%	100.0%

Source: Company records. Data obtained from marketing research report prepared by an independent research firm. Data represent a typical six month period.

and material costs are estimated to be 20 percent of the retail price. Overhead costs were approximately $50,000. Present suggested retail prices on Carapace products are shown in Exhibit 5.

Promotion

At this point, $1,000 has been spent to develop a brochure for Carapace. This brochure emphasized quality, service, product attributes, and the importance of remaining small:

> As a statement of business philosophy, it is our desire never to mass produce our CARAPACE bandage—to remain small enough so that we can continue to produce the best and the most inexpensive bandage available and still offer personal, fast service to our customers. Sure, we're small; but that is why we are so good.

Klintworth outlined Carapace's important selling points that could be selected for future promotional efforts:

- "Wetting out" is faster with Carapace bandages—that is, they absorb water faster when preparing the bandages for wrapping.
- Plaster loss is low. The use of adhesives in Carapace plaster reduces the amount of plaster melting off the gauze during application.

EXHIBIT 4
Annualized Cast Material Market Share
among Hospitals

Firm	Unit Shares		Dollar Shares	
	Volume (000s)	Percentage	Volume (000s)	Percentage
Johnson & Johnson	23,855.6	81.1	5,339	73.0
Parke-Davis	3,661.3	12.4	733	10.2
Solar	209.6	0.7	651	9.0
Kendall	1,128.7	3.8	263	3.6
Acme Cotton	567.9	1.9	173	2.4
Others	29.4	0.1	62	.9
Total	29,451.5	100.0%	7,221	100.0%

Source: Company records. Data obtained from marketing research report prepared by an independent research firm.

- Carapace is the "Cadillac of bandages" due to the high quality of chemicals used in the mixture.

- The initial setting time is faster—three to four minutes, as opposed to five to eight minutes.

- Eventual hardening time is faster than others. With Carapace, a foot cast can be walked on the next day, whereas other products require forty-eight hours to harden completely.

- Packaging: it is easier to remove the Carapace bandage from its plastic bag, as opposed to rival products that are heat-sealed in plastic.

- Carapace has an indefinite shelf life.

- Carapace doesn't delaminate in water.

- It's "organic," unlike Johnson & Johnson's bandage, which contains formaldehyde as a preservative. Therefore, Carapace plaster smells better and causes no skin irritation.

- It finishes out prettier, whiter, and smoother than other plaster casts.

- Carapace gives off less exothermic heat during the cast-hardening process.

- The delivery time is faster than Johnson & Johnson's.

- There is a 5 percent discount if payment is in by the tenth of the month.

EXHIBIT 5
Carapace Price List

	Bandages	
	Single-Case Quantity Case Price	*Price per Unit*
2 inches × 3 yds.—6 dozen to a case	$23.40	$.325
3 inches × 3 yds.—6 dozen to a case	27.30	.387
3 inches × 5 yds.—6 dozen to a case	39.30	.545
4 inches × 5 yds.—6 dozen to a case	40.20	.558
5 inches × 5 yds.—4 dozen to a case	32.60	.679
6 inches × 5 yds.—4 dozen to a case	37.20	.775

Source: Company records. A bondage is equivalent to a unit.

- Carapace won't "telescope"—that is, slide down the patient's limb.

Distribution

Klintworth was unsure of how to reach the cast material market with his plaster bandage. He had ruled out using his own sales group due to sales administration, recruiting, and training costs. Accordingly, he welcomed the interest of two nationally recognized orthopedic supply distributors.

On succeeding days, Klintworth was contacted by Miller Medical Associates and Continental, Inc. (disguised names). Both described their organizations and presented him proposals including exclusive rights to represent Carapace in the United States.

Miller Medical Associates (MMA)

MMA has sixty-two salespersons located throughout the United States except for the West South Central and East North Central regions (see Exhibit 6). In addition, MMA also services twenty-two established orthopedic dealers situated in major metropolitan areas in territories serviced by salespersons. MMA does not compete with its dealers for accounts.

For its sales effort, MMA would receive a 5 percent commission on retail sales below $500,000, 4 percent on retail sales up to $1 million, and 3 percent on retail sales over $1 million. This commission is obtained both from sales by MMA to final users (e.g., doctors, hospitals), and from retail sales through dealers. MMA dealers also receive a 20

EXHIBIT 6
Miller Medical Associates Sales Personnel

Region	Number of Sales Personnel
New England	5
Middle Atlantic	9
East North Central	0
West North Central	11
South Atlantic	11
East South Central	7
West South Central	0
Mountain	8
Pacific	11
Total	62

Source: Company records.

percent commission on their own sales. According to the MMA representative, sales volume of Carapace bandage would be split 70–30 percent between dealers and salesmen, respectively.

During the previous three months, MMA had been selling a new synthetic cast called Hexcalite. Since this cast could only be used for certain kinds of injuries, MMA sought out Carapace to complement this product. In addition to bandages, MMA is a distributor of hundreds of orthopedic products and related products. Its product mix contains a wide variety of items ranging from medical equipment priced in five figures to much smaller items such as bandages.

Continental, Inc.

Continental is a smaller distributor of orthopedic supplies than MMA. Continental has fifty salespersons operating in the United States in addition to fifteen established dealers in territories serviced by salespersons. Continental does not compete with dealers for accounts. Its sales organization has representatives in every region (see Exhibit 7). Continental's commission schedule indicates that it receives a 6 percent commission on sales less than $1 million and a 4 percent commission on sales of $1 million or more. This commission is obtained both from sales by Continental to final users and from sales through dealers. Dealers receive a 20 percent commission on their own sales and would account for 40 percent of Carapace bandage sales.

Continental, which does not currently handle a line of plaster bandages, sought out Carapace to fill a gap in its assortment, according to its representative. Continental carries a more limited product assort-

EXHIBIT 7
Continental, Inc., Sales Personnel

Region	Number of Sales Personnel
New England	4
Middle Atlantic	6
East North Central	3
West North Central	9
South Atlantic	9
East South Central	3
West South Central	3
Mountain	4
Pacific	9
Total	50

Source: Company records.

ment than MMA and does not represent manufacturers of medical equipment.

"Having two proposals is a mixed blessing," remarked Klintworth. "While it confirms our confidence in our product, we now have to figure out which one will most likely help us reach our objectives." Nooleen noted that MMA was the older more established distributor, but he wasn't sure about the attention MMA would give Carapace. Continental was more aggressive, but "it is spread pretty thin nationally," commented Nooleen.

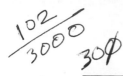

— CASE —

Frito-Lay, Inc.: GRANDMA'S® Brand Cookies

IN EARLY JUNE 1980, Frito-Lay, Inc., executives met to consider alternative sales and distribution approaches for the newly acquired GRANDMA'S® brand line of cookies and snack bars. At an earlier meeting these executives had identified three sales options and three delivery options for the new line. The sales options included (1) using the existing sales force, (2) augmenting the existing sales force, or (3) creating a separate sales force. The delivery options included using (1) the current "front-door" delivery system, (2) a "back-door" delivery system, or (3) a "warehouse" delivery system. At least tentative agreement on the sales and delivery effort was necessary at the meeting because October 1980 was the target date for launching the line in the southwestern and western United States by Frito-Lay, Inc.

READY-TO-EAT COOKIE MARKET

Cookies are either the number-one or number-two snack food in the United States, depending on industry source used. The cookie market divides into two distinct segments. The home-baked segment consists of boxed mixes and refrigerated and frozen bake-it-yourself products.

The cooperation of Frito-Lay, Inc., in the preparation of this case is gratefully acknowledged. This case was prepared by Ms. Megan Cochran, graduate student, under the supervision of Professor Roger A. Kerin, Edwin L. Cox School of Business, Southern Methodist University, as a basis for class discussion and is not designed to illustrate appropriate or inappropriate handling of administrative situations. Certain data are either disguised or approximations and are not useful for research purposes.

The ready-to-eat (RTE) segment consists of dry, shelf-packaged products, of which GRANDMA'S® brand line of cookies is a part. Although industry sources differ in their volume estimates, retail sales of RTE cookies were believed to be $1.87 billion in 1980, with 1.41 billion pounds sold. The RTE cookie dollar volume at manufacturers' prices was about $1.3 billion in 1980. The average annual increase in dollar volume had been 8 percent per year.

Competitors

Nabisco, Keebler, and Sunshine are the three major national brand producers of RTE cookies. In 1979 these three producers accounted for approximately 48 percent of RTE cookie tonnage sold and 53 percent of dollar volume. Nabisco, the acknowledged leader in RTE cookies, captured about 34 percent of this market based on dollar sales. Its well-known major brands are Oreos, Chips A'Hoy, Nilla Wafers, and Fig Newtons. Keebler, a wholly owned subsidiary of United Biscuits, Ltd., captures about 11 percent of dollar sales with such familiar brand names as Rich 'n Chips, Fudge Strips, and Double Nutty. Finally, Sunshine, a division of American Brands, accounts for about 8 percent of dollar sales. Its major well-known brands are Hydrox and Chiperoos. Three additional producers—Pepperidge Farms, Archway, and Mother's cookies—combined account for another 12 percent of dollar sales. The remaining 35 percent of the RTE cookie market dollar volume is captured by regional and private-label manufacturers. None of these manufacturers captures more than 2 percent of the RTE cookie market.

Distribution, Sales, and Delivery Systems

RTE cookies are distributed through a wide variety of outlets. However, industry sources estimate that approximately 89 percent of RTE cookie volume is sold through supermarkets and grocery stores. The remaining 11 percent is sold through other outlets, including convenience stores, commercial eating and drinking places, vending machines, and educational and business cafeterias.

Three kinds of sales and delivery systems are used to distribute RTE cookies. The majority (60 percent) of cookies are distributed by a *store delivery* method. Thirty-five percent of cookie volume is distributed using a *warehouse system*. The remainder of cookie volume (5 percent) is delivered through food brokers, independent distributors, and franchised distributors.

Store delivery systems come in two forms—front-door and back-door. In both systems, manufacturers' trucks transport the product from the plant to distribution centers. In a back-door system, a company sales representative visits a store owner or manager or a chain store buyer, receives an order or authorization to display products, and phones it in to a driver or delivery person. The driver delivers the product within twenty-four hours to the back door of the store and leaves it boxed. The sales representative returns within a day or two to shelve the goods. The method allows the sales representative to focus on merchandising only and relieves the representative of inventory management. Industry experience indicates that the back-door system cannot be used economically for small accounts, since small-volume outlets do not provide for cost-efficiencies with two individuals serving them.

A front-door system combines the duties of the delivery person and the sales representative. A driver/sales representative takes the order, unloads the product, and stocks the shelves during one stop. The main advantage of the front-door system arises from the use of fewer employees and consequent lower personnel costs. A counteracting cost disadvantage is that delivery trucks cover a much smaller territory in a given time period, since each individual call takes a substantially longer time. Also, recruiting good people for a sales representative's position is difficult, since the individual's job duties also include delivering and truck driving.

When a warehouse delivery system is used, the product is picked up at the plant and delivered to supermarket chain or grocery store warehouses. A manufacturer's delivery duties are over once the product has reached the warehouse. This system, though much easier to execute and less costly than a store delivery system, nevertheless has several drawbacks. First, a warehouse delivery system results in a loss of control by the manufacturer at the point of sale, since the manufacturer has no representative at the store. Second, the range of possible retail outlets through which the product can be sold is narrowed, because outlets that do not possess a warehouse cannot receive product deliveries. In many instances an independent warehouse, broker, or distributor must be used, at additional expense. Third, warehouse-delivered products tend to have a longer delay before being shelved, and therefore may become stale. Even though stales costs are absorbed by the store and not by the manufacturer as in store delivery, loss of freshness may produce negative consumer reactions.

The economics of the store delivery method and the warehouse method also differ. Industry experts generally agree that the warehouse method provides the retailer with a larger trade margin than the store delivery method. A store delivery method, however, provides a manufacturer with a higher gross profit, but because of higher distribution and selling expenses, the operating profit produced by each sales/delivery system is about the same. Exhibit 1 shows the economics of the two systems.

EXHIBIT 1
Economics of Store Delivery and Warehouse Delivery Methods for the Sale/Distribution of Cookies

	Store Delivery	Warehouse Delivery
Retail price (assuming $1.00/unit)	$1.00	$1.00
Trade margin	27%[a]	35%
Selling price to store	$0.73 (100%)	$0.65 (100%)
Cost of goods sold	0.40 (55%)	0.40 (62%)
Gross profit	0.33 (45%)	0.25 (38%)
Advertising and promotion	0.04 (5%)	0.05 (8%)
Distribution/selling expense[b]	0.18 (25%)	0.10 (15%)
Fixed overhead (administration)	0.05 (7%)	0.05 (8%)
Operating profit	$0.06 (8%)	$ .05 (7%)

Source: Industry interviews.

[a]21 percent + 6 percent in discounts.

[b]Includes trade deals.

The distribution and sales efforts of the three national brand producers of RTE cookies are generally similar, but differ in certain respects. Nabisco's sales approach is termed an *advance-man system.* Under the system, one of the company's three thousand sales representatives calls on an outlet or chain store headquarters for the purpose of gaining authorization to display products and obtain orders. If an order is obtained, the order (products) is brought to the store approximately two days later in a company-owned truck by a delivery person and left at the back door. The sales representative returns a day or two later and shelves, prices, replaces broken or stale product, and displays products on an ongoing basis. In addition, the sales representative is responsible for working with the direct store goods buyer in chain stores or with the owner-manager in small grocery stores on subsequent orders, including ideas for merchandising, shelf-space allotments and placements, and so forth. Nabisco distributes through about 100,000 supermarkets, grocery stores, and other outlets (e.g., vending machine companies), using a fleet of 1,500 trucks and 1,200 delivery people. Sales representatives receive a salary plus commission on sales; delivery personnel receive a straight salary.

Keebler's distribution system is similar to Nabisco's back-door approach. Its sales force, however, is approximately one-half the size, with thirteen hundred sales representatives and six hundred delivery people. Competition with Nabisco is the primary reason for Keebler's distribution system.

Sunshine uses a warehouse delivery system. Products are delivered directly to supermarket warehouses or to independent distributors, who sell and deliver products to retail outlets. Sunshine recently switched from a store delivery system because it could not meet the frequency of trade delivery demands (once or twice per week) as a result of its lower sales volumes. Sunshine provides an additional 8–10 percent discount to retailers since they provide the service otherwise performed by a direct sales force.

Advertising and Promotion

Advertising and promotion (A&P) expenditures for RTE cookies vary by manufacturer. Nabisco spent approximately $20 million (5 percent of sales) on its line—twice Keebler's expenditure (8 percent of sales) and about three times Sunshine's (6 percent of sales) in 1980. The mix of expenditures also varies somewhat by manufacturer. All three major RTE cookie manufacturers spend the majority of A&P funds on trade-oriented efforts such as off-invoice allowances, shelf tags, and cooperative advertising allowances. However, Keebler spends a significant percentage of its A&P budget on consumer advertising. Still, Keebler's dollar outlay is about the same as Nabisco's expenditure for consumer advertising. All three manufacturers allocate 5 percent of A&P dollars to consumer promotions (e.g., couponing). A breakdown of advertising and promotion expenditures for the three major manufacturers is shown in Exhibit 2.

FRITO-LAY, INCORPORATED

Frito-Lay, Inc., is a division of PepsiCo, Inc., a diversified consumer goods and services firm. Other PepsiCo, Inc., divisions in 1980 include

EXHIBIT 2
Advertising and Promotion Expenditures by Major RTE
Cookie Manufacturers
(millions of dollars)

Manufacturer	Total Expenditure	Expenditure Allocation		
		Advertising	Consumer	Trade
Nabisco	$20.4	$4.1	$1.0	$15.3
Keebler	$10.5	$4.2	$0.5	$5.8
Sunshine	$ 5.8	$0.9	$0.3	$4.6

Source: Company records.

Pizza Hut, Taco Bell, Wilson Sporting Goods, North American Van Lines, Lee Way Motor Frieght, PepsiCo Bottling Company, and PepsiCo Foods International. PepsiCo, Inc., recorded net sales of $5.9 billion in 1980.

Frito-Lay, Inc., is a nationally recognized leader in the manufacturing and marketing of salty snack foods. The company's major salty snack products and brands include potato chips (LAY'S,® RUFFLES®); tortilla chips (DORITOS,® TOSTITOS®); corn puffs (CHEETOS®); and pretzels (ROLD GOLD®). In addition, the company markets a line of cookies, nuts, peanut butter crackers, processed beef sticks, and assorted other snacks under the GO-B-TWEEN® trade name. Exhibit 3 shows the line of Frito-Lay products. Frito-Lay, Inc., net sales in 1980 exceeded $1.5 billion.

Competitive Position

Given the nature of its products, Frito-Lay primarily competes in what is termed the salty snack segment of the snack food market. In 1980 Frito-Lay captured approximately 50 percent of the dollar volume in the salty snack segment and 46 percent of the tonnage sold. Nevertheless, market shares by product category varied dramatically. For example, Frito-Lay's share of corn and tortilla chips pounds sold was over 81 percent. Its share of potato chips was 32 percent on a pound basis, and its pretzels accounted for 14 percent of pounds consumed. Similarly, market shares varied by region. Frito-Lay sold about 80 percent of the total salty snack food tonnage in the southwestern United States, but only 31 percent of the total salty snack tonnage in the northeastern U.S.

Distribution and Sales

Frito-Lay distributes its products through 33,000 accounts nationwide. In 1980, 11 percent of these 33,000 accounts were supermarkets and 13 percent were convenience stores. The remainder of Frito-Lay's accounts were small grocery stores, liquor stores, service stations, and a variety of institutional customers. Supermarket accounts produced 35 percent of sales, convenience stores produced 9 percent of sales, and the remaining accounts produced 56 percent of sales in 1980.

The 33,000 accounts represented approximately 300,000 outlets, since most of the supermarket and convenience store accounts were chain operations. About 20 percent of Frito-Lay accounts were chain accounts, and these accounts produced about 40 percent of Frito-Lay dollar sales in 1980.

Frito-Lay's distribution system is organized around six geographical zones that cover the entire United States. Each of the six

EXHIBIT 3
Frito-Lay, Inc., Product Line

Source: Courtesy of Frito-Lay, Inc.

zones is further subdivided into divisions. Each division is divided into regions, and each region is divided into districts. Districts, regions, and divisions are managed by a sales manager. Each zone is managed by a zone vice-president, who reports to the corporate vice-president of sales. Each zone contains distribution centers that inventory products for the Frito-Lay sales force.

The Frito-Lay sales force is composed of 9,000 individuals who make 80,000 sales and delivery calls in an average work day, or 400,000 calls in an average five-day work week. Timing of sales calls was not evenly spread throughout the week (e.g., 9 per day), nor were the calls made throughout the day. Rather, for big accounts and most supermarkets, sales and delivery calls were made on Fridays (to build stocks for weekend purchases) and on Mondays (to replenish stocks for weekly purchases). For some very large volume outlets, a third call was necessary. Furthermore, a sizable number of sales and delivery calls had to be made before noon, since operators (store managers or owner-managers) preferred to have shelves or displays stocked before the midday or after-work shoppers arrived.

The 400,000 calls during an average week were made on 33,000 supermarkets, 178,000 "big" (important) and "little" (low volume outlets, and 89,000 other customers. Each Frito-Lay salesperson, called a *route salesman,* follows an assigned route and is responsible for selling the full line of Frito-Lay products to present and potential customers on his or her route. Each route salesman was expected to gain profitable product distribution and sales volume by seeking out selling opportunities, meeting customer service requirements, building customer goodwill, and operating effectively and economically.

Frito-Lay uses a front-door store delivery system, whereby one person performs the sales and delivery function. However, experience indicated that sales calls on chain store accounts virtually always required participation by a region or division manager. Such participation was necessary because chain store buyers purchased for all outlets in the chain, so that the sales task and account servicing was more time-consuming and complex, though no less important, than that required for individual outlets (e.g., mom-and-pop grocery stores, liquor stores). Once a sales order was obtained from a chain buyer, individual outlets were assigned to route salespeople in accordance with the existing route network. Individual route salespeople then serviced these outlets and received an average 8 percent commission on net sales. In 1980 the average cost per route per year was $34,090, which included compensation (including commission), fringe benefits, and route truck expenses.

GRANDMA'S® BRAND COOKIES AND SNACK BARS

Frito-Lay, Inc., acquired GRANDMA'S® brand cookies in May 1980. The acquisition provided numerous potential benefits for Frito-Lay:

1. GRANDMA'S® Cookies were viewed as complementing the GO-B-TWEENS® product line currently sold by Frito-Lay.

2. GRANDMA'S® Cookies had an established consumer franchise in the southern and western United States.

3. GRANDMA'S® Cookies were viewed as providing an excel-

lent entry into supermarkets nationwide, even though they were currently being distributed only through vending machine outlets.

4. GRANDMA'S® Cookies provided significant sales potential. Preliminary estimates indicated that as much as $175 million in incremental sales was possible from GRANDMA'S® Cookies and snack bars once the line was introduced nationally.

Product Line

GRANDMA'S® Cookies and a companion line of GRANDMA'S® brand snack bars came in a variety of flavors. Cookie flavors included chocolate chip, apple spice, peanut butter, soft raisin, and molasses. The cookies are large (3 inches in diameter), round, and sold two to a package. Snack bars, also sold two to a package, come in cherry, apple, raspberry, fruit and spice, granola, and raisin and honey flavors. Exhibit 4 shows the line of GRANDMA'S® Cookies and snack bars. Market research on the RTE cookie market indicated that fruit-filled or flavored cookies and chocolate chip cookies accounted for about 35 percent of RTE cookie dollar and pound volume in 1980.

Preliminary Marketing Program

Preliminary discussions on the introduction of GRANDMA'S® Cookies focused on the product's target market, product positioning, advertising and promotion strategy, distribution strategy, and pricing strategy. Tentatively, there appeared to be general agreement that the introductory program would be as follows:

Target Market
The target consumer would be the active housewife twenty-five to fifty-four years old with one or more children living at home. The family-oriented woman would have at least a high school education and family income of $20,000 or more. Cookies purchased by this woman would serve as a snack or dessert item for the entire family.

Product Positioning
GRANDMA'S® Cookies would be positioned as a line of fresh, wholesome cookies with an "all-family" appeal. This position would be supported by the product's high-quality ingredients, soft and moist texture, and superior taste. Prior marketing research has shown consumer dissatisfaction with current hard and dry-textured RTE cookies, and the positioning intended to capitalize on this point.

EXHIBIT 4
GRANDMA'S® Brand Cookies Product Line

Source: Courtesy of Frito-Lay, Inc.

Advertising and Promotion

The introductory advertising campaign, tentatively named "Honest to Grandma," would communicate the positioning and create a positive image by showing warmth and human relationships between a real-life "Grandma" and young children. Trade and consumer promotions were also planned. Trade promotions would be designed to obtain authorizations to display the product in outlets. Consumer promotions were designed to stimulate consumer trial of the product. A preliminary budget contained a first-year expenditure of $17 million for advertising and promotion. About 60 percent of this amount would be for advertising; consumer and trade promotions were each allocated 20 percent of the budget.

Distribution

Preliminary discussions favored focusing on the 300,000 outlets currently served by route salesmen. Emphasis would be placed on obtaining authorizations to stock product in these outlets and gaining display space near the checkout counters of supermarkets and near cash registers in the "big/little" outlets. Permanent displays would be designed to get such placement at no cost to the outlet.

Pricing

The high-quality ingredients, superior taste, and homemade goodness (the result of no preservatives) led to a tentative decision to price GRANDMA'S® Cookies at the upper end of RTE cookie brands currently available. A gross margin in the range of 51 to 55 percent was set for the line.

Delivery and Sales Issue

An issue needing further discussion concerned the delivery and sales system for GRANDMA'S® Cookies. Recent trade surveys focusing on supermarkets had uncovered several points that had contributed to the issue. Results from the surveys indicated that:

1. All buyers preferred the margins provided by a warehouse delivery system, since buyers were evaluated on their ability to achieve high gross margins. When pressed on the subject, however, buyers accepted the reasons for smaller margins with a store delivery system and admitted that they did not have the personnel to service cookie inventory adequately.

2. Nabisco was universally cited as the supplier with which buyers worked best.

3. Services expected from a cookie manufacturer's representative at the buying office included prompt information on cookie category trends, normal account service and allowances, monthly sales figures, and annual business reviews and trends.

4. Services expected at the store level were inventory management, display building, and damaged and stale goods control.

5. A ten- to twenty-one-day supply of cookies was maintained at a warehouse to minimize stock-outs at the retail store level.

Based on these findings and earlier discussions, the decision making on the delivery and sales system for GRANDMA'S® Cookies was structured to address, first, the question of whether to use a warehouse system or a store delivery system like that used for salty snacks. If a store delivery system was chosen, then the specific form of delivery and sales system needed attention. Exhibit 5 shows the various options or combinations of delivery and sales systems scheduled for consideration at the meeting in early June 1980.

Warehouse versus Store Delivery Systems

The first issue raised was whether to use a warehouse or a store delivery system. A decision to adopt a warehouse system over a store delivery system would represent a radical change for Frito-Lay. The store delivery system used by Frito-Lay for its salty snack products was considered by the company and competitors alike to be one of Frito-Lay's major strengths. Nevertheless, a warehouse system had certain factors in its favor. First, supermarket chain store buyer surveys indicated some preference for this system. Second, this system would not dilute salty snack sales force selling time and would, in fact, leave the Frito-Lay store door delivery system intact. However, this system would also result in certain incremental costs. For example, incremental distribution costs to warehouses were estimated to be $5 million annually, assuming only chain supermarket warehouses were serviced. If Frito-Lay provided in-store service for its 33,000 supermarkets by a cookie representative, then cookie representatives would have to be hired. It was believed that a cookie representative would have two thousand hours of available selling time per year. A typical call on a supermarket would require one hour, and a minimum of fifty-two calls would be made on each supermarket per year. The cost of a cookie representative was estimated at $33,000 per year which included compensation, fringe benefits, and car expenses. If in-store service was provided by store personnel, this cost would be eliminated. However, some executives cautioned that cookie placement and upkeep could be a problem unless it was continually monitored by a cookie representative. For example, GRANDMA'S® Cookies might be placed among salty snacks, thus reducing shelf space for Frito-Lay's salty snacks, or given little attention in terms of replacing damaged or stale goods. Furthermore, there could be no assurances that the special displays designed for GRANDMA'S® Cookies would be properly placed and maintained.

EXHIBIT 5
GRANDMA'S® Brand Cookies Delivery and Sales Options

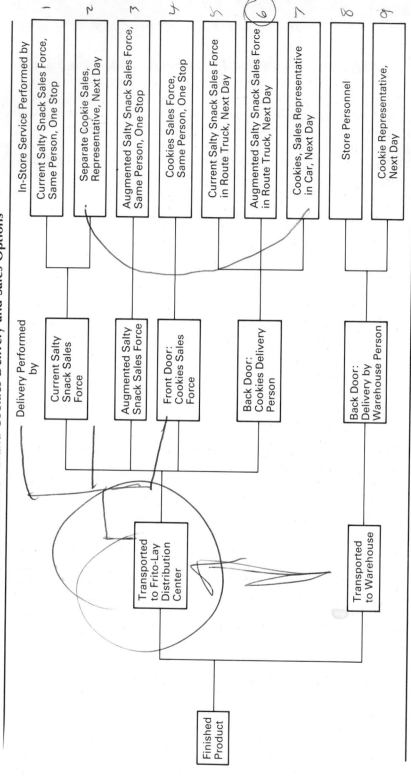

482

Alternatively, the current store delivery system or a modified one could be implemented. Apart from the advantages or disadvantages of the various forms it might take, a store delivery system had a number of factors in its favor. First, the majority of cookies were distributed in this manner. Second, Nabisco and Keebler—both major prospective competitors—used this system. Third, given the potential for stale or broken goods, continuous attention at the point of sale was critical. Fourth, Frito-Lay sales management personnel had intimate knowledge of such a system. However, a store delivery system also had some drawbacks. For example, store margins were typically lower than those associated with a warehouse system. Second, given the intricacies of scheduling and managing literally thousands of routes, significant effort and expense would be required to set up such a system and make it effective and efficient. Sunshine's decision to move to a warehouse system from a store delivery system highlights this point, as well as the need to have a sizable sales volume to cover the expenses incurred and generate a profit.

Alternative Store Delivery Methods

Several different store delivery methods were under consideration. First, current salty snack route salespeople could be given responsibility for the delivery and sale of cookies. Two immediate benefits were cited for this alternative. First, another product line would contribute to a salesperson's salary, particularly since the sales commission on cookies was tentatively set at 10 percent of net sales. Second, this option could be implemented quickly. Nevertheless, this option was questioned on three grounds. First, space availability on route trucks was questioned. A second question concerned the ability of route salespeople to sell to supermarket chain accounts without significant assistance from Frito-Lay sales management at all levels. A related issue was that the chain store buyer for salty snacks was often different from the cookie buyer. Third, given the additional time needed to service a new product, it was felt that routes might have to be restructured or shortened and that additional routes might be necessary. In addition to these points, it was estimated that the sales and delivery expense for this option would be 15 percent of sales, including sales commissions and chargeable truck expense.

A second alternative was to rely on the salty snack route salespeople to deliver cookies to the back door of supermarkets. A route salesperson would not be responsible for sales or in-store service. This option would be less time-consuming, since sales and in-store service would be eliminated, but it would not overcome potential problems with truck capacity. Sales and in-store service would be handled by a separate cookie sales representative, who would arrive the next day to shelve the product, maintain the display, and perform other tasks. Call frequency, call time, and cost of a cookie representative would be the same as those for a warehouse system. This option only applied to supermarkets and not to "big/little" and other accounts, where it was believed that salty snack route salespeople could handle both sales and delivery responsibilities through the front door. In addition to the cost of cookie representatives, a 5 percent truck expense would be charged against supermarket cookie sales, since the salty snack sales force would handle delivery. Delivery and sales expense to nonsupermarket outlets would be 15 percent of sales, including sales commissions and a chargeable truck expense.

A third alternative was to augment the salty snack sales force. A prior assessment of route structures, of time devoted to sales and delivery, and again of truck capacity indicated that 1,046 additional routes would be added to the existing 9,000. The incremental annual cost of each new route would be $35,745, which would be charged directly to the cookie line. The sales and delivery approach would be the same as for salty snacks.

The fourth alternative was to establish a separate cookie driver/delivery sales force who would handle sales and delivery responsibilities on their own route system. These individuals would have the same qualifications, training, and job description as salty snack route salespeople. Their route system would focus exclusively on the 33,000 supermarkets, with other outlets handled by the existing salty snack sales force. The cost per route (per cookie driver/delivery sales representative) per year would be $35,745. A typical supermarket call would require 75 minutes (1.25 hours) as a result of delivery responsibilities, and a minimum of fifty-two calls per year would be required to service a supermarket. Available selling time per year would be 2,000 hours. Sales and delivery cost for nonsupermarket accounts would be 15 percent of cookie sales volume for commissions and truck expenses.

The last three alternatives involved a back-door store delivery system using semitrailer trucks to service supermarkets. The estimated annual operating cost of the semitrailer truck fleet chargeable to the cookie line was $16.5 million. The figure included truck operating costs and salary (plus fringe benefits) of drivers and would be incurred regardless of how the in-store servicing was done. One approach for servicing supermarkets was to rely on current salty snack route salespeople who would arrive within twenty-four hours to shelve and price cookies and to maintain displays. Route salespeople would receive a 10 percent commission on sales to supermarkets. Salty snack salesmen would service nonsupermarket accounts and the sales and delivery cost would be 15 percent of sales. Another approach involved the augmented salty snack sales force option. However, since the delivery responsibilities for supermarkets were eliminated, the estimated average chargeable incremental cost of each route (i.e., 1,046 routes) was reduced to $32,300. Finally, cookie representatives could be responsible for in-store servicing in supermarkets. The number and cost of cookie representatives to be added would be the same as that required for a warehouse delivery system. Sales and delivery expenses associated with nonsupermarket accounts would be 15 percent of cookie sales to these accounts.

The Decision

Executives attending the June meeting realized that the sales and delivery issue was complex and far-reaching. Even though the planned introduction was limited to the southwestern and western United States, their decision had to be national in scope to provide the necessary lead time to implement a full-scale sales and delivery program. Therefore, they concluded that a long-term decision applicable to a nationwide program be considered first. Once that decision was made, then they would consider short-run actions to meet the October launch date.

41,250

Factors

Customer Service
(Buyers & Consumers)

Costs to Firm   *33,785,800*

Product Positioning (?)   *× 16, 500,000*
(Shelf space &
placement, promos, etc.)

41,250
2,145,000
1072

total

$50,285,1
800

Speer Electric Company

THE CORPORATE PLANNING PROCESS for Speer Electric Company had just concluded, and Mr. Richard Hawly, vice-president of marketing, was reviewing the corporate goals for 1987. Even though Mr. Hawly had participated in the deliberations and the drafting of the final document, he was impressed with the ambitious goals. For example, the corporate plan established a sales goal of $37 million for 1987; sales volume for 1986 was estimated to be $27 million.

During the planning process, a number of fellow executives had voiced concern over whether the distribution approach used by Speer Electric was appropriate for the expanded sales goals. Mr. Hawly felt that their concerns had merit and should be given careful consideration. Even though he had considerable latitude in devising the distribution strategy, the final choice would have to be consistent with the overall marketing program for the company in 1987. A recommendation and supporting documentation had to be prepared in a relatively short time to permit an integrated marketing program introduction in 1987.

[handwritten margin note: 10 mill increase in sales]

THE COMPANY

The Speer Electric Company was formed in 1961 by Mark Speerson, a Ph.D. in electrical engineering. The company introduced a stereo radio unit in 1964 and a line of television sets in 1966. By the early 1980s the company had expanded its product line to include a full line of home

This case was prepared by Professor Roger A. Kerin, Southern Methodist University, Dallas, as a basis for class discussion and is not designed to illustrate effective or ineffective handling of administrative situations. The company name and research data are disguised and are not useful for research purposes.

entertainment equipment. In addition to stereo radio and television units, Speer Electric produced ten to twelve different models of record players, AM-FM radio combinations, tape recorders, and video cassette recorders.

Speer Electric distributes its products directly to 425 independent specialty home entertainment dealers and fifty exclusive dealers of standard industry size in terms of selling space.[a] Combined, these 475 dealers serviced 150 markets nationwide. The exclusive dealers, however, were the sole Speer Electric representatives in fifty markets. According to Mr. Hawly, this disparity in market coverage had occurred as a result of Speer Electric's early difficulty in gaining adequate distribution.

The independent dealers typically carried ten or more brands of home entertainment equipment products, whereas the exclusive dealerships carried only Speer Electric products. Dealerships were located in market areas of approximately 250,000 population or less throughout the United States. In contrast, major competitors such as Zenith, RCA, and Admiral had been selling an increasing proportion of their products through mass merchants such as chain and discount stores in areas with a population of one million or more.

The company employed ten sales representatives, each responsible for a territory generally delineated by state boundaries. These representatives dealt primarily with the independent dealers and called on them twice a month on average.

A NOTE ON THE HOME ENTERTAINMENT INDUSTRY

The home entertainment industry has grown considerably with the rise in consumer disposable income, changes in life-styles, and product innovation in the last decade. Estimates of the actual dollar volume of the industry are extremely vague, partly because of the rapidly changing product mix encompassed by the general term *home entertainment* and the constant production innovation.

Despite the difficulty in estimating market size, it is generally accepted that RCA is the major domestic firm in the industry, followed by Zenith and Admiral and then by Sony and Toshiba, two Japanese corporations. Combined, these five firms are believed to account for

---

[a]"Exclusive dealerships" had chosen to operate in this manner. This was not the policy of Speer Electric Company.

67–77 percent of total dollar volume. Private brands, produced by several of these firms and many others, are also important in the industry. The total market was estimated to be growing at a rate of 12 percent annually.

Even though it is difficult to define specifically the product mix in the industry at any one time, eight general product categories exist: television, video disc players, video cassette recorders, radios, phonographs, tape recorders, tape decks, and high-fidelity stereo system components. Product categories varied dramatically in terms of saturation. For example, 99.9 percent of all electrically wired homes in the United States had television sets; 71.5 percent of all electrically wired homes have color television sets. Tape recorders, tape decks, and video cassette recorders have significantly lower saturation levels because of their recent popularity and recent advances in product technology (see Exhibit 1).

In 1985 the company commissioned a study on the socioeconomic characteristics and purchase behavior of home entertainment product buyers. Exhibit 2 shows selected demographic characteristics of buyers of selected home entertainment products. Furthermore, the study reported that home entertainment product purchasers had median household incomes above the median household incomes of the U.S.

EXHIBIT 1
First Purchase and Replacement Purchases for Selected Home Entertainment Products

	Percentage of Households Buying			
	For the First Time	*As a Replacement*	*In Addition to One Now Owned*	*Total Market*
Color console TV	37	49	14	100
Color portable TV	41	30	29	100
Color table TV	44	31	25	100
Console stereo	61	29	10	100
Stereo receiver/ amplifier	58	23	19	100
Stereo speakers	55	21	24	100
Stereo turntable	57	25	18	100
Tape deck	71	14	15	100
Tape recorder	61	15	24	100
Video cassette recorder	85	10	5	100

Source: Company records.

EXHIBIT 2
Demographic Characteristics of Heads of Households
Buying Selected Types of Home Entertainment Products

	For the First Time	Buying as a Replacement	In Addition to One Now Owned
Color console			
Median age	38	50	42
Median household members	3.3	3.3	4.3
College graduate	21.3%	15.4%	30.6%
Color table TV			
Median age	36	45	46
Median household members	3.4	3.2	4.3
College graduate	44.0%	22.5%	30.8%
Color portable TV			
Median age	41	43	43
Median household members	3.1	2.9	3.8
College graduate	24.2%	32.2%	33.9%
Console stereos			
Median age	39	NA	NA
Median household members	3.6	NA	NA
College graduate	20.5%	NA	NA
Stereo receiver/amplifier			
Median age	39	40	46
Median household members	3.6	3.3	4.3
College graduate	32.1%	43.8%	46.8%
Stereo speakers			
Median age	37	34	41
Median household members	3.5	3.0	4.1
College graduate	34.7%	48.8%	38.7%
Stereo turntable			
Median age	40	34	42
Median household members	3.5	3.0	4.2
College graduate	33.2%	40.4%	38.1%
Video cassette recorder			
Median age	39	39	NA
Median household members	3.2	3.4	NA
College graduate	42.1%	20.1%	NA

(continued)

EXHIBIT 2 (continued)

	For the First Time	Buying as a Replacement	In Addition to One Now Owned
Tape recorder			
Median age	43	44	43
Median household members	3.7	4.2	3.9
College graduate	28.1%	39.4%	39.1%
Tape deck			
Median age	40	34	49
Median household members	3.9	3.5	4.2
Median income	$16,130	$15,910	$22,610
College graduate	27.5%	20.5%	29.6%

Source: Company records.

population as a whole. Research on the purchasing behavior of home entertainment products revealed that:

1. In-store demonstration, friend or relative recommendation, dealer or salesperson, and advertising are dominant influences when buyers decide what brand of home entertainment products to purchase.

2. The median number of shopping trips made before purchasing home entertainment products was 2.4.

3. The most frequently shopped outlets for home entertainment products were radio/TV/music stores.

The vast majority of home entertainment products are distributed through five types of retail outlets: (1) home furnishings/furniture

EXHIBIT 3
Selected Data on Radio/TV/Music Stores

Year	Number of Establishments	Retail Sales Volume	Gross Margin
1977	38,434	$8,127 million	N.A.
1982	35,195	$13,813 million	N.A.
1985 (est.)	33,495	$19,410 million	25-30%

Source: Census of Retail Trade (selected years). Estimates of establishments and sales volume for 1985 reflect trends in the category. Gross margin data estimates made by Mr. Hawly.

stores, (2) housewares/hardware stores, (3) auto supply stores, (4) department stores/mass merchandisers, and (5) radio/TV/music stores. The volume of home entertainment merchandise sold by these outlets is unknown because of the variety of merchandise offered. However, selected data on the radio/TV/music store group with a more homogeneous product mix are available (see Exhibit 3). These types of dealers represent all of Speer Electric's accounts.

SPEER ELECTRIC CORPORATE POLICY FOR 1987

The following is an excerpted version of the company's statement of policy.

General Corporate Objective

Our customer is the discriminating purchaser of home entertainment products who makes the purchase decision in a deliberate manner. To this customer we will provide, under the Speer brand, quality home entertainment products in the higher-priced brackets that require specialty selling, retailed through reputable electronic specialists who provide good service.

Marketing Objectives and Strategy

The company's marketing objective is to serve the discriminating purchaser of home entertainment products who approaches his purchase in a deliberate manner with heavy consideration of long-term benefits. We will emphasize home entertainment products with superior performance, style, reliability, and value that require representative display, professional selling, trained service, and brand acceptance—retailed through reputable electronic specialists to those consumers whom the company can most effectively service.

This will be accomplished by:

1. A focused marketing effort to serve the customer who approaches the purchase of a home equipment product as an "investment"

2. Concentration on our areas of differential advantage: high-technology television, audio, and related home entertainment products with innovative features, superior reliability, and high performance levels, which generally sell for more than $600 at retail

3. Emphasis on products requiring display, demonstration, and product education, which must be delivered to and serviced in the home, to be sold through reputable merchants who specialize in home entertainment products and who provide good service

4. Concentration on distribution in existing markets, and general exclusion of large core city markets with populations of one million or more

5. Goal of developing Speer brand acceptance by obtaining in every market served a market position of at least $1.50 sales per capita, which our research indicates is possible

The new policy statement and marketing strategy for Speer Electric in 1987 represented a significant departure from the company's previous marketing posture. For many years the company manufactured and marketed good-quality, medium- and promotionally priced home entertainment products. In the last few years, however, the company had begun to emphasize more expensive and more luxurious home entertainment equipment.

Although this was not stated in the overall marketing strategy, the company had also become more aggressive in its advertising. The advertising budget for 1987 would include television advertising, which the company had previously eschewed in favor of local newspaper advertising on a cooperative basis with dealers. In 1987 television advertising would be directed at the 100 highest potential markets, with an expenditure level of $2.5 million.

THE DISTRIBUTION STRATEGY ISSUE

Mr. Hawly was well aware of the value Speer Electric placed on its dealers and the importance of developing a close linkage between the company and the dealers. The company has long emphasized that dealers are an asset that must be consistently strengthened.

Mr. Hawly saw his charge as reviewing the characteristics, the number, and the location of dealers that Speer Electric would need to meet its sales objective of $37 million in 1987. Initially this would involve identifying the types of dealers who would satisfy the kind of customer Speer Electric sought and who would work closely with the company in meeting corporate objectives.

A number of different viewpoints had been voiced by fellow executives. One viewpoint favored increasing the dealers in the 150 markets currently served by the company. The argument behind this position was that it would be difficult for existing dealers to generate the $37 million sales objective specified in the corporate plan. Executives expressing this view noted that the average sales volume per outlet was $63,529 at manufacturer's prices in 1986. To reach $37 million, an average outlet would have to sell $87,059 at manufacturer's prices—a 37 percent increase. These executives noted that even with a 12 percent increase in sales following the industry trend, 95 nonexclusive dealers would have to be added in the 100 markets not currently served by exclusive dealers. Adding additional outlets meant that Speer Electric would seek to gain shelf space in existing radio/TV/music stores that did not carry the company's line. These executives also recognized that this proposal would involve expanding the sales force that serviced nonexclusive dealers.

A second viewpoint favored the development of an exclusive franchise program, since 25 nonexclusive dealers had posed that possibility in the last year. These dealers were prepared to sell off competitive lines and to sell Speer home entertainment products exclusively. Speer Electric executives who supported this approach felt the company could give a limited number of dealers the right to sell Speer products exclusively in a specific market for a specified franchise fee in exchange for the dealer's premise to promote, merchandise, and service Speer products in a specified manner consistent with corporate objectives. If adopted, the franchise program would be instituted in 50 markets served by the television advertising program. The other 50 markets served by exclusive dealers would be unaffected, since this program was already being applied.

A third viewpoint called for a reduction in the number of dealerships in general without the exclusive franchise concept. Executives supporting this view cited a number of factors favoring this approach. First, analysis of dealers' sales indicated that 10.5 percent of Speer dealers (all exclusive dealers) produced 80 percent of company sales. Second, these executives emphasized the improvement in sales force effort due to the time that could be given to fewer dealers. Although a number had not been set, some consideration had been given to the idea of reducing the number from 475 dealers to 150 dealers in the 100 markets served by the television advertising program. In actuality, this meant that the 50 exclusive dealers would be retained and 100 nonexclusive dealers would operate in the remaining 50 markets served by the television program.

A fourth proposal voiced by several executives was not to change either the distribution strategy or the dealers. Rather, they believed that Speer Electric should do a better job with the current distribution system.

CASE

Thompson Respiration Products, Inc.

VICTOR HIGGINS, EXECUTIVE VICE-PRESIDENT for Thompson Respiration Products, Inc. (TRP), sat thinking at his desk late one Friday in April 1982. "We're making progress," he said to himself. "Getting Metro to sign finally gets us into the Chicago market . . . and with a good dealer, at that." "Metro" was, of course, Metropolitan Medical Products, a large Chicago retailer of medical equipment and supplies for home use. "Now if we could just do the same in Minneapolis and Atlanta," he continued.

However, getting at least one dealer in each of these cities to sign a TRP dealer agreement seemed remote right now. One reason was the sizable groundwork required; Higgins simply lacked the time to review the operations of the well over 100 dealers currently operating in the two cities. Another was TRP's lack of dealer-oriented sales information that went beyond the technical specification sheet for each product and the company's price list. Still another concerned two conditions in the dealer agreement itself; prospective dealers sometimes balked at agreeing to sell no products manufactured by TRP's competitors and differed with TRP in interpretations of the "best efforts" clause (the clause required the dealer to maintain adequate inventories of TRP products, contact four prospective new customers or physicians or respiration therapists per month, respond promptly to sales inquiries, and represent TRP at appropriate conventions where it exhibited).

This case was written by Professor James E. Nelson and D.B.A. candidate William R. Wooldridge, the University of Colorado. © 1983 by the Business Research Division, College of Business and Administration and the Graduate School of Business Administration, University of Colorado. Used by permission.

"Still," Higgins concluded, "we signed Metro in spite of these reasons, and twenty-one others across the country. That's about all anyone could expect—after all, we've been trying to develop a dealer network for only a year or so."

THE PORTABLE RESPIRATOR INDUSTRY

The portable respirator industry began in the early 1950s, when polio-stricken patients who lacked the control of upper-body muscles necessary for breathing began to leave treatment centers. They returned home with hospital-style iron lungs or fiberglass chest shells, both of which were large chambers that regularly introduced a vacuum about the patient's chest. The vacuum caused the chest to expand and thus the lungs to fill with air. However, both devices confined patients to a prone or semiprone position in a bed.

By the late 1950s TRP had developed a portable turbine blower powered by an electric motor and battery. When connected to a mouthpiece via plastic tubing, the blower would inflate a patient's lungs on demand. Patients could now leave their beds for several hours at a time and realize limited mobility in a wheelchair. By the early 1970s TRP had developed a line of turbine respirators that were more sophisticated in terms of monitoring and capability for adjustment to individual patient needs.

At about the same time, applications began to shift from polio patients to victims of other diseases or of spinal-cord injuries, most of which resulted from automobile accidents. Better emergency medical service, quicker evacuation to spinal-cord injury centers, and more proficient medical and rehabilitation treatment meant that people who formerly would have died now lived and went on to lead meaningful lives. Patients were frequently younger and strongly desired wheelchair mobility. Respiration therapists obliged by recommending a Thompson respirator for home use or, if unaware of Thompson, recommending a Puritan-Bennett or other machine instead.

Instead of a turbine, Puritan-Bennett machines used a bellows design to force air into the patient's lungs. The machines were widely used in hospitals but seemed poorly suited for home use. For one thing, Puritan-Bennett machines used a compressor pump or pressurized air to drive the bellows and were much more cumbersome than Thompson's electric motor. Puritan-Bennett machines also cost approximately 50 percent more than a comparable Thompson unit and were relatively large and immobile. On the other hand, Puritan-Bennett machines were viewed by physicians and respiration therapists as industry standards.

By the middle 1970s TRP was able to develop a portable piston-

and-cylinder design and place it on the market. The product lacked the sophistication of the Puritan-Bennett machines but was reliable, portable, and much simpler to adjust and operate. It also maintained TRP's traditional cost advantage. Another firm, Life Products, began its operations in 1976 by producing a similar design. A third competitor, Lifecare Services, had begun operations somewhat earlier.

Puritan-Bennett

Puritan-Bennett was a large, growing, and financially sound manufacturer of respiration equipment for medical and aviation applications. Its headquarters were located in Kansas City, Missouri. However, the firm staffed over forty sales, service, and warehouse operations in the United States, Canada, United Kingdom, and France. Sales for 1981 exceeded $100 million while employment was just over two thousand people. Sales for its Medical Equipment Group (respirators, related equipment and accessories, service and parts) likely exceeded $40 million for 1981; however, Higgins could obtain data only for the period 1977–1980 (see Exhibit 1). Puritan-Bennett usually sold its respirators through a system of independent, durable-medical-equipment dealers. However, its sales office did sell directly to identified "house accounts" and often competed with dealers by selling slower-moving products to all accounts. According to industry sources, Puritan-Bennett sales were slightly more than three-quarters of all respirator sales to hospitals in 1981.

EXHIBIT 1
Puritan-Bennett Medical Equipment Group Sales

Item	1977	1978	1979	1980
Domestic sales				
Model MA-1				
Units	1,460	875	600	500
($ millions)	8.5	4.9	3.5	3.1
Model MA-2				
Units	—	935	900	1,100
($ millions)	—	6.0	6.1	7.8
Foreign sales				
Units	250	300	500	565
($ millions)	1.5	1.8	3.1	3.6
IPPB equipment ($ millions)	6.0	6.5	6.7	7.0
Parts, service, accessories ($ millions)	10.0	11.7	13.1	13.5
Overhaul ($ millions)	2.0	3.0	2.5	2.5
Total ($ millions)	28.0	34.0	35.0	37.5

Source: Wall Street Transcript.

However, these same sources expected Puritan-Bennett's share to diminish during the 1980s because of the aggressive marketing efforts of three other manufacturers of hospital-style respirators: Bear Medical Systems, Inc., J. H. Emerson, and Siemens-Elema. The latter firm was expected to grow the most rapidly, despite its quite recent entry into the United States market (its headquarters were in Sweden) and a list price of over $16,000 for its basic model.

Life Products

Life Products competed directly with TRP for the portable respirator market. Life Products had begun operations in 1976 when David Smith, a TRP employee, left to start his own business. Smith had located his plant in Boulder, Colorado, less than a mile from TRP headquarters.

He began almost immediately to set up a dealer network and by early 1982 had secured over forty independent dealers located in large metropolitan areas. Smith had made a strong effort to sign only large, well-managed durable-medical-equipment dealers. Most dealers employed one or more respiration therapists who set up home respirators, adjusted respirators to the patient's needs, and provided both routine maintenance and emergency service. Representatives from all dealers were required to complete Life Product's service training school, held each month in Boulder. Life Products sold its products to dealers (in contrast to TRP, which both sold and rented products to both dealers and consumers). Dealers, in turn, typically rented products to consumers. Dealers received a 20–25 percent discount off suggested retail price on most products.

As of April 1982, Life Products offered two respirator models (the LP3 and LP4) and a limited number of accessories (such as mouthpieces and plastic tubing) to its dealers. Suggested retail prices for the two respirator models were approximately $3,900 and $4,800. Suggested rental rates were approximately $400 and $500 per month. Life Products also allowed Lifecare Services to manufacture a respirator similar to the LP3 under license.

At the end of 1981, Smith was quite pleased with his firm's performance. During Life Products's brief history, it had passed TRP in sales and now ceased to see the firm as a serious threat, at least according to one company executive:

> We really aren't in competition with Thompson. They're after the stagnant market and we're after a growing market. We see new applications and ultimately the hospital market as our niche. I doubt if Thompson will even be around in a few years. As for Lifecare, their prices are much lower than ours but you don't get the service. With them you get the basic product, but nothing else. With us, you get a complete medical care service. That's the big difference.

Lifecare Services, Inc.

In contrast to the preceding firms, Lifecare Services, Inc., earned much less of its revenues from medical equipment manufacturing and much more from medical equipment distributing. The firm primarily resold products purchased from other manufacturers, operating out of its headquarters in Boulder as well as from its sixteen field offices (Exhibit 2). All offices were stocked with backup parts and an inventory of respirators. All were staffed with trained service technicians under Lifecare's employ.

Lifecare did manufacture a few accessories not readily available from other manufacturers. These items complemented the purchased products and, in the company's words, served to "give the customer a complete respiratory service." Under a licensing agreement between Lifecare and Life Products, the firm manufactured a respirator similar to the LP3 and marketed it under the Lifecare name. The unit rented for approximately $175 per month. While Lifecare continued to service the few remaining Thompson units it still had in the field, it no longer carried the Thompson line.

Lifecare rented rather than sold its equipment. The firm maintained that this arrangement gave patients more flexibility in the event of their recovery or death and lowered patients' monthly costs.

THOMPSON RESPIRATION PRODUCTS, INC.

TRP currently employed thirteen people, nine in production and four in management. It conducted operations in a modern, attractive building (leased) in an industrial park. The building contained about six thousand square feet of space, split 75 percent/25 percent for production/management purposes. Production operations were essentially

EXHIBIT 2
Lifecare Services, Inc., Field Offices

Augusta, GA	Detroit, MI	Oakland, CA
Baltimore, MD	Grand Rapids, MI[a]	Omaha, NB
Boston, MA	Houston, TX	Phoenix, AR
Chicago, IL	Los Angeles, CA	Seattle, WA
Cleveland, OH	New York, NY	St. Paul, MN
Denver, CO		

Source: Trade literature.
[a]Suboffice.

job-shop in nature; skilled technicians assembled each unit by hand on workbenches, making frequent quality control tests and subsequent adjustments. Production lots usually ranged from 10 to 75 units per model and probably averaged around 40. Normal production capacity was about 600 units per year.

Product Line

TRP currently sold seven respirator models plus a large number of accessories. All respirator models were portable but differed considerably in terms of style, design, performance specifications, and attendant features (see Exhibit 3). Four models were styled as metal boxes with an impressive array of knobs, dials, indicator lights, and switches. Three were styled as less-imposing "overnighter" suitcases with less prominently displayed controls and indicators. (Exhibit 4 reproduces part of the sales specification sheet for the M3000, as illustrative of the metal box design.)

Four of the models were designed as *pressure machines,* using a turbine pump that provided a constant, usually positive, pressure. Patients were provided intermittent access to this pressure as breaths per minute. One model, however, the MV Multivent, could provide either a constant positive or a constant negative pressure (i.e., a vacuum, necessary to operate chest shells, iron lungs, and body wraps). No other portable respirator on the market could produce negative pressure. Three of the models were designed as *volume machines,* using a piston pump that produced intermittent, constant volumes of pressurized air as breaths per minute. Actual volumes were prescribed by each patient's physician on the basis of lung capacity. Pressures depended on the breathing method used (mouthpiece, trach, chest shell, and others) and on the patient's activity level. Breaths per minute also depended on the patient's activity level.

Models came with several features. The newest was an assist feature (currently available on the Minilung M25 but soon to be offered also on the M3000) that allowed the patient alone to "command" additional breaths without having someone change the dialed breath rate. The sigh feature gave patients a sigh, either automatically or on demand. Depending on the model, up to six alarms were available to indicate a patient's call, unacceptable low pressure, unacceptable high pressure, low battery voltage/power failure, failure to cycle, and the need to replace motor brushes. All models but the MV Multivent also offered automatic switchover from alternating current to either an internal or an external battery (or both) in the event of a power failure. Batteries provided for eighteen to forty hours of operation, depending on usage.

EXHIBIT 3
TRP Respirators

Model[a]	Style	Design	Volume (cc)	Pressure (cm H_2O)
M3000	Metal box	Volume Pressure (positive or negative)	300-3000	+10 to +65
MV Multivent	Metal box		NA[b]	−70 to +80
Minilung M15	Suitcase	Volume	200-1500	+5 to +65
Minilung M25 Assist (also available without the assist feature)	Suitcase	Volume Pressure	600-2500	+5 to +65
Bantam GS	Suitcase	Pressure (positive)	NA	+15 to +45
Compac CS	Metal box	Pressure (positive)	NA	+15 to +45
Compact C	Metal box	Pressure (positive)	NA	+15 to +45

Model[a]	Breaths per Minute	Weight (lbs.)	Size (ft.³)	Features
M3000	6 to 30	39	0.85	Sigh, four alarms, automatic switchover from AC to internal battery
MV Multivent	8 to 24	41	1.05	Positive or negative pressure, four alarms, AC only
Minilung M15	8 to 22	24	0.70	Three alarms, automatic switchover from AC to internal battery
Minilung M25 Assist (also available without the assist feature)	5 to 20	24	0.70	Assist, sigh, three alarms, automatic switchover from AC to internal battery
Bantam CS	6 to 24	19	0.75	Sigh, six alarms, automatic switchover to external battery

(continued)

EXHIBIT 3 (*continued*)

Model[a]	Breaths per Minute	Weight (lbs.)	Size (ft.³)	Features
Compact CS	8 to 24	25	0.72	Sigh, six alarms, automatic switchover to external battery
Compact C	6 to 24	19	0.50	Sigh, four alarms, automatic switchover to external battery

Source: Company sales specification sheets.

[a]Five other models considered obsolete by TRP could be supplied if necessary.

[b]NA=not applicable.

Higgins felt that TRP's respirators were superior to those of Life Products. Most TRP models allowed pressure monitoring in the airway itself rather than in the machine, providing more accurate measurement. TRP's suitcase-style models were often strongly preferred by patients, especially the polio patients who had known no other. TRP's volume models offered easier volume adjustments, and all TRP models offered more alarms. On the other hand, Higgins knew that TRP had recently experienced some product-reliability problems of an irritating—not life-threatening—nature. Further, he knew that Life Products had beaten TRP to the market with the assist feature (the idea for which had come from a Puritan-Bennett machine).

TRP's line of accessories was more extensive than that of Life Products. TRP offered the following for separate sale: alarms, call switches, battery cables, chest shells, mouthpieces, plastic tubing, pneumobelts and bladders (equipment for still another breathing method that utilized intermittent pressure on a patient's diaphragm), and other items. Lifecare Services offered many similar items.

Distribution

Shortly after Higgins had joined TRP, he and Thompson had decided to switch from selling and renting products directly to patients to selling and renting products to dealers. While it meant lower margins, less control, and infrequent communication with patients, the change had several advantages. It allowed TRP to shift inventory from the factory

EXHIBIT 4
The M3000 Minilung

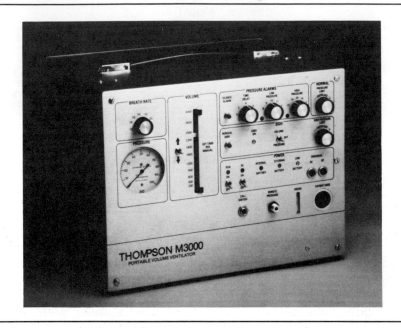

to the dealer, generating cash more quickly. It provided for local representation in market areas, allowing patients greater feelings of security and TRP more aggressive sales efforts. It shifted burdensome paperwork (required by insurance companies and state and federal agencies to effect payment) from TRP to the dealer. It also reduced other TRP administrative activities in accounting, customer relations, and sales.

TRP derived about half of its 1981 revenue of $3 million directly from patients and about half from the dealer network. By April 1982 the firm had twenty-two dealers (see Exhibit 5), with three accounting for over 60 percent of TRP dealer revenues. Two of the three serviced TRP products, as did two of the smaller dealers; the rest preferred to let the factory take care of repairs. TRP conducted occasional training sessions for dealer repair personnel, but distances were great and turnover in the position high, making such sessions costly. Most dealers requested air shipment of respirators, in quantities of one or two units.

Price

TRP maintained a comprehensive price list for its entire product line (Exhibit 6 reproduces part of the current list). Each respirator model

EXHIBIT 5
TRP Dealer Locations

Bakersfield, CA	Newark, NJ	Tampa, FL
Baltimore, MD	Oklahoma City, OK	Tucson, AZ
Birmingham, AL	Pittsburgh, PA	Washington, DC
Chicago, IL	Salt Lake City, UT	Worcester, MA
Cleveland, OH	San Diego, CA	
Fort Wayne, IN	San Francisco, CA	Montreal, Canada
Greenville, NC	Seattle, WA	Toronto, Canada
Indianapolis, IN	Springfield, OH	

Source: Company records

carried both a suggested retail selling price and a suggested rental rate that patients would pay. TRP applied these rates when it dealt directly with patients. The list also presented two net purchase prices for each model, along with an alternative rental rate paid by dealers. About 40 percent of the 300 respirator units TRP shipped to dealers in 1981 went out on a rental basis. The comparable figure for the 165 units sent directly to consumers was 90 percent. Net purchase prices allowed an approximate 7 percent discount for orders of three or more units of each model. Higgins had initiated this policy early last year with the aim of encouraging dealers to order in larger quantities. To date one dealer had taken advantage of this discount.

Current policy called for TRP to earn a gross margin of approxi-

EXHIBIT 6
Current TRP Respirator Price List

	Suggested Retail:			Dealer Price	
Model	Rent/ Month	Price	Dealer Rent/Month	1–2	3 or more
M3000	$380	$6,000	$290	$4,500	$4,185
MV Multivent	270	4,300	210	3,225	3,000
Minilung M15	250	3,950	190	2,960	2,750
Minilung M25	250	3,950	190	2,960	2,750
Bantam GS	230	3,600	175	2,700	2,510
Compact CS	230	3,600	175	2,700	2,510
Compact C	200	3,150	155	2,360	2,195

Source: Company sales specification sheets.

mately 35 percent on the dealer price for one to two units. All prices included shipping charges by United Parcel Service (UPS); purchasers requesting more expensive transportation service paid the difference between actual costs incurred and the UPS charge. Terms were net thirty days with a 1.5 percent service charge added to past-due accounts. Prices were last changed in late 1981.

CONSUMERS

Two types of patients used respirators, depending on whether the need followed from disease or from injury. Diseases such as polio, sleep apnea, chronic obstructive pulmonary disease, muscular dystrophy, and others annually left about 1,900 victims unable to breathe without a respirator. Injury to the spinal cord above the fifth vertebra caused a similar result for about 300 people per year. Except for polio, incidences of the diseases and injuries were growing at about 3 percent per year. Most patients kept one respirator at bedside and another mounted on a wheelchair. However, Higgins did know of one individual who kept eight Bantam B models (provided by a local polio foundation, now defunct) in his closet. Except for polio patients, life expectancies were about five years. Higgins estimated the total number of patients using a home respirator in 1981 as:

Polio	3,000
Other Diseases	6,500
Spinal-cord injury	1,000

Almost all patients were under a physician's care as well as that of a more immediate nurse or attendant (frequently a relative). About 95 percent paid for their equipment through insurance benefits (either private plans, government programs, or a combination) or foundation monies. About 90 percent rented their equipment. Almost all patients and their nurses or attendants had received instruction on equipment operation from respiration therapists employed by medical centers or by dealers of durable medical equipment.

The majority of patients were poor. Virtually none were gainfully employed, and all had seen their savings and other assets diminished to varying degrees by treatment costs. Some had experienced a divorce. Slightly more patients were male than female. About 75 percent lived in their homes, with the rest split between hospitals, nursing homes, and other institutions.

Apart from patients, Higgins thought that hospitals might be considered a logical new market for TRP to enter. Many of the larger and some of the smaller general hospitals might be convinced to purchase one portable respirator (like the M3000) for emergency and occasional other use with injury patients. Such a machine would be much cheaper to purchase than a large Puritan-Bennett and would allow easier patient trips to testing areas, X-ray, surgery, and the like. Even easier to convince should be the fourteen regional spinal-cord injury centers located across the country (Exhibit 7). Other medical centers that specialized in treatment of pulmonary diseases should also be prime targets. Somewhat less promising but more numerous would be public and private schools training physicians and respiration therapists. Higgins estimated the numbers of these institutions at:

General hospitals (100 beds or more)	3,800
General hospitals (fewer than 100 beds)	3,200
Spinal-cord injury centers	14
Pulmonary disease treatment centers	100
Medical schools	180
Respiration therapy schools	250

DEALERS

Dealers selling home-care medical products (as distinct from dealers supplying hospitals and medical centers) showed a great deal of diversity. Some were little more than small areas in local drugstores that rented canes, walkers, and wheelchairs in addition to selling supplies like surgical stockings and colostomy bags. Others carried nearly everything needed for home nursing care, renting everything from canes to hospital beds and selling supplies from bed pads to bottled oxygen. Still others specialized in products and supplies only for certain types of patients.

In this latter category, Higgins had identified dealers of oxygen and oxygen-related equipment as the best fit among existing dealers. These dealers serviced victims of emphysema, bronchitis, asthma, and

EXHIBIT 7
Regional Spinal-Cord Injury Centers

Birmingham, AL	Englewood, CO	Philadelphia, PA
Boston, MA	Fishersville, VA	Phoenix, AZ
Chicago, IL	Houston, TX	San Jose, CA
Columbia, MO	Miami, FL	Seattle, WA
Downey, CA	New York, NY	

other respiratory ailments, a growing market that Higgins estimated was about ten times greater than that for respirators. A typical dealer had begun perhaps ten years ago selling bottled oxygen (obtained from a welding supply wholesaler) and renting rather crude metering equipment to patients at home under the care of a registered nurse. The same dealer today now rented (and serviced) oxygen concentrators (a recently developed device that extracts oxygen from the air), liquid oxygen equipment and liquid oxygen, and much more sophisticated oxygen equipment and oxygen to patients cared for by themselves or by relatives.

Most dealers maintained a fleet of radio-dispatched trucks to deliver products to their customers. Better dealers promised twenty-four-hour service and kept delivery personnel and a respiration therapist on call twenty-four hours a day. They usually employed several respiration therapists who would set up equipment at the initial visit and provide operating instructions to victims and attendants. Dealers often expected their therapists to function as a sales force, calling on physicians and other respiration therapists at hospitals and medical centers, discharge planners at hospitals, service organizations such as muscular dystrophy associations and spinal-cord injury associations, and visiting nurse associations.

Dealers usually bought their inventories of durable equipment and supplies directly from manufacturers. They usually received a 20–25 percent discount off suggested list prices to consumers and hospitals. Only in rare instances might dealers lease equipment from a manufacturer instead. Dealers aimed for a payback on the purchase cost of equipment of one year or less, meaning that most products began to contribute to profit and overhead after twelve months of rental. Most products lasted physically for upwards of ten years but technologically for only three to five; every dealer's warehouse contained idle but perfectly suitable equipment that had been superseded by models demanded by patients, their physicians, or their attendants.

Most dealers were independently owned and operated. However, a number had recently been acquired by one of several parent organizations that were regional or national in scope. Such chains usually consisted of from ten to thirty retail operations located in separated market areas. However, the largest, Abbey Medical, had begun operations in 1924 and now consisted of over seventy local dealers. Higgins estimated 1981 sales for the chain (which was itself acquired by American Hospital Supply Corporation in April 1981) at over $60 million. In general, chains maintained a low corporate visibility and provided their dealers with working capital, employee benefit programs, operating advice, and some centralized purchasing. Higgins thought that chain organizations might grow more rapidly over the next ten years.

THE ISSUES

Higgins looked at his watch. It was 5:30 and really time to leave. "Still," he thought, "I should jot down what I see to be the immediate issues before I go—that way I won't be tempted to think about them over the weekend." He took a pen and wrote the following:

1. Should TRP continue to rent respirators to dealers?

2. Should TRP protect each dealer's territory (and how big should a territory be)?

3. Should TRP require dealers to stock no competing equipment?

4. How many dealers should TRP eventually have? Where?

5. What sales information should be assembled in order to attract high-quality dealers?

6. What should be done about the "best efforts" clause?

As he reread the list, Higgins considered that there probably were still other short-term-oriented questions he might have missed. Monday would be soon enough to consider them all.

Until then, he was free to think about broader, more strategic issues. Some reflections on the nature of the target market, a statement of marketing objectives, and TRP's possible entry into the hospital market would occupy the weekend. Decisions on these topics would form a substantial part of TRP's strategic marketing plan, a document Higgins hoped to have for the beginning of the next fiscal year in July. "At least I can rule out one option," Higgins thought as he put on his jacket. That was an idea to use independent sales representatives to sell TRP products on commission; a recently completed two-month search for such an organization had come up empty. "Like my stomach," he thought, as he went out the door.

COASTAL MILLS, INC.

IN JANUARY 1984 Ms. Suzanne Goldman was scheduled to meet Mr. Robert Meadows, president of Coastal Mills, Inc. Ms. Goldman knew that the meeting would relate to the recently completed board of directors' meeting. In her position as special assistant to the president, or "trouble-shooter," as she called herself, such meetings often led to a project of some type. Her expectations were met as Mr. Meadows began to describe what happened at the directors meeting.

> The directors are not pleased with the present state of affairs. The cyclical nature of carpet sales is again proving itself as disposable personal income and new house construction have plateaued and actually declined in many areas of the country. Our wholesalers are complaining about slow payments from retailers. In many cases their receivables are taking sixty days to collect and we are extending our receivables to satisfy them at a 15 percent annual carrying cost. Wholesalers are cutting back on inventory as costs of carrying inventory approach 15 percent annually. Our inventories have increased and our delivery costs have risen as we attempt to service them. Costs of servicing wholesalers are running about 4 percent of sales. I could go on, but you get the picture. The possibility of establishing our own warehouses or wholesale operation was raised, but I was unprepared to discuss it. Needless to say, I was somewhat embarrassed. Would you examine such a program for me and prepare a position paper for the May directors' meeting? Focus only on the retail sales business since we handle contract sales on a direct basis and assume the same sales level as 1983. Remember that our policy is to finance programs from internal funds. I'd like to see the same comprehensive job you did on the advertising and sales program last November.

This case was prepared by Professor Roger A. Kerin, Southern Methodist University. The case was prepared solely for use as a discussion vehicle and is not designed to illustrate appropriate or inappropriate handling of administrative situations.

THE INDUSTRY

The carpet and rug industry reported sales of $4.97 billion at manufacturer's prices in 1982. Estimated 1983 sales would reach $5.2 billion, according to Mr. Meadows. Industry sales are evenly divided between "contract" or commercial sales and retail sales for household use.

The industry is moderately concentrated. In 1982, 15 companies out of over 250 carpet and rug manufacturers accounted for approximately two-thirds of total industry carpet and rug volume. Burlington Industries is the industry leader.

Three major types of retail outlets account for the vast majority of carpet and rug volume in the retail segment. The latest statistics available indicate that floor covering specialty stores accounted for 58 percent of industry volume, department stores sold 21 percent, and furniture stores sold 19 percent. Although no statistics exist, industry observers believe that discount stores are increasing their share of carpet and rug volume.

Industry trends suggest that significant cost pressures arising from raw material prices will accelerate in the next five years. This trend is likely to compress profit margins since upwards of 80 percent of the typical producers' cost of goods sold is materials. A second trend is the increasing emphasis on nylon in carpet and rug manufacturing. Nylon was used in 75 percent of all carpet face yarn consumed. Nylon's popularity will continue because of its excellent bulk, flexible styling, easy printing and dyeing capabilities, and usefulness as a flame retardant. A third trend is the relatively strong market for higher-quality carpets and rugs despite potential sluggishness in the industry as a whole. Higher-quality products should experience better sales results than popular-priced lines over the next few years.

Carpet purchase for household use is important and often time consuming for the buyer. The purchase process is similar to that observed in furniture buying: (1) multiple store shopping, (2) joint decision making between a husband and wife, and (3) considerable ego involvement. Questionnaires completed by *Better Homes and Gardens* Consumer Panel members revealed that:

1. Almost one-half of panel members purchasing carpet in the past two years bought it to replace another carpet or rug. (Note: Industry estimates indicate a carpet replacement cycle of eight years.)

2. About three in five panel members said that the brand name of carpet was a very important or somewhat important consideration in determining quality.

3. Surface appearance, color, durability, soil resistance/
cleanability were designated as very important factors in
choosing a carpet/rug by over one-half of panel members re-
sponding.[a]

COASTAL MILLS, INC.

Coastal Mills, Inc., is a manufacturer of a full line of medium- to high-
priced carpet for household use. Contract sales to apartment and office
builders are also made but account for only 10 percent of total company sales. Total company sales in 1983 were $60 million with a net
profit before tax of $2.4 million. Exhibit 1 shows abbreviated financial
statements.

The company currently distributes its line through seven wholesalers located throughout the country. These wholesalers, in turn, supplied 4,000 retail accounts. Retail accounts included department stores,
furniture stores, and floor-covering specialty stores. Inspection of distribution records revealed that 80 percent of total company sales were
made through 50 percent of its retail accounts. This relationship ex-

[a]*INQUIRY: A Study on Home Furnishings from the Better Homes and Gardens
Consumer Panel.* Copyright Meredith Corporation.

EXHIBIT 1
Coastal Mills, Inc.—Abbreviated Financial Statements, 1983

Income statement	
Net sales	$60,000,000
Less: Cost of goods sold	45,000,000
Gross margin	$15,000,000
Distribution expense	$ 1,800,000
Selling and administrative expense	9,000,000
Other expenses	1,800,000
Net income before tax	$ 2,400,000
Balance sheet	
Current assets	$21,550,000
Fixed assets	19,200,000
Total assets	$40,750,000
Current liabilities	$ 8,250,000
Long-term debt and net worth	32,500,000
Total liabilities and net worth	$40,750,000

isted within all market areas served by Coastal Mills. Mr. Meadows commented that these sales-per-account percentages indicated that Coastal was gaining adequate coverage at the retail level, if not over-coverage.

Advertising used by Coastal Mills focused primarily on print advertisements in shelter magazines and newspapers. The emphasis in advertisements was on fiber type, colors, durability, and soil resistance. A cooperative advertising program also exists with retailers and was expanded on the basis of Ms. Goldman's recommendation. According to Ms. Goldman, "The coop program is being well received and has brought us into closer contact with retail accounts." The company employs two regional sales coordinators who act as a liaison with wholesalers, assist in managing the cooperative advertising program, and make periodic visits to large retail accounts. In addition, they are responsible for handling contract sales.

Independent wholesalers play a major role in the company's marketing strategy. Wholesalers maintained extensive sales organizations, with the average wholesaler employing ten sales people. Carpet manufacturers expect that retail accounts receive at least one call per month. Ms. Goldman's earlier evaluation of the sales program revealed that wholesale sales representatives performed a variety of tasks. These tasks included checking inventory and carpet samples, arranging point-of-purchase displays, handling retailer complaints, and taking orders. About 25 percent of an average salesperson's time involved nonselling activities (preparing call reports, liaison with manufacturers, travel, and so forth). About 40 percent of each sales call of one hour was devoted to Coastal Mills carpeting; 60 percent was devoted to selling noncompeting products such as furniture accessories, draperies, and other products. This finding disturbed Coastal Mills management, who felt that a full hour was necessary to represent them. In addition to sales, wholesalers also carried carpet inventory. Sufficient inventory to handle an inventory turnover of five times per year was typically carried by Coastal Mills wholesalers. Coastal Mills felt that inventory levels sufficient for four turns per year were necessary to service retailers properly. Finally, wholesalers extended credit to retail accounts. In return for these services, wholesalers received a 22 percent margin on sales billed at the price to retailers.

DIRECT DISTRIBUTION EXPERIENCE OF COMPETITORS

In February and March Ms. Goldman sought out information on competitor experience with direct distribution. Despite conflicting information between trade publications and knowledgeable industry observers, she was able to arrive at several important conclusions. First, competitors with their own warehousing operations located them in seven metropolitan areas: Atlanta, Chicago, Cleveland, Dallas–Fort Worth, Los Angeles, New York, and Philadelphia. Except for Dallas–Fort Worth and Atlanta, Coastal Mills had wholesalers already operating in these metropolitan areas. The company serviced these areas from wholesalers located in Houston, Texas, and Richmond, Virginia, respectively. Second, approximately $5 million in sales was necessary to operate a warehouse operation economically. The average warehouse operation could be operated at an annual fixed cost (e.g., rent, personnel, operations) of $700,000. Ms. Goldman was informed that suitable warehouse space was available in the metropolitan areas under consideration; therefore, Coastal Mills would not have to embark on an expansion program. Third, salaries, expenses, and fringe benefits of highly qualified sales representatives would be about $40,000 annually. One field sales manager would be needed to manage eight sales representatives. Salary, expenses, and fringe benefits would be approximately $50,000 per field sales manager per year. Finally, sales administration costs were typically 40 percent of the total sales force and management costs per year. Even though these figures represented rough approximations, these estimates were the best available in Ms. Goldman's opinion and the opinion of others with whom she conferred.

In March Ms. Goldman received a disturbing telephone call from a long-time and successful wholesaler of Coastal Mills's products. The wholesaler told her that he and others were aware of her inquiries about direct distribution possibilities. Through innuendo, the wholesaler threatened a mass exodus from Coastal Mills once the first Coastal Mills warehouse was opened. He implied that plans were already underway to establish a trade agreement with a competitor. This conversation would have a significant impact on her recommendation if direct distribution was deemed feasible. In short, a roll-out by market area looked less likely. A rapid transition would be necessary, which would require sizable cash outlays.

CHAPTER 9

Pricing Strategy And Management

WHETHER OR NOT it is so recognized, pricing is one of the most crucial decision functions of a marketing manager. To a large extent, pricing decisions determine the types of customers an organization will attract. Likewise, a single pricing error can effectively nullify all other marketing mix activities. Despite its importance, price rarely serves as the focus of marketing strategy. This is in part because pricing is the easiest marketing mix activity for the competition to imitate. Although pricing strategies need to be somewhat competitively oriented, it is unusual for one to take the extreme form of price cutting. Price cutting often leads to price warfare and in the long run is deleterious for all concerned.

It can be easily demonstrated that price is a direct determinant of profits (or losses). This is apparent from the fundamental *profit = revenues − costs* relationship. Revenue is a direct result of *unit price × quantity sold,* whereas costs are indirectly influenced by quantity sold, which in turn is partially dependent on unit price. Hence, price simultaneously influences both revenues and costs.

Yet, despite its importance, pricing remains one of the least understood marketing mix activities. This is true with respect to both its effects on buying behavior and its determination.

PRICING CONSIDERATIONS

Although the respective structures of demand and cost obviously cannot be neglected, there are numerous other factors that must be considered when determining pricing strategies.[1] Most important, pricing strategy has to be consistent with overall marketing strategy and broader organizational strategy. To treat the pricing objective solely as maximizing profits not only is a gross oversimplification, but may be in direct conflict with the broader objectives of an organization. Other pricing objectives include enhancing product or brand image, obtaining an adequate return on investment or cash flow, or maintaining price stability in an industry or market.

There are numerous factors—both internal and external to the organization—that must also be taken into account when pricing a product or service. The stage in the life cycle of the product or service being priced is one such factor. The effect of the pricing decision on competition is another factor, as is the impact on the intermediaries. In certain industries, products are so similar and competition so strong that an organization is forced to adhere to industry pricing standards. Likewise, pricing strategies may be effectively dictated by marketing channel members. Finally, the response of government—whether pricing will be perceived as deceptive, discriminatory, or anticompetitive—must be considered.

Price Elasticity of Demand

An important concept in understanding the intricacies of pricing and the nature of the price-quantity relationship is that of price elasticity of demand. The coefficient of price elasticity, E, is a measure of the relative responsiveness in the *quantity* of a product or service demanded as a function of a change in the *price* of that product or service. In other words, the coefficient of price elasticity measures the rate of percentage change in the quantity purchased of a product or service as compared to the corresponding percentage change in the price of the product or service. The formula for calculating the coefficient is:

$$E = \frac{(Q_1 - Q_2)/Q_1}{(P_1 - P_2)/P_1} = \frac{\Delta Q/Q_1}{\Delta P/P_1}$$

where

P_1 = initial price
Q_1 = quantity purchased at P_1
P_2 = final price
Q_2 = quantity purchased at P_2

If $E > 1$, demand is said to be *elastic*: a small reduction in price will result in a large increase in the quantity purchased; hence, total revenues will rise. Conversely, if $E < 1$, demand is termed *inelastic*, with a correspondingly opposite impact on revenues.

A number of factors influence the price elasticity of demand for a product or service. In general:

- The more *substitutes* a product or service has, the greater its price elasticity.
- The more *uses* a product or service has, the greater its price elasticity.
- The *greater* the relative price of the product or service to the income of the buyer, the greater its price elasticity.

In practice, it is common to apply the concept of price elasticity simultaneously to more than one product or service. By computing the *cross-elasticity* of, say, products A and B, it is possible to measure the responsiveness in quantity demanded of product A as a function of a price change in product B. A negative cross-elasticity coefficient indicates that the products are complementary; a positive coefficient indicates that they are substitutes. It is especially important to understand the implications of cross-elasticity for successful implementation of product-line pricing, in which product demand is interrelated and the goal is to maximize revenue for the entire line and not just for individual products or services.

Consider the marketer of cameras and films (or of copying machines and paper, or of personal computers and software). Should cameras be priced very low, perhaps close to or even below cost, in order to promote film sales? Film could then be marketed at relatively high prices. Or, should an opposite strategy be employed—high-priced cameras but low-priced film? Examples of each of these alternative tie-in pricing strategies are readily available. The important point is that for most organizations, products are not priced in isolation. In certain instances, individual products may be sold at a loss merely to entice buyers or to ensure that the organization can offer potential buyers complete product lines. In such situations, the price may bear little relationship to the actual cost of a product.

The concept of elasticity, though valuable, is often difficult to quantify in practice. However, the concept itself is invaluable as a framework for appraising the effects of price changes even in a qualitative sense.

PRICING STRATEGIES

Because of the difficulty in estimating demand, most pricing strategies have a decided reliance on cost as a basic foundation. To a great extent, price strategies can be termed as either *full-cost* or *variable-cost* strategies. Full-cost price strategies are those that consider both variable and fixed costs (sometimes termed *direct* and *indirect* costs). Variable-cost strategies employ only the direct costs associated with offering a product or service. A special case—the *experience curve*—is also introduced as a particular aspect of a cost-based pricing strategy.

Full-Cost Pricing

Full-cost pricing strategies generally take one of three forms: *markup pricing, break-even pricing,* and *rate-of-return pricing.* Markup pricing is a strategy by which the selling price of a product or service is determined by simply adding a fixed dollar amount to the (total) cost of the product. The fixed amount is usually expressed as a *percentage* of either the *cost* of the product or the *price* of the product. Hence, if it costs $4.60 to produce a product and the selling price is $6.35, the markup on *cost* would be 38 percent, and the markup on *price* would be 28 percent.

Markup pricing is frequently used in routine pricing situations, such as with grocery or clothing items, but it is also sometimes employed in pricing unique products or services—for example, military equipment or construction projects. Markup pricing may well be the most common type of pricing strategy. Although it possesses decided drawbacks (especially if a single percentage is applied across products without regard to their elasticities or competition), its simplicity, flexibility, and controllability make it highly popular.

As noted in Chapter 2 on financial aspects of marketing management, break-even analysis is a useful tool for indicating how many units of a product or service must be sold at a specific price for an organization to cover its total costs (fixed plus variable cost). On the other hand, by judicious use of break-even analysis, it is possible to calculate the break-even price for a product or service. Specifically, the break-even price of a product or service equals the per-unit fixed costs plus the per-unit variable costs.

A rate-of-return pricing strategy is slightly more sophisticated than either markup or break-even pricing. Still, it contains the basic ingredients of both of these strategies and can perhaps be viewed as an extension of them. In a rate-of-return pricing strategy, price is determined so as to obtain a prespecified rate of return on investment (capital) for the organization. Since rate of return on investment (ROI) equals profit (Pr) divided by investment (I).

$$\text{ROI} = \text{Pr.}/I = \frac{\text{Revenues} - \text{Cost}}{\text{Investment}} = \frac{P \cdot Q - C \cdot Q}{I}$$

where *P* and *C* are, respectively, unit selling price and unit cost, and *Q* represents the quantity sold.

By working backward from a predetermined rate of return, it is possible to derive a selling price that will obtain that return rate. Thus, if an organization desires an ROI of 15 percent on an investment of $80,000, while total costs per unit are estimated to be $0.175, and a demand of 20,000 units is forecast, then the necessary price will be

$$\frac{(\text{ROI}) \times I + CQ}{Q} = P = \frac{(0.15)\ \$80,000 + \$0.175 \times 20,000}{20,000} = 0.775$$

or roughly 78 cents.

This pricing strategy, popularized by General Motors, is most commonly used by larger firms and public utilities whose return rates are closely watched or are regulated by government agencies or commission. Like the other types of full-cost pricing strategies, rate-of-return pricing implicitly assumes a standard (linear) demand function and insensitivity of buyers with respect to price. This assumption often holds true only for certain price ranges, however.

Variable-Cost Pricing

An alternative to full-cost pricing strategies is a variable-cost, or contribution pricing, strategy. This type of strategy is sometimes used when an organization is operating at less than full capacity and fixed costs constitute a great proportion of total unit costs. The basic idea underlying variable-cost pricing is that, in certain short-run pricing situations, the relevant costs to consider are the *variable* costs, not the total costs. Specifically, in this strategy variable unit cost represents the minimum selling price at which the product or service can be marketed. Any price above this minimum then represents a contribution to fixed costs and profits.

Variable-cost pricing is a form of demand-oriented pricing. As such, it can serve two different purposes. Since variable-cost prices are lower than full-cost prices, the assumption is that a lower price will *stimulate demand* and increase revenues, and hence will lead to economies of scale, lower unit costs, and greater profits. This is why airlines offer different classes of fares, motels offer weekend rate specials, and movie theaters have discounts for senior citizens. Fixed costs are high relative to variable costs—the airline must still maintain its flight schedule regardless of whether there are any passengers; the motel or movie theater will still have to remain open even if it is only partially filled—and the incremental (variable) costs of serving one more customer are minimal.

Consider a bus line making a daily run from Minot to Fargo, North Dakota. The price of a one-way ticket is $8.00, and on an average trip the bus is 60 percent full. If unit fixed and variable costs are, respectively, $5.50 and $2.00, should the bus line offer a half-price fare for children under five years of age? Ignoring price elasticity and the like for the moment, the answer is yes, the reduced fare should be offered. The reduced fare ($4.00) covers the variable costs ($2.00) and still makes a contribution of $2.00 to fixed costs. Since the bus line will make the trip regardless of how many passengers there are, in the short run every reduced-fare ticket sold contributes $2.00 to fixed expenses. Such a pricing approach always assumes no more profitable use may be made of the revenue-generating activity.

In addition to stimulating demand, variable-cost pricing can be used to *shift* demand from one time period to another. Movie theaters sometimes have lower matinee ticket prices to encourage customers to switch from evening to afternoon attendance. Likewise, certain utilities (e.g., electric, telephone) have differing price schedules to shift demand away from peak load times and smooth it out over extended time periods.

Experience Curves, Costs, and Pricing

An emerging concept applicable to pricing strategy is the *experience curve* phenomenon, or experience effect. The experience curve is a representation of total unit cost reduction as volume produced increases. Specifically, the experience curve plots the constant percentage decline in total cost per unit each time the *cumulative volume* of a specific item doubles. The percentage decline in total cost per unit is reflected in the curve. Hence, if total cost unit drops by 15 percent each time the cumulative volume of production doubles, an 85 percent curve is indicated. In other words, the cost of the 100th unit produced will be about 85 percent of the cost to produce the 50th unit.

Experience curves are charted by plotting cost per unit on the vertical axis and cumulative production volume on the horizontal axis. An 85 percent curve is shown in Exhibit 9.1. In practice, experience curves are typically drawn on double log paper, in which both the horizontal and vertical axis are charted on a logarithmic scale. When presented in this manner, the "curve" appears as a straight line (see Exhibit 9.2).

The experience curve is a managed process, not a natural outcome of production volume. Decline in unit costs arises from a variety of factors. These are productivity improvements due to technological change, economies of scale, and labor specialization; product modifications designed to produce lower costs; and displacement of less effi-

EXHIBIT 9.1
A Typical Experience Curve (85 Percent) Displayed on Log-Log Scales

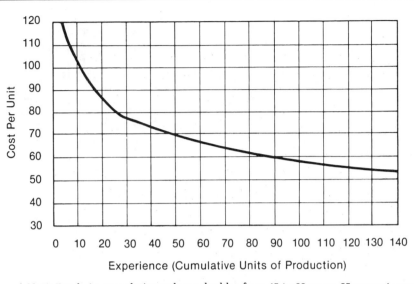

Experience (Cumulative Units of Production)

Note: Read: As cumulative volume doubles from 45 to 90 on an 85 percent curve, cost per unit declines from 70 to 60, or 15 percent.

cient production methods (e.g., labor-intensive versus capital-intensive production methods), among others. The fruits of these efforts are shown in the lower prices on a variety of commonly seen or purchased products. For example, a Sharp Electronics pocket calculator sold for $395 in 1971. In 1978 an even more sophisticated model produced by the same company sold for $10.95.[2] In a period of five years, digital watch prices declined from $2,000 per unit to $10 per unit.[3] Video cassette recorder (VCR) prices tumbled from $1,400 in 1975 to $400 in 1985 as a result of the effects of experience.[4]

Mechanics of the experience curve are described in the case entitled "Texas Instruments: Electronic Range Controls," in this chapter. However, the strategic message given by the experience curve phenomenon must be outlined here: The major-volume firm in a market has the greatest potential for the lowest unit costs and largest profits due to cumulative production volume. As costs decline, opportunities for price reductions become apparent and give the organization a lower price-cost advantage that is difficult for competitors (with little cumulative volume) to match and remain profitable.

EXHIBIT 9.2
An 85 Percent Experience Curve Displayed on Log-Log Scales

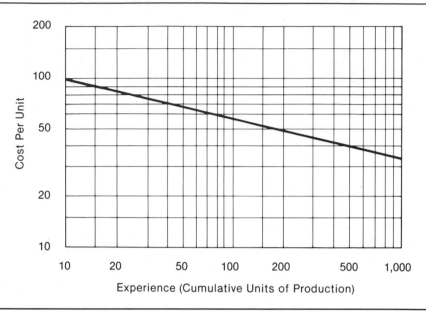

New-Offering Pricing Strategies

These pricing strategies are *technical strategies* that can be used when an organization initially sets or when it changes its prices. When pricing a new product or service, however, a manager has to consider other, more *conceptual* strategies.

When introducing a new product or service to the marketplace, an organization can employ one of three alternative pricing strategies. One is a *skimming* strategy. With this strategy, the price is initially set very high and is typically reduced over time. This high price is thought to create a high-quality image for the product or service and initially to attract price-insensitive buyers. This strategy is most often used

- When the organization wants to generate funds quickly so as to recover its investment or finance other developments
- When the product or service is unique enough to be protected from competition by patent or technical buyers

- When there is uncertainty about the potential demand for the product or service
- When production and distribution costs are uncertain

At the other extreme, the organization may use a *penetration* pricing strategy, whereby the organization introduces the product or service with a very low price. Such a strategy is typically used:

- To gain widespread rapid acceptance for the product or service, since potential buyers are assumed to be price-sensitive
- When the product or service is unprotectable and subject to strong competition
- When the organization has as a major objective the increasing or the obtaining of a large market share

Between these two extremes is an *intermediate* pricing strategy. As might be expected, this type of strategy is the most prevalent in practice. The other two types of introductory pricing strategies are, so to speak, more flamboyant; nevertheless, given the vagaries of the marketplace, the latter strategy is more likely to be used in the vast majority of initial pricing decisions.

Competitive Bidding

While the previous discussion has centered on *administered pricing* strategies, one additional form of pricing deserves brief mention. In certain situations, buyers prespecify in contract proposals characteristics of the products or services that they desire to purchase. Potential sellers then bid to obtain the contract. This proposal-bidding procedure is commonly known as *competitive bidding,* and it is especially prevalent when an organization is marketing to the government or to large industrial concerns.

Competitive bidding requires a highly specialized type of pricing strategy since (1) demand is known and constant and (2) other marketing mix elements are virtually uncontrollable or are inconsequential. For this reason, sophisticated mathematical bidding models have been developed to assist in submitting winning bids. Most of these models attempt to compute expected profits resulting from differing bid prices by associating each price with a probability of winning.

Determination of costs is a vital part of any competitive bidding proposal. For instance, depending on organizational goals, costs could be treated as either full or variable. Still, the most crucial aspect of competitive bidding is undoubtedly estimating the probabilities of award. Not only must the award probabilities take into account the needs of the organization, but they must also consider what the likely bids of the competitors will be.

NOTES

1. For examples of pricing decisions that incorporate factors beyond cost, see "Pricing of Products Is Still an Art, Often Having Little Link with Costs," *Wall Street Journal* (November 25, 1981): 25, and "Decontrol of Airlines Shifts Pricing from a Cost to a Competition Basis," *Wall Street Journal* (December 4, 1981): 25.

2. "The Age of Miracle Chips," *Time* (February 20, 1978): 44ff.

3. "The Great Digital Watch Shake-Out," *Business Week* (May 2, 1977): 78–80.

4. "Video Recorders Are Costing Less and Doing More," *Wall Street Journal* (July 15, 1985): 17.

ADDITIONAL READINGS

Day, George, and Montgomery, David. "Diagnosing the Experience Curve." *Journal of Marketing* (Spring 1983): 44–58.

Dean, Joel. "Pricing Policies for New Products." *Harvard Business Review* (November–December 1976): 141–153.

Ghemawat, Pankaj. "Building Strategy on the Experience Curve." *Harvard Business Review* (March–April 1985): 143–149.

Monroe, Kent B. *Pricing: Making Profitable Decisions.* New York: McGraw-Hill, 1979.

Rao, Vithala. "Pricing Research in Marketing: The State of the Art." *Journal of Business* (January 1984): 39–60.

Ross, Elliott B. "Making Money with Proactive Pricing." *Harvard Business Review* (November–December 1984): 145–155.

Walker, Kelly. "Software Economics 101." *Forbes* (January 28, 1985): 88.

Bristol-Myers Company: Datril

IN THE SPRING of 1975, Mr. Herbert Brotspies, a product manager in Bristol-Myers Products Division of the Bristol-Myers Company, was preparing the final marketing plan for the introduction of Datril, an acetaminophen analgesic product.[a] Datril would be the latest entry into the analgesic market for Bristol-Myers.

With the plan for Datril near completion, the question remaining to be answered for Bristol-Myers was how the competition and the market would react to the strategy when the product was introduced nationally. He was particularly concerned about the reaction to the pricing strategy for Datril.

THE COMPANY

Bristol-Myers is one of the larger producers and marketers of pharmaceutical and consumer products in the United States. The company holds a position of leadership in many product categories in the United

---

This case was prepared by Roger A. Kerin, Southern Methodist University, Dallas, as a basis for class discussion rather than to illustrate appropriate or inappropriate handling of administrative situations.

[a]*Analgesic:* A drug that produces a state of not feeling pain.

Acetaminophen: Generic name for principal active ingredient 4-hydroxy acetanilyde, which acts as an analgesic to raise the pain threshold and which acts as an antipyretic modifying the hypothalmatic heat-regulating center in the brain; sometimes referred to as "nonaspirin."

Aspirin: An analgesic that raises the pain threshold and alleviates fever; also has anti-inflammatory properties.

States and in over one hundred countries throughout the world. Domestic consumer products consist of such well-known brand names as Ban, Bufferin, Excedrin, Windex, Drano, Vitalis, Behold, and Clairol.

Bristol-Myers has shown consistent earnings growth over the past five years and in 1974 was ranked 125 in the *Fortune* 500. In 1974 the company recorded net sales of $1.59 billion and net earnings of $120.4 million, compared with $1.4 billion in sales and $102 million in net earnings in 1973. The company's expenditures for advertising and product promotion were $296 million in 1974. Bristol-Myers's income statement for 1974 is shown in Exhibit 1.

Bristol-Myers is divided into three major product groups: the Consumer Products Group; the Clairol Group; and the Pharmaceutical, Health Care, and International Group. The last group accounted for 51.8 percent of the company's total sales in 1974. The Consumer Products Group accounted for 25.8 percent of the company's sales in 1974. This product group consists of the Drackett and Bristol-Myers Products divisions. The Drackett division markets household products; the Bristol-Myers Products division is responsible for health and beauty aid products.

THE ANALGESIC MARKET

In 1974 the analgesic market produced sales of $680 million at wholesale prices. Almost 10 percent of the total analgesic market was attributed to the sale of acetaminophen products. From 1972 through 1974, "nonaspirin" sales increased almost 125 percent, while the sales of aspirin and aspirin compounds (the remainder of the analgesic market) increased about 13 percent. Exhibit 2 shows dollar sales volumes of the analgesic market for 1972 and 1974.

EXHIBIT 1
Bristol-Myers Company—Abbreviated Income Statement, 1974

Net sales	$1,590,949,000
Cost of products sold	603,398,000
Marketing, selling, and administrative expenses	422,630,000
Advertising and product promotion expenses	296,269,000
Research and development expenses	54,604,000
Earnings before income taxes	214,791,000
Provision for income taxes	94,388,000
Net earnings	120,403,000

Source: 1974 Bristol-Myers Company annual report.

EXHIBIT 2
Dollar Wholesale Sales

	Volume of Analgesic Market	
Year	Aspirin and Aspirin Compound Sales (000)	Acetaminophen Sales (000)
1972	$550,000	$27,500
1974	620,800	61,800

Source: Industry estimates.

Well-known analgesic products on the market are Bristol-Myers's Bufferin and Excedrin, and Bayer aspirin, marketed by Sterling Drug. The majority of the analgesic products are considered to be proprietary drugs, as opposed to ethical drugs.[b] Proprietary analgesic products are typically promoted by heavy consumer advertising and extensive point-of-purchase displays. For example, in 1974 Bristol-Myers spent over $30 million on measured media for Bufferin and Excedrin alone.

The accelerated growth in acetaminophen product sales reflects a growing acceptance by the U.S. public of a nonaspirin as an effective pain reliever, according to industry sources. In the early 1970s several publicized studies questioned consumers' almost blind dependence on aspirin as a pain reliever. These studies reported that one out of every one hundred people suffers stomach upset from aspirin. Even so, there were approximately 100 million aspirin tablets taken daily in the United States by a U.S. population of about 216 million people.

The acetaminophen analgesic product was originally developed as a prescription analgesic for those people who experienced side effects from aspirin. These side effects were generally an upset stomach, irritation of the stomach lining, or an allergic reaction. An acetaminophen analgesic product was specifically designed to be safer for people suffering from ulcers. Acetaminophen, like aspirin, raises the pain threshold and reduces fever, but it does not have the anti-inflammatory properties of aspirin and aspirin compounds.

There was only one widely sold nonprescription acetaminophen

---

[b]*Proprietary drug:* Requires no prescription and is marketed directly to the consumer; sometimes called an "advertised remedy."

Ethical drug: Legally available by prescription only and marketed directly to the medical profession.

product on the market in 1975—Tylenol. Tylenol was produced and marketed by McNeil Labs, a subsidiary of Johnson & Johnson. McNeil Labs introduced Tylenol about twenty years ago as a prescription analgesic. In the early 1960s Tylenol was reclassified as an over-the-counter drug and thus no longer required a prescription.[c] In 1974 Tylenol was on the shelves of 90 percent of food outlets and 98 percent of drug outlets.

Tylenol had an established niche in the analgesic market, with approximately 8 percent of the market in 1974. McNeil Labs typically sold Tylenol at about twice the price of aspirin. The typical cost to the trade for a 100-tablet bottle was estimated to be approximately $1.69.

Though categorized as ethical drugs, acetaminophen products were promoted only to the trade and to the medical profession. Therefore, the great majority of U.S. consumers were unfamiliar with acetaminophen products. Consumer awareness of these products came only from the recommendations of acetaminophens by physicians for specific cases. Even though the sale of Tylenol no longer required a prescription, McNeil Labs continued to promote its brand only to physicians. Sales continued to result largely from doctors' recommendations of the product to their patients. This strategy required promotion expenditures of less than $2 million a year by McNeil Labs, according to industry observers.

DATRIL PRODUCT DEVELOPMENT

The acetaminophen segment of the analgesic market had attracted little attention from the major drug companies before the 1970s. When sales of nonaspirin increased in the early 1970s, Bristol-Myers executives recognized an opportunity to develop their own acetaminophen product. They saw a major competitor with almost the entire growing acetaminophen business to itself. This growing market appeared to offer Bristol-Myers a chance to strengthen its position in the analgesic market. Consequently, the company began a careful study of the growing acetaminophen market and the potential product.

Initially, focus group sessions were conducted with Tylenol users to elicit their opinions about an acetaminophen product. The results of these sessions were used as a basis for concept testing of the product. Upon completion of this consumer research, Bristol-Myers Products executives were confident about completing the development of their own acetaminophen product. In early 1974 Datril—with acetamino-

---

[c] *Over-the-counter drug:* May be legally available without a prescription, but is promoted only to the medical profession as an ethical drug.

phen as its primary ingredient—was ready to be introduced into test markets. Datril was introduced to the market using a promotional campaign based solely on the benefits of a nonaspirin pain reliever. Sales results based on this approach were disappointing. In October 1974 Datril was reintroduced into test markets in Peoria, Illinois, and Albany, New York, for a five-month period. Datril was promoted on the basis of a price advantage to the consumer. It was advertised as costing one dollar less than the equivalent amount of Tylenol. The typical price difference was $2.85 for Tylenol and $1.85 for Datril at the consumer level.

In this market test, Datril captured the highest introductory share of any analgesic in the company's history. These positive results prompted the company to give the go-ahead for the introduction of Datril to the national market.

MARKETING PLANS FOR DATRIL

Bristol-Myers had the choice of two basic alternatives for establishing themselves in the acetaminophen market. They could present their product as identical with Tylenol and compete on a price basis. Alternatively, they could present their product as offering something different than Tylenol and therefore worth a price reflecting this difference. This price could be above, below, or identical to the price of Tylenol. The first alternative had been the most successful for the company in the test markets, and company executives interpreted it as proof that there "was room for a second product at a lower price." Bristol-Myers decided to base Datril tablets' introductory program on only one point of differentiation—a lower price.

The lower-price strategy was aimed at offering the greatest value to the consumer. The decision was made to implement an intensive promotional campaign for the introduction of Datril. The idea of talking directly to the consumer would mark a significant move from the traditional method of promoting an acetaminophen product. In the past, only proprietary drugs had been promoted to the consumer. Nevertheless, the price difference was viewed as most advantageous to the consumers; therefore, it was felt that they should be made aware of it.

Pricing
The suggested retail price for a 100-tablet bottle of Datril was to be $1.85. Bristol-Myers's selling price to the trade for a 100-tablet bottle would be $1.049. The company would also offer introductory trade deals that could possibly make the cost to a retailer as low as 70 cents for a 100-tablet bottle. One hundred tablets of an acetaminophen prod-

uct contain about 20 cents worth of acetaminophen and 20 cents worth of binders. There would be additional costs for the bottle, box, instruction sheets, and manufacturing.

Advertising

One month before the introduction of Datril, Bristol-Myers planned to present ads to the trade by way of a heavy advertisement campaign featuring commercials on all three TV networks. The campaign would also include ads in magazines such as *Reader's Digest* and *Ladies' Home Journal,* and newspaper ads and heavy TV spots in the top fifty markets for consumer products. Datril advertising would focus on the idea that "the 100-tablet bottle of Datril sells for as much as a dollar less than the same quantity of Tylenol. . . . Since they are both the same, there is no reason to keep paying more for Tylenol." The TV ads would show two women on a split screen, one holding a bottle of Datril and one, a bottle of Tylenol. The women would discuss the similar attributes of the two products; then one would point out the advantage of Datril's lower price. The ads for the magazines and the newspapers would show both products and point out price as the only significant difference between Datril and Tylenol (see Exhibit 3). This extensive comparative advertising would also represent a significant change from traditional forms of promotion in the drug industry. The cost of the advertising program was estimated to be $6 million for six months.

Other Promotion

In order to solidify support at the retail level, Bristol-Myers planned to offer introductory trade deals to retailers. Point-of-purchase displays for the retail outlets would also be included.

Although the majority of the promotion would be aimed directly at the consumer, the company would have some promotion for the medical profession. Plans were developed for advertising in medical journals, as well as for sending samples of Datril to approximately 125,000 physicians and 60,000 dentists.

EXHIBIT 3
Datril Print Advertisement

The difference between Tylenol and Datril is the price.

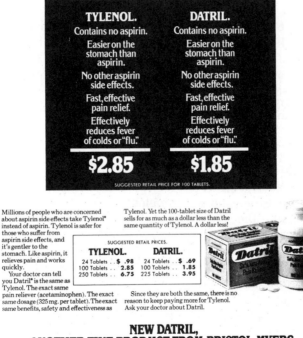

TYLENOL.	DATRIL.
Contains no aspirin.	Contains no aspirin.
Easier on the stomach than aspirin.	Easier on the stomach than aspirin.
No other aspirin side effects.	No other aspirin side effects.
Fast, effective pain relief.	Fast, effective pain relief.
Effectively reduces fever of colds or "flu."	Effectively reduces fever of colds or "flu."
$2.85	**$1.85**

SUGGESTED RETAIL PRICE FOR 100 TABLETS.

Millions of people who are concerned about aspirin side effects take Tylenol* instead of aspirin. Tylenol is safer for those who suffer from aspirin side effects, and it's gentler to the stomach. Like aspirin, it relieves pain and works quickly.

Your doctor can tell you Datril* is the same as Tylenol. The exact same pain reliever (acetaminophen). The exact same dosage (325 mg. per tablet). The exact same benefits, safety and effectiveness as

Tylenol. Yet the 100-tablet size of Datril sells for as much as a dollar less than the same quantity of Tylenol. A dollar less!

SUGGESTED RETAIL PRICES.

TYLENOL.		DATRIL.	
24 Tablets . . $ .98		24 Tablets . . $ .69	
100 Tablets . . 2.85		100 Tablets . . 1.85	
250 Tablets . . 6.75		225 Tablets . . 3.95	

Since they are both the same, there is no reason to keep paying more for Tylenol. Ask your doctor about Datril.

NEW DATRIL, ANOTHER FINE PRODUCT FROM BRISTOL-MYERS.

© 1974, BRISTOL MYERS CO.

Job No. BM-5833
This advertisement appears in:
Newspapers. . . . . 1000 lines. 1974
Ted Bates & Company / New York

CASE

Croft, Inc.

IN JANUARY 1987 the director of sales and the director of planning and administration of Croft, Inc., met to prepare a joint recommendation to the president on the pricing of the firm's line of asphalt shingles. Croft, Inc., had been a price leader over the years; when the firm announced its price on asphalt shingles, competitive manufacturers followed. Croft, Inc., had announced and implemented a price increase on January 1, 1985; however, this time competitors did not follow suit. The firm had since experienced a measurable decline in market share.

Approximately 80 percent of the homes in Croft, Inc.'s, region have asphalt shingles. About 90 percent of the homes contracting for new roofs use asphalt shingles. Nevertheless, the market for shingles has plateaued in recent years due to depressed conditions in new home construction and a lower incidence of reroofing due to uncertain economic conditions.

Sales and marketing efforts for asphalt shingles focus on roofing material distributors. Distributors provide a warehousing function for shingle manufacturers and sell shingles to roofing contractors or applicators who install the shingles.

Croft, Inc., is a major regional manufacturer of asphalt shingles for single-family houses. Company sales in 1986 were $10 million. The company's line of asphalt shingles was highly regarded by roofing material applicators in its region, and virtually all major distributors carried the company's line. None of its competitors had distribution through more than half of the distributors in the region.

The company had enjoyed a leadership position in its region because large, national producers of shingles (e.g., GAF Corporation, Georgia-Pacific Corporation) did not have manufacturing facilities in the region. Costs of freight due to the weight of asphalt shingles pre-

---

This case was prepared by Professor Roger A. Kerin, Edwin L. Cox School of Business, Southern Methodist University as a basis for class discussion and is not designed to illustrate appropriate or inappropriate handling of administrative situations. All information is disguised but useful for discussion purposes.

cluded national firms from shipping shingles into the region from their present plant sites.

In January 1985 Croft, Inc., raised its price per square of asphalt shingles from $18 to $20.[a] Although the company was strong financially, the price increase was prompted in part by a decision by the company's board of directors to embark on an extensive plant modernization and expansion program. The price increase was one of several changes directed by the board to improve the company's working capital position.

Contrary to past behavior, the five competitors of Croft, Inc., did not increase their prices. Rather, they held their prices at $18 per square. In 1986 Croft, Inc., recorded the same volume level as that achieved in 1978 (see Exhibit 1). The president of Croft, Inc., instructed the director of sales and the director of planning and administration to prepare a recommendation on the company's price policy and competitive posture soon after the end-of-year totals were recorded.

During the course of the initial meeting, the director of sales presented data on projected housing starts and the age of the existing housing stock (to estimate reroofing potential) in the region to arrive at a volume forecast of asphalt shingle squares. The figure both executives believed realistic was 1.2 million asphalt shingle squares for the region in 1987.

[a]*Square* is a unit of measurement used in the roofing industry. One square contains approximately eighty individual shingles. A rule of thumb in the industry holds that 25 squares are needed to roof an average single-family dwelling.

EXHIBIT 1
Volume and Price Behavior for Asphalt Shingle Squares: 1978–1986

| | Asphalt Square Volume (000s) | | Asphalt Shingle Square Price | |
| | Region Volume | Afton Industries Volume | Competitor Price | Afton Industries Price |
Year				
1978	830	500	$17	$17
1979	977	586	$17	$17
1980	1,085	651	$15	$15
1981	1,205	723	$15	$15
1982	1,339	803	$17	$17
1983	1,488	893	$18	$18
1984	1,600	960	$18	$18
1985	1,500	750	$18	$20
1986	1,250	500	$18	$20

A week later the executives met and discussed their options. After a lengthy discussion, they concluded that two options existed. They could recommend maintaining the price at $20 per square or reducing the price to $18. The option of recommending a price increase to $22 was dismissed on the grounds that the price differential between Afton Industries and its competitors would be entirely too great. In the sales director's opinion, it was unlikely that competitors would reduce their prices in the near future regardless of whether Croft, Inc., lowered its price or maintained the $20 price. He noted they were experiencing financial difficulties. However, he believed nothing was impossible and that a 10 percent chance of competitors lowering the price below $18 existed. The director of planning and administration felt the probability was conceivably higher but was unable to assign a probability estimate.

During the discussion on competitive response, the director of sales commented that if Croft, Inc., kept its price at $20, an additional loss of 10 percentage points in market share would result regardless of the actions by competitors. By comparison, he felt that lowering the price to $18 would lead to a gain of 10 percentage points in market share in 1987 if competitors stayed at the $18 price. If the price were reduced to $18 and competitors retaliated with an additional price cut, however, Croft, Inc., could expect a loss of 15 percentage points in market share in 1987. These assessments were based on discussions with the company's sales force indicating that a number of large construction contracts were locked into the $20 price and that the company's quality image would preclude a major downward movement in market share. Also, several sales representatives indicated that many applicators who purchased competitive shingles at the competitor

EXHIBIT 2
Croft, Inc., Estimated Per-Square Costs at 500,000 Square Volume: Asphalt Shingles

Direct labor	$ 8.00
Direct material	5.00
Scrappage	0.50
Product line expense	
Direct expenses[a]	0.50
Indirect expenses[b]	1.50
Selling and general administrative expenses[c]	2.00
Total cost per square	$17.50

[a]Includes supplies, repairs, power, etc. (all variable costs).

[b]Includes depreciation, supervision, etc. (all fixed expense).

[c]All costs were fixed, but allocated on a per-unit basis for expository purposes.

EXHIBIT 3
Selected Operating Data on Croft, Inc.'s Competitors: 1986

	Competitors				
	A	B	C	D	E
Unit (square) volume	200,000	190,000	150,000	150,000	60,000
Cost of goods sold/ unit	$15.00	$15.50	$16.00	$16.00	$16.25
Selling and general administrative expense	$500,000	$475,000	$425,000	$425,000	$350,000

price of $18 were marking up the product in such a manner that the installed price to homeowners and builders was equal to Croft, Inc.'s, installed price at typical markup levels. The installed price parity was annoying to competitors because they had no cost advantage at the point-of-sale or in the bidding process for new construction. In addition, it was believed that competitors had higher direct labor and material costs than Croft, Inc., had. The effect of this cost disadvantage was that competitor's contribution margins were lower than Croft, Inc.

Later in the same week, the accounting department submitted a cost breakdown on the company's line of asphalt shingles. These data are shown in Exhibit 2. In addition, the accounting department, in consultation with market research personnel, prepared a summary of the operating performance of the five competitors, shown in Exhibit 3. Croft, Inc., had planned to maintain selling and administrative expenses at 1986 levels.

CASE

Big Sky of Montana, Inc.

KAREN TRACY COULD FEEL the pressure on her as she sat at her desk late that April afternoon. Two weeks from today she would be called on to present her recommendations concerning next year's winter-season pricing policies for Big Sky of Montana, Inc.—room rates for the resort's accommodation facilities as well as decisions in the skiing and food service areas. The presentation would be made to a top management team from the parent company, Boyne USA, which operated out of Michigan.

"As sales and public relations manager, Karen, your accuracy in decision making is extremely important," her boss had said in his usual tone. "Because we spend most of our time in Michigan, we'll need a well-based and involved opinion."

It'll be the shortest two weeks of my life, she thought.

BACKGROUND: BIG SKY AND BOYNE USA

Big Sky of Montana, Inc., was a medium-sized destination resort located in southwestern Montana, forty-five miles south of Bozeman and forty-three miles north of the west entrance to Yellowstone National Park.[a] Big Sky was conceived in the early 1970s and had begun operation in November 1974.

The 11,000-acre, 2,000-bed resort was separated into two main areas: Meadow Village and Mountain Village. Meadow Village (elevation 6,300 feet) was located two miles east of the resort's main entrance

---

This case was written by Anne Senausky and Professor James E. Nelson, University of Colorado at Denver. Copyright © 1978 by the Endowment and Research Foundation at Montana State University.

[a]Destination resorts are characterized by on-the-hill lodging and eating facilities, a national market, and national advertising.

on U.S. 191 and seven miles from the ski area. Meadow Village had an 800-bed capacity in the form of four condominium complexes (ranging from studios to three-bedroom units) and a forty-room hostel for economy lodging. Additional facilities included an eighteen-hole golf course, six tennis courts, a restaurant, post office, a convention center with meeting space for up to 200 people, and a small lodge serving as a pro shop for the golf course in the summer and for cross-country skiing in the winter.

Mountain Village (elevation 7,500 feet), located at the base of the ski area, was the center of winter activity. In this complex was the 204-room Huntley Lodge offering hotel accommodations, three condominium complexes (unit size ranged from studio to three-bedroom), and an 88-room hostel for a total of 1,200 beds. The Mountain Mall was also located here, next to Huntley Lodge and within a five-minute walk of two of the three condominium complexes in Mountain Village. It housed ticket sales, an equipment rental shop, a skiers' cafeteria, two large meeting rooms for a maximum of 700 persons (regularly used as sack lunch areas for skiers), two offices, a ski school desk, and a ski patrol room—all of which were operated by Boyne. Also in this building were a delicatessen, drug store/gift shop, sporting goods store/rental shop, restaurant, outdoor-clothing store, jewelry shop, T-shirt shop, two bars, and a child day-care center. Each of these independent operations held leases, due to expire in one to three years.

The closest airport to Big Sky was located just outside Bozeman. It was served by Northwest Orient and Frontier Airlines with connections to other major airlines out of Denver and Salt Lake City. Greyhound and Amtrak also operated bus and train service into Bozeman. Yellowstone Park Lines provided Big Sky with three buses daily to and from the airport and Bozeman bus station (cost was $4.40 one way, $8.40 round trip), as well as an hourly shuttle around the two Big Sky villages. Avis, Hertz, National, and Budget offered car-rental service in Bozeman with a drop-off service available at Big Sky.

In July 1976 Boyne USA, a privately owned, Michigan-based operation, purchased Huntley Lodge, Mountain Mall, the ski lifts and terrain, the golf course, and the tennis courts for approximately $8 million. The company subsequently invested an additional $3 million in Big Sky. Boyne also owned and operated four Michigan ski resorts.

Big Sky's top management consisted of a lodge manager (in charge of operations within Huntley Lodge), a sales and public relations manager (Karen), a food and beverage manager, and an area manager (overseeing operations external to the lodge, including the mall and all recreational facilities). These four positions were occupied by persons trained with the parent company; a fifth manager, the comptroller, had worked for pre-Boyne ownership.

Business figures were reported to the company's home office on a daily basis, and major decisions concerning Big Sky operations were discussed and approved by "Michigan." Boyne's top management visited Big Sky an average of five times annually, and all major decisions, such as pricing and advertising, were approved by the parent company for all operations.

THE SKIING

Big Sky's winter season usually began in late November and continued until the middle of April, with a yearly snowfall of approximately 450 inches. The area had eighteen slopes between elevations of 7,500 and 9,900 feet. Terrain breakdown was as follows: 25 percent novice, 55 percent intermediate, and 20 percent advanced. (Although opinions varied, industry guidelines recommended a terrain breakdown of 20 percent, 60 percent, and 20 percent for novice, intermediate, and advanced skiers, respectively.) The longest run was approximately three miles in length; temperatures (highs) ranged from 15 to 30 degrees Fahrenheit throughout the season.

Lift facilities at Big Sky included two double chairlifts, a triple chair, and a four-passenger gondola. Lift capacity was estimated at 4,000 skiers per day. This figure was considered adequate by the area manager, at least until the 1980–1981 season.

Karen felt that the facilities, snow conditions, and grooming compared favorably with those of other destination resorts of the Rockies. "In fact, our only real drawback right now," she thought, "is our position in the national market. We need more skiers who are sold on Big Sky. And that is in the making."

THE CONSUMERS

Karen knew from previous dealings that Big Sky, like most destination areas, attracted three distinct skier segments: local day skiers (living within driving distance and not utilizing lodging in the area); individual destination skiers (living out of state and using accommodations in the Big Sky area); and groups of destination skiers (clubs, professional organizations, and so on).

The first category was typically comprised of Montana residents, with a relatively small number from Wyoming and Idaho. (Distances from selected population centers to Big Sky appear in Exhibit 1.) A

EXHIBIT 1

Population centers in proximity to Big Sky (distance and population)

City	Distance from Big Sky (Miles)	Population (U.S. 1970 Census)
Bozeman, Montana	45	18,670
Butte, Montana	126	23,368
Helena, Montana	144	22,730
Billings, Montana	174	61,581
Great Falls, Montana	225	60,091
Missoula, Montana	243	29,497
Pocatello, Idaho	186	40,036
Idaho Falls, Idaho	148	35,776

Approximate distance of selected major U.S. population centers to Big Sky (in air miles)

City	Distance to Big Sky[a]
Chicago	1275
Minneapolis	975
Fargo	750
Salt Lake City	375
Dallas	1500
Houston	1725
Los Angeles	975
San Francisco	925
New York	2025
Atlanta	1950
New Orleans	1750
Denver	750

[a]Per-passenger air fare can be approximated at 20 cents per mile (round trip, coach rates).

1973 study of four Montana ski areas, performed by the advertising unit of the Montana Department of Highways, characterized Montana skiers as:

1. In their early twenties and male (60 percent)
2. Living within seventy-five miles of a ski area
3. From a household with two skiers in it
4. Averaging $13,000 in household income
5. An intermediate- to advanced-ability skier
6. Skiing five hours per ski day, twenty days per season locally

7. Skiing four days away from local areas

8. Taking no lessons in the past five years

Karen was also aware that a significant number of day skiers, particularly on the weekends, were college students.

Destination, or nonresident skiers, were labeled in the same study as typically:

1. At least in their mid-twenties and male (55 percent)

2. Living in a household of three or more skiers

3. Averaging near $19,000 in household income

4. More likely to be an intermediate skier

5. Spending about six hours per day skiing

6. Skiing eleven to fourteen days per season with three to eight days away from home

7. Taking ski school lessons

Through data taken from reservation records, Karen learned that individual destination skiers accounted for half of last year's usage based on skier days.[b] Geographic segments were approximately as follows:

Upper Midwest (Minnesota, Michigan, North Dakota)	30%
Florida	20%
California	17%
Washington, Oregon, Montana	15%
Texas, Oklahoma	8%
Other	10%

Reservation records indicated that the average length of stay for individual destination skiers was six to seven days.

The individual destination skier was most likely to buy a lodging/lift package; 30 percent made commitments for these advertised packages when making reservations for 1977–1978. Even though there was no discount involved in this manner of buying lift tickets, Karen knew that it was fairly popular because it saved the purchaser a trip to

---

[b]A skier day is defined as one skier using the facility for any part of one day of operation.

the ticket window every morning. Approximately half of the individual business came through travel agents, who received a 10 percent commission.

The third skier segment, the destination group, accounted for a substantial 20 percent of Big Sky's skier-day usage. The larger portion of the group business came through medical and other professional organizations that held meetings at the resort, as this was a way to combine business with pleasure. These groups were typically comprised of couples and individuals between the ages of thirty and fifty. Ski clubs made up the remainder, with a number coming from Florida, Texas, and Georgia. During the 1977–1978 season, Big Sky drew thirty ski clubs with membership averaging fifty-five skiers. The average length of stay for all group destination skiers was about four to five days.

A portion of these group bookings were made through travel agents but the majority were made directly with Karen. The coordinator of the professional meetings or the president of the ski club typically contacted the Big Sky sales office to make initial reservation dates, negotiate prices, and work out the details of the stay.

THE COMPETITION

In Karen's mind, Big Sky faced two types of competition, that for local day skiers and that for out-of-state (i.e., destination) skiers.

Bridger Bowl was virtually the only area competing for local day skiers. Bridger was a "no-frills," nonprofit, smaller ski area located some sixteen miles northeast of Bozeman. It received the majority of local skiers, including students at Montana State University, which is located in Bozeman. The area was labeled as having terrain more difficult than that of Big Sky and thus was more appealing to the local expert skiers. However, it also had much longer lift lines and had recently lost some of its weekend business to Big Sky.

Karen had found through experience that most Bridger skiers usually "tried" Big Sky once or twice a season. Season passes for the two areas were mutually honored (by charging the half-day rate for an all-day ticket), and Big Sky occasionally ran newspaper ads offering discounts on lifts to obtain more Bozeman business.

Big Sky considered its competition for out-of-state skiers to be mainly the destination resorts of Colorado, Utah, and Wyoming. (Selected data on competing resorts appear in Exhibit 2.) Because Big Sky was smaller and newer than the majority of these areas, Karen reasoned, it was necessary to follow an aggressive strategy aimed at increasing its national market share.

EXHIBIT 2

**Competitors' 1977–1978 Package Plan Rates, [a] Number
of Lifts, and Lift Rates**

	Lodge Double (2)[b]	Two-Bedroom Condo (4)	Three-Bedroom Condo (6)	Number of Lifts	Daily Lift Rates
Aspen, CO	$242	$242	$220	19	$13
Steamboat, CO	230	230	198	15	12
Jackson, WY	230	242	210	5	14
Vail, CO	230	242	220	15	14
Snowbird, UT	208	none	none	6	11
Bridger Bowl, MT (no lodging available at Bridger Bowl)					

[a]Package plan rates are per person and include seven nights lodging and six lift tickets (high-season rates).

[b]Number in parentheses denotes occupancy of unit on which price is based.

PRESENT POLICIES

Lift Rates

It was common knowledge that there existed some local resentment concerning Big Sky's lift-rate policy. Although comparable to rates at Vail or Aspen, the price of an all-day lift ticket was $4 higher than the ticket offered at Bridger Bowl. In an attempt to alleviate this situation, management at Big Sky instituted a $9 "chair pass" for the 1977–1978 season, entitling the holder to unlimited use of the three chairs, plus two rides per day on the gondola, to be taken between specified time periods. Because the gondola served primarily intermediate terrain, it was reasoned that the chair pass would appeal to the local, more expert skier. A triple chair serving the bowl area was located at the top of the gondola; two rides on the gondola would allow those skiers to take ample advantage of the advanced terrain up there. Otherwise, all advanced terrain was served by another chair.

However, Karen believed that if Big Sky was to establish itself as a successful, nationally prominent destination area, the attitudes and opinions of all skiers must be carefully weighed. Throughout the season she had made a special effort to grasp the general feeling toward rates. A $12 ticket, she discovered, was thought to be very reasonable by destination skiers, primarily because Big Sky was predominantly an intermediate area and the average destination skier was of intermediate ability, and also because Big Sky was noted for its relative lack of lift lines, giving the skier more actual skiing time for the money. "Perhaps we should keep the price the same," she thought. "We do need more business. Other destination areas are likely to raise their prices and we should look good in comparison."

Also discussed was the possible abolition of the $9 chair pass. The question in Karen's mind was whether its elimination would severely hurt local business or would instead sell an all-lift $12 ticket to the skier who had previously bought only a chair pass. The issue was compounded by an unknown number of destination skiers who also opted for the cheaper chair pass.

Season pass pricing was also an issue. Prices for the 1977–1978 all-lift season pass had remained the same as last year's, but a season chair pass had been introduced that was the counterpart of the daily chairlift pass. Karen did not like the number of season chair passes purchased in relation to the number of all-lift passes and considered recommending its abolition as well as an increase in the price of the all-lift pass. "I'm going to have to think this one out carefully," she thought, "because skiing accounted for about 40 percent of our total revenue this past season. I'll have to be able to justify my decision not only to Michigan but also to the Forest Service."

Price changes were not solely at the discretion of Big Sky management. As was the case with most larger Western ski areas, the U.S. government owned part of the land on which Big Sky operated. Control of this land was the responsibility of the U.S. Forest Service, which annually approved all lift pricing policies. For the 1976–1977 ski season, Forest Service action had kept most lift-rate increases to the national inflation rate. For the 1977–1978 season, larger price increases were allowed for ski areas that had competing areas nearby; Big Sky was considered to be such an area. No one knew what the Forest Service position would be for the upcoming 1978–1979 season.

To help Karen in her decision, an assistant had prepared a summary of lift rates and usage for the past two seasons (Exhibit 3).

Room Rates

Room-rate pricing was particularly important because lodging accounted for about one-third of the past season's total revenue. It was also difficult because of the variety of accommodations (Exhibit 4) and the difficulty in accurately forecasting next season's demand. For example, the season of 1976–1977 had been unique in that a good portion of the Rockies was without snow for the initial months of the winter, including Christmas. Big Sky was fortunate in receiving as much snow as it had, and consequently many groups and individuals who were originally headed for Vail or Aspen booked in with Big Sky.

Pricing for the 1977–1978 season had been determined on the premise that there would be a good amount of repeat business. This came true in part, but not as much as had been hoped. Occupancy

EXHIBIT 3

Ticket	Consumer Cost	Skier Days[a]	Number Season Passes Sold
1977–1978 lift rates and usage summary (136 days operation)			
Adult all-day, all-lift	$12	53,400	
Adult all-day chair	9	20,200	
Adult half-day	8	9,400	
Child all-day, all-lift	8	8,500	
Child all-day chair	5	3,700	
Child half-day	6	1,200	
Hotel passes[b]	12/day	23,400	
Complimentary	0	1,100	
Adult all-lift season pass	220	4,300	140
Adult chair season pass	135	4,200	165
Child all-lift season pass	130	590	30
Child chair season pass	75	340	15
Employee all-lift season pass	100	3,000	91
Employee chair season pass	35	1,100	37
1976–1977 lift rates and usage summary (122 days operation)			
Adult all-day	10	52,500	
Adult half-day	6.50	9,000	
Child all-day	6	10,400	
Child half-day	4	1,400	
Hotel passes[b]	10/day	30,500	
Complimentary	0	480	
Adult season pass	220	4,200	84
Child season pass	130	300	15
Employee season pass	100	2,300	70

[a]A skier day is defined as one skier using the facility for any part of one day of operation.

[b]Hotel passes refer to those included in the lodging/lift packages.

experience had also been summarized for the past two seasons to help Karen make her final decision (Exhibit 5).

As was customary in the hospitality industry, January was a slow period, and it was necessary to price accordingly. Low-season pricing was extremely important because many groups took advantage of the lower rates. In addition, groups were often offered discounts in the neighborhood of 10 percent. Considering this, Karen could not price too high, with the risk of losing individual destination skiers, nor too low, such that an unacceptably low profit would be made from group business in this period.

EXHIBIT 4

Nightly Room Rates,[a] 1977–1978	Low-Season Range	High-Season Range	Maximum Occupancy
Huntley Lodge			
Standard	$42–62 *56*	$50–70	4
Loft	52–92 *72*	60–100	6
Stillwater Condo			
Studio	40–60 *52.5*	45–65	4
One-bedroom	55–75 *67.5*	60–80	4
Bedroom w/loft	80–100 *95*	90–110	6
Deer Lodge Condo			
One-bedroom	74–84 *82*	80–90	4
Two-bedroom	93–103 *101.5*	100–110	6
Three-bedroom	112–122 *121*	120–130	8
Hill Condo			
Studio	30–40 *37.5*	35–45	4
Studio w/loft	50–70 *62.5*	55–75	6
Nightly Room Rates, 1976–1977			
Huntley Lodge			
Standard	32–47 *41*	35–50	4
Loft	47–67 *58.5*	50–70	6
Stillwater Condo			
Studio	39–54 *45.5*	37–52	4
One-bedroom	52–62 *56*	50–60	4
Bedroom w/loft	60–80 *72.5*	65–85	6
Deer Lodge Condo			
One-bedroom	51–66 *60.5*	55–70	4
Two-bedroom	74–94 *87*	80–100	6
Three-bedroom	93–123 *223* *115.5*	100–130	8
Hill Condo			
Studio	28–43 *34.5*	30–45	4
Studio w/loft	42–62 *53.5*	45–65	6

[a]Rates determined by number of persons in room or condominium unit and do not include lift tickets. Maximums for each rate range apply at maximum occupancy.

Food Service

Under some discussion was the feasibility of converting all destination skiers to the American plan; each guest in Huntley Lodge would be placed on a package that included three meals daily in a Big Sky–controlled facility. There was a feeling both for and against this idea. The parent company had been successfully utilizing this plan for years at its destination areas in northern Michigan. Extending the policy to Big Sky should find similar success.

Karen was not so sure. For one thing, the Michigan resorts were

EXHIBIT 5

1977-78 lodge-condominium occupancy (in room-nights[a])

	December (26 Days Operation)	January	February	March	April (8 Days Operation)
Huntley Lodge	1,830	2,250	3,650	4,650	438
Condominiums[b]	775	930	1,350	100	90

1976–1977 Lodge-condominum occupancy (in room-nights)

	December (16 Days Operation)	January	February	March	April (16 Days Operation)
Huntley Lodge	1,700	3,080	4,525	4,300	1,525
Condominiums[c]	600	1,000	1,600	1,650	480

Lodge-condominium occupancy (in person-nights[d])

December 1977 (1976)	January 1978 (1977)	February 1978 (1977)	March 1978 (1977)	April 1978 (1977)
7,850 (6,775)	9,200 (13,000)	13,150 (17,225)	17,900 (17,500)	1,450 (4,725)

[a]A room-night is defined as one room (or condominium) rented for one night. Lodging experience is based on 124 days of operation for 1977–1978, while Exhibit 3 shows the skiing facilities operating 136 days. Both numbers are correct.

[b]Big Sky had ninety-two condominiums available during the 1977–1978 season.

[c]Big Sky had eighty-five condominiums available during the 1976–1977 season.

[d]A person-night refers to one person using the facility for one night.

primarily self-contained and alternative eateries were few. For another, the whole idea of extending standardized policies from Michigan to Montana was suspect. As an example, Karen painfully recalled a day in January when Big Sky "tried on" another successful Michigan policy of accepting only cash or check payments for lift tickets. Reactions of credit card–carrying skiers could be described as ranging from annoyed to irate.

If an American plan were proposed for next year, it would likely include both the Huntley Lodge dining room and Lookout Cafeteria. Less clear, however, were prices to be charged. There certainly would have to be consideration for both adults and children and for the two independently operated eating places in Mountain Mall (see Exhibit 6 for an identification of eating places in the Big Sky area). Beyond these considerations, there was little other than an expectation of a profit to guide Karen in her analysis.

EXHIBIT 6
Eating Places in the Big Sky Area

Establishment	Type of Service	Meals Served	Current Prices	Seating	Location
Lodge dining room[a]	A la carte	Breakfast	$2–5	250	Huntley Lodge
		Lunch	2–5		
		Dinner	7–15		
Steak House[a]	Steak/lobster	Dinner only	$6–12	150	Huntley Lodge
Fondue Stube[a]	Fondue	Dinner only	$6–10	25	Huntley Lodge
Ore House[b]	A la carte	Lunch	$0.80–4	150	Mountain Mall
		Dinner	5–12		
Ernie's Deli[b]	Deli/restaurant	Breakfast	$1–3	25	Mountain Mall
		Lunch	2–5		
Lookout Cafeteria[a]	Cafeteria	Breakfast	$1.50–3	175	Mountain Mall
		Lunch	2–4		
		Dinner	3–6		
Yellow Mule[b]	A la carte	Breakfast	$2–4	75	Meadow Village
		Lunch	2–5		
		Dinner	4–8		
Buck's T-4[b]	Road house restaurant/bar	Dinner only	$2–9	60	Gallatin Canyon (2 miles south of Big Sky entrance)
Karst Ranch[b]	Road house restaurant/bar	Breakfast	$2–4	50	Gallatin Canyon (7 miles north of Big Sky entrance)
		Lunch	2–5		
		Dinner	3–8		
Corral[b]	Road house restaurant/bar	Breakfast	$2–4	30	Gallatin Canyon (5 miles south of Big Sky entrance)
		Lunch	2–4		
		Dinner	3–5		

[a]Owned and operated by Big Sky of Montana, Inc.
[b]Independently operated.

Recs:
1) Up all prices
2) Up lift prices
3) Up food/lodging
4) Up food only
5) keep all steady

EXHIBIT 7
Ski Season Income Data (Percentage)

	Skiing	Lodging	Food and Beverage
Revenue	100.0	100.0	100.0
Cost of sales			
Merchandise	0.0	0.0	30.0
Labor	15.0	15.9	19.7
Maintenance	3.1	5.2	2.4
Supplies	1.5	4.8	5.9
Miscellaneous	2.3	0.6	0.6
Operating expenses	66.2	66.4	66.7
Net profit (loss) before taxes	11.9	7.1	(25.2)

THE TELEPHONE CALL

"Profits in the food area might be hard to come by," Karen thought. "Last year it appears we lost money on everything we sold" (see Exhibit 7). Just then the telephone rang. It was Rick Thompson, her counterpart at Boyne Mountain Lodge in Michigan. "How are your pricing recommendations coming?" he asked. "I'm about done with mine and thought we should compare notes."

"Good idea, Rick—only I'm just getting started out here. Do you have any hot ideas?"

"Only one," he responded. "I just got off the phone with a guy in Denver. He told me all of the major Colorado areas are upping their lift prices one or two dollars next year."

"Is that right, Rick? Are you sure?"

"Well, you know nobody knows for sure what's going to happen, but I think it's pretty good information. He heard it from his sister-in-law who works in Vail. I think he said she read it in the local paper or something."

"That doesn't seem like very solid information," said Karen. "Let me know if you hear anything more, will you?"

"Certainly. You know, we really should compare our recommendations before we stick our necks out too far on this pricing thing. Can you call me later in the week?" he asked.

"Sure, I'll talk to you the day after tomorrow; I should be about done by then. Anything else?"

"Nope—gotta run. Talk to you then. Bye," and he was gone.

"At least I've got some information," Karen thought, "and a new deadline!"

Texas Instruments: Electronic Appliance Controls

THE TELEPHONE WAS RINGING as Charles Ames, manager of appliance controls engineering, entered his office on the morning of June 21, 1976. The call was from the director of engineering for Electronic Cooking Incorporated (ECI), who told Ames that a competitor had underbid Texas Instruments for an order of electronic controls for microwave ovens. Mr. Ames was confident that the competitor's bid price was unrealistically low since Texas Instruments, with its accumulated experience, could meet the bid only by pricing with profit margins significantly less than those of the TI model for this product line.

While assembling his staff to discuss the ramifications of the competitive bid, Ames realized that a decision of this importance would significantly affect the direction of TI market growth. Accordingly, a meeting time that afternoon was agreed upon to bring together

The assistance of Texas Instruments Incorporated, in the preparation of this case, is gratefully acknowledged. This case was prepared by Mr. Bill Stearns, Texas Instruments, and Professor Roger A. Kerin, Edwin L. Cox School of Business, Southern Methodist University, as a basis for class discussion and is not designed to illustrate appropriate or inappropriate handling of administrative situations. Quantitative and financial data reported in this case have been disguised, as have relationships among these data, thus rendering them inappropriate for research purposes.

Ames, his staff, and their group vice-president to formulate a course of action, if any.

THE COMPANY

Texas Instruments Incorporated (TI) is a worldwide leader in electronic technology innovation, production, and applications. In 1975, 84 percent of TI's total business was electronics-based. TI is a major producer of hand-held calculators in terms of dollar volume.

Past and Future Performance

TI has experienced almost a threefold increase in net sales in the last decade. Net sales volume in 1975 was approximately $1.4 billion compared with net sales of about $580 million in 1966. TI was ranked 152 in *Fortune's* "500" in 1975. Abbreviated TI 1976 financial statements are shown in Exhibit 1.

Two years ago, TI had announced its goal to grow to $10 billion in net sales by the late 1980s. The guidelines for achieving the $10 billion goal were articulated in the *First Quarter and Stockholders Meeting Report, 1976:*

- We will model TI's business to self-fund growth.
- We intend to rely primarily on internal growth rather than on major acquisitions.
- We will optimize our resources to improve TI's share position.
- We will emphasize expansion of served markets into contiguous new segments, taking advantage of intra-TI shared experience.
- We will rely primarily on opportunities related to electronics, particularly those in which our semiconductor skills can be decisive.

The operating guidelines for reaching the $10 billion goal were also outlined in the 1976 document:

- We must meet TI's return on assets goals to allow the growth to be self-funded.
- We must meet the operating model parameters to generate adequate OST funds.[a]

---

[a]The TI objectives, strategies, and tactics (OST) system is described briefly in the OST budgeting procedure section of this case.

EXHIBIT 1
Abbreviated Texas Instruments Consolidated Financial
Statements for the Year Ended December 31, 1975
(thousands of dollars)

Income statement

Net sales		$1,367,621
Operating costs and expenses		
Cost of goods and services sold	1,004,133	
General, administrative, and marketing	227,515	
Employee's retirement and profits sharing plans	21,185	
Total		1,252,833
Profit from operations		$ 114,788
Other income (net)		11,971
Interest on loans		(10,822)
Income before provision for income taxes		$ 115,937
Provision for income taxes		53,795
Net income		$ 62,142

Balance sheet

Current assets	
Cash and short-term investments	$ 266,578
Accounts receivable	245,785
Inventories (net of progress billings)	142,880
Prepaid expenses	7,322
Total	$ 662,565
Property, plant, and equipment (net)	253,709
Other assets and deferred charges	25,203
Total assets	$ 941,477
Liabilities and stockholders' equity	
Current liabilities	$ 301,843
Deferred liabilities	54,346
Stockholders' equity	585,288
Total liabilities and stockholders' equity	$ 941,477

Source: Annual report.

- OST funds must be invested in TI's major growth thrusts—
  that is, products that serve markets with a high growth rate
  and in which TI can develop a profitable position.
- We must retain and build upon TI philosophies and methods
  to manage profitable growth. This is why the institutionalism
  of TI's management culture has been emphasized through

mechanisms such as the OST system, people and asset effectiveness, and design-to-cost.[b]

- TI must continue to increase its basic technological strength,
  especially in semiconductors. This includes not only the design and development of key components but also the application of these components to advanced systems and services.

- We must make success sharing work because it is the key to
  increased productivity.[c]

OST Budgetary Procedure

An OST program—objectives, strategies, and tactics—is the action
plan for a particular endeavor. An OST program states not only what a
particular endeavor expects to achieve, but also how it will be
achieved and the specific actions necessary to achieve it, including the
costs of engineering, marketing, and production. OST funding is derived from a portion of operating profits intended to support a new
business strategy and is controlled at the department (profit and loss
center) level. Funding for OST programs is competitive in that division
managers obtain inputs from each of the department managers and
subsequently submit funding requests to a budget committee. OST
programs are ranked according to their growth and profitability potential by the budget committee with funds allocated accordingly.

The annual budgeting procedure is highly refined and well controlled. Flexibility is retained, however, to modify a product or program definition operating within the OST system. Programs are
defined in the fourth quarter for the coming calendar year and are
reviewed monthly and quarterly. The flexibility of the process is illustrated by Mr. Ames's reflection on the Electronic Controls program:

> In 1973 the Oven Temp Sensor Program was funded $50,000 and the
> Electronic Control Program was allocated $10,000. In 1974 Oven Temp
> was allocated $60,000 while the Electronic Controls Department was al-
> located nothing. Then, in December 1974 a group of vice-presidents from
> a microwave oven manufacturer visited TI. The prospects outlined by
> these executives allowed for an improved Electronic Control Program to
> be developed. Funds from another program were immediately diverted
> to Electronic Controls, which marked the beginning of the program as it
> now stands.

---

[b]Design-to-cost is described briefly in the text on p. 552.

[c]Success sharing is a term used to designate the total package of TI employees'
pension, profit sharing, and stock option purchase plans.

Mr. Ames noted that this episode was not uncommon given TI's corporate position that OST funds should be invested in products that serve growth markets and in which TI could develop a profitable position. In the same vein, existing programs exhibiting poor performance could lose funding. Mr. Ames was very much aware of this fact: "The sequence of events that benefited the Electronic Controls Program could work against it unless the program could be made profitable."

DEVELOPMENT OF TACTICAL ACTION PROGRAM: ELECTRONIC CONTROLS

Pre-1975

Texas Instruments executives had decided to examine the electronic control market for microwave ovens in late 1972 in order to utilize and expand TI's semiconductor expertise. Microwave oven volume had grown substantially in the late 1960s and early 1970s. According to industry estimates, total industry sales in 1972 were 320,000 units compared with 20,000 units in 1968. Total industry sales in 1974 were approximately 785,000 units. During this period ECI held the major share of the market, accounting for about 40 percent of the microwave oven units sold.

Controls for microwave ovens prior to 1975 were produced by electromechanical companies. However, industry sources indicated that these companies were experimenting with electronic controls. Other firms with semiconductor technology were showing signs of interest in producing electronic controls; yet, no firm had openly entered the market. "But TI had the right product at the right time, the capacity to support the potential demand, and the recognized technological expertise from calculators and related products to enter the market," Ames noted.

January–June 1975

On January 27, 1975, Charles Ames was assigned as manager of TI's Electronic Controls Program, then called the Tactical Action Program (TAP). Ames was responsible for both the engineering and marketing functions associated with the electronic control. His role included responsibility for designing the product in addition to developing proposals for microwave oven producers.

Within two weeks of his appointment, Ames made his first presentation to ECI. The proposal was rejected in March. In April he presented a proposal to AMEX Ovens for electronic controls with a unit sales price of $55. AMEX made a verbal commitment in June for 50,000 units.

During this period, Ames's energies were devoted to designing the electronic controls to cost requirements imposed by the cost-conscious appliance industry. The idea of design-to-cost (DTC) is central to TI's production and marketing thrust. Briefly, this concept involves designing a product from the start to achieve specific performance, cost, and profit goals. This practice involves the reduction in product cost necessary to perform a function due to a lower material and labor content. The impact of the DTC process for a TI hand-held calculator serves as a typical illustration. In 1974 forty-seven total parts (including sixteen electronic parts) were required to build the TII9 model calculator. By 1976 the TII200 calculator, identical in function, required twenty-three parts, and only two parts were electronic. Mr. Ames's efforts were focused on similar DTC activities for electronic controls.

The guide used by Ames in charting cost reductions was the learning or experience curve phenomenon. In effect, Ames hoped that he could realize a 20 percent reduction in electronic control assembly labor cost each time his volume doubled for a new design. Similar curves would be developed for each proposal to microwave oven producers and would reflect Ames's ability to economize on material and labor content for each succeeding generation of controls. Mr. Ames realized, however, that a practical limit existed in how much he could reduce overall costs.

July–December 1975

On July 2 Mr. Ames received a call from a Superior Cooking Products (SCP) executive requesting that he prepare a proposal for them. This proposal included a bid price per unit of $45. On August 14 SCP placed the first confirmed order for 50,000 units.

Mr. Ames received a call from ECI on November 28 asking for a proposal. A new proposal was developed to the ECI specifications and a price of $36 per unit was bid. The difference in prices between the AMEX, SCP, and ECI prices arose from TI manufacturing cost savings due to order size (250,000 per year for ECI) and different control specifications.

During this period Ames consolidated and generated a variety of data pertaining to the appliance market and the electronic controls market for the purpose of forecasting TI's potential market growth and identifying possible areas of product superiority. These data would serve as inputs for his OST funding requests and preparation of financial planning and control indices.

Appliance Market and Microwave Ovens

Frequent discussions with marketing executives of appliance manufacturers revealed that technological innovation was the single most distinguishable factor separating competing products. Accordingly, appliance manufacturers were constantly seeking out new product features providing the costs of product innovation were commensurate with the benefits. One reason for the search for new product designs was the saturation level of appliances in American homes. According to industry estimates, about 70 percent of the 72.7 million electrically wired homes in the United States had electric ranges in 1975. Approximately, six of ten electric ranges sold in 1975 were replacement purchases rather than net new purchases.

Microwave oven unit volume had grown substantially since the early 1970s. This occurred in spite of unfavorable publicity regarding the potential for radiation emission. Exhibit 2 shows Ames's forecast of microwave oven unit sales and penetration of electronic controls in the total market through 1980 based on discussions with appliance manufacturer executives. Mr. Ames believed that these estimates might be optimistic because some industry observers were forecasting a 17 percent saturation level among U.S. homes by 1980. The annual rate of increase in the number of homes was about 2.3 percent, and the replacement cycle of microwave ovens had not been determined.

Also of interest to Ames was potential market shares held by major microwave oven producers. ECI had been a major supplier in the market prior to 1975. However, Home Appliance, Inc. (HAI), Superior Appliance, and AMEX had made competitive inroads and would continue to do so, according to industry sources. Despite some dis-

EXHIBIT 2
Forecast of Microwave and Electric Range Unit Volume and Penetration of Electronic Controls
(unit volume in millions)

	1977	1978	1979	1980
Microwave units	2	2.8	3.5	4
Percentage of microwave units with electronic controls	30%	45%	60%	80%
Electric ranges	2.9	2.87	2.85	2.8
Percentage of electric ranges with electronic controls	0%	3%	5%	10%

EXHIBIT 3
Estimated Market Shares of Microwave Producers,
1975, 1976, 1980

	1975 (%)	1976 (%)	1980 (%)
Electronic Cooking Inc.	25–33	25–30	15
Superior Appliance	16–25	20–25	15
Amex Ovens	10–18	15–25	12–20
Home Appliance Inc.	10	10–12	20–25
Other U.S. producers	5–7	7–8	15–20
Japanese producers	8–18	8–15	5–8

agreement among microwave oven producers as to their respective market share, Exhibit 3 shows the market share ranges described by industry observers.

Microwave Oven Controls Competition

Two major suppliers of controls existed in late 1975. These were electromechanical control producers. Relays and Wire, Inc. (R&W) and the Contact-Switch Company (C-S), in particular, were major producers. Both firms had made progress in designing electromechanical controls at competitive prices. However, Ames believed that inherent limitations in the electromechanical technology would prohibit them making major cost reductions or offer the innovative control features possible through semiconductor technology in the future. Nevertheless, in 1975, electromechanical technology was able to supply controls at a lower cost than semiconductor technology, and this competitive advantage was forecasted to exist until 1979. This would happen "provided semiconductor producers could penetrate the market, the microwave oven growth potential was realized, and so on and so forth," Ames opined. "A lot depends on how long semiconductor firms will stay with it, given very limited profit margins in the short run of maybe four to five years," Ames continued.

January–June 1976

On February 26, 1976, Ames was notified that ECI accepted his bid price. During the remaining spring months, Ames directed an increasing amount of his time toward DTC efforts for the second generation controls for TI customers and the ensuing production of first-generation controls. Time was also spent preparing OST funding and planning schedules.

On April 19, 1976, Ames was asked to bid on a second-generation control for ECI. Given the nature of the bid, including the specifications and quantity (150,000 units), Ames proposed a price of $44 (see the cost schedule in Exhibit 4 and supplementary material). Shortly thereafter, Ames was advised that the competitive bid level was $42 per unit, which TI met after considerable discussion. Then, on June 21, 1976, Ames was informed that TI had been underbid by a major semi-

EXHIBIT 4

ECI second-generation control cost estimate
The cost estimate developed by Ames is shown below:

$26.50	Yielded material cost
6.50	(0.45 hours/unit @ $14.45/hour)[a]
$33.00	Total material, labor and overhead or "manufactured cost"
11.00	25% gross margin
$44.00	Control selling price at 150,000 unit volume

Estimated labor learning curve for the ECI second-generation control

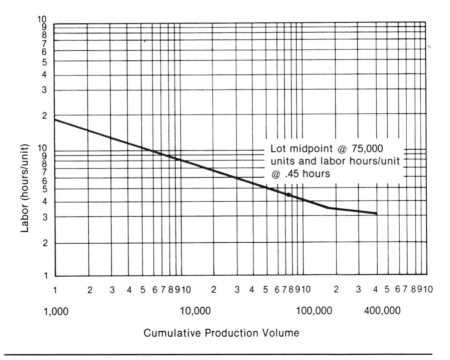

Cumulative Production Volume

[a]0.45 hours = lot midpoint of the 150,000 unit lot; $14.45 = hourly rate including factory overhead.

conductor manufacturing company at a price of $37. He assembled his staff to discuss the ramifications of the bid.

Ames had forecasted an 80 percent labor learning curve for this bid, as shown in the exhibit. The labor estimate early in the process was about 1.75 hours/unit, but would decrease to about 0.36 hours/unit at the 150,000th unit. The midpoint at 75,000 units was 0.45 hours/unit. Hence, one-half of the unit volume would require more than 0.45 hours/unit to build and one-half would require less.

Also shown in the exhibit is a 90 percent labor learning curve coresponding to the doubling of unit volume from 150,000 to 300,000. The flattening of the curve represented a "fact of life"—that learning gains would be less dramatic beyond 150,000 units without redesign and major change to the configuration. The labor hours/unit of the 300,000th unit would be 0.325 with the midpoint being approximately 0.34 labor hours/unit at the 225,000th unit produced.

Ames did not forecast reductions in material or yield cost since he did not plan an interim design change that would be fruitful in the short run. Furthermore, labor cost/unit reductions, assuming that he would bid for an additional 150,000 second-generation ECI controls, did not look promising.

Overshadowing the entire situation was the question of whether the competitor was also forecasting prices and costs on an 80 percent labor learning curve. If so, then Ames would have to consider how long his group would stay in the electronic range control business. This factor was critical if volume doubled again for the ECI account.

Ames was also plagued by other considerations. First, the future of cumulative microwave sales volume remained a question. Second, even if Ames received the contract, a possibility existed that all 150,000 units would not be shipped, since contingencies provided that the customer could stop shipment of controls at any time. In other words, as few as 50,000–75,000 units could be shipped and the order could be stopped. Third, TI policy held that every contract must achieve profit from operation objectives (8.4 percent of net sales) consistent with total company operations. Future OST funding for electronic appliance controls would depend, to a significant degree, on his ability to meet these objectives.

S. C. Johnson and Son, Limited

IN NOVEMBER 1980 George Styan was appointed Division Manager of INNOCHEM, at S. C. Johnson & Son, Limited (popularly known as "Canadian Johnson Wax") (SCJ), a Canadian subsidiary of S. C. Johnson & Son, Inc. INNOCHEM's sole product line consisted of industrial cleaning chemicals for use by business, institutions, and government. George was concerned by the division's poor market share, particularly in Montreal and Toronto. Together, these two cities represented approximately 35 percent of Canadian demand for industrial cleaning chemicals, but less than 10 percent of INNOCHEM sales. It appeared that SCJ distributors could not match the aggressive discounting practiced by direct selling manufacturers in metropolitan markets.

Recently, George had received a rebate proposal from his staff designed to increase the distributor's ability to cut end-user prices by "sharing" part of the total margin with SCJ when competitive conditions demanded discounts of 30 percent or more off the list price to end users. George had to decide if the Rebate Plan was the best way to penetrate price-sensitive markets. Moreover, he wondered about the plan's ultimate impact on divisional profit performance. George had to either develop an implementation plan for the Rebate Plan, or draft an alternative proposal to unveil at the 1981 Distributors' Annual Spring Convention, three weeks away.

This case was prepared by Roger A. More and Carolyn Vose, University of Western Ontario, as a basis for class discussion and is not intended to illustrate effective or ineffective handling of administrative situations. Used with permission.

THE CANADIAN MARKET FOR INDUSTRIAL CLEANING CHEMICALS

In 1980 the Canadian market for industrial cleaning chemicals was approximately $100 million at end-user prices. Growth was stable at an overall rate of approximately 3 percent per year.

"Industrial cleaning chemicals" included all chemicals products designed to clean, disinfect, sanitize, or protect industrial, commercial, and institutional buildings and equipment. The label was broadly applied to general-purpose cleaners; floor maintenance products (strippers, sealers, finishes, and detergents); carpet cleaners and deodorizers; disinfectants; air fresheners; and a host of specialty chemicals such as insecticides, pesticides, drain cleaners, oven cleaners, and sweeping compounds.

Industrial cleaning chemicals were distinct from equivalent consumer products typically sold through grocery stores. Heavy-duty industrial products were packaged in larger containers and bulk and were marketed directly by the cleaning chemical manufacturers or sold through distributors to a variety of end users. Exhibit 1 includes market segmentation by primary end-user categories, including janitorial service contractors and the in-house maintenance departments of government, institutions, and companies.

Building Maintenance Contractors

In Canada, maintenance contractors purchased 17 percent of the industrial cleaning chemicals sold during 1980 (end-user price). The segment was growing at approximately 10–15 percent a year, chiefly at the expense of other end-user categories. *Canadian Business* reported, "Contract cleaners have made sweeping inroads into the traditional preserve of in-house janitorial staffs, selling themselves on the strength of cost efficiency. . . ."[1] Maintenance contract billings reached an estimated $1 billion in 1980.

Frequently, demand for building maintenance services was highly price-sensitive, and since barriers to entry were low (small capitalization, simple technology), competition squeezed contractor gross margins below 6 percent (before tax). Variable cost control was a matter of survival, and only products bringing compensatory labor savings could command a premium price in this segment of the cleaning chemical market.

A handful of contract cleaners did specialize in higher-margin services to prestige office complexes, luxury apartments, art museums, and other "quality-conscious" customers. However, even contractors serving this select clientele did not necessarily buy premium cleaning supplies.

EXHIBIT 1
S.C. Johnson & Son Limited, Segmentation of the
Canadian Market for Industrial Cleaning Chemicals, by
End-User Category and by Product Category

End-User Category	Percentage of Total Canadian Market for Industrial Cleaning Chemicals (End-User Value)
Retail outlets	25
Contractors	17
Hospitals	15
Industrial and office	13
Schools, colleges	8
Hotels, motels	6
Nursing homes	5
Recreation	3
Government	3
Fast food	2
Full-service restaurants	2
All others	1
Total	100% = $95 million

Product Category	Percentage of Total Canadian Market for Industrial Cleaning Chemicals
Floor care products	40
General purpose cleaners	16
Disinfectants	12
Carpet care products	8
Odor control products	5
Glass cleaners	4
All others	15
Total	100% = $95 million

In-House Maintenance Departments

Government

In 1980, cleaning chemical sales to various government offices (federal, provincial, and local) approached $2 million. Typically, a government body solicited bids from appropriate sources by formally advertising for quotations for given quantities of particular cleaning chemicals. Although bid requests often named specific brands, suppliers were permitted to offer "equivalent substitutes." Separate competitions were held for each item and normally covered twelve months'

supply with provision for delivery "as required." Contracts were frequently awarded solely on the basis of price.

Institutions

Like government bodies, most institutions were price-sensitive as
a result of restrictive budgets and limited ability to pass on expenses to
users. Educational institutions and hospitals were the largest consumers of cleaning chemicals in this segment. School boards used an open
bid system patterned on the government model. Heavy sales time requirements and demands for frequent delivery of small shipments to
as many as 100 locations were characteristic.

Colleges and universities tended to be operated somewhat differently. Dan Stalport, one of the purchasing agents responsible for maintenance supplies at the University of Western Ontario, offered the
following comments:

> Sales reps come to UWO year 'round. If one of us (in the buying group)
> talks to a salesman who seems to have something—say, a labour-saving
> feature—we get a sample and test it. . . . Testing can take up to a year.
> Floor covering, for example, has to be exposed to seasonal changes in
> weather and traffic.
>
> If we're having problems with a particular item, we'll compare the
> performance and price of three or four competitors. There are usually
> plenty of products that do the job. Basically, we want value—acceptable
> performance at the lowest available price.

Hospitals accounted for 15 percent of cleaning chemical sales.
Procurement policies at University Hospital (UH), a medium-sized
(450-bed) facility in London, Ontario, were typical. UH distinguished
between "critical" and "noncritical" products. Critical cleaning chemicals (i.e., those significantly affecting patient health, such as phenolic
germicide) could be bought only on approval of the staff microbiolo-
gist, who tested the "kill factor." This measure of effectiveness was
regularly retested, and any downgrading of product performance could
void a supplier's contract. In contrast, noncritical supplies, such as
general-purpose cleaners, floor finishes, and the like, were the exclusive province of Bob Chandler, purchasing agent attached to the
Housekeeping Department. Bob explained that performance of noncritical cleaning chemicals was informally judged and monitored by
the housekeeping staff:

> Just last year, for example, the cleaners found that the floor polish was
> streaking badly. We (the Housekeeping Department) tested and com-
> pared five or six brands—all in the ballpark price-wise—and chose the
> best.

Business

The corporate segment was highly diverse, embracing both service and manufacturing industries. Large-volume users tended to be price-sensitive—particularly when profits were low. Often, however, cleaning products represented such a small percentage of the total operating budget that the cost of searching for the lowest-cost supplier would be expected to exceed any realizable saving. Under such conditions, the typical industrial customer sought efficiencies in the purchasing process itself—for example, by dealing with the supplier offering the broadest mix of janitorial products (chemicals, paper supplies, equipment, etc.). Guy Breton, purchasing agent for Securitech, a Montreal-based security systems manufacturer commented on the time economies of "one-stop shopping."

> With cleaning chemicals, it simply isn't worth the trouble to shop around and stage elaborate product performance tests. . . . I buy all our chemicals, brushes, dusters, towelling—the works—from one or two suppliers. . . . Buying reputable brands from familiar suppliers saves hassles—back orders are rare, and Maintenance seldom complains.

DISTRIBUTION CHANNELS FOR INDUSTRIAL CLEANING CHEMICALS

The Canadian market for industrial cleaning chemicals was supplied through three main channels, each characterized by a distinctive set of strengths and weaknesses:

1. Distributor sales of national brands
2. Distributor sales of private-label products
3. Direct sale by manufacturers

Direct sellers held a 61 percent share of the Canadian market for industrial cleaning chemicals, whereas the distributors of national brands and private label products held shares of 25 percent and 14 percent, respectively. Relative market shares varied geographically, however. In Montreal and Toronto, for example, the direct marketers' share rose to 70 percent and private labelers' to 18 percent, reducing the national brand share to 12 percent. The pattern, shown in Exhibit 2, reflected an interplay of two areas of channel differentiation—namely, discount capability at the end-user level and the cost of serving distant, geographically dispersed customers.

EXHIBIT 2
S. C. Johnson & Son Limited, Effect of Geography on
Market Share of Different Distribution Channels

Supplier Type	Percentage Share Nationwide	Percentage Share in Montreal and Toronto
Direct marketers	61[a]	70
Private label distributors	14	18
National brands distributors	25[b]	12

[a]Dustbane = 17%, G. H. Wood = 13%, and all others = 31%, for a total of 61%.
[b]SCJ = 8%, N/L = 4%, Airkem = 3%, and all others = 10%, for a total of 25%.

Distributor Sales of National Brand Cleaning Chemicals

National brand manufacturers, such as S. C. Johnson and Son, Airkem, and National Labs, produced a relatively limited range of "high-quality" janitorial products, including many special-purpose formulations of narrow market interest. Incomplete product range, combined with shortage of manpower and limited warehousing, made direct distribution infeasible in most cases. Normally, a national brand company would negotiate with middlemen who handled a broad array of complementary products (equipment, tools, and supplies) by different manufacturers. "Bundling" of goods brought the distributors' cost efficiencies in selling, warehousing, and delivery by spreading fixed costs over a large sales volume. Distributors were therefore better able to absorb the costs of after-hours emergency service, frequent routine sales and service calls to many potential buyers, and shipments of small quantities of cleaning chemicals to multiple destinations. As a rule, the greater the geographic dispersion of customers and the smaller the average order, the greater the relative economies of distributor marketing.

Comparatively high gross margins (approximately 50 percent of wholesale price) enabled national brand manufacturers to offer distributors strong marketing support and sales training along with liberal terms of payment and freight plus low minimum order requirements. Distributors readily agreed to handle national brand chemicals, and in metropolitan markets each brand was sold through several distributors. By the same token, most distributors carried several directly competitive product lines. George suspected that some distributor salesmen only used national brands to "lead" with and tended to offer a private label whenever a customer proved price-sensitive or a competitor handled the same national brand(s). Using an industry rule of thumb, George estimated that most distributors needed at least a 20 percent margin on retail sales to cover sales commission of 10 percent, plus delivery and inventory expenses.

Distributor Sales of Private Label Cleaning Chemicals

Direct-selling manufacturers were dominating urban markets by aggressively discounting end-user prices—sometimes below the wholesale price national brand manufacturers charged their distributors. To compete against the direct seller, increasing numbers of distributors were adding low-cost private-label cleaning chemicals to their product lines. Private labeling also helped differentiate a particular distributor from others carrying the same national brand(s).

Sizable minimum order requirements restricted the private-label strategy to only the largest distributors. Private-label manufacturers produced to order, formulating to meet low prices specified by distributors. The relatively narrow margins (30–35 percent wholesale price) associated with private-label manufacture precluded the extensive marketing and sales support national brand manufacturers characteristically provided to distributors. Private-label producers pared their expenses further still by requiring distributors to bear the cost of inventory and accept rigid terms of payment as well as delivery (net thirty days, FOB plant).

In addition to absorbing these selling expenses normally assumed by the manufacturer, distributors paid salespeople higher commission on private label sales (15 percent of resale) than on national brands (10 percent of resale). However, the incremental administration and selling expenses associated with private-label business were more than offset by the differential savings on private-label wholesale goods. By pricing private-label chemicals at competitive parity with national brands, the distributor could enjoy approximately a 50 percent gross margin at resale list while preserving considerable resale discount capability.

Private-label products were seldom sold outside the metropolitan areas where most were manufactured. First, the high costs of moving bulky, low-value freight diminished the relative cost advantage of private-label chemicals. Second, generally speaking, it was only in metro areas that distributors dealt in volumes great enough to satisfy the private labeler's minimum order requirement. Finally, outside the city, distributors were less likely to be in direct local competition with others handling the same national brand, reducing the value of the private label as a source of supplier differentiation.

For some very large distributors, backward integration into chemical production was a logical extension of the private labeling strategy. Recently, several distributors had become direct marketers through acquisition of captive manufacturers.

Direct Sale by Manufacturers of Industrial Cleaning Chemicals

Manufacturers dealing directly with the end user increased their gross margins to 60–70 percent of retail list price. Greater margins increased ability to discount end-user price—a distinct advantage in the price-competitive urban marketplace. Overall, direct marketers averaged a gross margin of 50 percent.

Many manufacturers of industrial cleaning chemicals attempted some direct selling, but relatively few relied on this channel exclusively. Satisfactory adoption of a full-time direct-selling strategy required the manufacturer to match distributor's sales and delivery capabilities without sacrificing overall profitability. These conflicting demands had been resolved successfully by two types of company, large-scale powder chemical manufacturers and full-line janitorial products manufacturers.

Large-Scale Powder Chemical Manufacturers

Economies of large-scale production plus experience in the capital-intensive manufacture of powder chemicals enabled a few established firms, such as Diversey-Wyandotte, to dominate the market for powder warewash and vehicle cleansers. Selling through distributors offered these producers few advantages. Direct-selling expense was almost entirely commission (i.e., variable). Moreover, powder concentrates were characterized by comparatively high value-to-bulk ratios and so could absorb delivery costs even where demand was geographically dispersed. Thus any marginal benefits from using middlemen were more than offset by the higher margins (and associated discount capability) possible through direct distribution. Among these chemicals firms, competition was not limited to price. The provision of dispensing and metering equipment was important, as was twenty-four-hour servicing.

Full-Line Janitorial Products Manufacturers

These manufacturers offered a complete range of maintenance products including paper supplies, janitorial chemicals, tools, and mechanical equipment. Although high margins greatly enhanced retail price flexibility, overall profitability depended on securing a balance of high- and low-margin business, as well as controlling selling and distribution expenses. This was accomplished in several ways, including:

1. Centering on market areas of concentrated demand to minimize costs of warehousing, sales travel, and the like

2. Increasing average order size, either by adding product lines that could be sold to existing customers or by seeking new large-volume customers

3. Tying sales commission to profitability to motivate sales personnel to sell volume, without unnecessary discounting of end-user price

Direct marketers of maintenance products varied in scale from established nationwide companies to hundreds of regional operators. The two largest direct marketers, G. H. Wood and Dustbane, together supplied almost a third of Canadian demand for industrial cleaning chemicals.

S. C. JOHNSON AND SON, LIMITED

S. C. Johnson and Son, Limited (SCJ) was one of forty-two foreign subsidiaries owned by the U.S.-based multinational S. C. Johnson and Son, Inc. It was ranked globally as one of the largest privately held companies. SCJ contributed substantially to worldwide sales and profits and was based in Brantford, Ontario, close to the Canadian urban markets of Hamilton, Kitchener, Toronto, London, and Niagara Falls. About three hundred people worked at the head office and plant, while another hundred were employed in field sales.

INNOCHEM Division

INNOCHEM (Innovative Chemicals for Professional Use) was a special division established to serve corporate, institutional, and government customers of SCJ. The division manufactured an extensive line of industrial cleaning chemicals, including general-purpose cleansers, waxes, polishes, and disinfectants, plus a number of specialty products of limited application, as shown in Exhibit 3. In 1980 INNOCHEM sold $4.5 million of industrial cleaning chemicals through distributors and $0.2 million direct to end users. Financial statements for INNOCHEM are shown in Exhibit 4.

EXHIBIT 3

S. C. Johnson & Son Limited, INNOCHEM Product Line

Johnson Wax is a systems innovator. Frequently, a new product leads to a whole new system of doing things—a Johnson system of "matched" products formulated to work together. This makes the most of your time, your effort, and your expense. Call today and see how these Johnson systems can give you maximum results at a minimum cost.

—for all floors except unsealed wood and unsealed cork

Stripper:	Step-Off—powerful, fast action
Finish:	Pronto—fast drying, good gloss, minimum maintenance
Spray-Buff Solution:	The Shiner Liquid Spray Cleaner or The Shiner Aerosol Spray Finish
Maintainer:	Forward—cleans, disinfects, deodorizes, sanitizes

—for all floors except unsealed wood and unsealed cork

Stripper:	Step-Off—powerful, fast stripper
Finish:	Carefree—tough, beauty, durable minimum maintenance
Maintainer:	Forward—cleans, disinfects, deodorizes, sanitizes

—for all floors except unsealed wood and unsealed cork

Stripper:	Step-Off—for selective stripping
Sealer:	Over & Under-Plus—undercoater-sealer
Finish:	Scrubbable Step-Ahead—Brilliant, scrubbable
Maintainer:	Forward—cleans, disinfects, sanitizes, deodorizes

General Cleaning:	Break-Up—cleans soap and body scum fast Forward—cleans, disinfects, sanitizes, deodorizes Bon Ami—instant cleaner, pressurized, or pump, disinfects
Toilet-Urinals Glass:	Go-Getter—"Working Foam" cleaner Bon Ami—spray-on foam or liquid cleaner
Disinfectant Spray:	End-Bac II—controls bacteria, odors
Air Freshener:	Glade—dewy-fresh fragrances
Spot Cleaning:	Johnson's Pledge—cleans, waxes, polishes Johnson's Lemon Pledge—refreshing scent Bon Ami Stainless Steel Cleaner—cleans, polishes and protects
All Purpose Cleaners:	Forward—cleans, disinfects, sanitizes, deodorizes Break-Up—degreaser for animal and vegetable fats Big Bare—heavy duty industrial cleaner
Carpets:	Rugbee Powder & Liquid Extraction Cleaner— Rugbee Soil Release Concentrate—for prespraying and bonnet buffing Rugbee Shampoo—for power shampoo machines Rugbee Spotter—spot remover

—for all floors except unsealed wood and cork

Stripper: **Step-Off**—powerful, fast stripper

Finish: **Easy Street**—high solids, high gloss, spray buffs to a "wet look" appearance

Maintainer: **Forward**—cleans, disinfects, deodorizes
Expose—phenolic cleaner disinfectant

—for all floors except unsealed wood and unsealed cork

Stripper: **Step-Off**—for selective stripping

Sealer: **Over & Under-Plus**—undercoater-sealer

Finishes: **Traffic Grade**—heavy-duty floor wax
Waxtral—extra tough, high solids

Maintainer: **Forward**—cleans, disinfects, sanitizes, deodorizes

—for all floors except asphalt, mastic, and rubber tile. Use sealer and wax finishes on wood, cork and cured concrete; sealer-finish on terrazzo, marble, clay and ceramic tile; wax finish only on vinyl, linoleum and magnesite.

Sealer: **Johnson Gym Finish**—sealer and top-coater, cleans as it waxes

Wax Finishes: **Traffic Wax Paste**—heavy-duty buffing wax
Beautiflor Traffic Wax—liquid buffing wax

Maintainers: **Forward**—cleans, disinfects, sanitizes, deodorizes
Conq-r-Dust—mop treatment

Stripper: **Step-Off**—stripper for sealer and finish

Sealer: **Secure**—fast-bonding, smooth, long-lasting

Finish: **Traffic Grade**—heavy-duty floor wax

Maintainer: **Forward**, or **Big Bare**

Sealer-Finish: **Johnson Gym Finish**—seal and top-coater

Maintainer: **Conq-r-Dust**—mop treatment

Furniture: **Johnson's Pledge**—cleans, waxes, polishes

Johnson's Lemon Pledge—refreshing scent

Shine-Up Liquid—general purpose cleaning

Disinfectant Spray: **End-Bac II**—controls bacteria, odors

Air Freshener: **Glade**—dewy-fresh fragrances

Glass: **Bon Ami**—spray-on foam or liquid cleaner

Cleaning: **Break-Up**—special degreaser designed to remove animal and vegetable fats

Equipment: **Break-Up Foamer**—special generator designed to dispense Break-Up Cleaner

General Cleaning: **Forward**—fast-working germicidal cleaner for floors, walls—all washable surfaces

Sanitizing: **Expose**—phenolic disinfectant cleaner
J80 Sanitizer—liquid for total environmental control of bacteria. No rinse necessary if used as directed

Disinfectant Spray: **End-Bac II Spray**—controls bacteria, odors

Flying Insects: **Bolt Liquid Airborne, or Pressurized Airborne,** P3610 through E10 dispenser

Crawling Insects: **Bolt Liquid Residual or Pressurized Residual,** P3610 through E10 dispenser

Rodents: **Bolt Roach Bait**
Bolt Rodenticide—for effective control of rats and mice, use with Bolt Bait Box

EXHIBIT 4
S. C. Johnson & Son Limited, Profit Statement
of the Division

Gross sales	$4,682
Returns	46
Allowances	1
Cash discounts	18
Net sales	4,617
Cost of sales	2,314
Gross profit	2,303
Advertising	75
Promotions	144
Deals	—
External marketing services	2
Sales freight	292
Other distribution expenses	176
Service fees	184
Total direct expenses	873
Sales force	592
Marketing administration	147
Provision for bad debts	—
Research and development	30
Financial	68
Information resource management	47
Administration management	56
Total functional expenses	940
Total operating expenses	1,813
Operating profit	490

INNOCHEM Marketing Strategy

Divisional strategy hinged on reliable product performance, product innovation, active promotion, and mixed channel distribution. Steve Remen, market development manager, maintained that "customers know our products are of excellent quality. They know that the products will always perform as expected."

At SCJ, performance requirements were detailed, and tolerances precisely defined. The Department of Quality Control routinely inspected and tested raw materials, work in process, packaging, and finished goods. At any phase during the manufacturing cycle, Quality Control was empowered to halt the process and quarantine suspect product or materials. SCJ maintained that nothing left the plant "without approval from Quality Control."

"Keeping the new product shelf well stocked" was central to divisional strategy, as the name INNOCHEM implies. Products launched over the past three years represented 33 percent of divisional gross sales, 40 percent of gross profits, and 100 percent of growth.

Mixed Distribution Strategy

INNOCHEM used a mixed distribution system in an attempt to broaden market coverage. Eighty-seven percent of divisional sales were handled by a force of 200 distributor salesmen and serviced from 50 distributor warehouses representing 35 distributors. The indirect channel was particularly effective outside Ontario and Quebec. In part, the tendency for SCJ market penetration to increase with distances from Montreal and Toronto reflected Canadian demographics and the general economics of distribution. Outside the two production centers, demand was dispersed, and delivery distances were long.

Distributor salesmen were virtually all paid a straight commission on sales and were responsible for selling a wide variety of products in addition to S.C. Johnson's. Several of the distributors had sales levels much higher than INNOCHEM'S.

For INNOCHEM, the impact of geography was compounded by a significant freight cost advantage: piggybacking industrial cleaning chemicals with SCJ consumer goods. In Ontario, for example, the cost of SCJ to a distributor was 30 percent above private-label, while the differential in B.C. was only 8 percent. On lower-value products, the "freight effect" was even more pronounced.

SCJ had neither the salesmen nor the delivery capabilities to reach large-volume end users who demanded heavy selling effort or frequent shipments of small quantities. Furthermore, it was unlikely that SCJ could develop the necessary selling and distribution strength economically, given the narrowness of the division's range of janitorial products (i.e., industrial cleaning chemicals only).

The Rebate Plan

The key strategic problem facing INNOCHEM was how best to challenge the direct marketer (and private-label distributor) for large-volume, price-sensitive customers with heavy service requirements, particularly in markets where SCJ had no freight advantage. In this connection George had observed:

> Our gravest weakness is our inability to manage the total margin between the manufactured cost and consumer price in a way that is equitable and sufficiently profitable to support the investment and expenses of both the distributors and ourselves.

EXHIBIT 5
S. C. Johnson & Son Limited, Distributors' Rebate Pricing Schedule

Code: 04055 Product Description: Pronto Fast Dry Fin Size: 209 Ltr Pack: 1

Eff. Date: 03-31-81
Resale List Price 71   613.750
Distributor Price List 74   349.837
Percentage Markup on Cost with Car Load & Rebate

Disc % (1)	Quote (FST) (Incl) (2)	Rebate % (3)	Dlrs (4)	2% Net (5)	2% MU-% (6)	3% Net	3% MU-%	4% Net	4% MU-%	5% Net	5% MU-%
30.0	429.63	8.0	27.99	314.85	36	311.35	38	307.86	40	304.36	41
35.0	398.94	12.0	41.98	300.86	33	297.36	34	293.86	36	290.36	37
40.0	368.25	17.0	59.47	283.37	30	279.87	32	276.37	33	272.87	35
41.0	362.11	17.5	61.22	281.62	29	278.12	30	274.62	32	271.12	34
42.0	355.98	18.0	62.97	279.87	27	276.37	29	272.87	30	269.37	32
43.0	349.84	18.5	64.72	278.12	26	274.62	27	271.12	29	267.63	31
44.0	343.70	19.0	66.47	276.37	24	272.87	26	269.37	28	265.88	29
45.0	337.56	20.0	69.97	272.87	24	269.37	25	265.88	27	262.38	29
46.0	331.43	20.5	71.72	271.12	22	267.63	24	264.13	25	260.63	27
47.0	325.29	21.0	73.47	269.37	21	265.88	22	262.38	24	258.88	26
48.0	319.15	21.5	75.21	267.63	19	264.13	21	260.63	22	257.13	24
49.0	313.01	22.0	76.96	265.88	18	262.38	19	258.88	21	255.38	23
50.0	306.88	23.0	80.46	262.38	17	258.88	19	255.38	20	251.88	22
51.0	300.74	24.0	83.96	258.88	16	255.38	18	251.88	19	248.38	21
52.0	294.60	25.0	87.46	255.38	15	251.88	17	248.38	19	244.89	20

53.0	288.46	26.0	90.96	251.88	15	248.38	16	244.89	18	241.39	19
54.0	282.33	28.0	97.95	244.89	15	241.39	17	237.89	19	234.39	20
55.0	276.19	30.0	104.95	237.89	16	234.39	18	230.89	20	277.39	21

1. Discount extended to end user on resale list price.
2. Resale price at given discount level (includes federal sales tax).
3. Percentage of distributor's price ($613.75) rebated by SCJ.
4. Actual dollar amount of rebate by SCJ.
5. Actual net cost to distributor after deduction of rebate and "carload" (quantity) discount.
6. Effective rate of distributor markup.

Our prime competition across Canada is from direct selling national and regional manufacturers. These companies control both the manufacturing and distribution gross margins. Under our pricing system, the distributors margin at end-user list on sales is 43 percent. Our margin (the manufacturing margin) is 50 percent on sales. When these margins are combined, as in the case of direct selling manufacturers, the margins are combined, as in the case of direct selling manufacturers, the margin becomes 70 percent at list. This long margin provides significant price flexibility in a price-competitive marketplace. We must find a way to profitably attack the direct marketer's 61 percent market share.

The rebate plan George was now evaluating had been devised to meet the competition head-on.

"Profitable partnership" between INNOCHEM and the distributors was the underlying philosophy of the plan. Rebates offered a means to "share fairly the margins available between factory cost and consumer price." Whenever competitive conditions required a distributor to discount the resale list price by 30 percent or more, SCJ would give a certain percentage of the wholesale price back to the distributor. In other words, SCJ would sacrifice part of its margin to help offset a heavy end-user discount. Rebate percentages would vary with the rate of discount, following a set schedule. Different schedules were to be established for each product type and size. Exhibits 5 and 6 outline the effect of rebates on both the unit gross margins of SCJ and individual distributors for a specific product example.

The rebate plan was designed to be applicable to new, "incremental" business only, not for existing accounts of the distributor. Distributors would be required to seek SCJ approval for end-user discounts of 30 percent or more off resale list. The maximum allowable end-user discount would rarely exceed 50 percent. To request rebate payments, distributors would send SCJ a copy of the resale invoice along with a written claim. The rebate would then be paid within 60 days. Currently, INNOCHEM sales were sold by distributors at an average discount of 10 percent off list.

Proponents of the plan maintained that the resulting resale price flexibility not only would enhance INNOCHEM competitiveness among end users, but would also diminish distributor attraction to private label.

As he studied the plan, George questioned whether all the implications were fully understood and wondered what other strategies, if any, might increase urban market penetration. Any plan he devised would have to be sold to distributors as well as to corporate management. George had only three weeks to develop an appropriate action plan.

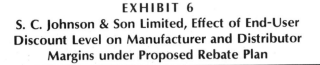

EXHIBIT 6
S. C. Johnson & Son Limited, Effect of End-User Discount Level on Manufacturer and Distributor Margins under Proposed Rebate Plan

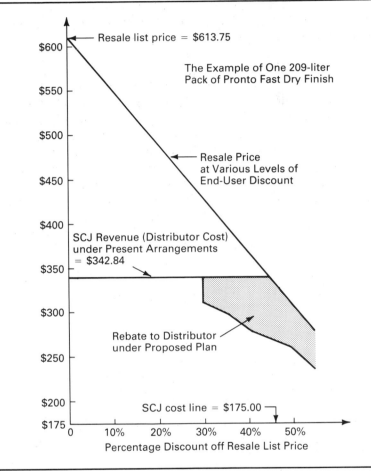

NOTE

1. "Contract Cleaners Want to Whisk Away Ring-Around-the-Office," *Canadian Business*, (1981): 22.

CHAPTER 10

Marketing Strategy Reformulation: The Control Process

MARKETING STRATEGIES ARE RARELY, if ever, timeless. As the environment changes, so must product-market and marketing mix strategies change. Moreover, as organizations strive for gains in productivity, constant attention must be given to improving the efficiency of marketing efforts.

The marketing control process serves as the mechanism for achieving strategic and operational adaptation to environmental change and productivity needs, respectively. Marketing control consists of two complementary activities. Strategic control is concerned with "doing the right things"; operations control focuses on "doing things right." Strategic control assesses the direction of the organization evidenced by its implicit or explicit goals, objectives, strategies, and capacity to perform in the context of changing environments and competitive actions. The ever-present issue of defining the "fit" between organization capabilities and objectives and environmental threats and opportunities is at the core of strategic control. Operations control assesses how well the organization performs marketing activities as it seeks to achieve planned outcomes. It is implicitly assumed that the direction of the organization is correct. Only improvements in how well the organization performs specific tasks are necessary.

The distinction between strategic and operations control is important to grasp. It has been noted that a "poorly executed plan can produce undesirable results just as easily as a poorly conceived plan."[1] Even though undesirable results may be identical (e.g., sales decline, market share erosion, sagging profits), remedial actions under the two types of control will differ. Remedial efforts drawn from an operations control perspective focus on heightening the marketing effort or identifying ways to improve *efficiency*. Alternatively, remedial efforts based on a strategic control orientation focus attention on the *effectiveness* of the organization in seeking opportunities and mitigating threats in its environment. Improper assessment of the need for strategic versus operations control could lead to a disastrous response in which an organization pours additional funds into an ill-conceived strategy only to realize further declines in profit.

STRATEGIC CHANGE

Strategic change is defined here as change in the environment that will affect the long-run well-being of the organization. Strategic change may represent opportunities or threats to the organization, depending on an organization's competitive posture. For example, the gradual aging of the U.S. population represents a potential threat to organizations that have catered to children, whereas this change represents an opportunity to organizations providing products for and services to the elderly.

Strategic change can arise from a multitude of sources.[2] One source is *market evolution*. Market evolution results from changes in primary demand for a product class and changes in technology. For example, the increased primary demand for "natural foods" prompted both General Foods and Quaker Oats to reposition Grape Nuts and 100% Natural brands, respectively, to take advantage of this resurgence in the popularity of natural foods. Technological change often prompts market evolution and changes in marketing techniques, as evidenced by the application of electronics to the watch industry.

Market redefinition is another source of strategic change. Market redefinition results from changes in the offering demanded by buyers or promoted by competitors. For example, firms that provided only automatic teller machines for banks saw the market redefined to electronic funds transfer, with total systems rather than equipment alone being the "offering" purchased. Firms with systems capabilities, such as IBM and NCR, thus gained a competitive advantage in the redefined market.

Change in *marketing channels* is a third source. Changes in marketing channels have been prompted by scrambled merchandising, a situation where intermediaries carry a wider assortment of merchandise than they have in the past (e.g., 7-11 stores offer gasoline in many locations). Scrambled merchandising has led many manufacturers to reevaluate channel relationships and potential outlets for goods and services. For example, in the late 1970s supermarkets accounted for over 20 percent of home improvement product sales. Firms seeing this trend benefited from the change; those that did not found themselves struggling to gain access to display space in supermarkets. Similarly, it is not uncommon to find various types of electronics products, such as hand-held calculators, television sets, tape recorders, and personal computers, in general-merchandise stores as well as specialty outlets.

Threat severity or opportunity potential is determined by the organization's business definition. In other words, does the threat or opportunity relate to the type of customer served by the organization, the needs of the customers, the means by which the organization satisfies these needs, or some combination of these factors?

The effects of strategic change are clearly apparent in the worldwide watchmaking industry.[3] Although Swiss watchmakers had dominated this industry for a century, market evolution, market redefinition, and marketing channel changes combined to spell disaster for the Swiss. Market evolution reflected in technological change (from jeweled watches to quartz and electronic watches) and changing channels (from select jewelry stores to mass merchandisers and supermarkets) eroded Swiss dominance. Moreover, a redefinition of the term *watch* occured. No longer was a watch defined only in terms of craftmanship or elegance as jewelry. It was now considered an economical and disposable timepiece. These changes, brought about by Timex in the United States and such Japanese firms as Seiko and Citizen, severely affected the Swiss watchmakers. Today, Swiss watchmakers have, for the most part, retreated to a highly specialized market niche, which can be identified as the prestige, luxury, artistry watch segment. For example, Swiss watches "tell you something about yourself" (Patek) and are "the most expensive in the world" (Piaget).

This example highlights how strategic change can affect an entire industry and its individual participants, and how Swiss watchmakers responded. In practice, several options exist to deal with strategic change.

1. An organization can attempt to marshal the resources necessary to fit market success requirement with technical or marketing capabilities. Swiss watchmakers did not do this but, rather, devoted modest research funds to perfecting their mechanical watches, where they had a distinctive competency.

2. An organization can shift its priorities to product markets where the match between success requirements and its distinctive

competence is clear and can cut back efforts in product markets where
it has been outflanked. Many Swiss watchmakers chose this option.

   3. An organization can leave the industry. Over a thousand selected this option.

OPERATIONS CONTROL

Operations control consists of techniques necessary for improving the
productivity of marketing efforts. Marketing cost analysis is a fundamental aspect of operations control. Accordingly, cost identification
and allocation are central to the appraisal of marketing effort and profitability. This section provides an overview of marketing cost analysis
and selected examples of product-service mix control, sales control,
and marketing channel control.

Nature of Marketing Cost Analysis

The purpose of marketing cost analysis is to assign or allocate costs
according to a specified marketing activity or entity (hereafter referred
to as a *segment*) in a manner that accurately displays the financial
contribution of activities or entities to the organization. Typical marketing segments to which costs may be allocated include: (1) elements
of the product-service offering; (2) type or size of customers; (3) sales
divisions, districts, or territories; and (4) different marketing channels.
Cost allocation is based on the principle that for every marketing segment, certain costs are directly or indirectly assignable to it.
   Several issues arise in regard to the cost-allocation question.

   1. How should costs be allocated to separate marketing segments? As a general rule, the manager should attempt to assign costs in
accordance with an identifiable measure of application to an entity.

   2. What costs should be allocated? Again, as a general rule, costs
arising from the performance of a marketing activity or charged to that
activity according to administrative policy are the costs that should be
allocated.

   3. Should all costs be allocated to marketing segments? The answer to this question will depend on whether the manager prefers a
"whole-equals-the-sum-of-parts" income statement. If so, then all
costs are fully allocated. However, if it appears that certain costs have
no identifiable measure of application to a segment, or that costs do
not arise from one particular segment, then such costs should not be
allocated.

The manager should follow two guidelines when considering the cost allocation question. First, when allocating costs, fundamental distinctions between cost behavior patterns should be maintained. Second, the exactness of cost allocations will depend on the existence and magnitude of joint costs—those costs that have no identifiable basis for allocation or that arise from a variety of marketing segments. In general, more useful information will be provided by greater detail in cost allocation.

Product-Service Mix Control

Proper control of the product-service mix consists of two interrelated tasks. First, the manager must assess the performance of offerings in the relevant markets. Second, the manager must appraise the financial worth of product-service offerings.

Sales volume, as an index of performance, can be approached from two directions. For example, growth or decline of unit sales volume provides a quantitative indicator of the acceptance of offerings in their relevant markets. Equally important is the *proportion of sales* coming from individual offerings in the product-service mix and how this sales distribution affects profitability. Many firms experience the "80-20 rule"—80 percent of sales or profits come from 20 percent of a firm's offerings. Such imbalance in the mix has a disastrous effect on overall profitability if sudden changes in competitive or market behavior threaten the viability of this 20 percent.

Market share complements sales volume as an indicator of performance. Market share is a means for determining whether an organization is gaining or losing ground in comparison with competitors.

Market share as a performance indicator is a valuable index, provided it is used properly. Several questions must be considered when using market share for control purposes. First, what is the relevant market on which the market share percentage is based, and has the market definition changed? In other words, market share can be computed by geographical area, product type or model, customer or channel type, and so forth. Note in the Carapace, Inc., case in this book that market shares for hospital cast material are reported by region, hospital size, and cost size, and for the competitors' total sales. Second, is the market itself changing? For example, high market share by itself may be misleading since overall sales in the market may be declining. Alternatively, high market share in a growth market is an entirely different story. Finally, the unit of analysis—dollar sales or unit sales— must be considered. Returning to the Carapace case, when Johnson & Johnson's market share was computed using unit sales, the figure was 81.1 percent. However, their market share in dollar volume was 73 percent. A useful guide is to use unit rather than dollar volume in examining market share due to price differentials.

A second aspect of product-service control consists of appraising the financial contribution of marketing offerings. An important step in this process is the assignment of costs to offerings in a manner that reflects their profitability. Unfortunately, this step is difficult and often requires managerial judgment. Moreover, the definition of an "offering" itself is illusive. For example, a "red-eye" flight (early morning or late evening) scheduled by an airline might be viewed as an offering. The decision by McDonalds and Jack-in-the-Box to open for the breakfast trade can be viewed as a marketing offering consisting not only of the costs of producing the menu items, but also of the cost of being open.

From a control perspective, the manager should examine the financial worth of marketing offerings using a *contribution margin approach*. This means that the relevant costs charged against an offering include direct costs and assignable overhead. How these costs are assigned should be determined by identifying the most meaningful unit of analysis corresponding to the behavior of these costs.

As an example, consider the situation where the owner of a chain of gasoline service stations is examining operating performance. Exhibit 10.1 shows the operating performance before and after cost allocation by department. Examination of the total yields little managerially relevant information. However, when costs are disaggregated by department, it becomes apparent that gasoline operates at a net loss, whereas general merchandise and automobile service operate profitably. Fortunately, each department "contributes" to overhead; that is, each department's revenue exceeds its allocated variable costs.

EXHIBIT 10.1
Disaggregating Costs for Product-Service Mix Control
(thousands of dollars)

| | | | Departments | |
	Total	Gasoline	General Merchandise	Automobile Service
Sales	$4,000	$2,000	$1,700	$300
Cost of goods sold and variable expenses	3,000	1,600	1,220	180
Contribution margin	$1,000	$ 400	$ 480	$120
Fixed expenses	900	500	310	90
Net income	$ 100	$ (100)	$ 170	$ 30

This analysis serves a useful purpose in identifying potential trouble spots. When the question of corrective action arises, however, several alternatives exist. If the owner decides to drop the unprofitable line and leave the selling space empty, then general merchandise and automobile service must cover the total fixed costs, which will continue. It is doubtful this would occur. (Note that gasoline does contribute to the payment of fixed costs.) Another possibility is that the manager might expand the other departments to use the empty space. Market demand and forecasts of revenue would be necessary for further consideration of this action. Moreover, a commitment of resources must occur that, in effect, significantly alters the nature of the business.

Sales Control

Sales control directs a manager's attention to both the behavioral and the cost aspects of sales activity. The behavioral element consists of sales effort and allocation of selling time. The cost aspect considers expenses arising from the performance and administration of the sales function.

A simplified example of the sales control process illustrates its use. Consider the situation in which a district sales manager has requested a quarterly performance review of two sales personnel in a territory within the district. These individuals had failed to achieve their sales, gross profit, and profit quota. Exhibit 10.2 displays the representatives' performance according to customer-volume account categories. These categories were established by the national sales manager on the basis of industry norms, as were the expected quarterly call frequencies that follow.

Account Definition	Expected Call Frequency
A: $1,000 or less in sales	2
B: $1,000–$1,999 in sales	4
C: $2,000–$4,999 in sales	6
D: $5,000 or more in sales	8

Both representatives had an equal number of A, B, C, and D accounts.

EXHIBIT 10.2
District Performance Summary

Account Category	(1) Potential Accounts in Sales District[a]	(2) Active Accounts[b]	(3) Sales Volume[c]	(4) Gross Profit[d]	(5) Total Calls[e]	(6) Selling Expenses[f]	(7) Sales Administration[g]
A	80	60	$ 48,000	$14,000	195	$18,400	
B	60	40	$ 44,000	$15,400	200	$17,900	
C	40	10	$ 25,000	$12,250	50	$11,250	
D	20	6	$ 33,000	$16,500	42	$ 9,000	
Totals	200	116	$150,000	$58,550	487	$56,550	$10,000

[a]Based on marketing research data identifying potential users of company products.

[b]Current accounts.

[c]Based on invoices.

[d]Based on invoice price for full mix of products sold.

[e]Based on sales call reports cross-referenced by customer name.

[f]Direct costs of sales including allocated salaries of two sales representatives.

[g]Costs not assignable on a meaningful basis; includes office expense.

EXHIBIT 10.3
Selected Operating Indexes of Sales Performance
(Based on District Performance Summary)

Sales Volume/ Active Account (Col. 3 ÷ Col. 4)	Gross Profit/ Active Account (Col. 4 ÷ Col. 2)	Selling Expenses/ Active Account (Col. 6 ÷ Col. 2)	Contribution to Sales Administration (Gross Profit − Selling Expenses)
A: $800	$240	$307	− $67
B: $1,100	$385	$448	− $63
C: $2,500	$1,225	$1,125	$1,375
D: $5,500	$2,750	$1,500	$1,250

Account Penetration (Col. 2 ÷ Col. 3)	Call Frequency/ Active Account (Col. 5 ÷ Col. 2)	Selling Expense per Call (Col. 6. ÷ Col. 5)	Gross Profit %/ Active Account (Col. 4 ÷ Col. 3)
A. 75%	3.25	$94.36	30%
B: 67	5.0	$89.50	35
C: 25	5.0	$225.00	49
D: 30	7.0	$214.29	50

Exhibit 10.3 shows various indexes prepared by the district sales manager from the performance summary shown in Exhibit 10.2. Among the principal findings evident from Exhibit 10.3 were the following:

1. The representatives' account penetration varied inversely with the size of accounts. While representatives had penetrated 75 percent of the smaller A accounts, only 30 percent of the potentially large D accounts were listed as active buyers.

2. Part of the reason for this performance appears to be in the call frequency of the representatives. The representatives exceeded the call norm on the smaller A and B accounts, but fell short on call frequency on the larger C and D accounts. Moreover, their "effort" level appears questionable (487 calls ÷ 90 days ÷ 2 representatives = 2.7 calls per day).

3. Furthermore, the gross profit percentage derived from sales to smaller accounts was considerably less than on the larger accounts, which in turn affected profitability.

4.   When account sales volume, gross profit, and selling ex-
     penses are matched against each other, it becomes apparent
     that the smaller accounts actually produced a net contribu-
     tion dollar loss.

The sales control process in this instance revealed that the two
representatives were not actively calling on accounts (2.7 calls per
day), and their allocation of call activity focused on smaller-volume,
less profitable accounts that were in fact contributing a *loss* to overhead. Redirection of effort is clearly needed in this instance.

Marketing Channel Control

Marketing channel control consists of two complementary processes.
The manager must first assess environmental and organizational factors that may alter the structure, conduct, and performance of marketing channels. These considerations were highlighted in Chapter 8.
Second, the manager must evaluate the profitability of marketing
channels.

Profitability analysis for marketing channels follows the same
general format outlined for product-service control. Cost identification
and allocation differ, however. Two types of costs—*order-getting* and
order-servicing costs—must be identified and allocated to different
marketing channels. Order-getting costs include sales expense and advertising allowances. Order-servicing expenditures include packing
and delivery costs, warehousing expenses, and billing costs.

Consider a hypothetical marketer of furniture polishes, cleaners,
and assorted furniture improvement products as an example. This firm
sells its products through three marketing channels using its own sales
force: (1) furniture stores, (2) department stores, and (3) home improvement stores. Exhibit 10.4 shows income statements for all three channels combined, as well as individually (general and administration
costs are not allocated or included). It is apparent that after costs and
revenues are identified and allocated by channel, furniture stores and
department store channels generate equal sales revenue; however, furniture stores incur a sizable loss and department stores account for
almost all of net income. Why has this occurred?

Inspection of disaggregated costs suggests the following:

1.   The gross margin percentage on the mix of products sold to
     department stores is 38 percent, whereas the gross margin
     percentage for furniture stores and home improvement stores

EXHIBIT 10.4
Disaggregated Costs for Marketing Channel Control
(thousands of dollars)

	Total	Marketing Channels		
		Furniture Stores	Department Stores	Home Improvement Stores
Sales	$12,000	$5,000	$5,000	$2,000
Cost of goods sold	8,000	3,500	3,100	1,400
Gross margin	$ 4,000	$1,500	$1,900	$ 600
Expenses				
Selling	$ 1,000	$ 617	$ 216	$ 167
Advertising	750	450	150	150
Packing and delivery	800	370	300	130
Warehouing	400	200	150	50
Billing	600	300	250	50
Total expenses	$ 3,550	$1,937	$1,066	$ 547
Net channel income (loss)	$ 450	$ (437)	$ 834	$ 53

is 30 percent. Thus lower-margin products are being sold through furniture and home improvement stores on the average.

2. Order-getting costs (selling and advertising) for furniture stores run about 21 percent of sales, but are only 7 percent of sales in department stores and 16 percent in home improvement stores.

3. Order-servicing costs for furniture stores are 17 percent of sales, 14 percent for department stores, and about 12 percent for home improvement stores.

In short, a manager might conclude that the effort (reflected in costs) necessary to generate sales and service in the furniture store channel is much greater than that needed for department and home improvement stores. Moreover, furniture stores purchase lower-gross-margin products. Now that these problems have been identified, efforts to remedy the situation might be explored in a more systematic fashion.

CONSIDERATIONS IN MARKETING CONTROL

Proper implementation of strategic and operations control requires that the manager be aware of several pertinent considerations. Three considerations are as follows.

Problems versus Symptoms

Effective control, whether at the strategic or operations level, requires that the manager recognize the difference between root problems and surface symptoms. This means that the manager must develop causal relationships between occurrences. For example, if there is evidence of a sales decline or poor profit margins, the manager must "look behind" the numbers to identify the underlying causes of such performance and then attempt to remedy them. This process differs little from the diagnostic role of a physician who first establishes patient symptoms to identify the ailment.

Effectiveness versus Efficiency

The difference between effectiveness and efficiency is a second consideration. Effectiveness addresses the question of whether the organization achieves its intended goals, given environmental opportunities and constraints and organizational capabilities. Efficiency concerns itself with productivity—the relationship between the levels of output, given a specified unit of input. A dynamic tension exists between effectiveness and efficiency considerations. Consider the situation where a sales representative has a high call frequency per day and a low cost-per-call expense ratio. From an efficiency perspective, the individual might be viewed favorably. However, if the emphasis of the organization is on customer service and problem solving, this person might be viewed as ineffective.

Data versus Information

A third consideration is the qualitative difference between data and information. Data are essentially *reports* of activities, events, or performance. Information, on the other hand, may be viewed as a *classification* of activities, events, or performance prepared in a manner that is interpretable and useful for decision making. The distinction between data and information has been shown in the discussion of marketing cost analysis techniques where data were organized into meaningful classifications and operating ratios.

NOTES

1. R. Paul, N. Donavan, and J. Taylor, "The Reality Gap in Strategic Planning," *Harvard Business Review* (May–June 1978): 126.

2. These concepts were drawn from D. Abell, "Strategic Windows," *Journal of Marketing* (July 1978): 21–26.

3. This example is adapted from D. Landes, "Time Runs Out for the Swiss," *Across the Board* (January 1984): 46–55.

ADDITIONAL READINGS

Strategic Control

Abell, D. "Strategic Windows." *Journal of Marketing* (July 1978): 21–26.

Harrigan, Kathryn R. "Managing Declining Businesses." *Journal of Business Strategy* (Winter 1984): 74–78.

Kotler, P.; Gregor, W.; and Rodgers, W. "The Marketing Audit Comes of Age." *Sloan Management Review* 18 (1976): 1–18.

Naylor, J., and Wood, A. *Practical Marketing Audits: A Guide to Increased Profitability.* New York: Wiley, 1978.

Operations Control

Dubinsky, A., and Hansen, R. "Improving Marketing Productivity: The 80/20 Principle Revisited." *California Management Review* 25 (1982): 96–105.

Dunne, P., and Wolk, H. "Marketing Cost Analysis: A Modularized Contribution Approach." *Journal of Marketing* 41 (1977): 83–94.

Hulbert, J., and Toy, N. "A Strategic Framework for Marketing Control." *Journal of Marketing* 41 (1977): 12–20.

Mossman, F.; Crissy, W. J. E.; and Fischer, P. *Financial Dimensions of Marketing Management.* New York: Wiley, 1978.

"Report of the Committee on Cost and Profitability Analysis for Marketing." *The Accounting Review Supplement* (1972): 575–615.

Shapiro, S. and Kirpalani, V. H. *Marketing Effectiveness: Insights from Accounting and Finance.* Boston: Allyn and Bacon, 1984.

——————— CASE ———————

Murphy Mud Service, Inc.

JAMES ASHLEY, PRESIDENT of Murphy Mud Service, Inc., leaned back in his chair and stared at the cover of the September 27, 1982, issue of *Business Week*. The feature article entitled "Oil-Field Suppliers: The Crash after a Boom—An Uncertain Future" wasn't news to him.[1] In the short span of twenty months, he had begun the operations of a drilling-fluids company, had built an organization from scratch, was overwhelmed by customers eager for his company's services, and had exceeded $3 million in sales in the first year of operations. Suddenly, in the summer of 1982, with the leveling of oil prices and drastic cutbacks in oil-exploration activity, oil-field supply firms, including Murphy Mud, were scrambling for customers. He unconsciously nodded his head as he reflected on a recent statement by the president of a major oil-field service firm: "Before [1980 and 1981] we had to run with what just came through the door. Now marketing strategy is important again."[2] Mr. Ashley knew that if the large firms were embracing marketing concepts and practices to succeed, he would need the same perspective just to survive.

DRILLING-FLUIDS INDUSTRY

The ultimate goal of drilling a well is either to locate or to exploit a commercially viable reservoir of oil, gas, or both. If the goal is reached, a well of casing extending from the earth's surface downward into an

This case is based on "Marran Mud and A Note on the Drilling Fluids Industry," prepared by Shelley Bessier, research assistant, under the direction of M. Edgar Barrett, director of the Maguire Oil and Gas Institute, Southern Methodist University. This version was prepared by Roger A. Kerin, Professor of Marketing, Edwin L. Cox School of Business, Southern Methodist University, as a basis for class discussion and is not intended to illustrate effective or ineffective handling of an administrative situation. Selected market and cost data have been disguised and are not useful for research purposes.

oil- or gas-bearing formation or reservoir, plus the necessary production equipment to extract the hydrocarbons, will be put into place.

The most popular drilling method is called rotary drilling. The advantage of rotary drilling over other drilling methods is that drilling fluids are circulated to remove the rock cuttings and cavings continuously. These drilling fluids are commonly called muds because of their mudlike appearance.

A rotary drilling rig, as the name implies, has a turning bit that bores into the earth. The rotary rig consists of four groups of components. The first set consists of the engines and power equipment. The second set of components is the hoisting equipment. The third set consists of rotating equipment including the steel shaft and drill bit.

The fluid-circulation equipment is the final component of the rotary rig. It accounts for a major portion of both the equipment needed for and the cost of drilling a well. Bulk storage of drilling-fluid materials, as well as pumps and mud mixing equipment, is placed at the start of the circulation system. At the other end are working mud pits and pits for reserve storage. Between the two is the actual fluid-circulating system with auxiliary equipment for drilling fluid maintenance and equipment for well pressure control. A diagram of the fluid-circulation system is shown in Exhibit 1.

The total volume of a mud system varies with the depth of the well and the size of the casing. For example, a 10,000-foot well of 9⅞-inch diameter uses 950 barrels of mud. A well of similar depth, but with a diameter of 12½ inches, would use 1,450 barrels. Generally a reserve supply of 400–500 barrels of mud is kept on the surface in the rig's storage pits.

Quantifying a mud system in terms of dollars is a complex process. The systems range from a simple "vanilla" mud consisting of water and bentonite up to an expensive oil mud. Transportation costs may then double the cost figures by the time the fluid reaches the well. Furthermore, as drilling needs become more complex, so do the demands on the drilling fluids and the need for more specialized, esoteric mud additives. Thus the escalating costs and volume used make drilling fluids an even more important consideration in the drilling of a well.

Functions of Drilling Fluids

The principal function of drilling mud is to remove the cuttings and cavings from the well bore. However, it serves many other important functions. Mud keeps the bit cool and lubricates it as it cuts and lubricates the hole itself to reduce drill-pipe rotational friction. Mud also inhibits corrosion of the drill pipe and casing. Furthermore, the drill pipe receives flotation support from the drill mud as it is being inserted into the well hole.

EXHIBIT 1
Rotary Rig Fluid-Circulation and Mud-Treating System

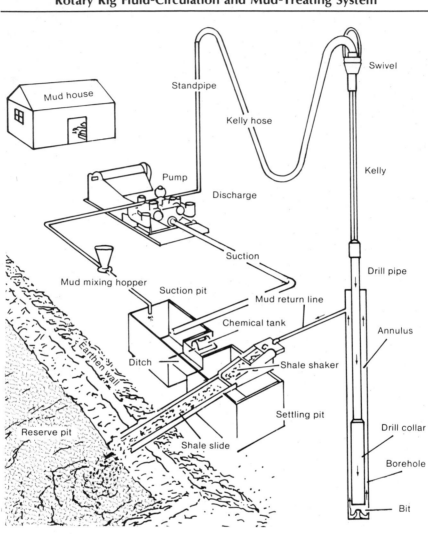

Source: Used with permission of Petroleum Extension Service, the University of Texas at Austin (PETEX).

Mud also plays a variety of roles in the formation of the hole. As the mud comes up between the drill pipe and the hole well, it is generally under heavy pressure. This results in the mud "plastering" the well with a hard and thick layer. The result is that the walls of the rotary hole stand up far better than holes drilled without the use of drilling mud.

This mud-cake layer also minimizes the adverse effects of fluid invasion of the hole. Any porous rock formations that have been drilled are slightly penetrated with mud, so the fluids these formations contain are thereby sealed out of the hole. Only water or gas under unexpectedly high pressure can enter the well hole. Furthermore, since the drilling fluids exert hydrostatic pressure, the mud "column" helps block the entry of rock formation fluids into the well.

A seemingly simple, but nonetheless crucial, function of the drilling mud is to suspend the cuttings and weighting materials when circulation is interrupted. Because a drill must be pulled up periodically to replace the bit, the gel property of the mud prevents the cuttings from settling to the bottom of the hole when the fluid stops circulating.

The Mud Engineer

The continuous monitoring of the mud mixture and its circulation system is generally supervised by a mud engineer, a specialist with expert knowledge of chemistry and engineering, an understanding of oil-drilling techniques, and a thorough understanding of petroleum engineering. The mud engineer's responsibilities include: testing the physical and chemical properties of the fluid; preparing a report that shows the mud weight and includes the materials, additives, and chemicals used; and supervising the mud mixing and use of equipment. The mud engineer is aided by drilling engineers and tool pushers (a rig supervisor) who do much of the routine mud testing and treating on the job. The mud engineer's report reads like a doctor's prescription, calling for various additives in terms of sacks per hour or pounds per ton.

The mud engineer may service many shallow or intermediate-level wells simultaneously. On a deep well, however, a mud engineer will probably be on site full time. Normally, this fluids specialist is employed by the mud company. For routine daily service checks, the cost of the mud-engineering services is generally covered by the cost of the mud system. However, the mud supply company will generally charge extra for services of a twenty-four-hour on-site mud engineer. The mud engineer's technical knowledge can have a significant impact on the drilling process. Deeper holes and faster drilling can both be facilitated by mixing the mud properly and by using the correct chemical additives to ensure that the mud performs the functions described earlier. Since oil- and gas-producing formations can vary tremendously in their composition and depth, the mud must be carefully mixed to suit the particular needs of each well.

The mud engineer can also help prevent tragic explosions and blowouts by regulating the pressures in the well. Well-pressure control is managed largely through the blowout preventer, which regulates the amount of mud that flows through the well and provides for release of gas that has become mixed with the mud.

Types of Mud Systems

The type of mud used depends on the requirements of the particular drilling operation. In a general sense, drilling muds are suspensions of solids in liquids or in liquid emulsions. An emulsion is a system containing two liquids that cannot be mixed, one dispersed in the other as small droplets. The major liquids used are water or oil. Thus, muds are classified as water-base or oil-base.

The original and most basic muds are water-base. Water alone, however, may not be dense enough to control formation pressures or thick enough to suspend the formation cuttings when drilling is interrupted. Thus, carefully chosen solids and chemicals must be added to the liquid base of the system, to perform collectively the drilling-fluid functions. Water-base systems are more frequently used in shallow wells than in deeper wells.

The use of oil muds has long been recognized as intuitively sound. However, oil-base muds were considered special-application fluids because of difficult control and high cost. Whereas water may be virtually free, a barrel of oil may cost $40 to $50.

As of 1981, however, technological advances had improved oil-base muds. The main advantage of oil-base has been the reduction of hydration (absorption of water) and the subsequent dispersion of cuttings. An oil-base mud coats the drilled cuttings with oil, and they remain intact, allowing for easier separation and analysis. Industry statistics show that total costs and total drilling time have been reduced in some cases by up to 50 percent with oil-base muds. These and other advantages can make oil-base systems advantageous, even though they are more costly than water-base systems.

A number of minerals are employed as additives in drilling fluids. In addition to these solids, various chemicals are added to control the mud. The additives are generally sold separately under a multitude of product trade-names by mud supply companies. The chemistry varies between water-base and oil-base systems. Rarely are mud engineers expert in the chemistry of both.

INDUSTRY STRUCTURE, COMPOSITION, AND CONCERNS

The petroleum industry as a whole has divided itself among many different types of organizations, both large and small, integrated and specialized. This is also reflected in the drilling-fluid industry. The drilling-fluid industry can be divided into a small number of large supply companies that have achieved a high degree of vertical integration, a large number of intermediate-size suppliers, and an extremely large number of "independents" such as Murphy Mud.

The major suppliers are all drilling-fluid subsidiaries of large firms specializing in providing goods and services for the oil and gas industry. They are integrated in that they may supply some of their own raw materials—such as mined barite or bentonite—and they provide a full range of marketing and technological services. The four majors, generally identified as industry leaders, are: (1) Baroid (NL Industries), (2) IMCO Services (Halliburton), (3) Magcobar (Dresser Industries), and (4) Milchem (Baker International). Magcobar and Baroid are the current contenders for the greatest share of the overall market. The general industry consensus as of 1982 appeared to assign an average 20 percent market share to each of these two mud suppliers. The drilling mud industry in 1982 was estimated to have about $3 billion in sales.

The intermediate-size suppliers are those with market shares just smaller than the majors'. Delta Mud and OBI Hughes are often identified as leaders in this intermediate range. The independents are characterized by their smaller size and generally narrower scope of production functions. Their market areas must be smaller and are more often regionally bounded. An independent will usually choose a particular basin or production area in which to specialize.

One alleged basis for competition in the drilling-fluids industry revolves around the constant flow of technological innovations and discoveries. In addition to technology, service has traditionally been a distinguishing factor in choosing a mud supplier. The mud supply company must not only provide the mud. It must also help install and service the system with a drilling-fluid engineer. The mud engineer's services for routine mixing and troubleshooting are generally included when a rig operator purchases a drilling mud system from a supplier.

In addition to product technology and service, suppliers differentiate themselves by price. Due to declining oil prices and rising drilling costs, price is becoming an increasingly important variable. Some major oil and gas companies have made efforts to choose a mud supplier strictly on a low-bid basis for aggregate services. This forces the mud company to make significant assumptions about the costs it will incur. Price has been cited as a more important variable on shallower wells where routine drilling does not require special mud additives or significant mud engineering. On the deeper wells, however, the services and consultation of a good mud engineer can easily pay for themselves through the provision of correctly functioning additives and through blowout prevention.

The drilling-fluids industry also had been forced to adapt to major changes in its environment over the past decade. These include new technological demands, substitutes for fluids, rising drilling costs, raw materials shortages, and changing industry structure.

The drilling of oil wells into increasingly deeper subterranean reservoirs has presented many new problems concerning the choice of drilling fluids. Formation composition at depths of 10,000 feet can differ drastically from that at 25,000 feet with regard to temperature, pressure, and formation stability. These formations may be undercompacted and more easily broken up unless the drilling fluid is carefully chosen. This is why oil-base muds were developed in the 1970s and proliferated in the early 1980s.

Some attention has also been given to substitutes for drilling fluids. Air or gas may be circulated to remove cuttings in formations. However, neither is a generally acceptable substitute for drilling fluids in most wells.

The supply of drilling-fluids additives is also a potential constraint on drilling activity. Three major products that equal half of the dollar market value for drilling-fluid companies are barite (weighting material), bentonite (thickener), and lignosulfate (thinner). The problems stem from shortages of these resources and more significantly from a shortage of grinding capacity to process the minerals and make them usable in drilling fluids. The greatest shortage, of barite, the principal weighting material used in muds, occurred in the late 1970s. The shortage occurred because of a dramatic increase in the number of operating rigs at that time, but as grinding capacity caught up with rig growth, the shortage eased. However, due to current economic conditions, another barite shortage looms. In 1982 NL Industries shut down several barite mines, plus facilities where barite was ground for drilling mud, in order to preserve capital.[3]

Finally, economic conditions in the oil and gas industry have severely reduced the number of independent drilling companies. Historically, independent operators have drilled the majority of the wells in the United States. More recently, however, the drilling activity of independent companies has declined, as has all drilling activity. As of September 1982, more than two thousand of the forty-five hundred operating wells were made idle by economic conditions. It was unlikely that a recovery in drilling activity would be forthcoming in the next year to eighteen months. Estimates of drilling activity in Murphy Mud's service area for the period 1981–1983 are shown in Exhibit 2. These estimates are considered to be rough since drilling activity data are not reported by well depth.

EXHIBIT 2

Estimated New Drilling Activity by Basin and Well Depth: 1981, 1982, 1983

Well depth	McKlintock Basin			New Horizon Basin			Midland Basin			Plains Basin		
	1981	1982	1983	1981	1982	1983	1981	1982	1983	1981	1982	1983
Shallow	72	40	30	85	51	32	40	35	40	29	32	30
Intermediate	40	40	35	15	33	27	60	65	49	35	40	42
Deep	14	15	23	2	10	27	74	60	60	45	45	48
Total	126	95	88	102	93	86	174	160	149	109	117	120

Note: Other basins are included in the total Texas drilling activity besides those shown here. However, Murphy Mud management was unable to service them for a variety of reasons including geographical proximity to the McKlintock Basin and New Horizon Basin, unfamiliar or difficult geology, or well depth. The total number of wells drilled in Texas, excluding offshore drilling, was 3,259 in 1981 and 3,149 (estimate) in 1982, which represented a decline of 3.4 percent (Oil & Gas Journal, July 26, 1982).

THE COMPANY

Murphy Mud opened its doors in January 1981, after incorporating late in 1980. The founders had similar backgrounds within oil-field services. Each had started as a mud engineer and had been trained by a major mud company and gained experience and contacts through these first few years. Each had some experience either as a mud engineer or as a manager.

James Ashley had worked for one of the largest independent mud companies for thirty years. He had held the position of vice-president–general sales manager for the past several years. Four of his associates quit their jobs to join Mr. Ashley to form their own independent mud company.

Mr. Ashley chose Mike Willard as vice-president. Willard, who had been in the oil business since 1952, was given responsibility for administrative services such as staffing and budgeting. Jack Rogers, operations manager, had worked closely with the distribution function for a mud supplier, so he was given warehousing responsibilities, which consisted of hiring warehouse managers and overseeing and coordinating the warehouses. Steve Aaker was assigned the title of technical services manager, carrying direct responsibilities for the mud engineers and their assignments. Orville Reed rounded out the management team as sales manager.

The Start-up Process

"Putting together a company of twenty people to sell mud is not that hard," said Mr. Ashley. "All you need is experienced men and contacts. We had both, plus customers on the first day we opened for business. Yes, 1981 was an incredible year."

Murphy Mud's capitalization came largely from Mr. Ashley, who put up almost 60 percent of the total capital of $300,000. The majority of the rest of the equity capital came from a group of investors solicited through a stock brokerage firm. A large Texas bank supplied further capitalization for the company in the form of long-term financing and lines of credit. A five-year term loan of $275,000 was issued at prime plus 2 percent. These funds were used to help purchase trucks and forklifts.

With financing well under way, the company's next step was to begin to draw together its assets. The main fixed assets required were "rolling stock" (trucks, forklifts, pickups, and cars) for distribution and field services and a warehousing system. The company purchased six trucks and a few forklifts and pickups. Five warehouses and eighteen cars were leased.

After the warehouses had been leased, the next step for the company was to locate field personnel, warehouse managers, and drilling mud engineers. Murphy Mud had little trouble luring good mud engineers away from the majors. "The engineers are just a number to the majors," Mr. Ashley said. "There's much more room for advancement and attention with us. Besides, we're going to need management within one to two years, and we intend to promote from within. With a major, it may take five to ten years to get to management level."

Mr. Ashley viewed the mud engineers as the company's greatest asset. Therefore, he felt the salaries paid to them had to be competitive and had to be increased quickly to keep the good engineers from being stolen. "In a sense," Mr. Ashley mused, "the mud engineers are our main asset. They may not be reflected on our books, but paying their salaries is just like a monthly lease payment for an expensive and highly vital asset."

The last asset-acquisition phase consisted of acquiring an inventory of drilling-fluids additives. Murphy Mud bought materials from wholesale distributors. A large portion of drilling-fluids additives were chemicals or minerals, available from a variety of companies and locations. Materials were generally purchased from many different locations and suppliers, depending on the price and payment and delivery terms.

Mr. Ashley stressed that, for a newly formed independent mud supplier like Murphy Mud, quality materials were crucial. "We could get a lower-grade barite and bentonite for less than we're paying now, but they wouldn't function as well. A shoddy mud system doesn't make sense. It would mean at least one customer lost forever. Customers were looking for mistakes from us. The majors said we had a lesser product, and we had to prove them wrong."

Murphy Mud's service area included the adjacent McKlintock and New Horizon basins in Texas. An average 10,000-foot well in these basins with a 9¾-inch diameter required about a thousand barrels of circulating mud, with five hundred barrels in reserve storage in case of an emergency or of excessive fluid loss into the formation walls. Such a system may use only $6,000 worth of inventory (at cost) to mix and install initially. But as the fluid circulates through the well, chemicals and additives are "lost" or absorbed into the formation walls. Therefore, the mud has to be "maintained" by constant addition of additives that have been lost. This maintenance could easily require up to another $18,000 of inventory per job.

Murphy Mud generally serviced shallow to intermediate-depth wells. The company had not entered the oil-base mud market but specialized in water-base systems. Oil-base muds were extremely expensive and were difficult for the company's mud engineers to use. If one of the company's regular customers needed an oil mud for a particular job, Murphy Mud would "lease" the oil-base system from a larger mud company. In this case, the mud system was supplied by the larger mudder directly to Murphy Mud.

Financial Control

A major consideration for Mr. Ashley was the use of cash to fund the growth experienced in 1981. A constant concern was the effect of cash inflows and outflows on the company's primary variable cost, additives. Additive inventories were purchased on a ninety-day trade accounts payable. Jobs were then contracted and completed on a sixty-day receivable basis. "Timing was critical because if the job dragged out, we would have to make payments before we were paid," noted Mr. Ashley.

Another major concern was fixed costs, which accounted for 34 percent of sales in 1981. The high fixed costs came primarily from equipment and salaries. The company owned six trucks and a few forklifts and pickups and leased eighteen company cars and five warehouses. The debt service and lease payments on this equipment had to be made periodically, sales or no sales. The salary expenses were also significant. Murphy Mud employed five drilling mud engineers, five warehouse managers, several truck drivers, and an administrative staff to support both the warehouses and well operations.

Raw material costs were also a concern since they accounted for 56 percent of sales and represented 96 percent of variable costs. These materials included mainly bentonite and additives. Fortunately, since water was viewed to a large extent as a "free good," it was not considered to be a significant, measurable cost. However, in those situations where oil-base mud systems were required, Murphy Mud found that the raw material costs increased to 60 percent of sales due to the increased additives required for those systems. The Murphy Mud income statement for 1981 is shown in Exhibit 3.

Sales and Marketing Effort

"We never thought much about sales or marketing when we formed the company," Mr. Ashley said. "Orville Reed's task as sales manager was to sift through the multiple requests for mud service and schedule jobs."

Murphy Mud adhered to the pricing strategy of its twenty competitors, four of which were the major mud companies. "Everyone in the industry knows what the price should be, and if you are too far off you lose the job," Mr. Ashley commented. Recently, however, the over-

EXHIBIT 3
Murphy Mud, Inc., Income Statement for the Year
Ending December 31, 1981

Revenues		$3,410,275
Cost of goods sold		1,892,703
Gross profit		$1,517,572
Operating expenses		
Mud engineering salaries	$272,988	
Lease payments, cars	125,820	
Warehouse rental	60,000	
Maintenance/gas	85,500	
Trucking salaries	192,000	
Depreciation	10,000	746,308
Total operating income		$ 771,264
General administrative expenses		
Executive and staff salaries	$348,000	
Office rental	60,000	
Interest expense	105,792	513,792
Profit before taxes		$ 257,472

all price level had dropped 10 percent across all types of jobs, except for deeper wells (those exceeding 20,000 feet). "Simple arithmetic shows that if we again worked fifty wells as we did in 1981, our gross revenues would have been over $300,000 less—and there goes our profit before tax," Mr. Ashley said.

As sales manager, Mr. Reed emphasized the matching of a mud engineer with the specific requirements of the proposed well. This matching process involved matching the technical requirements of the job, such as the geology, special additives, and the magnitude of on-site service, as well as the temperaments of the tool pusher. "The drilling business is not only strenuous, but stressful," Mr. Reed noted. "Given what's at stake out there and the minimum margin for error, tempers can flare up. I for one wouldn't want to face a disgruntled tool pusher or drilling crew."

Even with the insatiable demand for mud services, Murphy Mud had emphasized service in its dealings with customers. This policy was followed for two reasons. First, Murphy Mud management believed service reflected in the mud engineer, as opposed to price, was what a mud company offered. Second, a service orientation was particularly effective with independent drilling companies—Murphy Mud's primary customer group. Furthermore, since Murphy Mud was dealing with independent drilling companies (as opposed to major oil and gas companies), most of its contacts were with tool pushers or other individuals at the well site. Tool pushers were particularly sensitive to the importance of a well-qualified mud engineer, even with shallow, uncomplicated wells.

The Future

"In all my years in the business, I've never seen such rapid and radical change," said Mr. Ashley. "A day doesn't pass when I don't hear about another independent mud company failing."

Over the course of several conversations with his management team, Mr. Ashley received numerous recommendations on how Murphy Mud might "ride out" the downturn. Mr. Reed emphasized refocusing Murphy Mud's efforts by well depth (shallow versus deeper wells), mud system (water-base versus oil-base), customer type (major versus independent), or oil and gas basin. Each change would bring with it significant modifications in how Murphy Mud conducted its business. For example, a move toward deeper and more complex wells would entail devoting a mud engineer exclusively to the project. This action would probably require expertise in oil-base mud systems and dealings with majors as opposed to independents. "In short," Mr. Ashley noted, "we would have to fire a few mud engineers who couldn't work with oil-base mud systems and hire new engineers at $50,000 a crack. Furthermore, we know the geology in the McKlintock and New Horizon basins, and maybe the Midland Basin. But the Plains Basin is a no-man's-land since nobody has really figured it out. If we go after majors, then we will be dealing with purchasing agents, not tool pushers. Purchasing agents don't respond to service like tool pushers—they like price. Moreover, a major oil and gas company typically deals with a major mud company, not independents."

Mr. Aaker estimated that Murphy Mud was averaging thirty-five days plus or minus ten days per job in 1981, but that a single mud engineer worked more than one job at any one time. Mr. Rogers believed that deeper wells would require sixty or so days per job and a full-time mud engineer at the well-site.

Mr. Willard suggested cutting back on the company's overhead and "running a little leaner. Cutting people is the easiest," he said. "We could easily cut executive and staff salaries by 20 percent by each of us taking a lower salary and laying off some clerical support. At the end of September, our revenues for 1982 will be $2 million, and I figure we have another $500,000 coming in October through December. Our cost of goods sold is running about 57 percent of sales due to rising additive costs and more oil-base mud installations. Our salary expenses are up 10 percent across the board over last year; our lease, rental, depreciation, interest expenses remain unchanged." Murphy Mud would work forty wells in 1982.

NOTES

1. "Oil-Field Suppliers: The Crash after a Boom—An Uncertain Future," *Business Week* (September 27, 1982): 66–70.

2. "Slow Recovery Forecast for Oil Service Companies," *Dallas Times Herald* (September 20, 1982): Section D, p. 1, 4.

3. *Business Week* (September 27, 1982): 68.

CASE

Brand Pipe Company

MR. ALAN BUFORD, manager of the Brand Pipe Company, a division of the Arnol Corporation, was considering a directive he had just received from top management of the parent organization. He was told by Arnol management that he was to come up with a specific marketing strategy and plan to stop the losses of the division as soon as possible and to provide a base for continued growth in the future.

COMPANY BACKGROUND

Brand Pipe, located in the Puget Sound area of the state of Washington, was a plastic extruder serving the Pacific Northwest. The company began operations in the early 1950s and subsequently was acquired by Arnol Corporation, a large company in an unrelated field. Company sales were $1.8 million, making it the second-largest extruder in the Pacific Northwest. Profits, however, had declined, and the company had operated at a loss for the past year and a half.

The management staff at Brand Pipe consisted of Mr. Buford, who acts as both general manager and sales manager; Mr. George Timkin, the plant manager; Mr. Alan Britt, the plant engineer; and a plant foreman.

INDUSTRY BACKGROUND

Thermoplastic pipe was made from four types of plastic resins: polyvinyl chloride (PVC), rubber-modified styrene (styrene), acrylonitrile butadiene styrene (ABS), and polyethylene (poly). The resins differ in

This case is produced with the permission of its author, Dr. Stuart U. Rich, professor of marketing, and director, Forest Industries Management Center, College of Business Administration, University of Oregon, Eugene, Oregon.

chemical and physical characteristics, such as resistance to acids and bases, strength, melting point, and ease of extrusion. These plastic resins were bought from the large national petrochemical suppliers.

Plastic pipe competed with iron, aluminum, and asbestos-cement pipe in the Northwest market. In comparison with the other materials, plastic pipe was considered superior in terms of lower cost, ease of installation and maintenance, and lack of deterioration from environmental influences. Plastic pipe was considered inferior to the other materials in terms of crushability, strength, and melting temperature. Plastic pipe could not be extruded in sizes greater than ten inches in diameter and also had a high degree of thermal expansion that restricted its use in some applications.

A machine called an extruder was used to form plastic pipe by heating the resin to near its melting point, forcing the fluid mass through a die, and then cooling the formed pipe in a water bath. A relatively unsophisticated plant to manufacture plastic pipe could be built for approximately $150,000. In fact, one of the successful competitors in the ABS market in the Northwest, the PJ&J Company, had what was called a "backyard operation" and operated out of a converted garage.

The different resins could all be satisfactorily extruded on the same machine, with the possible exception of PVC, which required a stainless steel die instead of the usual mild steel die. All that is required to change resin type is to change the resin fed into the machine. A die change to make different-size pipe is even simpler. The extruder can be left hot and the pressure relieved so that the die can be changed.

BRAND PIPE COMPANY EXTRUDED PIPE

All four thermoplastic resins were being converted by Brand Pipe into plastic pipe ranging from one-half inch to eight inches in diameter. The final product had pressure ratings from 80 psi (pounds per square inch) to 600 psi. The company's pipe was of standard quality and was comparable to that produced by competing pipe extruders.

Brand Pipe Company had just completed capital expenditures for new resin-blending and pipe-extrusion equipment that executives described as "the most technically advanced in the industry." The company had a plant investment of over $2 million. In view of Brand Pipe's unprofitable operating performance, it was considered doubtful that the Arnol Corporation would agree to additional capital expenditure appropriations. Brand Pipe owned and operated four modern pipe-extruding machines as well as three older machines. Despite the modern production setup, a production problem arose from the firm's inability to maintain adequate control over pipe-wall thickness. Pipe production used 7 percent more resin material than was theoretically required to ensure a minimum pipe-wall thickness. The plant engineer was in control of quality control, but, because of substantial workload, he had spent little time on the costly material waste problem.

Since corporate management imposed tight limits on finished goods inventories, Brand Pipe had aimed at minimizing inventories. Rush orders, which frequently could not be filled from inventory, necessitated daily extrusion machine changeovers. However, a relative cost study conducted by the plant engineer showed that Brand Pipe could conceivably hold a much larger finished goods inventory and still not reach the point where costs of holding inventory would exceed machine changeover costs. Brand Pipe averaged seven machine changeovers per day, at an average loss to contribution to fixed overhead of $25 per changeover.

PLASTIC PIPE MARKET SEGMENTS

Brand Pipe Company produced some two hundred separate pipe products of varying sizes and resin types to supply eleven market segments. Mr. Buford felt that, in order to use plant capacity to the utmost, Brand Pipe had to reach all of these end-use segments. Brand Pipe's sales volume was highest in water transportation markets for PVC and styrene pipe. The company's total pipe production by resin type (in pounds) was as follows:

Poly	450,000
PVC	3,871,000
ABS	769,000
Styrene	1,032,000
Total	6,122,000

Arnol Corporation market researchers had concluded that demand for plastic pipe would increase during the next five years in all market segments in the states served by Brand Pipe—that is, in Oregon, Washington, Idaho, and northern California. A summary analysis of each market segment follows, including current consumption estimates and five-year growth projections for Washington alone and for the four-state region including Washington.

Agriculture Irrigation

This segment was the largest-volume plastic pipe market in the Pacific Northwest. Plastic pipe, however, accounted for only 11 percent of all pipe used for agriculture irrigation. Newly developed plastic component systems, particularly plastic-component sprinkler irrigation systems, were replacing many open-ditch and metal pipe water transportation systems. Arnol market researchers, in describing growth potential for this plastic pipe market, stated that the "pendulum is swinging from metal to plastic pipe as the primary water transportation method." PVC resin pipe was used almost exclusively to supply this segment. Total plastic pipe consumption in Washington was 8.25 million pounds. Total for the four-state market area (Washington, Oregon, Idaho, and northern California) was 16.5 million. Estimated growth for the next five years for Washington, as well as for the whole region, was 17 percent.[a]

Private Potable Water System Market

Building codes continued to favor copper and aluminum and to exclude plastic pipe from use for home water-supply systems. Although public utilities were utilizing PVC plastic pipe for public water systems, plumbing contractors shied away from using polyethylene pipe in private systems. Total plastic pipe consumption for Washington was 145,000 pounds. For the Northwest region it was 350,000 pounds. No growth was forecast for the next five years.

Mobile Home Market

Most ABS plastic pipe sold to this segment was used in plumbing fixtures. Most mobile home manufacturers sought to buy plastic fixtures on a national contract basis. It was a rare occasion when one of these national concerns purchased pipe from a local or regional extruder. Washington plastic pipe consumption was 130,000 pounds; regional consumption was 1.4 million pounds. A 90 percent growth figure was forecast for Washington, and 75 percent for the region.

Public Potable Water

Some public water utilities were using PVC plastic pipe for water service lines that connect households to main water distribution lines. Styrene pipe had given way in recent years to the stronger, less brittle, more inert PVC pipe. Washington consumption was slightly over 2 million pounds, and regional consumption over 5 million pounds. A 100 percent growth figure was projected for both the state and the region.

---

[a]Growth figures are for the five-year period. They are *not* annual growth rates. Therefore, a five-year growth figure of 61 percent is equivalent to a 10 percent average annual growth rate.

Industrial Market

Plastic pipe applications in processing, material supply, transfer, and waste disposal were severely limited in this segment. According to Mr. Buford, this was due to thermoplastic pipe's sensitivity to steam, sparks, and hot fluids. The most prominent industrial application was in copper mining, with minor applications in pulp and paper manufacturing, food processing, and seawater transfer. Total consumption in Washington was 600,000 pounds; for the region, slightly over 1 million pounds. Growth was projected at 45 percent for both the state and the region.

Turf Irrigation Market

Turf irrigation included applications such as public and private lawn-watering systems. Small-diameter PVC pipe was generally used by this market segment. Consumption in Washington was 3 million pounds; in the region it was 5.9 million. The projected five-year growth was 66 percent for Washington and 57 percent for the region.

Drain Waste and Vent Market

DWV was defined as all plumbing pipe running from and venting sinks, toilets, and drains to the structure drain. ABS pipe accounted for 86–90 percent of the market, with the remaining amount held by PVC. Plumbing unions had opposed the use of plastic pipe in favor of traditional materials, apparently because of the easy installation of plastic pipe with its resultant labor savings. Yet the unions claimed the traditional steel and iron pipes were superior. Consumption in Washington was slightly over 1 million pounds; regional consumption was 1.75 million. Washington growth was projected at 27 percent; regional growth at 35 percent.

Conduit

Electric conduit was used primarily to protect and insulate electric power lines and telephone lines, both underground and in buildings. Competitive materials included the traditional aluminum metals. Major users in this market were large contractors and utilities that bought on a competitive bidding system. Consumption in Washington was 465,000 pounds; regional consumption was 1 million pounds. A 75 percent growth figure was projected for Washington, and 50 percent growth was forecast for the region.

Sewer and Outside Drain

This market segment used plastic pipe for connections from house to septic tanks and sewer systems, downspout drainage, water drainage, and septic tank drainage. The primary resins used were styrene and PVC. The major competitive materials were asbestos fibers, cast iron, and vitrified clay; however, they were generally competitive only in the large sizes used in a public sewer system. The FHA had recently approved plastic pipe for rural homes. Washington consumption was 1.4 million pounds, and regional consumption was 2.8 million. A 90 percent growth figure was forecast for Washington, and 78 percent growth was predicted for the region.

Gas Transportation Market

Plastic pipe in this segment was used to distribute low-pressure natural gas from major terminals through distribution mains to residences, businesses, and industrial users. Gas companies, which bought the pipe in large lots or on a yearly basis, had tested the plastic pipe and were not entirely pleased with the results. They favored the traditional steel pipe and the new epoxy-coated steel pipe that combined the inherent advantages of both plastic and steel. Washington consumption was 123,000 pounds; regional consumption, 300,000 pounds. Growth projection was marginal.

Water Well Service and Stock Water

Plastic pipe was used in rural areas to bring water from the individual farm wells into the home and to distribute it to outlying farm buildings to water livestock. The primary resins used were PVC and polyethylene. Washington consumption was 400,000 pounds, and regional consumption was 900,000 pounds. Relatively little growth was projected.

The four types of plastic pipe varied in their availability to use in the various markets just described. Adaptability depended on the physical attributes of the resin type as well as cost advantages needed for low-grade applications. PVC was the most versatile and was used in all market segments. Poly was suitable for use in all markets except sewer and outside drain, mobile homes, and drain waste and vent. ABS was adaptable for use in six of the eleven markets public potable water, private potable water, turf irrigation, mobile homes, drain waste and vent, and gas transportation. Styrene was used for the most part in sewer and outside drain, drain waste and vent, and conduit markets.

PROMOTION AND SALES

Brand Pipe used a limited amount of advertising in promoting its plastic pipe, preferring to rely on personal selling as its main promotional device. In the past the company had advertised in trade journals and in agriculturally oriented magazines such as *Pacific Farmer*. It also sponsored early-morning farm radio programs on local stations, and utilized the usual product information folders and catalogs.

Recently Brand Pipe had used a mailer soliciting inquiries on a "spike sprinkler" coupling for irrigation. The spike sprinkler was a device to position a sprinkler in the field, and it was considered a superior pipe coupling. The company had contracted for exclusive distribution of the coupling to be used with its pipe, but did not itself produce the device. Brand Pipe had mailed 1,000 of the product folders and had received 200 inquiries. Mr. Buford was enthusiastic about the response and planned to increase mailer promotion in the future.

The company salesmen were assigned by geographic area, and they called on pipe distributors and large end-users in each area. They were responsible for sales of all company products in their respective areas. The three main sales areas were the Seattle–Puget Sound area, the Portland and eastern Oregon–eastern Washington area, and the southern Oregon–northern California area. Each of these areas was covered by one salesman. In addition, Mr. Buford had a number of working contacts and made visits to major accounts. This was relatively simple because most of the major distributors were located within short distances of the division office.

In addition to the field salesman, there was one in-house salesman who handled small "drop-in" business, short-notice orders, and customers requiring a quote on an order of pipe. Often, a distributor would phone in an order asking for a price quote and delivery at the end user's site the next day. If the company was not capable of meeting a price and delivery schedule, the customer would take his business elsewhere. The company tried its best to provide service on these accounts so that it could maintain plant capacity, even if it meant machine changeovers to produce the order.

Since the salesmen were assigned one to an area, they were responsible for missionary, maintenance, and service selling. They were compensated, according to corporate policy, by straight salary with no commissions paid for different product sales. They called on distributors and large end users and were expected to educate distributors on product knowledge and use and to handle field complaints. Often these complaints emanated from a do-it-yourself end user who had not followed the directions for joining pipe sections together correctly. At times the salesmen tried to stimulate sales by going to the end user and providing technical service such as product specification and pipe-system design.

DISTRIBUTION

Brand Pipe sold the majority of its plastic pipe through distributors, with 20 percent of the accounts contributing 75 percent of gross revenue. Only in the case of large end-users such as utilities and major contractors did the company try to sell directly. In such cases, the company paid the regular commission to the area distributor only if the distributor managed to learn of the sale and the distributor was of some importance to the company. Marketing terms were 2/10 net 30.

Pipe distributors, who were paid a commission of 5 to 10 percent of sales, performed several major functions: (1) they broke bulk and sold to many retailers in their area; (2) they used the pipe along with many other components in the piping systems that they installed, such as agricultural irrigation systems, plumbing systems, and turf irrigation systems; and (3) they provided financing and inventory service for their customers. Distributors held preparatory inventory in seasonal markets such as agricultural irrigation. In preparation for the seasonal demand, Brand Pipe would deposit "dated" shipments at the distributor's warehouse.

Pipe distributors in most market segments considered price to be the most important factor determining from whom they bought pipe. Most distributors agreed that one pipe was as good as another; they considered delivery service to be the next most important factor. They did not feel that technical service offered by the manufacturer was very important in their choice of suppliers. In fact, some distributors were very ambivalent about the usefulness of manufacturer's salespeople. They did not feel that technical service by the manufacturer was very important in the sale of pipe. Some felt that the best thing salesmen could do was stay out of the field. They disliked pipe salespeople "muddying the water" at the end-user level and making promises to the end-user that the distributor was unable or unwilling to fulfill. Other distributors, however, felt that pipe salespeople could and did help by providing product knowledge to the distributor salespeople. Under no circumstances did any of the distributors favor having pipe salespeople contact the end user.

Distributors generally viewed the price competition within the industry with disfavor. One reason was the lowered profit margin on sales of the pipe. Since distributors usually made a fixed percentage on sales, their income was reduced by lowered prices. Another reason was the distributor's concern that when he was making a bid on a system including plastic pipe, his competitor might get a more favorable quote on plastic pipe and therefore be able to quote a lower bid. The distributors wanted plastic pipe prices stabilized so that their bids could be based on their own competence and economic situation rather than on the pricing practices of the pipe manufacturers.

Although distributors disliked price competition, they were glad to see that Brand Pipe and other producers had lowered the price to the point where imported pipe was not a major source of market supply. Many were reluctant to handle shipload quantities of imported pipe with its resultant inventory and handling problems. They much preferred a convenient source of supply, which the local producers could provide.

Although some distributors had considered making their own plastic pipe, they did not at the time consider such production attractive. For the time being, they were content to buy pipe from suppliers. Brand Pipe had been a factor in this decision by improving service and by lowering prices.

In view of the continuing poor profit situation of his division, Mr. Buford had considered trying to integrate forward and capture the distributor's margin. One of the salesmen had felt that Brand Pipe salesmen could do as good a job selling plastic pipe to end users as the distributors did.

TRANSPORTATION

Approximately 75 percent of Brand Pipe's annual volume was shipped via common carrier, with the remaining 25 percent being delivered by company-leased trucks or through factory "will-call" by customers. Because of competitors' practices, most of Brand Pipe's shipments were either prepaid to Northwest destinations, or comparable freight allowances were made from gross sales price when pipe orders were picked up at the plant by customers. Because plastic pipe was so bulky, shipping costs averaged about 15 percent of the selling price. This meant that each competitor had a substantial advantage in selling in his own home market.

PRICING POLICY

Mr. Buford looked over the profit summary report (see Exhibit 1) and wondered whether changes in the present pricing policy might lead to improvements in the profit picture of his division. The present policy of "meeting or beating the price offered by any other supplier" had

EXHIBIT 1
Profit Summary Report, Per-Pound Basis

	Poly	PVC	ABS	Styrene
Gross sales price	.3625	2760	.3648	.2762
Less: discounts, freight, allowances	.0710	.0138	.0378	.0377
Net sale price	.2915	.2622	.3270	.2385
Less: variable cost (raw materials and conversion)[a]	.3050	.2230	.3392	.2110
Direct margin (contribution to fixed cost)	−.0135	.0392	−.0122	.0275
Less: fixed cost	.0397	.0375	.0501	.0314
Profit	−.0532	.0017	−.0623	.0039

[a]*Text authors' note:* For analysis purposes, treat conversion as *changeover costs* only. Other labor costs are included in fixed cost figure.

been initiated earlier when the Japanese began exporting large quantities of plastic pipe to the Pacific Northwest. Because of lower raw material costs and a suspected dumping policy, they were pricing their products below local suppliers. Even though there were disadvantages in the sales agreements offered by the Japanese (such as order sizes of shipload quantities only), the Japanese were able to capture a significant portion of the market due to their low price.

The effects of the Japanese entry into the Pacific Northwest market were immediately felt by Brand Pipe, since the Japanese were marketing PVC—the major resin type produced by Brand Pipe. At that time, Mr. Buford reasoned that the size of the Pacific Northwest market could not accommodate another supplier of plastic pipe. He felt that steps must be taken immediately to drive the Japanese out of the Pacific Northwest.

To achieve this goal, Brand Pipe adopted its present pricing policy, thus forcing the Japanese to compete on terms other than price, such as speed of delivery, where the Japanese were at a strict disadvantage. Soon after this, other suppliers followed suit. The average price levels gradually eroded from 28 cents per pound down to 26 cents per pound. With the decreased price the Japanese left the Pacific Northwest market, and Mr. Buford felt that they would not reenter it until the price came back to 28 cents per pound.

Recently, the Sierra Plastic Pipe plant had burned to the ground. This company had been the major supplier for southern Oregon and northern California. A number of the other suppliers including Brand

Pipe increased their plant capacity in anticipation of taking over the accounts that they were sure Sierra would lose. To prevent the loss of its accounts, Sierra bought plastic pipe on the open market and was thus able to maintain its customers while its plant was being rebuilt. Because Sierra was able to remain in business, and because the growth of the Pacific Northwest market was not up to expectations, a considerable overcapacity on the part of all suppliers soon developed in the Pacific Northwest. This overcapacity was estimated at 30–40 percent, but some suppliers were continuing expansion.

Because of the overcapacity and the desire on the part of executives to maintain market share, Brand Pipe had continued its present pricing policy. It was reasoned by Mr. Buford that a reduction in price would increase market share, which would increase production and narrow the gap between plant capacity and the production level, thus minimizing fixed cost per unit.

In evaluating the present pricing policy, Mr. Buford came to two conclusions. First, the profit picture for his division was most likely quite similar to that of the other regional suppliers. Second, although the distributors enjoyed the low price that was resulting from the fierce price competition, they were unhappy with the volatility of the price levels that was also generated.

COMPETITION

Domestic competition in Brand Pipe's marketing area came from six regional manufacturers and five to eight major national producers. The number of national producers varied because some of them moved in and out of the Northwest market, depending on economic conditions. The regional manufacturers had about 75 percent of the market, while the larger national firms and a few import firms controlled the rest. Three of the regional firms controlled 60 percent of the Northwest market. Sierra Plastics was a leader, although Brand Pipe and Tamarack Pipe closely followed. The three companies produced essentially the same products.

Tamarack Pipe was within fifty miles of Brand Pipe's plant and was a strong competitor in the Portland, Oregon, market and the Puget Sound market. Due to its location in southern Oregon, Sierra Plastics had a strong competitive position in the southern Oregon–northern California market, resulting from its lower transportation cost in this area compared with those of Brand Pipe and Tamarack.

Brand Pipe had tried to differentiate its product in the past, but had met with limited success. In an attempt at differentiation, Brand Pipe had changed the color of its PVC pipe from gray to white. Other competitors, especially the nationals, had made some progress in differentiating their products. Babbit Corporation, a national supplier of pipe and piping systems to industry, had added plastic pipe to its product line and advertised in such nationwide periodicals as *Chemical Engineering*. Babbit was very strong in the industrial segment of the market. Cable Company had distinguished its pipe by application to sump pump installations and had a virtual monopoly in this specialized application. PJ&J in northern California was the chief supplier of ABS pipe in the Pacific Northwest, primarily through being the least expensive marketer. For example, Brand Pipe was able to buy PJ&J pipe and resell it at less cost than could produce comparable pipe.

In recent months, Brand Pipe salesmen had reported that Tamarack had begun to concentrate more on the agricultural irrigation market, while Sierra was concentrating on being the primary supplier of plastic pipe for conduit. Even though this market was small, it was anticipated to mushroom when the housing market resumed its growth. The large national firms had concentrated on the mobile home industry and appeared to have the greatest number of manufacturers, since contracts are negotiated on a countrywide basis.

The large national manufacturers were either owned by or affiliated with national petrochemical companies. These companies usually adjusted to the prevailing market conditions and were a stabilizing influence in the market.

The competitive conditions that had prevailed in the Northwest had depressed the financial conditions of some of the smaller independent firms, and it was not known how much longer they could continue operations. The larger independent firms, although experiencing losses, were as well financed as Brand Pipe and were still battling for increased market share.

CONCLUSION

Mr. Buford realized that a number of changes were needed in many parts of his company's marketing program. He saw that some of these changes were interrelated; for example, decisions on pricing strategy might have an important impact on product policy, and vice versa. Certain decisions had to be made very soon if the company's profit position were to be improved, whereas other decisions could be postponed for a while.

Mr. Buford felt that his planning task was made more difficult by the limited size of the management staff in his division. Although the parent corporation provided help in market research and some coaching in general planning procedures, the actual planning and strategy determination was Mr. Buford's responsibility. Because of the need to keep division overhead expenses down to a minimum, Mr. Buford knew that no additional management staff could be hired at the present time.

   As he walked into his office, pondering what to do first in the way of planning, his phone rang and the in-house salesman asked him to okay a price quote on a drop shipment for the next day. Mr. Buford okayed the quote, and then sat down muttering, "How can I find time to plan for the months and years ahead when daily operating problems demand so much of my time?"

Universal Machine Company, Inc.

IN EARLY 1980 Mr. Frank Kirmss, chairman of the board of APO International and Universal Machine Company, Inc., and Mr. Dallas Smith, general manager of Universal Machine Company, returned triumphantly from a trip to New York City. They had just finalized a major sale to a large New York City bank.

Upon entering his office, Mr. Kirmss spotted the financial statements for 1979 lying on his desk. Turning to the year-end income statement, his excitement about the New York sale quickly turned to despair. Universal Machine Company had recorded its third consecutive year of declining sales volume and net profit before taxes.

"That's it," Mr. Kirmss murmured to himself. He called Dallas Smith and scheduled a meeting to, in his words, "rethink the business."

THE COIN-HANDLING INDUSTRY

The coin-handling industry in the United States consists of firms who manufacture equipment used in the wrapping, sorting, and verifying of coins. Total industry sales in 1979 was estimated to be $18.9 million which also includes sales of coin-wrap paper.

This case was prepared by Professor Roger A. Kerin, Southern Methodist University, Dallas, as a basis for class discussion and is not designed to illustrate appropriate or inappropriate handling of administration situations. All financial and market data are disguised and not useful for research purposes. The assistance of Universal Machine and APO International in the preparation of this case is gratefully acknowledged.

Coin Distribution in the United States

There are about 160 billion coins circulating daily in the United States with a total value of approximately $980 billion. The distribution of coins roughly follows the geographical distribution of population. The top fifty standard metropolitan statistical areas (SMSA) in the United States account for about 48 percent of the coins in circulation. Six SMSAs—New York City, Philadelphia, Chicago, Dallas, Los Angeles, and San Francisco—account for about 17 percent of the coins in circulation.

Users of Coin-Handling Equipment

Eight major users of coin-handling equipment exist in the United States. Exhibits 1 and 2 list these major users and show their market potential through 1982 expressed in retail prices.

Banks represent the largest market for coin-handling equipment and paper, accounting for 33 percent of industry sales. This market, including Federal Reserve Banks, which account for 20 percent of bank market volume, consists of approximately one thousand large banking institutions (greater than $100 million in assets) nationwide. Larger commercial banks in New York, California, Illinois, Texas, and Pennsylvania alone account for upwards of 40 percent of coin-handling

EXHIBIT 1
Coin-Processing Equipment—Market Segment Sales at
Retail Prices
(thousands of dollars)

Market Segment	Percentage of Total Sales	Equipment	Paper	Parts	Total
Banks	33.0%	$ 3,306	$2,620	$312	$ 6,237
Armored car	22.0	2,204	1,746	203	4,158
Casinos	18.0	1,803	1,429	170	3,402
Retailing	16.0	1,603	1,270	151	3,024
Vending	7.0	701	556	66	1,323
Public transportation	2.0	200	159	19	378
Tollway	1.0	100	79	9	189
Pay telephone	0.8	80	63	8	151
Miscellaneous	0.2	20	16	2	38
Total	100.0%	$10,017	$7,938	$945	$18,900

EXHIBIT 2
Forecast of Market Potential by Market Segment and New Versus Replacement Sales at Retail, 1980–1982
(thousands of dollars)

Segment	1980	1981	1982
Banks	$ 6,611	$ 7,008	$ 7,428
Armored cars	4,407	4,672	4,952
Casinos	3,606	3,822	4,052
Vending	1,402	1,487	1,576
Pay telephone	160	170	180
Public transportation	401	425	450
Tollway	200	212	225
Retailing	3,205	3,398	3,602
Miscellaneous	40	43	45
Total	$20,032	$21,237	$22,510
Current replacement market:			
Wrapper equipment	$ 5,257	$ 5,572	$ 5,906
Sorter/verifier equipment	2,629	2,787	2,954
Paper	7,721	8,184	8,675
Parts	820	870	922
Forecast of total annual replacement sales	$16,427	$17,413	$18,457
New sales (equipment only)	$ 3,605	$ 3,824	$ 4,053
Replacement sales	16,427	17,413	18,457
Total market potential	$20,032	$21,237	$22,510

equipment volume in the bank segment. The smaller commercial banks in the United States rely on correspondent banks to handle the coin-wrapping function for them. One-third of industry sales to commercial banks occurs in Federal Reserve cities.

According to Mr. Kirmss, "Bank executives are very sensitive about having adequate service for their equipment due to the volume of coins they process daily. Therefore, it is necessary to have a dealer located nearby in the event of an equipment failure; and this factor plays a major role in selling to them. We must be able to remedy the problem within six hours if a machine breaks down." Federal Reserve Banks, however, serviced their own machines.

Armored car companies represent the second largest user of coin-handling equipment, with 22 percent of industry sales. Four companies—Brinks, Purolator, Wells Fargo, and Loomis—account for over 90 percent of coin equipment volume. These companies operate in many cities nationwide and decisions on the choice of coin-handling equipment are made at each of 700 operating locations. Mr. Kirmss noted that each of these companies typically had its own maintenance capability in cities in which the companies operated, which numbered about 300. Typically, two firms would operate in each city. However, in the top one hundred SMSAs, three firms would operate offices. Federal Reserve cities and nearby areas are estimated to account for 30 percent of armored car coin equipment volume.

Gambling casinos represented the third largest user group for the coin-handling equipment industry. However, with the legalization of gambling in New Jersey and particularly Atlantic City, a spurt in volume is expected. "Our people worked Atlantic City very effectively; I hope we can establish a presence there as we've done in Las Vegas," Mr. Kirmss commented. UMC had 250 coin-wrapping machines in use out of an estimated 460 machines in Las Vegas.

"Casinos are the elephant's graveyard for coin-wrapping machines," says Mr. Kirmss. "For example, Harrah's Club in Reno, which operates forty-two UMC wrapping machines, recently bought fifteen 'old' UMC machines from some banks in Chicago. The banks used them five years; now Harrah's will get another five, maybe ten years out of them. The bankers are paranoid about breakdowns and thus account for a large percentage of new machines sold, whereas casinos and armored car companies maintain and overhaul old machines and purchase only equipment parts."

Retail stores nationwide account for 16 percent of the coin-handling industry volume. Despite the apparent dispersion of retail activity in the United States, industry sources have estimated that 15–20 percent of total national retail sales are generated in Federal Reserve Bank cities and upwards of 30 percent of coin equipment volume resides in these cities and immediate environs. Retail outlets typically do not service their equipment; rather, they rely on dealers. Remaining users of coin-handling equipment account for 11 percent of industry volume, of which 50 percent is in Federal Reserve city environs. These users rely on dealers for service.

Life Cycle of the Industry and Product Requirements

Approximately 82 percent of the annual sales volume in the coin-handling industry consists of replacement products; 18 percent of the volume represents new placements. Exhibit 3 describes estimated new and replacement sales by product category. Industry observers project this relationship will continue at least through 1982. The nature of the replacement market, in the words of Mr. Kirmss, "indicates that each manufacturer must constantly watch over his old customers and guard

EXHIBIT 3
Coin-Processing Equipment—New and Replacement Sales at Retail Prices

Product Category	New Sales	Replacement Sales	Total	Percentage of Total Sales
Wrappers	$1,088,460	$ 4,959,360	$ 6,048,000	32%
Paper	1,598,940	6,339,060	7,938,000	42
Sorters/verifiers	544,320	3,424,680	3,969,000	21
Parts	170,100	774,900	945,000	5
Total (round)	$3,402,000	$15,498,000	$18,900,000	100%

against attack from his competitors to maintain his share of market as little loyalty exists. Only a sales effort will suffice."

Aggressive pricing and threats from outside the industry have characterized the industry in recent years. The role of these factors vary by type and size of coin-handling equipment users, however. For example, pricing is not as important to banks as it is to casinos and armored car companies. Manufacturers have long realized that "value" pricing dominates the bank user, as members of this group will pay nearly any price to insure themselves protection from the inconvenience of equipment failure. Thus high-quality equipment (with attendant prices) and availability of service from manufacturers or dealers often determine the choice of equipment. Retailers exhibit similar preferences, but to a lesser degree. Casinos and armored car companies, on the other hand, are more cost-conscious than banks. Product features most appealing to them are those that are clearly cost-savings related. Therefore, factory-rebuilt equipment and overhauled machines are viewed favorably by these user segments due to their lower prices. Research commissioned by UMC indicated that product quality and the availability of fast and capable service from equipment manufacturers or dealers are key factors in the selling process. However, "prices and dollar margins overall have been depressed in recent years," according to Mr. Kirmss.

The major external threat to coin-handling industry manufacturers has been the erosion of coin-wrapper paper sales due to paper suppliers' direct sales to large users at lower prices. By selling direct, paper suppliers capitalize on the demand for paper created by equipment manufacturers. The large paper buyers, such as Federal Reserve Banks, the very large commercial banks, and the larger casinos such as Harrah's Club, typically purchase their paper on a bid basis and secure sizable volume discounts.

Competition and Dealer Network

Eight United States–based companies dominate the coin-handling equipment industry. All of them, except UMC, distribute foreign-made wrapping equipment under their own labels.

Brandt, Inc., is the industry sales leader with about 46 percent of industry sales. Brandt distributes a wrapping machine produced in Germany. The company is unique in the industry in that it operates its own network of 250 to 300 sales and service representatives. Other companies distribute and service its products through independent dealers.

Ameil Industries and Cummins-Allison Corporation both distribute wrapping equipment made in Japan. Industry sources estimate that these two companies account for about 36 percent of industry volume. Except for Brandt, Inc., and Cummins-Allison Corporation, which are public companies, and Ameil, which is an importer, UMC competitors in the industry are closely held, family-run organizations.

Competitor strength varies somewhat by user segment. For example, UMC is strong in the casino segment and maintains a presence in the bank segment due primarily to its placements in Federal Reserve Banks. Ameil Industries is also strong in the Federal Reserve System in addition to larger commercial banks because of its ability to place more sophisticated coin-handling systems in these banks. Cummins-Allison is also present in the Federal Reserve Banks and is a source of equipment for armored car companies. Brandt covers all segments; nevertheless, most of its business is in small coin-handling equipment (coin changers and the like). Moreover, Mr. Kirmss believed that a sizable percentage of Brandt's revenue came from service contracts on its equipment in place.

The Sales and Service Effort

The sales effort in the coin-handling industry is a lengthy process, often requiring six months to complete. The process is initiated through one of three sources: (1) an unsolicited inquiry from a user direct to a manufacturer, (2) a manufacturer's direct effort leading to an inquiry, or (3) a dealer contact. A manufacturer or dealer will then install demonstration units in a user's place of business and educate operators on how to use them. During this period the manufacturer or the dealer prepares "system procedures and equipment layout designs" necessary for the equipment to achieve its most productive use. Approximately one to two months is required for this step. Next, a two- to three-month review of the equipment is conducted by a user, during which time a decision is made. Throughout this process it is common for a manufacturer or dealer to visit the buyer occasionally to inspect the machines and overcome any buyer reticence about the decision to purchase a particular brand. This latter point is important since several manufacturer's demonstration units may be under review at the same time. Moreover, Mr. Kirmss noted that he has heard of situations in which one dealer would sabotage another's equipment, thus requiring vigilance on the part of equipment dealers or representatives.

Dealers perform the service function for manufacturers through the use of service contracts with the equipment buyer. Even though specifics of service contracts vary by equipment manufacturer and dealer, most contracts include a stated monthly service fee for a specified number of days of service. Service contracts provide a substantial revenue source for dealers. Although it is difficult to estimate how much revenue is provided through service, industry sources and UMC's experience suggest that a dealer makes two times his machine gross profit in service contract revenue per year. According to Mr. Kirmss: "Once a machine is sold, the dealer makes two times his gross margin on that machine every year for the life of the machine. On a $12,000 machine, the dealer makes $6,000 per year from that machine as long as the buyer owns it. We make about the same percentage as dealers when we sell direct through our own dealers.

"The service function in this business requires capable preventative maintenance," Mr. Kirmss noted. However, Mr. Kirmss was quick to praise his machines: "A UMC machine can run for years with little maintenance. But in the hands of an inept operator—a gorilla—a machine can be busted in five minutes and require hours of service."

THE COMPANY

Universal Machine Company, Inc., is a manufacturer of coin-handling equipment needed by a variety of firms, such as large banking institutions, casinos, and armored car companies in the United States and several foreign countries. The company was acquired by APO International in 1973. Prior to its acquisition, UMC served as a distributor of German-manufactured coin-handling equipment, operating from Falls Church, Virginia, since 1967. With the acquisition of UMC, APO acquired the rights to produce its own coin-handling equipment in the United States. UMC has the distinction of being the only firm in the United States that manufacturers its own coin-wrapping equipment. UMC recorded $1.1 million worldwide sales in 1979. Sales and service revenue in the United States was about $600,000 in 1979. UMC 1979 abbreviated financial statements are shown in Exhibit 4.

EXHIBIT 4
Universal Machine Company Abbreviated Financial
Statements, 1979

Income statement

Net sales	$1,100,000
Cost of goods sold	715,000
Gross profit	$ 385,000
Other income	$ 330,000
Marketing, general, and administrative expense	$ 285,000
Net profit before tax	$ 430,000

Balance sheet

Assets	
Current assets	$ 600,000
Plant and equipment	400,000
Total assets	$1,000,000
Liabilities and owners' equity	
Current liabilities	$ 350,000
Long-term debt	325,000
Owners' equity	325,000
	$1,000,000

Product Line and Product Placements

UMC has the broadest line of coin-wrapping equipment in the industry. The company has five equipment models, compared with one or two models provided by competitors. UMC's wrapping machines are the world's fastest—competitive models operate at 50 to 75 percent the speed of Universal's equipment. Selected examples of UMC equipment are reproduced in the Appendix. Selected specifications of equipment models are shown in Exhibit 5.

A recent survey of UMC customers conducted by an independent research group showed that the company's comparative performance with competitors' was quite favorable. UMC was above average on product application capability, equipment quality, and processing system design and average on price and product-line depth. Service-maintenance was rated above average to excellent, "due to our own efforts," Kirmss noted.

EXHIBIT 5
Selected Specifications of UMC Equipment

Counter/verifier	Operating Speed	Retail Price
#360	5,000 coins per minute	$ 4,850
Wrapper		
#500	960 rolls per hour	$ 9,830
#600	1,440 rolls per hour	$11,160
Wrapper/counter		
#2400[a]	1,440 rolls per hour	$12,500
#2800[a]	1,440 rolls per hour	$13,500
#3200	1,920 rolls per hour	$14,500

[a]Principal difference between #2400 and #2800 is that the #2800 incorporates a stack detector to avoid spills. The #2400 does not.

UMC has product placements throughout the world and generates about half of its volume from foreign sales. In addition, UMC has machines placed in thirty-nine of fifty states and in nine of the twelve Federal Reserve Banks.

Dealer Network in the United States

UMC has twenty dealer outlets in the United States. Eighteen dealers are independent office equipment businesses. These dealers typically carry such products as typewriters, filing cabinets, stationery, and the like. Two factory outlets, located in Las Vegas (established in 1974) and Dallas (established in 1975), are UMC-owned-and-operated and handle only UMC equipment. The Dallas office opening was prompted in part by its central location and excellent airline connections useful for shipping parts and demonstration equipment throughout the United States. The Las Vegas office opening was prompted by the number of machines located there, its potential, and its proximity to Reno.

Exhibit 6 shows the dealer locations, including the total sales of equipment, parts, and coin-wrapping paper sold through independent dealers and through UMC factory outlets plus 1980 potential in their respective markets. Dollar figures for independent dealers are at UMC prices; UMC dealers' figures are at retail. UMC makes 25 percent gross profit on equipment, 20 percent gross profit on parts sold through independents, and approximately 27 percent on coin-wrap paper sold by independents.[a] UMC gross profit on direct sales are 50 percent for

---

[a]*Casewriter's note:* The cost structure of the firm indicated that UMC gross profit figures incorporated virtually all variable costs of operations. Hence the gross profit is essentially identical to contribution margin.

EXHIBIT 6

Universal Machine Company Domestic Sales-Service Dealers—Sales Figures and Replacement Volume in Trade Areas

Independent Dealers	1979 Volume				1980 New and Replacement Market at Retail Prices (000)			
	Machines	Parts	Paper	Total	Equipment	Parts	Paper	Total
New York City (including Atlantic City, N.J.)					$ 750	$ 95	$ 775	$ 1,620
Los Angeles, Calif. (2 dealers)					375	48	412	835
Boston, Mass.					325	33	338	696
Washington, D.C.					295	20	143	458
Chicago, Ill.					390	40	435	865
Cramwell, Conn.					35	4	53	92
Little Rock, Ark.					55	6	82	143
Denver, Colo.					75	8	112	195
Jacksonville, Fla.					75	7	112	194
St. Louis, Mo.					215	22	172	409
Tulsa, Okla.					35	3	38	66
Billings, Mont.					15	3	38	66
Portland, Ore.					80	8	120	208
Reno, Nev.					850	96	600	1,546
Richmond, Va.					165	17	198	380
Casper, Wyo.						Unknown		
Total dealer sales	$157,825	$ 82,563	$ 8,864	$249,252	$3,735	$410	$3,628	$ 7,779
UMC factory outlets								
Dallas-Fort Worth, Tex. (includes Houston)	$ 53,347	$ 6,282	$13,773	$ 73,402	$ 360	$ 42	$ 218	$ 620
Las Vegas, Nev.	124,478	62,563	40,243	227,284	1,100	125	1,025	2,250
Total UMC and dealers	$335,650	$151,408	$62,880	$549,938	$5,195	$577	$4,871	$10,649

624

equipment, 40 percent for parts, and 33 percent on paper sales. Independent dealers receive a 25 percent gross profit on sales of equipment and parts to users and 10–15 percent gross profit on paper sales, depending upon competition. Mr. Dallas Smith estimates that UMC accounts for between 10 and 15 percent of a typical independent dealer's equipment and parts sales volume.

UMC dealers have been regarded as the firm's greatest asset. Therefore, UMC has developed a policy of dealer autonomy. In practice this means UMC does not contact potential customers in a dealer's territory unless asked by dealers, nor does UMC interfere with the operations of its dealers. The rationale for this policy is based on UMC management's belief that service is very important for customer relations and the ability to make sales. Even more basic is UMC's realization that it is difficult to find dealers who will carry the UMC line *and* represent the firm in a competent fashion. "Yet," according to Mr. Kirmss, "we can't get them [existing dealers] to sell and service customers without our insistence." He added that UMC spent about $60,000 in executive time, technician time, and travel expenses to assist dealers in sales efforts and maintenance work at no cost to dealers.

Despite the value placed on its dealers by UMC, recent events have led UMC executives to question dealer support reciprocity. Mr. Kirmss commented:

> The more we get out into the field, the more we hear about how we're represented. For example, a few years ago we heard that a dealer had made a deal with a competitor to service their equipment. Some dealers have misrepresented our warranty policy and thus got warranty service from us, but charged the customer at regular rates. On top of that, we found out that some dealers were squeezing us for price, delivery, warranty and service concessions but charging the full price to customers. They pocketed the difference. We have summarily dropped these dealers over the last three years, but it has hurt our market presence as well as sales.

Dealer sales effectiveness also varies. For example, sales records indicated that the Reno and one Los Angeles dealer would account for about 20 percent of UMC overall sales of equipment, parts, and paper in 1979. Dealers in New York City, Boston, and Washington, D.C., have contributed little to UMC sales in recent years. Estimated dealer sales by user groups are shown in Exhibit 7.

Sales Efforts

UMC has historically relied on its dealer network to perform the sales function. Recently, however, Mr. Kirmss noted that he and Dallas

EXHIBIT 7
Estimated Independent Dealer Sales by Type of User at UMC Prices

Market Segment	Equipment	Parts	Paper	Total
Banks	$ 59,165	$44,874	$5,662	$109,701
Armored cars	9,830	7,328	290	17,448
Casinos	67,557	20,173	2,000	89,730
Retailing	18,328	6,188	412	24,928
All other	2,945	4,000	500	7,445
	$157,825	$82,563	$8,864	$249,252

Smith have played an increasing role in sales efforts. This change in orientation was prompted by two factors. First, dealers have increasingly called on UMC personnel to become involved in the demonstration phase of the sales effort, including the preparation of "system procedures and equipment layout designs" and operator-education sessions. Second, Kirmss and Smith noted from their records that a majority of their sales leads were unsolicited contacts made directly to UMC due to favorable industry word-of-mouth. Few inquiries were due to dealer contacts. This low level of dealer sales activity prompted direct sales to large banks and particularly Federal Reserve Banks. Currently, the inquiry distribution is 65 percent unsolicited, 25 percent UMC initiated, and 10 percent dealer generated. Despite the distribution of sales leads, UMC has continued to provide the dealer with a 25 percent margin on equipment sales in his territory. This practice is currently under review. However, some UMC executives believe it serves as a "perk" for dealers and is a necessity. Moreover, they argued, eliminating this margin would lead to an erosion of the partnership concept UMC tried to develop with its dealers. According to one UMC executive, "You've got to realize that the dealers aren't costing us anything—it's all variable—and we get the service that is needed by our customers." Other executives countered that since dealers made their money on service contracts, they "do not sell accounts that service their own equipment anyway. Why should we pay them for nothing—sales or service?" These executives did admit that sales to casinos were not subject to this criticism.

THE MEETING

Kirmss and Smith met the next day to evaluate UMC's approach to marketing its coin-handling equipment. During the course of their discussion, they considered a number of alternatives.

First, the possibility of direct sales and service was considered. Both executives were acutely aware of the cost of switching over to a complete direct-to-customer program. However, on a limited basis in Las Vegas and Dallas–Fort Worth, this approach did seem to work. Mr. Smith estimated that the operation of a factory outlet would cost about $5,000 per month. This figure would include two UMC sales-service representatives plus other overhead costs. If this alternative were considered, Mr. Kirmss said that factory outlets would have to cover fixed costs from the sale of equipment, parts, and paper, since service revenue would take time to develop. Industry dealerships generally obtained 53 percent of their revenue from machines, 42 percent from paper, and 5 percent from parts apart from service revenue. Mr. Kirmss instructed Dallas Smith to examine where UMC factory outlets could operate and the decision rules for opening a factory outlet. UMC would have to finance the cost of company-owned outlets out of UMC funds.

Second, Kirmss and Smith considered the possibility of selling direct. UMC was already spending considerable funds annually for executive and technician time and travel for sales-related calls, and Kirmss thought that direct sales should be considered. The dealer network would not be affected. Kirmss's experience indicated that an initial sales call often required about one hour per customer. An equipment user should be called on at least once per year. However, about one-third of potential customers required additional sales attention each year to meet their equipment replacement needs. Therefore, one call and four more hours of sales time would be necessary for this group. About one in ten of these accounts requested demonstration and "on premises" capability by UMC or its dealers. This would require yet another four four-hour calls added to the sales effort. However, UMC technicians could and often do assist in performing this function. Mr. Kirmss instructed Dallas Smith to prepare alternative approaches for his review on the direct sales possibility, recognizing that the total cost of one UMC sales representative would be $30,000 annually. Mr. Smith, having anticipated the direct-sales-only possibility, prepared a sales mix estimate for a sales representative, which showed that 53 percent of dollar sales volume would come from equipment, 42 percent from paper, and 5 percent from parts. These estimates were derived from the industry sales volume mix shown in Exhibit 1.

Third, Mr. Kirmss again raised the issue of eliminating the margin on sales given to dealers when UMC produced an equipment sale without the assistance of a dealer. This issue would have to be considered in light of whatever program UMC adopted, although its effect on dealers would vary. Finally, questions concerning whether the dealers could be motivated to become more active in the sales process were raised.

Selected Examples of Universal Machine Company Equipment

EXHIBIT A.1
Universal Model 3600 Counter/Verifier

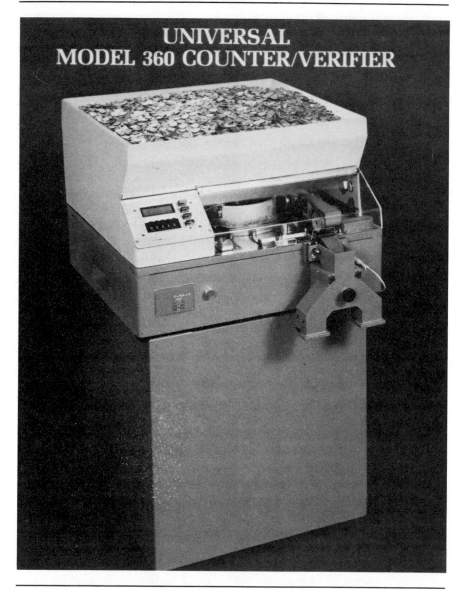

EXHIBIT A.2
Universal Model 600 Automatic Wrapper

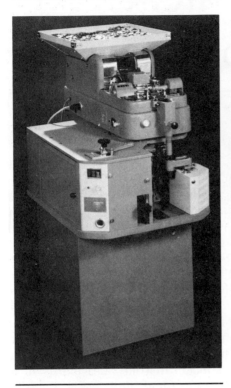

EXHIBIT A.3
Universal Model 2800 Automatic Wrapper/Counter

CASE

Hanover-Bates Chemical Corporation

JAMES SPRAGUE, NEWLY APPOINTED northeast district sales manager for the Hanover-Bates Chemical Corporation, leaned back in his chair as the door to his office slammed shut. "Great beginning," he thought. "Three days in my new job and the district's most experienced sales representative is threatening to quit."

On the previous night, James Sprague, Hank Carver (the district's most experienced sales representative), and John Follet, another senior member of the district sales staff, had met for dinner at Jim's suggestion. During dinner Jim had mentioned that one of his top priorities would be to conduct a sales and profit analysis of the district's business in order to identify opportunities to improve the district's profit performance. Jim had stated that he was confident that the analysis would indicate opportunities to reallocate district sales efforts in a manner that would increase profits. As Jim had indicated during the conversation, "My experience in analyzing district sales performance data for the national sales manager has convinced me that any district's allocation of sales effort to products and customer categories can be improved." Both Carver and Follet had nodded as Jim discussed his plans.

Hank Carver was waiting when Jim arrived at the district sales office the next morning. It soon became apparent that Carver was very upset by what he perceived as Jim's criticism of how he and the other district sales representatives were doing their jobs—and, more partic-

This case was prepared by Professor Robert E. Witt, The University of Texas, Austin. The case is intended to serve as a basis for class discussion rather than to illustrate effective or ineffective management.

ularly, how they were allocating their time in terms of customers and products. As he concluded his heated comments, Carver said:

> This company has made it darned clear that thirty-four years of experience don't count for anything . . . and now someone with not much more than two years of selling experience and two years of pushing paper for the national sales manager at corporate headquarters tells me I'm not doing my job. . . . Maybe it's time for me to look for a new job . . . and since Trumbull Chemical [Hanover-Bates's major competitor] is hiring, maybe that's where I should start looking . . . and I'm not the only one who feels this way.

As Jim reflected on the scene that had just occurred, he wondered what he should do. It had been made clear to him when he had been promoted to manager of the northeast sales district that one of his top priorities should be improvement of the district's profit performance. As the national sales manager had said, "The northeast sales district may rank third in dollar sales, but it's our worst district in terms of profit performance."

Prior to assuming his new position, Jim had assembled the data presented in Exhibits 1 through 6 to assist him in analyzing district sales and profits. The data had been compiled from records maintained in the national sales manager's office. Although he believed the data would provide a sound basis for a preliminary analysis of district sales and profit performance, Jim had recognized that additional data would probably have to be collected when he arrived in the northeast district (District 3).

EXHIBIT 1
Hanover-Bates Chemical Corporation: Summary
Income Statements, 1981–1985

	1981	1982	1983	1984	1985
Sales	$19,890,000	$21,710,000	$19,060,000	$21,980,000	$23,890,000
Production expenses	11,934,000	13,497,000	12,198,000	13,612,000	14,563,000
Gross profit	7,956,000	8,213,000	6,862,000	8,368,000	9,327,000
Administrative expenses	2,606,000	2,887,000	2,792,000	2,925,000	3,106,000
Selling expenses	2,024,000	2,241,000	2,134,000	2,274,000	2,399,000
Pretax profit	3,326,000	3,085,000	1,936,000	3,169,000	3,822,000
Taxes	1,512,000	1,388,000	790,000	1,426,000	1,718,000
Net profit	$ 1,814,000	$ 1,697,000	$ 1,146,000	$ 1,743,000	$ 2,104,000

EXHIBIT 2
District Sales Quota and Gross Profit Quota
Performance, 1985

District	Number of Sales Reps	Sales Quota	Sales— Actual	Gross Profit Quota[a]	Gross Profit— Actual
1	7	$ 3,880,000	$ 3,906,000	$1,552,000	$1,589,000
2	6	3,750,000	3,740,000	1,500,000	1,529,000
3	6	3,650,000	3,406,000	1,460,000	1,239,000
4	6	3,370,000	3,318,000	1,348,000	1,295,000
5	5	3,300,000	3,210,000	1,320,000	1,186,000
6	5	3,130,000	3,205,000	1,252,000	1,179,000
7	5	2,720,000	3,105,000	1,088,000	1,310,000
		$23,800,000	$23,890,000	$9,520,000	$9,327,000

[a]District gross profit quotas were developed by the national sales manager in consultation with the district managers and took into account price competition in the respective districts.

In response to the national sales manager's comment about the northeast district's poor profit performance, Jim had been particularly interested in how the district had performed on its gross profit quota. He knew that district gross profit quotas were assigned in a manner that took into account variation in price competition. Thus he felt that poor performance in the gross profit quota area reflected misallocated sales efforts either in terms of customers or in the mix of product line items sold. To provide himself with a frame of reference, Jim had also requested data on the north-central sales district (District 7). This district was generally considered to be one of the best, if not the best, in the company. Furthermore, the north-central district sales manager, who was only three years older than Jim, was highly regarded by the national sales manager.

THE COMPANY AND INDUSTRY

The Hanover-Bates Chemical Corporation was a leading producer of processing chemicals for the chemical plating industry. The company's products were produced in four plants located in Los Angeles, Houston, Chicago, and Newark, New Jersey. The company's production process was, in essence, a mixing operation. Chemicals purchased from a broad range of suppliers were mixed according to a variety of user-based formulas. Company sales in 1985 had reached a new high of $23.89 million, up from $21.98 million in 1984. Net pretax profit in 1985

EXHIBIT 3
District Selling Expenses, 1985

District	Sales Rep Salaries[a]	Sales Commission	Sales Rep Expenses	District Office	District Manager Salary	District Manager Expenses	Sales Support	Total Selling Expenses
1	$177,100	$19,426	$56,280	$21,150	$33,500	$11,460	$69,500	$ 388,416
2	143,220	18,700	50,760	21,312	34,000	12,034	71,320	351,346
3	157,380	17,030	54,436	22,123	35,000[b]	12,382	70,010	368,529
4	150,480	16,590	49,104	22,004	32,500	11,005	66,470	348,153
5	125,950	16,050	42,720	21,115	33,000	11,123	76,600	326,558
6	124,850	16,265	41,520	20,992	33,500	11,428	67,100	315,655
7	114,850	17,530	44,700	22,485	31,500	11,643	58,750	300,258
								$2,398,915

[a]Includes cost of fringe benefit program, which was 10 percent of base salary.

[b]Salary of Jim Sprague's predecessor.

EXHIBIT 4
District Contribution to Corporate Administrative
Expense and Profit, 1985

District	Sales	Gross Profit	Selling Expenses	Contribution to Administrative Expense and Profit
1	$ 3,906,000	$1,589,000	$ 388,416	$1,200,544
2	3,740,000	1,529,000	351,346	1,177,654
3	3,406,000	1,239,000	368,529	870,471
4	3,318,000	1,295,000	348,153	946,847
5	3,210,000	1,186,000	326,558	859,442
6	3,205,000	1,179,000	315,376	863,624
7	3,105,000	1,310,000	300,258	1,009,742
	$23,890,000	$9,327,000	$2,398,636	$6,928,324

EXHIBIT 5
Northeast (#3) and North-Central (#7)
District Sales and Gross Profit Performance
by Account Category, 1985

District	(A)	(B)	(C)	Total
	Sales by Account Category			
Northeast	$915,000	$1,681,000	$810,000	$3,406,000
North-central	751,000	1,702,000	652,000	3,105,000
	Gross Profit by Account Category			
Northeast	$356,000	$623,000	$260,000	$1,239,000
North-central	330,000	725,000	255,000	1,310,000

EXHIBIT 6
Potential Accounts, Active Accounts, and Account Call
Coverage: Northeast and North-Central Districts, 1985

District	Potential Accounts			Active Accounts			Account Coverage (Total Calls)		
	(A)	(B)	(C)	(A)	(B)	(C)	(A)	(B)	(C)
Northeast	90	381	635	53	210	313	1,297	3,051	2,118
North-central	60	286	499	42	182	218	1,030	2,618	1,299

had been $3.822 million, up from $3.169 million in 1984. Hanover-Bates had a strong balance sheet, and the company enjoyed a favorable price-earnings ratio on its stock, which traded on the OTC market.

Although Hanover-Bates did not produce commodity-type chemicals (e.g., sulfuric acid and others), industry customers tended to perceive minimal quality differences among the products produced by Hanover-Bates and its competitors. Given the lack of variation in product quality and the industrywide practice of limited advertising expenditures, field sales efforts were of major importance in the marketing programs of all firms in the industry.

Hanover-Bates's market consisted of several thousand job-shop and captive (in-house) plating operations. Chemical platers process a wide variety of materials including industrial fasteners (e.g., screws, rivets, bolts, washers, and others), industrial components (e.g., clamps, casings, couplings, and others), and miscellaneous items (e.g., umbrella frames, eyelets, decorative items, and others). The chemical plating process involves the electrolytic application of metallic coatings such as zinc, cadmium, nickel, brass, and so forth. The degree of required plating precision varies substantially, with some work being primarily decorative, some involving relatively loose standards (e.g., 0.0002 zinc, which means that anything over two ten-thousandths of an inch of plate is acceptable), and some involving relatively precise standards (e.g., 0.0003–0.0004 zinc).

Regardless of the degree of plating precision involved, quality control is of critical concern to all chemical platers. Extensive variation in the condition of materials received for plating requires a high level of service from the firms supplying chemicals to platers. This service is normally provided by the sales representatives of the firm(s) supplying the plater with processing chemicals.

Hanover-Bates and the majority of the firms in its industry produced the same line of basic processing chemicals for the chemical plating industry. The line consisted of a trisodium phosphate cleaner (SBX), anesic aldahyde brightening agents for zinc plating (ZBX), cadmium plating (CBX) and nickel plating (NBX), a protective post-plating chromate dip (CHX), and a protective burnishing compound (BUX). The company's product line is detailed as follows:

Product	Container Size	List Price	Gross Margin
SPX	400-lb. drum	$ 80	$28
ZBX	50-lb. drum	76	34
CBX	50-lb. drum	76	34
NBX	50-lb. drum	80	35
CHX	100-lb. drum	220	90
BUX	400-lb. drum	120	44

COMPANY SALES ORGANIZATION

Hanover-Bates's sales organization consisted of forty sales representatives operating in seven sales districts. Sales representatives' salaries ranged from $14,000 to $24,000 with fringe-benefit costs amounting to an additional 10 percent of salary. In addition to their salaries, Hanover-Bates's sales representatives received commissions of 0.5 percent of their dollar sales volume on all sales up to their sales quotas. The commission on sales in excess of quota was 1 percent.

In 1983 the national sales manager of Hanover-Bates had developed a sales program based on selling the full line of Hanover-Bates products. He believed that if the sales representatives could successfully carry out his program, benefits would accrue to both Hanover-Bates and its customers:

1. Sales volume per account would be greater and selling costs as a percentage of sales would decrease.

2. A Hanover-Bates's sales representative could justify spending more time with such an account, thus becoming more knowledgeable about the account's business and becoming better able to provide technical assistance and identify selling opportunities.

3. Full-line sales would strengthen Hanover-Bates's competitive position by reducing the likelihood of account loss to other plating chemical suppliers (a problem that existed in multiple-supplier situations).

The national sales manager's 1983 sales program had also included the following account call-frequency guidelines:

A accounts (major accounts generating $12,000 or more in yearly sales)—two calls per month
B accounts (medium-sized accounts generating $6,000–$11,999 in yearly sales)—one call per month
C accounts (small accounts generating less than $6,000 yearly in sales)—one call every two months

The account call-frequency guidelines were developed by the national sales manager after discussions with the district managers. The national sales manager had been concerned about the optimum allocation of sales effort to accounts and felt that the guidelines would increase the efficiency of the company's sales force, although not all of the district sales managers agreed with this conclusion.

It was common knowledge in Hanover-Bates's corporate sales office that Jim Sprague's predecessor as northeast district sales manager had not been one of the company's better district sales managers. His attitude toward the sales plans and programs of the national sales manager had been one of reluctant compliance rather than acceptance and support. When the national sales manager succeeded in persuading Jim Sprague's predecessor to take early retirement, he had been faced with the lack of an available qualified replacement.

Hank Carver, who most of the sales representatives had assumed would get the district manager job, had been passed over in part because he would be sixty-five in three years. The national sales manager had not wanted to face the same replacement problem again in three years and also had wanted someone in the position who would be more likely to be responsive to the company's sales plans and policies. The appointment of Jim Sprague as district manager had caused considerable talk, not only in the district but also at corporate headquarters. In fact, the national sales manager had warned Jim that "a lot of people are expecting you to fall on your face . . . they don't think you have the experience to handle the job, in particular, and to manage and motivate a group of sales representatives, most of whom are considerably older and more experienced than you." The national sales manager had concluded by saying, "I think you can handle the job, Jim. . . . I think you can manage those sales reps and improve the district's profit performance . . . and I'm depending on you to do both."

CHAPTER 11

Linking Corporate and Marketing Strategy

INCREASINGLY, MARKETING EXECUTIVES are confronted with two parallel and often conflicting decision responsibilities. On the one hand, marketing executives must make short-term operating decisions that implement marketing programs and effectively use allocated resources. On the other hand, they must contribute to strategic decisions that guide the firm's financial, managerial, and productive resources to effect long-term linkages with its social, technological, and competitive environments in a manner that preserves the organization's vitality—indeed, its survival. This latter responsibility is growing in significance as marketing executives play an expanding role in the design of corporate strategy.

The development of corporate strategy, or *strategic management,* as the process is now called, requires a manner of thinking that integrates broadly defined strategic and operating viewpoints with decisions in order to direct resources toward opportunities consistent with an enterprise's distinctive competency to achieve a sustainable differential advantage.

PURSUIT OF A SUSTAINABLE DIFFERENTIAL ADVANTAGE

The ultimate goal of corporate strategy is to secure a sustainable differential advantage for the firm. The process involved in identifying an opportunity for differential advantage is intellectually demanding and requires a careful appraisal of where a company *is, should be, can be,* and *must be* within a competitive environment. In addition, the question of *how* a differential advantage can be achieved and sustained must be addressed.

The concept of differential advantage is important to grasp, given its centrality to corporate strategic management. *Differential advantage* refers to the creation of competitive situations in which a firm's distinctive competency matches the requirements for success in one or several product-market settings, whereas competitors can acquire such capabilities only over an extended time period or through extensive investment.

The actual pursuit of a sustainable differential advantage depends on the imagination and skill of top management, including marketing professionals, in all functional areas of the firm. The pursuit begins with a strategic definition of the firm, an objective assessment of its strengths and weaknesses, and the identification of competitive situations where these strengths can be brought to bear, as was indicated in Chapter 1. Consider the words of Thornton Bradshaw, chairman of the board of RCA, as he draws on these concepts in explaining RCA's possible course of action in the 1980s: "What I have been doing is spending a lot of time finding out what kind of a company this is so that we can decide where we are going to go." He concluded that RCA's principal strengths are in entertainment (RCA owns NBC) and communications. In his words:

> The strength is there. We have enormous strength in marketing; we are a leader in satellite communications; we have strength in entertainment programming. Match all that against the communications explosion that is coming in the 1980s, and we have got some tremendous opportunities.[1]

How Mr. Bradshaw plans to marshal the resources to pursue these opportunities is discussed next.

THE LINK BETWEEN CORPORATE AND PRODUCT-MARKET STRATEGY

The link between corporate and product-market strategy is evident in the management of the firm's product-market relationships and the view that these relationships are investment units. As Boyd and Larréché note:

> They [product-markets], are, in essence, the firm's *basic investment* units because the firm's income streams derive from the coupling of specific

products with specific markets. The yield of the investment made in each is largely a function of the fit between the product and the needs and wants of the target market(s), the size and growth of the market, and the firm's relative competitive market position. Clearly, how these domains are defined and analyzed is critical, not only because of the obvious organizational implications, but because of the potential synergistic effects of an investment made in one domain on the outcome of another.[2]

In theory, the corporate strategist seeks to achieve a differential advantage for the organization through (1) the analysis and choice of the firm's product-market relationships with a view toward developing the "best-yield" configuration in terms of financial performance and (2) the formulation of management strategies that create and support viable product-market relationships consistent with enterprise capabilities and objectives. Therefore, two types of related decisions must be made.[3] First, product-market *investment decisions* must be made that involve determining where and how resources should be invested. These decisions address the question: What product-markets should we be in? Second, *management* strategies must be designed to implement investment decisions. Decisions made at this level address the question: How should we compete in these product-markets? The product-market strategies and marketing mix strategies described throughout the book have dealt with these topics.

In practice, the product-market investment perspective means that some products or businesses are managed to produce cash either to support the firm's other, higher-yielding businesses or to acquire new businesses that have better growth prospects. In some instances, divestment (sale or liquidation) rather than investment is necessary. In other instances, businesses or products are selectively managed and some investment may be justified on a case-by-case basis.

Several recent examples illustrate this investment approach to managing diverse product-market entries. B. F. Goodrich has decided to use the profits generated by its tire business to finance ventures in chemicals, plastics, and industrial products.[4] American Can Company has announced its plan to sell its capital-hungry wood and paper products business in the hope of raising $1 billion for new business acquisition purposes.[5] RCA has sold its interests in Random House publishing and will sell or use funds from some of its other businesses to provide cash for ventures in its entertainment and communications businesses, where it sees the most growth in the 1980s.[6] Examples of firms selectively managing businesses include Esmark, Inc., which has divested some but not all of its Swift and Company meat-packing business.[7] In other situations, firms realize they have inadequate resources to fund growth businesses, as was evident in Computervision Corporation's sale of a division that required extensive capital outlays for research and development to remain competitive in a high-technology market.[8] Finally, some firms divest themselves of businesses that do not fit their strategic thrust or whose method of operation or industry is foreign to them. Such was the case when Colgate-Palmolive Company announced plans to divest businesses that did not fit the company's future growth strategy. According to the company's president, the long-term strategy is to focus on products and businesses that "we know best and in which our market position, expertise and technology create the best opportunity."[9]

PORTFOLIO ANALYSIS

Product or business portfolio analysis has emerged as a useful tool for making the resource-allocation decisions described here. Portfolio analysis explicitly evaluates the organization's present products or businesses to determine when (1) new products or businesses should be added to existing operations, (2) existing products or businesses should be modified, or (3) existing products or businesses should be deleted or divested. The principal factors considered in making these decisions often include product or business sales growth, competitive strength, profitability, risk, and resource demands.[10]

A variety of product or business portfolios have been developed.[11] A common element in the different approaches is that the firm's business or product is related to external industry or market conditions in a two-dimensional matrix. The approaches differ in terms of the number of factors used for evaluating products or businesses. The two most common portfolio approaches are the *Growth/Share Matrix* developed by the Boston Consulting Group, an international management consulting firm, and various forms of a *Business Position Matrix* developed by a number of firms, including General Electric and Shell International.

Growth/Share Matrix

The Growth/Share Matrix uses two factors for evaluating a firm's businesses or products. These factors are market growth and the business or product relative market share. The underlying rationale of the Growth/Share Matrix lies in the experience curve phenomenon described in Chapter 9 and the belief that cash flow is a critical concern in corporate strategy. The relationships between market growth, market share, and cash flows is apparent from a quote by the originator of the Growth/Share Matrix, Bruce Henderson of the Boston Consulting Group:

> If cost is a function of experience, and experience a function of volume, and volume is a function of market share, then cost is a function of market share. But cash is a function of cost, so it too must be a function of market share. That led to the conclusion that if you have high market share, you must be generating cash, but if you're also growing, you must have high cash use.[12]

In short, *cash use* is a function of *market growth* since incremental investments are necessary to fund growth. *Cash generation* is a function of *market share* since the experience curve phenomenon suggests that the business or product(s) with the largest volume has the greatest potential for lowest costs and higher profits due to accumulated experience.

Given the two factors of market growth and relative market share, the Boston Consulting Group has developed a four-cell matrix, shown in Exhibit 11.1.[13] Each cell in the matrix describes a product or business as being a star, cash cow, problem child, or dog, depending on its placement. Furthermore, a product's or business's placement in the matrix indicates a particular strategy, according to the Boston Consulting Group. For example, stars (high market growth/high share) generate sizable cash flows given their high share; however, this cash flow is necessary to fund rising volume spurred by a high market growth. These products or businesses represent the future for the firm and must be maintained and protected through aggressive marketing strategies designed to hold market share. As the product or business matures (i.e., market growth slows), *and* assuming the market share remains high, the star becomes a cash cow. Cash cows (low market

EXHIBIT 11.1
Growth/Share Matrix

Market Growth		High Market Share	Low Market Share
	High	star (modest + or − cash flow)	problem child (large negative cash flow)
	Low	cash cow (large positive cash flow)	dog (modest + or − cash flow)

High | Low
Market Share

growth/high share) produce more cash than is necessary to maintain them in the marketplace. Therefore, they can generate cash that other existing products or businesses in the portfolio need to grow, fund research and development efforts, or provide capital to acquire new products or businesses. A firm's cash cows must be protected from market share erosion caused by competitors seeking to gain additional market share for their products or businesses. Problem children (high market growth/low share) require a large infusion of cash because of the market growth; unfortunately, their low market share generates little or no cash to fuel this growth. Accordingly, problem children must be subsidized by cash cows in the hope of building market share and turning them into stars. If this cannot be done, then the firm should consider divesting itself of the product or business. Finally, dogs (low market growth/low share) produce little cash and require little cash to maintain their market position. These products or businesses typically have little to offer the firm in terms of future profits. Accordingly, firms often attempt to sell them or harvest them in the manner described in Chapter 6. Occasionally a firm will attempt to reposition a dog by seeking out a growth market, as when General Foods attempted to reposition its Grape Nuts ready-to-eat cereal brand in the rapidly growing "natural" cereal market.[14]

Business Position Matrix

A second approach to portfolio analysis involves the construction of a two-dimensional matrix using multiple criteria for arraying products or businesses. A Business Position Matrix is shown in Exhibit 11.2. The two dimensions are typically market or industry attractiveness and competitive strength. The attractiveness dimension is a composite rating of such factors as market size and growth rate, industry profitability, number and strength of competitors, rate of social and technological change, and the like. A "high" composite rating on attractiveness might include a large, rapidly growing, and profitable industry with a limited number of small or weak competitors. The competitive strength dimension is a composite rating of such business or product factors as unique strengths in marketing, image in the marketplace, market share, cost advantage, and leading edge in technology. A "high" composite rating on competitive strength might include a high market share, a favorable customer franchise, and a decisive cost advantage.

Investment strategies derived from the product or business placement in the matrix typically include (1) invest resources, (2) harvest or divest, and (3) selectively manage. In short, a firm should invest additional resources where competitive strengths exist and the market is

EXHIBIT 11.2
Business Position Matrix

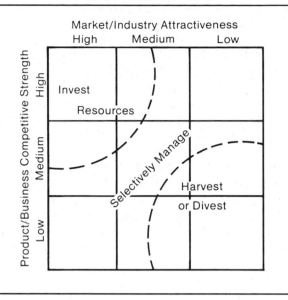

attractive and should harvest or divest products or businesses where either competitive strengths are not apparent or the market is unattractive. These clear-cut prescriptions are blurred when competitive strengths are apparent but the market is unattractive or when the market is attractive but competitive strengths do not exist. In these situations, almost surgical precision is necessary to distinguish those products or businesses that have potential from those that do not. The decision by Esmark, Inc., to divest some but not all of its Swift and Company meat-packing business illustrates this type of decision making.

Additions to the Product Portfolio

A special case in the management of product or business portfolios is the addition of new investment units. These new investments may take the form of cash cows acquired to produce cash flow for the acquirer. This strategy appears to underlie the decision by Gillette to acquire Liquid Paper Corporation in the 1970s.[15] Liquid Paper Corporation held a dominant market share in the typewriter correction fluid market, which was in the mature (low-growth) stage. Alternatively, a firm might acquire a star business. This appeared to be the case when Warner Communications acquired Atari, a leader in the then rapidly expanding electronic games industry.[16] In both examples, the acquisitions were designed to enrich the sales or profit yield of the acquirer's overall portfolio.

Acquisitions differ from the internal product-development process because the acquirer is adding an *existing* business or product line to the portfolio. Therefore, different issues are raised for consideration by the strategist. For example, it is important to consider the financial status of the acquired business, including a detailed analysis of sales and profits over time, in addition to cash flow and working capital requirements. Second, a detailed analysis of the acquired business's competitors and market franchise, in addition to its product's positioning by market segments, is necessary. Third, marketing strategy issues, including an analysis of marketing channels and sales and promotional efforts, must be addressed. Fourth, considerations in the physical merger of operations, including people and policies, are necessary. Finally, and at a broader strategic level, the acquirer must consider the requirements for success in the acquired business's market and objectively assess what, if any, synergy can be created by merging the two businesses.

FINANCIAL CONSIDERATIONS

The investment strategy adopted by the firm, as these examples show, also requires a fundamental understanding of basic concepts developed in the finance literature beyond those discussed in Chapter 2. Concepts such as *sustainable growth* and *discounted cash flow* are frequently applied in product-market investment decision making. Each concept will now be introduced.

Sustainable Growth

Sales and asset growth are two common corporate objectives. Growth, however, requires financial resources, and these resources are produced through the firm's marketing and financial policies. It is important to recognize that a firm's ability to grow results from an interdependent system of variables that, if not synchronized, can negatively affect the financial soundness of the firm.

Four variables are used to determine a firm's ability to grow in sales or assets:[17] (1) net profit margin after tax (P), (2) earnings retention ratio (E), (3) total (short- and long-term) debt-to-equity ratio (D/E), and (4) ratio of total assets to net sales (A/S). The interdependency between these variables is shown in the following formula:

$$\text{Sustainable growth} = \frac{P(E)\,(1 + D/E)}{A/S - P(E)\,(1 + D/E)}$$

Consider a situation where a firm has a net profit margin after tax of 7 percent, an earnings retention ratio of 50 percent (i.e., $1 out of every $2 earned is retained and $1 is distributed to shareholders), a total debt-to-equity ratio of 50 percent, and a total assets-to-sales ratio of 65 percent (i.e., $0.65 of assets is needed to produce $1 of sales). The sales growth attainable is:

$$\text{Sustainable growth} = \frac{0.07(0.50)\ (1 + 0.5)}{0.65 - 0.07(0.50)\ (1 + 0.5)} = \frac{0.0525}{0.5975} = 8.8\%$$

This means that, given the marketing and financial policies of the firm, a sustainable growth rate of 8.8 percent is possible. If actual sales fall below this amount, then the firm has more than enough capital to meet its investment needs, and the excess capital can be used to reduce debt or increase dividends. If sales growth exceeds this amount, however, the firm will have to adjust its marketing and financial policies. Financial adjustments include increasing debt and reducing dividends. Marketing policy adjustments might include raising the net profit margin through average price increases or cost reductions (reflected in a changed product mix, for example) or attempting to reduce the assets necessary to generate a particular sales level (i.e., change the assets-to-sales ratio by increasing asset turnover).

The implication of these interdependencies is important to grasp: *growth must be managed.* Excessive growth will often necessitate increased debt or additional funding through equity markets unless internally generated cash from operations can fund growth. Unfortunately, increased debt and access to equity markets (selling shares) are not always possible. Such was the case with Tenneco, Inc., a large diversified firm.[18] Rapidly growing businesses in the energy field required large infusions of cash to fund the growth, but other businesses could not satisfy their cash needs. Additional debt was incurred at high interest costs, which in turn required cash to meet interest commitments. The final result was that Tenneco management sought to divest some of its businesses to provide the cash necessary to fund the growth businesses and retire existing debt.

Discounted Cash Flow

A second concept from finance is discounted cash flow. Discounted cash flow incorporates the theory of the time value of money, or present-value analysis. The idea behind the present value of money is that a dollar received next year is not equivalent to a dollar received today because the use of money has a value. To illustrate, if $500 can be invested today at 20 percent, $600 will be received a year later ($500 +

20% of $500). In other words, $600 to be received next year has a present value of $500 if 20 percent can be earned ($600 ÷ 120% = $500). Following this line of reasoning, the estimated results of an investment (e.g., a business) can be stated as a cash equivalent at the present time (i.e., its present value).

The discounted cash flow method employs this reasoning by evaluating the present value of a business's *cash flows* (cash inflows minus cash outflows). A simplified view of cash flow is "cash flow from operations," which is net income plus depreciation charges, since depreciation is a noncash charge against sales to determine net income.

The present value of a stream of cash flows is obtained by selecting an interest rate at which they are to be valued, or discounted, and a time period. The interest or discount is often defined by the *opportunity cost* of capital—the cost of earnings opportunities foregone by investing in a business as opposed to investing in securities such as Treasury Bills. In the mid-1980s, the opportunity cost ranged from 10 percent to 20 percent.

An application of discounted cash flow analysis illustrates the mechanics involved. Suppose, for example, that a firm is considering investing $105,000 in one of two businesses. The firm has forecast cash flows for each business over the next five years. The discount rate adopted by the firm is 15 percent.

Given the discount rate of 15 percent, the cash flow when the investment is made is a negative $105,000 (no cash inflows, only outflows). The first-year cash flow for business A is discounted by the factor $1/(1 + 0.15)^1$, or $25,000 × 0.870 = $21,700. The second-year cash flow for business A is discounted by the factor $1/(1 + 0.15)^2$, or $35,000 × 0.756 = $26,460, and so forth. Exhibit 11.3 shows the complete analysis for businesses A and B for the five-year planning horizon.

Three points are of particular interest. First, the key series of numbers is the *cumulative cash flow*. This series shows that the cumulative cash flows from business B are greater than from business A. Second, the *payback period* is two years for business B, as opposed to about three years for business A. In other words, business B will recover its investment sooner than business A. Finally, the *time value of money* is clearly indicated. Business A will produce a higher cash flow in later years than business B. However, the present value of these cash flows five years in the future, when discounted, is less than the value of the cash flows in the near future that business B will produce.

A valuable characteristic of present-value analysis is that the discount rates are additive. If the projected cash flows from an investment are equal over a specified time period, summing the discount rates for

EXHIBIT 11.3
Application of Cash Flow Analysis with a 15 Percent Discount Factor

Year	Discount Factor	Business A			Business B		
		Cash Flow	Cumulative Cash Flow	Discounted Cash Flow	Cash Flow	Cumulative Cash Flow	Discounted Cash Flow
0	1.000	($105,000)	($105,000)	($105,000)	($105,000)	($105,000)	($105,000)
1	0.870	25,000	(80,000)	21,750	50,000	(55,000)	43,500
2	0.756	35,000	(45,000)	26,460	55,000	0	41,580
3	0.658	50,000	5,000	32,900	60,000	60,000	39,480
4	0.572	70,000	75,000	40,040	65,000	125,000	37,180
5	0.497	90,000	165,000	44,730	70,000	195,000	34,790
Totals			$270,000	$17,380		$300,000	$44,010

649

each of the time periods (say three years) and multiplying this figure by the annual cash flow estimate will give the present value.

Suppose, for example, that a firm can expect a constant cash flow of $10 million per year for three years, and the discount rate is 10 percent. The present value of this cash flow can be computed as follows (in millions of dollars):

$$
\begin{aligned}
0.870 \times \$10 &= \quad\$8.70 \\
0.756 \times \$10 &= \quad\$7.56 \\
\underline{0.658 \times \$10} &= \quad\underline{\$6.58} \\
2.284 \times \$10 &= \$22.84
\end{aligned}
$$

Most basic finance textbooks contain tables that provide these numbers.

NOTES

1. "His Master's New Voice," *Time* (January 18, 1982), p. 49.

2. H. W. Boyd, Jr., and Jean-Claude Larréché, "The Foundations of Marketing Strategy," in R. Kerin and R. Peterson, eds., *Perspectives on Strategic Marketing Management*, 2nd ed. (Boston: Allyn and Bacon, 1983).

3. This view of strategy formulation is based on the works of C. Hofer and D. Schendel, *Strategy Formulation: Analytical Concepts* (St. Paul: West Publishing Company, 1978), and W. E. Rothchild, *Putting It All Together* (New York: AMACOM, 1976).

4. "Goodrich's Cash Cow Starts to Deliver," *Business Week* (November 14, 1977): 78–84.

5. "American Can's Big Shakeout," *Fortune* (August 24, 1981): 74–80.

6. "His Master's New Voice."

7. "Asset Redeployment," *Business Week* (August 24, 1981): 68–74.

8. Ibid.

9. "Colgate to Sell Non-Core Lines, Buy Back Stock," *Wall Street Journal* (August 1, 1985): 4.

10. Y. Wind, *Product Policy: Concepts, Methods and Strategy* (Reading Mass.: Addison-Wesley, 1982), pp. 108–148.

11. For a review of different portfolio approaches, see Y. Wind and V. Mahajan, "Designing Product and Business Portfolios," *Harvard Business Review* (January–February 1981): 155–165.

12. W. Kiechel III, "Playing by the Rules of the Corporate Strategy Game," *Fortune* (September 24, 1979): 110–115.

14. W. E. Cox, Jr., "Product Portfolio Strategy, Market Structure, and Performance," in H. Thorelli, ed., *Strategy + Structure = Performance* (Bloomington: Indiana University Press, 1977).

15. See the Liquid Paper Corporation case in this text.

16. "Atari Sells Itself to Survive Success," *Business Week* (November 15, 1976): 58.

17. This formulation of the sustainable growth model is described in R. Higgins and R. Kerin, "Managing the Growth-Financial Policy Nexus in Retailing," *Journal of Retailing* (Fall 1983): 19–48.

18. "Energy Growth Fuels Problems for a Conglomerate," *Business Week* (November 23, 1981): 80–91.

ADDITIONAL READINGS

Day, George. *Analysis for Strategic Market Decisions.* St. Paul: West, 1986.

Donaldson, Gordon. "Financial Goals and Strategic Consequences." *Harvard Business Review* (May–June 1985): 56–66.

Gluck, Frederick. "A Fresh Look at Strategic Management." *Journal of Business Strategy* (Fall 1985): 4–21.

Gupta, Anil, and Govindarajan, V. "Build, Hold, Harvest: Converting Strategic Intentions into Reality." *Journal of Business Strategy* (Winter 1984): 34–47.

Hamermesh, R. G., and White, R. E. "Manage beyond Portfolio Analysis." *Harvard Business Review* (January–February 1984): 103–109.

Haspeslagh, Philippe. "Portfolio Planning: Uses and Limits." *Harvard Business Review* (January–February 1982): 58–73.

Jacobson, Robert, and Aaker, David A. "Is Market Share All That It's Cracked Up to Be?" *Journal of Marketing* (Fall 1985): 11–22.

Kerin, Roger A., and Peterson, Robert A. *Perspectives on Strategic Marketing Management,* 2nd ed. Boston: Allyn and Bacon, 1983.

Wind, Yoram, and Mahajan, Vijay. "Designing Product and Business Portfolios." *Harvard Business Review* (January–February 1981): 155–165.

———— CASE ————

Zale

Corporation

THE ASSIGNMENT GIVEN Jack Olsen's marketing management class sounded easy enough when the instructor outlined the task. The assignment was as follows:

1. Choose a large, diversified corporation and prepare a description of its operations from published documents.

2. Describe the social, economic, technological, and competitive opportunity and threat environments in which it operates.

3. Outline a resource-allocation and market strategy statement for the corporation, with particular emphasis on the firm's growth opportunities in the context of the overall portfolio of businesses.

Jack selected the Zale Corporation for two reasons. First, having worked part time for a large, diversified retailing firm for two years, he was interested in a career in retailing. Second, he had just become engaged and had purchased the engagement ring at Zales Jewelers. The professionalism evident at Zales and the liberal credit terms provided him as a struggling student had impressed him.

This case was prepared from published sources, including Zale Corporation annual reports and 10-K reports. The information presented in the case does not necessarily depict the explicit situation faced by Zale Corporation or past operating procedures but is introduced only for the purpose of class discussion. Financial data referenced from noncompany sources have not been validated as to accuracy. Data presented on the retailing environment are based on a variety of sources including U.S. census data and the author's extrapolation of these data. The discussion of the retailing environment should not be interpreted as reflecting any research or views of the Zale Corporation. This case was prepared by Professor Roger A. Kerin, Edwin L. Cox School of Business, Southern Methodist University, solely as a basis for class discussion and is not designed to illustrate appropriate or inappropriate handling of administrative situations.

Shortly after he began to piece together published information on the Zale Corporation, he realized that the assignment and firm were much larger than he had expected. Zale Corporation sales exceeded $1 billion and had operations spanning the globe. The corporation was indeed a diversified firm with a variety of businesses ranging from drug stores to jewelry stores. "This is the kind of firm I would enjoy working for," he thought, "and now I'm going to chart its strategy for the 1980s."

ZALE CORPORATION

Zale Corporation is one of the largest diversified specialty retailing firms in the United States and the world's leading retailer of jewelry merchandise. Sales for combined operations exceeded $1 billion during the 1980 fiscal year ending March 31, 1980. A three-year financial summary is shown in Exhibit 1.

Company Background

The present-day Zale Corporation traces its beginnings to 1924, when Morris B. Zale and William Zale opened Zales Jewelers in Wichita

EXHIBIT 1
Zale Corporation Consolidated Financial Statements
(thousands of dollars)

Abbreviated Income Statements
(Year Ended March 31)

	1980	1979	1978
Sales	$1,041,699	$904,464	$790,556
Costs and expenses:			
Cost of goods sold	662,359	600,856	527,939
Administrative, publicity, and selling	279,531	229,304	200,283
Interest	12,698	9,398	7,173
Amortization of gain on sale of corporate office building	1,950	10,549	—
Earnings from continuing operations before income taxes	89,061	75,455	55,161
Income taxes	35,036	32,450	26,808
Net earnings	$ 54,025	$ 43,005	$ 28,353

(continued)

EXHIBIT 1 *(continued)*

Abbreviated Balance Sheets

	1980	1979	1978
Assets			
Current assets			
Cash	$ 13,043	$ 15,166	$ 19,070
Trade receivables	175,106	131,331	115,143
Less allowance for doubtful accounts	(11,022)	(4,804)	(3,553)
Merchandise inventories	396,235	324,947	292,475
Other current assets	9,679	36,580	4,024
Total current assets	$ 583,041	$504,220	$427,159
Other assets	$ 33,536	23,198	19,088
Property and equipment (at cost), less accumulated amortization and depreciation	101,425	82,448	87,919
Total assets	$ 718,002	$609,866	$534,166
Liabilities and shareholders investment			
Current liabilities	$ 234,729	$173,012	$138,759
Long-term debt	103,433	55,046	54,745
Deferred gain from sale of corporate office building	10,287	12,237	—
Shareholders investment	369,553	369,571	340,662
Total liabilities and shareholders investment	$ 718,002	$609,866	$534,166

Falls, Texas. Both men remain as emeritus officers in the Zale Corporation.

From its beginnings, the company philosophy has rested on three pillars. Its merchandising philosophy held that Zales Jewelers would carry many types of goods other than jewelry.[a] Thus Zales Jewelers carried a brand line of merchandise—small appliances, cameras, cookware, and other complementary items—that set it apart from many competitors.

Its marketing philosophy emphasized two factors: heavy advertising and credit. On its opening day in Wichita Falls, Texas, Zales Jewelers recorded sales of $427.25, and of that amount $368.50 was on credit. Finally, the company has always placed great trust in its em-

---

[a]This strategy was modified in the late 1970s, when Zale Corporation removed nonjewelry merchandise from jewelry stores. Nonjewelry merchandise is now carried by other divisions.

ployees. This philosophy was and is unique in the jewelry business since jewelry, and particularly diamond goods, is exceptionally vulnerable to theft.

The company experienced a steady thirty-six-year growth in sales volume following a strategy focused on jewelry and related items. However, in 1960 General Electric announced it had discovered a process for manufacturing synthetic diamonds. The possibility of a market glutted with synthetic diamonds prompted a diversification program in the 1960s aimed at acquiring firms engaged in specialized retailing in other fields.

The first acquisition was Skillern Drug Company, a regional specialty drug store chain, in 1965. The diversification program continued during the 1960s to include Butler Shoe Company, a specialty shoe store chain, and a number of sporting goods firms, including Cullum and Boren, Cook, Zinik, and Housport. Levine's, a budget-fashion–merchandising store chain, was also acquired, as was Karotkin's, a furniture store chain. Zale Corporation subsequently sold Levine's in 1977 and Karotkin's in 1978.

In 1978 Zale Corporation formally articulated its mission, which emphasized a focus on specialty retailing and outlined its framework for long-range planning that promoted:

1. Strengthening and improving existing lines of business
2. Pursuing additional lines of business
3. Expanding in the international market
4. Taking opportunism as a business attitude

In 1979 the Zale Corporation prepared a detailed introspective study to assess its competitive position, and in 1980 the company exceeded $1 billion in sales and achieved record earnings of $50 million. In addition to acquisitions of thirty-four additional jewelry units in 1980, the Zale Corporation recorded the largest increase in net new stores through internal expansion in a decade.

Current Operating Divisions

Zale Corporation has four primary lines of business as of March 31, 1980: (1) jewelry, (2) footwear, (3) drug, and (4) general merchandise. The corporation currently operates 1,845 retail stores in forty-nine states, the District of Columbia, Puerto Rico, Guam, and the United Kingdom. A brief description of each line of business follows:

Jewelry
The jewelry business produced sales of $692.4 million, or 66.5 percent of total Zale Corporation sales, in fiscal 1980. About 11,000

EXHIBIT 2
Financial Summary of the Jewelry Business
(thousands of dollars)

	1980	1979	1978	1977
Sales	692,411	581,318	485,778	411,156
Operating profit	109,757	80,932	61,820	65,938
Assets	579,277	450,352	388,039	359,584
Net capital expenditures	24,373	14,774	7,002	10,461
Amortization and depreciation	10,035	7,655	6,626	5,840

Source: Zale Corporation annual reports.

Notes:

1. Operating profit and assets of the jewelry business on March 31, 1979 (end of fiscal year) reflect the change in pricing of certain nondiamond jewelry inventories from the FIFO (first in, first out) to the LIFO (last in, first out) method. This change had the effect of reducing operating profit and merchandise inventories by $2,004,000.

2. Operating profit and assets of the jewelry business at March 31, 1978, reflect the change in pricing of substantially all diamond merchandise inventories from the FIFO to the LIFO method. This change had the effect of reducing operating profit and diamond merchandise inventories by $27,379,000.

3. Operating profit was determined as follows. *Operating profits are those con-*tributed by the various merchandise groups without allocation of interest income, interest expense, profit-sharing contribution, corporate general and administrative expense, and income taxes. All significant intercompany sales and profits have been eliminated from the above calculations (Zale Corporation 1977 annual report). This definition of operating profit applies to all lines of business.

persons are employed in the jewelry-related business. A four-year summary of the financial performance of the jewelry business is shown in Exhibit 2.

The business is divided into retail operations and "other" operations. Retail operations consist of five divisions, each of which markets diamonds, gold jewelry, watches, silver, fine china, glassware, and complementary merchandise. The Zale Jewelers Division operates 760 outlets in forty-eight states and Puerto Rico, with the average store size being 2,000 square feet. The merchandise carried is principally in the medium price range. This division accounted for 51 percent of the sales of the jewelry business. The Fine Jewelers Guild Division operates 305 stores and one leased department in thirty-seven states and Guam under various trade names (Corrigans; Selco, Inc.; Wiss & Lamberg; and Litwin Co.). The average store size is 3,200 square feet. The merchandise carried is in the higher price range. The Leased Jewelry Division operates seventy-five units in fourteen states under the names of the stores in which they are located. This division also operates eighteen stores under the name Mission Jewelers in five states. Merchandise in this division is principally in the popular price range, and the average store size is 2,000 square feet. The Catalog Division operates thirteen showrooms (average showroom size is 30,000 square feet) in six states under the O. G. Wilson name. This division sells sporting goods, appliances, electronics, cameras, luggage, and other items in addition to items marketed through other jewelry divisions. The merchandise carried is in the medium to higher price range. Zales Jewellers Limited operates sixty stores in the United Kingdom under the names Zales Jewellers, Maxwell Jewellers, and Leslie Davis Jewellers and sells merchandise principally in the medium price range. The average store size is 1,200 square feet.

Zale Corporation also engages in the purchasing, processing, and assembling of diamond and other jewelry-related merchandise. The corporation operates facilities in New York, Puerto Rico, and Tel Aviv for cutting and polishing diamonds and assembling jewelry items. The Ross Watch Case Division manufactures watch cases and other components for the company and sells to retailers and watch assemblers. In addition, the company, through its International Diamond Division, sells precious gems to retailers and suppliers throughout the world.

Drug

The drug business produced sales of $148.7 million in fiscal 1980, which represented 14.3 percent of total corporation sales. Approximately 3,000 persons were employed in this business. A four-year summary of the drug business is shown in Exhibit 3.

EXHIBIT 3
Financial Summary of the Drug Business
(thousands of dollars)

	1980	1979	1978	1977
Sales	148,704	126,257	111,568	97,445
Operating profit	(291)	543	2,462	4,659
Assets	43,841	38,393	33,714	31,183
Net capital expenditures	933	1,864	630	2,619
Amortization and depreciation	1,160	1,051	1,010	820

Source: Zale Corporation annual reports.

Note: Operating profit and assets of the drug business on March 31, 1979, reflect the change in pricing of drug merchandise from the FIFO to the LIFO method. This change had the effect of reducing the operating profit and merchandise inventories by $1,379,000.

The drug business consists of two divisions. The Skillern Drug Division operates 146 drug stores in New Mexico and Texas. The average store contains 3,100 square feet. Skillern Drug Stores sell prescription and over-the-counter drugs, cosmetics, health and beauty aids, candy, tobacco, photographic supplies, and numerous complementary products. An article in the *Wall Street Journal* (October 15, 1980) stated that sales of this division were about $142.2 million in fiscal 1980. The Aeroplex Division operates fifteen news, tobacco, and gift stands in the Dallas-Fort Worth Regional Airport. The average unit contains 800 square feet.

Footwear

The footwear business employed 4,000 persons and recorded sales of $136.8 million, or 13.1 percent of total corporation sales, in fiscal 1980. Exhibit 4 gives a four-year summary of the footwear business financial performance.

The footwear business is composed of two divisions. The Butler Shoe Division has 385 stores in thirty-five states, Washington, D.C., and Puerto Rico. The stores are variously named Butler's, Hot Feet, or Maling Brothers, and the average store size is 3,100 square feet. The merchandise in these units consists of ladies' and children's shoes, ladies' hosiery and handbags, and shoe cleaners. The Self-Service Shoe Division operates in twelve states with thirty leased departments under the name of the stores in which they are located. The typical size of a shoe department is 3,000 square feet. This division sells popular-price shoes for the entire family.

General Merchandise

The general-merchandise business employed 1,000 persons and achieved sales of $63.8 million, or 6.1 percent of total corporation sales,

EXHIBIT 4
Financial Summary of the Footwear Business
(thousands of dollars)

	1980	1979	1978	1977
Sales	136,827	123,089	116,927	98,001
Operating profit	17,567	15,486	15,696	11,499
Assets	56,083	47,850	41,382	36,669
Net capital expenditures	6,615	3,671	3,588	4,906
Amortization and depreciation	2,666	2,178	1,942	1,610

Source: Zale Corporation annual reports.

EXHIBIT 5
Financial Summary of the
General Merchandise Business
(thousands of dollars)

	1980	1979	1978	1977
Sales	63,757	73,800	76,283	71,225
Operating profit	939	(788)	1,163	2,949
Assets	28,385	25,589	35,387	38,263
Net capital expenditures	1,472	(989)	746	357
Amortization and depreciation	743	796	861	849

Source: Zale Corporation annual reports.

Note: During October 1978, Zale Corporation sold the inventory, receivables, and certain other assets of the Home Furnishing Division at a loss of approximately $700,000.

in fiscal 1980. Exhibit 5 gives a four-year summary of the general merchandise business financial performance.

The general-merchandise business consists of two divisions. The Sporting Goods Division operates thirty-seven stores in nine states under a variety of store names (e.g., Cullum and Boren). The average store carries a complete assortment of sporting goods, including sportswear, and contains 14,000 square feet. According to a *Wall Street Journal* article (September 22, 1982), the sporting goods division had about $35 million in sales in 1980. The Sugarman Division is a wholesaler of consumer electronics, jewelry, optical goods, and military insignia and accessories. The Home Furnishing Division, consisting of eleven stores in Texas, was divested in 1978. This division produced sales of $29.556 million in 1977.

The number of stores operated by the Zale Corporation in fiscal 1977 through fiscal 1980 is shown in Exhibit 6. Approximately 62 percent of the stores in the United States are located in the southern tier of states and California known as the Sunbelt.

Zale Corporation sales are seasonal, with peaks coinciding with major holidays such as Christmas, Easter, and Mother's Day and with the back-to-school selling season. The seasonality in sales requires large inventory levels to meet the demand at these sales peaks.

Selected Performance Measures

Zale Corporation strives for balanced performance in three areas: (1) operating results, (2) asset management, and (3) investment perform-

EXHIBIT 6
Number of Operating Stores

Division	1980	1979	1978	1977
Zale Jewelers Division	760	722	692	671
Fine Jewelers Guild Division	306	261	245	244
Leased Jewelry Division	93	65[a]	117	111
Catalog Division	13	12	11	13
Zales Jewellers, Ltd. (United Kingdom)	60	51	42	37
Home Furnishings Division	—	—	11	11
Sporting Goods Division	37	32	36	33
Aeroplex Division	15	14	13	13
Butler Shoe Division	385	359	349	351
Self-Service Shoe Division	30	45	47	48
Skillern Drug Division	146	143	117	112
Total	1,845	1,704	1,680	1,644

Source: Zale Corporation 10-K reports.

[a]The number of leased jewelry operations was reduced as the division completed its planned strategy of lessening its involvement in discount stores and placing more emphasis on department stores. Most of the discount store departments were in Woolco stores. Jewelry departments were subsequently opened in Dillard's Department Stores in the southwestern United States.

EXHIBIT 7
Selected Zale Corporation Performance Measures

Operating results	1978	1979	1980
Sales growth	16.6%	14.4%	15.2%
Gross margin	33.2%	33.6%	36.4%
Operating expense ratio (percent of sales)	25.3%	25.4%	26.8%
Return on sales	3.6%	4.8%	5.2%

Asset management	1978	1979	1980
Accounts receivable turnover	2.3	2.1	2.0
Inventory turnover	1.8	1.9	1.8
Long-term debt (millions)	$54.7	$55.0	$103.4

Investment performance	1978	1979	1980
Dividends per share	$.91	$.98	$1.06
Earnings per share	$2.11	$3.21	$4.50
Return on shareholder's investment	8.5%	12.1%	14.6%

Source: Zale Corporation annual report, fiscal 1980.

ance. A summary of published performance measures is shown in Exhibit 7 for the 1978, 1979, and 1980 fiscal years.[b]

During the 1980 fiscal year, Zale Corporation, like all businesses, was faced with unprecedented interest costs. On March 31, 1980, the interest rate was 19.5 percent. These costs are reflected in the corporation's income statement. Furthermore, Zale Corporation, again like all businesses that provide extensive credit, experienced a sizable increase in bad debts. Furthermore, the collection time on accounts receivable increased.

THE RETAILING ENVIRONMENT

The retailing environment of the late 1970s and for the foreseeable future can be characterized as turbulent. The combination of recession, continuing inflation, and high interest rates during 1980 produced a bleak retail sales picture. Retail sales in the United States rose from an estimated $886 billion in 1979 to an estimated $948 billion in 1980—a 7 percent increase. By comparison, the Consumer Price Index increased 12 percent during the 1979–1980 period.

Inventory—typically a major current asset of retailers—has become a costly asset with rising interest rates. Accordingly, retailers have emphasized inventory turnover as a performance measure. The principal retailing strategy in recent years has been the move toward high-turnover and high-markup merchandise and away from slow-moving, low-markup products in an effort to increase sales per square foot and, ultimately, return on assets.

This retailing strategy is apparent in the growth of specialty retail stores and the popularity of leased departments in full-line department

---

[b]The Zale Corporation adopted the LIFO (last-in, first-out) method of inventory valuation in 1978 fiscal year. Prior to 1978, the FIFO (first-in, last-out) method of inventory valuation was used. LIFO inventory valuation is based on the assumption that the last items acquired in inventory are the first items sold. FIFO is based on the assumption that the first items added to inventory are the first items sold. LIFO more closely matches current costs of inventory items with current revenues during periods of rising prices. LIFO is used for jewelry and drug merchandise inventories; FIFO is still used for footwear and general merchandise.

The effect of this change in inventory valuation during periods of rising prices (inflation) is to increase the cost of goods sold, thereby decreasing the gross margin percent. This in turn will decrease the return on sales percent. Inventory turnover is increased due to these changes. Fully 77 percent of all company inventories are valued using the LIFO method.

Therefore, performance measures such as gross margin percent, inventory turnover, return on sales, and return on shareholders investment for the 1979 and 1980 fiscal years are not comparable with those of previous fiscal years. Other performance measures discussed here are not materially affected by the method of inventory valuation.

EXHIBIT 8
Selected Performance Measures of Specialty Retailers
Arranged by the Geographical Scope of Operations

Operating Characteristic	Geographical Scope[a]		
	Local	Regional	National
Gross margin	36.6%	30.0%	42.2%
Inventory turnover (sales cost of goods sold ÷ average inventory)	3.1	4.2	2.8
Sales/store (thousands) (annual sales ÷ number of stores)	$2,608	$820	$883
Sales/total assets (annual sales ÷ total assets)	2.2	2.7	2.2
Return on sales (annual net profit after tax ÷ annual sales × 100)	0.23%	2.42%	4.45%
Return on assets (annual net profit ÷ total assets)	2.41%	5.81%	7.90%

Source: Richard Miller, "Strategic Pathways to Growth in Retailing," *Journal of Business Strategy,* (Winter 1981):16–29. Reproduced with permission of the author.

[a]*Local specialty retailers* were those operating in up to five contiguous states whose markets and demographics were reasonably homogeneous. *Regional specialty retailers* were those who operated beyond five contiguous states or served demographically heterogeneous markets but did not serve all major regions and the top twenty SMSAs. *National specialty retailers* were defined as those firms that served all major regions and had representation in the top twenty SMSAs.

stores. The results of a recent study, examining the performance of local, regional, and national specialty stores for the period 1974–1978, are shown in Exhibit 8. The results reported include firms in a variety of retailing specialties. Leased departments currently account for about 6 percent of total department store sales. The most popular leased departments are sewing machines, wigs and hair goods, shoes, and watches and fine jewelry. About 65 percent of the 2,047 traditional department store companies in the United States lease out their shoe operation.[1]

Jewelry Retailing

Jewelry retailing faced a variety of shocks during the 1979–1980 period. The price of gold increased from $300 per ounce in June 1979 to $850 per ounce in January 1980. The escalating price of gold sparked widespread consumer interest in gold and gold jewelry, and jewelry retailers generally recorded extraordinary sales dollar gains even though unit volume remained stable or declined for many retailers. The price of gold continued to rise until the autumn of 1980, which made the financing of inventories at rising interest rates very costly. As the price of gold declined, jewelers were forced to offer substantial markdowns. A similar, though less dramatic, change occurred in silver prices. Silver was priced at $6–$8 per ounce during most of 1979, but rose rapidly to $50 per ounce in January 1980, before falling to $10.80 per ounce in March 1980.

The uncertain economic picture resulted in greater popularity of "hard assets" among the buying public, however. The extent to which consumers will retain this hard-asset mentality is not known.

There are an estimated 35,000 jewelry stores in the United States. These stores accounted for $8 billion in retail sales. The Zale Corporation is purported to be the world's leading retailer of jewelry merchandise.

Drugstore Retailing

Three major drugstore chains in 1979 were Walgreens, Eckerd Drug, and Revco Discount Drug Centers. Walgreens operates approximately 690 drugstores, with a high percentage located in the Midwest. Eckerd Drug operates about 1,000 drugstores located primarily in Florida, North Carolina, and Texas. Revco Discount Drug Centers operates some 1,200 discount drugstores in a twenty-four-state area, ranging from New York to Florida and from the eastern seaboard to Arizona.

Drugstores in the United States produced retail sales of approximately $30 billion. Drugstores affiliated with chains accounted for over half of this total (*Drug Store News*, May 1979). Texas and New Mexico alone accounted for about 2 percent of total drugstore sales. There were approximately 50,000 drugstores in the United States in 1977.

An evolution in drugstore retailing is under way.[2] The movement is away from the conventional drugstore concept toward the super drugstore or combination food stores and drugstores. The conventional drugstore chain unit operates with 7,500 square feet, generates annual sales of $1 million per unit, and has as its principal market focus health care and general merchandise. The super drugstore operates with 25,000 square feet, generates annual sales of $5 million per unit, and has as its principal market focus broad general merchandise at low prices. The combination food store and drugstore located in or adjacent to a supermarket emphasizes one-stop shopping for a wide variety of food and general merchandise. The average size of a new drugstore exceeds 15,000 square feet (*Chain Store Age Executive*, August 1980).

Sporting Goods and Footwear Retailing

Sporting goods retailers are divided into two groups. General-line sporting goods stores carry a variety of merchandise including athletic equipment, sportswear, footwear, and related items. General-line sporting goods retailers number about 8,000 and produce sales of about $3 billion. Specialty sporting goods stores carry limited lines of merchandise and typically focus on a particular sport or complementary sports. These stores include golf shops; ski-related stores; and tennis, handball, and racketball stores. Specialty sporting goods retailers number about 10,000 and produce sales of about $2.3 billion.

The estimated shoe store volume is $8 billion; approximately 30,000 shoe stores operate in the United States. Kinney Shoe Corporation, a division of F. W. Woolworth, is the largest shoe store chain under one name in the United States. The Melville Corporation is also a major competitor in footwear retailing with footwear departments in K-Mart stores throughout the United States. The company also operates the popular-priced Thom McAn specialty shoe stores. The average size of new shoe stores is approximately 3,000 square feet.

Both sporting goods and footwear retailing practices are evolving, but in a direction directly opposite to drug retailing, Rather than broadened lines and larger units, as evident in drug retailing, sporting goods and footwear retailing is experiencing the "superspecialist." For example, Tennis Lady is a superspecialist store selling only ladies' expensive, high-fashion tennis apparel. The Foot Locker and Athlete's Foot are superspecialists in footwear retailing.

DRAFTING A RESOURCE ALLOCATION AND MARKET STRATEGY

Having completed the first two parts of his assignment, Jack began to consider how he might draft a resource-allocation and market strategy for Zale Corporation. His reading indicated that all Zale Corporation businesses were in specialty retailing of one form or another. Furthermore, all businesses were in retailing sectors or geographical areas that were growing. He estimated that the annual growth of the U.S. retail jewelry business was about 13 percent; the retail drug business, 10 percent (12 percent in the Southwest); the retail footwear business, 10 percent; and the retail sporting goods business, 14 percent.[c] But the

---

[c]These growth rates were determined from the *1977 Census of Retail Trade.* Growth rates were extrapolated to 1980. The growth rates are not adjusted for inflation. All figures are based on total U.S. sales, except where indicated.

various businesses of Zale Corporation were quite different, he thought. For example, jewelry retailing was characterized by high retail margins and low inventory turnover when compared with drug retailing, which seemed to be a lower-margin, higher-turnover business. Jack had not decided how to include this factor in his analysis.

More important, Jack knew that whatever resource-allocation and market strategy he recommended, it would have to include where and how Zale Corporation might grow in the 1980s. Was it in the jewelry business, the drug business, the footwear business, the general-merchandise business, or in some combination of businesses? Where were the growth opportunities? Moreover, how could growth be accomplished? For example, should geographical expansion be considered since the majority of Zale Corporation store units were situated in the southern tier of states?

Underlying these considerations and others he had noted was the need for a clear understanding of Zale Corporation's distinctive competency before any recommendations could be made. Finally, he knew that any recommendation would necessitate all the financial documentation he could produce from the published data he had before him.

NOTES

1. L. Spalding, "Footwear: To Lease or Own?" *Stores* (July 1979): 16.

2. A. Bates, "Three New Store Formats Will Soon Dominate Drug Retailing," *Marketing News* (March 7, 1980): 9.

Norton Company

Subject to the business cycle swings of the capital goods industry, Norton Company experienced the usual drop in sales during the economic downturn of 1975. What was unusual for Norton was its ability on this occasion to sustain profits compared to the customary plunge in earnings whenever the economy dipped. Robert Cushman, president and chief executive officer of Norton Company, saw this performance as evidence of the growing effectiveness of Norton's strategic planning.

As of 1976, five years' efforts had gone into developing planning activities that specifically could help top management shape strategies for the firm's diversified business operations. Mr. Cushman was pleased with the results of these efforts:

> Our strategic planning has made a tremendous difference in the way the company is now managed. It gives us a much-needed handle to evaluate strategies for each of our many businesses.

One of the difficult strategic planning decisions faced by top management in 1976 concerned a reevaluation of the long-term strategy for the coated abrasives business operations in the United States. This situation is described following a general explanation of the strategic planning process at Norton Company and how it came to be.

THE COMPANY

Norton Company, headquartered in Worcester, Massachusetts, was a multinational industrial manufacturer with 85 plant locations in 21 countries. The firm employed almost 19,000 persons.

This case was prepared by Professor Francis Aguilar with the assistance of Norton Company to serve as a basis for class discussion rather than to illustrate either effective or ineffective handling of an administrative situation. Copyright © 1979 by the President and Fellows of Harvard College.

As the world's largest abrasives manufacturer, Norton produced both abrasive-grain raw materials and finished products. The latter included such items as sandpaper and grinding wheels. The company also produced a wide range of other industrial products, including industrial ceramics, sealants, catalyst carriers, and tower packings for the chemical process industries; engineered plastic components, tubing, and related products for medical applications and for food processing; and industrial safety products. In 1975 these other products accounted for about 27 percent of the reported total sales of $548 million.[a] Exhibit 1 contains a five-year summary of financial results.

Organization

Norton Company was organized into "low growth" and "high growth" product groups. This organizational structure reflected two basic corporate objectives. The first was to remain the worldwide leader in abrasives. The second was to improve profitability through "a limited number of diversified product lines and without conglomeration."[b]

When introducing this structure in 1971, Cushman had remarked:

> As you look at Norton Co. you see two major areas of business: our traditional abrasives products, which are good cash generators but have low growth, and our newer nonabrasive lines, which need cash but have high growth potential. We need a different type of manager to run each area.

Harry Duane, age forty-five, headed the abrasives group. His job was characterized as that of "running a large, cyclical-prone, slow-growth business with stiff competition in many different markets." Successful performance in this business was said to depend on careful cost control, keeping products up to date, and holding established markets. Duane had had experience in the abrasives business abroad as well as in the United States since joining Norton in 1957.

Donald R. Melville, age fifty, headed Norton's diversified products business group. He had joined the company in 1967 as vice-president of marketing after having served in various marketing capacities

---

[a]On September 9, 1976, Norton Company announced an agreement in principle to merge with Christensen, Inc., for stock valued at $100 million. Christensen, with 1975 sales of $118 million and net income of $9.5 million, manufactured diamond-drilling bits and coring bits for the petroleum and mining industries. With Christensen, nonabrasive products would account for about 40 percent of total sales.

[b]The *Norton Company Annual Report* for 1975 also highlighted three other corporate objectives: (1) to maintain responsible corporate citizenship, which at times means accepting lower profits; (2) to maintain a superior employee working environment; and (3) to enhance the value of Norton stock.

EXHIBIT 1
Norton Company: Five-Year Financial Summary

	1971	1972	1973	1974	1975
Net sales ($ millions)	346	374	475	558	548
Net income ($ millions)[a]	11.4	14.5	25.4	21.6	20.9
Net income, excluding effect of foreign currency exchange rate changes ($ millions)[a]	10.3	15.0	21.3	25.1	24.8
By line of business (%):					
Abrasives					
Sales	70	75	75	75	73
Net income	85	87	89	76	70
Diversified products					
Sales	30	25	25	25	27
Net income	15	13	11	24	30
By subsidiaries outside the United States (%):					
Sales (%)	41	41	42	45	49
Net income (%)	39	33	56	56	40
Working capital ($ millions)	148	151	155	159	200
Total debt ($ millions)	69	65	66	102	112
Shareholders' equity ($ millions)	211	218	232	244	255
Operating and financial ratios:					
Net income as percentage of sales	3.3	3.9	5.3	3.9	3.8
Net income as percentage of equity	5.4	6.7	10.9	8.8	8.2
Current ratio	3.7	3.6	2.9	2.3	3.3
Percentage total debt to equity	33	30	29	42	44
Per share statistics[b]					
Net income[a]	2.12	2.70	4.70	4.02	3.85
Net income, excluding effect of foreign currency exchange rate changes[a]	1.92	2.80	3.94	4.68	4.57
Dividends	1.50	1.50	1.50	1.575	1.70
Stock price (NYSE)	27–37	32–39	23–36	19–29	21–29

Source: Annual reports and Moody's Industrial Manual, 1975.

[a]Exchange gains and losses resulting from the translation of foreign currency financial statements were included for the first time in the 1975 annual report in determining net income in accordance with a new procedure recommended by the Financial Accounting Standards Board (FASB). The net income results excluding foreign currency effects conform to prior reporting practices at Norton and generally throughout industry.

[b]The average number of shares of common stock outstanding varied between 5.37 million and 5.67 million during this period.

with Continental Can Company, Scott Paper Company, and Dunlop Tire & Rubber. As reported in *Business Week:*

> Melville's management style relies on creating an entrepreneurial atmosphere that will allow people to operate where they are not bogged down by a formal line-management reporting system. "In the case of abrasives," says Melville, "you compensate your people on the basis of whether or not they make that month's budget. In diversified products, you don't care as much about a month's budget—you try to double your sales in 12 months."[c]

The 1976 company organization structure is shown in Exhibit 2.

CONCEPTS FOR STRATEGIC PLANNING

In 1967, as executive vice-president in charge of companywide operations, Cushman faced the problem of assessing the role each of some seventy-five product lines was to play in Norton's future. The conventional corporate long-range planning then in use at Norton was found wanting for this task. Mr. Cushman consequently began to search for more appropriate ways to plan multibusiness operations. He later remarked:

> During the early sixties, Peter Drucker, widely known spokesman, critic, and analyst to business, began to describe business in terms of certain variables which seemed to determine a company's future. But it was Fred Borch, marketing vice-president of the highly diversified General Electric, who in 1960 asked the key question and then assigned two members of his staff, Jack McKitterick and Dr. Sidney Schoeffler, to find the answer. "Why is it," he said, "that through the years some of our businesses fail while others succeed? There must be certain decisions, strategies, or factors which lead to certain results. With hundreds of products ranging from electric pencil sharpeners to diesel engines and nuclear plants, it is difficult to do an effective job of planning. It is, in fact, impossible for management to have a direct, personal feeling and knowledge about so many business environments. We need better guidelines."

In 1967 Dr. Schoeffler was invited to Norton to describe the results of GE's "profitability optimization" study. Based on sophisticated multiple regression analyses covering ten years' experience for 150 product lines at General Electric, Dr. Schoeffler had been able to identify some 37 factors that accounted for more than 80 percent of the variations in profit results. The findings showed how profitability var-

EXHIBIT 2
Partial Organization Chart, June 1976

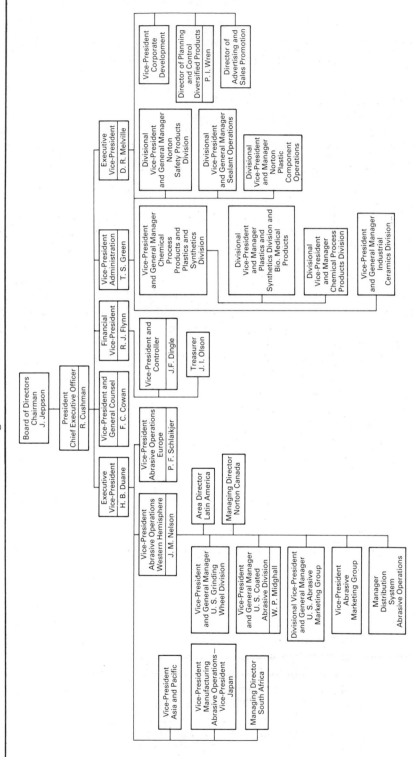

ied with respect to such factors as market share, market growth rate, and the level of investments required. The findings also showed how profitability varied with respect to policies on such matters as research and development as a percentage of sales, marketing expenditures, product quality, and pricing.[d] Mr. Cushman was struck with the relevance and concreteness of the resulting guidelines.

In his search for better guidelines, Mr. Cushman also became interested in the work of Bruce Henderson, founder and president of the Boston Consulting Group. Based on the premise that costs decreased with experience in a predictable manner, Henderson held that the firm with the greatest volume should have the lowest costs for a given product line. Market share served as a measure of relative volume for planning purposes.

The cash flows associated with growth and mature industries constituted a second element of Henderson's approach. Product lines with leading market shares in mature industries were generators of surplus cash; those in growth industries represented the potential cash generators for future years. For diversified business operations, Henderson urged that attention be given in strategic planning to the creation of a portfolio in which some product lines could generate sufficient cash throw-off to nourish the development and growth of other product lines in growing markets.

STRATEGIC PLANNING AT NORTON

The basic building block for planning continued to be the strategy analysis for individual product lines. This analysis considered a wide range of business factors such as competitive conditions, technology, and future trends, and concluded with a proposed course of action over time. Each strategy was prepared by the manager holding profit responsibilty for the product line and was evaluated by group and corporate line management. The customary analysis and review of strategy were extended to include two additional tests based on the somewhat related sets of concepts described earlier.

One of these additional tests concerned the intrinsic profit potential for a business. Based on experiential data for a wide range of businesses (such as had been generated for General Electric), Norton was able to ascertain a measure of the profit level appropriate for a business as it existed. It was also able to ascertain the extent to which

---

[d]Examples of profit determinants would include: (1) high marketing expenditures damage profitability when product quality is low; (2) high R&D spending hurts profitability when market share is small but increases ROI when market share is high; and (3) high marketing expenditures hurt ROI in investment-intensive businesses.

profits and cash flows might be increased under alternative strategies. These financial norms helped management to evaluate how well a business was being run and how much additional potential it had.

A business strategy was also evaluated in the context of total corporate cash flows. The strategy had to conform to the overall avail-abilities of, or needs for, cash. For this purpose, market share perform-ance served as a major controlling device. In broad terms, businesses were assigned the task of building, holding, or harvesting market share. *Building strategies* were based on active efforts to increase mar-ket share by means of new product introductions, added marketing programs, and the like. Such strategies customarily called for cash in-puts. *Holding strategies* were aimed at maintaining the existing level of market share. Net cash flows might be negative for rapidly growing markets and positive for slowly growing markets. *Harvesting strat-egies* sought to achieve earnings and cash flows by permitting market share to decline.

In line with this approach, Norton's operations had been divided into some sixty businesses whose characteristics were sufficiently dif-ferent to warrant the development of individual business strategies. These subdivisions were known as substrategic business units. Combi-nations of these substrategic business units were grouped into about thirty strategic business units for purposes of top-management review.

Strategy Guidance Committee

In April 1972 Cushman formed a top-management committee to assist in the evaluation of these business strategies. As Cushman later re-ported to the Norton Board:

> The function of the Strategy Guidance Committee is to review at appro-priate levels the strategy of each business unit, to make certain it does fit corporate objectives, and to monitor how effectively its strategy is being carried out. It provides the executive, regional, and division manager an opportunity for an "outside" peer group to examine and advise.
>
> The committee totals 12: the president, the executive vice president, the regional vice presidents, the financial vice-president, the controller, the vice president of corporate development, and Graham Wren as secre-tary. Depending on the circumstances, business units are reviewed on a two-year cycle. Well-documented strategies along standard lines are sent to members for review before meetings.

Each strategic business unit was responsible for preparing a strat-egy book for review. Copies of this book were distributed to members of the Strategy Guidance Committee at least one week prior to the scheduled review. To focus attention on the critical issues, Cushman had set the following ground rules for the review session:

No formal presentation is required at the meeting because each committee member is expected to have thoroughly studied the strategy book.

Discussion during the meeting will generally center around these questions:

1. Questions of facts, trends, and assumptions as presented in the strategy book.
2. Questions as to the appropriateness of the mission of the business in terms of *build, maintain,* or *harvest.*
3. Questions as to the appropriateness of the strategy in the context of the facts and mission.
4. Questions suggested by Profit Impact of Marketing Strategies [PIMS] analysis.
5. How does the business unit and its strategy fit and relate to similar businesses within Norton (e.g., coated abrasives Europe versus coated abrasives worldwide)?
6. How does the business unit and its strategy fit within the corporate portfolio and strategy?

INVOLVEMENT OF LINE MANAGERS

The involvement of key line managers in the Strategy Guidance Committee and the methodology used in generating the strategy books gave a distinct line orientation to planning at Norton. Management for each business unit had to take a position concerning its mission, strengths and weaknesses, likely competitive developments, trends, and finally its strategy. The analysis and recommendations had to stand the test of critical evaluation by an experienced and involved top management.

Although Cushman was pleased with the planning tools Norton had developed, he felt that the deep involvement of line managers in both the formulation and review of strategies served to prevent a mechanical or otherwise undue reliance on the planning tools themselves. He believed it highly desirable that an operating manager's "gut feel" remain an important input to strategic planning.

Other Elements Related to Strategic Planning

In 1976 detailed cash flow models that could be used to support and extend the analysis described earlier were being completed. Several Norton managers remarked that these models would contribute importantly to the strategic planning efforts.

Also, Norton's incentive system was designed to motivate managers in carrying out their assigned strategic moves—whether to build, maintain, or harvest their business. Cushman reported the use of over fifty different custom-tailored plans for this purpose.

Finally, Cushman's deep-seated involvement in the strategic planning process and the respect he commanded from other senior-level managers at Norton undoubtedly influenced this process in major ways.

COATED ABRASIVES DOMESTIC

One of the difficult cases for consideration by the Strategy Guidance Committee in 1976 concerned a reevaluation of the strategy to be followed for the U.S. coated abrasives business.[e] Coated Abrasives Domestic (CAD), one of Norton's larger operating divisions, had had a recent history of declining market share and profitability.

In 1974 Norton management had decided to stem further loss of market share by a major restructuring of the CAD division. During the ensuing two years, market share and profitability continued to decline. These unfavorable results raised important questions about the merits of the earlier decision. The case for holding market share (the current strategy) was further challenged by the recommendations resulting from the PIMS regression analysis. The PIMS report had concluded that the CAD business should be moderately harvested (market share permitted to decline) for its cash throw-off.

The remainder of this case presents excerpts from information presented to the Strategy Guidance Committee or otherwise known by its members concerning CAD.

The Abrasives Market

Abrasive finished products were generally classified as bonded or coated. Bonded abrasives were basic tools used in almost every industry where shaping, cutting, or finishing of materials was required. Some of the major uses were in foundries and steel mills for rough grinding of castings and surface conditioning of steels and alloys, in metal fabrication for such products as automobiles and household appliances, in tool and die shops, in the manufacture of bearings, and in the paper and pulp industry. Norton produced more than 250,000 types and sizes of grinding wheels and other bonded abrasive products.

Coated abrasives (popularly referred to as sandpaper) were widely used throughout the metalworking and woodworking industries, in tanneries, and in service industries such as floor surfacing and automobile refinishing. Norton produced more than 38,000 different items in the form of sheets, belts, rolls, discs, and specialties. The most common form of coated abrasives was the endless belt, some major applications of which included the grinding and finishing of automobiles and appliance parts; the precision grinding and polishing of

---

[e]Numbers for the remainder of the case are disguised.

stainless and alloy steel; and the sanding of furniture, plywood, and particle board.

The overlap of customers' requirements for bonded and coated abrasives varied from industry to industry. For example, the woodworking industry used coated abrasives almost exclusively. In contrast, the auto industry purchased large quantities of both bonded abrasives (e.g., for grinding engine parts) and coated abrasives (e.g., for finishing bodies). Industrial distributors, which accounted for a large portion of Norton's abrasive sales, usually carried both bonded and coated abrasive products. Both Norton and Carborundum offered full lines of bonded and coated abrasive products; 3M competed only in coated abrasives.

In management's opinion, the principal factors that contributed to a favorable market position in this included quality and reliability of product, completeness of product line, nonpatented technological "know-how," substantial capital investment, length of experience in the business, familiarity and reputation of name, strength of marketing network, technical service, delivery reliability, and price. In 1975 no single customer, including the U.S. government, accounted for as much as 5 percent of Norton's net sales.

CAD in the Corporate Context

As was customary, the meeting of the Strategy Guidance Committee to review the CAD strategy was opened by Mr. Graham Wren, secretary of the committee, with a short presentation showing where the product line in question fitted in the Norton portfolio of businesses. The first chart he presented contained an overview of the market share strategies for 31 strategic business units, as summarized in Exhibit 3.

including CAD

EXHIBIT 3
Summary of Market Share Strategies for the Norton
Portfolio of Businesses

Market Share Strategy	Sales ($ millions)	Abrasive Operations	Diversified Products
Build	96		
Build/maintain	135		
Maintain	257		
Maintain/harvest	60		
Harvest	0	—	—
Total	548	400	148

Note: In the actual presentation, each strategic business was listed under its appropriate category. For example, CAD and 15 other business units were listed in the abrasives column for the "maintain" strategy.

Separate charts showed the ranking of all business units with respect to return on net assets (RONA), return on sales (ROS), and asset turnover ratio for 1974 and 1975, and the average for the two years. CAD placed in the ranking as follows:

	Rank among 31	Value for 1974–1975 Average	Norton Average Operations
RONA	27	6.0	10
ROS	26	3.5	6
Asset turnover	23	1.7	1.9

A growth share matrix showed CAD to lie well in the undesirable low-growth/smaller-than-competitor quadrant (see Exhibit 4). A product experiencing both low growth and low market share (relative to the industry leader) would likely be a net user of cash with little promise for future payoff.

Finally, the committee's cash generations versus market share corporate test was applied to the CAD proposed strategy. As shown in Exhibit 5, the combination of maintaining market share at its present level and generating cash was acceptable.

CAD STRATEGY PLAN

Paul Midghall, vice-president and general manager for Norton's U.S. Coated Abrasives Division, was the principal architect of the strategic plan to maintain market share. His reasoning, as laid out in the 1976 strategy book for CAD, began with a statement of the division's role and strategy:

Mission: Cash Generation

Norton's long-term objective is to allocate resources to high-growth opportunities while maintaining total world abrasives leadership. CAD's role within that corporate objective is: to be a long-term cash generator; to act as the technical focal point for coated abrasives operations worldwide.

Strategy: Restructure and Maintain

To meet that objective, CAD has in the last two years radically restructured its operations. Its strategy now is to complete the restructur-

EXHIBIT 4
Norton Portfolio of Businesses on Growth Share Matrix
(Balloon Areas Proportional to Sales)

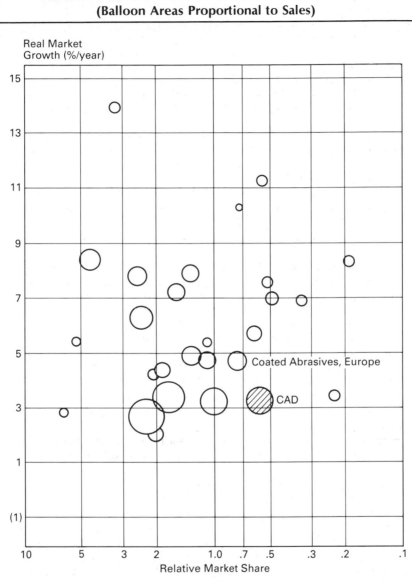

ing; to consolidate the organization into a confident, coherent team; and to pursue market segmentation based on the strengths which have emerged from restructuring. To understand how this strategy evolved, one must turn to CAD's history.

EXHIBIT 5
The Cash Generation/Market Share Strategy Test

Cash Generation	Market Share Strategy		
	Build	Maintain	Harvest
Uses cash	A/?	U	U
Provides own cash	A/?	U	U
Disengages cash	A	(A) ↖CAD	A

Notes:
A = The combination is an acceptable strategy.
? = The combination is a questionable strategy.
U = The combination is an unacceptable strategy.

The strategy report went on to identify the reasons for the earlier deterioration of market share and profitability. These included:

1. Inadequate reinvestment in the basic coated abrasives business in favor of investments which attempted to build allied businesses.[f]

2. High wage rates and fringe benefits coupled with low productivity and poor work conditions.
3. High overheads.
4. Premium pricing without compensating benefits to the customer.
5. A labor strike in 1966.

Serious attempts to reverse the negative trends for CAD had proved unsuccessful, and in late 1973 management decided a major change had to be made to the business. The current strategy report reviewed the alternative strategies that had been considered earlier:

By late 1973, CAD's condition demanded positive action; share had dropped to 26 percent and RONA to 7.5 percent. A fundamental change had to occur. The principal options were:

---

[f]According to Mr. Duane, coated abrasives and the other allied businesses had been organized in a single profit center at that time. The focus of attention had been on the total unit's overall performance. With the current approach to strategy analysis, each major product line was examined separately.

1. Sell, liquidate, or harvest. These alternatives were eliminated because: (a) a viable coated abrasives business was deemed important to worldwide coated abrasives business: (b) a viable coated abrasives business was judged important to U.S. bonded abrasives business.
2. Attempt to regain lost share and with it volume to cover fixed expenses. In a mature industry, with the major competitors financially secure and firmly entrenched, such a strategy was judged too expensive.
3. Greater price realization. We already maintained a high overall price level, and 3M was the price leader in the industry. In later 1974, Norton tried to lead prices up dramatically to restore profitability but the rest of the industry did not follow.

Alternative: Comprehensive Cost Reduction

A new cost structure was the only reasonable choice for a radical change. We had to scale down to a cost level consistent with our volume and our position in the industry.

In 1974 a decision to restructure the CAD business by making major cost reductions was made by Norton's Executive Committee and approved by its board of directors. This move was intended to make CAD more competitive so that it could prevent further erosion of its market share.

Restructuring

The strategy review of 1974 had identified many areas for cost reduction. These touched on almost every segment of operations and included: moving labor-intensive manufacturing operations from New York to Texas; combining the coated abrasives sales force with that for bonded abrasives (e.g., grinding wheels); and reducing fixed assets. The product line was also to be reduced. Earlier, about 4,000 product items out of some 20,000 (that is, 20 percent) had accounted for 87 percent of sales.

During the two-year period 1974–1975, over $2 million had been invested to implement the restructuring. The changes were eventually expected to result in over $9 million annual direct recurring savings, raising RONA by about 8 percentage points to a total of 14 percent.[8] The number of employees for CAD had declined from 2,000 to 1,300 by 1976.

---

[8]It was estimated that 3M had a RONA of 17 percent of 20 percent in coated abrasives.

CAD'S FUTURE ENVIRONMENT

The U.S. coated abrasives industry was expected to experience low growth and gradual changes as a rule. The strategy book forecast long-term growth at 2.5 percent per annum. Industrial markets, which constituted 75 percent of Norton's CAD business, were to grow even more slowly. Because of the depressed level of business operations in early 1976, annual growth for industrial markets was forecast to spurt to about 7 percent until 1980.[h]

Product technology was expected to change slowly, but in important ways. The strategy book noted:

> The advent of Norzon grain, new resin bonds, and synthetic backings illustrates the fact that although coated abrasives may be a mature product, it is not a commodity product. Technological evolution is slow but continuous, and a competitor who fails to keep abreast cannot survive.
>
> While product development exhibits highly visible evolution, process development is inconspicuous. No major changes have occurred, or are expected, in manufacturing technology.
>
> Capacity in all segments of manufacturing will be adequate to fill demand well into the 1980s.

The U.S. coated abrasives market was said to have "healthy, strong, rational competition." With the exception of 3M, the return of most competitors was thought to be below the U.S. industrial average. Exhibit 6 shows sales and market shares for the principal competitors.

CAD STRATEGY FOR 1976

The proposed strategy for CAD contained two principal elements. One element was a continuation of the restructuring and cost cutting that

---

[h]An investment advisory report issued by Loeb Rhoades some months later (August 1976) had this to say about future prospects for the industry as a whole (bonded and coated products):

> We have believed for some time that there were fair prospects for higher profitability in abrasives on a secular and not just a cyclical basis, merely because profitability had been poor for a long enough (seven to nine years) time. In a product that is basic to economic activity and that is capital intensive, and where no unusual reason can be discerned for the poor return on investment, such as foreign competition or technological change, etc., a lengthy period of poor profitability generally will lead to changes by industry factors designed to improve returns. . . . At some point supply and demand come into a better balance, which then supports firmer pricing. And in fact . . . pricing had improved significantly since late 1974 despite declining demand in real terms.

EXHIBIT 6
U.S. Coated Abrasives Market Share Estimates

	1975 Sales ($ millions)	Total Market Share	
		1975	1973
3M	$ 99	34%	32%
Norton	76	26	27
Carborundum	40	14	15
Armak	23	8	8
Other U.S. manufacturers	35	12	12
Foreign	21	7	7
Total industry	$294	100%	100%

	Market Segment		
	Metal-working[a]	Wood-working	General Trade[b]
Market potential, 1975 ($ millions)	$130	$36	$81
Estimated market share, 1975			
3M	30%	27%	65%
Norton	29	26	20
Carborundum	22	10	11

[a]Includes primary metals, fabricated metals, and transportation equipment (autos, aircraft) industries.

[b]Includes hardware retail and automobile finishing businesses.

had begun in 1974. CAD management estimated that about 75 percent of this program had been put into effect and that two more years would be required to complete the steps under way.

The second element of the strategy was to focus on those market segments where Norton had competitive advantage. Detailed share/growth balloon charts, such as shown in Exhibit 7, were used to identify specific sectors for attention.

To foster product innovation, the 1976 plan had introduced a recommendation to expand R&D efforts. Twenty-two men had been assigned to CAD product development in 1975.

These strategic moves were predicted to produce favorable results. The CAD report identified the units' future strengths to include: variable costs to be among the lowest in the industry; distribution channel relations to be among the best, especially with the close tie

EXHIBIT 7
CAD Growth Share Matrices (Balloon Areas
Proportional to Norton's Sales)

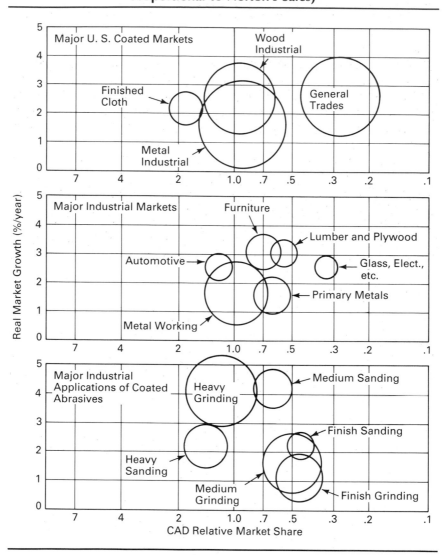

between coated and bonded abrasives; and a technological edge on new products (e.g., Norzon). The ultimate result, the report forecast, would be the generation of more than $7 million cash during 1977–1980. Excerpts from the summary of financial results are shown in Exhibit 8.

EXHIBIT 8
Summary of Financial Results (Numbers Disguised)

	Actual					*Expected*				
	1971	*1972*	*1973*	*1974*	*1975*	*1976*	*1977*	*1978*	*1979*	*1980*
Market share (%)	29	28	27	26	25.5	26	27	27.5	27.5	27.5
Net sales (index)	77	90	107	120	100	108	128	150	160	180
Net income (index)	215	220	310	230	100	140	480	760	810	950
Percent return on sales	4.4	3.9	4.6	3.0	1.6	2.0	6.0	8.0	8.0	8.0
Percent RONA	8	8	7.5	7	5	4.5	8	13	13	13
Funds generated ($ millions)						(4.7)	0.5	2.5	3.4	1.3

^a7 percent inflation per annum assumed.

THE PIMS REPORT

The PIMS analysis for CAD had resulted in a recommendation at variance with that made by Mr. Midghall.[i] A summary of these findings was included in the strategy book submitted to the Strategy Guidance Committee. The remainder of this section presents excerpts from the PIMS analysis:

> The 1975 PAR report[j] indicates that the Coated-U.S. business is a below-average business in a weak strategic position with a *pretax* PAR-ROI of 12.0 percent. The business' operating performance has been very close to PAR with a 1973–75 average *pretax* actual ROI of 12.2 percent.

---

[i]As a subscriber to the services of the Strategic Planning Institute, Norton received on a regular basis analysis reports for several of its major businesses. These reports were circulated to divisional and corporate managers concerned with the business in question.

[j]The PAR report specified the return on investment that was normal for a business, given the characteristics of its market, competition, technology, and cost structure.

Working Capital

The major factors impacting on PAR-ROI and their individual impacts are listed below.[k]

| *Major Negative Factors* | *Major Positive Factors* |

(1.5)   Marketing only expense/sales   1.8   Sales direct to end users
(1.7)   Capacity utilization
(4.1)   Effective use of investments

During the three-year period, the *marketing less sales force expenses/ sales* ratio averaged 6 percent compared to the 4.1 percent PIMS average. PIMS findings acknowledge that high marketing expenses hurt profitability when relative product quality is low; i.e., it doesn't pay to market heavily a product with equivalent or inferior product quality. The average relative product quality for the business over the three years was estimated as follows: 10 percent superior, 75 percent equivalent, and 15 percent inferior.

For the Coated-U.S. business, the positive impact indicates that selling through distributors instead of direct should lower customer service costs.

Whether the Coated-U.S. business objective is to optimize cash flow or ROI over the long term, the Strategy Sensitivity Report (SSR) suggests a *moderate harvest* strategy. The SSR is based upon how other participating businesses with similar business characteristics have acted to achieve their objectives.

The SSR suggests that the following strategy should be pursued to optimize either cash flow or ROI over the long term.

1. *Prices.* Prices relative to competition should be maintained.
2. *Working capital/sales.* The SSR suggests that this ratio be lowered significantly to about 25 percent through primarily reduced inventory levels.
3. *Vertical integration.* Over the long term, the degree of vertical integration should be reduced.
4. *Fixed capital.* Don't add large segments of capacity, and maintain capacity utilization at the 80 percent level.
5. *R&D marketing expenses.* The SSR recommends that R&D expenditures should be reduced; and consequently, the relative product quality remains inferior. Also, the products should be marketed less energetically during the implementation phase.

The results from this strategy are (1) a gradual loss of market share from 26 percent to 21 percent; (2) an average ROI of 24 percent versus the current PAR-ROI of 12 percent; and (3) a 10-year discounted cash flow value of $2.33 million.

---

[k]The figures represent the impact of that factor on PAR-ROI. For example, the higher marketing (excluding sales force) expenses/sales ratio noted in the following paragraphs when comparing CAD to all PIMS businesses was said to have an effect of reducing the PAR-ROI by 1.5 percent. In contrast, by selling directly to the end users, PAR-ROI was increased by 1.8 percent compared to all PIMS businesses.

A study was undertaken to compare the PAR-ROI of this business in its steady-state environment (after the recommended strategy has been implemented—1978–80) with the 1973–75 PAR-ROI. The results indicate that the strategy is successful in moving this business into a much better strategic position. The pretax PAR-ROI increases from 12 percent to 24 percent.

The major factors that had a significant impact on the improved PAR-ROI are *relative pay scale* and *use of investments*. These two factors account for a majority of the 12 percentage point increase in PAR-ROI.

The general message from the SSR for the *restructured* Coated-U.S. business is the same as for the *current* business; i.e., if the objective is to manage the business for cash flow or ROI, a *moderate harvest strategy* is recommended by PIMS.

MANAGEMENT CONSIDERATIONS

Norton's top managers recognized how difficult it was for them to remain objective when deciding the fate of a core part of the company's traditional business. As Mr. John Nelson, vice-president abrasive operations Western Hemisphere, remarked:

> There is no question that this decision had been an emotional one for me and probably for others as well. It would be difficult to turn our backs on CAD. Yet, if the business cannot produce the target return on net assets, I think we are prepared to take the appropriate actions.
>
> I do not think that we are likely to close shop on U.S. coated abrasives. It is too important to other parts of our business to go that far. For example, coated abrasives strengthens our sales of bonded abrasives and is a plus to our distribution system in the United States. It also provides us with a bigger base for R&D on coated abrasives. This benefits our overseas coated abrasives operations. Nonetheless, whether to stay with our earlier decision to maintain market share or to harvest the business was and still is very much at issue.

Both Mr. Duane and Mr. Nelson remarked that the choice of strategy in 1973–1974 had been predicated on the belief that the industry could support a profitable number two and that Norton could play that role with its existing market share. The continued loss of market share was a cause of concern to them and to other members of the Strategy Guidance Committee. As noted in the minutes for the CAD review session of June 7, 1976:

> In the shorter term period of late 1973 to the first quarter 1976, CAD market share dropped from 27 percent to 25 percent. Some of this drop was due to intentional de-emphasis of the general trades segment. However, there was also an unintentional loss in the industrial segment. The key question is whether this short-term market share decline in the industrial area can be stopped and reversed.

The PIMS recommendations for an alternative strategy also served to raise questions about the soundness of the present approach. One Norton executive put in context the relative impact of PIMS with the following observation: "We are still learning how to use PIMS. At present, we consider it a useful input, among many, to our thinking. We would not reverse divisional management's position on the basis of PIMS alone."

Mr. Donald Melville, executive vice-president, diversified products, made the following comment about the CAD issue:

> You have to consider the dynamics of Norton's situation in 1976. We have done a lot to restructure the company, and the results in 1975—a bad recession year for abrasives—show our progress. But we are not yet in a position where we can harvest a major segment of our abrasives business, because that is the major guts of our company.
>
> By the early 1980s our restructuring should be complete and we will not be so dependent on abrasives. If we were faced with the decision in, say, 1982, instead of 1976, we could and probably should be willing to harvest CAD. In the meantime, we might as well repair CAD, because if we succeed, then we won't have to harvest it in the 1980s. And if we fail, we will have lost very little.

A relative newcomer to the top management ranks at Norton, Mr. Richard Flynn, financial vice-president, made the following comments about Norton's approach to strategic planning:[1]

> However the Strategy Guidance Committee finally decides on this matter, I think they are at least addressing the right issues, and that itself is something.
>
> The wide use of profit centers in large U.S. corporations has often led to bad analysis when different products were lumped together. Corporate-wide planning did not help the situation. Looking at a single product line family, as we are doing for U.S. coated abrasives, gives management much more meaningful data to work with.
>
> The other thing I like about Norton's strategic planning is that we are doing it repeatedly during the year. This means that we are always called on to think strategy. Looking at different businesses at different times enables us to take on different perspectives to our strategic thinking. This sometimes helps us to gain new insights for other businesses.
>
> All in all, the strategic planning sessions have been very effective in helping top management to think about and to deal with business strategies.

---

[1]Richard J. Flynn joined Norton Company in January 1974 as financial vice-president and as a member of the board of directors and the executive committee. He had been president of the Riley Stoker Corporation, a subsidiary of the Riley Company, manufacturers of steam generating and fuel burning equipment. He previously held executive positions with Ling-Temco Vought and Collins Radio.

CASE

Marion Laboratories, Inc.

MICHAEL E. HERMAN, senior vice-president of finance of Marion Laboratories, had just received word that the board of directors was planning to meet in three days to review the company's portfolio of subsidiary investments. In particular, he and his senior financial analyst, Carl R. Mitchell, were to prepare an in-depth analysis of several of the subsidiaries for the board. The board would be considering these subsidiaries' compatability with Marion's overall long-run strategic objectives. The analysis was part of a continuing process of self-assessment to assure future growth for the company. At the upcoming meeting the board was interested in a review of Kalo Laboratories, Inc.,[a] a subsidiary that manufactured specialty agricultural chemicals.

Marion's future had been the subject of careful study following the first two years of earnings decline in the company's history. In fiscal 1975 the company's net earnings were 12 percent lower than in 1974. In fiscal 1976 Marion faced a more serious problem, as earnings fell 30 percent below 1974 levels while sales decreased 4 percent and cost of goods sold rose by 12 percent above 1974 levels.

Kalo was profitable and in sound financial shape for the fiscal year just ended (see Exhibit 1). But Kalo was unique for Marion, and Mr. Herman knew that Kalo's long-term status as a Marion subsidiary would depend on more than just profitability.

This case was prepared by Kenneth Beck and Marilyn Taylor of the University of Kansas.

[a]Kalo Laboratories, Inc., was utilized as the case subject because of the singular nature of the segment information available in Marion Laboratories, Inc., SEC submissions, and does not reflect Marion's intentions as to its investment in Kalo or any of its other subsidiary operations. Materials in this case were generally gathered from publicly available information.

EXHIBIT 1
Sales Profits and Identifiable Assets by Industry Segments
(thousands of dollars)

	1978	1977	1976	1975	1974[a]
Sales to unaffiliated customers:					
Pharmaceutical and hospital products	$ 84,223	$ 72,299	$ 59,236	$ 64,613	$ 54,165
Specialty agricultural chemical products	9,302	5,227	2,880	4,522	4,044
Other health-care segments	23,853	22,605	18,722	14,961	13,569
Consolidated net sales	$117,378	$100,131	$ 80,838	$ 84,096	$ 71,778
Operating profit:					
Pharmaceutical and hospital products	$ 27,900	$ 23,439	$ 18,941	$ 28,951	$ 25,089
Specialty agricultural chemical products	905	382	(328)	881	620
Other health-care segments	929	1,251	(593)	686	871
Operating profit:	29,734	25,072	18,020	30,518	26,580
Interest expense	(1,546)	(1,542)	(898)	(97)	(83)
Corporate expenses	(5,670)	(4,474)	(3,106)	(2,795)	(2,475)
Earnings before income taxes	$ 22,518	$ 19,056	$ 14,016	$ 27,626	$ 24,022
Identifiable assets:					
Pharmaceutical and hospital products	$ 75,209	$ 69,546	$ 60,376	$ 43,658	$ 35,103
Specialty agricultural chemical products	3,923	3,805	1,801	1,942	1,790
Other health-care segments	14,635	14,875	13,902	14,229	12,217
Corporate	5,121	3,424	4,518	3,928	3,770
Discontinued operations	—	—	—	3,370	6,865
Consolidated assets	$ 98,888	$ 91,650	$ 80,597	$ 67,127	$ 59,745

Source: 1978 annual report.
[a]*Year ended June 30.*

BACKGROUND

As a result of the interruption in the earnings growth pattern, Marion had sought to reexamine its corporate portfolio of investments. By fiscal year 1977 some results were seen as earnings rose 28 percent from the previous year. Although sales continued to climb, earnings had not yet recovered to the 1974 level by the end of fiscal year 1978. Marion's long-range planning was an attempt to define what the company was to become in the next ten-year period. Current analysis of subsidiaries and investments were analyzed within the ten-year framework. As part of this long-range planning, Marion's corporate mission was defined as follows:

1. To achieve a position of market leadership through marketing and distribution of consumable and personal products of a perceived differentiation to selected segments of the health care and related fields.

2. To achieve long-term profitable growth through the management of high risk relative to the external environment.

3. To achieve a professional, performance-oriented working environment that stimulates integrity, entrepreneurial spirit, productivity, and social responsibility.

In addition to these more general goals, Marion also set a specific sales goal of $250 million. No time frame was established to achieve this goal as the major emphasis was to be placed on the stability and quality of sales, but it was well understood that to meet stockholders' expectations, the company would have to grow fairly rapidly. For example, on June 8, 1978, in a presentation before the Health Industry's analyst group, Fred Lyons, Marion's president and chief operating officer, emphasized Marion's commitment to growth. In his remarks he stated:

> We expect to grow over the next ten years at a rate greater than the pharmaceutical industry average and at a rate greater than at least twice that of the real gross national product. Our target range is at least 10 to 15 percent compounded growth—shooting for the higher side of that, of course. Obviously we intend to have a great deal of new business and new products added to our current operations to reach and exceed the $250 million level.
>
> Our licensing activities and R&D expenditures will be intensified. . . . At the same time we'll undertake some selective in-house research business into Marion through the acquisition route. It is our intention to keep our balance sheet strong and maintain an "A" or better credit rating, to

EXHIBIT 2
Ten-Year Financial Summary
(thousands of dollars except per-share data)

	1978	1977	1976	1975	1974	1973	1972	1971	1970	1969
Sales										
Net sales	$117,378	$100,131	$80,838	$84,096	$71,778	$57,937	$49,066	$41,692	$35,322	$30,188
Cost of sales	43,177	37,330	29,315	26,078	21,715	18,171	14,932	12,262	10,622	8,985
Gross profit	74,201	62,801	51,523	58,018	50,063	39,766	34,134	29,430	24,700	21,203
Operating expenses	51,718	43,397	37,292	31,699	26,991	21,155	19,164	17,181	13,828	12,453
Operating income	22,483	19,404	14,231	26,319	23,072	18,611	14,970	12,249	10,872	8,750
Other income	1,581	1,194	683	1,404	1,033	722	709	599	630	328
Interest expense	1,546	1,542	898	97	83	109	116	88	198	260
Earnings:										
Earnings from continuing operations before income taxes	22,518	19,056	14,016	27,626	24,022	19,224	15,563	12,760	11,304	8,818
Income taxes	10,804	8,404	5,628	13,295	11,791	9,297	7,730	6,364	5,899	4,493
Earnings from continuing operations	11,714	10,652	8,388	14,331	12,231	9,927	7,833	6,396	5,405	4,325
Earnings (loss) from discontinued operations	—	—	—	(3,617)	(120)	76	488	—	—	—
Net earnings	$ 11,714	$ 10,652	$ 8,388	$10,714	$12,111	$10,003	$ 8,321	$ 6,396[a]	$ 5,405	$ 4,325

Common share data:

Earnings (loss) per common and common equivalent share:										
Continuing operations	$ 1.38	$ 1.23	$ .96	$ 1.65	$ 1.40	$ 1.14	$ .90	$ .76	$ .65	$ .52
Discontinued operations	—	—	—	(.42)	(.01)	.01	.06	—	—	—
Net earnings	$ 1.38	$ 1.23	$ .96	$ 1.23	$ 1.39	$ 1.15	$ .96	$ .76[a]	$ .65	$ .52
Cash dividends per common share	$ .59	$ .53	$ .52	$ .48	$ .28	$ .21	$ .20	$ .16	$ .12	$ .12
Stockholder's equity per common and common equivalent share	$ 7.87	$ 6.63	$ 6.63	$ 6.29	$ 5.52	$ 4.16	$ 3.16	$ 2.52	$ 2.01	$ 1.47
Weighted average number of outstanding common and common share equivalents	8,475	8,640	8,707	8,708	8,689	8,715	8,651	8,396	8,377	8,354

Source: 1978 annual report.

[a]Before extraordinary charge of $916,000, equal to $0.11 per common share resulting from the disposition of investment in affiliated companies.

EXHIBIT 3
Consolidated Balance Sheet, 1977 and 1978

	June 30	
Assets	1978	1977
Current assets		
Cash	$ 381,116	$ 961,588
Short-term investments, at cost which		
approximates market	2,561,660	10,028,297
Accounts and notes receivable, less		
allowances for returns and doubtful		
accounts of $1,845,466 and $2,305,793	28,196,199	20,576,412
Inventories	19,640,945	15,568,170
Prepaid expenses	2,305,403	1,461,367
Deferred income tax benefits	757,585	895,110
Total current assets	53,842,908	49,490,944
Property, plant, and equipment, at cost		
Land and land improvements	2,832,588	2,935,671
Buildings	24,458,746	25,224,652
Machinery and equipment	19,671,607	18,110,907
Aircraft and related equipment	1,670,904	1,670,904
Construction in progress	365,311	357,338
	48,999,156	48,299,472
Less accumulated depreciation	10,725,533	8,585,190
Net property, plant and equipment	38,273,623	39,714,282
Other assets		
Intangible assets	4,774,055	2,042,762
Notes receivable (noncurrent)	890,692	11,589
Marketable equity securities, at market value	688,914	—
Deferred income tax benefits (noncurrent)	318,434	249,647
Miscellaneous	99,597	141,232
Total other assets	6,771,692	2,445,230
Total assets	$98,888,223	$91,650,456

(continued)

EXHIBIT 3 (*continued*)

	June 30	
	1978	*1977*
Current liabilities		
Current maturities of long-term debt	$ 82,102	$ 95,004
Accounts payable, trade	3,979,341	4,224,105
Accrued profit sharing expense	1,752,515	243,096
Other accrued expenses	3,864,168	3,008,238
Dividends payable	1,260,612	1,198,938
Income taxes payable	4,391,252	5,030,219
Total current liabilities	15,329,990	13,799,600
Long-term debt, excluding current maturities	15,580,072	15,661,399
Deferred income taxes payable	1,107,000	733,000
Deferred compensation	177,975	172,889
Stockholders' equity		
Preferred stock of $1 par value per share Authorized 250,000 shares; none issued	—	—
Common stock of $1 par value per share Authorized 20,000,000 shares; issued 8,703,346 shares	8,703,346	8,703,346
Paid in capital	3,474,358	3,475,443
Retained earnings	58,358,925	51,604,550
	70,536,629	63,783,339
Less:		
293,153 shares of common stock in treasury, at cost (189,500 shares in 1977)	3,819,213	2,499,771
Net unrealized loss on noncurrent marketable equity securities	24,200	—
Total stockholders' equity	66,693,186	61,283,568
Commitments and contingent liabilities		
Total liabilities and stockholders' equity	$98,888,223	$91,650,456

Source: 1978 annual report.

achieve a return on investment in the 12 to 15 percent range, and to produce net after-tax earnings compared to sales in the 8 to 12 percent range.

See Exhibits 2 and 3 for financial statements.

To finance this growth in sales, Marion was faced with a constant need for funds. Most of these funds in the past had come from the company's operations. To finance a $25 million expansion in its pharmaceutical facilities, the company, in fiscal year 1976, found it necessary to borrow $15 million in the form of unsecured senior notes. The notes were to mature on October 1, 1980, 1981, and 1982, with $5 million due on each of those dates.

In regard to possible future financing, Mr. Herman made the following comments before the Health Industry's analyst group: "Most of you realize that industrial companies have debt-equity ratios of 1:1, and if we desired to lever ourselves to that level, we could borrow $66 million. However, we would keep as a guideline the factor of always maintaining our "A" or better credit rating, so we would not leverage ourselves that far."

Although Marion was fairly light on debt, the potential for future borrowing was not unlimited. Besides maintaining an "A" credit rating, it was felt that a debt-to-equity ratio greater than 0.4:1 would be inconsistent with the pharmaceutical industry.

To analyze Kalo's future as well as the futures of the other non-pharmaceutical subsidiaries, Mr. Herman realized that he and his analysts would have to consider the impact of these financing constraints on Marion's future growth. With unlimited financing in the future, he would have needed only to make a "good" investment decision. However, to balance the goals of a strong balance sheet and a high growth rate, Mr. Herman was faced with making the optimal investment decision. It was with these constraints that Mr. Herman would eventually have to make his recommendation to the board of directors.

COMPANY BACKGROUND AND ORGANIZATION

In 1979 Marion Laboratories, Inc., of Kansas City, Missouri, was a leading producer of ethical (prescription) pharmaceuticals for the treatment of cardiovascular and cerebral disorders (see Exhibit 4). Marion also owned subsidiaries that manufactured hospital supplies, proprietary (nonprescription) drugs, eyeglasses, optical accessories, electrical home-stairway elevators, and specialty agricultural chemicals.

EXHIBIT 4
Marion's Major Ethical Pharmaceutical Products

Product	Product Application	Estimated Market Size ($ Millions)	Marion's Product	Share of Market (%)
Cerebral and peripheral vasodilators	Vascular relaxant to relieve constriction of arteries	90–100	PAVABID®	22
Coronary vasodilators	Controlled release nitroglycerin for treatment of angina pectoris	90–100	NITRO-BID®	12
Ethical and OTC plain antacids	Tablets for relief of heartburn	37	GAVISCON®	26
Androgens-estrogens	Product for treatment of calcium deficiencies	12	OS-CAL®	46
Topical burn antimicrobials	Ointment for prevention of infection in third-degree burns	8	SILVADENE®	57
Urologic antispasmodies	Product for treatment of symptoms of neurogenic bladder	10	DITROPAN®	10

Source: Smith, Barney, Harris, Upham and Company research report (January 19, 1978).

Marion Laboratories was founded in 1950 by Ewing Marion Kauffman. Prior to establishing his own company, Mr. Kauffman had held a job with the field sales force of a Kansas City pharmaceutical company. After four years on the job, Kauffman was so successful in his sales efforts that his commissions were greater than the company president's salary. When the company cut his commission and reduced his sales territory, Kauffman quit to establish his own firm.

From the company's inception, its major emphasis was on sales and marketing. Mr. Kauffman was successful in developing an aggressive, highly motivated sales force. During the mid-1960s the company's sales effort was concentrated on developing Pavabid, introduced in 1962, into the leading product in the cerebral and peripheral vasodilator market.

While other drug companies were spending large amounts on research and development, hoping to discover new drugs, Marion concentrated on the sales effort, spending very little on basic research. Nearly all of its research expenditures were directed at improving its current products or further developing products licensed from other drug companies. This approach to product development was still being followed in 1979.

Beginning in the late 1960s, Marion decided to reduce its dependence on Pavabid, which accounted for more than half of Marion's sales. In the pharmaceutical area, the company continued to minimize basic research and worked to develop new drug sources. Marion also began diversifying into the hospital and health products sector primarily by acquiring existing firms in those areas (see Exhibit 5). Taking advantage of the high market value of its common stock, the company acquired several subsidiaries engaged in fields other than pharmaceuticals.[b]

In 1979 Marion's operations were divided into two separate groups, the Pharmaceutical Group and the Health Products Group. The Pharmaceutical Group's operations were a continuation of the original ethical drug line of the company. The Health Products Group was composed of subsidiaries purchased by Marion in hospital and health-related fields.

As a matter of operating policy, Marion made some of its operating decisions in small group or task force settings that brought together corporate personnel from several different disciplines. The process of approving certain capital expenditures was an example of the review and analysis process.

Marion had a formal capital expenditure review program for expenditures on depreciable assets in excess of $10,000. At the option of the group president, the review program could also be applied to ex-

---

[b]Price-earnings ratios for Marion in 1968 and 1969 were 46 and 52, respectively.

EXHIBIT 5
Diagram of Marion's Pharmaceutical
Distribution System

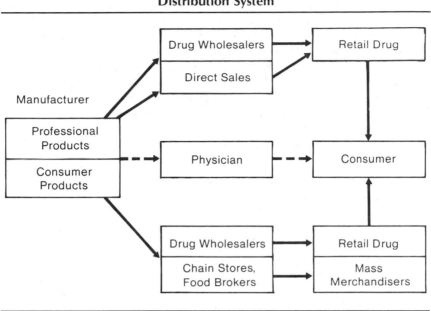

penditures of less than $10,000, with the modification that in these cases only the group president was involved in the review process.

A form that forced the requesting individual to discount the cash flows of the project was required to be completed and submitted, if the net present value of cash flows was positive, to a corporate planning group. This group consisted of corporate accounting and facilities-planning personnel who, since the company was operating with limited funds, decided which projects, on the basis of financial and strategic considerations, should be forwarded to Fred Lyons for final approval or rejection. This process occurred after the planning period and prior to the purchase of the asset. The capital expenditure review program was used for expenditures in both the Pharmaceutical Group and the Health Products Group.

PHARMACEUTICAL GROUP

Marion's ethical and over-the-counter drug operations were the major components of the Pharmaceutical Group. These operations were split into two divisions, the Professional Products Division and the Consumer Products Division. James E. McGraw headed the Pharmaceutical Group, which included research and development, administration, operations, and government compliance. Although Marion had been exclusively an ethical drugmaker prior to diversification efforts, the company had recently increased its operations in the proprietary drug area.

In 1978 Marion formed the Consumer Products Division from what had been International Pharmaceutical Corporation (IPC) to market its growing nonprescription product line. This market area, previously untapped for Marion, was expected to be a major ingredient for near-term growth. To aid in the marketing of its nonprescription line, Marion hired a full-scale consumer advertising agency for the first time in the company's history.

The Consumer Products Division's sales were boosted when, in fiscal 1978, Marion purchased the product Throat-Discs from Warner-Lamberts's Parke-Davis division. In addition, Marion also purchased two Parke-Davis ethical products, Ambenyl cough-cold products and a tablet for the treatment of thyroid disorders. Because of the timing of the acquisition, most of the sales and earnings were excluded from that year's earnings results. Sales of these three lines were expected to be nearly $8 million in 1979.

Marion's ethical pharmaceutical products were marketed by its Professional Products Division. The company sold its ethical products with a detail sales force of about two hundred who called on physicians, pharmacists, and distributors within their assigned territories. The sales force was very productive by industry standards and was motivated by intensive training and supervision and an incentive compensation system. There was very little direct selling to doctors and pharmacists, the main purpose of a salesperson's visits being promotion of Marion's products. In addition, Marion had an institutional sales force that sold directly to hospitals, institutions, and other large users.

In fiscal 1978, 80 percent of Marion's pharmaceutical products were distributed through 463 drug wholesalers. All orders for ethical drug products were filled from the Kansas City, Missouri, manufacturing plant. Marion's pharmaceutical distribution system is shown in Exhibit 5.

During 1978 the company decided to use its improved liquidity position to aid its wholesale drug distributors. Many wholesalers used outside financing to purchase their inventories and were unable to maintain profit margins when interest rates rose. By extending credit on key products, Marion helped its distributors maintain higher inventories and gave the company a selling edge over competitors.

One of Marion's major goals for each of its products was for the product to hold a market-leadership position in the particular area in which it competed. This goal had been accomplished for most of the company's leading products (see Exhibit 6).

EXHIBIT 6
Summary of Subsidiary Acquisitions and Divestitures

Name of Subsidiary	Type of Product(s)	Date Acquired	Date Divested
Marion Health & Safety	First aid and hospital products	1968	—
American Stair-Glide	Home stairway lifts and products to aid the handicapped	1968	—
Kalo Laboratories	Specialty agricultural chemicals	1968	—
Rose Manufacturing	Industrial fall-protection devices	1969	Sold, 1978
Mi-Con Laboratories	Ophthalmic solutions	1969	Merged into MH&S, 1973
Pioneer Laboratories	Sterile dressings	50% in 1970	Sold out, 1971
Signet Laboratories	Vitamin and food supplements	1971	Discontinued operations, selling some assets, 1975
Optico Laboratories	Eyeglasses, hard contact lenses, and related products	1973	—
Certified Laboratories	IPC products (manufacturer)	1969	Sold, 1978
IPC	IPC products (marketer)	1969	Merged into Pharmaceutical Division, 1979
Marion International	Pharmaceutical products distributor	Incorporated 1971	—
Inco	Industrial creams	1972	Merged into MH&S, 1974
Occusafe	Consulting services for OSHA regulation and compliance	Incorporated 1972	Discontinued operations, 1973

(continued)

EXHIBIT 6 (*continued*)

Name of Subsidiary	Type of Product(s)	Date Acquired	Date Divested
Nation Wide	Specialty AG- Chem products	1973	Merged into Kalo
Marion Scientific	Manufacturer and distributor of scientific devices	Acquired by MH&S, 1973	—
Colloidal	Specialty agricultural products	1973	Merged into Kalo, 1974
WBC	Holding company for IPC	Incorporated 1976	Sold, 1978
SRC	Specialty AG- Chem products	1977	Merged into Kalo

Capturing a large share of a market had worked particularly well for Marion's leading product, Pavabid, which in 1978 accounted for 18 percent of the company's entire sales. Marion was decreasing its reliance on Pavabid (see Exhibit 7). Through the 1960s Pavabid had been responsible for almost all of Marion's growth. In recent years, as the product market matured, sales growth had slowed, forcing the company to become less dependent on Pavabid. The 3.9 percent decrease in sales in fiscal year 1976 was due primarily to previous overstocking of Pavabid and the subsequent inventory adjustments at the distributor level.

In April 1976 the Food and Drug Administration (FDA) had requested that makers of papaverine hydrochloride (sold by Marion as Pavabid) submit test data to support the safety and efficacy of the drug. Many small manufacturers were not able to submit the data and dropped out of the market. Marion complied with the request and had not yet been notified by the FDA of the outcome of the review by early 1979. A negative action by the FDA was not expected since it had taken so long for a decision and papaverine had been used safely for decades. However, if the FDA ruled that compounds such as Pavabid could not be marketed, because they were either unsafe or ineffective, Marion would lose its leading product.

In August 1977 the FDA requested that manufacturers of coronary vasodilators, including nitroglycerin compounds like Marion's Nitro-

EXHIBIT 7
Changing Product Mix

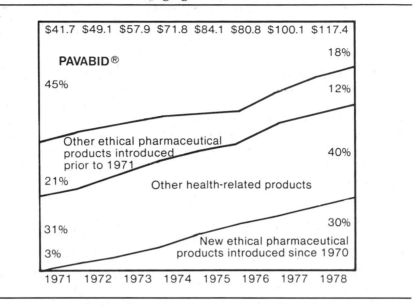

| $41.7 | $49.1 | $57.9 | $71.8 | $84.1 | $80.8 | $100.1 | $117.4 |

PAVABID®

45%   18%

12%

Other ethical pharmaceutical
products introduced
prior to 1971

21%   40%

Other health-related products

31%   30%

New ethical pharmaceutical
products introduced since 1970

3%

1971   1972   1973   1974   1975   1976   1977   1978

Source: 1978 annual report.

Bid, submit test data to prove product safety and efficacy. This review was the same process to which Pavabid was subject, and a negative ruling, although not expected, would adversely affect the company.

Proving its products to be safe and effective was only one area in which the company dealt with the FDA. Before any ethical drug product could be marketed in the United States, Marion had to have the approval of the FDA. Under the system effective at that time, the company was required to conduct extensive animal tests, file an Investigational New Drug Application, conduct three phases of clinical tests on humans, file a New Drug Application, and submit all its data to the FDA for final review. With the FDA's approval, the drug firm could begin marketing the drug.

The approval process from lab discovery and patent application to FDA approval took from seven to ten years. Often a company had only seven or eight years of patent protection left in which to market its discovery and recover the average $50 million it had taken to fully develop the drug from the initial discovery stages.

To avoid the R&D expenses necessary to develop fully a new drug entity into a marketable product, Marion's source for new products was a process the company called "search and development." Marion licensed the basic compound from other drug manufacturers large enough to afford the basic research needed to discover new drugs. Generally the licensors, most notably Servier of France and Chugai of Japan, were companies lacking the resources or expertise necessary to obtain FDA approval and marketing rights in the United States. Marion's R&D effort then concentrated on developing a product with an already identified pharmacological action into a drug marketable in the United States. By developing existing drug entities, Marion was able to bring a new drug to market in a shorter development time and at a lower cost than discovering its own drugs required. This strategy enabled Marion to compete in an industry dominated by companies many times its own size (see Exhibits 8 and 9 for drug industry information).

In addition to the FDA, federal government activities that promoted generic substitution also affected the drug industry. In early 1979 forty states had provisions for generic substitution that allowed nonbranded drugs to be substituted for branded, and often more expensive, drugs. The U.S. Department of Health, Education, and Wel-

EXHIBIT 8
Selected Ethical Drug Companies, 1977
(thousands of dollars)

	Net Sales	Cost of Goods Sold	R&D Expenses	Net After-Tax Income
Pfizer, Inc.	$2,031,900	$978,057	$ 98,282	$174,410
Merck & Co.	1,724,410	662,703	144,898	290,750
Eli Lilly & Co.	1,518,012	571,737	124,608	218,684
Upjohn, Inc.	1,134,325	—	102,256	91,521
SmithKline Corp.	780,337	299,338	61,777	89,271
G. D. Searle & Co.	749,583	345,224	52,645	(28,390)
Syntex Corp.	313,604	132,710	27,648	37,643
A. H. Robbins Co.	306,713	122,374	16,107	26,801
Rorer Group, Inc.	186,020	59,606	5,174	18,143
Marion Laboratories	100,131	37,330	5,907	10,652

Source: Drug and Cosmetic Industry (June 1978).

EXHIBIT 9
Ethical Drug Industry, Composite Statistics

	1978	1977	1976	1975
Sales ($ millions)	12,450	10,859	10,033	9,022
Operating margin (%)	22.5	22.2	21.9	22.1
Income tax rate (%)	36.5	36.4	36.2	36.7
Net profit margin (%)	11.8	11.7	11.7	11.6
Earned on net worth (%)	18.5	17.9	18.2	18.4

Source: *Value Line Investment Survey.*

fare and the Federal Trade Commission had also recently proposed a model state substitution law and a listing of medically equivalent drugs. Under another federal program, the maximum allowable cost (MAC) guidelines, reimbursement for Medicaid and Medicare prescriptions was made at the lowest price at which a generic version was available.

Generics accounted for 12 percent of new prescriptions being written and were likely to increase in relative importance. To combat the decreasing profit margins that were expected, the industry was looking to its ability to develop new drugs to offset the expected shortfall that was expected in the 1980s caused by a loss of patent protection on many important drug compounds.

The effect that generic substitution laws would have on Marion was unclear. The company had always concentrated on products with a unique pharmacological action rather than those that were commodity in nature. Generic substitution required an "equivalent" drug to be substituted for the brand-name drug, and there were uncertainties about how equivalency would be defined.

Marion's pharmaceutical operations had not produced a major new product for several years. Products that were in various stages of development were diltiazen hydrochloride, an antianginal agent; sucralfate, a nonsystematic (does not enter the bloodstream) drug for the treatment of ulcers; and benflourex, a product that reduced cholesterol levels in the blood.

HEALTH PRODUCTS GROUP

Subsidiaries selling a wide range of products used in health care and related fields made up Marion's Health Products Group. The company had bought and sold several subsidiaries since beginning to diversify in 1968 (see Exhibit 5). By 1978 the group of subsidiaries was responsible for 39 percent of total company sales and 22 percent of earnings before taxes.

Several times, after purchasing a company, Marion had decided to sell or discontinue operations of a subsidiary. The divestment decision in the past had been based on such considerations as weak market position, low growth position, excessive product liability, or poor "fit" with the rest of Marion.

In his presentation before the Health Industry's analyst group, Fred Lyons noted the importance of a subsidiary's fit with the rest of Marion in his explanation of the company's decision to sell Rose Manufacturing: "You may have noticed that during this past year we determined through our strategic planning that Rose Manufacturing, in the fall-protection area of industrial safety, did not fit either our marketing base or our technology base. Therefore we made a decision to spin off Rose, and we successfully culminated its sale in November 1977. Rose, like Signet Laboratories three years ago, just did not fit."

In adjusting its corporate profile, Marion was always searching for companies that provided good investment potential and were consistent with the company's goals. To provide a framework within which to evaluate potential acquisitions and to avoid some of the mistakes made in past purchases, Marion developed the following set of acquisition criteria to be applied to possible subsidiary investments:

Product Area	Health Care
Market	$100 million potential with 8% minimum growth rate
Net sales	$3–$30 million
Tangible net worth	Not less than $1 million
Return on investment	Not less than 20% pretax
Method of payment	Cash or stock

The board of directors made the ultimate decisions on the acquisitions and divestment of Marion's subsidiaries. At the corporate level, Mr. Herman was responsible for evaluating changes in the corporate portfolio and, on the basis of his analysis, making recommendations to the board. Since Mr. Herman was also on the board of directors, his recommendations were heavily weighted in the board's final decision.

In early 1979 Marion had four subsidiaries in its Health Products Group: Marion Health and Safety, Inc., Optico Industries, American Stair Glide, and Kalo Laboratories. A brief description of each follows.

Marion Health and Safety, Inc., sold a broad line of hospital and industrial safety products through its Marion Scientific Corporation and Health and Safety Products Division. Recently introduced Marion

Scientific products (a consumer-oriented insect-bite treatment and a device for transporting anaerobic cultures) both showed good acceptance and growth in their respective markets. Distribution was generally through medical/surgical wholesalers and distributors, who in turn resold to hospital, medical laboratories, reference laboratories, and so forth. Health and Safety Division manufactured or packaged safety-related products (hearing protection, eye-wash, and so on) and first-aid kits and kit products, such as wraps, band-aids, and various OTC products. Sale of these products was made to safety equipment wholesalers/distributors who resold to hospitals, industry, and institutions. Sales of Marion Health and Safety, Inc., were estimated, by outside analysts, to have increased about 17 percent to a level estimated at $19.0 million. Pretax margins were about 10 percent in this industry. Marion Health and Safety, Inc., was headquartered in Rockford, Illinois.

Optico Industries, Inc., participated in the wholesale and retail optical industry. Its main products were glass and plastic prescription eyeglass lenses and hard contact lenses. Outside analysts estimated this subsidiary recorded sales gains of about 26 percent for 1978 for sales estimated to be about $8 million. Optico had reduced profitability during 1978 because of expansion of its retail facilities. Pretax margins for 1978 were estimated at 6 percent, but this was expected to improve when the expansion program was completed. Optico's headquarters were located in Tempe, Arizona.

American Stair Glide Corporation manufactured and marketed home stairway and porch lifts and other products to aid physically handicapped individuals. These products were principally sold to medical/surgical supply dealers for resale or rental to the consumer. In some instances distribution was through elevator companies. Sales were estimated at about $5 million annually by outside analysts. This subsidiary was expected to grow slowly and steadily, and its historical earnings pattern was very stable. The trend for greater access to buildings for the handicapped was expected to have a favorable impact on this Grandview, Missouri–based subsidiary.

KALO LABORATORIES, INC.

Kalo Laboratories operated in the specialty agricultural chemical market and provided products to meet specialized user needs. In the past, Kalo had been successful in marketing its line of specialty products (see Exhibit 10). There were many risks to consider in assessing Kalo's future. These risks included competition from large chemical companies, governmental regulatory actions, and uncertain future product potentials.

EXHIBIT 10
Kalo Laboratories Sales, Investment, and Expense Information

	Dollars (millions)					
	1978	*1977*	*1976*	*1975*	*1974*	*1973*
Sales	$9	$5	$2	$4	$3	$2
Total assets	$5.0	$4.0	$2.0	$2.0	$2.0	$1.0
Total investment[a]	$3.0	$3.0	$1.0	$1.0	$1.0	$0.5
	Expenses as Percentage of Sales					
	1978	*1977*	*1976*	*1975*	*1974*	*1973*
COGS	43%	54%	61%	53%	55%	48%
R&D expense	8%	7%	7%	5%	5%	3%
Marketing, selling, and general administrative expenses	37%	31%	42%	23%	24%	27%

[a]Includes Marion's equity in Kalo and funds lent on a long-term basis. Authors' estimates.

Competition and Industry

The U.S. and Canadian agricultural chemical market was estimated to be $3.2 billion in 1978 and to grow at more than 15 percent a year.[c] The industry was dominated by large chemical manufacturers, including Dow Chemical, DuPont, Stauffer Chemical, and Gulf Oil. The market was also shared by large ethical drug manufacturers, including Eli Lilly, Pfizer, and UpJohn (see Exhibit 11). Economies of scale allowed the larger companies to produce large amounts of what might be perceived as a commodity product (herbicides, insecticides, and fungicides) at a much lower cost per unit than the smaller companies could. Diversification of and within agricultural product lines assured the larger manufacturers even performance for their agricultural divisions as a whole.

Since smaller chemical companies like Kalo could not afford to produce large enough amounts of their products to match the efficiency and prices of the large companies, these firms concentrated on specialty markets with unique product needs. By identifying specialty chemical needs in the agricultural segment, Kalo was able to produce its products and develop markets that were very profitable but not large enough to attract the bigger firms.

[c]1979 DuPont annual report and 1979 Upjohn annual report.

EXHIBIT 11
Total and Agriculture-Related Sales, Selected Companies, 1979

		Agriculture-Related	
	Total Sales (millions)	*Sales (millions)*	*Earnings (before Tax)*
Eli Lilly	$2,520	$920[a]	28.6%
Pfizer	3,030	480[a]	9.8
Upjohn	1,755	280[a]	9.2
Marion (1978)	100	9	9.0

Source: *Value Line Investment Survey.*
[a]Includes international sales.

Products

Since the larger chemical companies dominated the large product segments, Kalo's products were designed to meet the specialized needs of its agricultural users. Kalo's product line was divided into four major classes—seed treatments, adjuvants, bactericides, and herbicides.

Seed treatments for soybeans accounted for the majority of Kalo's sales. One product in this area was Triple Noctin. Products in the seed-treatment class are intended to act on soybean seeds to increase their viability once in the ground. Kalo manufactured seed treatments for soybeans only.

Adjuvants are chemicals that, when added to another agricultural product, increased the efficacy of the product or made it easier to use. For instance, Biofilmo prevents liquid fertilizer from foaming, which makes it easier to apply, and Hydro-Wet enhances the soil's receptiveness to certain chemicals, which reduces runoff into surrounding areas.

Kalo's newest product was the adjuvant EXTEND, a chemical compound added to fertilizer that made it bind chemically with the soil or the plant. The binding process helped retain the fertilizer where it was applied, making each application longer lasting and more effective. EXTEND was only recently introduced, and its success was difficult to assess at such an early stage. Kalo's management was planning to build a family of products around EXTEND. Sales projections showed EXTEND contributing between 60 to 70 percent of Kalo's future growth through 1987.

Bactericides and herbicides were the final two product classes at Kalo. Bactericides were applied to the soil to either inhibit or encourage the growth of selected bacteria. One product, ISOBAC, was used to control boll rot in cotton. Herbicides, mainly for broadleaf plants, were used to control or kill unwanted weeds, leaving the desirable crop unharmed.

In the past Kalo had acquired several of its products by acquiring the company that manufactured the product. When it purchased a going concern intact, Kalo was able to gain both manufacturing facilities and an existing distribution system. In the future Kalo expected to diversify its product line in a similar fashion. Kalo was planning to use both internal and contract R&D to enlarge its existing product lines. An example of enlarging the product family was the planned adaptation of its products to different numerous crop applications.

Because Kalo did not have a well-diversified product line, its operations were more cyclical than those of the overall agricultural sector. Two major factors beyond Kalo's control—the weather and spot prices for commodities—made its annual performance extremely unpredictable.

Kalo's operating results were seasonal as its products were intended to be applied primarily in the spring months. It was not unusual for the subsidiary to show a net loss from operations for the nine months from July until March and then to show a large profit in April, May, and June, when the products were being purchased for immediate application. If the spring months were particularly rainy, Kalo's profitability was adversely affected. Heavy farm equipment couldn't operate on wet fields without getting stuck, and application was impossible until the fields dried out. Once the fields were dry, Kalo's agricultural users often did not have time to apply the herbicides or other products even though it would have been economically advantageous to do so.

The other factor that affected the demand for Kalo's products was the spot pricing of commodities. The price of commodities relative to each other had a large effect on the total amount of each type of crop planted. Because the producer was free to switch crops yearly on the basis of spot prices, Kalo's demand for the upcoming planting season was uncertain and variable. Kalo was particularly vulnerable to swings in demand caused by the substitutability of crops since many of its products were applicable only to soybeans.

Distribution and Marketing

The end user of Kalo's products was usually the individual farmer. Kalo and the rest of the agricultural chemical industry had a distribution system like the one shown in Exhibit 12.

EXHIBIT 12
Diagram of Kalo's Distribution System

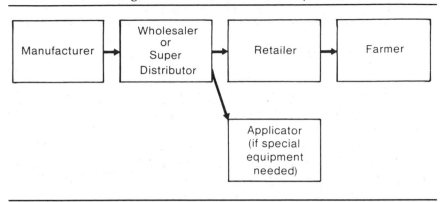

Kalo promoted its products with a sales force of about thirty. The main task of these salesmen was to call on and educate wholesalers/distributors on the advantages, unique qualities, and methods of selling Kalo's products. In addition, some end-user information was distributed to farmers, using "pull" advertising to create demand. A limited amount of promotion was done at agricultural shows and state fairs, but because of the expense involved this type of promotion was not used often.

Kalo's Future

Sales forecasts prepared by the staff analysts for Mr. Herman looked very promising; they predicted sales gains of from $4 to $6 million in each of the next nine years (see Exhibit 13). There were, however, some important assumptions on which the forecasts were based.

EXHIBIT 13
Kalo Laboratories, Forecasted Sales and Asset Turnover

	1979	1980	1981	1982	1983	1984	1985	1986	1987
Net sales ($ million) (current dollars)	12	16	20	25	30	35	40	45	50
Asset turnover	1.8x	1.8x	1.9x	1.9x	1.9x	1.9x	1.9x	1.9x	1.85x

Note: After-tax margin expected to increase to 7 percent by 1984. Authors' estimates.

EXHIBIT 14
Kalo Laboratories, Balance Sheet, June 30, 1978
(millions of dollars)

Current assets:	$2.5	Current liabilities:	$1.4
PP&E (net)	1.9	Long-term debt	1.0
Other	.2	Capital	2.2
Total	$4.6	Total	$4.6

Note: Authors' estimates.

As mentioned earlier, 60 to 70 percent of the forecasted growth was to come from a product family based on the new product EX-TEND. A great deal of uncertainty surrounded the product, however. Since it was new, the current success of EXTEND was difficult to measure, particularly in determining how current sales translated into future performance. If the market evaluations for EXTEND and related products were correct, and if a family of products could be developed around EXTEND, then the sales potential for the proposed product family was very promising—provided Kalo was able to exploit the available sales opportunities.

Additional growth projected in the sales forecasts was to come from existing products and undefined future products that were to be developed or acquired. Approximately 20 percent of the growth was to come from the existing products in the next four to five years. Ten to 20 percent of the growth in the later years of the forecast was expected to come from currently unknown products.

For Kalo to realize the forecasted growth, Marion would have to provide financing. It was going to be impossible for Kalo to generate all the required funds internally. Kalo had been a net user of cash, provided by Marion, since 1976. (See Exhibits 9 and 14.) Marion's management did not consider the amount of cash provided through the first part of 1979 to be excessive so long as Kalo maintained adequate profitability and steady growth rates. In addition to the long-term funds provided by Marion, Kalo also required short-term financing of inventory during each year because of the seasonality of its sales.

Government Regulation

Another major uncertainty in Kalo's future was an unpredictable regulatory climate. Regulation of agricultural chemicals was under the jurisdiction of the Environmental Protection Agency (EPA). Compliance with the EPA was similar to compliance with the FDA. The process of developing and introducing a new chemical product took from eight to ten years, which included the two to five years necessary to obtain EPA approval. The costs of developing and bringing a new product to market were generally from $5 to $10 million.

Once a product was on the market, the EPA had powers of recall similar to the FDA's and could require the company to do additional research after the product was introduced. The prospect of having a product removed from the market was an added element of risk for Kalo if any of its products were affected. No problems were expected for Kalo, although several of the subsidiary's products (particularly its herbicides and bactericides) had a relatively high potential for environmental problems if not applied correctly.

THE DECISION

Mr. Herman knew that in making his recommendation he would have to balance the immediate and long-term resource needs and the goals of Marion. Although Kalo looked promising from the forecasts, there were many uncertainties surrounding these subsidiaries' futures that had to be considered.

Since Marion had no new drug products ready to be introduced soon, the company would have to rely on other areas to reach its growth goals. Kalo was growing, but it was also requiring a constant input of funds from its parent.

One possibility for growth was to purchase another drug manufacturer and add its products to Marion's to take advantage of any distribution synergies that might exist. To make such a purchase, the company would need more resources. Selling a subsidiary could provide needed resources, but to do so quickly under less than optimum conditions would surely result in a significantly lower price than could be realized under normal conditions. The income and cash flow impact of this approach would be undesirable.

With the board meeting coming up so soon, Mr. Herman was faced with analyzing the complex situation quickly. In three days he would have to make his recommendation to the board of directors.

Preparing a Written Case Analysis: Republic National Bank of Dallas NOW Accounts

Chapter 3 outlined an approach for marketing decision making and case analysis. The purpose of this appendix is to provide a more detailed description of what is involved in a thorough written case analysis through the use of an example. The following case—Republic National Bank of Dallas NOW Accounts—describes an actual problem encountered by bank executives. The case is accompanied by a student analysis of the case using the format described in Chapter 3. The student analysis shows how to organize a written case and the nature

The cooperation of Republic National Bank of Dallas in the preparation of this case is gratefully acknowledged. This case was prepared by Professor Roger A. Kerin, Edwin L. Cox School of Business, Southern Methodist University, as a basis for class discussion and is not designed to illustrate appropriate or inappropriate handling of administrative situations. Certain nonpublished data in the case are either disguised or approximations.

and scope of the analysis, which includes both qualitative and quantitative analyses. It is recommended that the reader first read and analyze the case before examining the student analysis.

INTRODUCTION TO CASE

In early 1977 Ms. Ruth Krusen, marketing officer for Republic National Bank of Dallas (RNB), was asked to assess the impact on Republic Bank of offering NOW accounts if they became legal nationwide. Specifically, she was asked to:

1. Determine the impact on profits that Republic National Bank could anticipate from NOW accounts.

2. Recommend a NOW account marketing strategy.

NOW accounts "(negotiable order of withdrawal"), which are effectively interest-bearing checking accounts, have been in effect since 1972 in New England. However, in early 1977 a bill was introduced into Congress that would allow commercial banks and thrift institutions in all fifty states to provide this service.[a] Despite some opposition in Congress, observers were of the opinion that NOW account enabling legislation would be passed by the first quarter of 1978 and would become effective January 1979.

BANKING IN TEXAS

Texas is a "unit banking" state. This means that individual banks cannot operate branch banks. This regulation, which limits a bank to a single location, was specified in the state constitution of 1876. However, in 1971 amendments to the Bank Holding Act allowed individual banks to acquire smaller institutions, while still maintaining the identity of the acquired bank. Since 1971 large banks in Texas have formed holding companies to improve their lending capability to better serve large commercial accounts. By 1977 thirty-three bank holding companies operated in Texas. Holding companies owned 250 of the state's 1,360 banks and held about 55 percent of the state's total bank deposits in 1977.

---

[a]Thrift institutions include mutual savings banks, cooperative banks, credit unions, and savings and loan associations. Thrift institutions differ from commercial banks in that only banks have the authority to accept demand deposits or checking accounts or offer commercial loans.

Three of the largest bank holding companies in Texas are based in Dallas. Each operates its largest bank in downtown Dallas. First International Bancshares, which operates First National Bank, is the largest bank holding company in Texas. Republic of Texas Corporation operates the Republic National Bank of Dallas and is the second-largest holding company. Mercantile Texas Corporation operates Mercantile National Bank and is the fifth-largest bank holding company in terms of total assets.

Banking activity in Texas generally corresponds to pockets of urban and commercial growth. Accordingly, banking activity is concentrated in the Dallas–Fort Worth and Houston metropolitan areas. The San Antonio metropolitan area has also shown a dramatic increase in banking activity due in part to population growth and increased economic growth.

DALLAS COMPETITIVE SITUATION

The Dallas banking market consists of fifty-seven banks in the city of Dallas and an additional forty-three banks in Dallas County. By the end of 1977, the fifty-seven banks in the city of Dallas recorded total deposits of $13.27 billion. The forty-three banks in Dallas County recorded deposits of about $1.25 billion.

Three large downtown banks dominate the Dallas banking market. By the end of 1977, Republic National Bank, First National Bank, and the Mercantile National Bank accounted for approximately 78 percent of total bank deposits in the city of Dallas and 71 percent of Dallas County bank deposits. Republic National Bank was the leader with approximately $4.6 billion in deposits, followed closely by First National Bank with $4.4 billion. Mercantile National Bank recorded total deposits of about $1.3 billion by the end of 1977. These three banks are located within walking distance of each other, in addition to some twelve other banks.

Competitive activities of Dallas banks have historically focused on retail (consumer) bank accounts or wholesale (business) bank account development. Banks located in suburban areas typically emphasized the retail business while downtown banks have emphasized the wholesale business. Nevertheless, the Dallas competitive environment in recent years has been characterized by aggressive bank marketing efforts on both fronts. According to one observer of the Dallas banking scene:

> The competitive marketing furor is fierce, and it's not just the catchy advertising themes. . . . There's a scramble going on to repackage con-

sumer services, put forth new services, cross-sell services and woo corporate customers. There's Saturday banking, extended hours banking, twenty-four-hour tellers, foreign currency sales, cash machines, no-charge checking package deals, automatic payroll deposits, pension fund management services, computer billing services, specially arranged travel tours, traveler's checks to spend on travel tours, equipment leasing, credit card loans, loan syndications, lock boxes, and on and on. First National Bank in Dallas alone lists more than 400 different bank "products" in its inventory of services.[b]

Ms. Krusen confirmed the observation that the Dallas banking market was competitive. She noted that RNB continues to be competitive in banking services, but "the question of how aggressive we should be has not been resolved at least as regards retail account marketing." RNB has at least as many bank services for customers as competitors, if not more services than the vast majority of commercial banks in Dallas.

In addition to the competitive activity of commercial banks, savings and loan associations also compete for passbook savings accounts among Dallas County residents. By the end of 1977, deposits of the twenty-two Dallas County-based savings and loan associations were $2.85 billion. Dallas Federal Savings was the largest savings and loan association with about $909.6 million in deposits, or about 32 percent of total deposits. Texas Federal Savings and First Texas Savings combined accounted for approximately $992 million in deposits, or 35 percent of total deposits. Dallas-based savings and loan associations operated approximately 150 offices in Dallas County. Savings and loan associations based outside Dallas County also operated offices—which numbered about fifty by the end of 1977—in the county.

Savings and loan associations have also aggressively sought deposits in recent years. Dallas-based associations have historically outpaced the national average for savings and loan deposit volume growth. Savings associations have emphasized two competitive advantages in their passbook savings marketing programs. First, they could pay 5¼ percent on passbook savings, whereas commercial banks were limited by law to 5 percent on passbook savings. Second, they could develop branch operations with a common name whereas commercial banks were limited to a single location in Texas.

Savings and loan associations have placed greater emphasis on consumer or installment loans in recent years. Texas is unique among states in that savings associations are allowed to provide installment

---

[b]Dave Clark, "A Big Pitch for Bucks," *Dallas–Fort Worth Business Quarterly* 1, no. 2.

loans, and some associations have used this opportunity to attract deposit volume. According to an industry observer,

> S&L's have historically attracted older customers. Installment loans are a
> useful service to bring in younger customers, introduce them to S&L's,
> and open a passbook savings account.

Credit unions also represent a competitive force in the Dallas market. By the end of 1977, 218 credit unions were located in the city of Dallas and immediate environs. These credit unions operated 232 offices. Combined, credit unions held over $666 million in assets and served almost one-half million members.

Credit unions compete effectively in the Dallas market in three ways. First, they offer consumer or installment loans to their members at competitive interest rates. They hold a significantly large share of the automobile loans in the Dallas market. Second, credit unions hold substantial funds in member savings accounts. Third, credit unions provide *share drafts* to their members. A share draft is a withdrawal document that permits credit union members to make payments from the interest-bearing savings accounts. These drafts resemble checks, but are actually drafts drawn on a credit union and payable through a bank.

REPUBLIC NATIONAL BANK

Republic National Bank was founded in 1920. At that time, the bank's name was Guaranty Bank and Trust, and it held a state banking charter. After several name changes, the present name was adopted in 1937 and RNB obtained a national bank charter. Today, RNB is the largest member of the Republic of Texas Corporation bank holding company system. By the end of 1977, RNB would be ranked twenty-first in the United States in total assets and deposits and would be the largest bank in Texas and the South in total assets, deposits, loans, and equity capital. Also by the end of 1977, RNB would be ranked one hundred fiftieth among the 500 largest banks in the non-Communist world according to *American Banker* magazine. RNB had total assets exceeding $6 billion and a net income of approximately $36.3 million by the end of 1977.

Retail Account Marketing

Although figures are not available for competing banks, RNB is considered to have one of the largest, if not the largest, retail account bases in

EXHIBIT 1
Estimated Distribution of Personal Checking Account Balances in Early 1977

Account Size	Percentage of Accounts	Percentage of Total Checking Account Deposits
Under $200	32	3
$200–$499	23	3
$500–$999	14	4
$1,000–$4,999	18	13
$5,000–$9,999	7	11
$10,000–$24,999	3	13
$25,000–$100,000	2	20
Over $100,000	1	33
	100	100

Number of personal checking accounts: 45,000
Personal checking account deposits: $150 million

Note: Figures reported in this exhibit reflect approximations drawn from 1977 *District Bank Averages: Functional Cost Analysis* (Dallas: Federal Reserve Bank of Dallas).

the Dallas area. According to Ms. Krusen, this has occurred as a result of RNB's historic position of "taking chances on the little guy and community service." In 1977 it was estimated that about 55 percent of RNB's retail checking accounts were under $500. Exhibit 1 shows the distribution of accounts by account size.

This philosophy is also communicated in RNB advertising. Beginning in the late 1960s with its "Silver Star Service" campaign and subsequently with the "Star Treatment" advertising campaign, RNB communicated to present and potential customers that they were special and that RNB had a number of special services to provide them. In early 1977 the "Republic National Bank *Is* Dallas" campaign was launched with Orson Welles narrating television and radio advertising spots and the Dallas Symphony playing the theme music. This campaign was designed to reflect the mutual traditions of RNB and Dallas residents as progressive and growth-oriented as well as emphasizing the interdependence of banking leadership and service with the prosperity and quality of Dallas life. Marketing research has shown that RNB has had the highest "top-of-mind awareness" of any bank in the Dallas area since 1975.

Retail Account Services

RNB retail account marketing efforts have resulted in a variety of traditional as well as innovative bank services for its customers. For example, RNB provides its Teller 24® Service for customers, which is an automatic bank teller/cash machine. This service operates twenty-four hours a day at twenty-six locations around the city of Dallas and in six other Texas cities. Another innovation, the *Starpak* Account, is a complete package of banking services provided customers for a fixed monthly fee of $3. Exhibit 2 gives a description of this service. RNB personal checking is also highly competitive in the Dallas market, with no service charge for accounts that maintain a minimum monthly balance of $400. A $1 charge accrues to accounts with a minimum monthly balance of $300, a $2 charge with a minimum monthly balance of $200, and a $3 charge with no minimum balance requirement.

Retail Checking Account Revenue and Cost Estimates

In the course of preparing her report, Ms. Krusen contacted the RNB Controllers Division to obtain revenue and cost data on retail checking accounts. The Controllers Division report, based largely on Federal Reserve statistics, indicated that approximately 85 percent of retail checking account deposits were investable. In other words, about 15 percent of checking account deposits must be held in reserve. Ninety-six percent of savings account balances were investable.

  The Controllers Division also indicated that RNB would realize an average yield on loans and securities of about 7.5 percent in 1977. Ms. Krusen noted that this figure was the lowest experienced by RNB in recent years. RNB realized an average yield of 10.59 percent in 1974. Other figures obtained directly from Federal Reserve statistical averages for commercial banks with total deposits of over $200 million were as follows:

Service and handling charge revenue per account per month: $1.56

Account cost per month (including checks, deposits and other assignable overhead): $5.24

NOW ACCOUNTS

NOW accounts came into being as the result of the attempt of a Massachusetts mutual savings bank to circumvent the prohibition against

EXHIBIT 2
Components of Republic National Bank
Starpak Account

1) *Unlimited Checking*—There's no minimum balance requirement, no per check charge, and no limit on the number of checks you write when you have a Starpak personal checking account.

2) *Free Personal Checks*—They're prenumbered; personalized with your name, address, and phone number; and you can order as many as you need any time you need them.

3) *Reduced Loan Rates*—With this feature alone, many people make Starpak pay for itself. At the end of the loan period, we'll refund 10 percent of the total interest you paid on installment loans of $1,000 or more, when the loan has been repaid as agreed. Of course, your loan is subject to normal credit approval.

4) *No Bank Charge for Traveler's Checks*—Or for Money Orders and Cashier's Checks when you show us your Starpak Account Card.

5) *Free Safe Deposit Box*—We'll give you the $5 size free. Or, take $5 off the rent for a larger size.

6) *Combined Monthly Statement*—Your monthly statement can include status reports on any or all of the accounts you and your spouse have at Republic. You select the accounts you want the Combined Statement to cover. We can include your checking, savings, personal certificates of deposit, and even personal loans. Yes, you'll also receive separate regular statements on each of your Republic accounts you include in the Combined Statement.

7) *Numerical Check Listing*—Your monthly statement will report each check in the order written. That makes it much easier to reconcile your statement each month.

8) *Automatic Overdraft Protection*—This optional service gives you additional peace of mind. And the opportunity to take advantage of an exceptional bargain. It works this way. If the checks you write exceed your balance, we'll cover the overdrafts up to the limit of your Republic Master Charge or VISA Credit. Finance charges for deferred payment will apply at the normal rate. Repayment will be through your monthly Master Charge or VISA account payment.

9) *Teller 24® Service*—You can get cash from your Starpak Checking Account, or your Republic Master Charge or VISA Card, at any of twenty-six Teller 24 machines located in Dallas and six other Texas cities, and at 12,000 banks nationwide. With Teller 24 your money is available twenty-four hours a day, seven days a week.

10) *Automatic Loan Repayment*—If you have an installment loan at Republic, we will, at your request, withdraw your monthly loan payment from your Starpak Checking Account. It's a good way to make sure you can take advantage of the 10 percent interest refund.

(continued)

EXHIBIT 2 *(continued)*

11) *Automatic Savings Account Deposits*—If you've never been able to save before, this plan solves the problem. Just tell us how much and on what day of the month. On the date you specify, we'll automatically transfer the amount you select from your checking to your savings account. Then, to help your savings grow even faster, we'll pay the highest interest rates allowable.

12) *Starpak Account Card*—It identifies you as a preferred customer of Republic National Bank, entitled to the privileges and special savings available with your Starpak Account.

13) *No Separate Charges*—All these Starpak services are available for the flat monthly fee of $3. There's no separate charge.

Plus these other services available to all Republic National Bank customers—We pay postage both ways when you bank by mail. We'll validate your in-bank parking stub when you bank. And you'll have a personal banker assigned to your accounts to call for advice or assistance with any banking need.

Source: Bank brochure.

thrift institutions offering checking accounts. After a two-year regulatory and legal battle, Consumer Savings Bank of Worcester, Massachusetts, won its case and in June 1972 began to offer a savings account on which checklike instruments called negotiable orders of withdrawal could be written. Other mutuals in Massachusetts and New Hampshire soon followed suit.

Although regulatory authorities persist in regarding the NOW account as a savings account on which checks can be written, from a consumer point of view (and from an operational point of view) it is a checking account that pays interest. As consumers gradually became educated about NOWs, commercial banks began to lose customers to this attractive type of account, with which they were unable to compete. In response, federal and state laws were passed permitting commercial banks as well as mutuals and savings and loans in Massachusetts and New Hampshire to offer NOW accounts starting in January 1974. As of March 1976, financial institutions in the other New England states were granted the same powers. In two of the states (Connecticut and Maine), state-chartered thrifts had been empowered to offer checking accounts a few months earlier.

In New England, NOW accounts may be offered to individuals and nonprofit organizations (except that in Connecticut, thrifts can offer NOWs only to individuals).[c] A uniform rate ceiling of 5 percent applies to all institutions. Excerpts from a report prepared by the RNB

---

[c]At the time of this case and for analysis purposes, only retail (personal and nonprofit) checking accounts were affected by NOW accounts in the Dallas area.

Marketing Division on the development of NOW accounts in New England is presented in Appendix B at the end of this case.

NOW ACCOUNT MARKETING STRATEGY

The task facing Ms. Krusen was difficult for a number of reasons. First, the only NOW account information available pertained to the New England experience. Although this information would be useful in gauging the rate of adoption of NOW accounts, it was not entirely clear how the Dallas-area banks and thrift institutions would react. Second, she realized that several contingency plans would have to be charted. If NOW accounts were not deemed appropriate for RNB by top management, then she would have to recommend a strategy to maintain the RNB customer base. This strategy would depend on whether a "free" NOW account program became popular in the Dallas area or a more conservative approach was adopted by competitors. If the NOW account was adopted by RNB, she realized, the NOW account package (separate account or part of an existing bank service) and the price (i.e., service charges if any) would have to be defined. The package and price would be, in part, determined by the competitive environment that developed and the cost of NOW accounts.

Timing was a third consideration. Should RNB be a leader and set the competitive tenor in the market or take a "wait and see" stance? Finally, she realized that if RNB decided to adopt the NOW account, then a question of communications arose. For example, should RNB quietly inform present customers of NOW account availability or actively communicate availability to the Dallas market as a whole via an advertising program?

APPENDIX: NOW ACCOUNTS IN NEW ENGLAND: A REPORT PREPARED BY THE MARKETING DIVISION OF REPUBLIC NATIONAL BANK OF DALLAS

The objectives of this investigation of NOW accounts in New England were:

1. To learn the speed and magnitude of NOW account impact as a basis for estimating the impact on RNB

2. To identify and evaluate various marketing strategies and their possible relevance to our own market

Penetration of NOWs

Reaction of New England financial institutions given the power to offer NOWs is shown in Exhibit A.1. It indicates the percentages of thrifts and commercial banks that were offering NOWs by August 1976 and the market shares of commercial banks. By August 1976 mutual savings banks in Massachusetts and New Hampshire had been able to offer NOWs for fifty months, commercial banks for thirty months. In the other states, all institutions had been able to offer them for only six months.

Despite the resistance and delay of commercial banks in Massachusetts and New Hampshire to offering NOWs, Exhibit A-1 shows that a substantial majority are now providing them. In the other New England states, commercial banks have moved more quickly to adopt NOW accounts. This is one of the reasons that they have a larger share of NOW accounts and balances than do commercial banks in Massachusetts and New Hampshire. Nevertheless, even in the latter states, commercial banks have captured more of the total NOW balances than have thrifts.

One conclusion supported by the data is that the competitiveness

EXHIBIT A.1
NOW Account Adoption in New England
as of August 1976

| | Percentage of Institutions Offering | | Commercial Banks' Share of NOW Market | |
	Thrifts	Commercial Banks	Percentage of Accounts	Percentage of Balances
Massachusetts	94[a]	72	32	52
New Hampshire	81[a]	64	43	62
Connecticut	69	53	35	74
Maine	32	40	68	81
Vermont	23	29	89	93
Rhode Island[b]	25	75	83	85

[a]Mutual savings banks only; in each state two-thirds of the savings and loans also offer NOWs.

[b]Rhode Island has a unique situation of affiliated mutual savings banks and commercial banks. Figures in table refer only to unaffiliated thrifts and commercial banks. NOWs are offered by 66 percent of the affiliated group.

of financial institutions is directly related to the degree to which the state's population is concentrated in large urban markets.

The additional data on Massachusetts and New Hampshire shown in Exhibit A-2 indicate the substantial impact of NOWs in the personal payment account market. Exhibit A-2 shows that after four years, 72 percent of checking account balances in New Hampshire have been converted to NOWs and 44 percent have been converted in Massachusetts. Thrifts have captured 27 percent of this market in New Hampshire and 21 percent in Massachusetts.

Marketing Strategies

Massachusetts and New Hampshire

As simple as the concept of an interest-bearing checking account appears to be, NOW account introduction in New England produced an initial confusion of positioning, pricing, and marketing strategies.

Positioning For a variety of reasons, thrifts initially positioned NOWs as savings accounts with a special convenience feature in getting access to funds. Consumers who opened them did not regard them as checking accounts and there was relatively low account activity. Adding to the confusion, when banks began to offer NOWs, some of them were very negative in their presentations. They told customers, in effect, "We have NOW accounts, but you don't really want to spend your savings, do you?"

In time, thrifts and then banks became more daring in presenting NOWs as accounts that were identical in function to checking accounts but paid interest. NOWs are by now recognized as a substitute for checking accounts, are opened instead of checking accounts (or an existing checking account is closed when it is realized that it is no

EXHIBIT A.2
Personal Payment Accounts, August 1976

	Personal Payment Balances	
	Percentage in NOWs	*Percentage in Thrifts*
New Hampshire	72	27
Massachusetts	44	21

Note: Personal payment accounts consist of all checking balances plus 80 percent of NOW balances. The 20 percent of NOW balances estimated to have come from savings accounts have been deducted.

longer needed), and have virtually the same level of activity as checking accounts.

Pricing   Pricing was initially fairly conservative. In New Hampshire NOWs were usually offered at a lower rate of interest than a savings account, while in Massachusetts per-item charges were prevalent. Then a price war began and increasing numbers of institutions offered free NOWs—that is, maximum rate of interest, no service or item charges, and no minimum balance requirements.

The proportion of institutions offering free NOWs increased until mid-1975, but since then the trend has been reversed, largely because late entrants into the field have offered less generous terms. It has also been true that some institutions that previously offered free NOWs have imposed charges or minimum balance requirements.

The free NOW resulted from a variety of causes and motives:

1. At the time of introduction, money market rates were so high that the cost of NOW funds might still allow a margin of profit.

2. Thrifts were inexperienced in the costs involved in servicing checking accounts.

3. Some thrifts were determined to establish a good market share early, regardless of short-run lack of profitability.

4. In the major market areas, there was a free checking environment.

Price and Service Package   Pricing structures on NOWs in New England are as varied as checking account charges have historically been. The possibility of competing through the interest rate paid is the only new element. When NOW accounts are not free, some variant of the following occurs:

1. *Interest rates.* Initially, some institutions paid less than the maximum rate on savings accounts. However, under competitive pressure rates rose to the 5 percent ceiling in all major markets. However, some institutions do not pay on a day-of-deposit to day-of-withdrawal basis. While very few now pay only on collected balances, several large banks are contemplating going in that direction. A few banks pay only on minimum balances.

2. *Balance requirements.* Balances above which the NOW account is "free" range from $200 to $1,000. In most cases, this is the

minimum balance, although one large bank, Shawmut, has an average balance requirement.

What happens when the balance goes below the minimum varies. In some cases, no interest is paid; in others, a transaction or service fee is imposed; and in some cases, both. In some isolated markets, fees are imposed on all accounts, but in competitive major markets, NOWs become free at some balance level.

3. *Transaction charges.* Charges per check range from 10 to 25 cents. Usually, the charge is levied on all checks if the balance is below the required level. In some cases, a certain number of checks are free (five to fifteen per month), and in some other cases the number of free checks is related to balances (e.g., five checks per $100 of average balance).

4. *Service charge.* Some banks charge flat fees rather than per-transaction charges. Fees generally are $1 or $2.

Other New England States

By the time NOW accounts were authorized in the other New England states, both thrift and commercials had had the opportunity to assess the cost and competitive impact of NOWs in the two original states, and money market conditions had changed. These facts are reflected in the response of financial institutions in offering NOWs. Commercial banks have moved more rapidly than they did in Massachusetts and New Hampshire. At the same time, both thrifts and commercial banks have been more conservative in pricing.

Connecticut Thrifts have moved aggressively to offer both checking accounts and NOWs. Although free checking prevails in major Connecticut markets and although about one-third of the thrifts offer free NOWs, large Connecticut banks have offered NOWs on conservative terms (high minimum balances with transaction charges for lower-balance accounts). The effect of this strategy is reflected in the high average balances of commercial bank NOWs—over $4,000.

Rhode Island The financial market is highly concentrated in a very few institutions. Six months after NOWs became legal, six of the nine commercial banks affiliated with thrift institutions, six of the eight unaffiliated banks, and one of the four unaffiliated thrifts were offering NOWs. None of them offered free NOWs. As in the checking account market in this state, relatively high minimum balances are required. It should be noted that because of the thrift commercial bank

affiliations, a majority of thrifts have in effect been able to offer checking accounts to their customers.

   Maine   Thrifts have concentrated harder on selling checking accounts than on offering NOWs. Neither thrifts nor commercial banks
have moved very fast to offer NOWs. Few offer them free.

   Vermont   This state shows the slowest gain in institutions offering NOWs. None offers them free.

Student Analysis of Republic National Bank of Dallas NOW Accounts

STRATEGIC ISSUES AND PROBLEMS

Ms. Ruth Krusen, marketing officer for RNB, has been given responsibility for (1) determining the profit impact RNB could anticipate from NOW accounts and (2) recommending a contingency plan for a NOW account marketing strategy. Her task involves a number of important factors. She must assess the likelihood that the Dallas competitive environment will be liberal or conservative in its marketing of NOW accounts. An important consideration is RNB's role in affecting this environment, given its dominant position in the Dallas market and its posture regarding aggressiveness in retail account marketing. Ultimately, she must make a "go–no go" decision. A "go" decision requires a recommendation on the form of the service, its target market, its price reflected in service charges, and promotion. A "no go" decision must consider RNB's competitive position without NOW accounts and measures to minimize their impact. The problem facing RNB is how to retain its dominant competitive position given an environment threat (NOW accounts) while at the same time preserving profitability and its customer base.

DALLAS RETAIL BANK MARKETING

Financial institutions compete with each other—or avoid direct competition—in terms of primary markets served and the character of the marketing mixes employed. Banks either emphasize the wholesale (business) market or the retail (individual market). Savings and loan institutions (S&Ls) and credit unions focus on the retail market.

The *product-service* element of a bank's marketing mix consists of (1) the variety of accounts provided (checking, savings, savings certificates); (2) the sources of funds for customers (installment, commercial loans); (3) frills (package accounts such as RNB's Starpac, safety deposit boxes); and (4) service delivery systems (statements, speed of banking service, accuracy in recording transactions, friendliness of personnel, and the like). S&Ls and credit unions use the same product-service elements, although the nature of the mix varies. S&Ls do not offer checking accounts, yet credit unions provide share drafts, which have similarities with checking accounts. Both offer savings accounts, and S&Ls offer savings certificates. S&Ls and credit unions provide funds for installment loans; S&Ls are also major sources of mortgage loans. Frills are less apparent in S&Ls and credit unions than in banks.

The *distribution* element is reflected in the number of locations at which financial institutions can operate. Banks in Texas are limited to a single location by the unit banking regulation. However, S&Ls and credit unions have multiple locations. The case notes that about 200 S&L offices existed in Dallas County; 232 credit union offices operated in Dallas County. *Convenience* in personal finance is influenced by the distribution factor. The *price* element is evident in interest rates and service charges on personal accounts. Regulations limit banks to 5 percent interest on savings; S&Ls can offer 5 ¼ percent. Service charges vary between banks. The *communication* element includes advertising, sales efforts of bank officers and tellers, gifts, and promotion gimmicks.

In short, banks, S&Ls, and credit unions compete through their primary market focus and marketing mix. However, NOW accounts will change the way financial institutions compete. To a large extent, NOW accounts will transform S&Ls and credit unions into banks!

INSIGHTS FROM THE NEW ENGLAND EXPERIENCE

The NOW account experience, based on the data in Appendix A, reveals the following:

1. The faster commercial banks move to adopt NOW accounts, the larger their share of NOW accounts and NOW account balances.

2. Cannibalization of checking accounts occurs when NOW accounts are available: 72 percent of checking account balances in New Hampshire have been converted to NOW accounts, and 44 percent of checking accounts in Massachusetts have converted to NOWs. These figures developed over fifty months (four years) after the NOW introduction (see Exhibit A.2).

3. Exhibit 1 provides some evidence that NOW account balances are high. This could mean that those individuals with high checking account balances are more likely to switch to NOWs. Alternatively, the Connecticut experience would indicate that minimum balance requirements increase the NOW account balances. Yet Massachusetts and New Hampshire data—where both states experienced "free NOWs"—would tend to support the point that individuals with high account balances convert to NOWs.

4. NOW account usage activity approaches checking account activity; hence checking account costs are merely transferred to managing NOW accounts.

5. Competitive activity, reflected in the NOW package provided, reveals that "free NOWs" were initially provided. However, financial institutions subsequently offered less generous terms.

6. NOW account packages differ greatly according to minimum balances, service charges, and positioning against checking and savings accounts.

Results from the New England experience suggest that three scenarios are possible in the Dallas market.

Environment	*Environment Description*
No NOW adoption:	Financial institutions refrain from adoption
Liberal NOW adoption:	NOWs adopted with no minimum balance, service charges, 5% interest, active promotion/communication program
Conservative NOW adoption:	NOWs adopted with some form of minimum balance, service charges, less than 5% interest, little promotion/communication

EXHIBIT 1
RNB Retail Account Profit Analysis
(based on Exhibit 1 in the case)

Account Size	Average Interest Revenue Account[a] +	Average Service Handling Revenue/ Account[b] =	Average Revenue Per Account −	Account Cost[b] =	Profit/(Loss)
< $200	$ 19.92	$18.72	$ 38.64	$62.88	$ (24.24)
$200–$499	27.72	18.72	46.44	62.88	(16.44)
$500–$999	60.71	18.72	79.43	62.88	16.55
$1,000–$4,999	153.47	18.72	172.19	62.88	109.31
$5,000–$9,999	333.93	18.72	352.65	62.88	289.77
$10,000–$24,999	920.83	18.72	939.55	62.88	876.67
$25,000–$100,000	2,125.00	18.72	2,143.72	62.88	2,080.84
> $100,000	7,083.00	18.72	7,101.72	62.88	7,038.84

[a]Computed as follows: $\dfrac{\text{Account size deposit volume}}{\text{Number of accounts in category}} \times 85\% \times .075$

For account size of $200 using Exhibit 1 data: $\dfrac{\$4.5 \text{ million}}{14,400} \times .85 \times .075 = \$19.92$

[b]Annualized average account revenue and cost given in the case where:
Service/handling charge revenue/account/month = $1.56
Account cost per month = $5.24

Numerous factors will affect the likelihood of each environment developing in the Dallas market.

Two factors in favor of a no-NOW environment are:

1. The New England experience suggests that a no-win possibility exists for all financial institutions. For example, banks will have to pay interest on previously interest-free funds. S&Ls and credit unions will incur costs not previously encountered.

2. Money market rates are quite low at present, suggesting little spread to make an adequate profit margin.

Three factors in favor of a NOW environment are:

1. The New England experience suggests that where NOWs are legalized, they are adopted in some form, by someone.

2. If the Dallas market is competitive *and* various financial institutions are vying for deposits, then NOWs offer a means to attract deposits. Moreover, the New England experience suggests that "getting in first" is crucial. "Followership" is not rewarded.

3. S&Ls are poised to take some advantage of NOWs in that their interest rate paid on deposits will fall from 5 1/4 percent to 5 percent, assuming a 5 percent ceiling level.

Three factors in favor of a liberal NOW environment are:

1. Thrifts might view NOWs as a way of gaining deposits quickly.

2. S&Ls will benefit from NOWs even if 5 percent interest is offered on NOW accounts, since they are currently paying 5 1/4 percent on savings.

3. Share drafts provided by credit unions have characteristics similar to NOWs; NOW accounts would seem like logical extension.

Two factors in favor of a conservative NOW environment are:

1. This appears to be the trend in New England states.

2. Dallas banks do not generally offer free checking.

3. Money market rates are low.

It would seem that a potential determinant of how the NOW environment evolves will be determined by RNB, given their dominance in the Dallas banking market. RNB's dominant position would seem to affect the environment *only* if RNB acts immediately with a well-thought-out NOW account program. NOWs are probably inevitable (that is, the no-NOW environment seems unlikely). The question, then, is whether a liberal or a conservative NOW environment will develop. The environment could be influenced by RNB.

REPUBLIC NATIONAL BANK

RNB dominates the Dallas financial market. RNB's assets alone ($6 billion) are almost ten times *total* assets of all credit unions ($666 million). RNB's deposits ($4.6 billion) exceed the total for *all* S&Ls ($2.85 billion). RNB has the largest deposit base of all Dallas banks *and* the largest retail account deposit base in Dallas.

Nevertheless, RNB management apparently has not resolved how aggressive the bank should be in retail account marketing efforts. The aggressiveness issue would seem to be related to the bank's emphasis on the wholesale business rather than the retail business.

Exhibit 1 in the case indicates that about 55 percent of RNB's checking accounts are under $500. However, 96 percent of total checking account balances are accounted for by accounts $500 and up; 53 percent of total deposits are accounted for by account sizes over $25,000. The average account size is $3,333 ($150 million in deposits ÷ 45,000 accounts). A profitability analysis of checking account sizes reveals the RNB loses money on accounts that are less than $500.00 on an annual basis (see Exhibit 1 in this analysis). This profitability analysis indicates that accounts below $500 produce a *loss* of $519,210 annually:

Accounts under $200: 14,400 accounts × ($24.24) = ($349,056)
Accounts $200–$499: 10,350 accounts × ($16.44) = ($170,154)
Loss = ($519,210)

More important, this analysis provides important data on the pricing of NOW accounts and the form of the service, as I will discuss later.

PLAN OF ACTION

There are two primary alternatives open to RNB: either to offer NOWs or not to offer NOWs. If NOWs are considered, then the form, price, and NOW promotion must be determined. The alternatives are:

1. Do not offer NOW accounts.

2. Offer NOW accounts with no conditions and promote heavily/modestly.

3. Offer NOW accounts with conditions and promote modestly/heavily.

The advantages and disadvantages of the options available to RNB can be outlined as follows.

1. *Advantages/disadvantages of RNB not offering NOW accounts:*

   Advantages
   - RNB is dominant and has the resources to wait and see what will happen.
   - The impact on revenue will be too severe. Assuming that *all accounts* are cannibalized by NOWs and the interest yield drops from 7 1/2 percent to 2 1/2 percent because of 5 percent interest on NOWs, then the interest revenue lost is estimated to be about $6.0 million.

Checking Deposits	Investable %		Investable Deposits
$150 million	×	85%	= $ 127.5 million
$127.5 million	×	.075	= 9,562,500 = Interest revenue
$144 million[a]	×	.025	= −3,600,000 = Interest revenue
Interest revenue lost			$5,962,500

   Disadvantages
   - RNB will lose an opportunity to be an innovator or "first-to-market," which has been shown in New England to be advantageous.
   - Erosion of accounts may occur as individuals switch to institutions offering NOW accounts. This factor is particularly important if *large* accounts switch. They are most likely to do so since they would benefit most from NOW accounts.

2. *Advantages/disadvantages of offering NOW accounts with no conditions:*

   Advantages
   - Will have a dramatic impact on Dallas banking market.

---

[a]Note that NOW accounts are viewed as savings accounts and 96 percent of deposits are investable.

- Will most likely attract deposits and accounts in great numbers, particularly since this is a better deal than checking accounts with minimum balances or service charges, *plus* interest!
- Will set competitive tenor of market; retail banks will likely be unable to compete.
- Will keep current accounts from being attracted to competitors (preemptive cannibalism).

Disadvantages
- This strategy could be very expensive. As noted earlier, a loss of interest of $6.0 million is possible, *plus* the service/handling revenue/account costs.
- This strategy will cannibalize checking accounts almost totally.

3. *Advantages/disadvantages of offering NOW accounts with conditions:*

Advantages
- A minimum-balance condition would allow RNB to accept only those accounts on which RNB can make money.
- A service/handling charge condition would also result in greater account selectivity.
- A break-even analysis shows how RNB can determine a minimum balance given current service charge and account costs per year. The break-even says that total revenues (interest plus handling/service charges) minus total costs (account cost per month) equals zero. Since RNB will net 2.5 percent in account interest revenue, has an $18.72 handling and service revenue per account per year ($1.56 x 12 months) and has an annual account cost of $62.88 ($5.24 x 12 months), I solved for the minimum account balance as follows:

Profit = Acct. Interest Revenue + Handling/Service Chg. − Acct. Cost
0 = .025 (X) + $18.72 − $62.88
$44.16 = .025 (X)
$1,766.40 = X

Thus RNB breaks even at an account size of $1,766.40, given existing handling/service revenue per account and account maintenance costs. At this minimum balance level, RNB could impose a condition that from 80 percent to 90 percent of account balances could meet (see case Exhibit 1).

Disadvantages
- This leaves RNB open to being undercut by competitors if conditions are too stringent.
- Overly complex conditions and the likelihood of customers being unexpectedly hit with service charges could hurt goodwill, particularly among larger-balance account holders.

NOW ACCOUNT MARKETING STRATEGY

The previous analysis indicates to me that RNB should offer NOW accounts immediately to set a competitive tone in the market and create a "rational" NOW environment. By doing so, RNB will assume a leadership position.

The principal *target market* should be current customers with large account balances. The emphasis should be on preemptive cannibalism. There is probably little to gain from new customers. The RNB *NOW account should be offered with conditions.* It is recommended that RNB set a minimum balance of about $1,500. Moreover, RNB should incorporate NOWs into one of their package accounts such as the Starpak account. The promotional effort should be modest and directed. Specifically, direct mail to current customers is recommended.